D1616091

W. H. AUDEN AND
CHESTER KALLMAN

LIBRETTI

THE COMPLETE

WORKS OF

W. H. AUDEN

POEMS

PLAYS (WITH CHRISTOPHER ISHERWOOD)

LIBRETTI (WITH CHESTER KALLMAN)

ESSAYS AND REVIEWS

W. H. AUDEN AND
CHESTER KALLMAN

_____

LIBRETTI

_____

AND OTHER DRAMATIC
WRITINGS BY
W. H. AUDEN

□

1939–1973

EDITED BY

Edward Mendelson

PRINCETON UNIVERSITY
PRESS

CONTENTS

TEXTUAL NOTES

PREFACE

THIS volume, the second to be published in a complete edition of Auden's works, includes his libretti and other dramatic writings from his arrival in America in 1939 until his death in 1973. Auden collaborated with other writers on most of his works intended for performance. In his first years in America he wrote radio and stage plays together with James Stern and Bertolt Brecht. After 1947 he wrote his libretti with Chester Kallman. This volume and the volume of Auden's *Plays, 1928–1938,* contain Auden's complete dramatic writings. Later volumes will present his complete essays and reviews and his complete poems. The texts of this edition are newly edited from Auden's manuscripts, and the notes report variant readings from all published versions.

ACKNOWLEDGEMENTS

BEFORE his death in 1975, Chester Kallman made this edition possible by recalling obscure details of his collaborations with Auden and by giving me free access to his manuscripts. Hans Werner Henze provided copies of typescripts and letters, and was generous with other information. A. R. Braunmuller wrote an expert account of Auden's collaboration with Bertolt Brecht on *The Duchess of Malfi*. Nicholas Jenkins once again gave expert critical attention to every word of the text and notes. Cheryl Mendelson's expert criticism was always indistinguishable from warm encouragement.

I could not have begun this volume without the scholarship and encouragement of B. C. Bloomfield, and I could not have finished it without the learning and intelligence of John Fuller. Lincoln Kirstein, who helped bring many of Auden's libretti into being and made possible many of their productions, was a generous and bracing source of knowledge and wisdom. Over the course of many years Benjamin Britten, John Gardner, Donald Mitchell, Peter Pears, James Stern, and Tania Stern labored to provide information, letters, and manuscripts. Robert Craft, who provided the same ready assistance, also responded generously to dozens of queries about small details. Andrew Porter was an unfailing fount of scholarship and judgement. The notes and appendices reflect the generous labors of Betty Bean, Humphrey Carpenter, Toni Greenberg, Wendell Stacy Johnson, Monroe K. Spears, Francis Thompson, Susana Walton, and Eric Walter White. For recollections of the creation of *Paul Bunyan* I am grateful to Mordecai Bauman, William S. Hess, Hugh Ross, and Milton Smith. For help with Auden's writings for film, radio, and television I am grateful to Thomas C. Daly at the National Film Board of Canada, John Houseman, J. William Nelson at the United States Department of Commerce, Davidson Taylor, and Francis Thompson. Auden's contribution to *Rosina* was clarified by, among others, Marlies K. Danziger, Shane Devine, Clare Goldfarb, Elizabeth Gallaher von Klemperer, and Robert Petersson.

Auden's collaboration with Bertolt Brecht on *The Duchess of Malfi* is one of the great quagmires of textual scholarship. A. R. Braunmuller and I were kept on a solid footing by Dr Michael Voges, who provided an advance copy of his critical edition of Brecht's version of the play and much additional aid. We also received help from Elisabeth Bergner, Michael Jeske, James K. Lyon, and John Willett. Various mysteries elsewhere in this volume were solved by Katherine Bucknell, Stewart R. Craggs, James

Gindin, Newell Jenkins, Mitt Jones, J. D. McClatchy, James Merrill, Maria Rich, Maureen Sullivan, and Robert A. Wilson. For other help with the text I am grateful to Antonella Antelli and Francesco Binni. Ulysses d'Aquila and Glenn Horowitz made possible the inclusion of Auden's masque in celebration of Chester Kallman's twenty-second birthday. Dale Wasserman made available the full texts of Auden's lyrics written for *Man of La Mancha* and generously offered his recollections of his talks with Auden.

This entire edition stands as an inadequate tribute to the late Lola Szladits, who gathered an unparalleled collection of Auden's books and manuscripts for the Henry W. and Albert A. Berg Collection of the New York Public Library. I am indebted to Cathy Henderson and Heather Moore at the Harry Ransom Humanities Research Center at the University of Texas at Austin. Rosamund Strode, Philip Reed, and everyone else at the Red House and the Britten-Pears Library at Aldeburgh provided hospitality and assistance. The expert staff at the Stiftung Paul Sacher in Basel, especially Harriet Leander and Ingrid Westin, transformed arduous research into pleasure. Valuable information came from M.-A. Ziprian and Karin Pfotenhauer at the Bertolt-Brecht-Archiv in Berlin. Among many who provided help at the Library of Congress I am indebted especially to John Wayne and Ronald Wilkinson. David Farneth at the Kurt Weill Foundation for Music, Thomas F. Kilfoil at the Brander Matthews Dramatic Museum at Columbia University, and Margery N. Sly at Smith College were kind and resourceful. I am grateful also to the staff of the Columbia University Library, the Music Collection and Theatre Collection of the New York Public Library, the Museum of Broadcasting, and the Poetry Collection at the State University of New York at Buffalo.

For scripts and other information on Auden's broadcasts I relied on the intelligence and tirelessness of John Jordan, Cedric Messina, and J. P. Mullins at the BBC Written Archives Centre; Dorothy S. Boyle and Bernard S. Krause at the Columbia Broadcasting System; and Debra Levinson and Cathy Lim at the National Broadcasting Company. I received valuable help from Dr Horst Goerges at the Bayerische Staatsoper, Claus H. Henneberg at the Deutsche Oper Berlin, Erich Breitweiser at the Österreichischer Rundfunk, Dr Werner Rainer at the Salzburger Festspiele, and Christine Waltisbühl at the Opernhaus Zürich.

Nicholas Jenkins translated an essay from the Italian, and Stanley Corngold provided drafts of translations from German. Auden and James Stern's adaptation of D. H. Lawrence's "The Rocking-Horse Winner" appears through the kind permission of the late Laurence Pollinger. I am especially grateful to Sylvia Goldstein of Boosey & Hawkes for her help in untangling matters of copyright. I am grateful also to Petra Hensel and the Bonn office of Boosey & Hawkes, Sally Groves at Schott & Co., and Louise T. Guinther at *Opera News*.

This volume has profited variously and extensively from the advice of David Bromwich, Edward Callan, Martin Meisel, Charles H. Miller, Michael Seidel, and Natasha Staller.

Jane Lincoln Taylor, who edited the manuscript for Princeton University Press with sympathy and concentration, caught errors that had escaped all earlier editors. Auden's readers will continue to share my gratitude to Jan Lilly for the clarity and elegance of the design of this edition.

INTRODUCTION

AUDEN called opera "the last refuge of the High style" among the arts that use words, the only one in which the grand manner had survived the ironic levellings of modernity.* Unlike poetry, which always stops to reflect on the emotions that gave rise to it, the verse of an opera libretto, he said, gives immediate expression to wilful feeling. For Auden, the unique combination of artifice and intensity in opera made it the ideal dramatic medium for both archetypal comedy and tragic myth. His libretti, most of them written in collaboration with Chester Kallman, present their mythical actions with a directness unlike anything in even his greatest poems. In their use of the simplest language of song to dramatize the most complex issues of history, psychology, and religion they surpass everything written for the musical theatre in English and have few equals in the richer operatic traditions of Italian, German, and French.

Opera gave Auden the solution to a problem of dramatic poetry that he had been unable to solve in his early poetic plays, the problem of the proper voice for a poet who wants to write a public and heroic art as well as a private and intimate one. Poetry, he wrote in 1961, "cannot appear in public without becoming false to itself"; this was the conviction Auden had reached after his attempts to write public poetry in the 1930s. Yet public poetry is precisely what dramatic poetry must be:

> Dramatic poetry, to be recognizable as poetry, must raise its voice and be grand. But a poet today cannot raise his voice without sounding false and ridiculous. The modern poetic dramatist seems faced with these alternatives: either he writes the kind of verse which is natural to him, in which case he produces little closet dramas which can only make their effect if the audience is a small intimate one, or, if he wishes to write a public drama, he must so flatten his verse that it sounds to the ear like prose. Neither alternative seems to me satisfactory.

Because opera, like ballet, is a virtuoso art, it can still be public. An audience regards a great singer or dancer as "a heroic superhuman being, even if the music or the choreography is sub-human trash". The grand heroic art of the singer allows the librettist to write in service of heroism without claiming heroism for himself.

*Sources for quotations are listed on p. xxxi.

When Auden renounced as dishonest the grand style he had used in his public poems of the 1930s, he renounced only his use of that style in lyric and personal poetry, not the grand style itself. He still hoped to use it if he could find the proper vehicle. Around 1950, in "We, too, had known golden hours", the dedicatory poem to his book *Nones,* he wrote that "we" (the poem implicitly speaks for all who value the private realm) had known all the feelings that the grand style is best suited to express, "And would in the old grand manner / Have sung from a resonant heart". But the modern era had transformed the public realm from one of personal choice and action to one of mass necessity, where the grand manner now could do nothing more than endorse popular sentiment and political lies. The only authentic tones of voice that remained for poetry were private and quiet ones: "the wry, the sotto-voce, / Ironic and monochrome". The poem ended with an apparently rhetorical question:

> And where should we find shelter
> For joy or mere content
> When little was left standing
> But the suburb of dissent.

The unstated answer, for Auden as poet, was in the grand style still possible in opera, and in libretti of the kind he had begun to write a few years before.

Auden's early plays included songs and choruses written to be set to music, but he took almost no interest in opera until shortly after he moved to America in 1939. He settled in New York where, that spring, when he was thirty-two, he fell in love with Chester Kallman, an eighteen-year-old Brooklyn College student who was passionately knowledgeable about opera. When the Metropolitan Opera season began in the autumn, Auden and Kallman attended regularly. Early in 1940 they heard at least five of Wagner's operas in a series of matinées. In February 1940 Auden wrote to a friend in England, "My chief luxury is the opera". In September he told a lecture audience that Wagner "seems to me the greatest and the most typical modern artist, the forerunner, and in many ways the creator, of both the high-brow and the low-brow tastes of our time". Sometime after 1942 his operatic loyalties shifted from Wagner to Verdi, and in the late 1950s to Strauss and Hofmannsthal, but his sense of opera's significance and value remained constant. In an introduction to an anthology of Greek literature published in 1948 he wrote that "as a period of sustained creative activity in one medium, the seventy-five-odd years of Athenian drama, between the first tragedies of Aeschylus and the last comedy of Aristophanes, are surpassed by the hundred and twenty-five years, between Gluck's *Orpheus* and Verdi's *Othello,* which comprise the golden age of European opera".

Because the golden age of opera had ended, the composers of new operas, Auden wrote, "can not carry on from where their predecessors left off, but must start anew from the beginning". When he wrote his first libretto, in 1939, he characteristically started anew by updating a work from the distant past. In the autumn of 1939 Benjamin Britten, recently arrived in America, was commissioned by his publisher to compose an operetta suitable for high schools. Auden, who had collaborated with Britten on films, song cycles, and poetic drama since 1935, suggested that they write a work about Paul Bunyan, the legendary logger hero of the American frontier. Auden apparently found a model for his semi-mythical libretto about the consolidation of America in Dryden's *King Arthur,* a extravagant semi-mythical libretto, set by Purcell, about the consolidation of Britain. Auden's choice of this model may have been motivated in part by his sense of his and Britten's place in literary and musical history. *King Arthur* was the first and still the only libretto written by a major English poet for a major English composer. *Paul Bunyan* would be the second.*

Both libretti are set in a legendary past and end with a prophecy of the present day; both have scenes in which trees speak and in which (as described in Dryden's stage direction) "Airy Spirits appear in the Shapes of Men and Women". Dryden's loosely organized sequence of spoken dialogue interspersed with arias and choruses, some of them marginally relevant to the action, corresponded closely enough to the conventions of American musical comedy to encourage Auden to join his mythical subject and historical theme with characterization and diction suitable to Broadway. Auden was gratified when Britten responded with a sweepingly melodic score that combined the immediate appeal of the Broadway musical with a sometimes exotic sophistication.

Most of Paul Bunyan's exploits that Auden found in published versions of the story have the quality of frontier legends invented in the city, and Auden dispensed with them in a few stanzas of ballad narration. He used the essential elements of the story as the deliberately lightweight dramatic vehicle for the historical vision that he had begun to sketch in a book of pensées, *The Prolific and the Devourer,* which he wrote in the summer of 1939 and abandoned a few weeks before beginning *Paul Bunyan.* The

---

*In his quasi-dramatic radio work *Hadrian's Wall* two years earlier, Auden quoted from memory two stanzas of "Fairest Isle", the only widely known lyric from *King Arthur.* The context of the quotations makes clear that Auden knew the lyric was part of a play about ancient Britain.

machine, he wrote in this book and elsewhere, had destroyed the old so-
cial order based on community, "the association of people to place, regu-
lated by the disciplines of nature"; the machine had also destroyed the
chance relations of neighbors, and "left only personal relations of choice
united by the automobile and telephone". In Europe this change was ob-
scured by a still-vigorous past; in America it was inescapably clear. *Paul
Bunyan* is a mythical version of the vast historical development that ended
with this change. The libretto traces that history from the birth of human-
ity (under the name Paul Bunyan) in the Prologue, through the introduc-
tion of crafts and trades in Act I and the differentiation of society in Act
II, to the advent of urbanism, free movement, and mass publicity in the
final scene. Before he departs, in his apotheosis as a quasi-divine principle
of the inevitable sequence of events that brought about the era when
events are not inevitable but chosen, Paul Bunyan summarizes the
change: "Gone the natural disciplines / And the life of choice begins."

A planned Broadway production by George Balanchine and Lincoln
Kirstein's Ballet Caravan failed to materialize, and *Paul Bunyan*, after
many delays, was first performed in May 1941 by a mostly student cast at
Columbia University. Auden and Britten took obvious pleasure in making
wholesale revisions until the last minute. They added a new lyric for an
unexpectedly accomplished singer and dropped the first-act finale be-
tween the preview performance and the official opening night. The pro-
duction was enthusiastic but rougher than the work deserved, and the
American story showed too many English traces of tone and content to
satisfy most reviewers.*

By the time of the premiere, Auden's sense of America was much more
secure than it was when he finished most of the libretto around the end of
1939. In January 1940 he had begun his long poem *New Year Letter,* which
elaborates on *Paul Bunyan*'s historical vision and adapts metres and ideas
from Bunyan's allegorical meditations, but, unlike the libretto, localizes
them in convincing details of culture and history and has an exact com-
mand over its American material. After the week-long first production
closed, Auden rewrote much of the libretto with a sharper and more lo-

---

*The loggers sound like English schoolboys complaining about their food, and Bunyan
sometimes sounds like an idealized headmaster. This headmasterly manner fits easily with the
operetta's traces of an American inspirational style borrowed from the patriotic cantata *Ballad
for Americans,* written by John Latouche and set by Earl Robinson, and first broadcast, while
Auden was working on his libretto, on 5 November 1939. When Bunyan is asked, in the final
scene, "who are you?" the question is the same one asked repeatedly of the solo bass voice
(Paul Robeson) that, in the cantata, contains multitudes and represents all Americans. How-
ever, when the stage director of *Paul Bunyan* asked for a rousing patriotic conclusion, Auden
replied "I don't want to sound like John Latouche". This and other modern sources for *Paul
Bunyan* are explored in Donald Mitchell's essay in his 1988 edition of the libretto.

cally specific political moral about Communist pressure groups, and reduced much of the whimsy of the earlier text. (The revised version is printed for the first time in the notes to this edition.) But when hopes of further productions fell through, Britten abandoned the work without setting Auden's new lyrics. In 1974, after Auden's death, Britten returned to the version produced in 1941, made small cuts and changes, and authorized a new production. This lightly revised version successfully entered the operatic repertory.

Auden also used American themes in two brief works for film. The first was a scenario he devised with Christopher Isherwood, probably early in 1939, for a film to be titled *The Life of an American,* in which the viewpoint of the camera and the viewpoint of an ordinary American would be the same. What the camera saw would be what the American saw in scenes of his life from childhood to old age. The image on screen would not always be naturalistic; the object of his calf love would appear not as a young girl but as a pillar of blazing light. The other work was Auden's verse commentary for a documentary, *US,* produced during 1967 and 1968 for the American pavilion of an international exposition. The film, shown on multiple screens, consisted of representative scenes of American life. Like *Paul Bunyan,* the commentary moved from a celebration of America's possibilities to a warning against its dangers to itself.*

After finishing the draft of *Paul Bunyan,* Auden wrote two radio plays for the Columbia Broadcasting System. The first was a half-hour monologue broadcast in June 1940 under the title *The Dark Valley,* but probably submitted under the title *The Psychological Reactions of the Woman Who Killed the Goose Who Laid the Golden Egg,* or something similar. This was a greatly expanded version of the cabaret sketch "Alfred" that Auden had written in 1936 as a satire on "certain prominent European figures". The expanded version, which was perhaps the first extended monologue of its kind written for radio, included foreboding lyrics set by Britten. The second radio play, written in collaboration with James Stern and broadcast in May 1941, was *The Rocking Horse Winner,* an adaptation of D. H. Lawrence's story, with the psychology of the doomed visionary boy dramatized by choral voices, again set to Britten's music. These radio plays are among the most concentrated and unconventional works in their medium—which may explain why, when CBS commissioned Auden to do the journeyman task of extracting dialogue from *Pride and Prejudice* for a radio version, Auden's choices had to be replaced by a more professional selection.

---

*Auden's only other film work after his move to America was the commentary for a Canadian documentary, *Runner,* in 1962. Auden provided a modern version of Pindar's praises of athletic prowess.

While America was at war Auden wrote almost nothing for the stage, although nearly all his poetry during those years was dramatic in form. From late 1941 to 1946 he wrote three long poems composed of dramatic monologue or versified debate. The first was his Christmas oratorio *For the Time Being,* which Auden and Britten conceived as a work for solo voices and chorus, to be performed without costumes or staging. The oratorio retold the story of the Nativity through speeches for Gabriel, Mary, Joseph, Simeon, Herod, wise men, shepherds, and various collective and allegorical voices unknown to more traditional versions. When Auden finished it in 1942, Britten, who had since returned to England, found it too long and too literary to set, and he had begun to resent what he took to be Auden's dominant role in their relations. The collaboration between the two, which had begun in 1935, now quietly ended, and Britten decisively broke off their friendship in the early 1950s.

The second of Auden's dramatic poems, *The Sea and the Mirror,* written from 1942 to 1944, took the form of dramatic monologues spoken by the characters of *The Tempest* after the close of the play. The third poem, *The Age of Anxiety,* written from 1944 to 1946, was a "baroque eclogue" set in a wartime New York bar. Many of the speeches of its four quasi-allegorical characters are monologues comparable to those in the two earlier poems, but the characters also engage in dialogue of a kind that a poet might write who hoped to write again for the stage. Auden included these three works in his volumes of collected poems but always allowed them to be performed. For a staged production of *The Age of Anxiety* at Princeton in 1960 he appeared on film reading some of the framing prose narrative.

In contrast to these three ambitious poems, the work Auden did for the stage during the war years was occasional and slight. In 1943 he wrote a brief comic masque for Chester Kallman's friends to perform privately on Kallman's birthday. From 1944 to 1946 he worked intermittently on an adaptation of Webster's *The Duchess of Malfi* commissioned by the Viennese actress Elisabeth Bergner. Bertolt Brecht had also labored over this ill-starred adaptation since 1943, although he worked mostly on his own or, until Auden joined the project, with one of his American translators, H. R. Hays. Auden rearranged some scenes and wrote a few new speeches, partly to introduce an incest motive for the Duchess's murder, but most of his changes were discarded by the director by the time the play started its ignominious run on Broadway in October 1946. Britten, who had revisited America a few months before, supplied some incidental music but did not set any of the verse.

Auden wrote his three long poems of the war years partly as experiments in dramatic poetry. In 1947 he received a letter from Igor Stravinsky who, at Aldous Huxley's suggestion, invited him to write the libretto for *The Rake's Progress*, an opera to be based on Hogarth's series of engravings. Auden now had a chance to apply on stage the lessons he had learned from his dramatic poems. He visited Stravinsky in California where they devised a scenario that supplemented Hogarth's eight scenes with a pastoral opening interrupted by the Devil (in the guise of a servant who tempts the Rake from the garden) and a moralizing epilogue borrowed from *Don Giovanni* for use in a Mozartean score. When Auden returned to New York he asked Kallman to collaborate. The finished libretto displays Kallman's skill at local dramatic effects and his light but sharp-edged exuberance of tone, combined with Auden's structural intelligence and the anachronistic allegory he had perfected in his longer poems. Stravinsky was unsettled when told of the fait accompli of the collaboration but came to value Kallman as a librettist and a friend.

Auden and Kallman worked together on terms more equal than critics and reviewers imagined. Kallman wrote half of *The Rake's Progress* and at least half of most of his later collaborations with Auden. In *The Rake's Progress,* where he worked from an existing scenario, Kallman gave deeper resonance to the plot by replacing the Rake's three sighs, which the scenario specified as the cues for the Devil's entrances, with the three traditional wishes of folktales. He helped replace the Ugly Duchess, whom the Rake marries in the scenario, with the more comic and disturbing figure of the bearded Baba the Turk. Auden wrote that the partners in a successful literary collaboration "must surrender the selves they would be if they were writing separately and become one new author; though, obviously, any given passage must be written by one of them, the censor-critic who decides what will or will not do is this corporate personality." The notes to this volume identify the authorship of different passages and scenes on the basis of Auden's and Kallman's letters and the evidence of manuscript drafts.*

---

*Kallman wrote one libretto of his own, *The Tuscan Players*, for Carlos Chávez, in 1953 (performed as *Panfilo and Lauretta* in 1957). Auden suggested to Kallman that he use a story from Boccaccio and helped him through a difficulty in the second act by contributing six lines (see p. 500). Kallman was a prolific translator of libretti. In addition to the translations he made in collaboration with Auden (see Appendix VII), he translated Bartók's *Bluebeard's Castle* (performed and published in 1952), Stravinsky's *The Nightingale* (translated as *The Chinese Nightingale* in 1953, apparently never performed or published), Rossini's *La Cenerentola (Cinderella)* (published under this double title in 1953), Verdi's *Falstaff* (performed and published in 1954), Monteverdi's *Coronation of Poppea* (performed in 1954), Mozart's *Abduction from the Seraglio* (performed in 1956), Donizetti's *Anne Boleyn* (performed and published in 1959), Vieri Tossati's *The Prize Fight* (published in 1959), Schubert's *The Twin Brothers* (performed in 1962), and probably others. He also translated most of the arias in *Milton Cross' Favorite Arias from the Great Operas* (1958). He reviewed music for the *Michigan Daily* in 1942 and reviewed opera for *Commonweal* in 1945–46. He, Auden, and Noah Greenberg of the New York Pro Musica collaborated on *An Elizabethan Song Book* (1955). Kallman also published three books of poems.

In *The Rake's Progress* the librettists transformed Hogarth's moral episodes into a philosophical and religious fable. Tom Rakewell (the first initial and surname are taken from Hogarth) yields to three temptations that embody three philosophical errors. The first error is a childlike egoism built on Rakewell's trust in the sympathy of Nature's amoral powers. The second is an existential *acte gratuit* (a free, motiveless act of the kind much in philosophical fashion in the 1940s) that leads him to marry Baba the Turk precisely because neither desire nor duty compels him to do so. The third is his belief that the ills of the world can be cured by material change—which he imagines can be brought about by a machine that he is credulous enough to think can turn stones into bread; that is, it offers something for nothing. In the metaphysical dimension of the libretto, each of these errors lets Rakewell believe he can evade the responsibilities of time. He pursues a world where time is malleable (the Devil turns back the clock), irrelevant (Rakewell ignores his promises to his first love), or unreal (the stone-into-bread machine promises instant riches). Anne Trulove, abandoned by Rakewell, uses Kierkegaard's religious vocabulary when she offers Rakewell the opportunity to return; Nick Shadow (the Jungian name adopted by the Devil when he becomes Rakewell's servant) borrows from the same source when he teaches Rakewell to fear repetition, and to believe that no return is possible. Kierkegaard called repetition a recollection that looks forward, and wrote that the true repetition is eternity. Rakewell finally renews his life by a leap of faith in which he calls on Love to return and to assume eternal reign. He first recollects his love for Anne; his recollection is answered when he hears a miraculous repetition of her vow. He can then defeat the Devil by repeating his recollection: in the card game he plays with the Devil for his soul he names the Queen of Hearts a second time after seeing the Devil throw away the card when Rakewell named it the first time. Repetition cannot reverse time: Anne's love can save Rakewell from death, but his acts allow the Devil to condemn him to madness.

This elaborate scheme is drawn finely enough to be unnoticeable in the opera house. But the libretto also conceals a second allegorical pattern, a simpler and more personal allegory about the librettists themselves. Anne Trulove's active and protective faithfulness to Rakewell, her conviction that "it is I who was unworthy" when he marries so unrewarding a substitute as Baba the Turk, corresponds to Auden's sustained emotional loyalty to Kallman after Kallman ended their sexual relationship in 1941. Anne's "vow / Holds ever", even in Rakewell's final madness; Auden, who wore a wedding ring in his first years with Kallman, felt himself bound to Kallman by a marriage vow of the kind that he made the subject of his poem "In Sickness and in Health" in 1940. The personal allegory of the libretto is slightly, and characteristically, complicated by Kallman's author-ship of the scene in which Anne swears her vow.

In 1949, a year after finishing the libretto of *The Rake's Progress,* Auden and Kallman sketched a scenario for an opera to be titled *On the Way.* Three of its main characters represent Berlioz, Mendelssohn, and Rossini. The fourth is their Muse. A prefatory note described the subject of the opera as "the romantic sensibility of the post-Napoleonic period in Europe as exhibited by its artists, in particular by its musicians". The finished work would have been a comedy of disguises and of quick entrances and exits, but the text would evidently have explored the egoism of the romantic artist, a theme Auden had used a few years earlier in Prospero's and Cal-iban's speeches in *The Sea and the Mirror* and one he explored again in the more caustic terms of *Elegy for Young Lovers* ten years later. When Stravinsky showed little interest in the idea, the scenario was abandoned.

Plans for the premiere of *The Rake's Progress* foundered when various opera houses and theatres found it unsuitable (the New York City Center Opera rejected it because of the perverse sexuality implied by Baba the Turk), but a production was finally scheduled at La Fenice, in Venice, in September 1951, with chorus and orchestra from La Scala. Auden and Kallman had the often frustrating task of coaching the chorus in English pronunciation during rehearsals. The weeks of rehearsals were frustrat-ing in other ways, mostly because of inequitable arrangements for the composer and the librettists. Stravinsky lived in luxury while Auden and Kallman were installed first in a brothel, later in scarcely better quarters. Auden and Kallman had allowed Stravinsky's publisher to copyright the text of their libretto; after *The Rake's Progress* they took the trouble to copyright their libretti in their own names. At the premiere, as Auden reported to a friend, the staging (by a director, Carl Ebert, chosen "over our screams" by Stravinsky) was disastrous, but the music was "wonderful beyond belief." Despite the staging, the opera was an overwhelming suc-cess, and further productions followed quickly throughout Europe and America.

Stravinsky almost immediately asked Auden and Kallman to write an-other libretto for him, perhaps in the form of a seventeenth-century masque in celebration of the Goddess of Wisdom. The one-act libretto they gave him in 1952, *Delia, or, A Masque of Night,* celebrated instead the wisdom of the Goddess of Nature. The work is a compressed fairy tale in often deliberately naïve verse, interrupted at its center by a solemn pag-eant of Time, Mutability, Toil, Age, Pain, and Death. The title page de-scribes the masque as "suggested by George Peele's play, *The Old Wives' Tale*" (Auden had borrowed a song from this play when adapting *The Duchess of Malfi*), but, in Auden and Kallman's hands, most of Peele's incidents and characters disappeared.* All that remained was the broad out-line of the plot and a sufficient number of details to let Auden and Kall-man reshape the story into a seventeenth-century version of *The Magic Flute*. Orlando's quest for Delia corresponds to Tamino's quest for Pam-ina, but the contest between the mage Sacrapant who holds Delia captive and the Goddess of Nature (who identifies herself also as Diana, Dame Kind, and the Queen of Night and Elfland) has an entirely different out-come from the contest between Sarastro and the Queen of the Night. In *Delia* the Queen lets the knight defeat the mage—although afterward she rescues and rekindles the mage's light. The marriage of Orlando and Delia is blessed by the energy of Nature from whom wisdom was born, not, as in *The Magic Flute*, by a wisdom that defeats Nature's unruly passion.

Stravinsky's interests had shifted by the time he read *Delia*, and he chose not to set it. He maintained a strong friendship with Auden and Kallman, but never worked with them again on anything longer than a setting of Auden's brief "Elegy for J.F.K." in 1964. *Delia*, meanwhile, out-lived its abandonment. Echoes of its central theme resonate through all of Auden and Kallman's later libretti: their reordered and reinterpreted translation of *The Magic Flute; Elegy for Young Lovers* and *The Bassarids*, both written for Hans Werner Henze; and their libretto based on *Love's Labour's Lost*, written for Nicolas Nabokov. In the introduction to their translation of *The Magic Flute*, in 1956, they described this theme as "the story of a change in relation between the Dionysian principle and the Apollonian, Night and Day, the instinctive and the rational, the uncon-scious and the conscious". Whenever, in their libretti, one principle tri-umphs over the other—as calculation triumphs over love in *Elegy for Young Lovers* or as instinctive violence triumphs over enlightenment in *The Bassarids*—the result is tragedy and death. When the two principles are reconciled—as in the rewritten *Magic Flute* and *Love's Labour's Lost*—the result is comedy and marriage.

In adopting this elemental theme as the focus of the libretti he wrote with Kallman, Auden also altered his ideas about opera. In the essays he wrote on music and opera around the time of *The Rake's Progress* he em-phasized that opera is "about *wilful* feeling", that "it is rooted in the fact that we not only have feelings but insist on having them at whatever cost to ourselves. The moment a person starts to sing, he becomes a mono-maniac". Auden argued at that time, in 1951, that "The quality common to all the great operatic roles . . . is that each of them is a passionate and

*Auden and Kallman took at least one detail from *Friar Bacon and Friar Bungay*, the play that follows *The Old Wives' Tale* in the edition that they probably used, the Everyman's Library volume, *Minor Elizabethan Drama*. A would-be magician in the masque is named Bungay.

wilful state of being". But in his next essay on opera, ten years later, after absorbing the experience of writing *Delia* and his later libretti, he argued instead that "It has, I believe, always been the case that, to be operatic, the principal characters have a certain mythical significance which transcends their historical and social circumstances". Both the earlier and the later essays accurately describe the characters in Auden's libretti, but his emphasis has shifted from energy to archetype. His new interest in myth as an organizing principle in opera was partly the result of his recognition of the mythically dense operas of Strauss and Hofmannsthal as potential models for his own.

This shift in emphasis allowed Auden and Kallman to create more precise characterizations in their later libretti than in their earlier ones. Tom Rakewell and Anne Trulove are defined largely by the simple intensity of their changing feelings, an intensity too strong to let any coherent details of personality show through. Gregor Mittenhofer in *Elegy for Young Lovers* and Pentheus in *The Bassarids* are conceived securely as unchanging archetypes (the romantic artist-genius and the enlightened Apollonian ruler), so securely that their characterizations can, without any loss to their intensity of feeling, be refined by means of idiosyncratic social and psychological details.

In 1955, when the National Broadcasting Company commissioned them to translate *The Magic Flute* for television, Auden and Kallman interpreted their brief freely enough to let them reshape Schikaneder's confused Masonic symbols into a clear archetypal pattern. They had used the triumph of the female principle of Nature at the end of *Delia* as an implicit correction to the treatment of the same principle in *The Magic Flute*. Now, in their translation, they explicitly corrected the original by adding a soliloquy for Sarastro in which he acknowledges that his defeat of the Queen of the Night must bring about his own death as well. Sarastro does not enjoy his triumph; his ancient enmity toward the Queen must yield to the concord of Tamino and Pamina's marriage. Auden and Kallman also replaced or expanded much of the spoken dialogue (and characterized the Second Priest as a reformed drunk), and they drastically rearranged the second act to bring logic to the plot. Traditionalists complained about the disruption of Mozart's key-sequences, but the new version produced enough interest to stimulate plans (which later fell through) for a German production that would use a retranslation of Auden and Kallman's English version. The broadcast production in January 1956 cut many of the additional passages, but Auden and Kallman were so pleased with the costumes and staging by Rouben Ter-Arutunian that they used his drawings as illustrations when they published their version in book form a few months later. The book included three poems written as prologue, "metalogue", and epilogue to the opera. The metalogue, written as a bicentennial celebration of Mozart's birth, lamented on his behalf, and on Auden's, the pestilence of operatic productions in which the words and music are forced to endure the "small vanities" of the stage director ("who with ingenious wit / Places the wretched singers in the pit / While dancers mime their roles") and the designer ("Who sets the whole thing on an ocean liner, / The girls in shorts, the men in yachting caps"). *The Magic Flute* was the only original or translated libretto that Auden published through the ordinary book trade. His other libretti either remained unpublished in his lifetime or appeared only in the form of pamphlets sold mostly in the opera-house lobby.*

Auden's next work for performance, which he wrote in 1957 without Kallman's collaboration, was a verse narrative for the New York Pro Musica's production of the thirteenth-century liturgical drama *The Play of Daniel.* The alliterative metre that Auden had last used in *The Age of Anxiety* provided a suitably archaic tone. Auden had recited Elizabethan poetry in earlier programs of the New York Pro Musica, and when the production of *The Play of Daniel* came to Oxford, during a European tour two years after the first performance in January 1958, he took the role of the monk who read the verse narrative from the pulpit.†

Auden and Kallman had since 1948 summered in Ischia, where in 1953 they met Hans Werner Henze. In 1957 Henze asked them to write a libretto for a "chamber" opera with a small orchestra and no chorus. In working with Henze they followed the model of Hofmannsthal's relations with Strauss: "the choice of dramatic subject and its style of treatment was to be the librettist's business, not the composer's who must wait patiently till the librettist finds a subject which excites his imagination". For some time, Auden and Kallman's attempts to find a subject went nowhere—until, as Auden wrote, "we had our mythical figure". In *Elegy for Young Lovers,* written in 1959 and 1960 (its Austrian settings and characters, like its Austrian stylistic master Hofmannsthal, reflect Auden and Kallman's move to a summer house in Kirchstetten in 1958), Gregor Mittenhofer embodies the romantic myth of the artist-genius who stands above ordinary moral standards and obligations. According to the myth, "if it should prove necessary in order to create a masterpiece, the artist must be prepared ruthlessly to sacrifice his own life and happiness and those of

---

*NBC commissioned a second translation, of *Don Giovanni,* in 1957; it was published in G. Schirmer's series of pamphlet libretti and reprinted in a collection of Mozart libretti compiled from these pamphlets, but Auden had nothing to do with this reprinting in book form.

†In his only other appearance onstage in his own work, in a Swarthmore College production of his and Christopher Isherwood's play *The Ascent of F 6* in 1945, he also played the part of a monk—the cowled silent figure who carries a visionary crystal.

others". Mittenhofer (whom the librettists first named Hinterhofer, after their Austrian electrician) is a great artist who is also a monster, one who can knowingly bring about the death of the young lovers for the sake of the elegy he will write about them. His lesser monstrosities include hatred of his poetic rivals and childish greed—qualities Auden and Kallman introduced as deliberate shocks to the idealism about artists that is encouraged by the same romantic myth that gave rise to Mittenhofer. The theme combines the egoism of the artist with Auden's earlier theme in *The Ascent of F 6,* where the climber hero sacrifices himself and his friends to his neurotic wish for power. In both play and libretto, the tragic deaths occur in a blizzard on a mountain, and are followed in the final scene by a conscious misinterpretation of those deaths in an address to the public.

The libretto links its romantic myth with a more ancient one that resonates again in *The Bassarids.* The lovers, as Mittenhofer learns from the madwoman's visions that he uses as material for his poem, are "'sacrificed' to the old gods"—whose unknowing messenger is the Alpine guide who, alone among the characters, always speaks rather than sings. The theme of the archaic gods is sketched lightly in the libretto, so lightly that Kallman felt obliged to identify it to Henze. An ancient dramatic model that underlies the realistic early-twentieth-century texture of the dialogue is sketched even more lightly. "The management of the action will owe something to the Noh plays", Auden told a friend; Kallman told Henze that the presence of the same character on stage at the end of one act and the start of the next "gives the opera a visual 'flow' which I feel intrinsic to our adaptation of the Noh technique".

In his character and historical setting Mittenhofer recalls Stefan George; in his exploitation of a woman's visions as matter for his poetry, and his use of injections to keep himself vigorous, he resembles W. B. Yeats. But as Auden noted in a brief essay printed with the libretto, "the only things about him which were suggested to us by historical incidents were drawn from the life of a poet—no matter whom—who wrote in English". That poet was Auden. The misreading of "poet" for "port" in one of Mittenhofer's manuscripts repeats Isherwood's misreading of Auden's poem "Journey to Iceland" (mentioned in Auden and MacNeice's *Letters from Iceland,* chapter 2). Other incidents in the libretto serve as vehicles for Auden's characteristically oblique and severe self-rebuke. The relation between Mittenhofer and his patroness Carolina echoes the relation between Auden and the heiress Caroline Newton, who gave him money, nominally in exchange for manuscripts, in the early 1940s. (Her possessiveness and his revulsion against accepting her patronage eventually led to a break.) The triangle of Mittenhofer, his young mistress, and his mistress's new lover echoes the triangle of Auden, Kallman, and Kallman's temporary lover at the time when Kallman broke off sexual relations with Auden. Mittenhofer's manipulation of his mistress's emotions is a more pointed gloss on Anne Trulove's bitter statement that it was she who was unworthy in her relation to Tom Rakewell. The temptations to which Mittenhofer yields in the libretto are the same temptations to power and authority that Auden had confronted in his life. Yet Auden believed himself subject to judgement even for having opened himself to temptations that he finally refused.

Kallman supervised the rehearsals of the premiere of *Elegy for Young Lovers* at the Schwetzingen Festival in May 1961. He and Auden felt the opera was largely successful, except for the disastrous set. During rehearsals for a Glyndebourne production the same year (a production that Auden said "could have been worse"), Auden suggested to Henze that he compose an explicitly mythical grand opera based on *The Bacchae*. Henze read the play the next year, and Auden and Kallman wrote the libretto of *The Bassarids* in 1963. (The title refers to both male and female followers of Dionysus, in contrast to the exclusively female bacchants in Euripides.) In adapting the myth Auden and Kallman elaborated the psychology of the existing characters, added new ones, and gave all of them costumes taken from the historical eras that best represented their separate points of view. Tiresias, who adjusts his religion to policy and fashion, appears as an Anglican archdeacon; Dionysus makes his apotheosis in the style of Beau Brummel; Agave adopts the skeptical and sensual style of the French Second Empire. In some of these details, and in many other ways, the libretto draws on E. R. Dodds's commentary to his Oxford edition of the play.

The Bassarids gives special emphasis to Euripides' portrayal of the arbitrary injustice of the gods, and the final confrontation of Cadmus and Agave with Dionysus, with the great laments that follow, is the summit of Auden's art as a librettist. In one of her last speeches Agave warns the Olympians that they too must follow Uranus and Chronos to destruction. For a post-classical audience her speech points toward a different relation between divinity and humanity than the one assumed in Euripides' myth. In conversation Auden spoke of *The Bacchae* as *The Magic Flute* without Christianity, and he and Kallman appended to their version of the play an epigraph from Gottfried Benn: "The myth lied".

Despite its changes in emphasis, the action of *The Bassarids* conforms closely to the action of *The Bacchae*, with one striking innovation. Auden and Kallman introduced at the center of the libretto a play-within-a-play that dramatizes Pentheus's sexual fantasies about the bacchants. Pentheus is a philosophical ascetic who misjudges the reality and power of Dionysus because he has repressed his own sexuality. His repression causes his fantasies to take the superficial aestheticized form of a rhymed charade of the Judgement of Calliope, performed in eighteenth-century dress, with Roman names substituted for the Greek equivalents. When Auden lectured about his libretti in 1967 he said that this comic intermezzo derived from the custom in the early days of opera "to sandwich a one-act opera buffa between the two acts of an opera seria".* The contrast between eighteenth-century and archaic styles owed something to the contrast between the eighteenth-century prologue and archaic main action of Strauss's *Ariadne auf Naxos*. But a more exact model for the intermezzo was the dream-play that Auden added to the center of his first poetic drama, *Paid on Both Sides*, when he rewrote it a few months after finishing the first draft in 1928. *Paid on Both Sides*, like *The Bassarids*, is an archaic tragedy of revenge, written for actors and chorus. John Nower's dream at the center of the play was written in a phantasmagorical style entirely different from the stark, sagalike action around it. Pentheus's vision is written as a rococo fantasy entirely different from the Attic solemnity in which it is framed. Both John Nower and Pentheus are deceived by their visions, and wake unprepared for the lethal atavistic violence that follows. Like *Elegy for Young Lovers*, with its echoes of *The Ascent of F 6*, *The Bassarids* returns to the theme and structure of one of Auden's poetic plays from the early part of his career. A few months before the first performance of *The Bassarids* Auden told an interviewer that his early plays "seem to me now to be libretti *manqués*".† After the premiere at the Salzburg Festival in August 1966 he was even more satisfied with the result than he was after *The Rake's Progress*. He told a friend that Henze had, "without question, written a masterpiece", and that everything about the production was "perfect, except for the stage-direction, which was a mess". He was especially impressed by the sets and costumes designed by Filippo Sanjust, who became a close friend and illustrated Auden's *Academic Graffiti* in 1971.‡

After finishing *The Bassarids* Auden made one last attempt to work in the conventional theatre. In 1963 he wrote some lyrics intended for the musical version of Dale Wasserman's play *Man of La Mancha*. When these lyrics failed to provide the kind of uplift Wasserman preferred, the collaboration ended, and the play was produced with lyrics by another hand. A

---

*Auden's vocabulary is anachronistic but his history is correct. In the seventeenth and eighteenth centuries, the two parts of a comic intermezzo were often performed after the first and second acts of a serious opera.

†Auden was not the first to sense this. In "Some Notes on Auden's Early Poetry" (*New Verse*, November 1937), Isherwood wrote of their collaborations: "If Auden had his way, he would turn every play into a cross between grand opera and high mass."

‡*The Magic Flute* and *Academic Graffiti* were Auden's only books that included drawings, in each case provided by the designer of one of his libretti.

similar project had come to nothing after Isherwood and Auden exchanged intermittent letters during 1960 and 1961 about the possibility that they and Kallman might collaborate on a musical version of Isherwood's Berlin stories. Other writers later devised the musical *Cabaret* by adapting an existing stage play based on these stories.

The Bassarids portrayed the triumph of instinctual passion over rational thought in a mood of tragedy. Not long after finishing it, Auden began to contemplate an opera that would portray the same triumph in a mood of comedy fulfilled in reconciliation. Around 1964 he began to remark to friends that *Love's Labour's Lost* was the only one of Shakespeare's plays that could be turned into a libretto written in English. Henze (who in 1966 asked Auden and Kallman for an unstaged work for solo and chorus, and in 1967 received and set "Moralities", fables after Aesop by Auden alone) was now turning toward a Marxist aesthetic of commitment that made any further operatic collaboration with Auden and Kallman impossible. Auden's idea found no takers until 1969, when Lincoln Kirstein urged Nicolas Nabokov, who had known Auden for many years, to visit Auden and propose a collaboration. Auden and Kallman's libretto, written later that year, follows the central action of the play and stitches Shakespearean phrases into its dialogue and arias. But the libretto drastically simplifies the plot and texture of the play, omits characters and incidents, and treats its most formal and conventional elements in mythical and archetypal terms. Only the opening and closing arias are taken from Shakespeare without change. Moth becomes a cross between Cupid and Puck. The men's renunciation of love, and the women's power to confound that renunciation, are set within the recurring cycle of the seasons. The Deutsche Oper agreed to produce the premiere in February 1973 but moved the first performance to Brussels to avoid presenting a Berlin premiere in a language other than German. Auden and Kallman, who had usually attended rehearsals of their earlier libretti, arrived in Brussels only a few days before the performance. Auden wrote to a friend: "I liked the music very much, the singers were good, but the stage-direction sheer hell". Nabokov's pastiches of familiar musical styles received a polite but unenthusiastic reception, and the opera was not heard again after a few performances in Berlin later that year. The artifice of the libretto remains appealing on the page.

A few weeks before the premiere of *Love's Labour's Lost* Auden accepted a commission from John Gardner to write the libretto for an anti-masque to be interpolated in a performance of John Shirley's seventeenth-century masque *Cupid and Death*. Working in collaboration with Kallman, he wrote *The Entertainment of the Senses*, in which the five senses are represented by singers dressed as apes; Shirley had called for two real apes in the scene that the anti-masque was designed to replace. Each ape described the modern and unnatural pleasures now available to the senses, and ended its monologue with a reminder that even these synthetic pleasures end at death. The archetypal contest between instinct and reason recurred in the libretto, but as satire rather than as tragedy or comedy. *The Entertainment of the Senses* was reason's ironic celebration of its impending defeat by the irrational forces of instinct. On 26 September 1973 Auden mailed the libretto to the composer. He died three days later.

REFERENCES

Page xv

the last refuge "The World of Opera", in *Secondary Worlds* (1968), p. 116.

cannot appear in public "A Public Art", *Opera,* January 1961, pp. 13–14.

Page xvi

My chief luxury Letter to A. E. Dodds, 26 February 1940 (Bodleian Library).

seems to me the greatest "Mimesis and Allegory", *English Institute Annual, 1940,* p. 5.

as a period of sustained Introduction to *The Portable Greek Reader* (1948), p. 7.

Page xvii

can not carry on "Opera Addict", *Vogue,* July 1948, p. 65.

Airy Spirits appear *King Arthur,* Act III.

Page xviii

the association of people Letter to E. R. Dodds, 16 January 1940 (Bodleian Library).

Page xxi

must surrender the selves "Translating Opera Libretti", in *The Dyer's Hand* (1962), p. 483. The essay is described as "Written in collaboration with Chester Kallman", but the paragraph from which this passage is quoted is written in the first-person singular by Auden.

Page xxiii

over our screams Letter to Lincoln Kirstein, 2 September 1951.

Page xxiv

about wilful *feeling* "Opera Addict", p. 65.

it is rooted "Some Reflections on Opera as a Medium", *Tempo,* Summer 1951, p. 7; also, without the sentence beginning "The moment a person", in "Some Reflections on Music and Opera", *Partisan Review,* January–February 1952, p. 14, and *The Dyer's Hand* (1962), p. 470.

The quality common   "Some Reflections on Opera as a Medium", p. 8; "Some Reflections on Music and Opera", p. 15; *The Dyer's Hand,* p. 470.

Page xxv

It has, I believe   "A Public Art", p. 14.

Page xxvi

the choice of dramatic   "A Marriage of True Minds", *Times Literary Supplement,* 10 November 1961, p. 797 (unsigned); quoted here from the revised, signed version in *The Mid-Century,* March 1962, p. 4; slightly revised again in Auden's *Forewords and Afterwords* (1973), p. 347.

We had our mythical   "The World of Opera", p. 102.

if it should prove   "The World of Opera", p. 103.

Page xxvii

"sacrificed" to the old gods   Letter from Kallman to Henze, 13 January 1960 (Stiftung Paul Sacher).

The management of   Letter to Lincoln Kirstein, 13 October 1959.

gives the opera   Letter from Kallman to Henze, 13 January 1960.

Page xxviii

could have been worse   Letter to Elizabeth Mayer, 8 August 1961 (Berg Collection).

Page xxix

to sandwich a one-act   "The World of Opera", p. 113.

seem to me now   BBC radio interview with Peter Porter, recorded 27 August 1965, broadcast 29 April 1966 (BBC Written Archives Centre).

without question   Letter to Lincoln Kirstein, 19 August 1966.

Page xxx

I liked the music   Letter to Lincoln Kirstein, 22 March 1973.

THIS volume contains all of Auden's original dramatic writings from 1939 to 1973. It also contains his and Kallman's English version of *The Magic Flute,* which is as much a new work as a translation of an old one and, uniquely among Auden's libretti, was issued in book form by the publishers of his poems and prose. The works in this volume were written for staged performance or for broadcast or film; with the exception of *The Magic Flute,* the only work included here that Auden published in one of his books is the brief narrative for the film *Runner.* In contrast, Auden collected in book form all the works that he wrote for unstaged or minimally staged musical performance, and those works will appear in the volumes of Auden's poems in this complete edition. Those unstaged works include "Song for St Cecilia's Day", the Christmas oratorio *For the Time Being,* and the separate poems in the sequence *Our Hunting Fathers,* all set, or written to be set, by Benjamin Britten; "Moralities", set by Hans Werner Henze; "The Twelve", set by William Walton; "United Nations Hymn", set by Pablo Casals; and "The Ballad of Barnaby", written to be set by the students of the Wykeham Rise School under the supervision of Charles Turner. A comparable work for performance that Auden collected in book form was "A Reminder", spoken as a prologue to the 1968 Son et Lumière at Christ Church, Oxford.

In all the volumes of this collected edition Auden's works are presented in the versions that he prepared and revised around the time of their publication. Works that he published in books appear here in the versions that he prepared for publication or that he revised shortly thereafter; revisions that he made many years later for his retrospective collected editions appear in the notes.* Works that Auden abandoned before book publication, or that he never considered for inclusion in a book, appear in their last revised versions. For works with complex or unusual publishing histories, these same general principles have determined the choice of text. An essay, for example, that Auden first published in book form thirty years after he printed it in a magazine appears in this edition in the earlier version, and the later revisions are listed in the notes.

*This volume notes the revisions Auden made in different versions of each of the libretti as a whole and in different versions of separate scenes. When he excerpted some of the lyrics from these libretti for inclusion in his later volumes of collected and selected poems, he sometimes made minor revisions in the texts. These later printings are mentioned in the notes to this volume, but the details of any revisions belong more properly in the forthcoming edition of Auden's complete poems.

All the libretti in this volume present slightly different editorial problems and require slightly different editorial solutions. Most of the libretti that appeared in print appeared only in versions that were heavily revised or cut by the composer. Auden wrote in 1951 that the verses written by a librettist "are really a private letter to the composer" ("Some Reflections on Opera as a Medium", *Tempo*, Summer 1951, p. 9). The main texts in this volume present Auden's libretti in the texts that he gave to the composer, with the revisions that he and Kallman gave to the composer after the initial presentation. These versions include the full stage directions that often appeared in truncated form in the printed editions. Cuts and changes made by the composer are mentioned briefly in the notes, as are abridgements made by the librettists in response to a composer's request for a shorter text. Auden wrote to Henze in 1964, "Whatever cuts are made in the setting—and, of course, we have always known that there would have to be many—we want our text to be *printed* as is" (see p. 682). The notes also include a history of the composition, publication, and production of each libretto; a detailed description of the sources of the text, and the variants in all earlier editions; and the texts of letters and other material that figured in the composition of the libretti.

The text of *Paul Bunyan* in this edition is based on Auden's early manuscripts and typescripts, and includes much material dropped during rehearsals in 1941. It also restores Auden's preferred sequence of the final speeches, which is superior in dramatic terms to the sequence Britten set. The revised version that Auden prepared after the 1941 production appears in the notes. The only previously available text, first published in 1976, was based on the shortened and modified version produced in 1941 and the cuts and changes Britten made after Auden's death. Similarly, the text of *The Rake's Progress* in this edition is based on the typescripts that Auden gave Stravinsky, with subsequent revisions. These typescripts contain extensive headings and stage directions dropped by Stravinsky's publishers when they published the libretto as a pamphlet. Auden and Kallman prepared their version of *The Magic Flute* for publication, and the published text is reproduced in this edition. No typescript survives for *Elegy for Young Lovers*, which is printed in this edition on the basis of the printed libretto, but the text of *The Bassarids* restores the page layout, stage directions, and full dialogue of the typescript that Auden and Kallman hoped to see printed "as is". *Love's Labour's Lost* is printed in full for the first time from the text of the typescript.

I have made no attempt to impose a rigorous consistency on Auden's spelling and punctuation, or to bring his usage into conformity with Kallman's. Kallman, who was more careful than Auden was about such matters, apparently prepared for the typist or printer the manuscripts of his collaborations with Auden, so these works appear more polished on the page than do the works Auden wrote alone.

Although Auden paid little or no attention to spelling, there seems to be no compelling reason to correct his inconsistencies or to tidy up nonstandard usages such as "alright". Auden's mix of British and American spellings has been retained in work he wrote alone, and the largely American style of the typescripts (generally prepared by Kallman) has been retained in works he wrote in collaboration. I have restored from the typescripts some spellings that earlier printers or publishers had treated as errors, but that are not inconsistent with common practice.

Some typescripts of *Delia* (and part of a lost typescript of *Elegy for Young Lovers*) used red ribbon to indicate spoken dialogue. When Henze asked whether to use a typographic means of indicating a similar distinction in *Elegy for Young Lovers*, Kallman replied:

> I don't really think it's necessary or desirable. On a small page, different kinds of print look fussy and are distracting to the reader. Also, I always think that an element of surprise should be added by not indicating divisions to the reader that will be revealed to him when he hears the work. [See p. 670]

Although the use of red ribbon for spoken passages was, in a very few typescripts, an element of the librettists' "private letter to the composer", its omission here reflects Kallman's preference. In many of the libretti the stage directions indicate spoken dialogue, and the notes indicate the spoken text when the main text does not make the distinction clear.

Except for simple misspellings or slips of the pen, Auden's errors in transcribing or remembering passages quoted from other authors are left uncorrected in the main text of this edition, as the errors may be regarded as minor acts of authorship. In passages quoted in the notes, however, square brackets indicate the readings that Auden mistranscribed.

When Auden and his collaborators divided a dramatic work into both acts and scenes he occasionally included in his manuscripts and typescripts a separate part-title page for each act, bearing only a heading in the form "Act One". These separate titles for each act are omitted in this edition.

Some brief essays on their operas by Auden and Kallman survive only in the form of translations made by other hands for publication in Italian and German. These essays appear in this edition in their translated form, but retranslations into English are supplied in the notes.

The music publishers who first printed some of these libretti imposed their various house styles on each. Speech headings, stage directions, and other design elements in this volume have been set in the same style used for Auden's *Plays* in this collected edition. This style differs from that of surviving typescripts in only one notable way: Kallman's typescripts of the later libretti do not use square brackets around stage directions. Auden, however, tended to use square brackets around handwritten stage directions, and parentheses around typed ones, and this edition's use of square brackets reflects his practice. One convention has been added: where an open square (□) appears at the foot of a page, it indicates a break between stanzas or verse paragraphs that might not otherwise be evident.

LIBRETTI

Paul Bunyan

An Operetta in Two Acts

LIBRETTO BY W. H. AUDEN
MUSIC BY
BENJAMIN BRITTEN

[1939–1941]

CAST

PAUL BUNYAN   *A Voice*

Soloists

THREE WILD GEESE (Prologue)	*High Soprano and*
doubling	*two Mezzo-sopranos*
FIDO, a dog	*High Soprano*
MOPPET, a cat	*Mezzo-soprano*
POPPET, a cat	*Mezzo-soprano*
TINY, daughter of PAUL BUNYAN	*Soprano*
HEL HELSON, foreman	*Bass*
JOHNNY INKSLINGER, bookkeeper	*Tenor*
HOT BISCUIT SLIM, a good cook	*Tenor*
NARRATORS	*Contralto and Baritone*

Ensembles

FOUR YOUNG TREES	*Soprano, Soprano, Tenor, Tenor*
THE DEFEATED (Blues)	*Alto, Tenor, Bass, Bass*
LAME SHADOWS AND ANIMAS	*Soprano, Soprano, Tenor, Tenor*
TWO VOICES	*Soprano and Alto*

Characters from Chorus

FOUR LUMBERJACKS	*Tenor, Tenor, Bass, Bass*
FOUR SWEDES	*Tenor, Tenor, Bass, Bass*
WESTERN UNION BOY	*Tenor*
SAM SHARKEY	*Tenor*
AND ⎬ two bad cooks	*and*
BEN BENNY	*Bass*
JOHN SHEARS, a farmer	*Bass*
FOUR CRONIES OF HEL HELSON	*Bass, Bass, Bass, Bass*

Prologue

SEMI-CHORUS I. Since the birth
Of the earth
Time has gone
On and on:
Rivers saunter,
Rivers run,
Till they enter
The enormous level sea
Where they prefer to be.

SEMI-CHORUS II. But the sun
Is too hot
And will not
Let alone
Waves glad-handed
Lazy crowd,
Educates them
Till they change into a cloud,
But can't control them long.

SEMI-CHORUS I. For the will
Just to fall
Is too strong
In them all;
Revolution
Turns to rain
Whence more solid
Sensible earth-creatures gain:
In falling thcy scrve life.

CHORUS. Here are we
Flower and tree,
Green, alive,
Glad to be,
And our proper
Places know:
Winds and waters
Travel; we remain and grow;
We like life to be slow.

3 Young Trees. No. No. No.
Chorus. O.
Young Tree. We do *Not* want life to be slow.
1st Old Tree.   Reds.
2nd Old Tree. It's only a phase.
Young Tree. We're *bored* with standing still,
    We're *bored* with the whole idea of bigness.
    We want to go places and see things.
1st Old Tree. We never heard such nonsense.
2nd Old Tree. He's sick.

[*Enter two* Wild Geese.]

Duet of Geese.   O how terrible to be
                  As old-fashioned as a tree:
                  A dull stick that won't go out;
                  What on earth do they talk about?
                      An unexpressive
                      An unprogressive
                  Unsophisticated lout.
                  How can pines or grass or sage
                  Understand the Modern Age?

[*Enter* 3rd Wild Goose.]

Trio.   Tell us. What's the latest news,
                  What do you think, my dear, * —
                  — * — * — * —
                  — * — * — * —
                      — * — *
                      That's the most
                  Wonderful thing I've ever heard,
                  Shall we tell them? — * But
                  You ought to — * Shall I? — *

1st Goose. You are all going to leave here.
Young Tree. What.
Old Tree.   It's a lie.
Young Tree.   Hurrah.
Old Tree.   Don't listen.
Young Tree.   How?
1st Goose. Far away from here
    A mission is going to find a performer.
Old Tree. What mission?

1ST GOOSE.   To bring you into another life.
YOUNG TREE. What kind of performer?
1ST GOOSE.   A man.
YOUNG TREE. What is a man?
1ST GOOSE.   A man is a form of life
    That dreams in order to act
    And acts in order to dream
    And has a name of his own.
ALL TREES.   What is that name?
1ST GOOSE. Paul Bunyan.
OLD TREE.   How silly.
YOUNG TREE. When are we to see him?
1ST GOOSE. He will be born at the next Blue Moon.
OLD TREE. She's lying. It isn't true,
    O I'm so frightened.
OLD TREE.   Don't worry
    There won't be a Blue Moon in our lifetime.
OLD TREE. Don't say that. It's unlucky.

                             [The Moon begins to turn Blue.]

YOUNG TREE. Look at the moon. It's turning blue.
OLD TREE. I don't believe it.

TRIO OF GEESE.
      It isn't very often the Conservatives are wrong,
      To-morrow normally is only yesterday again,
      Society is right in saying nine times out of ten
      Respectability's enough to carry one along.

         But once in a while the odd thing happens,
            Once in a while the dream comes true,
         And the whole pattern of life is altered,
            Once in a while the Moon turns Blue.

TRIO OF YOUNG TREES.
      I want to be a ship's mast sailing on the sea,
      I want to be a roof with a house under me,
      I've always longed for edges—I'd love to be square—
      How swell to be a dado—Swell to be a chair.

CHORUS OF OLD TREES.
      We can't pretend we like it, that it's what we'd choose,
      But what's the point of fussing when one can't refuse

And nothing is as bad as one thinks it will be,
The children look so happy—Well, well, we shall see.

TRIO OF GEESE.

Attempts at revolution are a failure as a rule,
The eccentric or unusual isn't likely to succeed,
Successful new experiments are very rare indeed,
And nearly every rebel is a silly little fool.

TUTTI CHORUS.

But once in a while the odd thing happens,
Once in a while the dream comes true,
And the whole pattern of life is altered,
Once in a while the Moon turns Blue.

CURTAIN

Interlude

The cold wind blew through the crooked thorn
Up in the North a boy was born.

His hair was black, his eyes were blue,
His mouth turned up at the corners too.

A fairy stood beside his bed;
"You shall never, never grow old", she said,

"Paul Bunyan is to be your name";
Then she departed whence she came.

You must believe me when I say,
He grew six inches every day.

You must believe me when I speak,
He gained 346 pounds every week.

He grew so fast, by the time he was eight,
He was as tall as the Empire State.

The length of his stride's a historical fact;
3.7 miles to be exact.

Years later a famous professor swore
His footprints were those of a dinosaur.

When he ordered a jacket, the New England mills
For months had no more unemployment ills.

When he wanted a snapshot to send to his friends,
They found they had to use a telephoto lens.

But let me tell you in advance,
His dreams were of greater significance.

His favourite dream was of felling trees,
A fancy which grew by swift degrees.

One night he dreamt he was to be
The greatest logger in history.

He woke to feel something stroking his brow,
And found it was the tongue of an enormous cow,

From horn to horn or from lug to lug,
Was forty-seven axe-heads and a baccy plug.

But what would have most bewildered you
Was the colour of her hide which was bright bright blue.

But Bunyan wasn't surprised at all;
Said, "I'll call you Babe, you call me Paul".

He pointed to a meadow, said, "Take a bite
For you're leaving with me for the South to-night".

Over the mountains, across the streams
They went to find Paul Bunyan's dreams.

The bear and the beaver waved a paw,
The magpie chattered, the squirrel swore.

The trappers ran out from their lonely huts
Scratching their heads with their rifle-butts.

For a year and a day they travelled fast
"This is the place", Paul said at last.

The forest stretched for miles around,
The sound of their breathing was the only sound.

Paul picked a pine-tree and scratched his shins,
Said, "This is where our work begins.

But first of all I need some men."
Now it's time for the curtain to rise again.

Act I Scene 1

[*A clearing in the forest. Music background.*]

VOICE OF PAUL BUNYAN *off* [*quiet and meditative*]. It is a Spring morning
   without benefit of young persons.
   It is a sky that has never registered weeping or rebellion.
   It is a forest full of innocent beasts. There are none who blush at
      the memory of an ancient folly, none who hide beneath dyed
      fabrics a malicious heart.
   It is America but not yet.
   Wanted. Disturbers of public order, men without foresight or fear.
   Wanted. Energetic madmen. Those who have thought themselves a
      body large enough to devour their dreams.
   Wanted. The lost. Those indestructibles whom defeat can never
      change. Poets of the bottle, clergymen of a ridiculous gospel,
      actors who should have been engineers, and lawyers who
      should have been sea-captains, saints of circumstance,
      desperados, unsuccessful wanderers, all who can hear the
      invitation of the earth. America, youngest of her daughters,
      awaits the barbarians of marriage.

[LUMBERJACKS' *song. Starting off.*]

LUMBERJACKS' SONG

CHORUS.   Timber-rrr. Down the Line. Timber-rrr.

1ST LUMBERJACK.
   My birthplace was in Sweden, it's a very long way off
   My appetite was hearty but I couldn't get enough;
   When suddenly I heard a roar across the wide blue sea,
   "I'll give you steak and onions if you'll come and work for me".

CHORUS.   We rise at the dawn of day
            We are handsome and free and gay
                  We're lumberjacks,
                  With saw and axe
            Who are melting the forests away.

2ND LUMBERJACK.
   In France I wooed a maiden with an alabaster skin
   But she left me for a fancy chap who played the violin;
   When just about to drown myself a voice came from the sky,
   "There's no one like a shanty boy to catch a maiden's eye".

CHORUS.   We rise at the dawn *etc.*

3RD LUMBERJACK.

>   O long ago in Germany when sitting at my ease,
>   There came a knocking at the door and it was the police
>   I tiptoed down the backstairs and a voice to me did say
>   "There's freedom in the forests out in North America".

CHORUS.   We rise at the dawn *etc.*

4TH LUMBERJACK.

>   In Piccadilly Circus I stood waiting for a bus
>   I thought I heard the pigeons say "Please run away with us;
>   To a land of opportunity with work and food for all
>   Especially for shanty-boys in Winter and in Fall".

CHORUS.   We rise at the dawn *etc.*

PAUL BUNYAN. Welcome and sit down: we have no time to waste.
>   The trees are waiting for the axe and we must all make haste
>   So who shall be the foreman to set in hand the work
>   To organise the logging and see men do not shirk.

QUARTET OF SWEDES

4 SWEDES. I. I. I. I.

CHORUS. Why?

4 SWEDES. Swedish born and Swedish bred
>   Strong in the arm and dull in the head.
>   Who can ever kill a Swede
>   His skull is very thick indeed
>   But once you get an idea in
>   You'll never get it out again.

PAUL BUNYAN. What are your names?

4 SWEDES. Cross Crosshaulson.
>   Jen Jenson.
>   Pete Peterson.
>   Andy Anderson.

PAUL BUNYAN.
>   In your opinion which of you, which one would be the best
>   To be the leader of the few and govern all the rest?

4 SWEDES [*fighting*]. I.
>   Why?
>   Who?

You?
O.
No.
Me.
He?
Yah.
Bah.

PAUL BUNYAN. None of you, it seems will do
    We must find another.
CHORUS.   Yes, but who?

                               [*Enter a* WESTERN UNION BOY.]

WESTERN UNION BOY.
                A telegram, a telegram,
                  A telegram from oversea
                Paul Bunyan is the name
                  Of the addressee.   [*Exit across stage.*]

CHORUS. Bad News? Good News? Tell us what you're reading.
PAUL BUNYAN. I have a message that will please you from the King of
      Sweden.
  [*Reads.*] Dear Paul
    I hear you are looking for a head-foreman, so I'm sending
    you Hel Helson. He is the finest logger in my kingdom. He
    doesn't talk much. Wishing you every success.
                            Yours sincerely
                            Nel Nelson. King.

             [*Enter while he is reading* HEL HELSON.]

PAUL BUNYAN. Are you Hel Helson?
HEL HELSON. Aye tank so.
PAUL BUNYAN. Do you know all about logging?
HEL HELSON. Aye tank so.
PAUL BUNYAN. Are you prepared to be my head-foreman?
HEL HELSON. Aye tank so.
PAUL BUNYAN. Then I think so too.
    Now for one to cook and bake
    Flapjacks, cookies, fish, or steak.

             [*Enter* SAM SHARKEY *and* BEN BENNY.]

SAM SHARKEY. Sam Sharkey at your service. Sam for Soups.
BEN BENNY. Ben Benny at your service. Ben for Beans.

Duet

SAM. Soups feed you.
BEN.   Beans
     For Vitamins.
SAM. Soups satisfy
     Soups gratify.
BEN. Ten beans a day
     Cure food-delay.
SAM. Soups that nourish
     Make hope flourish.
BEN. Beans for nutrition
     Beans for ambition.
SAM. The Best People are crazy about Soups.
BEN. Beans are all the rage among the Higher Income Groups.
SAM. Do you feel a left-out at parties, when it comes to promotion are
     you passed over, does your wife talk in her sleep, then ask our
     nearest agent to tell you about Soups for Success.
BEN. You owe it to yourself to learn about Beans and how this delicious
     food is the sure way to the Body Beautiful. We will mail you a
     fascinating booklet Beans for Beauty by return of post if you
     will send us your address.

                                          [*Enter* INKSLINGER.]

INKSLINGER. Did I hear anyone say something about food.
SAM. What about a delicious bowl of soup?
BEN. What would you say to a nice big plate of beans?
INKSLINGER. I'll have a double portion of both, please.

                              [*Exeunt* SAM SHARKEY *and* BEN BENNY.]

PAUL BUNYAN. Good-day stranger. What's your name?
INKSLINGER. Johnny Inkslinger.
PAUL BUNYAN. Can you read?
INKSLINGER. Think of a language and I'll write you its dictionary.
PAUL BUNYAN. Can you handle figures?
INKSLINGER. Think of an irrational number and I'll double it.
PAUL BUNYAN. You're just the man I hoped to find
     For I have large accounts in mind.
INKSLINGER. Sorry. I'm busy.
PAUL BUNYAN. What's your job?
INKSLINGER. O, just looking around.
PAUL BUNYAN. Who do you work for?

INKSLINGER. Myself, silly. This is a free country. [COOKS *enter.*] Excuse
    me.
SAM SHARKEY. Your soup.
BEN BENNY. Your beans.
BOTH. Just taste them.
PAUL BUNYAN. Wait a minute. [COOKS *stand back.*] Have you any money?
INKSLINGER. Search me.
PAUL BUNYAN. How are you going to pay for your supper?
INKSLINGER. Dunno. Never thought of it.
PAUL BUNYAN. If you work for me
    You shall eat splendidly.
    But no work, no pay.
INKSLINGER. No sale. Good-day. [*Exit* INKSLINGER.]
CHORUS. Now what on earth are we to do
    For I can't keep accounts, can you?
PAUL BUNYAN. Don't worry, he'll come back
    He has to feed.
    Now what else do we lack
    Who else do we need?
SAM SHARKEY. I'd like a dog to lick up all the crumbs
    And chase away the salesmen and all the drunken bums.
BEN BENNY. I'd like a pair of cats
    To catch the mice and rats.

> [PAUL BUNYAN *whistles. Enter* FIDO, MOPPET,
> POPPET.]

TRIO

FIDO.   The single creature lives a partial life,
               Man by his eye and by his nose the hound;
               He needs the deep emotions I can give,
               Through him I sense a vaster hunting-ground.

MOPPET AND POPPET.
               Like draws to like, to share is to relieve,
               And sympathy the root bears love the flower;
               He feels in us, and we in him perceive
               A common passion for the lonely hour.

               We move in our apartness and our pride
               About the decent dwellings he has made;
FIDO.   In all his walks I follow at his side,
               His faithful servant and his loving shade.

PAUL BUNYAN. Off to supper and to bed
    For all our future lies ahead
    And our work must be begun
    At the rising of the sun.

                               [Exeunt to Lumberjack chorus.]

PAUL BUNYAN. Now at the beginning.
    To those who pause on the frontiers of an untravelled empire,
        standing in empty dusk on the eve of a tremendous task, to you
        all a dream of warning.

BLUES

QUARTET OF DEFEATED [1, 2 *and* 4 *men;* 3 *a woman*].
1.   Gold in the North came the blizzard to say
        I left my sweetheart at the break of day,
        The gold ran out and my love grew grey.
           You don't know all, sir, you don't know all.

2.   The West, said the sun, for enterprise,
        A bullet in Frisco put me wise,
        My last words were, God damn your eyes.
           You don't know all, sir, you don't know all.

3.   In Alabama my heart was full,
        Down to the river bank I stole,
        The waters of grief went over my soul.
           You don't know all, mam, you don't know all.

4.   In the streets of New York I was young and swell
        I rode the market, the market fell,
        One morning I found myself in hell.
           I didn't know all, sir, I didn't know all.

2.   In the saloons I heaved a sigh
1.   Lost among deserts of alkali
        I cursed myself and lay down to die
ALL.   *We didn't know all, sir, we didn't know all.*

3.   There is always a sorrow can get you down
        On the mountain-top or right in town
4.   All the world's whiskey can never drown,
ALL.   *You don't know all, sir, you don't know all.*

2.   Some think they're strong, some think they're smart,
3.   Like butterflies they're pulled apart,

1.   America can break your heart.
ALL.   *You don't know all, sir, you don't know all.*

[Enter INKSLINGER.]

PAUL BUNYAN. Hello Mr Inkslinger. Lost anything?
INKSLINGER. I want my supper.
PAUL BUNYAN. What about my little proposition?
INKSLINGER. You win. I'll take it. Now where's the kitchen, Mr Bunyan?
PAUL BUNYAN. Call me Paul.
INKSLINGER. No. You're stronger than I, so I must do what you ask. But
    I'm not going to pretend to like you. Good night. [*Exit.*]
PAUL BUNYAN. Good night, Johnny and good luck.

CURTAIN

Interlude

The Spring came and the Summer and the Fall;
Paul Bunyan sat in his binnacle.

A thousand feet up with a spy-glass
Watching the trees mown down like grass.

Regarding like a lighthouse lamp
The work going on in the lumber camps.

Dreaming dreams which now and then
He liked to tell his lumber men.

His phrases rolled like waves on a beach
And during the course of a single speech

Young boys grew up and needed a shave,
Old men got worried they'd be late for the grave.

He woke one morning feeling unwell,
Said to Babe: "What's the matter? I feel like Hell".

Babe cocked her head, said: "Get a wife;
One can have too much of the bachelor life".

And so one morning in the month of May
Paul went wife-hunting at the break of day.

He kept a sharp look-out but all
The girls he saw were much too small.

But at last he came to a valley green
With mountains beside and a river between.

And there on the bank before his eyes
He beheld a girl of the proper size.

The average man if he walked in haste
Would have taken a week to get round her waist.

When you looked at her bosom you couldn't fail
To see it was built on a generous scale

And wherever she bought her size of shoe
It wasn't on Fifth Avenue.

You'd have liked her mouth if you like a cave;
And when she laughed she could crack a safe.

They eyed each other for an interval;
Then she said "I'm Carrie" and he said "I'm Paul".

What happened then I've no idea
They never told me and I wasn't there

But whatever it was she became his wife
And they started in on the married life.

And in a year a daughter came
Tiny she was and Tiny was her name.

I wish I could say that Carrie and Paul
Were a happy pair but they weren't at all.

It's not the business of a song
To say who was right and who was wrong.

Perhaps he thought about his work too much
Perhaps he hadn't the tactful touch.

Perhaps she was too obstinate
Or liked to go out or stay up late.

Perhaps they were both too set upon
Having their way to get along

But whatever the reason both day and night
Their married life was a constant fight

Both said the bitter things that pain
And wished they hadn't but said them again.

Till Carrie said at last one day:
"It's no use, Paul, I must go away".

Paul struck a match and lit his pipe,
Said: "It seems a pity but perhaps you're right".

So Carrie returned to her home land
Leading Tiny by the hand

And Paul stayed in camp with his lumbermen
Though he paid them visits now and then.

One day Tiny telegraphed him: "Come quick.
Very worried. Mother sick".

But the doctor met him at the door and said:
"I've bad news for you, Paul; she's dead".

He ran upstairs and stood by the bed:
"Poor Carrie", he murmured and stroked her head.

"I know we fought and I was to blame
But I loved you greatly all the same".

He picked up Tiny and stroked her hair,
Said: "I've not been much of a father, dear.

But I'll try to be better until the day
When you want to give your heart away.

And whoever the lucky man may be
I hope he's a better man than me".

So they got ready to return
To the camp of which you now shall learn.

Act I Scene 2

[*The camp.* CHORUS *with* JOHNNY INKSLINGER.]

1.   Nothing but soup and beans
2.   Mondays, Wednesdays, and Fridays soup
3.   Tuesdays, Thursdays, and Saturdays beans
1.   Sundays, soup *and* beans.
2.   Soup gives me ulcers
3.   I'm allergic to beans.
1.   Have you seen the chief about it, Johnny?

JOHNNY. He's not back yet from his wife's funeral.
2.   Well, something's gotta be done about it, and done quick.
3.   You'll have to speak to them, yourself.
ALL. Things have gone too far.

FOOD CHORUS (*with* INKSLINGER)

1.   Do I look the sort of fellow
             Whom you might expect to bellow
                 For a quail in aspic, or
             Who would look as glum as Gandhi
             If he wasn't offered brandy
                 With a Lobster Thermidor.

2.   Who would howl like a lost sinner
             For a sherry before dinner
                 And demand a savoury
3.   Who would criticise the stuffing
             In the olives, and drink nothing
                 But Lapsang Souchong tea.

CHORUS.   Our digestion's pretty tough
             And we're not particular
             But when they hand us out to eat
             A lump of sandstone as a sweet
             Then things have gone too far.

1.   O, the soup looks appetising
             Till you see a maggot rising
                 Like Venus from the sea;
2.   And a beetle in the cauli-
             Flower isn't very jolly
                 Or so it seems to me;

3.   Flies have interesting features
             And, of course, they're all God's creatures,
                 But a trifle out of place
             In a glass of drinking water
             And it makes my temper shorter
                 To meet one face to face.

CHORUS.   Our digestion's pretty tough
             And we're not particular.
             But when we're asked to crunch
             A large cockroach with our lunch
             Then things have gone too far.

1.	Iron, they say, is healthy,
	And even wood is wealthy
	    In essential vitamins;
	But I hate to find a mallet
	Tucked away in the fruit salad
	    Or a hammer in the greens.

3.	There are foods, so doctors tell you,
	With a high nutritious value
	    The Middle Ages never knew;
	But I can't secrete saliva
	At the thought of a screw-driver
	    Or a roasted walking shoe.

CHORUS.	Our digestion's pretty tough And we're not particular But when the kitchen offers one A rusty thumb-tack underdone Then things have gone too far.

[*Enter* SAM SHARKEY *and* BEN BENNY.]

SAM AND BEN. Anything wrong?

JOHNNY. Please don't think for a moment we want to criticise. Your cooking's wonderful. We all know that Sam's soups are the finest in the world and, as for Ben's beans, why there isn't a dish like them anywhere. But don't you think that just occasionally, say once a month, we could have something different?

SAM SHARKEY. I can't believe it.

BEN BENNY. It's not possible.

SAM AND BEN. After all we've done for them.

SAM SHARKEY. Haven't you stayed awake all night thinking how to please them?

BEN BENNY. Haven't you worked your fingers to the bone?

SAM SHARKEY. Day in, day out.

BEN BENNY. Week after week, month after month.

SAM SHARKEY. Year after year.

BEN BENNY. Not a word of thanks.

SAM SHARKEY. Just grumble, grumble, grumble.

BEN BENNY. Treating us like dogs.

SAM SHARKEY. I can't bear it any longer.

BEN BENNY. You don't know how much you've hurt us.

SAM SHARKEY. My nerves.

BEN BENNY. My art.

SAM AND BEN. Very well. Very well. From now on you shall do the cook-
    ing yourselves.
JOHNNY. O but please. We didn't mean to upset you.
SAM SHARKEY. It's alright. We understand perfectly.
JOHNNY. Sam. Ben. Please listen. I'm sorry if . . .
BEN BENNY. Don't apologise. We're not angry.
SAM SHARKEY. Just a little sad, that's all.
BEN BENNY. One day perhaps you'll realise what you've done. Come,
    Sam.
SAM SHARKEY. Come, Ben.

[*Exeunt.*]

CHORUS. There now look what you have done.
JOHNNY. What I did, you asked me to.
1.   You know I only spoke in fun.
2.   I never understood what you
      Meant to do.
3.   I said it wouldn't do.
      You heard me, didn't you?
JOHNNY. What would you have done instead?
CHORUS. Never mind. Beyond a doubt
      You have put us in the red
      So you'd better get us out.

[*Voice of* HOT BISCUIT SLIM, *off.*]

SLIM.   In fair weather and in foul
                      Round the world and back,
                  I must hunt my shadow
                      And the self I lack.

[*Enter* SLIM.]

JOHNNY. Hullo stranger. What's your name?
SLIM. Slim.
JOHNNY. You don't look like a logger. Where do you come from?

                    SLIM'S SONG

SLIM.   I come from open spaces
                      Where over endless grass
                  The stroking winds and shadows
                      Of cloud and bison pass;
                  My brothers were the buffalos,
                      My house the shining day,

I danced between the horse-hoofs like
　　A butterfly at play.

One winter evening as I sat
　　By my camp fire alone,
I heard a whisper from the flame,
　　The voice was like my own:
"O get you up and get you gone,
　　North, South or East or West,
This emptiness cannot answer
　　The heart in your breast.

"Horse, buffalo and bison
　　Like water vaguely roam,
All places are the same to them
　　For Nowhere is their home;
But every man remains a child
　　Uncertain and afraid
Until he find his destiny
　　And all his ghosts be laid.

"O ride, ride till a mountain
　　Get up like a woman's thigh,
Or a lake corner the image
　　From which you must not fly;
O ride till woods or houses
　　Provide the narrow place
Where you can force your fate to turn
　　And meet you face to face".

SLIM, FIDO, MOPPET, POPPET.
　　In fair weather and in foul
　　　　Round the world and back

$\left.\begin{array}{l}\text{I}\\\text{Men}\end{array}\right\}$ must hunt $\left\{\begin{array}{l}\text{my shadow}\\\text{their shadows}\end{array}\right.$

And the $\left\{\begin{array}{l}\text{self I}\\\text{selves they}\end{array}\right\}$ lack.

JOHNNY. Say, you can't cook by any chance?
SLIM. Sure.
CHORUS. Can you cook flapjacks?
SLIM. Yes.
CHORUS. Cookies?
SLIM. Yes.

CHORUS. Fish?
SLIM. Yes.
CHORUS. Steaks?
SLIM. Yes.
CHORUS. Are you telling lies?
SLIM. Yes. No. No. No.
CHORUS. You're an angel in disguise
    Sam and Benny get the sack.
1.   Look, look, the Chief is back
2.   And look. Can I believe my eyes
    Is that a girl he's got with him?
3.   Gosh, she's pretty
4.   And young
5.   And trim.
CHORUS. O boy.

[Exeunt all but FIDO *and* JOHNNY.]

JOHNNY. Hello, Fido. Staying to keep me company? That's mighty nice of you. Say Fido, I want to ask you a question. Are you happy? [FIDO *shakes his head.* JOHNNY *goes to the door and looks to see if anyone is listening.*] Then I'll tell you a secret. Neither am I. May I tell you the story of my life? [FIDO *nods.*] You're sure it won't bore you? [FIDO *shakes his head but when* JOHNNY *is not looking stifles a yawn with a paw.*]

JOHNNY INKSLINGER'S SONG

JOHNNY.   It was out in the sticks that the fire
            Of my existence began
      Where no one had heard the Messiah
            And no one had seen a Cézanne.
      I learned a prose style from the preacher
            And the facts of life from the hens
      And fell in love with the teacher
            Whose love for John Keats was intense.
      And I dreamed of writing a novel
            With which Tolstoi couldn't compete
      And of how all the critics would grovel
            But I guess that a guy gotta eat.

      I can think of much nicer professions
            Than keeping a ledger correct
      Such as writing my private confessions
            Or procuring a frog to dissect

  Learning Sanskrit would be more amusing
    Or studying the history of Spain.
  And, had I the power of choosing
    I would live on the banks of the Seine
  I would paint St Sebastian the Martyr
    Or dig up the Temples of Crete
  Or compose a D Major sonata
    But I guess that a guy gotta eat.

  The company I have to speak to
    Are wonderful men in their way
  But the things that delight me are Greek to
    The Jacks who haul lumber all day.
  It isn't because I don't love them
    That this camp is a prison to me
  Nor do I think I'm above them
    In loathing the sight of a tree.
  Yet I dream of a day when employment
    Will be not such a difficult feat,
  When by doing what gives him enjoyment
    A guy gets sufficient to eat.

             [Enter CHORUS.]

1. I never knew he had a daughter.
2. She's much lovelier than I thought her.
3. Tiny, what a pretty name.
1. I am delighted that she came.
2. Her eyes
3.   Her cheeks
1.   Her lips
2.   Her nose
3. She's a peach
2.   A dove
3.   A rose
CHORUS. But how do you think we should address her
  What can we do to impress her?
JOHNNY. You must sing her a love song.
CHORUS. That's too hard and takes too long.
JOHNNY. Nonsense. It's quite easy, and the longer it is, the more she'll
  like it. Use the longest words you can think of. Like this:

THE LOVE SONG

In this emergency
Of so much urgency,
    What can I do
Except wax lyrical?
Don't look satirical;
I have empirical
    Proof I love you.

Like statisticians, I
Distrust magicians, I
    Think them a crew,
That is, collectively;
Speaking objectively
If not effectively,
I feel protectively
    Mad about you.

Speaking with deference,
I have a preference
    For a nice view:
Your look of spaciousness,
Your manner's graciousness,
Your limb's vivaciousness,
Your mind's herbaceousness
Your whole palatiousness
    Makes me love you.

Some force mysteriously
But most imperiously
    Warms my heart through:
I on detecting it,
After inspecting it
Find that correcting it
Will mean reflecting it,
Back and convecting it,
In fact connecting it
    Firmly with you.

You must receive it: a
Natural naiveté
    Tells me to woo:
Please don't sarcastically

Iconoclastically
Say I'm bombastically
Telling a drastic lie;
Hardly monastically,
Quite orgiastically
I dream phantastically
    Often of you.

My dreams compulsively,
Almost convulsively
    Show, it is true,
No animosity,
Only precocity:
Eyes' luminosity
Ears' curiosity
Nose's monstrosity
Cheeks' adiposity
And lips' verbosity
All with velocity
    Bear down on you.

[*Spoken*]. Got the idea? Right. Now this time you join in. When I think of a word, you think of another word to rhyme with it.

	All nouns are dedicate
	To this one predicate,
	Adjectives too:
	Appendicectomy
CHORUS.	's a pain in the neck to me
JOHNNY.	Anthropomorphosis
CHORUS.	Owns several offices
JOHNNY.	Psychokinesia
CHORUS.	Never gets easier
JOHNNY.	Papal Encyclicals
CHORUS.	Are full of pricklicles
JOHNNY.	Plenipotentiaries
CHORUS.	Endure for centuries
JOHNNY.	Supralapsarians
CHORUS.	Aren't vegetarians
JOHNNY.	Hendecasyllable
CHORUS.	Makes me feel illable
JOHNNY.	Icthyosauruses
CHORUS.	Won't sing in choruses

JOHNNY.	Septuagesima
CHORUS.	Ate less and lessima
JOHNNY.	Occi-parietal
CHORUS.	O DO BE QUIET
JOHNNY.	all
	Mean:
CHORUS.	I LOVE YOU.

[Enter TINY.]

CHORUS 1. Look at me, Miss Tiny: I'm six feet tall.
2.   Look at me, Miss Tiny: I've the bluest eyes you ever saw.
3.   Feel my biceps, Miss Tiny.
4.   I can ride a bicycle.
5.   I can spell parallelogram.
6.   I've got fifty dollars salted away in an old sock.
1.   I'll run errands for you.
2.   I'll bring you your breakfast in bed.
3.   I'll tell you stories before you go to sleep.
4.   I'll make you laugh by pulling faces.
5.   I'm husky. You need someone to look after you.
6.   You need someone to look after. I'm sick.

JOHNNY. Leave her alone, you fools. Have you forgotten her mother's just
     died?

TINY'S SONG

TINY.   Whether the sun shine upon children playing,
             Or storms endanger sailors on the sea,
             In a solitude or a conversation,
             Mother, O Mother, tears arise in me.

             For underground now you rest who at nightfall
             Would sing me to sleep in my little bed;
             I turn with the world but grief has no motion;
             Mother, O Mother, too soon you were dead.

             O never again in fatigue or fever
             Shall I feel your cool hand upon my brow;
             As you look after the cherubs in Heaven,
             Mother, O Mother, look down on me now.

             Should a day come I hear a lover whisper,
             Should I stay an old maid whom the men pass by,
             My heart shall cherish your guardian image,
             Mother, O Mother, till the day I die.

CHORUS.   The white bone
                          Lies alone
                          Like the limestone
                          Under the green grass.

                          All time goes by
                          We, too, shall lie
                          Under death's eye
                          Alas. Alas.

                                                    [*Enter* SLIM.]

SLIM. Supper's ready.
TINY. Excuse me, are you the cook?
SLIM. Yes, mam.
TINY. I'm Miss Tiny. Father said I was to help you in the kitchen.
SLIM. I'm sure you'll be a great help, Miss Tiny. This way please.
CHORUS 1 [*as they exeunt*]. Did you see how he looked at her?
2.   Did you see how she looked at him?
3.   I shall take cooking lessons.
REST OF CHORUS. Don't chatter so. Let's go and eat. [*Exeunt.*]

                          JOHNNY'S REGRET

JOHNNY [*alone*]   All the little brooks of love
                          Run down towards each other
                    Somewhere every valley ends
                          And loneliness is over
                    Some meet early, some meet late,
                          Some, like me, have long to wait.

VOICE OF PAUL BUNYAN. Johnny.
JOHNNY. Yes, Mr Bunyan.
PAUL BUNYAN. Has anything happened since I've been away?
JOHNNY. Keep an eye on Hel Helson. He broods too much by himself and
    I don't like the look on his face. And the bunch he goes around with
    are a bad bunch.
PAUL BUNYAN. Poor Hel. He was born a few hundred years too late.
    Today there is no place for him. Anything else?
JOHNNY. Some of the men say they are tired of logging and would like to
    settle down. They'd like to try farming.
PAUL BUNYAN. John Shears?
JOHNNY. He's the chief one but there are many others.
PAUL BUNYAN. I'll look into it. And what about yourself, Johnny?
JOHNNY. I'm alright, Mr Bunyan.

PAUL BUNYAN. I know what you want. It's harder than you think and not
    so pleasant. But you shall have it and shan't have to wait much longer.
    Good night, Johnny.
JOHNNY. Good night, Mr Bunyan.
PAUL BUNYAN. Still *Mr* Bunyan?
JOHNNY. Good night, Paul.

[*Exit* JOHNNY.]

CHORUS [*off*]. Good night, Mr Bunyan.
PAUL BUNYAN. Good night. Happy dreams.

[*Music.*]

CHORUS 1. Ah that music. How lovely it is. Louder. More. More.
2.   Let me dream I am the master of a goddess.
3.   Let me dream I am the little owner of a luxurious garden.
4.   Let me land on a calm shore where I have been long expected.
5.   Let me be a drowned hero without a wish.

LULLABY

[*Enter* LAME SHADOWS AND ANIMAS
(*Film Stars and Models*).]

LAME SHADOWS AND ANIMAS.
                Say O say farewell
                Now is yesterday
                But the tolling of a bell
                On a fading, fading shore:
                Gaze and fear no more
                Into sleep's translucent wave
                Deeper, deeper, deeper still;
                All the motions of your will
                Given to its oceans, hear
                Like the drumming of an ear
                Sorrows homing to their grave.

[*Sound of snores.*]

1ST LAME SHADOW. All O.K.
2ND ANIMA. Ssh. No so loud.
VOICE OFF. Go on singing, ma.
2ND ANIMA. O damn. Excuse me. [*Runs off stage.*] Go to sleep this minute
    or I'll give you such a nightmare. [*Returns.*] Phew.
1ST LAME SHADOW. A moment's peace at last.

2ND ANIMA. O these men.
1ST ANIMA. They seem to think we enjoy entertaining them.
2ND LAME SHADOW. Gosh. I could do with a vacation.

CHORUS (FILM STARS AND MODELS)

CHORUS.   You've no idea how dull it is
                  Just being perfect nullities,
                        The idols of a democratic nation;
                  The heroes of the multitude
                  Their dreams of female pulchritude:
                        We're very very tired of admiration.

FILM STAR L.S. The cut of my moustache and lips,
FILM STAR A.   My measurement around the hips,
BOTH.   Obey the whims of fashion;
                  In our embraces we select
                  Whatever technique seems correct
                  To give the visual effect
                        Of an Eternal Passion.

MODELS A.   On beaches or in night-clubs I
                  Excel at femininity,
MODELS L.S.   And I at all athletics;
                  I pay attention to my hair,
MODELS A.   For personal hygiene I've a flair,
MODELS L.S.   The Hercules of underwear,
MODELS A.   The Venus of cosmetics.

CHORUS.   We're bored with being glamourous,
                  We're bored with being amorous,
                        For all our fans we don't give a banana;
                  Who wants to be exhibited
                  To all the world's inhibited
                        As representative Americana.

ANIMAS.   The things a man of eighty-two
                  Will ask of his dream ingenue
                        I shouldn't like to retail;
                  Unless you tried to play mama,
                  You can't think how particular
                  Young men who miss their mothers are
                        About each little detail.

LAME SHADOWS. Rescuing girls from waterfalls
          Or shooting up the sheriff, palls,
             Like any violent action;
          We never want to fly again
          Or throw a custard pie again
          To give the decent citizen
             Vicarious satisfaction.

QUARTET OF ANIMAS AND LAME SHADOWS.
          The growth of social consciousness
          Has failed to make our problems less,
             Indeed, they grow intenser;
          And what with Freud and what with Marx
          With bureaucrats and matriarchs
          The chances are our little larks
             Will not get past the censor.

          You'd hate it if you were employed
          To be a sin in celluloid
             Or else a saint in plaster;
          O little hearts who make a fuss,
          What pleasure it would give to us
          To give the bird to Oedipus,
             The raspberry to Jocasta.

CHORUS. You've no idea how dull it is
          Just being perfect nullities,
             The idols of a democratic nation;
          The heroes of the multitude,
          Their dreams of female pulchritude;
             We're VERY VERY tired of admiration.

                    [*Sound of heavy snores.*]

              [*Lullaby again but sung off by* CHORUS.]

PAUL BUNYAN. Now let the complex spirit dissolve in the darkness
    Where the Actual and the Possible are mysteriously exchanged.
    For the saint must descend into Hell; that his order may be tested
        by its disorder
    The hero return to the humble womb; that his will may be pacified
        and refreshed.
    Dear children, trust the night and have faith in to-morrow

That these hours of ambiguity and indecision may be also the hours
of healing.

CURTAIN

Act II Scene 1

[*A clearing.*]

VOICE OF PAUL BUNYAN. The songs of dawn have been sung and the
night watchmen are already in the deep beginnings of sleep.

Leaning upon their implements the hired men pause to consider
their life by the light of mid-morning and of habits already
established in their loosened limbs. And the aggressive will is no
longer pure.

Much has been done to prepare a continent for the rejoicings and
recriminations of all its possible heirs. Much has been ill done.
There is never enough time to do more than one thing at a
time, and there is always either too much of one thing or too
little.

Virtuosos of the axe, dynamiters and huntsmen, there has been an
excess of military qualities, of the resourcefulness of thieves,
the camaraderie of the irresponsible, and the accidental
beauties of silly songs.

Nevertheless you have done much to render yourselves unnecessary.
Loneliness has worn lines of communication.
Irrational destruction has made possible the establishment of a
civilised order.
Drunkenness and lechery have prepared the way for a routine of
temperance and marriage.
Already you have provoked a general impulse towards settlement
and cultivation.

[*Enter* CHORUS.]

CHORUS. What does he want to see us for,
I wonder what he has in store,
I never did a thing I shouldn't,
I couldn't. I wouldn't.
I'll do my work. I'll never shirk.
I'll never never grumble any more.

PAUL BUNYAN. I've been thinking for some time that we needed some farmers to grow food for the camp, and looking around for a nice piece of country, the other day I found the very place. A land where the wheat grows as tall as churches and the potatoes are as big as airships. Now those who would like to be farmers: Stand out.

JOHN SHEARS. It has always been my dream
           Since I was only so high
     To live upon a farm and watch
         The wheat and barley grow high.
FARMERS' CHORUS. The wheat and barley grow high.

PAUL BUNYAN. Hel Helson.

HEL HELSON. Yes.

PAUL BUNYAN. You are in charge while I take our friends to the Land of Heart's Desire. I want you to start to-day clearing the Topsy-Turvey Mountain. Now boys, if you're ready we'll start as we have a thousand miles to go before noon. But if you think farming is a soft job you'd better stay right here.

If there isn't a flood, there's a drought,
If there isn't a frost, there's a heatwave,
If it isn't the insects, it's the banks.
You'll howl more than you'll sing,
You'll frown more than you'll smile,
You'll cry more than you'll laugh.
    But some people seem to like it.
    Let's get going.

FARMERS' SONG

CHORUS.   I hate to be a shanty-boy
         I want to be a farmer
     For I prefer life's comedy
         To life's crude melodrama.

     The shanty-boy invades the wood
         Upon his cruel mission
     To slay the tallest trees he can
         The height of his ambition.

     The farmer heeds wild Nature's cry
         For Higher Education,
     And is a trusted friend to all
         The best in vegetation.

The shanty-boy sleeps in a bunk
    With none to call him Dad, sir,
And so you cannot wonder much
    If he goes to the bad, sir.

The farmer sees his little ones
    Grow up like the green willow
At night he has his Better Half
    Beside him on the pillow.

The shanty-boy puts back the back the wealth
    Of nature he has taken;
The farmer by investing it
    Sees it bring home the bacon.

[The others watch them go and all except HELSON *and his four* CRONIES *exeunt.]*

CRONIES 1. The Topsy-Turvey Mountain. It's impossible.
2.   He's nuts.
3.   Just another of his crazy ideas.
4.   You are not going to take him seriously, are you, Hel?
1.   Why do you go on taking orders from a dope like that?
2.   Why don't you run this joint yourself? We'd support you.
3.   Sure we would.
4.   Hel for Boss.
1.   Tell him where he gets off.
2.   And that stooge of his, Johnny Inkslinger.
3.   You said it. We'll take him for a ride.
4.   Stand up for your rights, Hel. You're the only boss around here.
HEL HELSON. Get out.
1.   Of course, Hels.
2.   Anything you say, boss.
3.   We were just going anyway.
4.   Don't forget what we think of you.

[Exeunt FOUR CRONIES.]

*[*HELSON *is left sitting moodily alone.]*

THE MOCKING OF HEL HELSON

[All voices off. Questions and answers come from different places.]

Q.
Heron, heron winging by
Through the silence of the sky,
What have you heard of Helson the Brave?

A.
O I heard of a hero working for wages,
Taking orders just like a slave.

CHORUS.
I'm afraid it's too late,
He will never be great.

Q.
Moon, moon shining bright
In the deserts of the night,
What have you heard of Helson the Fair?

A.
Not what one should hear of one so handsome,
The girls make fun of his bashful air.

CHORUS.
I'm afraid it's too late,
He will never be great.

Q.
Wind, wind as you run
Round and round the earth for fun,
What have you heard of Helson the Good?

A.
Just the old sad story of virtue neglected
Mocked at by others, misunderstood.

CHORUS.
I'm afraid it's too late,
He will never be great.

Q.
Beetle, beetle as you pass
Down the avenues of grass,
What have you heard of Helson the Wise?

A.
O it's sad to hear of all that wisdom
Being exploited by smarter guys.

CHORUS.
I'm afraid it's too late,
He will never be great.

Q.
Squirrel, squirrel as you go
Through the forests to and fro,
What have you heard of Helson the Strong?

A.
Not what one likes to hear of a fighter,
They say he's a coward, I hope They're wrong.

CHORUS.
Too late, too late, too late,
He will never never never be great.

[*Enter* FIDO, MOPPET *and* POPPET.]

MOPPET. Did you really?

POPPET. Yes, I says, excuse me, I says, but this is my roof, what of it, he says, you're trespassing, I says, and if I am, he says, who's going to stop me, yours truly, I says, scram alley cat, he says, before I eat you, I don't know about alley cats, I says, but one doesn't need to be a detective to see who has a rat in his family tree, and the fight was on.

FIDO. There now, just look. Helson has got the blues again. Dear O dear, that man has the worst inferiority complexes I've ever run across. His dreams must be amazing. Really I must ask him about them. Excuse me.

MOPPET. Nosey prig.

POPPET. He can't help it. Dogs are like that. Always sniffing.

FIDO'S SYMPATHY

FIDO [*looking up at Helson, sings*].
> Won't you tell me what's the matter,
> I adore the confidential role,
> Why not tell your little troubles
> To a really sympathetic soul.

[HELSON *lunges a kick at him and he bolts.*]

POPPET. Dogs have no savoir-faire.

MOPPET. Serve him right. I hate gush.

THE CATS' CREED

POPPET AND MOPPET [*duet*].
> Let Man the romantic in vision espy
> A far better world than his own in the sky
> As a tyrant or beauty express a vain wish
> To be mild as a beaver or chaste as a fish.
>
> Let the dog who's the most sentimental of all
> Throw a languishing glance at the hat in the hall,
> Struggle wildly to speak all the tongues that he hears
> And to rise to the realm of Platonic ideas.
>
> But the cat is an Aristotelian and proud
> Preferring hard fact to intangible cloud;
> Like the troll in Peer Gynt, both in hunting and love,
> The cat has one creed: "To thyself be enough".

POPPET. Let's go and kill birds.

MOPPET. You've heard about Tiny and Slim. Fido caught them necking in the pantry after breakfast.

POPPET. Yes, he told me. No one can say I'm narrow-minded, but there are *some* things that just aren't done till after dark.

[*Exeunt.*]

VOICE OF PAUL BUNYAN. Helson. Helson.

[*Enter* FOUR CRONIES.]

CRONIES 1. He's back.

2. He's mad at you.

PAUL BUNYAN. Helson. I want to talk to you.

3. Don't pay any attention to him.

4. Go and settle with him.

PAUL BUNYAN. Helson.

1. You're not going to do what he tells you, are you?

2. Go on, wipe the floor with him.

3. Don't let him think you're a cissy.

4. Show him you're an American. Give him the works.

HELSON. I'll kill him.

[*Exit* HELSON.]

CRONIES. Atta boy.

THE FIGHT

[CHORUS *rush in.*]

CHORUS. What's happening?
    A fight.
    Helson
    He's haywire,
    He's fighting mad,
    A killer,
    They're heaving rocks,
    Gee, that was close
    Look out
    That's got him
    No, missed
    Did you see that?
    Helson is tough
    But Paul has the brains.

[*They stream out to watch the fight.*]

[Enter SLIM *and* TINY.]

LOVE DUET

TINY. Slim.
SLIM. Yes, dear.
TINY. Where has everybody gone?
SLIM. I don't know, but I'm glad.
TINY. Darling.

[They embrace. Thunder and shouts off.]

DUET.   Move, move from the trysting stone,
                   White sun of summer depart
                   That I may be left alone
                   With my true love close to my heart.

[Thunder and shouts off.]

SLIM. Tiny.
TINY. Yes, dear.
SLIM. Did you hear a funny noise?
TINY. I did, but I don't care.
SLIM. Darling.

[They embrace.]

DUET.   The head that I love the best
                   Shall lie all night on my breast.

TINY. Slim.
SLIM. Yes, dear.
TINY. How do people really know
    They really are in love?
SLIM AND TINY. Darling.

DUET.   Lost, lost is the world I knew,
                   And I have lost myself too;
                   Dear heart, I am lost in you.

                   [Enter CHORUS *carrying the unconscious body of*
                   HEL HELSON.]

                   MOCK FUNERAL MARCH

CHORUS.   Take away the body and lay it on ice,
            Put a lily in his hand and beef-steaks on his eyes;
            Tall white candles at his feet and head;
            And let this epitaph be read.

□

Here lies an unlucky picayune;
He thought he was champ but he thought too soon:
Here lies Hel Helson from Scandinavia,
Rather regretting his rash behaviour.

CRONIES 1. We told him not to
We never forgot to
2. Be careful to say
He should obey
3. Helson, we said,
Get this in your head
4. Take orders from Paul
Or you'll have a fall.
1 AND 3. We are all put here on earth for a purpose. We all have a job to
do and it is our duty to do it with all our might.
2 AND 4. We must obey our superiors and live according to our station
in life, for whatever the circumstances, the Chief, the Company and
the Customer are always right.
HELSON. Where am I? What happened? Am I dead?
Something struck me on the head.
CHORUS. It's alright, Hel, you are not dead,
You are lying in your bed.
HELSON. Why am I so stiff and sore?
I remember nothing more.
CHORUS. Alright Hel, don't be a sap
You had a kind of little scrap.
Don't worry now but take a nap.
HELSON. Who was it hit me on the chin?
VOICE OF PAUL BUNYAN. I'm sorry, Hels, I had to do it,
I am your friend if you but knew it.
HELSON. Good Heavens, what a fool I've been.
PAUL BUNYAN. Let bygones be bygones. Forget the past,
We can now be friends at last.
Each of us has found a brother,
You and I both need each other.
CRONIES. That's what we always told you, Hels.
HELSON. How could I ever have been so blind
As not to recognise your kind.
Now I know you. Scram. Or else.
CHORUS. Scram. Or else.
CRONIES. Ingratitude
A purely selfish attitude
And inability to see a joke
Are characteristic of uneducated folk.

CHORUS. Scram.
CRONIES. Don't argue with them. They're sick people.

[*Exeunt* CRONIES.]

HYMN

CHORUS.   Often thoughts of hate conceal
                       Love we are ashamed to feel;
                       In the climax of a fight
                       Lost affection comes to light.
                       And the prisoners are set free,
                       O great day of discovery.

CURTAIN

Interlude

So Helson smiled and Bunyan smiled
And both shook hands and were reconciled.

And Paul and Johnny and Hel became
The greatest partners in the logging game.

And every day Slim and Tiny swore
They were more in love than the day before.

All over the States the stories spread
Of Bunyan's camp and the life they led.

Of fights with Indians, of shooting matches
Of monster bears and salmon catches.

Of the Whirling Whimpus Paul fought and killed
Of the Buttermilk Line that he had to build.

And a hundred other tales were known
From Nantucket Island to Oregon.

From the Yiddish Alps to the Rio Grande,
From the Dust Bowl down to the Cottonland.

In every dialect and tongue
His tales were told and his stories sung

Harsh in the Bronx where they cheer with zest,
With a burring R in the Middle West,

And lilting and slow in Arkansas
Where instead of Father they say Paw.

But there came a winter these stories say
When Babe came up to Paul one day

Stood still and looked him in the eye;
Paul said nothing for he knew why.

Babe said, "Although it breaks your heart
Your work is done and you must depart.

Shoulder your axe and leave this place
Let the clerk move in with his well-washed face.

Let the architect with his sober plan
Build a residence for the average man.

Till in hollows dug by your giant heel
Families lunch by their automobile.

Till laundry caper in the summer breeze
That could hardly stir the heavy trees

And garden birds not bat an eye
When the locomotive whistles by.

And telephone wires go from town to town
For lovers to whisper sweet nothings down.

We must depart but it's Christmas Eve
So let's have a feast before we leave."

And that is all I have to tell.
The curtain rises; friends, farewell.

Act II Scene 2

[*Christmas Eve. A full-size pine-tree lit up as a Christmas tree in background. Foreground a big table with candles.* CHORUS *eating dinner. Funny hats, streamers, noises.*]

CHRISTMAS PARTY

CHORUS.   Another slice of turkey,
                        Another slice of ham,
            I shall feel sick to-morrow, but I don't give a damn.
            Take a quart of whiskey and mix it with your beer,
            Pass the gravy, will you,
                        Christmas comes but once a year.

MOPPET AND POPPET.
    Men are three parts crazy and no doubt always were,
    But why do they go mad completely one day in the year.

CHORUS.
    Who wants the Pope's nose?
                  I do.
                        French fried if you please
    I've a weakness for plum pudding
                      Would you pass the cheese
    Wash it down with Bourbon
                  I think I'll stick to Rye
    There's nothing to compare with an old-fashioned apple pie.

FIDO. Seeing his temper's so uncertain as a rule, it's very queer
    He should always be good-tempered on one day in the year.

CHORUS. Cigars
          Hurrah
              Some nuts
                  I'm stuffed to here
  Your health
          Sköl
            Prosit
              Santé
                Cheer
  A merry merry Christmas and a happy New Year.

                [JOHNNY INKSLINGER *bangs on the table and
                rises.*]

JOHNNY.   Dear friends, with your leave this Christmas Eve
        I rise to make a pronouncement;
    Some will have guessed but I thought it best
        To make an official announcement.

    Hot Biscuit Slim, you all know him,
        As our cook (or coquus in Latin)
    Has been put in charge of a very large
        Hotel in Mid-Manhattan.

                                [*Cheers.*]

    But Miss Tiny here, whom we love so dear,
        Has recently consented
    To share his life as his loving wife
        I must say they look contented.

CHORUS.   Carry her over the water
                     And set her down under the tree
                 Where the culvers white all day and all night
                     And the winds from every quarter
                 Sing agreeably agreeably agreeably of love.

                 Put a gold ring on her finger
                     And press her close to your heart
                 While the fish in the lake their snapshots take
                     And the frog that sanguine singer
                 Sings agreeably agreeably agreeably of love.

                 The preacher shall dance at your marriage
                     The steeple bend down to look
                 The pulpit and chairs shed suitable tears
                     While the horses drawing your carriage
                 Sing agreeably agreeably agreeably of love.

SLIM [*rising*].
                 Where we are is not very far
                     To walk from Grand Central Station,
                 If you ever come east, you will know at least
                     Of a standing invitation. [*Sits down.*]

JOHNNY.   And Hel so tall who managed for Paul
                     And had the task of converting
                 His ambitious dreams into practical schemes
                     And of seeing we all were working

                 Will soon be gone to Washington
                     To join the Administration
                 As a leading man in the Federal plan
                     Of Public Works for the nation.

                                         [*Cheers.* HELSON *rises.*]

HELSON.   I hope that some of you will come
                     To offer your assistance
                 In installing turbines and High Tension lines
                     And bringing streams from a distance.

                                                 [*Cheers.*]

JOHNNY.   And now three cheers for old John Shears
                     Who has taken a short vacation
                 From his cattle and hay, to be with us to-day
                     On this important occasion.

[*Cheers.* SHEARS *rises.*]

SHEARS [*stammering*].
>I am. I'm not. Er which er what
>>As I was saying, the—er
>The er, the well. I mean. O Hell,
>>I'm mighty glad to be here. [*Sits down.*]

[*Enter* WESTERN UNION BOY.]

WESTERN UNION BOY.
>>A telegram, a telegram,
>>>A telegram from Hollywood.
>>Inkslinger is the name;
>>>I think the news is good.

JOHNNY [*reading*]. Technical Advisor required for all-star lumber picture stop your name suggested stop if interested wire collect.

>>A lucky break. Am I awake?
>>>Please pinch me if I'm sleeping.
>>It only shows that no one knows
>>>The future of book-keeping.

CHORUS.
>>We always knew that one day you
>>>Would come to be famous, Johnny.
>>When you're prosperous remember us
>>>And we'll all sing Hey Nonny Nonny.

JOHNNY.
>>And last of all I call on Paul
>>>To speak to us this evening,
>>I needn't say how sad to-day
>>>We are that he is leaving.

>>Every eye is ready to cry
>>>At the thought of bidding adieu, sir,
>>For sad is the heart when friends must part,
>>>But enough—I call upon you, sir.

VOICE OF PAUL BUNYAN.
>>Now the task that made us friends
>>In a common labour, ends;
>>For an emptiness is named
>>And a wilderness is tamed
>>Till its savage nature can
>>Tolerate the life of man.
>>All I had to do is done,

You remain but I go on,
Other kinds of deserts call
Other forests whisper Paul,
I must hasten in reply
To that low instinctive cry
There to make a way again
For the conscious lives of men.

Here, though, is your life, and here
The pattern is already clear
That machinery imposes
On you as the frontier closes,
Gone the natural disciplines
And the life of choice begins.
You and I must go our way
I have but one word to say:
O remember, friends, that you
Have the harder task to do
As at freedom's puzzled feet
Yawn the gulfs of self-defeat;
All but heroes are unnerved
When life and love must be deserved.

LITANY

CHORUS.
The campfire embers are black and cold,
The banjos are broken, the stories are told,
The woods are cut down and the young are grown old.

TRIO. From a Pressure Group that says I am the Constitution,
From those who say Patriotism and mean Persecution,
From a Tolerance that is really inertia and disillusion
            Save animals and men.

TINY AND SLIM. Bless us, father.
PAUL BUNYAN.   A father cannot bless.
May you find the happiness that you possess.

CHORUS.
The echoing axe shall be heard no more
Nor the rising scream of the buzzer saw
Nor the crack as the ice-jam explodes in the thaw.

TRIO. From entertainments neither true nor beautiful nor witty,
From a homespun humour manufactured in the city,

> From the dirty-mindedness of a Watch Committee
> Save animals and men.

HELSON. Don't leave me, Paul. Where am I? What's to become of America
now?

PAUL BUNYAN.

> Every day America's destroyed and re-created
> America is what you do,
> America is I and you,
> America is what we choose to make it.

TRIO. From children brought up to believe in self-expression,
From the theology of plumbers or the medical profession,
From alcohol as the way to self-respect and self-possession
> Save animals and men.

JOHNNY. Paul, who are you?
PAUL BUNYAN.

> Where the night becomes the day
> Where the dream becomes the Fact
> I am the Eternal Guest
> I am Way
> I am Act.

CHORUS.

> No longer the logger shall hear in the Fall
> The pine and the spruce and the sycamore call.

PAUL BUNYAN.

> Good-bye, dear friends.

CHORUS.   Good-bye, Paul.

CURTAIN

The Rake's Progress

A Fable

────────────────

LIBRETTO BY W. H. AUDEN
AND CHESTER KALLMAN
MUSIC BY IGOR STRAVINSKY

[*1947–1948*]

CHARACTERS

TOM RAKEWELL
NICK SHADOW
TRULOVE
SELLEM, an Auctioneer
A KEEPER

ANNE, daughter to TRULOVE
BABA THE TURK
MOTHER GOOSE

ROARING BOYS, WHORES, SERVANTS, CITIZENS, MADMEN

ACT ONE

Scene 1: The garden of TRULOVE's country cottage. Spring afternoon.
Scene 2: MOTHER GOOSE's, a London brothel. Summer.
Scene 3: The garden of TRULOVE's cottage. Autumn night.

ACT TWO

Scene 1: The morning room of RAKEWELL's house in London. Autumn morning.
Scene 2: The street before RAKEWELL's house. Autumn dusk.
Scene 3: Morning room of RAKEWELL's house. Winter morning.

ACT THREE

Scene 1: The morning room of RAKEWELL's house. Spring afternoon.
Scene 2: A Churchyard. The same night.
Scene 3: Bedlam.

EPILOGUE

The action takes place in an Eighteenth Century England.

Act I Scene 1

[Garden of TRULOVE's *home in the country. Afternoon in spring.]*

> *[House R, Garden Gate center back, Arbor L down-stage in which* ANNE *and* RAKEWELL *are seated.]*

DUET

ANNE.   The woods are green and bird and beast at play
For all things keep this festival of May;
With fragrant odors and with notes of cheer
The pious earth observes the solemn year.

RAKEWELL.
Now is the season when the Cyprian Queen
With genial charm translates our mortal scene,
When swains their nymphs in fervent arms enfold
And with a kiss restore the Age of Gold.

> *[Enter* TRULOVE *from house and stands aside.]*

TRIO

ANNE.   How sweet within the budding grove
       To walk, to love.
RAKEWELL.   How sweet beside the pliant stream
       To lie, to dream.

TRULOVE   O may a father's prudent fears
       Unfounded prove,
And ready vows and loving looks
       Be all they seem.

In youth we fancy we are wise,
       But time hath shown,
Alas, too often and too late,
       We have not known
The hearts of others or our own.

ANNE AND RAKEWELL.
       Love tells no lies
       And in Love's eyes
       We see our future state,
       Ever happy, ever fair:
       Sorrow, hate,
       Disdain, despair,

Rule not there
But Love alone
Reigns o'er his own.

TRULOVE [*coming forward*]. Anne, my dear.
ANNE. Yes, Father.
TRULOVE. Your advice is needed in the kitchen.

[ANNE *curtsies and exits into house.*]

Tom, I have news for you. I have spoken on your behalf to a good
friend in the City and he offers you a position in his counting house.
RAKEWELL. You are too generous, sir. You must not think me ungrateful
if I do not immediately accept what you propose, but I have other
prospects in view.
TRULOVE. Your reluctance to seek steady employment makes me uneasy.
RAKEWELL. Be assured your daughter shall not marry a poor man.
TRULOVE. So he be honest, she may take a poor husband if she choose,
but I am resolved she shall never marry a lazy one. [*Exits into house.*]
RAKEWELL. The old fool.

ORCHESTRAL RECITATIVE

Here I stand, my constitution sound, my frame not ill-favored, my
wit ready, my heart light. *I* play the industrious apprentice in the
copybook? *I* submit to the drudge's yoke? *I* slave through a lifetime to
enrich others, and then be thrown away like a gnawed bone? Not *I*!
Have not grave doctors assured us that good works are of no avail for
Heaven predestines all? In my fashion, I may profess myself of their
party and herewith entrust myself to Fortune.

ARIA

Since it is not by merit
We rise or we fall,
But the favor of Fortune
That governs us all,
Why should I labor
For what in the end
She will give me for nothing
If she be my friend?
While if she be not, why,
The wealth I might gain

For a time by my toil would
At last be in vain.
Till I die, then, of fever,
Or by lightning am struck,
Let me live by my wits
And trust to my luck.
My life lies before me,
The world is so wide:
Come, wishes, be horses;
This beggar shall ride.

[RAKEWELL *walks about. Orchestra plays. Then: spoken:*]

I wish I had money.

[SHADOW *appears immediately at the garden gate.*]

RECITATIVE SECCO

SHADOW. Tom Rakewell?

RAKEWELL [*startled, turning around*]. I—

SHADOW. I seek Tom Rakewell with a message. Is this his house?

RAKEWELL. No, not his house, but you have found him straying in his thoughts and footsteps. In short—

SHADOW. You are he?

RAKEWELL [*laughing*]. Yes, surely. Tom Rakewell, at your service.

SHADOW. Well, well. [*Bows.*] Nick Shadow, sir, and at *your* service for, surely as you bear your name, I bear you a bright future. You recall an uncle, sir?

RAKEWELL. An uncle? My parents never mentioned one.

SHADOW. They quarreled, I believe, sir. Yet he— Sir, have you friends?

RAKEWELL. More than a friend.

[SHADOW *looks questioningly.*]

The daughter of this house and ruler of my heart.

SHADOW [*bows*]. A lover's fancy and a lovely thought. Then call her, call her. Indeed, let all who will make their joy here of your glad tidings.

[*As* RAKEWELL *rushes into the house, the orchestra begins to play, and* SHADOW *reaches over the garden gate, unlatches it, enters the garden and walks forward.* RAKEWELL *re-enters from the house with* ANNE *and* TRULOVE.]

ORCHESTRAL RECITATIVE *and*
RECITATIVE SECCO

SHADOW [*bows*]. Fair lady, gracious gentlemen, a servant begs your pardon
for your time, but there is much to tell. Tom Rakewell had an uncle,
one long parted from his native land. Him I served many years,
served him in the many trades he served in turn; and all to his profit.
Yes, profit was perpetually his. It was, indeed, his family, his friend,
his hour of amusement—his life. But all his brilliant progeny of gold
could not caress him when he lay dying. Sick for his home, sick for a
memory of pleasure or of love, his thoughts were but of England.
There, at least, he felt, his profit could be pleasure to an eager youth;
for such, by counting years upon his fumbling fingers, he knew that
you must be, good sir. Well, he is dead. And I am here with this
commission: to tell Tom Rakewell that an unloved and forgotten un-
cle loved and remembered. You are a rich man.

ORCHESTRAL RECITATIVE *and* QUARTET

RAKEWELL. I wished but once, I knew
That surely my wish would come true,
That I
Had but to speak at last
And Fate would smile when Fortune cast
The die.
I knew. [*To* SHADOW.] Yet you, who bring
The fateful end of questioning,
Here by
A new and grateful master's side,
Be thanked, and as my Fortune and my guide,
Remain, confirm, deny.
SHADOW [*bowing*].
Be thanked, for masterless should I abide
Too long, I soon would die.
ANNE [*reverently, as though startled from a trance*].
Be thanked, O God, for him, and may a bride
Soon to his vows reply.
TRULOVE. Be thanked, O God, and curb in him all pride,
That Anne may never sigh.

*   *   *

[RAKEWELL *puts one arm around* ANNE *and ges-
tures outward with other.*]

RAKEWELL. My Anne, behold, for doubt has fled our view,
 The skies are clear and every path is true.
ANNE. The joyous fount I see that brings increase
 To fields of promise and the groves of peace.
ANNE AND RAKEWELL. O clement love!
TRULOVE.   My children, may God bless you
 Even as a father. . . .
SHADOW.   Sir, may Nick address you
 A moment in your bliss? Even in carefree May
 A thriving fortune has its roots of care:
 Attorneys crouched like gardeners to pay,
 Bowers of paper only seals repair;
 We must be off to London.
RAKEWELL.   They can wait!
TRULOVE. No, Tom, your man is right, things must be done.
 The sooner that you settle your estate,
 The sooner you and Anne can be as one.
ANNE. Father is right, dear Tom.
SHADOW.   A coach in wait
 Is down the road.
RAKEWELL.   Well then, if Fortune sow
 A crop that wax and pen must cultivate,
 Let's fly to husbandry and make it grow.

* * *

SHADOW. I'll call the coachman, sir.
TRULOVE [*to* SHADOW].   Should you not mind,
 I'll tell you of his needs.
SHADOW.   Sir, you are kind.

[SHADOW *and* TRULOVE *exit by garden gate.*]

DUET

ANNE.   Farewell for now, my heart
       Is with you when you go,
       However you may fare.

RAKEWELL.   Wherever, when apart,
       I may be, I shall know
       That you are with me there.

[TRULOVE *and* SHADOW *re-enter by garden gate.*]

RECITATIVE SECCO

SHADOW. All is ready, sir.

RAKEWELL. Tell me, good Shadow, since, born and bred in indigence, I am unacquainted with such matters, what wages you are accustomed to receive.

SHADOW. Let us not speak of that, master, till you know better what my services are worth. A year and a day hence, we will settle our account, and then, I promise you, you shall pay me no more and no less than what you yourself acknowledge to be just.

RAKEWELL. A fair offer. 'Tis agreed. [*Turning to* TRULOVE.]

ORCHESTRAL RECITATIVE

Dear father Trulove, the very moment my affairs are settled, I shall send for you and my dearest Anne. And when she arrives, all London shall be at her feet, for all London shall be mine, and what is mine must of needs at least adore what I must with all my being worship.

> [RAKEWELL *and* TRULOVE *shake hands affectionately.* RAKEWELL *kneels and kisses* ANNE's *hand. Pause. He rises.* ANNE *brings her hand quickly to her eyes and turns her head away. Pause.* RAKEWELL *steps forward.*]

TRIO *and* FINALE

RAKEWELL [*aside*].
      Laughter and light and all charms that endear,
        All that dazzles or dins,
      Wisdom and wit shall adorn the career
        Of him who can play, and who wins.

ANNE [*aside*]. Heart, you are happy, yet why should a tear
        Dim our joyous designs?

TRULOVE [*aside*].
      Fortune so swift and so easy, I fear,
        May only encourage his sins.

*   *   *

TRULOVE. Be well, be well advised.

ANNE.   Be always near.

> [*During the last lines,* ANNE, RAKEWELL *and* TRU-
> LOVE *move toward the garden gate.* SHADOW *holds it
> open for them and they pass through.*]

ANNE, RAKEWELL AND TRULOVE. Farewell.
SHADOW [*turning to audience*].
>> The PROGRESS OF A RAKE begins.

QUICK CURTAIN

Orchestral Interlude

Act I Scene 2

[MOTHER GOOSE'*s Brothel, London.*]

> [*At a table, downstage R, sit* RAKEWELL, SHADOW
> *and* MOTHER GOOSE *drinking. Backstage L a
> Cuckoo Clock.* WHORES, ROARING BOYS.]

CHORUS

ROARING BOYS. With air commanding and weapon handy
>> We rove in a band through the streets at night,
>> Our only notion to make commotion
>> And find occasion to provoke a fight.

WHORES.   In triumph glorious with trophies curious
>> We return victorious from Love's campaign;
>> No troop more practiced in Cupid's tactics
>> By feint and ambush the day to gain.

ROARING BOYS. For what is sweeter to human nature
>> Than to quarrel over nothing at all,
>> To hear the crashing of furniture smashing
>> Or heads being bashed in a tavern brawl?

WHORES.   With darting glances and bold advances
>> We open fire upon young and old;
>> Surprised by rapture, their hearts are captured,
>> And into our laps they pour their gold.

TUTTI.   A toast to our commanders then
                         From their Irregulars;
                     A toast, ladies and gentlemen:
                         To VENUS and to MARS.

RECITATIVE SECCO

SHADOW. Come, Tom, I would fain have our hostess, good Mother Goose,
    learn how faithfully I have discharged my duties as a godfather in
    preparing you for the delights to which your newly-found state of
    manhood is about to call you.
                         So tell my lady-Bishop of the game
                         What I did vow and promise in thy name.
RAKEWELL.   *One aim in all things to pursue:*
                    My duty to myself to do.
SHADOW [*to* MOTHER GOOSE]. Is he not apt?
MOTHER GOOSE.   And handsome too.
SHADOW.   What is thy duty to thyself?
RAKEWELL.   *To shut my eyes to prude and preacher*
                    And follow Nature as my teacher.
MOTHER GOOSE. What is the secret Nature knows?
RAKEWELL.   *What Beauty is and where it grows.*
SHADOW.   Canst thou define the Beautiful?
RAKEWELL.   I can.
                    That source of pleasure to the eyes
                    Youth owns, wit snatches, money buys,
                    Envy affects to scorn, but lies:
                    One fatal flaw it has. It dies.
SHADOW.   Exact, my scholar!
MOTHER GOOSE.   What is Pleasure then?
RAKEWELL.   *The idol of all dreams, the same*
                    Whatever shape it wear or name;
                    Whom flirts imagine as a hat,
                    Old maids believe to be a cat.
MOTHER GOOSE. Bravo!
SHADOW.   One final question. Love is . . .
RAKEWELL [*aside*].   Love!
                    That precious word is like a fiery coal,
                    It burns my lips, strikes terror to my soul.
SHADOW.   No answer? Will my scholar fail me?
RAKEWELL [*violently*].   No,
                    No more.
SHADOW.   Well, well.

MOTHER GOOSE.	More wine, love?
RAKEWELL.	Let me go.
SHADOW.	Are you afraid?

[*As the Cuckoo Clock coos ONE,* RAKEWELL *rises.*]

RAKEWELL.	Before it is too late.
SHADOW.	Wait.

[SHADOW *makes a sign and the clock turns backward and coos TWELVE.*]

See. Time is yours. The hours obey your pleasure.
Fear not. Enjoy. You may repent at leisure.

[RAKEWELL *sits down again and drinks wildly.*]

CHORUS

ROARING BOYS AND WHORES.
    Soon dawn will glitter outside the shutter
    And small birds twitter; but what of that?
    So long as we're able and wine's on the table
    Who cares what the troubling day is at?

    While food has flavor and limbs are shapely
    And hearts beat bravely to fiddle or drum
    Our proper employment is reckless enjoyment
    For too soon the noiseless night will come.

RECITATIVE SECCO

SHADOW [*rising to address the company*]. Sisters of Venus, Brothers of Mars, Fellow-worshippers in the Temple of Delight, it is my privilege to present to you a stranger to our mysteries who, following our custom, begs leave to sing you a song in earnest of his desire to be initiated. As you see, he is young; as you shall discover, he is rich. My master, and, if he will pardon the liberty, my friend, Mr Tom Rakewell.

ARIA

RAKEWELL [*coming forward to sing*].
    Love, too frequently betrayed
    For some plausible desire
    Or the world's enchanted fire,
    Still thy traitor in his sleep
    Renews the vow he did not keep,
      Weeping, weeping,
    He kneels before thy wounded shade.

□

Love, my sorrow and my shame,
Though thou daily be forgot,
Goddess, O forget me not.
Lest I perish, O be nigh
In my darkest hour that I,
        Dying, dying,
May call upon thy sacred name.

ENSEMBLE FINALE

WHORES [*in turn*]. How sad a song.
                            But sadness charms.
                How handsomely he cries.
        Come drown your sorrows in these arms.
                Forget it in these eyes.
        Upon these lips . . .
MOTHER GOOSE [*pushing them aside and taking* RAKEWELL'*s hand*].
                            Away. To-night
        I exercise my elder right
                And claim him for my prize.

> [*The* CHORUS *form a lane with the men on one side
> and the women on the other, as in a children's game.*
> MOTHER GOOSE *and* RAKEWELL *walk slowly be-
> tween them to a door backstage.* SHADOW *stands
> down stage watching.*]

CHORUS.   The sun is bright, the grass is green:
                      Lanterloo, lanterloo.
                 The King is courting his young Queen.
                      Lanterloo, my lady.

MEN.   They go a-walking. What do they see?
WOMEN.   An almanack in a walnut tree.

WOMEN.   They go a-riding. Whom do they meet?
MEN.   Three scarecrows and a pair of feet.

MEN.   What will she do when they sit at table?
WOMEN.   Eat as much as she is able.

WOMEN.   What will he do when they lie in bed?
CHORUS.   *Lanterloo, lanterloo.*
MEN.   Draw his sword and chop off her head.
CHORUS.   *Lanterloo, my lady.*

SHADOW [*raising his glass*].
  Sweet dreams, my master. Dreams may lie,
  But dream. For when you wake, you die.

SLOW CURTAIN

Act I Scene 3

[*Same as Scene 1. Autumn night, full moon.*]

[ANNE *enters from house in travelling clothes.*]

ORCHESTRAL RECITATIVE

ANNE. No word from Tom. Has Love no voice, can Love not keep
  A Maytime vow in cities? Fades it as the rose
  Cut for a rich display? Forgot! But no, to weep
  Is not enough. He needs my help. Love hears, Love knows,
  Love answers him across the silent miles, and goes.

ARIA

  Quietly, night, O find him and caress,
      And may thou quiet find
    His heart, although it be unkind,
        Nor may its beat confess,
  Although I weep, it knows of loneliness.

  Guide me, O moon, chastely when I depart,
      And warmly be the same
    He watches without grief or shame;
        It cannot be thou art
  A colder moon upon a colder heart.

RECITATIVE SECCO

    [TRULOVE'S *voice is heard calling from the house—*
    "Anne, Anne."]

My father! Can I desert him and his devotion for a love who has
deserted me? [*Starts walking back to the house. Then she stops suddenly.*]
No, my father has strength of purpose, while Tom is weak, and needs
the comfort of a faithful hand.

ORCHESTRAL RECITATIVE

[*She kneels.*] O God, protect dear Tom, support my father, and strengthen my resolve. [*She bows her head, then rises and comes forward with great decision.*]

CABALETTA

I go to him.
Love cannot falter,
Cannot desert;
Though it be shunned
Or be forgotten,
Though it be hurt
If love be love
It will not alter.
O should I see
My love in need
It shall not matter
What he may be.

[*She turns and starts toward the garden gate.*]

QUICK CURTAIN

Act II Scene 1

[*The morning room of* RAKEWELL'*s house in a London square.*]

[*A bright morning sun pours in through the window, also noises from the street.* RAKEWELL *is seated at breakfast table. At a particularly loud outburst of noise he rises, walks quickly to the window and slams it shut.*]

ARIA

RAKEWELL [*reseated at the table—with a quiet, but semi-agitated despair*].
Vary the song, O London, change!
Disband your notes and let them range;
Let Rumor scream, let Folly purr,
Let Tone desert the flatterer.
Let Harmony no more obey
The strident choristers of prey—

Yet all your music cannot fill
The gap that in my heart—is still.

ORCHESTRAL RECITATIVE

O Nature, green unnatural mother, how I have followed where you led. Is it for this I left the country? No ploughman is more a slave to sun, moon and season than a gentleman to the clock of Fashion. City! City! What Caesar could have imagined the curious viands I have tasted? They choke me. And let Oporto and Provence keep all their precious wines. I would as soon be dry and wrinkled as a raisin as ever taste another. Cards! Living Pictures! And, dear God, the matrons with their marriageable girls! Cover their charms a little, you well-bred bawds, or your goods will catch their death of the rheum long before they learn of the green sickness. The others too, with their more candid charms. Pah! [*Pause.*] Who's honest, chaste or kind? One, only one, and of her I dare not think. [*He rises.*]

Up, Nature, up, the hunt is on; thy pack is in full cry. They smell the blood upon the bracing air. On, on, on, through every street and mansion, for every candle in this capital of light attends thy appetizing progress and burns in honor at thy shrine.

ARIA [*reprise*]

Always the quarry that I stalk
Fades or evades me, and I walk
An endless hall of chandeliers
In light that blinds, in light that sears,
Reflected from a million smiles
All empty as the country miles
Of silly wood and senseless park;
And only in my heart—the dark.

[*He sits down. Pause. Then: spoken:*]

I wish I were happy.

[*Enter* SHADOW. *He has a broadsheet in his hand.*]

RECITATIVE SECCO

SHADOW. Master, are you alone?
RAKEWELL. And sick at heart. What is it?
SHADOW [*handing* RAKEWELL *the broadsheet*]. Do you know this lady?
RAKEWELL. Baba the Turk! I have not visited St Giles Fair as yet. They say that brave warriors who never flinched at the sound of musketry have

swooned after a mere glimpse of her. Is such a thing possible in Nature?

SHADOW. Two noted physicians have sworn that she is no imposter. Would you go see her?

RAKEWELL. Nick, I know that manner of yours. You have some scheme afoot. Come, sir, out with it.

SHADOW. Consider her picture.

RAKEWELL. Would you see me turned to stone?

SHADOW. Do you desire her?

RAKEWELL. Like the gout or the falling sickness.

SHADOW. Are you obliged to her?

RAKEWELL. Heaven forbid.

SHADOW. Then marry her.

RAKEWELL. Have you taken leave of your senses?

SHADOW. I was never saner. Come, master, observe the host of mankind. How are they? Wretched. Why? Because they are not free. Why? Because the giddy multitude are driven by the unpredictable Must of their pleasures and the sober few are bound by the inflexible Ought of their duty, between which slaveries there is nothing to choose. Would you be happy? Then learn to act freely. Would you act freely? Then learn to ignore those twin tyrants of appetite and conscience. Therefore I counsel you, master,—Take Baba the Turk to wife.

ORCHESTRAL RECITATIVE

Consider her picture once more, and as you do so reflect upon my words.

ARIA

> In youth the panting slave pursues
>   The fair evasive dame;
> Then caught in colder fetters, woos
>   Wealth, Office, or a name;
> Till, old, dishonored, sick, downcast
>   And failing in his wits,
> In Virtue's narrow cell at last
>   The withered bondsman sits.
>
> That man alone his fate fulfills,
>   For he alone is free
> Who chooses what to will, and wills
>   His choice as destiny.

No eye his future can foretell,
No law his past explain
Whom neither Passion may compel
Nor Reason can restrain.

[*Pause.*]

Well?

[RAKEWELL *looks up from the broadsheet. He and*
SHADOW *look at each other. Pause. Then suddenly*
RAKEWELL *begins to laugh. His laughter grows*
louder and louder. SHADOW *joins in. They shake*
hands. During the finale SHADOW *helps* RAKEWELL
get dressed to go out.]

DUET-FINALE

[*Prestissimo. Voices in canon.*]

RAKEWELL.	SHADOW.
My tale shall be told	Come, master, prepare
Both by young and by old,	Your fate to dare,
A favorite narration	Perfumed, well-dressed
Throughout the nation	And looking your best,
Remembered by all	A bachelor of fashion,
In cottage and hall	Eyes hinting passion,
With song and laughter	Your carriage young
For ever after.	And upon your tongue
For tongues will not tire	The gallant speeches
Around the fire	That Cupid teaches
Or sitting at meat	With Shadow to guide
The tale to repeat	Come, seek your bride,
Of the wooing and wedding	Be up and doing,
Likewise the bedding	Attend to your wooing
Of Baba the Turk,	On Baba the Turk
That masterwork	Your charms to work.
Whom Nature created	What deed could be as great
To be celebrated	As with this gorgon to mate?
For her features dire,	All the world shall admire
To Tom Rakewell Esquire.	Tom Rakewell Esquire.

My heart beats faster.
Come, Shadow,

Come, master,
And do not falter

RAKEWELL AND SHADOW [*in unison*].
>   To Hymen's Altar.
>   Ye Powers, inspire
>   Tom Rakewell Esquire.

>   [*Exeunt.*]

QUICK CURTAIN

Act II Scene 2

[*Street in front of* RAKEWELL'*s house. London.*]

> [*The entrance, stage center, is led up to by a flight of semi-circular steps. Servants' entrance L, Tree R. Autumn. Dusk.*]

> [*Enter* ANNE. *She looks anxiously at the entrance for a moment, walks slowly up the steps and hesitatingly lifts the knocker. Then she glances to the left and, seeing a* SERVANT *beginning to come out of the servants' entrance, she hurries down to the right and flattens herself against the wall under the tree, her hand held against her breast, until he passes and exits to the right. Then she steps forward.*]

ORCHESTRAL RECITATIVE

ANNE. How strange! Although the heart for love dare everything,
>   The hand draws back to it and finds
>   No spring of courage. London! Alone! seems all that it can say.
>   O heart, be stronger, that what this coward hand
>   Wishes beyond all bravery, the touch of his,
>   May bring its daring to a close, unneeded;
>   And love be all your bounty.

ARIA

[*with an elevated and quiet determination*]
No step in fear shall wander nor in weakness delay;
Hear thou or not, merciful Heaven, ease thou or not my way;
A love that is sworn before Thee can plunder Hell of its prey.

> [*As she turns again towards the entrance, a noise from the right causes her to turn in that direction—*

MARCHE COMIQUE

*—and come forward, as a procession of servants carry-
ing wrapped, yet obviously strangely shaped, packages,
starts crossing the stage from the right and exiting into
the servants' entrance. While this is going on, night be-
gins to fall. At its close the stage is dark.*]

[*watching as they go by in back of her: parlando against the march*]
What can this mean? . . . A ball? . . . A journey? . . . A dream?
How evil in the purple dark they seem . . .
Loot from dead fingers . . . Living mockery . . .
I tremble with no reason . . .

[*As the procession is completed, a sedan chair is carried
in from the left, preceded by two* SERVANTS *carrying
torches.* ANNE *turns suddenly towards it.*]

Lights! . . .

[*The chair is set down before the steps.* RAKEWELL
steps from it into the light.]

. . . 'Tis he!

[ANNE *hurries to him, and he takes a few steps for-
ward to meet her and holds her gently away from
himself.*]

DUET

RAKEWELL [*confused and agitated*].
    Anne! Here!
ANNE [*with self-control*].
            And, Tom, such splendor.
RAKEWELL.   Leave pretences,
    Anne, ask me, accuse me—
ANNE [*interjecting*].   Tom, no—
RAKEWELL. —Denounce me to the world, and go;
    Return to your home, forget in your senses
    What, senseless, you pursue.
ANNE [*quietly*].   Do you return?
RAKEWELL [*violently*]. I!
ANNE.   Then how shall I go?
RAKEWELL.   You must!
        [*Aside.*] O wilful powers, pummel to dust
    And drive into the void, one thought—return!

ANNE [*aside*].
      Assist me, Heaven, since love I must
      To calm his raging heart, his eyes that burn.

RAKEWELL [*turning to* ANNE *and addressing her with a more measured tone*].
      Listen to me, for I know London well:
          Here Virtue is a day coquette,
          For what night hides, it can forget,
      And Virtue is, till gallants talk—and tell.
      Then, only let it gild its ruined fame,
          Perfume its obvious decay,
          It sallies forth into the day,
      Corrupting all again in Virtue's name.
      O Anne, that is the air we breathe; go home,
      'Tis wisdom here to be afraid.

ANNE.   How should I fear, who have your aid
      And all my love for you beside, dear Tom?

RAKEWELL [*bitterly*]. My aid? London has done all that it can
      With me. Unworthy am I, less
      Than weak. Go back.

ANNE [*simply*].   Let worthiness,
      So you still love, reside in that.

RAKEWELL [*touched, stepping towards her with emotion*].
                       O Anne!—

> [BABA *suddenly puts her head out through the curtains of the sedan-chair window. She is very elaborately coiffed, and her face is, below the eyes, heavily veiled in the Eastern fashion.*]

ORCHESTRAL RECITATIVE

BABA [*interrupting with vexation*]. My love, am I to remain in here forever? You know that I am *not* in the habit of stepping from sedan chairs unaided. Nor shall I wait, unmoved, much longer. Finish, if you please, whatever business is detaining you with this person. [*She withdraws her head.*]

RECITATIVE SECCO

ANNE [*surprised*]. Tom, what—?

RAKEWELL. My wife, Anne.

ANNE. Your wife! [*Pause. Then, with slight bitterness.*] I see, then, that it is I who was unworthy. [*She turns away.* RAKEWELL *again steps towards her, then checks himself.*]

TRIO

[*during which* BABA's *interjected interruptions become more and more frequent and gradually both faster and louder, until by the climax of the ensemble her complaints are going on continuously against the slower melody taken by* RAKEWELL *and* ANNE.]

ANNE [*aside*].   Could it then have been known
          When Spring was love, and love took all our ken,
                    That I and I alone
                    Upon that forsworn ground,
                         Should see love dead?
          O promise the heart to winter, swear it bound
                    To nothing live, and you shall wed;
                    But should you vow to love, O then
                    See that you do not feel again—
                         O never, never, never—
                    Lest you, alone, your promise keep,
                    Walk the long aisle, and walking weep
                         Forever.

TOM [*aside*].   It is done, it is done.
          I turn away, yet should I turn again,
                    The arbor would be gone
                    And on the frozen ground,
                         The birds lie dead.
          O bury the heart there deeper than it sound,
                    Upon its only bridal bed;
                    And should it, dreaming love, ask—When
                    Shall I awaken once again?
                         Say—Never, never, never;
                    We shall this wint'ry promise keep—
                    Obey thy exile, honor sleep
                         Forever.

BABA.   I'm waiting, dear . . . Have done
          With talk, my love . . . I shall count up to ten . . .
                    Who is she? *One* . . .
                    Hussy! . . . If I am found
                         Immured here, dead,
          I swear . . . *Two* . . . I'll haunt you . . . *Three* . . . You know
                    you're bound
                    By law, dear . . . *Four* . . . Before I wed

Could I . . . *Five, Six* . . . have . . . *Seven* . . . then
Foreseen my sorrow? . . . *Eight, Nine* . . . *Ten* . . .
O never, never, never . . .
I shall be cross, love, if you keep
Baba condemned to gasp and weep
Forever.

ORCHESTRAL RECITATIVE *and* FINALE

[ANNE *exits R hurriedly.*]

BABA [*from the carriage*]. *I* have not run away, dear heart. Baba is still
waiting patiently for her gallant.
RAKEWELL [*squaring his shoulders and approaching the chair*].
I am with you, dear wife.

[*He helps her from her chair with a gallant bow.*]

BABA [*patting him affectionately on the cheek*].
Who was that girl, my life?
RAKEWELL [*ironically*].
Only a milkmaid, pet,
To whom I was in debt.

[*As* RAKEWELL *takes his wife's hand and lifts it to
begin conducting her up the steps, the entrance doors
are thrown open,* SERVANTS *carry off the sedan chair
R,* SERVANTS *appear from the entrance and line the
sides of the steps carrying torches, and voices are heard
off crying:*]

VOICES. Baba the Turk is here! Baba the Turk is here!

[*At this* BABA, *as she begins her ascent, draws herself
up with obvious pride—and the* CROWD *pours on to
the stage from both sides.*]

CROWD [*facing the house—covering the whole front of the stage—in the
darkness*].
Baba the Turk, Baba the Turk, before you retire,
Show thyself once, O grant us our desire.

[BABA *and* RAKEWELL *have reached the top of the
steps. He exits into the house, and she, with an elo-
quent gesture, sweeps around to face the crowd, re-
moves her veil and reveals a full and flowing black
beard. As the* CROWD, *entranced, chants:*]

Ah! Baba, Baba, Baba. Ah!

> [—*she blows them a kiss and keeps her arms out-
> stretched with the practiced gestures of a great artiste.
> Tableau.*]

CURTAIN

Act II Scene 3

[*The same room as Act II, Scene 1, except that now it is cluttered up with every
conceivable kind of object, stuffed animals and birds, cases of minerals, china,
glass, etc.*]

> [RAKEWELL *and* BABA *are sitting at breakfast, the
> former sulking, the latter breathlessly chattering.*]

ORCHESTRAL RECITATIVE (*or* ARIA)

BABA [*très vite without stopping*].
  As I was saying both brothers wore moustaches,
  But Sir John was the taller; they gave me the musical glasses.
  That was in Vienna, no, it must have been Milan
  Because of the donkeys. Vienna was the Chinese fan
—Or was it the bottle of water from the River Jordan?—
  I'm certain at least it was Vienna and Lord Gordon.
  I get so confused about all my travels.
  The snuff boxes came from Paris, and the fluminous gravels
  From a cardinal who admired me vastly in Rome.
  You're not eating, my love. Count Moldau gave me the gnome,
  And Prince Obolovsky the little statues of the Twelve Apostles,
  Which I like best of all my treasures except my fossils.
  Which reminds me I must tell Bridget never to touch the mummies.
  I'll dust them myself. She can do the wax-work dummies.
  Of course, I like my birds, too, especially my Great Auk;
  But the moths will get in them. My love, what's the matter, why
      don't you talk?

                                                    [*Pause.*]

RECITATIVE SECCO

  What's the matter?
RAKEWELL.   Nothing.

BABA.   Speak to me!
RAKEWELL.   Why?

> [BABA *rises and puts her arm lovingly round*
> RAKEWELL's *neck. She sings, unaccompanied.*]

SONG UNACCOMPANIED

BABA. Come, sweet, come
    Why so glum?
    Smile at Baba who
    Loving smiles at you.
    Do not frown,
    Husband dear. . . .

RAKEWELL [*pushing her violently away*].
                     Sit down.

> [BABA *bursts into tears and rage. During her aria she
> strides about the stage and, at each of the four words
> in the first lines of both stanzas, picks up some object
> and smashes it.*]

ARIA

BABA.   Scorned! Abused! Neglected! Baited!
            Wretched me!
            Why is this?
            I can see.
            I know who is
        Your bliss, your love, your life
        While I, your loving wife,—
            Lie not!—am hated.

> [*With increased vocal ornamentation of melodic line.*]

    Young, demure, delightful, clever
            Is she not?
            Not as I. [*Shoving her face into* RAKEWELL's.]
            That is what
            I know you sigh.
        Then sigh! Then cry! For she [*She sits down.*]
        Your wife shall never be—
            Oh No! no, ne . . . . (ver)

[*With the last word she begins a cadenza.* RAKEWELL *rises suddenly, seizes his wig and plumps it down over her head, back to front, cutting her run off suddenly in the middle.* BABA *remains silent and motionless in her place for the rest of the scene.* RAKEWELL *walks moodily about with his hands in his pockets, then flings himself down on a sofa backstage.*]

ORCHESTRAL RECITATIVE

RAKEWELL. My heart is cold, I cannot weep;
   One remedy is left me—sleep.

[*He sleeps. A short pause.*]

PANTOMIME WITH ORCHESTRA

[*A door R opens and* SHADOW *peeps in. Seeing all clear he withdraws his head and then enters wheeling in front of him some large object covered by a dust sheet. When he has brought it to the front centre of stage he removes dust sheet, disclosing a phantastic baroque machine. He looks about, picks a loaf of bread from the table, opens a door in the front of the machine, puts in the loaf and recloses the door. Then he looks round again and picks off the floor a piece of a broken vase. This he drops into a hopper on the machine. He turns a wheel and the loaf of bread falls out of a chute. He opens the door, takes out the piece of china, replaces it by the loaf and repeats the performance, so that the audience see that the mechanism is the crudest kind of false bottom. The second time he ends with the loaf in the machine and the piece of china in his hand. Then he puts back the dust sheet and wheels the machine backstage near* RAKEWELL's *sofa and takes up a position near* RAKEWELL's *head. During all this he sings a gay ironic little aria to himself on the words* fa-la-la.]

RAKEWELL [*stirring in his sleep. Spoken voice against orchestra*]. O I wish it
   were true.

RECITATIVE SECCO

SHADOW. Awake?

Orchestral Recitative

RAKEWELL [*starting up*].
    Who's there?

Recitative Secco

SHADOW.   Your shadow, master.

Orchestral Recitative

RAKEWELL.   You!
    O Nick, I've had the strangest dream. I thought—
    How could I know what I was never taught
    Or fancy objects I have never seen?—
    I had devised a marvellous machine,
    An engine that converted stones to bread
    Whereby all peoples were for nothing fed.
    I saw all want abolished by my skill
    And earth become an Eden of good-will.

Recitative Secco

SHADOW [*with a conjurer's gesture, whipping the dust sheet off the machine*].
    Did your machine look anything like this?

Orchestral Recitative

RAKEWELL. I must be still asleep. That *is* my dream.

Recitative Secco

SHADOW. How does it work?

Orchestral Recitative

RAKEWELL [*very excited*].   I need a stone.

Recitative Secco

SHADOW [*handing him the piece of vase*].   Try this.

Orchestral Recitative

RAKEWELL. I place it here. I turn this wheel and then—
    The bread!

[*The loaf falls out.*]

Recitative Secco

SHADOW [*picking up the bread, breaks off a piece and hands it to* RAKEWELL].
    Be certain. Taste!

Orchestral Recitative

RAKEWELL [*after tasting it, falls on his knees*].
O miracle!

O may I not, forgiven all my past
For one good deed, deserve dear Anne at last?

Duet

RAKEWELL [*beside his machine. Très exalté and oblivious to his surroundings*].
> Thanks to this excellent device
> Man shall re-enter Paradise
> From which he once was driven.
> Secure from want, the cause of crime,
> The world shall for the second time
> Be similar to heaven.

SHADOW [*downstage. In a worldly-wise manner and taking the audience into his confidence*].
> A word to all my friends, where'er you sit,
> The men of sense, in boxes or the pit.
> My master is a fool as you can see,
> But you may do good business with me.

RAKEWELL. When to his infinite relief
> Toil, hunger, poverty and grief
> Have vanished like a dream,
> This engine Adam shall excite
> To hallelujahs of delight
> And ecstasy extreme.

SHADOW. The idle drone and the deserving poor
> Will give good money for this toy, be sure.
> For, so it please, there's no fantastic lie
> You cannot make men swallow if you try.

RAKEWELL. Omnipotent when armed with this,
> In secular abundant bliss
> He shall ascend the Chain
> Of Being to its top to win
> The throne of Nature and begin
> His everlasting reign.

SHADOW. So, you who know your proper interest,
> Here is your golden chance. Invest. Invest.
> Come, take your shares immediately, my friends,
> And praise the folly that pays dividends.

SHADOW. Forgive me, master, for intruding upon your transports; but your dream is still a long way from fulfillment. Here is the machine, it is true. But it must be manufactured in great quantities. It must be advertised, it must be sold. We shall need money and advice. We shall need partners, merchants of probity and reputation in the City.

RAKEWELL. Alas, good Shadow, your admonitions are only too just; and they chill my spirit. For how am I, who am become a byword for extravagance and folly, to approach such men? Is this dream, too, this noble vision, to prove as empty as the rest? What shall I do?

SHADOW. Have no fear, master. Leave such matters to me. Indeed, I have already spoken with several notable citizens concerning your invention; and they are as eager to see it as you to show.

RAKEWELL. Ingenious Shadow! How could I live without you? I cannot wait. Let's visit them immediately.

> [RAKEWELL *and* SHADOW *begin wheeling the machine out. Just as they reach the door,* SHADOW, *who is pulling in front, turns.*]

SHADOW. Oh, master.
RAKEWELL. What is it?
SHADOW. Should you not tell the good news to your wife?
RAKEWELL. My wife? I have no wife. I've buried her.

> [*Exeunt.*]

QUICK CURTAIN

Act III Scene 1

[*The same as Act II, Scene 3, except that everything is covered with cobwebs and dust.* BABA *is still seated motionless at the table, the tea cosy over her head, also covered with cobwebs and dust. Afternoon. Spring.*]

> [*Before the curtain rises a great choral cry of* "Ruin. Disaster. Shame." *is heard from behind it. When the curtain rises two groups of the* CROWD *of Respectable Citizens are examining the objects. Two other groups enter as the scene progresses.*]

CHORUS

GROUP I. What curious phenomena are up today for sale.
GROUP II. What manner of remarkables.
GROUP III [*entering. In the doorway, horrified*]. What squalor!
GROUP I [*crowded around some object, admiringly*].   What detail!
GROUP IV [*entering*]. I *am* so glad I didn't miss the auction.
GROUP II.   So am I.
GROUP III. I can't begin admiring.
GROUP IV.   O fantastic!
TUTTI.   Let us buy!

> [*Again the cry of* "Ruin. Disaster. Shame." *is heard
> from offstage. The* CROWD *pauses in its examina-
> tion, looks at each other, then comes forward and ad-
> dresses the audience with hushed voices that barely
> conceal a tinge of complacency.*]

CHORUS

CROWD. Blasted!   Blasted!   so many hopes of gain:
    Hundreds   of sober   merchants are insane;
    Widows   have sold their   mourning-clothes to eat;
    Herds of   pale orphans   forage in the street;
    Many   a Duchess,   divested of gems,
    Has crossed the   dread Styx   by way of the Thames.
    O stricken,   take heart   in placing the blame—

> [*They begin to disperse again into groups examining
> the objects.*]

Rakewell.   Rakewell.   Ruin. Disaster. Shame.

> [*Enter* ANNE. *She looks about quickly and then ap-
> proaches the* CROWD *group by group.*]

CHORUS *with* SOLO VOICE

ANNE. Do *you* know where Tom Rakewell is?
GROUP I.   America. He fled.
GROUP II. Spontaneous combustion caught him hurrying. He's dead.
ANNE. Do *you* know what's become of him?
GROUP III.   Tom Rakewell? How should we?
GROUP IV. He's Methodist.
GROUP III.   He's Papist.

GROUP IV.   He's converting Jewery.
ANNE. Can *no* one tell me where he is?
TUTTI.   We're certain he's in debt;
    They're after him, they're after him, and they will catch him yet.
ANNE [*aside*]. I'll seek him in the house myself. [*Exit.*]
GROUPS I & II.   I wonder at her quest.
GROUPS III & IV. She's probably some silly girl he ruined like the rest.

> [*They return to their examination unconcernedly.
> Then the door is flung open and* SELLEM *enters with
> a great flurry followed by a few* SERVANTS *who begin
> clearing space and setting up a dais.*]

CHORUS *with* SOLO VOICE

SELLEM. Aha!
CROWD.   He's here,
    The auctioneer.
SELLEM [*to the* SERVANTS]. No! over there.

> [*They begin nervously setting it up again in another
> spot.*]

    Be quick. Take care.
CROWD [*to each other*]. Your bids prepare.
    Be quick. Take care.

> [SELLEM *mounts the dais and bows.*]

ORCHESTRAL RECITATIVE

SELLEM. Ladies, both fair and gracious: gentlemen: be all welcome to this
    miracle of, this most widely heralded of, this—I am sure you follow
    me—ne plus ultra of auctions. [*Pause.*] Truly there is a divine balance
    in Nature: a thousand lose that a thousand may gain; and you who
    are the fortunate are so not only in yourselves, but also in being Na-
    ture's very missionaries. You are her instruments for the restoration
    of that order we all so worship, and it is granted to, ah! so few of us to
    serve. [*He bows again. Applause.*]

RECITATIVE SECCO

Let us proceed at once. Lots one and two: which cover all objects
subsumed under the categories—animal, vegetable and mineral.

ARIA *with* CHORUS (I)

[During the Aria, which is sung very rapidly with strong rhythmical accentuation, SELLEM *is continually on the move, indulging in elaborate by-play, holding up objects;* SERVANTS *are rushing on and off the dais with objects; the* CROWD *is eager and attentive.]*

Who hears me, knows me; knows me
A man with value; look at this—*[holding up the stuffed auk]*
What is it?—Wit
And Profit: no one, no one
Could fail to conquer, fail to charm,
Who had it by
To watch. And who could not be
A nimble planner, having this *[holding up a mounted fish]*
Before him? Bid
To get them, get them, hurry!

[During the next seven lines various individuals and groups in the CROWD *are bidding excitedly:* "One. Two. Three. Four. Etc."]

La! come bid.
Hmm! come buy.
Aha! the auk.
Witty, lovely, wealthy. Poof! go high!
La! Some more.
Hmm! Come on.
Aha! the pike. *[Silent pause.]*
Bid, bid, going at twenty-three, going, going, gone.
CROWD. Hurrah! *[Pause.]*
SELLEM *[holding up a marble bust].*
Behold it, Roman, moral,
The man who has it, has it
Forever,—yes! *[holds up a palm branch]*
And holy, holy, curing
The body, soul and spirit;
A gift of—God's!
And not to mention this or   *[Holding up*
The other, more and more and—   *various*
So help me—more!   *objects.]*
Then bid, O get them, hurry!

[CROWD, *during the next seven lines, bids as before.*]

 La! come bid.
 Hmm! come buy.
 Aha! the bust.
Feel them, life eternal: Poof! go high!
 La! some more.
 Hmm! come on.
 Aha! the palm. [*Silent pause.*]
Bid, bid, going at seventeen, going, going, gone.
CROWD. Hurrah! [*Pause.*]

RECITATIVE SECCO

SELLEM. Wonderful. Yes, yes. And now for the truly adventurous—

ARIA *with* CHORUS (II)

  [*walking over slowly to the covered* BABA, *and chang-
  ing his voice to a suggestive whisper*]

An unknown object draws us, draws us near.
A cake? An organ? Golden Apple Tree?
A block of copal? Mint of alchemy?
Oracle? Pillar? Octopus? Who'll see?
O you, whose houses are in order, hear!
Be brave! Perhaps an angel will appear. [*Pause for effect.*]

  [*During the next seven lines the* CROWD *bids as be-
  fore, but this time gets so excited that they almost
  drown out* SELLEM, *and they begin fighting among
  themselves.*]

 La! come bid.
 Hmm! come buy.
 Aha! the it.
This may be salvation. Poof! go high!
 La! be calm.
 Hmm! come on.
 Aha! the what.

  [*At this point the* CROWD *is so raucous that* SELLEM
  *is practically shouting by the time he ends the next
  phrase.*]

Bid, bid, going at ninety, going at a hundred, going, going, gone.

> [*In order to quiet the* CROWD, SELLEM, *as he shouts his last* "Gone," *snatches the tea cosy off* BABA'S *head. The effect quiets them immediately and she, for the moment completely impervious to her surroundings, finishes the cadenza she began in the last scene.*]

BABA. . . . . . ever.

> [*Then she looks quickly around, snatches up a veil that is lying on the table, stands up indignantly and during the next verse of her aria brushes herself off while the* CROWD *and* SELLEM *murmur in the background over and over:*]

CROWD AND SELLEM. It's Baba, his wife. It passes believing.

ARIA (II)

(See Act II, Scene 3, p. 70)

BABA.   Sold! Annoyed! I've caught you!—thieving!
               If you dare
               Touch a thing,
               Then beware
               My reckoning;
            Be off, be gone, desist:
            I, Baba, must insist
               Upon—your leaving.

> [*The voices of* RAKEWELL *and* SHADOW *are heard giving a street-cry from off stage:*

Old wives for sale, old wives for sale!
Stale wives, prim wives, silly and grim wives,
       Old wives for sale!]

ORCHESTRAL RECITATIVE

SELLEM AND CROWD. Now what was that?
BABA [*aside*].   The pigs of plunder!

> [*Enter* ANNE *hurriedly. She rushes to the window.*]

ANNE. Was that his voice?
SELLEM AND CROWD.   What next, I wonder?
BABA [*aside*]. The milk-maid haunts me.
ANNE [*at the window*].   Gone!
BABA [*reflectively—after glancing about*].   All I possessed
     Seems gone.

[*Shrugging her shoulders.*] Well, well.

[*To* ANNE, *a bit imperiously and indulgently.*] My dear!

ANNE [*turning*].   His wife!

BABA.   His jest—

No matter now. Come here, my child, to Baba.

[ANNE *goes over to her.*]

SELLEM [*obviously under a strain*]. Ladies, the sale, if you could go out—

BABA [*impatiently*].   Robber,

Don't interrupt.

CROWD [*to him as he walks desperately to a corner of the room*].

Don't interrupt or rail;

A scene like this is better than a sale.

TRIO *with* CHORUS

BABA [*to* ANNE]. You love him, seek to set him right:
He's but a shuttle-headed lad:
Not quite a gentleman, nor quite
Completely vanquished by the bad:
Who knows what care and love might do?
But good or bad, I know he still loves you.

ANNE.   He loves me still! Then I alone
In weeping doubt have been untrue:
O hope, endear my love, atone,
Enlighten, grace whatever may ensue.

SELLEM AND GROUPS I & II. He loves her.

GROUPS III & IV.   Who?

SELLEM AND GROUPS I & II.   That isn't known.

GROUPS III & IV. He loves her still.

SELLEM AND GROUPS I & II.   The tale is sad—

GROUPS III & IV.   —if true.

BABA.   So find him, and his man beware!
I may have made a bad mistake
Yet I can tell who in that pair
Is poisoned victim and who snake!
Then go—

ANNE.   But where shall you—?

BABA [*lifting her hand to gently interrupt*].   My dear,
A gifted lady never need have fear.
I shall go back and grace the stage,

Where manner rules and wealth attends.
Can I deny my time its rage?
My self-indulgent intermezzo ends. [*With an all-inclusive
gesture.*]

ANNE.   Can I for him all love engage
And yet believe her happy when love ends.
GROUPS III & IV.   She will go back.
GROUPS I & II.   Her view is sage.
GROUPS III & IV.
        That's life.
GROUPS I & II.   We came to buy.
TUTTI.   See how it ends.
SELLEM [*despondently*].
        Money farewell. Who'll buy? The auction ends.

[*At the climax of the ensemble, the voices of* RAKE-
WELL *and* SHADOW *are again heard from the street.
All on stage pause to listen.*]

RAKEWELL AND SHADOW [*off; to ballad tune*].
        If boys had wings and girls had stings
        And gold fell from the sky,
        If new-laid eggs wore wooden legs
        I should not laugh or cry.

STRETTO TRIO *and* FINALE *with* CHORUS

ANNE.   It's Tom, I know!
BABA.   The two, then go!
SELLEM AND CROWD.   The thief, below!

ANNE.   I go to him,
                        O love, be brave,
                        Be swift, be true,
                        Be strong for him and save.

BABA.   Then go to him,
                        In love be brave,
                        Be swift, be true,
                        Be strong for him and save.

SELLEM AND CROWD.   They're after him.
                        His crime was grave;
                        Be swift if you
                        Want time enough to save.

ANNE [*pausing for a moment—to* BABA].
　　　　　　　May God bless you.
ALL [*but* ANNE].　　　Be swift if you
　　　　　Want time enough to save. [ANNE *rushes out.*]

> [*The voices of* RAKEWELL *and* SHADOW *are heard disappearing in the distance.*]

RAKEWELL AND SHADOW.
　　　　Who cares a fig for Tory or Whig
　　　　　Not I, not I, not I.

> [*Pause, then* BABA *turns and addresses* SELLEM *with lofty command.*]

BABA. You! Summon my carriage!

> [*He, impressed in spite of himself and certainly forgetting he came to auction off her carriage, bows, goes to the door and opens it for her.*]

[*To the* CROWD.]　　　　Out of my way!

> [CROWD *falls back and she starts to leave—turning at the door.*]

The next time *you* see Baba you shall pay!
CROWD. We've never been through such a hectic day.

CURTAIN

Orchestral Interlude

Act III Scene 2

[*A starless night. A churchyard. Tombs. Front centre a newly-dug grave. Behind it a flat raised tomb against which is leaning a sexton's spade. On the right a yew-tree.*]

> [*Enter* RAKEWELL *and* SHADOW *left, the former out of breath, the latter carrying a little black bag.*]

DUET

*[to be sung to one or more ballad tunes in the
traditional manner without expression.]*

RAKEWELL. How dark and dreadful is this place.
    Why have you led me here?
There's something, Shadow, in thy face
    That fills my soul with fear!

SHADOW. A year and a day have passed away
    Since first to thee I came.
All things you bid, I duly did
    And now my wages claim.

RAKEWELL. Shadow, good Shadow, be patient; I
    Am beggared as you know
But promise when I am rich again
    To pay thee all I owe.

SHADOW. 'Tis not thy money but thy soul
    Which I this night require.
Look in my eyes and recognise
    Whom,—Fool! you chose to hire.

        *[Pointing out grave and taking the objects mentioned
        out of his bag.]*

Behold thy waiting grave, behold
    Steel, halter, poison, gun.
Make no excuse, thine exit choose:
    Tom Rakewell's race is run.

RAKEWELL. O let the wild hills cover me
    Or the abounding wave.
SHADOW. The sins you did may not be hid
    Think not thy soul to save.

RAKEWELL. Why did an uncle I never knew
    Select me for his heir?
SHADOW. It pleases well the damned in Hell
    To bring another there.

Midnight is come; by rope or gun
    Or medicine or knife
On the stroke of twelve you shall slay yourself
    For forfeit is thy life.

[A clock begins to strike.]

> Count one, count two, count three, count four,
> Count five and six and seven,

RAKEWELL. Have mercy on me, Heaven.
SHADOW.   Count eight,—
RAKEWELL. Too late.
SHADOW.   No, wait. *[He holds up his hand and the clock stops after the ninth stroke. So does the orchestra.]*

RECITATIVE SECCO

SHADOW *[urbanely]*. Very well then, my dear and good Tom, perhaps you impose a bit upon our friendship; but Nick, as you know, is a gentleman at heart, forgives your dilatoriness and suggests—a game.
RAKEWELL. A game?
SHADOW. A game of chance to finally decide your fate. Have you a pack of cards?
RAKEWELL *[taking a pack from his pocket]*. All that remains me of this world,—and for the next.
SHADOW. You jest. Fine, fine. Good spirits make a game go well. I shall explain. The rules are simple and the outcome simpler still: Nick will cut three cards. If you can name them, you are free; if not, *[he points to the instruments of death]* you choose the path to follow me. You understand. *[RAKEWELL nods.]* Let us begin. *[SHADOW shuffles the cards, places the pack in the palm of his left hand and cuts with his right, holding then the portion with the exposed card towards the audience and away from RAKEWELL.]* Well, then.

DUET with SECCO ACCOMPANIMENT

RAKEWELL. My heart is wild with fear, my throat is dry,
      I cannot think, I dare not wish.
SHADOW.   Come, try.
      Let wish be thought and think on one to name,
      You wish in all your fear could rule the game
      Instead of Shadow.
RAKEWELL *[aside]*.   Anne! *[Silent pause.]*
                              [Calmly.] My fear departs;
      I name—the Queen of Hearts.

RECITATIVE SECCO

SHADOW *[holding up the card toward RAKEWELL]*. The Queen of Hearts.
      [He tosses it to one side. The clock strikes once.] You see, it's quite a simple

game. [*As* RAKEWELL *lifts his head in silent thanks,* SHADOW
addresses the audience:]
To win at once in love or cards is dull;
The gentleman loves sport, for sport is rare;
    The positive appals him:
He plays the pence of hope to yield the guineas of despair.
[*Turning back to* RAKEWELL.] Again, good Tom. You are my master
    yet. [*He repeats the routine of shuffling and cutting the cards.*]

DUET *with* SECCO ACCOMPANIMENT

RAKEWELL. What shall I trust in now? How throw the die
    To win my soul back for myself?
SHADOW.   Come, try.
Was Fortune not your mistress once? Be fair.
Give her at least the second chance to bare
The hand of Shadow.

                [*The spade falls forward with a great crash.*]

RAKEWELL [*startled, cursing*].
                   The deuce!   [*Silent pause.* RAKEWELL *looks at
                                        what fell.*]
                    [*Calmly.*] She lights the shades
And shows—the two of spades.
SHADOW [*with scarcely concealed anger throwing the card aside*].
                  The two of spades. [*The clock strikes once.*]
    Congratulations. The Goddess still is faithful. [*Changing his tone.*]
But we have one more, you know, the very last. Think for a while, my
Tom, where you have come to. I would not want your last of chances
thoughtless. I am, as you may have oftentimes observed, really com-
passionate. Think on your hopes.
RAKEWELL. Oh God, what hopes have I? [*He covers his face in his arm and
leans against the tomb.* SHADOW *reaches deftly down, picks up one of the
discarded cards and holds it up while he addresses the audience.*]
SHADOW. The simpler the trick, the simpler the deceit;
That there is no return, I've taught him well,
    And repetition palls him:
The Queen of Hearts again shall be for him the Queen of Hell.
[*He slips the card into the pack and then turns to* RAKEWELL.]
Rouse yourself, Tom, your travail soon will end. [*Routine with cards.*]

TRIO *with* SECCO ACCOMPANIMENT

SHADOW. Come, try. [*Pause.*]
RAKEWELL.   Now in his words I find no aid.
  Will Fortune give another sign?
SHADOW.   Now in my words he'll find no aid
  And Fortune gives no other sign.

[*Pause.* RAKEWELL *looks nervously about him.*]

Afraid,
  Love-lucky Tom? Come, try.
RAKEWELL [*frightened, looking away from the ground*].
                    Dear God, a track
  Of cloven hooves.
SHADOW [*sardonic*].   The knavish goats are back
  To crop the spring's return.
RAKEWELL [*stepping forward, agonized*].
                    Return! and Love!
  The banished words torment.   Return O Love—   [*He breaks
                                                    off, startled,
                                                    when he
                                                    realizes he is
                                                    singing with
                                                    ANNE.
                                                    SHADOW
                                                    stands as
                                                    though
                                                    frozen.*]
SHADOW. You cannot now repent.
ANNE [*off. Unaccompanied*].   *A love*
  That is sworn before thee can plunder hell   [*See Act II, Scene 2, p. 64.*]
  Of its prey. [*Silent pause, then—*]
RAKEWELL [*spoken*].
                    I wish for nothing else.
  [*Sung. Exalté.*] Love, first and last, assume eternal reign;
  Renew my life, O Queen of Hearts, again.

[*As he sings* "O Queen of Hearts, again" *he
snatches the exposed half-pack from the still motionless*
SHADOW.]

[*The twelfth stroke strikes. With a cry of joy* RAKE-
WELL *sinks to the ground senseless. Orchestra re-
sumes.*]

SHADOW [*resuming the ballad*].
>   I burn! I freeze! in shame I hear
>   My famished legions roar:
>   My own delay lost me my prey
>   And damns myself the more.
>
>   Defeated, mocked, again I sink
>   In ice and flame to lie,
>   But Heaven's will I'll hate and till
>   Eternity defy.
>
>   [*Looking at* RAKEWELL.] Thy sins, my foe, before I go
>   Give me some power to pain:
>   [*With a magic gesture.*] To Reason blind shall be thy mind;
>   Henceforth be thou insane!
>
>>   [*Blackout. Then slowly* SHADOW *sinks into the grave.
>>   The dawn comes up. It is spring. The open grave is
>>   now covered with a green mound upon which* RAKE-
>>   WELL *sits smiling, putting grass on his head and sing-
>>   ing to himself in a child-like voice.*]

RAKEWELL.
>   With roses crowned, I sit on ground;
>   Adonis is my name,
>   The only dear of Venus fair:
>   Methinks it is no shame.

SLOW CURTAIN

Act III Scene 3

[*Bedlam. Back stage centre on a raised eminence a straw pallet.*]

>>   [RAKEWELL *stands before it facing the chorus of*
>>   MADMEN *who include a blind man with a broken
>>   fiddle, a crippled soldier, a man with a telescope and
>>   three old hags.*]

ORCHESTRAL RECITATIVE *and* CHORUS

RAKEWELL [*quasi arioso*]. Prepare yourselves, heroic shades. Wash you and make you clean. Anoint your limbs with oil, put on your wedding garments and crown your heads with flowers. Let music strike. Venus, Queen of Love, will visit her unworthy Adonis.

CHORUS.   Madmen's words are all untrue.
                          She will never come to you.
RAKEWELL. She gave me her promise.
CHORUS.   Madness cancels every vow;
                          She will never keep it now.
RAKEWELL. Come quickly, Venus, or I die.

> [*He sits down on the pallet and buries his face in his hands. The* CHORUS *dance before him with mocking gestures.*]

CHORUS *and* DANCE

CHORUS.   Leave all love and hope behind;
                          Out of sight is out of mind
                          In these caverns of the dead.
                          In the city overhead
                          Former lover, former foe
                          To their works and pleasures go
                          Nor consider who beneath
                          Weep and howl and gnash their teeth.
                          Down in Hell as up in Heaven
                          No hands are in marriage given,
                          Nor is honor or degree
                          Known in our society.
                          Banker, beggar, whore and wit
                          In a common darkness sit.
                          Seasons, fashions never change;
                          All is stale yet all is strange;
                          All are foes, and none are friends
                          In a night that never ends.

> [*The sound of a key being turned in a rusty lock is heard.*]

Hark! Minos comes who cruel is and strong:
Beware! Away! His whip is keen and long.

> [*They scatter to their cells. Enter* KEEPER *and* ANNE.]

RECITATIVE SECCO

KEEPER [*pointing to* RAKEWELL, *who has not raised his head*]. There he is.
     Have no fear. He is not dangerous.
ANNE. Tom!

> [RAKEWELL *still does not stir.*]

KEEPER. He believes that he is Adonis and will answer to no other name. Humor him in that, and you will find him easy to manage. So, as you desire, I'll leave you.

ANNE [*giving him money*]. You are kind.

KEEPER. I thank you, lady. [*Exit* KEEPER.]

> [ANNE *goes up and stands close to* RAKEWELL, *who still has not moved. A moment's pause.*]

ORCHESTRAL RECITATIVE

ANNE [*softly*]. Adonis.

RAKEWELL [*raising his head and springing to his feet; quasi arioso*]. Venus, my queen, my bride. At last. I have waited for thee so long, so long, till I almost believed those madmen who blasphemed against thy honor. They are rebuked. Mount, Venus, mount thy throne. [*He leads her to the pallet on which she sits. He kneels at her feet.*] O merciful goddess, hear the confession of my sins.

DUET

> In a foolish dream, in a gloomy labyrinth
> I hunted shadows, disdaining thy true love;
> Forgive thy servant, who repents his madness,
> Forgive Adonis   and he shall faithful prove.

ANNE [*rising and raising him by the hand*].

> What should I forgive? Thy ravishing penitence
> Blesses me, dear heart, and brightens all the past.
> Kiss me Adonis: the wild boar is vanquished.

RAKEWELL. Embrace me, Venus: I have come home at last.

RAKEWELL AND ANNE.

> Rejoice, belovèd: in these fields of Elysium
> Space cannot alter, nor time our love abate;
> Here has no words for   absence or estrangement
> Nor Now a notion   of Almost or Too Late.

> [RAKEWELL *suddenly staggers.* ANNE *helps him gently to lie down on the pallet.*]

ORCHESTRAL RECITATIVE

RAKEWELL [*quasi arioso*]. I am exceeding weary. Immortal queen, permit thy mortal bridegroom to lay his head upon thy breast. [*He does so.*] The Heavens are merciful, and all is well. Sing, my belovèd, sing me to sleep.

SOLO *and* CHORUS

ANNE.   Gently, little boat,
                         Across the ocean float,
                         The crystal waves dividing:
                              The sun in the west
                              Is going to rest;
                                   Glide, glide, glide
                         Toward the Islands of the Blest.

CHORUS [*off in their cells*].
     What voice is this? What heavenly strains
     Bring solace to tormented brains?

ANNE.   Orchards greenly grace
                              That undisturbèd place,
                              The weary soul recalling
                                   To slumber and dream,
                                   While many a stream
                                        Falls, falls, falls,
                              Descanting on a childlike theme.

CHORUS. O sacred music of the spheres!
     Where now our rages and our fears?

ANNE.   Lion, lamb and deer,
                              Untouched by greed or fear
                              About the woods are straying:
                                   And quietly now
                                   The blossoming bough
                                        Sways, sways, sways
                              Above the fair unclouded brow.

CHORUS. Sing on! For ever sing! Release
     Our frantic souls and bring us peace!

                                        [*Enter* KEEPER *with* TRULOVE.]

RECITATIVE SECCO

TRULOVE. Anne, my dear, the tale is ended now.
     Come home.
ANNE.   Yes, Father. [*To* RAKEWELL.] Tom, my vow
     Holds ever, but it is no longer I
     You need. Sleep well, my dearest dear. Good-bye.

                              [*Anne comes down stage and joins* TRULOVE.]

DUET

ANNE.
> Every wearied body must
> Late or soon return to dust,
> Set the frantic spirit free.
> In this earthly city we
> Shall not meet again, love, yet
> Never think that I forget.

TRULOVE.
> God is merciful and just,
> God ordains what ought to be,
> But a father's eyes are wet.

> [*Exeunt* ANNE *and* TRULOVE *and* KEEPER. *A short pause. Then* RAKEWELL *wakes, starts to his feet and looks wildly around.*]

FINALE, ORCHESTRAL RECITATIVE *and* CHORUS

RAKEWELL. Where art thou, Venus? Venus, where art thou? The flowers open to the sun. The birds renew their song. It is spring. The bridal couch is prepared. Come quickly, belovèd, and we will celebrate the holy rites of love. [*A moment's silence. Then with a shout.*] Holla! Achilles, Helen, Eurydice, Orpheus, Persephone, Plato, all my courtiers. Holla! [*The* CHORUS *enter from all sides.*] Where is my Venus? Why have you stolen her while I slept? Madmen! Where have you hidden her?

CHORUS. Venus? Stolen? Hidden? Where?
Madman! No one has been here.

RAKEWELL [*quasi arioso*]. My heart breaks. I feel the chill of death's approaching wing. Orpheus, strike from thy lyre a swan-like music, and weep, ye nymphs and shepherds of these Stygian fields, weep for Adonis the beautiful, the young; weep for Adonis whom Venus loved. [*He falls back on the pallet.*]

FUGAL CHORUS [*funèbre*]. Mourn for Adonis, ever young, the dear
Of Venus: weep, tread softly round his bier.

SLOW CURTAIN

Epilogue

[*Before the curtain. House Lights up. Enter* BABA, RAKEWELL, SHADOW, ANNE, TRULOVE, *the men without wigs,* BABA *without her beard.*]

RECITATIVE (SECCO *or* ORCHESTRAL)

ALL IN UNISON.
Good people, just a moment:
Though our story now is ended,
There's the moral to draw
From what you saw
Since the curtain first ascended.

ANNE.
Not every rake is rescued
At the last by Love and Beauty;
Not every man
Is given an Anne
To take the place of Duty.

BABA.
Let Baba warn the ladies:
You will find out soon or later
That, good or bad,
All men are mad;
All they say or do is theatre.

RAKEWELL.
Beware, young men who fancy
You are Vergil or Julius Caesar,
Lest when you wake
You be only a rake.

TRULOVE.
I heartily agree, sir!

SHADOW.
Day in, day out, poor Shadow
Must do as he is bidden
Many insist
I do not exist.
At times I wish I didn't.

QUINTET [*with orchestra*].
So let us sing as one.
At all times in all lands
Beneath the moon and sun,
This proverb has proved true,
Since Eve went out with Adam:
For idle hands
And hearts and minds

The Devil finds
A work to do,
A work, dear Sir, fair Madam,
For you and you.

[*Bow and exeunt.*]

FINIS

Delia

or

A Masque of Night

(Suggested by
George Peele's play,
The Old Wives' Tale)

BY W. H. AUDEN AND
CHESTER KALLMAN

[1952]

Prologue

[Before the curtain on which is painted a wood and crossroads. It is just before sunset. Enter ORLANDO.*]*

ARIA

ORLANDO. Long, long, by an image have I been haunted,
    Fair, fair, of a maiden in a wood enchanted,
    O when, O when shall my desire be granted?

> Dreaming on winter night,
>   Clearly I saw her,
> Seized was my heart at sight
>   With longing for her:
> "Who art thou, fair maid?", I cried,
>   Joyful and astonished;
> "I am Delia", she replied,
>   "Thy true love", and vanished.

On, on, a pilgrim with one purpose only,
    Far, far, in a passage perilous and lonely,
    O still, O still I seek my Delia vainly.

[Enter, unperceived by him, the CRONE.*]*

CRONE. A penny, kind sir, out of charity,
    For I am old and in poverty.
ORLANDO [*startled*]. God save thee, crone, I saw thee not.
    What dost thou here in this wild spot?
CRONE. Hips and haws I gather for food,
    A penny, kind sir, for the crone of the wood.
ORLANDO. A penny, crone, thou shalt surely have
    To spend in the ale-house, God thee save
    And if I prosper in my quest
    Of silken gowns thou shalt have the best.
CRONE. Is she so fair?
ORLANDO.   Thou hast rightly guessed.
    Fair she is above all the rest,
    Red as blood and white as snow,
    Seeking her through the world I go.

[During the CRONE's *speech the lights begin dimming: sunset glow, gradually darkened.]*

CRONE. Kind, Sir Knight, hast thou been to me;
    This willow twig I will give to thee,
    To guide thee when thine eyes are blind,
    If thou lose thy love, it will her find.
    But once, only once, it used may be
    So keep it for thy time of need.
    Farewell, and to my words pay heed
        He that in the savage wood
        To stranger and wild beast is good,
        He that, when his love he woos,
        Compels her not but lets her choose,
        He that, taunted by a foe,
        Answers not with blow for blow
        Nor in anger draws his sword,
        Shall obtain a great reward.
  Wilt thou swear, Sir Knight, by this holy willow
  My counsel faithfully to follow?
ORLANDO. Crone, I swear it.
    Stay. Who art thou? She is gone.
    I am alone and night comes on.

RECITATIVE

Blind wood, deaf wood, dumb wood, O would you could grant my will.
                                ECHO. I will.
A voice? Do I dream? Then again. Dost thou know where Delia is?
                                ECHO. Yes.
Shall I see her face and pour in her ears my orison?
                                ECHO. Aye, soon.
O joy! Away! Which path shall I take, that or this?
                                ECHO. This.

ARIA

    As the hoped-for moment nears,
      As this wood I enter,
    Premonitions, sudden fears,
      Shake my being's centre.
  "Fickle is a woman's mind,
    Delia well may prove unkind",
      Whispers Doubt, the traitor.
  Shall I be unwelcome now?
        FIRST ECHO. Come now!
        SECOND ECHO.   Come now!

O, if that should be, then how,
How shall I persuade her?
FIRST ECHO. Aid her!
SECOND ECHO.   Aid her!

[*Exit.*]

[*Darkness. Then, during the following chorus,* THE CURTAIN SLOWLY RISES *to reveal a semi-circular clearing in the enchanted wood. Moonlight. Stage left, the entrance to a cave; further up stage, an entrance into the clearing, revealing a view of thickly wooded forest; stage center, at the back, an enormous rock which blocks off any view of what is behind it; the base of the rock is reached by a slight incline; stage right is a platform connected with the stage level by a ramp that descends towards the back along the semi-circle; on the platform is the entrance to a ruined tower; of the tower itself enough can be seen to show a small balcony above the entrance; between the tower and the rock, the forest and scattered trees.* BUNGAY *is seen at the rise of the curtain seated on a tree stump near the cave entrance. During the chorus, various wood animals walk about or, if possible, execute a dance.*]

CHORUS.   As the moon rises we come a-dancing
             About in a spiral or round in a ring.
             Softly the white weirs murmur

             As the dew falls on the hawthorn-tree
             All night long we foot it lightly.
             Softly the white weirs murmur

             About in a spiral or round in a ring,
             With linked hands all to our liking.
             Softly the white weirs murmur

             All night long we foot it lightly
             On the hill, in the wood, by the shore of the sea.
             Softly the white weirs murmur

             With linked hands all to our liking,
             While the owl whoops and the bat takes wing.
             Softly the white weirs murmur

             On the hill, in the wood, by the shore of the sea,
             Without heart-longing or heart-envy.
             Softly the white weirs murmur

             While the owl whoops and the bat takes wing,
             As the moon rises we come a-dancing.
             Softly the white weirs murmur.

[*The stage is empty now, except for* BUNGAY, *still reading.*]

[*Enter* XANTIPPE.]

XANTIPPE.

Here, then, you hie to hide from me, here to the woods you come
To seek out your sure perdition in idleness and folly
While a husband and a father are wanting at home.

BUNGAY. Peace, woman, peace! The ground you tread is holy:
I have come here to nurse my melancholy.

XANTIPPE.

Then think on your home neglected, your good-wife nigh gone mad,
Bare cupboard, ingle cold, wantons wailing for your return,
And you will need no sorcery, I trow, to make you sad.

BUNGAY. Peace, woman, peace! Here we are under Saturn.
I must have quiet to unveil the pattern.

DUETTINO

BUNGAY AND XANTIPPE [*aside*].
Woe, the day we were plighted,
Alas, the day we wed,
And I for life united

BUNGAY.   To a rasping shrew,
XANTIPPE.   To an empty head.

XANTIPPE. Bungay, Bungay, why must you always stray from home?
BUNGAY. Good Xantippe, I stray not, but seek out wisdom
In its dwelling with the high Magus Sacrapant;
This is no woman's matter.

XANTIPPE.   Our children be, God grant!
Think, Bungay, on sweet Margaret and rosy Isobel,
Fat Philip, small Robin, gay Mary, blithely singing Nell,
Pink saintly James, frolicsome George and wise little Geoffrey . . .

BUNGAY. A magus has no children and a magus I would be.
XANTIPPE. A magus thou! O caitiff I that did not under lock
My husbnd keep, a plague . . .

BUNGAY [*finding spell in his book*].   Eureka! This opens the rock.
Now. A little peace, a little reverence,
Woman, and you shall see I stray not. I commence.

[*Draws a diagram on the ground with a stick and intones.*]

Hic. Haec. Hoc.
The fiddle and . . .

[*A man-sized* OWL *walks on the stage.*]

XANTIPPE. By all the saints!
BUNGAY. Well, if it a bird be, let us be bold
And quickly strike that it for us may lay an egg of gold.
[*Intoning.*] Eeta, theeta,
Lo and behold,
Pie-upsey, pie-upsey,
An egg of pure gold.

[*Pause.*]

Well, bird, the egg!
OWL. Tu-whit.
BUNGAY. The egg, I say.
OWL. Tu-whoo.
BUNGAY. What shall I do?
[*Consulting his book.*] Ah, now I see, that spell is but for geese!
OWL. Tu-whit. Tu-whoo.

[*Exit* OWL.]

BUNGAY [*depressed*]. I was not melancholy enough, pure enough,
Single in thought enough;—an unworthy caitiff.
XANTIPPE. Come home, then.
BUNGAY. I must try again.
XANTIPPE. I shall be off.

[*Exit* XANTIPPE *angrily.*]

BUNGAY. At last, properly alone in manly silence . . .
XANTIPPE [*returning, from the side of the stage*]. Bungay, come back
with me.
BUNGAY [*without looking up*]. Peace, woman.

[XANTIPPE *leaves in utter exasperation.*]

Once more I commence.

[*Intoning.*] Hic, haec, hoc,
The fiddle and the stock,
Horum, quorum, high cockalorum,
Open, rock.

[*A series of loud explosions.* BUNGAY *claps his hands
to his ears.*]

Mother of mercy, help! I perish!

> [SACRAPANT *appears from his tower and holds up his hand.*]

SACRAPANT.   Cease!
What rumorous fool intrudes on my peace?
BUNGAY. Sacrapant! [*He kneels.*]

ARIA

Master of wisdom magical,
Both sub-lunary and angelical,
Mighty and high one,
Forgive my intrusion.

> [*Pause.* BUNGAY *gets slowly and nervously to his feet.*]

Master. I, too, . . . *ardor divinarum* . . .
You understand me . . . *rerum* . . .
Humbly . . . but she . . .
Wife . . . in her jealousy
Of high philosophy . . .
Vita contemplativa . . .
Would not let me leave her . . .
You see . . . here . . . a man
I did what I can . . .
Bo! and she ran.

> [*Pause.* BUNGAY *laughs nervously.*]

Now that she is gone,
We men can get on,
For it is impossible
To procure a miracle
With such a manacle;
Call the Heavenly Venus
To guide us, to clean us;
Should *amor ferinus*—
—My wife you understand—
Be always at hand
With gabbles and hisses
And cloying kisses,
I wants and I wisses,
Tittling and tattling

And pots rattling
And ba-ba and 'sblood,
By the rood,
Shall not and should,
Till, help me God,
I must finally say,
From all women, *libera me.*

[*Pause. He kneels.*]

Accept a poor disciple who in wisdom wants a master,
And I will serve you well—by Simon and by Zoroaster.

[*Pause.*]

RECITATIVE

SACRAPANT. To know high mystery, do you so yearn?
BUNGAY. Master, much more—I faint, I freeze, I burn.
SACRAPANT. You shall.
BUNGAY.   Grammercy!

[SACRAPANT *makes a gesture and animals come out
of the wood and carry* BUNGAY *off.*]

SACRAPANT.   Thus, fools of magic learn.

[*Suddenly laughs.*]

You have come opportunely,
Delia doth crave
A pet-bear to have;
Her bear you shall be.

[*He makes a magic gesture. A yelp is heard from*
BUNGAY *off-stage.*]

[*During the end of the foregoing the* CRONE *has en-
tered and stands at the opposite side of the stage to*
SACRAPANT, *who turns and notices her after a
moment.*]

My old antagonist, my true-sworn foe.
CRONE [*mockingly*]. What mighty runes to work such simple ends.
SACRAPANT. The base and stupid work their proper woe.

[CRONE *laughs.*]

Yes, mock me, thy quaint mockery offends
The night with lunacy; and yet, thou too
Knowest I speak the truth.
CRONE.   That none contends;
But here is more, truth also; to woo
Fair Delia, enchanting Delia, thy delight,
A prince comes, gallant, handsome, brave and true,
And that which drives him, mightier than might,
Wiser than runes, will find her finally;
To bar him helps thee not; he comes to-night.
SACRAPANT. What drives him dwells in mere mortality;
Find her he may, woo her he can; to her
Content is certain here: she will stay with me,
The life she knows.
CRONE.   Like thou she would know more.
The flame-lit globe, the hidden crystal sphere
That holds thy life immortal and the lore
Beyond learning, that it be quenched, no fear
Hast thou?
SACRAPANT.   Nor force nor magic can.
CRONE.   Who lit
The flame for thee? Knowest thou, mighty seer?
SACRAPANT [*dream-like at first, then gradually stronger*].
So long it is that I have studied it,
Almost, meseems, that always it was mine,
Always my life enclosing sure, and yet,
Finding it here and knowing it divine,
O dimly I recall. With steadfastness
I read its secrets by its potent shine
And read that none but a son born motherless,
A thing impossible, can put it out!
CRONE. A son born motherless? Haply thou?
SACRAPANT.   Thy guesses
For sextons keep!
CRONE.   The flame, who lit it?
SACRAPANT.   What
Matters that, old mockery?
CRONE.   Nought, sweet foe,
If thou art certain, but—thou knowest not.
SACRAPANT. Mocker, be gone!
CRONE [*exiting slowly*].   The mortal prince may know.
SACRAPANT. Be still!

CRONE.   Who lit the flame? Who lit the flame?
SACRAPANT.   Go!

QUASI ARIOSO

Go. Slip through the night, quicksilver thief
Who robs me of my peace. Eternity!
    Means it eternal grief?
    Delia! Delia!
The time of choice has come, will she
    Give me the answer?

Yes. She must, she will; my life awaits
Fulfillment of the heart that I would own
    Beyond the meddling fates:
    Delia! Delia!
My light! O leave me not alone!
    What is the answer?

[*Enters the tower.*]

[*Enter* XANTIPPE *precipitously.*]

ARIA

XANTIPPE.   Not here? O I fear he has fled me,
    No wonder! It is all my blame,
For in truth I knew at our wedding
I took his follies with his name.

    But I forgot
    All that he is
    That brought me bliss
    And saw, I wiss,
    All he is not:
    Now he is gone,
    Untended, alone.

A scold and a shrew to my coney
    I was and did ever reprove;
From where'er you may be, O call me
And I will answer you with love.

[SACRAPANT *enters on his tower aloft with light.*]

XANTIPPE. What's that? God preserve me, but to-night is a wicked night.
I had best hide me quickly there. [*Runs into a cave.*]

ARIA

SACRAPANT.   O my immortal light!
            My best of lore that fends me from the day
                And change's appetite.
            There's none who may thy mystery and worth,
                Like mine, consign to earth,
            No gaudiness that in our wisdom may
                Breed folly or decay.
            What! Shall this heart and brain be common food?
                Cold, rotten solitude?
            Never I swear, and cry to the mocks of doubt,
            As nothing lit thee, nothing shall put thee out!
                No, we shall be renewed:
            When time has put the elements to rout,
            Into the sea of night we two shall dive
            To pass like flame beyond the stars—alive!

                                        [*Re-enters tower.*]

XANTIPPE [*peeping out*].
            That is most hellish Sacrapant. Perdy I understand;
            Surely in peril magical is my good husband.
            I must remain.

                    [*Retires.* SACRAPANT *comes out of tower and ap-
                    proaches rock in centre.*]

SACRAPANT.   The time to see my Delia is at hand.

    [*Intones.*]   In the name of Noname who
                    Guards the Everlasting Yew
                    Of the Uttermost Abyss,
                    Rock, fly open to my hiss.

                        [*The rock splits open revealing a perspective of
                        Graeco-Egyptian columns; also lit Tudor "chande-
                        liers".* DELIA *enters followed by an animal entourage,
                        including three* OWLS *and* BUNGAY, *now a bear,
                        who holds her train with one hand and his book of
                        magic with the other.*]

                    DUET

SACRAPANT.   Welcome, my child, the fair night welcomes
                    Delia, its fairest ornament.

DELIA.   Good master, welcome.
SACRAPANT. Then, Delia, tell
               If I have laboured well
               To form slave-bear and furnish your content.
DELIA.   Ah yes, I am content.

SACRAPANT. Wish on, my child, for your sweet wishes,
               Delia, shall here be deified.
DELIA.   I have no wishes.
SACRAPANT. May, Delia, I dare
               To wish you wish to share
               At last my life eternal? O decide!
DELIA.   Ah yes, I must decide.

               Alone, a child and lost, you saved me,
               Master, my life is in your debt.
SACRAPANT. More would I save you.
DELIA.   All I could want
               It is your will to grant,
               Now you would honor me, I know, and yet . . .
SACRAPANT. Ah, yes, my child, . . . and yet?

DELIA.   A green field do I see betimes in memory,
               All fair with flowers pranked and an air melodious,
               Making of green a green more live, that calls to me
               "*Want!*" and I see no more; "*Want*" and all fair is
                    treacherous;
               Weeping again, I am lost and you so bountiful
               Find me again, and I know that green impossible.

SACRAPANT. Fancies, my child, to still such fancies,
               Delia, consent, and future good
               Shall take your fancies.
DELIA.   Ah yes, I know,
               And I would have it so,
               Almost, I think . . . I'm hungry: fetch me food.
SACRAPANT. My child shall have her food.

               [*As* SACRAPANT *recites, a table rises out of the earth
               and animal servants bring in food.* DELIA *toys with
               her food, occasionally feeding* BUNGAY.]

SACRAPANT [*intoning*]. Spread the table, lay the dishes,
               Filled with all that Delia wishes,
               Slices of the whitest bread

Thick with honey overspread,
Custards, sugar-plums and cake
Such as emperors' kitchens bake,
Scarlet strawberries in cream,
Syrups soothing as a dream,
Lemon curd, crab-apple jelly,
Pleasing to her little belly,
While to please her little ear,
She a merry round shall hear.

ROUND

THREE OWLS.   On a snowy bank one Christmastide
A mouse and an owl sat side by side:
"O! O!" cried the mouse,
"If you spare my life,
  I'll run to my house
  And fetch you my wife."
"No! No!" cried the owl,
"I'm a hungry fowl,
And she's thinner, she's thinner." . . .
"Thinner than who?"
"Thinner than you!"
And gobbled him up for her dinner,
With a hoo, hoo, hoo, hoo, hoo.

DELIA. Master, no more. Have them all sent away.
All but my page; my page can stay;
And I wish someone new to speak with.

ECHOES [*alternating from either side of the stage, at first far off, then gradually
nearer and more frequent*].
Delia . . . Delia, Delia, Delia, *etc.*
SACRAPANT [*indicating the voices*].   As you say.

[*During the following, the table sinks, the servants
vanish, leaving only* SACRAPANT, DELIA *and* BUN-
GAY.]

D U E T

SACRAPANT [*aside*].	DELIA [*aside*].
The prince comes	Who is it comes
To woo Delia;	Calling Delia?
Does he indeed	Ah, shall I hide
Bring an answer?	Or shall I answer?
Use him I shall	What wisdom shall
Her longings to still.	Direct my will?

SACRAPANT. One to speak with: could wish be granted faster?
    I go. Call if you wish me.
DELIA.   Thank you, master.

[Exit SACRAPANT to tower.]

ECHOES [*near*]. Delia . . . Delia . . . Delia . . .

DELIA.   What now shall guide me?
                    I had best hide me,
                    From there to see
                    What this may be.

[Hides behind tree.]

ORLANDO [*bursting in*]. Delia!
    [*Seeing* BUNGAY.]   A bear! [*Reaches for his sword.*]
No, I have sworn,
    My sword shall not this night be drawn.
    Must I then die before the morn?
BUNGAY [*throwing himself at* ORLANDO's *feet*].
    Mercy, good Prince! Have mercy!
ORLANDO.   What's here?
    A meek, mild bear, a new-born bear,
BUNGAY. Late an apprentice sorcerer;
    Bungay, my name. O charity!
ORLANDO. Fear not.
BUNGAY.   Fear you the sorcery
    Of Sacrapant; be thanked—and flee.
DELIA [*behind tree*].   Ah, fair to see!
    Gentle, brave and kind is he.
ORLANDO. This is the place, yet where is she?
DELIA [*stepping forth*]. You have been sent to speak with me.

[Pause. ORLANDO and DELIA look at each other.]

TRIO

ORLANDO.

O mine own true love,
  My vision, then, was true;
Far, far have I journeyed,
  Led by a dream of you:
Ah, lovelier than a vision,
  Than any dream more bright
Reject not your Orlando,
  Accept your true knight.

DELIA.

Kind sir, your words bewilder,
  Though, surely they mean well;
My heart they make uneasy,
  Though why I cannot tell.

My love, my life are subject
  Unto your love's command;
Reject not your Orlando,
  Say that you understand.

Say, say, that you can love me,
  End you a lover's woe,
And from this wood together,
  For aye we two shall go.

BUNGAY.

His words of love remind me
  Of my Xantippe, Woe!
That once we were together
  And I have let her go.

From here, my shaded castle,
  Into the distant day,
You would that I should follow?
  What is this you say?

O strange enchantment!
  She understands me not;
O Love, lend me thy power
  Against this charmed spot!

O strange awakening,
  I understand you not;
O what may be his power
  To move me? Love? O what
Brings me so near to weeping,
  Yet sadness cannot be?

O who can break the power
  Of this accursed spot?
Eyes, be not done with weeping
  Lost is our Xantippe!

Come, come with your Orlando
  To felicity.

[BUNGAY *bursts into floods of tears. As an answer to* ORLANDO, DELIA *stamps her foot and points to* BUNGAY.]

DELIA. Why have you come? What do you here?
  See, you have saddened my poor bear!
BUNGAY. Good Prince, simple am I and weak;
  You, you alone can help me.
ORLANDO.   Speak.

ARIETTA

BUNGAY.
  My wife, my good wife, alas!, but I did not heed her,
      And now this guise
      Unto all eyes
        I wear;
  While she, my good wife, who knows where the spells may lead her
      That fill this wood;
      You, brave and good,
        May dare
  To find my good wife, and tell her I so do need her,
      Her husband, now a bear.

TRIO

ORLANDO.	DELIA.	BUNGAY.
To hear him plead	To hear one plead	
Of wife, of need	Of wife, of need,	
Moves me to cede	Is strange indeed,	
My willow wand	Past my command	Will she understand
Into his hand;	To understand;	I am her husband,
Yet dare I?	Why care I?	Though a bear I?

ORLANDO. Here. Take this wand: its true direction heed you.
  And to your wife, your true love, it will lead you.

[BUNGAY *takes the wand which leads him to the cave. He enters. A scream is heard.* XANTIPPE *rushes out and takes refuge behind* ORLANDO. BUNGAY *re-enters and starts to cry again.*]

QUARTET

BUNGAY.   My heart must break. She knows me not. Why should she?
                        O grief! O pain!
                Yet even if she did me know, then would she
                        Love me again?

XANTIPPE.   O night insane!
                Where mages, bears, sprite lamps in one place woody
                        Hold evil reign!

DELIA.   Poor bear, he weeps the more; to find his lady
                        Was but in vain.
ORLANDO.   I must explain.

ORLANDO [*to* XANTIPPE]. Be not afeard, good dame; this bear you see
    Your husband is, changed by vile sorcery.
XANTIPPE [*to* BUNGAY]. Bungay? In truth?

                        [BUNGAY *nods and hangs his head.*]

                        Poor silly, come to me!

                        [XANTIPPE *sits on a tree-stump.* BUNGAY *buries his
                        head in her lap. She comforts him.*]

                        ARIETTA

            Rest you, rest you, have no fear:
            Love is love and I am near.
            Folly ends, magic fails, finally:
                    Let the world still
                    See what it will,
                    Our world is here
            Where I my only loved one see.

                        QUARTET

DELIA.   How, even in adversity,
               They happy seem, as though distress
               Were nought beside togetherness.

ORLANDO.   O God of Love, enlighten me,
               For, should I lose her, my distress
               Would make my world a wilderness.

BUNGAY AND XANTIPPE.

> I was wrong as wrong could be:
> But that is over; now we bless
> Our mishap with togetherness.

DUET

ORLANDO. O Delia, hear me, know that evil is this wood:
> Trust you my love, my love is true, I swear!
> To the day, to the light, to the green and the good,
> Together let us repair!

DELIA.   Now I am certain, I see it again, ah! clear.
> The green, green field, it bids me love! I go

DELIA AND ORLANDO.
> From the night, from the wood, from the magic and fear
> Together let us . .

DELIA [*pushing* ORLANDO *violently away*]. Ah! No!

> [ORLANDO *stares at her in surprised alarm.* BUN-
> GAY *and* XANTIPPE *get to their feet.* DELIA *con-
> tinues in a semi-trance oblivious of them.*]

DELIA.   Air treacherous . . . lost . . . wanting
> Tears, tears . . . impossible . . .
> Find me and save me!

ORLANDO.   Delia!

DELIA.   O fancies . . . eternal,
> Bountiful, save me!

ORLANDO.   Delia!

DELIA.   Too bright! Too far! Too wild!

ORLANDO.   Delia!

DELIA.   Come to me, master.

SACRAPANT [*appearing instantly*].   You called me, my child?

> [DELIA *runs to* SACRAPANT. ORLANDO *stands de-
> fiant, facing them.* XANTIPPE *puts her arms round*
> BUNGAY *and also looks defiantly at* SACRAPANT.
> SACRAPANT *appears to notice no one but* DELIA.]

DELIA. Master, I need your help.

SACRAPANT.   I know.
> Is it, my child, you wish to go?

DELIA. Yes, master, yet I am afraid.
> Love was not to be disobeyed,

Love that unto the long unseen
Delirium of remembered green
Would take me; then, I know not why,
Came fear. Explain.
SACRAPANT [*to* ORLANDO].
                                        What want you?
ORLANDO.   I
Obeyed a dream and came to woo.
SACRAPANT.
You did what you were meant to do.
ORLANDO [*to* DELIA].
Do you not, Delia, hear the call
Of the bright day?
SACRAPANT.   And is that all
You have to tell?
ORLANDO.   I told my love.
SACRAPANT. Green princeling, that is not enough!
Delia, I shall explain what laws obey
The lovers and the fields of gaudy day.
Show you I shall of Time and of his slaves:
This life you know. Decide! Does he that craves
Your love—since you are free—allow that you may choose
Between us?
ORLANDO.   Yes.
DELIA.   I am prepared.
SACRAPANT AND ORLANDO [*aside*]. I cannot lose!

QUINTET

SACRAPANT.   Spirits of darkness, rouse ye in full accord!
                  Spew your illusion forth, O rocks and trees and caves!
                  Let all nocturnal magic spread abroad!

ORLANDO [*aside*].
                  Spirits of daylight, give me your full accord!
DELIA [*aside*].   May I choose well!
BUNGAY AND XANTIPPE [*aside*].   Protect us, thou, O light that saves!
ORLANDO, DELIA, BUNGAY AND XANTIPPE [*aside*].
                  For all nocturnal magic is abroad!

                              [*They take their places about the stage.*]

SACRAPANT.   Behold the world of Time and of his slaves.

(THE PAGEANT BEGINS)

> [*Funeral March. Enter* TIME *on a chariot drawn by human slaves of both sexes, followed by* MUTABILITY, TOIL, AGE, PAIN *and* DEATH. TIME *(masc.) has a wooden leg and carries an hour-glass,* MUTABILITY *(fem.) a wheel,* TOIL *(masc.) an ox-goad,* AGE *(fem.) a rosary,* PAIN *(masc.) an instrument of torture and* DEATH *(fem.) a crepe-covered drum.*]

TIME.

I, Time, of all things that are made am king
 Sovereign supreme over every element;
Without me is no causative happening,
 Sun, moon and stars to me are obedient,
 Likewise all creatures moving and sentient,
And man, proud man, that knoweth he is alive,
Is thrall to me and to my children five.

CHORUS.

  By Word mysterious
  Of the One-in-Three
  So is it with us,
  So ever to be.

MUTABILITY.

Some Chance me call, some Mutability;
 All things I alter that none may have rest,
To one I bring joy, to another misery,
 My secrets may by no Solomon be guessed,
 I turn my wheel as liketh me best,
And man, proud man, that would be permanent,
Is unstable, varying from moment to moment.

CHORUS.

  As the rivers various
  Flow to one sea,
  So is it with us,
  So ever to be.

TOIL.

I am Toil. The ploughman I prod with my goad
 To delve in poor soil for a crop scanty,
I lay on the housewife many a grievous load,
 Oppose worn sailors with winds contrary
 And clerks with points of great perplexity,
And man, proud man, wishing the long day ended,
With sweat shall earn, in tears shall eat his bread.

CHORUS.   As the hot sun luminous
                               Scorcheth the lea,
                               So is it with us,
                               So ever to be.

AGE.   I am Age. None shall bribe me with silver or gold.
                  Forgotten by youth in the May of his lust,
             But after short summer there cometh my cold;
                  The primrose I wither, the treasure I rust,
                  Palace and temple I crumble to dust,
             And man, proud man, shall weep and be dismayed,
             Seeing his wit, strength, beauty fail and fade.

CHORUS.   Round castles ponderous
                               Cold winds blow free,
                               So is it with us,
                               So ever to be.

PAIN.   I am Pain. I burn, I twist, I pierce, I break,
                  The tender flesh dispiteously I assail
             With sudden pang and dull unending ache;
                  The lord sore wounded, the lady in her travail,
                  Each calleth for mercy but to no avail,
             And man, proud man, paleth and cryeth "Alack!",
             When that his body I bind to my rack.

CHORUS.   Since Eve rebellious
                               Robbed the high tree,
                               So it hath been with us,
                               And so is to be.

DEATH.   I am Death. My wanton look causeth great fear;
                  Though my breath stinketh and my skin be loathsome
             From my embrace no heart may recover;
                  My music is harsh, grim and unwelcome,
                  Yet all that liveth must follow my drum,
             And man, proud man, to his hurt and grievance
             Must leave his friends alone with me to dance.

CHORUS.   Till the trump ominous
                               End our history,
                               As it hath been with us,
                               So is it to be.

(THE PAGEANT ENDS)

SACRAPANT. Well, Delia, has this pageant of your doubts relieved you?
DELIA. It cannot be. I never will believe you.
SACRAPANT. Ask your knight if I deceive you.

QUINTET

SACRAPANT.	DELIA.	ORLANDO.
See, it is so.	Can it be so?	Yes, it is so,
Dare you then go	If I should go	Yes, if you go
Out of my night	Out of his night	Out of this night
To his day bright,	To your day bright,	To the day bright
There to endure	Must I endure	You will endure
These ills for sure?	These ills for sure?	These ills for sure
Well may you fear.	I shake with fear.	Well may you fear,
Stay, Delia, here	Orlando, dear,	My Delia, dear,
Where, as you know,	Say No, say No,	Alas, I know
It is not so.	It is not so.	That it is so.

BUNGAY AND XANTIPPE.
Great Magus,
Please let me (him) go
Pity my (his) plight
With spell or rite
Restore my (his) nature
To human feature.
Who wander (wanders) here
As a brown bear.
Your mercy show,
Pleast let me (him) go.

SACRAPANT. Now you have heard this knight admit the truth
And seen the gifts he offers for your youth,
Will you go with him to the griefs of day
Or here be safe with me? What should she say,
Sir Knight?
DELIA.   Speak!
SACRAPANT.   Nothing?
ORLANDO.   Only this
That I will love you both in bale and bliss.

SACRAPANT.	DELIA.	ORLANDO.
Here are no chains.	I dread these chains,	Without these chains,
Afflictions, pains,	Afflictions, pains.	Afflictions, pains,
No grief need be,	Cannot I be	Mortality,
Wishes are free	Both sorrow-free	No will is free,
And dreams come true;	And loving too?	No heart is true.
Let me for you	I dare not. You	Ah, I love you
Be wise and make	Are stronger: Make	But cannot make
This choice for your sake:	This choice for my sake,	This choice for your sake:
Do what I say.	And I will obey.	You, you must say;
I warn you—Stay!	Shall I go? Shall I stay?	I will go. I will stay.

BUNGAY.
We beg in vain.
I must remain
A bear verily
Without liberty.
What shall I do?
        XANTIPPE.
This will I do:
Xantippe he shall make
A she-bear for your sake,
With you alway
In the wood to stay.

SACRAPANT. We wait, we listen, Delia.
ORLANDO.   Delia, choose!

TRIO

DELIA.   Must I choose to divide us? Division is pain.
                Why, my Orlando, should you not remain?
                To dwell in this forest, how glad would I be
                With my Knight and my Magus together all three!
SACRAPANT. He cannot love you, or he would remain.
ORLANDO.   Delia, that can never be.
                Yours the wooing, warned the crone,
                But hers the choice and hers alone;
                You may ask but not demand.
DELIA.   I begin to understand:
                Take, Orlando, take my hand.

ARIA

How joyful, clear, and loud and fast
My heart I hear, my doubts are past.
Away all fear! The die is cast.
Orlando, dear, my mind at last
    I know.
    Come death, come grief,
    Sacrapant will I leave,
    To Orlando cleave,
    With you will I go.

SACRAPANT. No! No! She shall stay, I say. She shall not go.
    Battle to battle I challenge you, Sir Knight,
    Battle to battle for Delia to fight.
XANTIPPE. Battle to battle give him; Sir Knight,
    Battle to battle the tyrant to smite.
ORLANDO. Peace be with you, Sir Sacrapant.
    Battle to battle I may not grant.
BUNGAY. Beware, beware of Sacrapant!
    Battle to battle do not grant!
SACRAPANT. No peace! If my sword you fear to brave,
    Coward I call you, caitiff and knave.
ORLANDO. Peace be with you, for I have sworn
    My sword this night shall not be drawn.
SACRAPANT. No peace. Your cheek with my glove I will smite
    That Delia may know you are no true knight.

DELIA.   O! O!
ORLANDO.   God's bones I will show
            If I be knight or no.
            I have wished you peace
            By the mass, truly . . .

                        [He draws his sword.]

A TORRENT OF ECHOES.
        You lie, you lie, you lie, you lie, *etc.*
ORLANDO [*he totters*].   I . . .
MORE ECHOES.   I, I, I, I, I, *etc.*
ORLANDO [*he falls*].   Die.
MORE ECHOES.   Die, die, die, die, die, *etc.*

        [The noise crescends and accelerates. Lights flash.
        Black out. The echoes die away. A pause of utter

silence. When the lights come on again, the MAGUS
and DELIA *have disappeared,* ORLANDO *lies on the
ground unconscious, watched anxiously by* BUNGAY
and XANTIPPE.]

DUET LEADING TO TRIO

BUNGAY.   *Kyrie eleison*
XANTIPPE.   We are undone.
BUNGAY.   *Plangere* of no avail is
XANTIPPE.   All hopes are vain.
BUNGAY.   *Magus crudelis*
                   Our knight hath slain.
XANTIPPE.   Still as a stone is
                   He lieth here dead.
BUNGAY.   *In os leonis*
                   He put his sweet head.
BUNGAY AND XANTIPPE.
                   Requiem aeternam toll
                   For Orlando's soul.

          [ORLANDO *comes to, looks round, remembers, rises to
          his feet, clutching his head.*]

ORLANDO.   Ah woe! Ah woe!
BUNGAY AND XANTIPPE.
                   Gloria!
                   It is not so.
                   Dormiebat in a swound.
ORLANDO.   With shame I am sore vexèd.
BUNGAY AND XANTIPPE.
                   Nunc resurrexit
                   He standeth on ground.
ORLANDO.   O grief! O bitter wound!

                        [*The* CRONE *approaches.*]

CRONE. Met again, Sir Knight. Why weepest thou?
    Ill hath fared thy quest, I trow.
ORLANDO. Good Beldame, for shame I dare not tell.
CRONE. Enough, enough, I know full well.
    Hadst thou not drawn thy sword, my son,
    Delia were already won.
ORLANDO. Help me, good Beldame, once more I pray,
    And I will in all things thee obey.

BUNGAY AND XANTIPPE. Help him, good Beldame, we beg of thee,
  This knight hath shown us much charity.
CRONE. With a promise, Sir Knight, thou art always ready.
  If I aid thee once more thy love to free
  The cost, I warn, will be full heavy.
  Wilt thou pay the price that I ask of thee?
ORLANDO. If I pay not the price thou shalt ask of me
  May I sweet Delia never see.
CRONE. Sweet Delia then thou shalt never see
  Unless, unless thou marry me.
ORLANDO [aside]. O cruel choice! Woe, woe is me!
  That sentence is indeed full heavy.
BUNGAY [to XANTIPPE]. I'faith, by Him that died on tree
  That sentence is indeed full heavy.
CRONE. Come! Yea or Nay? Wilt thou be mine
  Or in the rock shall Delia pine?
XANTIPPE [to BUNGAY]. Fie! Fie! That lechery should be
  In one so old and foul to see!
ORLANDO [aside]. Though Delia never shall be mine
  I cannot leave her here to pine
  [To CRONE.] So be it. Yea. Set Delia free
  And this very night I will marry thee.
CRONE. Approach, Sir Knight, my mouth to kiss
  In courteous earnest of thy promise.
BUNGAY [to XANTIPPE]. Her bed is no rosy bower, I wiss.
XANTIPPE [to BUNGAY]. If I clout her not, may I Heaven miss.

> [Solemn music. The CRONE throws back her hood
> and mask, revealing herself as a Goddess. Mysterious
> Light. The others fall on their knees.]

CRONE. Fear not, dear mortals. The Lady of the Green
  I am, of Night and Elfland the high Queen,
  Whom some Diana, some Dame Nature call,
  To all that live wise mother original.
  Fear not, Sir Knight, and set thy mind at peace;
  From thy late vow I do thee straight release.
  I did but try thee, thine inmost heart to prove,
  If thou thy Delia didst most truly love,
  Which by thine answer thou hast plainly shown,
  Her liberty preferring to thine own.
  My children three, now listen and mark well.

One alone shall never thrive,
Three in concert must contrive;
One knows where and one knows what,
One can do what two cannot,
One can find and one can tell,
One can overcome the spell.
In the fury of the fray
Illusion shall itself betray.
My children dear, in whom I am well pleasèd
Depart in peace, your pains shall soon be easèd.

[*Exit* CRONE.]

TRIO

ORLANDO, XANTIPPE, AND BUNGAY.
What did she mean? What did she mean?
XANTIPPE.   Lady, Dame or Elfland Queen,
Whatsoever, whosoever,
Might have been a jot more clear.
ORLANDO.   One knows where and one knows what.
BUNGAY.   Never shall we solve it, never,
Though we had a million year.
XANTIPPE.   Which we have not.
O where? O what?
ORLANDO, XANTIPPE, AND BUNGAY.
Shall we conquered be by night?
Give us light, O give us light.

[*Pause.*]

XANTIPPE.
The light, the light, Sacrapant's light, the globe he keeps in there.
That must be it, I know it is, for only I know where!

ORLANDO, XANTIPPE, AND BUNGAY.
What does it mean? What does it mean?
If the light that *you* have seen
Be the subject of the riddle
We its wicked what must weigh.
XANTIPPE.   One can find and one can tell.
ORLANDO.   Though I search my mind, it little
Helps, for it will nothing say.
BUNGAY.   The book of hell
Perhaps can tell.

ORLANDO, XANTIPPE, AND BUNGAY.
> Tome reluctant, clear our sight!
> Give us light, O give us light!

BUNGAY [*consulting book*].
A mage's light . . . A mage's light his life eternal is
Within a globe enspherèd, safe from all his enemies.

ORLANDO, XANTIPPE, AND BUNGAY.
> Then it must mean, then it must mean . . .

ORLANDO.   I the chosen one have been,
> I, the third one, the predicted
> One who does what two cannot.

BUNGAY.   One can overcome the spell.
XANTIPPE.   Sacrapant is well protected.
> Hard, unlucky is your lot.

ORLANDO.   I must compel
> His wicked spell.
> Great Dian, protect thy wight

XANTIPPE AND BUNGAY.
> Great Dian, protect this knight;

ORLANDO, XANTIPPE, AND BUNGAY.
> Quench the light! O quench the light!

> [ORLANDO *starts out boldly for the tower.* SACRA-
> PANT *appears at the door, holding the light.*]

SACRAPANT. You wish the light, Sacrapant's light? Then take it if you can.
ORLANDO. Quench it I shall, and Delia free, or else I am no man.

> [*He steps forward, touches the light and springs back
> with a cry of pain.*]

SACRAPANT. You cannot touch it, mortal friends,
And now your pretty story ends;
Delia, who does not know her mind,
Remains with me, in time to find
That here is best for her.

ORLANDO.   You lie!
SACRAPANT. Think what you will. Prepare to die.
You only live because tonight
The Crone said you an answer might
Bring to me when you came to woo.
She lied. No doubt she lied to you.
You, moonstruck fools, the Standing One

Thought to defy; then know that none,
Nothing, but a thing impossible,
Can his matter make corruptible,
Nought can work to his distress
But a son born motherless.

ORLANDO. Then, Sacrapant, prepare to die;
Torn from a mother dead was I!

> [*He blows out the light.* SACRAPANT *sinks to the ground with a cry. The rock splits open.* DELIA *is standing there. Semi-darkness.*]

DUETTO

ORLANDO.   Vision, descend, be true, be mine, be Delia!
DELIA [*joins* ORLANDO].
            Ended is all that dream, O brave Orlando!
ORLANDO AND DELIA.
            Right be our loves, our loves in grace abide;
            A bridegroom takes his bride.

RECITATIVE A CAPELLA

BUNGAY.   Gentle people, look at me,
            Bungay, who is still within
            What is nothing but a skin. [*Steps out of bear-skin.*]
            Magic disbelieved must be
            If . . .
XANTIPPE.   Enough! The time is late
            And our little children wait.

> [*A cock crows. The cleft in the rock brightens and now, instead of an enchanted bower, a vista is seen, leading away to green open fields, and a village on a hill, very bright and sharp. During the following* BUNGAY *hangs his bear-skin on a tree and leaves his Book of Magic by* SACRAPANT'S *body.*]

QUARTET

ORLANDO, DELIA, BUNGAY AND XANTIPPE.
            We are safe. We are sound.
            Our loves we have found.
            Well in the end
            Was all that happened;

                                    In peace and confidence
                                    Let us go hence.

ORLANDO [*solus*].   But first it is meet we extol,
                                    With a full heart and soul,
                                    Diana, the Goddess good
                                    Of Night and the dark wood,
                                    Who wrought for our deliver.
DELIA, BUNGAY AND XANTIPPE.
                                    To her be glory ever.

TUTTI.   Unseemly it were
                                    Longer to linger.
                                    Take my hand, so,
                                    So, so, on tiptoe,
DELIA.   Each with her dear one
ORLANDO.   Each with his dear one
BUNGAY AND XANTIPPE. Back to our dear ones
                                    Home let us run.

                                    [*Exeunt through cleft in rock.*]

                        [*As the* CHORUS *sings, various animals come out,
                        and, if possible, dance.*]

CHORUS.   Among the leaves the small birds sing,
                        The crow of the cock commands our going.
                        Day breaks for joy and sorrow.

                        Bright shines the sun on creatures mortal,
                        Of good and ill all men are capable.
                        Day breaks for joy and sorrow.

                                    [*Enter* CRONE.]

CRONE.   Sylvan spirits, leave your sport,
                        To your duties; time is short.
                        These events must leave no trace,
                        All must be restored to place.
                        Close the rock, repair the flower,
                        Bear the mage into his tower,
                        But his crystal bring to me;
                        In your motions reverent be.

                                    [*An animal brings her the mage's light, while the
                                    others tidy up.*]

All that must be comes about,
Love unknown could put thee out,
Love unknown rekindles thee;
This much is permitted me.

[*She kisses the lamp which lights up again.*]

Child of my sorrow, through this day,
Take your rest while rest you may;
Soon, too soon, will set the sun
And our wars be rebegun,
Night by night till Jove descend
In glory and our cycles end:
All dreams and darkness, then, He will away
And raise us up to His Eternal Day.

[*Handing the lamp to an animal.*]

Go, set it safely in the mage's room.
Spirits, my thanks: your caroling resume.

[*Exit* CRONE.]

[*Dawn brightens.*]

CHORUS.   The crow of the cock commands our going,
Already the mass-bell goes dong-ding.
Day breaks for joy and sorrow.

Of good and ill all men are capable,
God bless the Queen, God bless the people.
Day breaks for joy and sorrow.

Already the mass-bell goes dong-ding,
The dripping mill-wheel is again turning.
Day breaks for joy and sorrow.

God bless the Queen, God bless the people,
God bless this green world temporal.
Day breaks for joy and sorrow.

The dripping mill-wheel is again turning,
Among the leaves the small birds sing.
Day breaks for joy and sorrow.

SLOW CURTAIN

The Magic Flute

An Opera in Two Acts

English version after the
Libretto of Schikaneder
and Giesecke

BY W. H. AUDEN AND

CHESTER KALLMAN

MUSIC BY

W. A. MOZART

[1955]

TO

ANNE AND IRVING WEISS

This Tale where true loves meet and mate,
Brute, Brave, Grave, Laughter-loving, Great,
Wee, Wise and Dotty translate
To Music, we dedicate.

Preface

Probably no other opera calls more for translation than *Die Zauberflöte*, and for a translation that is also an interpretation. This does not demand nor excuse transporting the action to that hospitable and mythical Dixie which has had to put up with guests as unlikely as *Carmen, Aïda* and *The Cherry Orchard*. *Die Zauberflöte* must remain in its own Never-Never Land, but that land itself cries out for sharper definition.

Even the most ardent opera fans, who can easily take such absurdities as the plot of *I Puritani,* are apt to find the libretto of *Die Zauberflöte* hard to swallow, and with some justification; though they may not always be certain what it is that upsets them. So long as an opera libretto is just that and no more, we ask of it only that it provide lyrical characters and lyrical situations; but if, whether by accident or design, it should have a significance in itself, apart from anything the composer may do with it, then any muddle or contradictions in the story cannot be covered up by the music, even music by Mozart.

It is highly dangerous for a librettist, unless he knows exactly what he is doing, which Schikaneder and Giesecke certainly did not, to make use of fairy-story material, for such material almost always expresses universal and profound human experiences which will make a fool of anyone who ignores or trivializes them. Yet its very confusions, perhaps, give this libretto a fascination it might lack had the librettists stuck to what was, ostensibly, their original intention: to write a straight fairy-tale about the rescue of a young girl from a wicked sorcerer.

If their libretto also seems peculiarly silly, it is because a proper treatment of its material would have made it one of the greatest libretti ever written. It is not surprising that, even as it stands, it inspired Goethe to write a sequel (though not, it must be confessed, a very good one).

It is rare for the story of a successful opera to be interesting in itself. Even Don Juan, a character of profound extramusical significance, cannot be said to have a story since, by definition, he cannot or will not change himself; he can only be shown as triumphant and invulnerable (the Duke in *Rigoletto*), or in his fall (*Don Giovanni*). He cannot be shown as both in the same opera, for the transition from triumph to ruin depends not on him but on the will of Heaven. The characters in *Die Zauberflöte*, on the other hand, have a real history in which what happens next always depends upon what they choose now.

To discover what, if anything, can be done to improve the libretto, one must begin by trying to detect the basic elements of the story. This story combines two themes, both of great interest. The first and most basic of these is the story of a change in relation between the Dionysian principle and the Apollonian, Night and Day, the instinctive and the rational, the unconscious and the conscious, here symbolized as female and male, respectively.

What has been a relationship of antagonism, the war between the Queen and Sarastro, is finally replaced by a relationship of mutual affection and reconciliation, the marriage of Pamina and Tamino. (Who Pamina's father was, we are never told; we only learn that he was the maker of the flute.) Though the conscious and rational must take the responsibility for the instinctive, and hence be the "superior" partner, neither can exist without the other. What the libretto fails to make clear is that, though the Queen must be defeated in order that the New Age may come, her defeat completes Sarastro's task: he must now hand on the crown to Tamino and pass away like Prospero in *The Tempest*. The Freemasonry of the authors may be partly responsible for their vagueness on this point, but what is most surprising is that they should have allowed the Queen to play such a positive part: she saves Tamino's life, she shows him Pamina's portrait and even gives him the magic flute without which he could never have gotten through the trials successfully. Again, whether by sheer luck or by sound instinct, the librettists showed the Messengers of the Gods, the three Boy Spirits, as equally at home in the Queen's realm and in Sarastro's. This is surprising, because to allow the Night a creative role is very untypical of the Enlightenment doctrines for which they stood and, had they denied it to the Queen, they would have spared themselves the most obvious criticism which is always brought against them, namely, that without any warning the audience has to switch its sympathies at the end of the First Act.

Their other defect in the handling of this theme is one of taste rather than understanding: a perfectly proper symbolization of the two opposing Principles as male and female gave them an opportunity—which, alas, they could not resist—to make cheap vaudeville jokes about women.

The second theme is an educational one: how does a person discover his vocation and what does the discovery entail? When the opera opens, Tamino has been wandering about the desert without aim or direction, driven by some vague dissatisfaction, and is therefore, like all adolescents, in danger from forces in the depth of his nature which he cannot understand or control (the serpent). Saved from this, he is shown Pamina's picture and falls in love with her, i.e., he believes that he has discovered his future vocation, but only time will show if his belief is genuine or fantastic; he has, as yet, no notion of what this vocation will involve.

That is what Sarastro has to teach him, namely, that any vocation demands faith, patience and courage. For each of these, then, he has to be tested: he must endure the false doubts of the Queen's three Ladies, the pain of making Pamina suffer though his silence, and, finally, the terrors of Fire and Water.

Pamina, the representative of the emotions, has also to learn through suffering to endure the unwelcome attentions of Monostatos, Tamino's incomprehensible silence, her mother's curse and, finally, together with her lover, the trial by Fire and Water; for emotion has to learn that there are other values besides its own.

In Act Two, as written, Pamina's troubles with Monostatos and the Queen precede the trial of Tamino's silence and departure. We have reversed this order for the following reasons. It does not seem natural that, having seen her fall into Tamino's arms at the end of Act One, she should appear, when we see her next, to have forgotten his existence. Secondly, the effect of Monostatos and her mother upon her would be a much greater temptation to suicidal despair if she had to endure them after she imagines her lover has deserted her rather than before, when she could console herself with the thought of him and even call on him for help and guidance. Thirdly, we wished to make her appearance in the Finale with a dagger more plausible and more dramatic.

In the original libretto, the Queen gives her this dagger, Monostatos takes it away from her, a long interval elapses during which we have forgotten all about the instrument, and then, suddenly, there she is with it again. How did she get it back?

Here is the order of the numbers in Act Two as arranged by us, with the original order in figures on the right.

Aria and Chorus: *O Isis und Osiris.*	1
Duet: *Bewahret euch.*	2
Quintet: *Wie, wie, wie.*	3
Trio: *Seid uns zum zweiten Mal.*	7
Aria: *Ach, ich fühl's.*	8
Trio: *Soll ich dich, Teurer.*	10
Aria: *Alles fühlt der Liebe.*	4
Aria: *Der Hölle Rache.*	5
Aria: *In diesen heil'gen Hallen.*	6
Chorus: *O Isis und Osiris.*	9
Aria: *Ein Mädchen oder Weibchen.*	11
Finale:	12

Naturally, a change in order involves a change in key relationships. Were the music continuous, this would probably be a fatal objection, but it is not. If there are ears which can carry through each passage of spoken dialogue a memory of the last chord before it began, while anxiously anticipating the first chord after it has ended, they are more sensitive and less attentive than ours.

Over against Tamino, the Quest Hero, who has to *become* authentic,

stands Papageno, the uncorrupted child of Nature, for whom authen-
ticity means accepting the fact that he *is* what he is. Quite properly, his hut
lies in the Queen's realm, not Sarastro's. He successfully passes his trial
and is rewarded with his mirror image, Papagena: but this is so casually
treated in the original libretto that the audience does not always notice
what the trial is. Asked if he is prepared to endure the trials by Fire and
Water like his master, he says No, they are not for the likes of him.
Threatened then by the Priest that if he refuses he will never win Papa-
gena, he replies, ". . . In that case, I'll remain single." It is by this last
answer that his humility is revealed, and for which he receives his reward.

This clear division between the Hero who must be brave enough to
dare and the Hero who must be humble enough to stay home is smudged
in the original due to the actor's vanity of Schikaneder, who wanted to be
on stage and get laughs as much as possible.

For example, it is absurd and embarrassing to have Papageno present
and being "funny" during the pathetic scene *Ach, ich fühl's.* Also, Tamino
can take vows because for him they have meaning, and for the audience
they have the dramatic excitement of causing it to wonder whether he will
keep them. But a child of Nature cannot take vows because they apply to
the future, and he exists in a continuous present; there is no interest in
hearing Papageno take a vow of silence which we know perfectly well in
advance he will not keep because the notion of a vow is incomprehensible
to him.

The only trial, therefore, that we have allowed him to share with Tam-
ino is that of being frightened by the three Ladies in the *Wie, wie, wie*
Quintet, from which, anyway, he cannot, for musical reasons, be absent.
This fright, then, confirms his decision not to accompany Tamino; he is
officially excused from doing so, and the two say good-bye to each other.
As we now have it, it is only after he has left, and shortly before Pamina's
entrance, that the vow of silence is imposed upon Tamino.

There is historical evidence that Mozart found Schikaneder's horseplay
in the role of Papageno excessive and irritating (there is practically none
in the musical sections), yet the horseplay has remained "traditional."
And it may be that audiences, vexed by a lack of any clear narrative
thread, have seized upon this one consistent wrong note and helped, by
their overdelighted reactions, to keep this tradition alive.

Papageno must be comic, but he should not be low farce. A Noble Sav-
age, he enjoys a happiness and self-assurance which Tamino, and even
Sarastro, cannot share; one might even say that he is the unlettered aristo-
crat, they but learned clerks. This presents the translator with a stylistic
problem. Fortunately, pastoral, a literary genre created by Theocritus and
Virgil for just such characters, with its paradox of humble concerns and

sophisticated diction, has been popular in English literature since the six-teenth century; in Germany, there are few examples, and even these are an imitation of French models rather than an indigenous product.

Opposed to Papageno, the uncorrupted child of Nature, stands Mono-statos, his corrupted twin. Like Papageno, he is incapable of enduring the trials; unlike the former, however, he lacks the humility that would accept a variety of Papagena. No, he demands the heroine, Pamina. He is clearly another version of Caliban.

We have written the dialogue in verse, because it seemed to us the right medium for the spoken word in an *opera magica*; it obliterates any trace of *verismo*, and it keeps the comic passages within decent bounds.

Translation is a dubious business at best and we are inclined to agree with those who believe that operas should always be given in their native tongue. However, if audiences demand them in their own, they must ac-cept the consequences. Obviously, the texture and weight of the original words set by the composer are an element in his orchestration and any change of the words is therefore an alteration of the music itself. Yet the goal of the translator, however unattainable, must be to make audiences believe that the words they are hearing are the words which the composer actually set, which means that a too-literal translation of the original text may sometimes prove a falsification.

Assuming that he is a competent versifier and can read a score, the translator can copy the original prosody and rhyme schemes and know that his version will fit the notes, but it does not necessarily follow that he should be content with this. In doing an aria, for example, it is often better, once he has grasped its emotional mood and general tenor, to put the actual words out of his mind and concentrate upon writing as good an English lyric as possible. His real headaches, of course, begin when he comes to nonlyrical connecting passages where the meaning of what is being sung has an informative or dramaturgical importance. Some of the stumbling blocks we encountered in translating this opera we have de-scribed in the end-notes.

We have every sympathy for those who are distressed by the slightest deviation from a score they know so well and have loved for so long, just as a British ear is jarred every time Americans pray "Our Father *who* art in heaven" instead of the "Our Father *which*" it has heard since childhood, but if they wish to enjoy the advantages of opera in English, they must put up with the drawbacks.

W. H. A.
C. K.

DRAMATIS PERSONAE

SARASTRO, *a High Priest*
TAMINO, *a Prince*
PAPAGENO, *a bird-catcher*
MONOSTATOS, *servant to Sarastro*
FIRST PRIEST
SECOND PRIEST
TWO MEN IN ARMOR
THREE SLAVES

ASTRAFIAMMANTE, *Queen of the Night*
PAMINA, *her daughter*
PAPAGENA
THREE LADIES, *attendants on the Queen*

THREE SPIRITS

CHORUS

Proem

Queen Astrafiammante, she
*   Long ruled the primal Night,*
In realms of dream had reigned supreme,
*   Until there came the Light.*

But she defied that civil guide,
*   Refused to share her throne,*
With the High Gods became at odds
*   And fled to dwell alone,*

Deep underground a refuge found,
*   Hating all love and joy,*
And, plotting there in her despair
*   Sarastro to destroy,*

That high priest good whose Brotherhood
*   Adored the rising Sun,*
With female wile she did beguile
*   Among his Order one.*

A daughter she bore to her paramour,
*   Pamina was her name,*
Gentle and fair beyond compare
*   Despite her birth in shame.*

Commanded by the Gods on high
*   This maiden to instruct,*
Sarastro then from her mother's den
*   Pamina did abduct.*

Predestined she, as you will see,
*   To serve the High Gods' plan,*
That through this child might be reconciled
*   The Dark and Light in Man.*

Requiring too a bridegroom who
*   Their purpose shall effect,*
A noble youth in love with truth,
*   Tamino, they select.*

Beginning now, our play shows how
*   What the High Gods intend*
Through peril and doubt is brought about
*   That all things well may end.*

Act I Scene 1

[*A rocky desert. In the background a great cliff. Enter* TAMINO *in the last stages of exhaustion and terror.*]

TAMINO. O save me, have mercy, ye gods, or I perish!
  Have mercy and save me, ye Heavenly Powers!
  A venomous serpent pursues me with jaws open wide to devour me!

[*Serpent appears.*]

  With glittering eye he slowly draws nigh.
  Ah, pitiless! Am I to die in agony?
  Have mercy, mercy, save me, save . . . [*Falls.*] I die! [*Faints.*]

[*Enter the* THREE LADIES *of The Queen carrying silver javelins with which they slay the serpent.*]

TRIO

LADIES.   Die, monster, die! Pernicious bane!
  'Tis done, 'tis done, the deed is done,
  The serpent slain.
  From terror free and mortal harm,
  The hero lies, saved by a woman's arm.

[*They inspect the unconscious* TAMINO.]

1ST LADY.   What grace of feature, how manly a mien!
2ND LADY.   Such noble beauty I have never seen.
3RD LADY.   So fair a form . . . to paint, I mean.
LADIES.   Should I submit to bonds of love,
  How soon would he my captor prove.
  Now to the palace haste we all, then,
  To tell the Queen what has befallen;
  Perhaps this handsome youth can cure
  Her burning grief, her joy restore.
1ST LADY.   You bring the Queen our news;
  I ought to stay with him.
2ND LADY.   You two go, if you choose;
  I want to stay with him.
3RD LADY.   Excuse me, I refuse;
  I mean to stay with him.
LADIES [*aside*]. I see their plan!
  Do they believe they can deceive me so?
  They want to be alone, I know,

Alone with him, I know, I know:
No, no, that shan't be so.

How sweet with him all day to dally
Alone in some secluded valley;
The thought brings rapture to my heart.
It cannot be: 'tis best we part.
The pleasing vision is in vain.
Fair youth, farewell; our idylls end:
Farewell; I stay your unknown friend
Until we meet again.
Your friend I shall remain,
Though moons may wax and wane,
In pleasure or in pain,
In sunshine or in rain.

[*Exeunt* LADIES.]

TAMINO [*coming to*]. How is it possible? Before my eyes,
Stretched out in death, the dreadful serpent lies,
And here I stand alive, preserved by Fate,
But for what purpose? How long must I wait
A vision of the future She intends?

[*The sound of pan-pipes approaching.*]

What uncouth shepherd now the path descends?

[*He hides. Enter* PAPAGENO.]

SONG[a]

PAPAGENO.   The lark, the ruddock and the willow-wren
And the jolly nightingale I ken;
In vain do all the pretty little creatures fly
When they the tall bird-catcher spy.
With a whistle I their ears decoy
And many a cunning snare employ,
So that I can merry merry-hearted be,
For all the birds belong to me.

For the snipe, the partridge, cock and hen,
The melodious mavis, too, I ken;
In vain do all the pretty little creatures fly

[Notes begin on p. 184—Ed.]

When they the tall bird-catcher spy.
Had I a maiden-catching net,
Fair maids by dozens I should daily get;
Had I a cage to keep them in,
I would lock it with a golden pin.

If all the pretty girls on earth were mine,
On spice and sugar they should dine,
And she that was the prettiest
Should get more sugar than the rest.
How sweetly would we bill and coo
As married turtledoves may freely do:
When at night she laid herself beside me, I
Would rock her with a lullaby.

TAMINO [*coming out*]. Good friend!
PAPAGENO [*startled*].   Who's there?
TAMINO.   Stop! Do not run away,
    But help a stranger who has lost his way.
PAPAGENO. A stranger here is a lost stranger since
    There *are* no strangers here. Who are you, pray?
TAMINO. Tamino is my name, my title Prince.
PAPAGENO [*bowing*]. This man is Papageno, known as Me,
    Bird-catcher to Her Glorious Majesty
    Queen Astrafiammante, She who reigns
    Unseen. What brings a prince to her domains?
TAMINO. Dream voices that I could not understand
    Called me and bade me leave my native land:
    By perilous and solitary ways,
    Through forest, fen and desert many days
    My feet have wandered with uncertain aim,
    Driven by longings which I cannot name,
    Seeking I know not what. Today it seemed
    The grave must be the quest of which I dreamed,
    But I was rescued by some giant's hand.
PAPAGENO. What giant? There are no giants in this land.
TAMINO. What man could such a mighty deed have done?
    Is this a land of heroes?
PAPAGENO.   There are none;
    This is a realm of women, but for me.
TAMINO [*embracing* PAPAGENO].
    Then . . . then . . . it must be . . . [*Aside.*] But how can it be?
    [*To* PAPAGENO.] Dear friend, my friend forever, it was you
    That saved my life and this great serpent slew.

PAPAGENO. Where? [*Sees corpse.*] Help! [*Tries to run.* TAMINO *holds him.*]
TAMINO.   Your hand!
PAPAGENO.   It's quite dead?
TAMINO.   You should know
    That slew it. The knightly modesty you show
    Is equal to your valor. Tell me how,
    Swordless, you did it.
PAPAGENO [*aside*].   What shall I say now?
    [*To* TAMINO.] O, it's quite simple once you know the way;
    I've slain far bigger serpents in my day.

> [*The* THREE LADIES *appear and advance with
> threatening looks.*]

LADIES. Papageno!
PAPAGENO.   Ah,
    Here come my friends with bread and figs and wine
    To pay me for these pretty birds of mine.
TAMINO [*aside*]. To me they neither look nor sound like friends!
LADIES. Papageno!
PAPAGENO. Ladies, good day! The Queen was pleased, I trust,
    With the white owl I sent her.
1ST LADY.   The Queen is just,
    And to her servant, Papageno, sends . . .
PAPAGENO [*aside*]. What have I done? I do not like her tone.
1ST LADY. Not wine, but water,
PAPAGENO.   Oh!
2ND LADY.   Not bread, but stone.
3RD LADY. No figs . . .
PAPAGENO.   O! gentle lady! No! No!
3RD LADY [*putting a padlock on his mouth*].   . . . but
    This padlock . . .
PAPAGENO.   Hm!
3RD LADY.   . . . his lying mouth to shut.
LADIES. So shall all be punished who
    Boast of deeds they did not do.

> [*Exit* PAPAGENO.]

3RD LADY. 'Twas we who saved you, Prince: enough of that.
    Your coming known, the Queen is pleased thereat:
    Whereof in token now she sends you this,

> [*Hands* TAMINO *a miniature.*]

The dearest of her treasures, for it is
The portrait of Pamina, her adored
And only daughter. May this face reward
The act of your beholding, your desire
Find its true image. We will now retire.

[*Exeunt* LADIES.]

ARIA

TAMINO.   True image of enchanting grace!
            O rare perfection's dwelling-place
            Where beauty is with virtue shown
            More noble than itself alone.

            Is she the dream to which I waken,
            The pursuit where I am overtaken,
            Body and mind and heart and soul?
            She is! To love her is my goal.

            How do I speak as though I knew her,
            When I must find her first and woo her?
            O tell me, image, grant a sign—
                 Am I her choice?

            She will be won—O sweet occasion!—
            By gentle force and warm persuasion,
            And with her love will answer mine.

I know she is, but that is all I know.
Where is the palace? Thither will I go
To ask the Queen what I must do to find
Her who engages heart and soul and mind.

[*Thunder.*]

LADIES [*off-stage*]. She comes! Fire in her eyes, with sceptered hand
     The dark instinctive powers to command.
     She comes! She comes! Invincible her might!
     Hail, Astrafiammante, hail, great Queen of Night!

[*Lightning. The cliff splits open, revealing* ASTRA-
FIAMMANTE.]

RECITATIVE AND ARIA

ASTRAFIAMMANTE. Brave Prince, approach: we welcome you.
     We know you gentle, courteous, true,

A young knight born for deeds of love and glory;
My son, hear now a mother's doleful story.

> Forlorn, despairing, broken-hearted,
> I mourn a daughter night and day;
> By evil fate our lives were parted:
> A murderer, a heartless fiend stole her away.
> O day dark with horror,
> Dismay, despair and terror!
> I see it still before my eyes,
> I hear her loud heart-rending cries.
> The thief ignored all supplication—
> O help! O help!
> She cried and cried again:
> But vain her pitiful rogation,
> My protestation all in vain,
> My frantic weeping all in vain.

> You, you, you
> Are the hero, her predestined saviour!
> Forth, to my daughter's rescue ride!
> To the victorious hero I will give her,
> And you shall take her for your bride.

[The cliff closes again.]

TAMINO [*dazed*]. Vision of awe and wonder! Who will guide
The eager bridegroom to the promised bride?

[Enter PAPAGENO.]

QUINTET

PAPAGENO.	Hm, hm, hm, hm, etc.
TAMINO.	His wits, by lack of words unwitty,
	Express what he is sentenced to:
	By words I can express my pity,
	But that is all my words can do.

[Enter the THREE LADIES.]

1ST LADY [*removes the padlock*].	
	Our gracious Queen declares through me
	She pardons you and sets you free.
PAPAGENO.	Good Papageno's tongue can wag now.
2ND LADY.	Remember, do not lie or brag now!

PAPAGENO.   The truth is wiser, I agree.
ALL.   Let this to all false tongues a warning be.

     So shall the Truth all untruth banish,
     And Evil yield before the Good,
     And denigrating Envy vanish
     Within the light of Brotherhood.

1ST LADY [*giving a flute to* TAMINO].
     Hail, Prince! Our Queen who favors few,
     As favor sends this flute to you.
     This magic flute will well defend you
     And in your darkest hour befriend you.
LADIES.   On moods of doubt and desolation,
     Its notes can work a transformation;
     The moping soul will dance and sing,
     And wintry hearts respond to spring.
ALL.   O, this flute has greater worth
     Than jeweled crowns or kingdoms, then,
     For it can bring good will to men,
     Peace, prosperity and mirth,
     Good will to all on earth.
PAPAGENO.   Lovely nightingales, no doubt you . . .
     Want me . . . now to disappear? [*Starts to leave.*]
LADIES.   We would gladly do without you
     But the Prince requires you here:
     He will daunt Sarastro's power
     While you find Pamina's bower.
PAPAGENO.   Do you want to see me dead!
     For Sarastro, you have said,
     Is a wild and savage beast,
     That without the slightest pity
     He would roast me, he would broil me,
     He would bake me, he would boil me:
     On my bones his dogs will feast!
LADIES.   The Prince shall your protector be,
     But you must serve him faithfully.
PAPAGENO.   The Devil take him: he'll deceive me:
     As sure as I draw breath
     The Prince'll sneak away and leave me
     To be tortured to death.
1ST LADY [*giving him chimes*].
     This, Papageno, is for you.

PAPAGENO.   For me? Does it make music, too?
LADIES.   Now we will set its bells a-chiming!
PAPAGENO.   And can I also set them chiming?
LADIES.   The gift is yours, the bells to play.
ALL.   Flute and bells have magic powers
                   To protect you (us) in threatening hours:
                   So farewell, we must away,
                   We shall meet another day.
TAMINO.   Fair ladies, for one moment stay
PAPAGENO.   And tell us how to find our way.

                                              [*The* THREE SPIRITS *enter.*]

LADIES.   These pages three shall walk beside you
                   Along your path to guard you and to guide you.
                   If you their counsel faithfully obey
                   Never, O never will you go astray.
TAMINO AND PAPAGENO.
                   These pages three shall walk beside us
                   Along our path to guard us and to guide us.
                   By duty called no longer to remain,
                   We bid farewell until we meet again.
LADIES.   Your duty calls "no more remain."
                   Farewell, farewell until we meet again.

                              [TAMINO *and* PAPAGENO, *led by the* THREE SPIR-
                              ITS, *leave.*]

Act I Scene 2

[PAMINA's *bower: two slaves working.*]

1ST SLAVE [*hurriedly entering*]. Have you heard? Pamina has escaped!
2ND SLAVE.   No!
1ST SLAVE. Indeed!
3RD SLAVE.   How happy I am!
2ND SLAVE.   This will show
        Sarastro how Monostatos behaves
        To that poor child.
1ST SLAVE.   I hope he's whipped!
MONOSTATOS [*off-stage*].   Ho! Slaves!
3RD SLAVE. Monostatos!
MONOSTATOS [*off-stage*]. Bring chains!

2ND SLAVE.   She has been caught!
1ST SLAVE. And will be chained!
3RD SLAVE.   I cannot bear the thought!

> [*The* SLAVES *retire.* MONOSTATOS *enters, dragging* PAMINA *along with him.*]

TRIO

MONOSTATOS.   Ah, pretty bird, so white and pure!
PAMINA.   How long must I these wrongs endure!
MONOSTATOS.   Prepare to die or love me!
PAMINA.   No fear of death can move me,
                But spare me for my mother's sake:
                Her heart of grief and pain would break.
MONOSTATOS [*to* SLAVES].
                Bring chains of steel and manacles!
                [*To* PAMINA.] If you your life still cherish . . . [*Tries to embrace her.*]
PAMINA [*struggling*]. No, rather let me perish
                Than seek to move a heart as hard as stone! [*Faints.*]
MONOSTATOS [*to* SLAVES]. Go! Go! Away! Leave her with me alone!

> [PAPAGENO *peers through a window.*]

PAPAGENO.   Well, here I am! I don't know where.
                I thought . . . I heard some voices . . .
                Dare I? . . . I think I dare! [*Jumps in.*]
                On a river bank all alone
                I espied a fair pretty maiden . . .

> [PAPAGENO *and* MONOSTATOS *catch sight of each other.*]

PAPAGENO AND MONOSTATOS. Hoo!
                It is the devil, without doubt.
                Don't touch me! Don't look at me!
                Boo!

> [*Exeunt,* MONOSTATOS *through door,* PAPAGENO *through window.*]

PAMINA [*coming to*].
                O mother . . . mother . . . hold me . . . where? again
                Must I endure the daylight of my pain?
                O let me dream! [*Buries her face in her hands.*]

PAPAGENO [*peering around door*].
                  The jackdaw must have flown.
    What's more, there *is* a maiden here. Alone.
    Can it be? It could be. She seems young. Sighing.
    That's logical. Well, there's no harm in trying.
    Excuse me!
PAMINA.   Oh!
PAPAGENO.   It is! That is, I mean,
    You are . . . Pamina, the daughter of Queen
    Astrafiammante, aren't you?
PAMINA.   Alas,
    I am. And weep the years that I must pass
    Without a mother's love.
PAPAGENO.   Weep not. You see . . .
    Your mother sent me. Well, it's not quite me
    She sent. I keep another company.
    I'm but an amiable bird-catching zero,
    A history of nothing, *he* is a hero,
    I, Papageno: he, Prince Tamino.
    By visions moved . . . and by your portrait too . . .
    He is approaching now to rescue you,
    Sent, as I said, by your mother, and spurred—
    If you follow—need I mention the word?—
    By love, his love for you.
PAMINA.   Love! What happiness!
    O tell me, is he near?
PAPAGENO.   I must confess
    That, stopping on the way to quench my thirst,
    I somehow lost him. [*Aside.*] Still, I got here first.
    [*To* PAMINA.] But he should soon be here.
PAMINA.   He will, I know!
    And I shall love him! Mother, be thanked!
PAPAGENO [*starts to cry*].   O!
PAMINA. Kind Papageno in tears? Tell me why.
PAPAGENO. Your lives and mine contrasted make me cry.
    He has a mind in which dreams are created,
    That please and that prosper and soon come true;
    You have a mother who cares if you're mated,
    And kindly arranges the details for you:
    I have no family, no mate, no art . . .
PAMINA. All will be well: you have love in your heart.

DUET[b]

PAMINA.   When Love in his bosom desire has implanted,
               The heart of the hero grows gentle and tame;
PAPAGENO. And soon from his passion enkindled, enchanted,
               The nymph receives the impetuous flame.
BOTH.   In all our days we mortals can prove
               No greater joy than mutual love.

PAMINA.   For Love's dear dominion extends to all nature
               And all to her kindly compulsion must yield;
PAPAGENO. Love solaces every sensible creature,
               The birds in air and the beasts of the field.
BOTH.   The highest goal of Nature's life
               Is the sweet joy of man and wife.
               Man and wife and wife and man
               Follow their Creator's plan.

Act I Scene 3

[*Outside the gates of the Temple City at sunset. Enter* TAMINO, *led by the* THREE SPIRITS.]

SPIRITS. Your journey's end is now in sight,
    Your quest no longer may engage us;
    On, on to glory, valiant knight:
    Be patient, courteous and courageous.
TAMINO. Immortal children, tell me how
    I am to save Pamina now.
SPIRITS. No further we your way can see:
    Be patient, courteous and courageous
    As knight should be. Faint not nor flee!
    On, on to glory, on to victory!

[*Exeunt* SPIRITS.]

TAMINO. So wise and comforting a counsel[c]
    Shall be engraved upon my heart.*
    Where am I now? What lies before me?*
    Is this the dwelling-place of gods?
    The pillars, the arches, all seem to bear witness
    To Reason and Beauty and Wisdom and Virtue.
    Where Greed and Sloth are banished
    And Art and Labor reign,

There all the temptations of Vice are in vain.
Now let me be fearless as any true knight,
Defending the helpless, upholding the Right,
To overthrow a tyranny,
To save Pamina, or to die!

[*Approaches one of the three gates.*]

VOICE. Beware!
TAMINO. "Beware!" "Beware!" I'll try the second door.
VOICE. Beware!
TAMINO. Again the cry "Beware!" I see one opening more.
    Am I allowed to enter there?

[*Gate opens.* PRIEST *appears in the doorway.*]

PRIEST. What purpose, pilgrim, leads you here?
    Why have you sought this holy place?
TAMINO. To learn where Love and Virtue dwell.
PRIEST. The words you speak are noble words.
    But, friend, what hope have you of learning?
    It was not Love that led you here:
    Revenge and murder in your heart are burning.
TAMINO. Revenge upon a murderer!
PRIEST. Within this land you will not find him.
TAMINO. But is this not Sarastro's kingdom?
PRIEST. It is; Sarastro is our king.
TAMINO. Not of your holy temple too?
PRIEST. He rules our holy temple too.
TAMINO. Then it is all a painted lie! [*Starts to leave.*]
PRIEST. Are you departing now?
TAMINO. Yes, I will go. Now. At once. Never to see you more!
PRIEST. You speak in ignorance; or you have been deceived.
TAMINO. Sarastro is your king: for me, that is enough!
PRIEST. Now, as you love your life, obey me! Do not move!
    You hate Sarastro, then?
TAMINO. I hate, I scorn him, yes!
PRIEST. Can you explain your hate to me?
TAMINO. He is a monster! He is vile!
PRIEST. My son, is what you say well proven?
TAMINO. Well proven by a weeping woman
    Whose pure and loving heart he broke!
PRIEST. Whose wiles have well bewitched your mind!
    Beware of women: woman's tongue

Can make-believe that foul is fair.
O, could you but Sarastro meet,
You would not doubt his purposes.
TAMINO. His purposes are all too clear.
Did he not steal, did he not ravish
Pamina from her mother's arms?*
PRIEST. He took her from her mother's arms.
TAMINO. Where is she? Fettered and confined?
Or has he made away with her?
PRIEST. Our temple secrets, noble knight,
I am forbidden to reveal.
TAMINO. Enough of riddles! Speak the truth!
PRIEST. My tongue a sacred vow obeys.
TAMINO. When will these clouds of darkness vanish?
PRIEST. As soon as you a vow will swear
Our Holy Brotherhood to share.

[PRIEST *withdraws. Gate closes.*]

TAMINO. O starless night! Unending sorrow!
When, when will come your golden morrow?
VOICES [*off-stage*]. Soon or never, either—or.
TAMINO. No! No! Torture me not with doubt!
Unfeeling spirits, answer me!
Is Pamina still alive?*
VOICES [*off-stage*]. Pamina is alive.
TAMINO. Alive! Alive! You turn my night to day!
Tell me with what celestial phrases,
Angelic Ones, to sing your praises!
No tongue has wit that grateful all to utter
That its heart would say.

[*He plays the flute. Wild animals come out to listen.*]

O how soft, enchanting, the magic tone,
Some celestial pleasure voicing;
Such a strain would melt a heart of stone,
Set the creatures in the wilderness rejoicing.
O how soft yet how insistent is the magic tone,
Angelic harmony, celestial pleasure voicing!
Such a strain would melt a heart of stone,
Set the creatures in the wilderness . . . Yes,
But Pamina, but Pamina cannot hear me,
But Pamina does not hear.

Pamina! Pamina! Hear me! Answer me!
Not there. Not there. Where? There? Here?
Alas, my love is nowhere near.

[*Pan-pipes heard as an echo to his flute off-stage.*]

Ah! I hear a familiar sound!
Can it mean Pamina has been found?
Can it mean that she is waiting there?
Could it be? It could be already she is waiting there.

[*Exit.*]

Act I Scene 4

[*An open court within the City. In the background a temple with great bronze doors. Enter* PAPAGENO *and* PAMINA *in flight.*]

PAPAGENO AND PAMINA. Walk on tiptoe! Hold your breath!
 To be captured would mean a painful death.
 All about are watchful eyes
 Who would catch us, who would catch us in a trice.
PAMINA. Tamino!
PAPAGENO. Softer, softer, softer! I know something better.

[*Plays his pipes.* TAMINO's *flute is heard in answer.*]

PAPAGENO AND PAMINA. O for friends what joy is greater,
 O what pleasure more complete,
 Than for parted friends to meet
 And relate what they have seen and done:
 Let us hurry, hurry, hurry, let us run.*d

[*Enter* MONOSTATOS *with* SLAVES.]

MONOSTATOS. Let us hurry, hurry, hurry, let us run!*
 Now! . . . Now we shall have some fun!
 Into irons I mean to throw you,
 A good lesson need to show you:
 All my kindness proved an error,
 I shall tame you now by terror!
 [*To* SLAVES.] Bring me chains to bind them with!
PAPAGENO AND PAMINA. All is done and over with!
PAPAGENO. Now it's all, all or nothing, I know well:
 Chime, my pretty silver bell!

Let all ears be now enchanted,
Dreaming that their dreams are granted.

> [*He plays.* MONOSTATOS *and* SLAVES *dance away enchanted.*]

MONOSTATOS AND SLAVES.
   Let us follow the music, let us caper away!
      Fa la la
   Over mountain and valley to dance night and day.
      Fa la la.

> [*Exeunt* MONOSTATOS *and* SLAVES.]

PAPAGENO AND PAMINA.
               Friends who such a music make
                  Cannot be divided;
               Anger to his heels will take,
                  Fear cannot abide it.

               Music makes us frank and free,
               Joined in peaceful harmony.
               Rich men, poor men, all agree,
                  So do men of learning,
               Music, Love and Sympathy
                  Keep our green world turning.

> [*From within the temple comes the sound of singing.*]

CHORUS [*within*]. Give praise to Sarastro, devoutly praise him!
PAPAGENO. What's that? What's that pudder?
   I shiver, I shudder.
PAMINA. Too late! Too late! I hear the drums
   Announcing that Sarastro comes.
PAPAGENO. O would I were a mouse
   Safe in the church's keeping,
   A snail securely sleeping
   Inside his tiny house!
   But now . . . what are we to say?*
PAMINA. The Truth now, Truth, let come what may!*ᵉ

> [*The temple doors and out comes a procession preceding* SARASTRO, *flanked by* 1ST *and* 2ND PRIESTS.]

CHORUS. Give praise to Sarastro, devoutly adore him,
   The proud and ungodly lie prostrate before him;

His word is redeeming, his counsels are wise;
Let praise of Sarastro ascend to the skies.

PAMINA [*kneeling before* SARASTRO]. Ah! Guilty at your feet I lie,
Who from your kingdom sought to fly.
Not all the guilt falls on my head:
Your traitor liege would have compelled me
To loveless love: therefore I fled.
SARASTRO. Arise and weep no more, Pamina!
I, too, the truth alone would tell you,
The secret of whose heart I know.
There is a name already written on your heart:
He commands your heart.
To love I never will compel you,
But still I may not let you go.
PAMINA. A daughter's longing bade me go
To see my mother.
SARASTRO.   Child, you do not know
How warped and loveless you would grow
Were I to leave you in her keeping.
PAMINA. Yet still for her my eyes are weeping.
SARASTRO. Passion rules her life.
A man must rule your education:
Without man's guidance women grow too vain and proud,
Forget their station.

[*Enter* MONOSTATOS *with captured* TAMINO.]

MONOSTATOS. Down, down, young man, upon your knees:
Sarastro's frown your blood will freeze.

[TAMINO *and* PAMINA *catch sight of each other and
fly into each other's arms.*]

TAMINO AND PAMINA. 'Tis He! 'Tis She! But do I dream?
'Tis She! 'Tis He! I do not dream.
Within his (her) fond embraces, I
Both death and torment will defy.
CHORUS. Mountains and Marvels!
MONOSTATOS.   Shameless and insolent!
Let go before I strike you! For this you shall repent!

[MONOSTATOS *comes forward and kneels before*
SARASTRO.]

My Lord, I bring you information,
Against this youth lay accusation,
Who with audacity unheard,
Assisted by this artful bird [*pointing to* PAPAGENO]
Of Fair Pamina tried to rob you
And would have done, had I not stopped him . . .
My service . . . My deserts you know.
SARASTRO. For these a recompense I owe.
    Toward your just reward shall go . . .
MONOSTATOS. Your favor sets my heart aglow!
SARASTRO. Full seventy with the bastinado.
MONOSTATOS. Ah, no! How can you treat your servant so!
SARASTRO. Away! Or I my wrath will show.
CHORUS. Give praise to Sarastro, give glory and praise,*
    For just are his dealings and righteous his ways.*f
SARASTRO. Cover their faces piously, their feet toward the temple guide.
    None may our sacred rites behold until he has been purified.

> [*The* 1ST PRIEST *takes charge of* TAMINO, *the* 2ND
> *of* PAPAGENO. *The procession retires toward the tem-*
> *ple,* SARASTRO *with* PAMINA, *followed by* 1ST
> PRIEST *with* TAMINO *and* 2ND *with* PAPAGENO.
> *As they reach the doors,* PAPAGENO *tries to bolt, but is*
> *firmly held by the* 2ND PRIEST. *The doors close be-*
> *hind them.*]

CHORUS. To Justice and to Righteousness
    We pray, that soon may come the day
    When Truth shall be revealed to all
    And every vain idol fall.

CURTAIN

Metalogue

[*To be spoken by the singer taking the rôle of* SARASTRO.]

> *Relax, Maestro, put your baton down:*
> *Only the fogiest of the old will frown*
> *If you the trials of the* Prince *prorogue*
> *To let* Sarastro *speak the Metalogue,*
> *A form acceptable to us, although*

Unclassed by Aristotle *or* Boileau.
No modern audience finds it incorrect,
For interruption is what we expect,
Since that new god, the Paid Announcer, rose
Who with his quasi-Ossianic prose
Cuts in upon the lovers, halts the band
To name a sponsor or to praise a brand.
Not that I have a product to describe
That you could wear or cook with or imbibe;
You cannot hoard or waste a work of art:
I come to praise but not to sell Mozart,
Who came into this world of war and woe
At Salzburg *just two centuries ago,*
When kings were many and machines were few
And open Atheism something new.
(It makes a servantless New Yorker sore
To think sheer Genius had to stand before
A mere Archbishop with uncovered head:
But Mozart *never had to make his bed.)*

The history of Music as of Man
Will not go cancrizans, and no ear can
Recall what, when the Archduke Francis *reigned,*
Was heard by ears whose treasure-hoard contained
A Flute *already but as yet no* Ring:
Each age has its own mode of listening.
We know the Mozart *of our fathers' time*
Was gay, rococo, sweet, but not sublime,
A Viennese Italian: that is changed
Since music-critics learned to feel "estranged";
Now it's the Germans he is classed amongst,
A Geist *whose music was composed from* Angst,
At International Festivals enjoys
An equal status with the Twelve-Tone Boys;
He awes the lovely and the very rich,
And even those Divertimenti *which*
He wrote to play while bottles were uncorked,
Milord chewed noisily, Milady talked,
Are heard in solemn silence, score on knees,
Like quartets by the deafest of the B's.
What next? One can no more imagine how,
In concert halls two hundred years from now,

When the Mozartian sound waves move the air,
The cognoscenti will be moved than dare
Predict how high orchestral pitch will go,
How many tones will constitute a row,
The tempo at which regimented feet
Will march about the Moon, the form of suite
For piano in a Post-Atomic Age,
Prepared by some contemporary Cage.

An opera composer may be vexed
By later umbrage taken at his text:
{ *Even* Macaulay's *schoolboy knows today*
{ *What* Robert Graves *or* Margaret Mead *would say*
{ *About the status of the sexes in this play,*
Writ in that era of barbaric dark
'Twixt Modern Mom and Bronze-Age Matriarch.
Where now the Roman Fathers and their creed?
"Ah, where," sighs Mr Mitty, *"where indeed?"*
And glances sideways at his vital spouse
Whose rigid jaw-line and contracted brows
Express her scorn and utter detestation
For Roman views on Female Education.
In Nineteen Fifty-six we find the Queen
A highly paid and most efficient Dean
(Who, as we all know, really runs the College),
Sarastro, *tolerated for his knowledge,*
Teaching the History of Ancient Myth
At Bryn Mawr, Vassar, Bennington *or* Smith;
Pamina *may a* Time *researcher be*
To let Tamino *take his Ph.D.,*
Acquiring manly wisdom as he wishes
While changing diapers and doing dishes;
Sweet Papagena, *when she's time to spare,*
Listens to Mozart *operas on the air,*
Though Papageno, *one is sad to feel,*
Prefers the juke-box to the glockenspiel,
And how is—what was easy in the past—
A democratic villain to be cast?
Monostatos *must make his bad impression*
Without a race, religion or profession.

A work that lives two hundred years is tough,
And operas, God knows, must stand enough:

What greatness made, small vanities abuse.
What must they not endure? The Diva *whose*
Fioriture *and climactic note*
The silly old composer never wrote,
Conductor X, *that overrated bore,*
Who alters tempi and who cuts the score,
Director Y *who with ingenious wit*
Places the wretched singers in the pit
While dancers mime their roles, Z *the Designer*
Who sets the whole thing on an ocean liner,
The girls in shorts, the man in yachting caps,
Yet genius triumphs over all mishaps,
Survives a greater obstacle than these,
Translation into foreign Operese.
(English sopranos are condemned to languish
Because our tenors have to hide their anguish.*)*
It soothes the Frank, *it stimulates the* Greek:
Genius surpasses all things, even chic.
We who know little—which is just as well—
About the future can, at least, foretell,
Whether they live in air-borne nylon cubes,
Practice group-marriage or are fed through tubes,
That crowds, two centuries from now, will press
(Absurd their hair, ridiculous their dress),
And pay in currencies however weird
To hear Sarastro *booming through his beard,*
Sharp connoisseurs approve if it is clean
The F in alt of the nocturnal Queen,
Some uncouth creature from the Bronx *amaze*
Park Avenue *by knowing all the K's.*

How seemly, then, to celebrate the birth
Of one who did no harm to our poor earth,
Created masterpieces by the dozen,
Indulged in toilet humor with his cousin,
And had a pauper's funeral in the rain,
The like of whom we shall not see again;
How comely, also, to forgive: we should,
As Mozart, *were he living, surely would,*
Remember kindly Salieri's *shade,*
Accused of murder and his works unplayed,
Nor, while we praise the dead, should we forget

We have Stravinsky, *bless him, with us yet.*
{ Basta! *Maestro, make your minions play!*
{ *In all hearts, as in our finale, may*
{ *Reason and Love be crowned, assume their rightful sway.*

Act II Scene 1

[*A hall in the Temple City of the Sun.*]

SARASTRO. A joyful purpose and occasion dear
    Have brought us, brethren, to assemble here:
    The High Prince, avid of the highest good,
    Desires to join our Holy Brotherhood,
    Let him approach.

                [*Three trumpet blasts.* TAMINO *is led forward by* 1ST
                PRIEST.]

              Prince, knowing what you speak
    The gods will hear, confess the goal you seek:
    What does your mind desire, your heart demand?
TAMINO. The light of Wisdom and Pamina's hand.
SARASTRO. Are you prepared to risk your life for these
    And lose them both if so the gods should please?
TAMINO. I am.
SARASTRO. Do you, Tamino, choose of your free will
    To face the rites that purify or kill?
TAMINO. I do.
SARASTRO. Will you, without complaining or delay,
    The orders of the Brotherhood obey?
TAMINO. I will.
SARASTRO. Escort him hence; in ways of holiness
    Instruct him further: pray for his success.

                [*Exeunt* TAMINO *and* 1ST PRIEST.]

ARIA AND CHORUS

SARASTRO.   O Isis and Osiris, hear him,
        Accept this vow that he has made,
    In hours of trial and grief be near him,
        Comfort his heart when sore afraid,
        And guide him through the dreadful shade.

□

> May love be born of tribulation,
>> Show him the path to his salvation,
> And when this mortal life shall cease,
>> From vain desire the soul release,
>> Grant him your everlasting peace.

Act II Scene 2

[*A large hall in the Temple of the Sun.*]

PAPAGENO [*to* 2ND PRIEST]. No thank you, no: I overheard
 The whole proceedings word by word.
 Does Papageno choose of his free will
 To face the rites that purify or kill?
 I don't!
 Will he without complaining or delay,
 The orders of the Brotherhood obey?
 I won't!
 What does his mind desire, his heart demand?
 Good food, good drink, a girl who's not too grand,
 A girl whom he can understand,
 Someone like me.
2ND PRIEST.   Supposing such a maid,
 Some rose-cheeked, tender, merry-hearted maid,
 Called Papagena, shall we say, should be
 Awaiting you . . .
PAPAGENO.   Lucky her and happy me!
 Where is she? Let me see her!
2ND PRIEST.   Suppose, I said.
PAPAGENO [*aside*]. I know her smile and how she tilts her head!
2ND PRIEST. To marry if you choose . . .
PAPAGENO.   Of course I choose.
2ND PRIEST. The way of trial.
PAPAGENO.   The way where I might lose
 My life?
2ND PRIEST. That way.
PAPAGENO. Supposing I refuse.
2ND PRIEST. You'll never meet her.
PAPAGENO.   Never?
2ND PRIEST.   Never.

PAPAGENO.   Then,
 Supposing friend, you must suppose again:
 I'll remain single. Ah, the Prince at last!

[*Enter* TAMINO *and* 1ST PRIEST.]

 My Prince, my dear good friend, why choose so fast?
 There must be other means by which to gain
 Wisdom and Love without such toil and pain.
TAMINO. No, Papageno, there's no other way.
PAPAGENO. That's only what you've heard Sarastro say.
 You think him honest?
TAMINO.   That is my belief.
PAPAGENO. How honest when Sarastro is a thief?
2ND PRIEST. Beware, rash fool, and hold your tongue!
PAPAGENO.   He took
 Both flute and bells away: then, by the Book,
 He stole them, for they were not his but ours.
1ST PRIEST. Till purified from all unhallowed powers
 These instruments could work you harm and sorrow:
 Sarastro will return them both tomorrow.
PAPAGENO. Sarastro *says*.
2ND PRIEST.   Sarastro never lies.
PAPAGENO [*aside*]. Ergo, Sarastro is not always wise.
1ST PRIEST [*to* TAMINO]. The sun has set; the night comes on apace,
 And Night is the first trial you must face,
 The lying voices of the dark to hear,
 The cries of lust, doubt, accusation, fear.
 For which in preparation listen to our teaching.
PAPAGENO. No nightmare could be worse than old men preaching.

DUET

PRIESTS.   A woman's heart on manly reason
                Its ardent Virtue can bestow,
             Unless man make of warmth a treason,
                Conspiring Virtue's overthrow.

             For Lust, that treacherous deceiver
                Can counterfeit the sacred flame,
             But then betrays the fond believer,
                Leaves him to self-approach and shame.

[*The lights start to dim, the* PRIESTS *to leave.*]

PAPAGENO. I'll come with you. No trials, please, for me.
    No power can compel me.
2ND PRIEST.   You are free
    To do without me.

> [*Door shuts behind them. Total darkness.*]

PAPAGENO.   But it's dark! I won't!
    Don't leave me! Let me out! Help! I'm betrayed!
    Where is your hand, Tamino? I'm afraid.

QUINTET

LADIES [*appearing suddenly*]. Why? Why? Why
    Do you rashly linger on?
    Fly! Fly! Fly
    From your peril and be gone!
    This teeming pit of deadly error
    Is monstrous with deforming terror.
PAPAGENO.   This I find alarming news!
TAMINO.   I continue as I choose.
    Their pretended trepidation
    Is but folly and temptation.
PAPAGENO.   But are you certain you are right?
TAMINO.   Hold your tongue and do not fear!
PAPAGENO.   Do not talk and do not hear
    And do not there and do not here!
LADIES.   Prophetic creatures of the night,
    We know the dreadful doom in sight.
PAPAGENO.   What doom? Is it avoidable?
TAMINO.   Do not hear them, and be still!
    Or you never will attain a
    Rank deserving Papagena.
LADIES.   Believe not here what may be sworn you:
    Where all is false, can vows be made?
    The Queen who sent us here to warn you,
    You have, for lying words, betrayed.
TAMINO.   Who has the light of wisdom seen
    Will not avow your vengeful Queen,
    Nor be misled, nor be afraid.
LADIES.   The love you shall not win is dear,
    For with your lives you pay the price!
PAPAGENO.   So then if I fulfill each trifle here

And stifle fear, no wife'll still appear!
You hear, Tamino! Is that nice?

TAMINO.   Believe not those to whom the breath
Of Love and Wisdom speak of Death!

PAPAGENO.   But if the Queen says we shall die?

TAMINO.   Her passions drive the Queen to lie.
And you are driving me away!
If you go on, I shall not stay!

LADIES.   Why yearn for love when we are pleasant,
Compliant, unattached . . . and present?

PAPAGENO [*aside to* LADIES]. You mustn't think me rude . . .

TAMINO.   Stop!

PAPAGENO [*aside to* LADIES]. But threats of solitude . . .

TAMINO.   Stop!

TAMINO AND PAPAGENO. A man must learn how to be lonely
Although the discipline be hard.

LADIES.   What can we do if they will only
Ignore us in their self-regard?

TAMINO AND PAPAGENO. What can they do if we will only
Ignore them and their self-regard?

ALL.   In bright formalities of art,
In fearful shadows of the heart,
With open manner, open eyes,
With stratagem and mean disguise,

1ST AND 2ND LADIES. Alas, that even in our lies,

TAMINO, PAPAGENO AND 3RD LADY. A man can study to be wise:

1ST AND 2ND LADIES. Though soon by our revenge he dies,

TAMINO, PAPAGENO AND 3RD LADY. A man can study to be wise.

CHORUS [*off-stage*]. Brave Chanticleer crows up the morning,
To spirits of darkness a warning.

LADIES.   Away! Away! Away! [*They flee.*]

PAPAGENO.   I die! I faint! I fai . . . (l)! [*Falls to the ground.*]

[*Dawn.*]

TAMINO. Papageno, Papageno, open your eyes.
Already morning brightens in the skies
And all is over.

PAPAGENO.   Have those witches gone?

TAMINO. Yes.

PAPAGENO.   Promise?

TAMINO.   Yes. Get up!

PAPAGENO.   I daren't.

TAMINO.   Come on!
PAPAGENO [*getting up*].
    What a nightmare! Tamino, Weren't you frightened?
TAMINO. I was.
PAPAGENO.   But then you want to be enlightened,
    I don't. I'm cold. I'm hungry. Why, why, why
    Did I leave my cosy hut? My birds will die.
    I want to go home.
TAMINO.   But not without a wife?
PAPAGENO. I've never been so hungry in my life.
    O that I had the bells Sarastro took!
    My! What a spread I'd conjure.
TAMINO.   Listen! Look!

> [*Enter the* THREE SPIRITS *with food, wine and the
> flute and bells.*]

TRIO

SPIRITS.   So for the second time we meet you,
      This time where grave Sarastro dwells;
    He has commanded us to greet you
      And to return your flute and bells.

    Also with food we may provide you;
      Eat, then, and drink to your content:
    May we a third time stand beside you,
      Join in your feasting and merriment.

    Tamino, forth: Well fares your quest.
    Back, Papageno: Safety is the best.

> [*Exeunt* SPIRITS.]

PAPAGENO. Wine is a friend with whom I never quarrel;
    He warms my spirits and he points no moral.
    Were I in search of wisdom I should look
    Not to Sarastro but Sarastro's cook.
    Tamino, tell me, do you still intend
    To face these trials to the very end?
TAMINO. I must be faithful to my chosen fate.
PAPAGENO. I feared so. Then our paths must separate.
TAMINO. But still as friends we'll walk them. May each find
    The honor that is proper to his kind.
    To each his mystery: the gods bless all! [*Drinks.*]

PAPAGENO. The gods bless birds and maidens, one and all! [*Drinks.*]

[*Enter the* TWO PRIESTS.]

Here come our bearded elders: mine looks glum.

1ST PRIEST. Hail, Prince, who have so bravely overcome
　　The night's alarms; we hail your victory.
　　Sarastro is well pleased.

PAPAGENO.　　　　　　　　But not with me.

2ND PRIEST [*to* PAPAGENO]. You, feather-witted clod of common clay,
　　Have leave to go your own unworthy way.

PAPAGENO. Long live Sarastro! And, dear Prince, farewell.
　　Let common clay turn prophet. I foretell
　　Pamina shall be yours.

TAMINO.　　　　　　　　Farewell, good friend,
　　And may we meet together at the end.

PAPAGENO. And all be feasting and fun. [*To* 2ND PRIEST.] Come, my old
　　　　supposer,
　　Lead me to Papagena and disclose her.

[*Exeunt* PAPAGENO *and* 2ND PRIEST.]

1ST PRIEST. Courageous Prince, I must prepare you now
　　To face your second trial. You must vow
　　Yourself to silence; henceforth you may speak
　　With none but your instructors and in meek
　　Obedience hold your tongue, appear to all
　　Both deaf and dumb, responding to no call,
　　No cry, no offer, order or request
　　By friend or foe. Beware, Tamino, lest
　　Pity or love betray you. You must keep
　　This vow no matter who may sigh and weep
　　For just one word, whose loving heart mistake
　　Your silence for indifference and break.

TAMINO. I will endure this for Pamina's sake.

1ST PRIEST. The gods be with you!

[*Exit* 1ST PRIEST. PAPAGENO *peers round the
corner.*]

PAPAGENO [*aside*].　　　　　　　　Virtue quits the scene,
　　[*To* TAMINO.] Tamino! Tamino! O what fools we've been.
　　We've got our flute and bells back. They will find
　　Pamina for you. Quickly! Never mind
　　Sarastro and his trials! Come with me!

Tamino! Are you deaf? Ah, now I see!
Hm, hm, hm, hm, hm, hm, hm.
Fancy a Prince, so anxious to be wise
Struck dumb like me, a Prince caught telling lies!
[*Sings.*]   By words I can express my pity
                    But that is all my words can do.ᵍ
                 Hm, hm, hm, hm.

PAMINA [*off-stage*]. Tamino!
PAPAGENO.   Though I'm not a clever bird
    I do know better than to make a third
    When lovers meet. Take wing!

                              [*Exit* PAPAGENO *as* PAMINA *enters.*]

PAMINA.   My love, how long
    The time has been without you.
                            What is wrong?
    My love, Tamino, do you know me not?
    Pamina speaks to you.
                     Have I been forgot
    So soon?
              Do you love me no more?
                            O say
    You love me still!
                  Tamino!
                       See! I pray
    [*Kneels.*] Your grace.
                     I love you.
                          Love!
                     He turns away.

                              ARIA

PAMINA.   Hearts may break, though grief be silent,
               True hearts make their love their lives,
               Silence love with ended lives:
               Love that dies in one false lover
               Kills the heart where love survives.

               O Tamino, see the silence
               Of my tears betray my grief,
               Faithful grief: If you flee
               My love in silence, in faithless silence,
               Let my sorrow die with me.

> If you can betray Pamina,
> If you love me not, Tamino,
> Let my sorrow die with me,
>   And silent be.

[*As* PAMINA *is leaving,* SARASTRO *enters and leads her gently back.*]

SARASTRO. Prince, for the last time, do you still desire
    To face the test by water and by fire?
    If you have changed your mind, you still are free
    To go no further.
PAMINA.   Tamino, stay with me.
SARASTRO. From former promise or from future task
    I will straightway release you if you ask.
PAMINA. Ask, for my sake, before it is too late!
SARASTRO. Speak, then.
TAMINO.   I reaffirm my chosen fate.
SARASTRO. Then for your trial you must now prepare
    With study, fasting, solitude and prayer,
    Forsaking beauty for a hermit's cell.
PAMINA. Do not forsake me!
SARASTRO.   Bid this world farewell . . .
PAMINA. Beloved, stay!
SARASTRO.   As one who knows not when,
    If ever, he will see its face again.

TRIO

PAMINA [*to* TAMINO]. O we shall never meet again!
SARASTRO [*aside*]. In triumph they shall meet again.
PAMINA [*to* TAMINO]. For death, not love, is your election.
TAMINO AND SARASTRO. I (he) trust(s) the gods and their protection.
PAMINA [*to* TAMINO]. Your peril, say my premonitions,
        Is greater, deadlier than you know.
TAMINO [*aside*]. The gods decree without conditions,
        And where they bid me, there I go.
SARASTRO [*to* PAMINA]. The gods decree without conditions
        And where they bid, there he must go.
PAMINA. You would not act in such a fashion
        If you felt love as deep as mine.
TAMINO AND SARASTRO [*aside*]. I (he) feel(s) no less profound a passion
        And would my (his) life for her resign.

PAMINA [*to* TAMINO]. O bitter grief of parting!
    Tamino, why must you be gone?
    Why must you go, Tamino?
    O golden morning, dawn so beautiful,
    Soon return, let all be well!

TAMINO [*aside*]. O bitter grief of parting!
    Pamina, I must now be gone.
    I have to go, Pamina.
    O golden morning, dawn so beautiful,
    Soon return, let all be well!

SARASTRO [*to* PAMINA]. The hour strikes; he must be starting.
    [*To* TAMINO.] Tamino, you must now be gone.
    [*To* PAMINA.] He has to go.
    [*To* TAMINO.] You must away, no more delay, Tamino!
    The hour strikes! [*Aside.*] His Quest will end well!

                  [*Exeunt* TAMINO *and* SARASTO.]

PAMINA. Tamino! [*Weeps.*]

                  [*Enter* PAPAGENO.]

PAPAGENO.   Papagena! Papage . . . [*Seeing* PAMINA.]
                        No!
    Not in tears again! Love's a dreadful woe.
    Perhaps it's just as well I never find
    Her who engages heart and soul and mind . . .
    Or such mind as I have . . . if Love has in it
    Such power to distress my lovely linnet. [*Goes to* PAMINA.]
    Pamina, dear!
PAMINA.   Tamino!
PAPAGENO.   Please! A tear
    In a woman's eye unnerves me. Please my dear,
    Don't cry! I'm sure it's not his fault. The best
    Advice I know seems heartless:—Try to rest.
    It's all Sarastro's doing, crazy man!
    I wish that I could help. Perhaps I can.

               [*Takes his chimes and sings.*][h]

        Go to sleep, do not weep,
        Go to sleep where all is well:

Listen to the silver bell!
Let your ears be now enchanted,
Dreaming that your dream is granted.

[PAMINA *falls asleep.*]

2ND PRIEST [*off-stage*]. Papageno! Hither, fool!
PAPAGENO [*aside*].   My learned owl!
    More lessons!
2ND PRIEST.   Come!
PAPAGENO [*loudly to* PRIEST].
                I come, sagacious fowl.

[*Exit* PAPAGENO. *Enter* MONOSTATOS.]

MONOSTATOS. Now here's a chance too good to miss! My lot
    Has quite improved to send me this. By what
    Sweet luck is she alone, asleep? A kiss? Why not?

ARIA

Every animal and human
Comes on earth to make a pair;
For each man there is a woman,
So, should anybody care
If I take my little share?
With a kiss I will but sample
What all people take and I
Must not to myself deny.
With all Nature for example,
Why should ugliness be shy?

And her beauty in relation
To my ugliness is right:
In the order of creation
Only opposites excite
The contrasting appetite.
She is frank and I am scheming,
I am warm and she is cold;
She is young and I am old,
I'm awake and she is dreaming:
So, Monostatos, be bold!

[MONOSTATOS *creeps stealthily toward the sleeping*
PAMINA. *Thunder and lightning.* ASTRAFIAM-
MANTE *and the* THREE LADIES *appear suddenly.*
The QUEEN *stands immobile, in her hand a dagger.*][i]

3RD LADY. Back!

> [MONOSTATOS *jumps back and cowers in a corner.*
> PAMINA *wakes, leaps to her feet, startled, and then,*
> *with arms outstretched, runs toward her mother.*]

PAMINA. Mother, I . . .
3RD LADY [*intercepting her*]. The Queen is not pleased.
1ST LADY. Her heart is in pain.
2ND LADY. She would have it eased
By proofs of your devotion.

> [ASTRAFIAMMANTE *hands dagger to* 1ST LADY,
> *who hands it to* PAMINA.]

1ST LADY. In your hands
She places this.
2ND LADY. A daughter understands
The gift.
3RD LADY. Sarastro dies!
PAMINA. Dies!
3RD LADY. Silence! She commands.

ARIA

ASTRAFIAMMANTE. Avenging fury lacerates my spirit,
Rage at Sarastro darkly throbs and wild
Blood cries for blood, O may my own blood hear it!
Impale his heart or you are not my child.

Sarastro has betrayed me! Tamino now betrays me:
My daughter would betray me and a mother's love deny.
Tormented, impassioned Nature sways me
As the heartless I defy!
My pain is deep, Sarastro's blood allays me:
Swear! Swear! Swear to avenge me! Or accursèd die!

> [ASTRAFIAMMANTE *and the* LADIES *disappear.*]

PAMINA [*wildly*]. Die. Who shall die? Kill. Who shall kill? O why
Does all the love I know command me: Die?
Merciful gods!
MONOSTATOS [*coming up softly behind her*].
Give your love to me.
PAMINA. You!
MONOSTATOS. Or would you rather that Sarastro knew
What you have been commanded? Come, my sweet,
Refusal would be very indiscreet.

PAMINA. Never!

MONOSTATOS. You force me then . . .

SARASTRO [entering]. Who speaks of force?

MONOSTATOS [immediately kneeling].
My lord, if you but knew . . .

SARASTRO. I know the source
Of your concern.

MONOSTATOS. My love for you.

SARASTRO. Your lust
For one I placed unwisely in your trust.
The gods forgive me!
O vile! that with your soul corrupt your dust
Which might, without a soul, have found the good
Of animals, at least. With brotherhood,
Our Holy Order, we had hoped to win
Your mind and soul from what we found them in—
A savage state; but you are of the lost:
Like the enfeebled asp, undone by frost,
Some kindly peasant puts before his fire
Only to find that light and warmth inspire
A graceless nature to renew its venomed ire.
Enough! I banish you! If you are seen
Within these walls again: Death!

MONOSTATOS [exiting; aside]. To the Queen!

SARASTRO [sadly]. Then Wisdom must use force: that is the worst.
[To PAMINA.] My dear child—

PAMINA [clutching the dagger to her breast; wildly].
Come not near! I am accurs'd!

[She runs out.]

SARASTRO. Spirits of Good, protect the noble child!
[Pause, then reflectively.]
Spirits of Good . . . and, still unreconciled,
Spirits of Evil. Day and Night. And all
Our forces wage a war perpetual.
I have grown old in combat, and I fear
Passionless. Can Wisdom be too dear?
Can she, the Queen of superstitious Night,
In her extremities of heart, be right?
No, no. We need each other. May we learn
Of music how to serve each other's turn:
For music, from the primal darkness sprung,
Speaks an undifferentiating tongue,

Yet, tamed by harmony, the beast can tame,
And every elemental passion name.

[*He lifts his hands in invocation.*]

O light of Wisdom, do not blind our eyes:
That Mind may love, and Heart may civilize.

[*He brings his hands down and lowers his head in prayer.*]

ARIA

SARASTRO. In holy rites, in labor,
  We join and learn to bear
The burden of our neighbor,
  His joys and woes to share.
He who forgives another's wrong
Shall hear the stars' triumphant song,
He who another's need supplies
Already dwells in Paradise.

By freeing one another
  We learn ourselves to free,
For man must love his brother
  Or cease a man to be.
The homely shepherds when they love
A green and social pasture rove,
The tyrant on his golden throne
Dwells in a desert all alone.

[*Enter* 1ST *and* 2ND PRIESTS.]

1ST PRIEST. Sire!
The charge you laid upon me is fulfilled.
Never before so apt, so eager-willed
A novice have I taught. My years of learning
He compassed into hours, and with such discerning
Questions searched out my understanding that
Soon at his feet a doting pupil sat.
SARASTRO. How as a lover has he borne our ban,
The absence of Pamina?
1ST PRIEST.   Like a man
He hides his grief; but I have heard him groan
At moments when he thought himself alone,
Who, when he saw me, smiled as if no care
Had ever touched him.

SARASTRO.   It is well. Prepare
    The Caves of Fire and Water, and with songs
    Escort him to the test for which he longs.

                                        [*Exit* 1ST PRIEST.]

2ND PRIEST. What of the silly bird-catcher, my lord?
    He cannot, will not learn.
SARASTRO.   Let his reward
    Be Papagena.
2ND PRIEST [*shocked*].
                    But . . .
SARASTRO.   If you see fit
    That he to some ordeal should submit,
    Let this be trifling. He, too, is a child of grace
    Who knows his nature and who keeps his place.

                    [*Exit* 2ND PRIEST. SARASTRO *comes forward and
                    addresses the audience.*]

                    Now my task is almost done:
                    When tomorrow's rising sun
                    Sees the Queen of Night's defeat
                    Shall my mission be complete,
                    And in that victorious hour
                    I must also lose my power,
                    Gratefully my throne resign
                    To a happier strength than mine.
                    In one wedding Day and Night,
                    Light and Darkness shall unite,
                    And their long wars ended be
                    In a mutual sympathy:
                    Blessing them, may I be blest,
                    Bid this world farewell and rest.

Act II Scene 3

[*A grove; sundown. In the background a procession of priests winds through the
trees, escorting* TAMINO *to the Trials. In the foreground, watching it pass, stand*
PAPAGENO *and the* 2ND PRIEST.]

                    CHORUS

CHORUS. O Isis and Osiris, great and gracious,
            The pathless shade inform with light sagacious

When all the unchecked elements deride him,
Down through their realm of hostile chaos guide him:
Inspire his heart, instruct his youth,
Soon, soon,
May he be soon reborn in Truth,
Light and Truth.[j]

PAPAGENO. Well, aren't you glad that you're not in his shoes?
2ND PRIEST. I wish that I were worthy.
PAPAGENO.   What's the use
Of trying to make friends? Once in a while
You might relax and even laugh or smile.
2ND PRIEST [*sadly*]. Laughter does not become me, I am told.
Some of the Brethren say I'm getting old.
I know I can't read quickly. I'm not clever.
But they needn't keep on sneering. [*Sniffs.*]
PAPAGENO.   Well, I never!
How stupid of me! But who would have thought
That you, at heart, were Papageno's sort?
Laugh at them! Look at me! I cannot spell
But I can find my way about as well
As any Brother. I trust my eyes and nose
To know a fungus from a guelder-rose.
2ND PRIEST [*pulling himself together*].
Beware, young man, beware! The louder the boast
The harder the fall.
PAPAGENO.   We're back!
2ND PRIEST.   I have been most
Remiss. I beg you to forget my indiscretion.
We were discussing . . .
PAPAGENO.   Not another session!
2ND PRIEST. What is the Good?
PAPAGENO.   The Good would now be wine,
If wine there were.

> [2ND PRIEST *claps his hands. A slave appears with
> wine and exits.*]

2ND PRIEST [*nostalgically*]. Tell me, is it a mere sign,
Or does it participate in the Divine?
PAPAGENO. This is a day of wonders without end,
The wine delicious, you my dear new friend.
Let's drink confusion to all fools who read.
Where is your glass?

2ND PRIEST. Water is all I need.
 Fermented juices of whatever kind
 Inflame the passions and perturb the mind.
PAPAGENO. But that is what we take them for.
2ND PRIEST. I know.
 I was notorious many years ago
 As an imbiber.
PAPAGENO. Bless you, ancient Druid. [*Drinks.*]
2ND PRIEST. I'll leave you now to your pernicious fluid.

           [*Exit* 2ND PRIEST.]

PAPAGENO. What a day! I feel so strange. I'd like to fly
 Up like a lark, up, up into the sky,
 Singing, singing of . . . Virtue? Surely not.
 Of Money? I don't think so. Then . . . of what?

      ARIA

PAPAGENO. Could I but once discover
     Some soft congenial She,
   How kindly would I love her
     And how happy I should be.
   My heart it would glow like a taper,
   How nimbly my two legs would caper.
   If such were to happen I would
   Be always exceedingly good.

   If, like in dreams and fancies,
     Some soft congenial She
   Would throw me tender glances
     O how happy I should be.
   A maid is the crown of creation
   But none look at me with elation.
   I never can find one to wed,
   O sometimes I wish I were dead.

   If maiden or if matron,
     Some soft congenial She,
   Would take me for her patron,
     O how happy I should be.
   My body grows thin as a cleaver,
   I'm wasting away with a fever;
   I'm half in the grave as it is,
   But I could be cured by a kiss.

[*To be spoken alla battuta.*]
Heartless gods! Must I remain alone?

[*Enter* PAPAGENA, *disguised as an old woman.*]

Who's *this?* What shall I say?
Though she's not my Papagena, still she's company. Good day!
PAPAGENA. I am looking for my true love. Do you know where he can be?
PAPAGENO. Does the gentleman that *you* love know that your true love is he?
PAPAGENA. No, he doesn't, but he *will* know. Do you seek your true love too?
PAPAGENO. Yes, I do but I have still no notion where she is. Have you?
PAPAGENA. Does the maiden you love truly know that truly you love her?
PAPAGENO. No, not yet but she will duly when our meeting can occur.
PAPAGENA. If you ask me more I *may* know how to show you when to meet.
PAPAGENO. And if *you* help Papageno, he may help you find *your* sweet.
    Does he want to be your lover?
PAPAGENA.   Yes, but doesn't know it yet.
PAPAGENO. *When* will he his love discover?
PAPAGENA.   When he can his creed forget.
PAPAGENO. I believe I know who *he* is.
PAPAGENA.   Yes, I know you *think* you know.
PAPAGENO. Do you think you know who *she* is?
PAPAGENA.   No, I *know* I know her.
PAPAGENO.   O!
    Is she pretty?
PAPAGENA.   Why deny it?
PAPAGENO.   Is she young?
PAPAGENA.   As young as you.
PAPAGENO. Is he old?
PAPAGENA.   As old as I, it seems.
PAPAGENO.   I know him?
PAPAGENA.   Yes, you do.
PAPAGENO.
    Now I'm certain. You need say no more. I know your love must be . . .
2ND PRIEST [*off-stage*]. Papageno! Papageno!
PAPAGENA.   You are right.
PAPAGENO.   'Tis he, 'tis he!

[*Enter* 2ND PRIEST.]

Well, dear guardian and guide, you are the person that we need.
Come, relax, there's love inside you if you can forget your creed.
I know whom you love.
2ND PRIEST.   Whom *I* love?

PAPAGENO.   *You,* but you don't know it yet.
　　You love *her.*
2ND PRIEST.   She is not *my* love. *You* love her.
PAPAGENO.   Come, come, my pet.
2ND PRIEST. She loves *you.*
PAPAGENO.   You're very stupid. *She* loves *you.*
2ND PRIEST.   You've lost your mind.
PAPAGENO. *You're* no person to play Cupid.
2ND PRIEST.   Maybe not. I am not blind.

　　　　　　　　　[*They turn their backs on each other.*]

PAPAGENA. I love *him.* I don't love *you.*
PAPAGENO.   You see.
2ND PRIEST.   You see.
PAPAGENA.   And *he* loves *me.*
PAPAGENO. *I* don't love you.
2ND PRIEST.   Don't you?
PAPAGENA.   Do you? I love *you.*
PAPAGENO.   You see.
2ND PRIEST.   You see.
PAPAGENO. *I* know whom I love.
2ND PRIEST.   You think so?
PAPAGENO.   And whom I love *not.*
2ND PRIEST.   Recall . . .
PAPAGENO. Really, sir, I think you drink so much you cannot see at all.
2ND PRIEST. *I* drink!
PAPAGENO.   You!
2ND PRIEST.   And you!
PAPAGENO.   Well, *I* know *how* and still know truth from lies.
　　Nose and ear and hand and eye know how to make a person wise.
　　That's what *I* believe the most.
2ND PRIEST.   The creed you must forget. Recall
　　This: the louder that you boast, the harder then shall be your fall.
　　Senses oft deceive . . .
PAPAGENO.   One minute! Talk of boasting, old imbiber!
　　You vowed *me* a lovely linnet, went so far as to describe her;
　　Now you *dare* suppose—in *vain*—a *new* love for me, old supposer!
　　If there *is* a Papagena, stop your boasting and disclose her
　　Now! Delay no more, old feigner!
2ND PRIEST [*leading* PAPAGENA *to him*].
　　　　　　　　　　　　Here!
PAPAGENO.   Not *her!*

2ND PRIEST [*removing* PAPAGENA's *disguise*].   Look well and love her!
PAPAGENA. Papageno!
PAPAGENO.   Papagena!
2ND PRIEST.   Back! You are not worthy of her!

[PRIEST *whisks* PAPAGENA *away*.]

PAPAGENO.
　Woe is me! I cannot bear it. Those three witches warned me. Where
　Has she gone to? Do I merit such a fate for taking care?
　Is it *fair*? It isn't fair. It *isn't* fair. It isn't *fair*!

Act II Scene 4

[*Same as Scene 2. Moonlight.*]

SPIRITS.
　Soon dawn, on earth and ocean breaking,
　　Will drive all shadows far away,
　And men from their illusions waking
　　Salute with grateful joy the candid day.
　Come, holy ray, our darkness brighten
　　And with thy wisdom our foolish hearts enlighten,
　That truth may be revealed to all
　　And every vain idol fall.
1ST SPIRIT. But O, Pamina may not hearken.
2ND AND 3RD SPIRITS. Though light is near . . .
1ST SPIRIT.   Her senses darken.
SPIRITS. While all await the joyous morrow.
　She grieves her yesterday of sorrow
　With disillusionment and fear.
　O that Tamino could be here!
　She comes, her stainless aspect wild.
　We must protect the noble child.

[*Enter* PAMINA, *holding the dagger before her*.]

PAMINA. You are my love, my love's reward,
　My mother's sorrow, my future lord.
SPIRITS. Her words are dark with sad intent.
　We dare not understand their bent.
PAMINA. My life, my traitor, hold with me—
　O heart of steel,

The fatal rites are soon to be;
My hears shall wed eternity.
SPIRITS. Furies of the night pursue her;
Desperation will undo her.
Fair Pamina, stay your hand!
PAMINA. Do not hold me! Love's command
To this heart where love was stronger
Is that it shall beat no longer;
By this hand will heart comply.
SPIRITS. Damned all self-destroyers die!
PAMINA. Life you gave and in my keeping
Gave this charm to still my weeping,
O my mother. Through darkness she calls
And her curse upon me falls!
SPIRITS. Hear us! Die not in despair!
PAMINA. Take, for nought remains to tell,
Faithless lover, my farewell.
Let Pamina seek release,
By this steel I find my peace.
SPIRITS [*taking the dagger from her*]. Dear unfortunate, forbear!
With one death would come a second:
From your grave would love have beckoned
And have slain Tamino there!
PAMINA. Love? But if he loved me would he
Turn away from me or could he
By his silence, love deny?
Or desert me? Tell me why?
SPIRITS. We may give no explanation.
You shall meet, and revelation
At the sight of him ensue.
Know that he, at love's command,
Faces death to win your hand.
Come with us and find him true!
PAMINA. Faithful love, I come to you!
PAMINA AND SPIRITS. When lovers to their lover tender
The lives that they may not surrender,
Then Love their safety will provide,
The gods their footsteps guard and guide.

[*Exeunt.*]

Act II Scene 5

[*Before the Caves of Fire and Water, the entrances to which are guarded by two men in armor.*]

CHORALE

ARMED MEN.

> Now shall the pilgrim tread a valley dark and dire,
> Face death by air and water, earth and fire.
> Who shall this dreadful passage to the end endure,
> He his salvation shall thereby secure,
> In mansions of the Light forever dwell;
> Isis her mysteries to him shall fully tell.

TAMINO. No fear of death shall daunt or bate me
> The gates of hell already wait me;
> I hear their dreadful hinges groan
> My feet must dare the path alone.

PAMINA [*off-stage*]. Tamino, stay! I come with you.

TAMINO. Do I hear Pamina calling?

ARMED MEN. You hear, you hear Pamina calling.

TAMINO AND ARMED MEN. The gods permit that she come too:
> Now nothing can our (your) lives divide
> Though Fate a mutual death decide.

TAMINO. My vow? Am I released from silence?

ARMED MEN. Henceforth you are released from silence.

TAMINO AND ARMED MEN. What joy a common fate to share,
> Thus hand in hand the way to dare!
> A love that death for love defies
> Is matchless, dear in Heaven's eyes.

PAMINA [*entering*]. Forever mine, in life, in death.

TAMINO. Forever mine, in life, in death.

> With threatening sad faces
> Grim spectres beckon me.

PAMINA. In savage and in dismal places
> Beside you I shall be.
> No harm can us betide
> For Love shall be our guide
> And Love can make the desert bloom,
> Can turn to spring the winter's gloom.
> Your flute shall also play its part
> Defending us by magic art.

With spell and runes of secret power
'Twas fashioned in a moonless hour,
Was carved from immemorial oak
To flash of lightning, thunderstroke.
So take the magic flute and play,
To make of night a cheerful day.
TAMINO, PAMINA AND ARMED MEN.
We (they) wander through the horrid shade,
Of death and darkness unafraid.

> [TAMINO, *playing the flute, leads* PAMINA *through the Cave of Fire.*]

TAMINO AND PAMINA [*emerging*].
Sweet notes that with your soft compulsion
Retired the elemental flame,
Rebuke the watery convulsion,
The flood in all its fury tame.

> [*They enter the Cave of Water.*]

Act II Scene 6

[TAMINO *and* PAMINA *emerge before the Temple, which is brightly lit.*]

TAMINO AND PAMINA. O dazzling splendor of the light!
O world so lovely, green and bright!
CHORUS. 'Tis done, 'tis done, your Quest is done.
The Crown of Wisdom you have won.
Come to the Temple, happy pair,
Advance. Advance.
Gods and men your triumph share.

Act II Scene 7

[*Same as Scene 4—Night. Enter* PAPAGENO *with a noose.*]

PAPAGENO. Papagena! Papagena! Come be near me!
Linnet! Pippit! Can you hear me?
No answer. Ah! All is predestined:
Can my unlucky stars be questioned?
Should I have shown bravery? It's not for me:

Love-birds can no more eagles be
Than a she can be a he.

I am not certain she was real.
The Order may have played a trick.
Yet I am certain how I feel:
I am in love; and I am sick.
Papagena, lovely linnet!
Papagena, pretty pippit!
O that wine had something in it!
What a fool I was to sip it,
For it made me love and I
Am unloved and want to die.

                                        [*Pointing to a tree.*]

I shall hang there like a letter,
For my body will say better
Than my mind could ever spell:
O you wicked world, farewell!
To the forceful and the forceless
You are equally remorseless.
I am sorry I was born.
Tell the pretty girls to mourn.

Will not one of them take pity?
Even if she's not so pretty
She could win me from my woe:
Is it Yes? Or is it No?

I hear nothing, no replying.
Was it worth my trying?
No one cares that I am dying.

Like a bird I must through air
Fly the grounds of my despair;
So, you broken-hearted dove,
Be a man and die for love.

Come, my rescuer, to me.
I'm waiting here. Come. I'll be
Waiting till . . . I . . . count . . . to . . . three.
One. Two. Three.
No reply—O futile plea!—
No reply to constancy.

Love can find no place to dwell;
So, you wicked world, farewell.
O you wicked world, farewell.

SPIRITS [*appearing suddenly*].
Forbear, forbear, O Papageno! If you choose
To throw away your life now, you will lose
The only life you'll ever have to use.
PAPAGENO. You boyish Spirits are well-spoken,
But you have no hearts to be broken.
If I were disembodied too
I'd miss nobody as I do.
SPIRITS. Pick up your chimes and set them ringing
To bring your lovely linnet winging.
PAPAGENO. Now how could I have thought of swinging?
Forgotten chimes, you start me singing!
Ring out, and with your ting-a-linging
Remind my absent sweetheart of
Her Papageno and her love.

Tingle, chimes, a summons, bring my dear to me.
Tingle, chimes, a summons! Bring her here to me.
Bring her back, my only love, the love for me.

SPIRITS [*ushering in* PAPAGENA]. Now, Papageno, turn and see!

[*Exeunt* SPIRITS.]

PAPAGENO. Pa-pa-pa-pa-papagena!
PAPAGENA. Pa-pa-pa-pa-papageno!
PAPAGENO. Are you mine to love completely?
PAPAGENA. Yours forever, yours completely!
PAPAGENO. Will you be my loving linnet?
PAPAGENA. I will be your faithful pippit!
PAPAGENO AND PAPAGENA. Heaven will augment our joys,
Will approve our love by sending
To our nest a dear, unending
Lovely brood of girls and boys,
An unending brood of girls and boys.
PAPAGENO. First, first a little Papageno.
PAPAGENA. Then, then a little Papagena.
PAPAGENO. Then, then another Papageno.
PAPAGENA. Then, then another Papagena.

PAPAGENO AND PAPAGENA. What better blessings to have more of?
    A score of
    Papagenos,
    Papagenas,
    To be the comforts of our life,
    To make us truly man and wife.

Act II Scene 8

[*A rocky place. Night.* ASTRAFIAMMANTE *and her* LADIES *enter, led by* MONOSTATOS.]

MONOSTATOS. We must be quiet, quiet, quiet
    If we are not to be espied.
ASTRAFIAMMANTE AND LADIES.
    We must be quiet near the temple
    And in familiar darkness hide.
MONOSTATOS. Your Highness, shall I wed Pamina?
    You swore I should, were we allied.
ASTRAFIAMMANTE. You had our word, impassioned ally,
    We swore our child should be your bride:
    The Queen will by her oath abide.
3RD LADY. The Queen will keep her promise,
    Will by her oath abide.
1ST AND 2ND LADIES.
    The Queen of Night will by her oath abide.
MONOSTATOS. But what is quickening the darkness?
    What can that ruthless roaring be?
ASTRAFIAMMANTE AND LADIES.
    O dreadful seems the pregnant darkness,
    Each lawless element set free.
MONOSTATOS. In rites convening is the Order.
ALL. Upon their rites shall rain disorder,
    Upon their gaudy Day descend
    A moonless Midnight without end.
MONOSTATOS AND LADIES.
    Astrafiammante, Queen of Night!
    May we achieve our vengeance tonight!

                        [*Thunder and lightning.*]

ALL. What blinds us with lightning! What binds us with fright?
We sink to the chaos of infinite Night!

> [*They sink into the ground.*]

Act II Scene 9

[*Throne Room in the Temple.*]

SARASTRO. The sun's golden glory has conquered the night:
Original Darkness gives way to the Light.

> [SARASTRO *takes off his crown and places it on*
> TAMINO's *head.*]

CHORUS. Glory to the Holy Ones,
Everlasting glory,
Our guardians and our guides! Amen!
Isis and Osiris! Amen!

> [SARASTRO *leads* TAMINO *and* PAMINA *up to two
> thrones.*]

Unfurl your brave banners, let trumpets be blown,
For Wisdom and Beauty are mounting the throne.

> [PAPAGENO *and* PAPAGENA *appear from behind the
> thrones and sit at their feet.*]

Unfurl your brave banners, let trumpets be blown,
For Wisdom and Beauty have mounted the throne.

CURTAIN

Postscript

[ASTRAFIAMMANTE *to the Translators.*]

"For Wisdom and Beauty have mounted the throne"
May be your *parting words, but the last is* Our *own:*
It is We *who dismiss, as you ought to have known.*

In Act Two, We observed, you saw fit to contrive
A later appearance for Us and deprive
Our rage of its dialogue: We shall survive

To laugh, unimpressed, at your liberal correction
Of conservative views about women's subjection;
Male vanity's always been Our best protection.

You may think, if you will, your New Order excuses
Putting Us in Our place, but it merely amuses:
Little men, have you any idea who your Muse is?

As for Wisdom and Beauty in heart-warming bliss,
Upon whom do they call every time that they kiss
But the blood-curdling Queen of the Kingdom of Dis?

To that realm We descend when Our cue has been sounded
(Obedient to music) and there rule unbounded
Where your loves are enforced and your fantasies founded.

Schikaneder and Giesecke clung to the hope a
Stage trap-door would bury this dark interloper,
But We'll never lack friends back in Mittel-Europa.

We were Goethe's Die Mütter, *an understage chorus,*
Then for Wagner We half-rose as Erda, now for Us
Freud adds a blunt synonym to the thesaurus.

So english, remodel Our lines as you please,
Unscramble the drama and jumble the keys:
That will serve for the rest of the cast—and your fees.

Let the Press laud your language as sharper and purer
Than the German can boast: when We strike in Our furor,
You won't hear a word in Our high tessitura.

And it won't be with diction, industrialized dull sirs,
Who with graph, daylight-saving and stop-watch repulse Us,
That We strike, but with hangover, sinus and ulcers.

Though translated to Hell, We still govern, a light
That wanes but to wax; whether shrouded or bright,
We are always Queen Astrafiammante:—Good night!

Notes

An asterisk following a line in the text indicates that a slight musical change is required in the score.

ᵃThe German is written in regular octosyllabics.

> Der Vogelfänger bin ich ja,
> Stets lustig heissa hop-sa-sa!
> Ich Vogelfänger bin bekannt
> Bei alt und jung im ganzen Land, *etc.*

In this song and in several places throughout the text, we have taken the liberty of writing more syllables than exist in the original when our ears so advised. The English language has fewer syllables than the German which sound well when spread over more than one note. If it be asked: "Is the effect the same?" the answer, of course, is "No. The English sounds more staccato than the German." We believe, however, that *The Magic Flute* should sound more staccato than *Die Zauberflöte*.

ᵇThe German lyric is written in iambic rhythm, i.e., in 4/4 time. This Mozart has set to a tune in 6/8, so that certain syllables have to be spread over two notes, linked by a slur, thus:

$$1 \quad \overbrace{2} \quad 1 \quad \overbrace{2} \quad 1 \quad \overbrace{2} \; 1 \quad 1 \quad 1$$
Bei Männern, welche Liebe fühlen,

$$1 \quad \overbrace{2} \quad 1 \quad \overbrace{2} \; 1 \quad \overbrace{2} \; 1 \quad 1$$
Fehlt auch ein gutes Herze nicht.

$$1 \quad \overbrace{2} \; 1 \quad \overbrace{2} \; 1 \quad \overbrace{2} \; 1 \quad 1 \quad 1$$
Die süssen Triebe mitzufühlen

$$1 \quad 1 \quad 1 \quad \overbrace{2} \; 1 \quad \overbrace{2} \quad 1 \quad 1$$
Ist dann der Weiber erste Pflicht.

In translating this, we found that the English language cried out for an anapestic rhythm, similar to that of the notes. If the original relation of syllables to notes is not an accident of the German prosody but a profound musical idea, then, of course, we are wrong, so he who is pedantic, let him be pedantic still and sing instead:

> When Love his dart has deep implanted,
> The Hero's heart grows kind and tame,
> And by his passion soon enchanted,
> The nymph receives the impetuous flame,.
> In all our days, *etc.*

> For Love is Lord throughout all nature
> And all to his command must yield;
> He comforts every living creature,
> The birds in air, the beasts of the field.
>   The highest goal, *etc.*

  ^cIn translating recitative, as contrasted with arias or ensembles, the actual sense and dramatic intensity of what is said must take precedence over the form. This particular passage of recitative is rhymed in the German, e.g.:

> Die Weisheitslehre dieser Knaben
> Sei ewig im mir ins Herz gegraben.
> Wo bin ich nun? Was wird mit mir?
> Ist dies der Sitz der Götter hier?

Naturally, it is technically possible to copy this, but the result must almost inevitably be operese, not English, since the feminine rhymes so common in German are rare in our own tongue and the majority of those which do exist are comic.

  Take for instance, the couplet

> Riss nicht der Räuber ohn Erbarmen
> Pamina aus der Mutter Armen.

  One can fiddle about with this in such a way that the second line ends on a rhymable feminine ending like *mother*, but all dramatic force will be lost unless this line is rendered literally, which means a masculine ending. In lieu of rhymes, we have tried to link the questions and answers of this recitative by repeating key words, a device common in the stichomythia of Greek tragedy. Thus, to Tamino's question

> Did he not steal, did he not ravish
> Pamina from her mother's arms?

the priest replies

> He took her from her mother's arms.

A similar difficulty arises with Tamino's anguished demand to the invisible spirits

> Lebt denn Pamina noch?

Nothing will do here but the direct and simple

> Is Pamina still alive?

Any exact prosodic equivalents of the German like *O does Pamina live?* or *Lives then Pamina still?* are stylistically and emotionally impossible. To preserve the essentials of the musical phrase, a strong accent must be thrown upon the first syllable, thus:

Ĭs Pᾱmĭnᾰ stĭll ᾱlῐve?

ᵈThe German word *geschwinde* when spoken ends in a trochee, but as set here is turned into a spondee. The trouble about any appropriate English equivalent like *hurry* is that it cannot be sung as a spondee without sounding distorted. Seeing that, a page earlier, Mozart sets to the same musical phrase a line with a masculine ending

sonst erwischen sie uns noch

we believe that he would have no profound objection to a change.

ᵉ   Mein Kind, was werden wir nun sprechen?
           Die Wahrheit, die Wahrheit! wär' sie auch Verbrechen.

Alas, what can a translator do with this, one of the most beautiful moments in the opera? There is nothing Pamina can possibly say in English but *The Truth* and that is a syllable short. *Be truthful* and *The whole Truth* are flat. One cannot spread *Truth* over two notes and sing *troo-hooth* without sounding funny. But whatever word one adds detracts from the intensity of the original.

ᶠ   Es lebe Sarastro, der göttliche Weise!
           Er lohnet, er strafet in ähnlichem Kreise.

Again, the old problem of the feminine ending. If they so wish, the fussy may sing:

           Give praise to Sarastro; his word shall perséver,
           For just are his dealings, enduring forever.

ᵍSee page 141, lines 27–28.

ʰSee page 149, line 28; page 150, lines 1–2.

ⁱIn the German dialogue, the Queen appears alone and speaks herself. We have introduced her three ladies to speak on her behalf for two reasons. It is more seemly that a semi-divine character like the Queen never descend from the heights of song to mortal speech, and the speaking voice of a coloratura soprano is rarely majestic.

ʲ*Light and Truth.* The German is set thus:

Würdi-ig sein.

The English syllables, it seems to us, should be differently distributed:

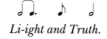

Li-ight and Truth.

Elegy for Young Lovers

Opera in Three Acts

BY W. H. AUDEN AND
CHESTER KALLMAN
MUSIC BY
HANS WERNER HENZE

[*1959–1960*]

*To the memory of
Hugo von Hofmannsthal, Austrian,
European and Master Librettist, this work is
gratefully dedicated by its three makers.*

W. H. AUDEN

CHESTER KALLMAN

HANS WERNER HENZE

DRAMATIS PERSONAE

GREGOR MITTENHOFER, a Poet	*Baritone*
DR WILHELM REISCHMANN, a Physician	*Bass*
TONI REISCHMANN, his Son	*lyric Tenor*
ELIZABETH ZIMMER	*Soprano*
CAROLINA VON KIRCHSTETTEN, Mittenhofer's secretary	*Contralto*
HILDA MACK, a Widow	*Soprano leggiero*
JOSEF MAUER, an Alpine Guide	*Speaker*
Servants at "Der Schwarze Adler"	*silent*

Act I
The Emergence of the Bridegroom

I. FORTY YEARS PAST

[*The scene represents the parlor and terrace of "Der Schwarze Adler", an inn in the Austrian Alps. The terrace, approached by steps from the parlor, runs backstage and stage left: deckchairs, terrace furniture and, near the front, a telescope. The two walls dividing it from the parlor are represented by a framework in which there are two doors, up and downstage, on the left. Right is a solid wall with three doors leading to various places in the inn. The door farthest upstage is reached by a few steps and a small landing. The parlor is sparsely but typically furnished: a porcelain stove in the right wall, a large grandfather clock, plants and flowers in pots, chairs, and a large desk downstage just right of center. The inn is approached from outside by steps leading up the angle of the terrace: people entering this way appear head first. At the right end of the terrace a short flight of wooden steps leads to a landing and from there to an outdoor exit right. Behind the terrace one sees the snow-capped peak of the Hammerhorn. The curtain rises on an inner curtain on which a view of the peak, as it might appear from the back terrace, is represented. HILDA MACK, a white-haired lady in her sixties, her make-up and clothes that of a young woman of the 1870s, is seated there left of center, a very large reticule next to her chair.*]

HILDA. At dawn by the window in the wan light of to-day
    My bridegroom of a night, nude as the sun, with a brave
    Open sweep of his wonderful Samson-like hand
    Pointed to Hammerhorn's glittering peak:
    "I shall conquer it, my honey-sweet bride, my comfort,
    For you!" he cried. His cry is to-day. Yearning
    For night, I lay in the litter of our cravings, naked,
    Dawdled in the grave of my gradual yesterdays,
    Of my maidenhood, its behest obeyed, in my marriage
    Bed by his want unweighed after his good-bye.
    It was. It is. I am not unless I wait.
    I rose. I dressed in this dress. From the peak my ravisher
    Undespondently speaks to me; and all
    To-morrow shall be and bear is known and has meaning
    In his words alone. My lord, my yearning, as you will it
    And will need me like toddy on returning, I stay as you knew me
    On leaving to-day—your dove. Have no fear to be late.
    My hero, I am. I hear. My love, I wait.

            [*A chime sounds from behind the curtain. HILDA rises; and at a gesture from her right hand, the*

> *inner curtain goes up on the scene . . .* CAROLINA,
> GRÄFIN VON KIRCHSTETTEN, *a strong-looking*
> *woman in her fifties, dressed simply in a practical but*
> *expensive suit, is seated at the desk sorting papers. It is*
> *a spring morning in 1910.*]

Each to her knitting on mountain and plain.
Again to-day begins again.

II. THE ORDER OF THE DAY

[HILDA *picks up her reticule and goes out to the terrace. A servant enters right*
front, places her chair near the wall, and exits. During the following scene HILDA
either knits or looks through the telescope. CAROLINA *suddenly rises and angrily*
throws down a review she's been reading.]

CAROLINA. How vile! How dare he!

> [DOCTOR WILHELM REISCHMANN *enters right*
> *front. Like Carolina he is in his fifties and is a perma-*
> *nent accessory of Gregor Mittenhofer's retinue; unlike*
> *Carolina, he is dressed anything but simply. His elab-*
> *orately worked Tyrolean jacket and short Lederhosen*
> *obviously represent his idea of the proper costume for*
> *staying anywhere that is not a capital city, in spite of*
> *the fact that they accentuate his bald head, modest*
> *height and fairly immodest girth. His good nature has*
> *become so habitual, it deceives even himself, and is*
> *noticed by no one.*]

DOCTOR.   Hard at work already, Lina? Well,
What do the critics say this time?
CAROLINA.   At last they see the truth
That anyone with sense has known from the beginning.

> [*A bell rings backstage right.*]

                        Oh!
He's ready for his second egg. Here, read them for yourself.

> [*She hands him a bunch of cuttings, takes a small cov-*
> *ered tray from a maid who has come in right front,*
> *and exits right back. The maid leaves.*]

DOCTOR [*reading reviews*].
   "In these new songs he strikes a note of passionate delight
   And shows a force no other poet of our time can match."

"Again we recognize in him the Master of us all."
"The peak of his achievement . . .", "flawless verse . . .",
    "authentic . . .", "grand . . ."
We have our fair Elizabeth to thank, in part, for that:
I shouldn't wonder if my pills had also done their share.

[CAROLINA re-enters.]

He should be pleased.
CAROLINA.   If they were men, they would apologize
For having been so blind.

[DOCTOR picks up the review she threw aside when
he entered, and begins to read it.]

DOCTOR.   Who is myopic still?
CAROLINA. Don't read it.
DOCTOR.   Really, Lina dear,
I'm not the Master. Let me guess! Who would it be? I know!
That fellow in "Die Fackel" who likes no one but himself.
The Master always was his bête-noire . . .
[Reading.] "The erotic dreams
Of impotent old age . . ."
CAROLINA.   The vulgar beast! He should be whipped!
DOCTOR. Well, as the Master's doctor, I could tell him different.
Wouldn't the Master laugh? Perhaps not. Better tear it up.

[The bell rings twice.]

Two rings. That's me. Injection time. Erotic dreams indeed! [Exits.]
CAROLINA [reading the instructions for the day she had brought in from
Mittenhofer].
"One. Who was Pelops' father? Two.
Check spelling of 'reveille.' Three. Important. Don't forget.
I'm running out of edelweiss; Mauer must pick me more
The next day he goes climbing. Four. That Monstrous Hag, Frau M.
How long am I supposed to wait? We've been here for a week
And she's not had one vision yet. In all the years we've come
She never has behaved like this. Do something! Make her tight.
Give her a laxative. Insult dead hubby. Anything.
But get her in the proper mood! She must perform to-day!"
To-day! What shall I do? To-day, just when I'm feeling ill.

[DOCTOR re-enters, rubbing his hands.]

DOCTOR. Now, that should make him full of beans . . . Lina, my dear,
    what's up?
    You don't look well.
CAROLINA.   It's nothing. Just a headache.
DOCTOR.   Let me feel
    Your pulse. I thought so. Feverish. You ought to be in bed.
CAROLINA.
    And who would do my work? Besides, you know he cannot bear
    Sick people near him: He believes they do it out of spite.
DOCTOR. But all the same, I wish you'd let me take your temperature.
CAROLINA. Later, perhaps. But please, I beg, don't say a word to him.

> [CAROLINA, *after tidying her papers, takes out her
> purse, extracts some gold coins and hides them in
> a flower-pot near the door.* DR REISCHMANN *is
> fascinated.*]

DOCTOR. So that is how you help him out! I've always longed to know.
CAROLINA. Promise to never tell a soul!
DOCTOR.   You never give him cheques?
CAROLINA. No.
DOCTOR.   How does he know where to look?
CAROLINA.   At first I always chose
    A place that He was bound to find: behind his bedroom clock.
    But presently I realized that what he most enjoys
    Is playing hide-and-seek. So now I change it every day.
    Great poets are like children.
DOCTOR.   Yes, and what would poets do
    Without their nannies? They'd be lost. What, even, but for you—,
    —What would the Master be to-day? A simple postman still.
CAROLINA.
    And he'd have died ten years ago, but for your care and skill.
DOCTOR. Come, let us blow our trumpets, for, if we don't, no one will.

> Blow where It will, the Spirit blows in vain
> Until It finds a healthy human brain:
> Poems are bodies and by bodies made;
> A mortal poet needs a doctor's aid.
> > Tooth decay,
> > Muse away;
> > Blood-pressure drops,
> > Invention stops;
> > Upset tum,

No images come;
Kidney infected,
Diction deflected;
Joints rheumatic,
Rhythm erratic;
Skin too dry,
Form awry;
Muscle tense,
Little sense;
Irregular stools,
Inspiration cools.
To wed Him to the Muse has been my mission,
By keeping him in physical condition.

CAROLINA. When young, the Poet cannot earn his bread
And someone has to give it him instead:
Then, when he triumphs, someone in his name
Must bear the burden of his world-wide fame.
Deal with mail
From lads in jail
Or ladies in
The looney-bin;
Answer pests
Who make requests
For a definition
Of man's condition;
Then, worse,
Those volumes of verse,
Thick and slim,
Inscribed to him,
And envelopes
Into which Young Hopes
Have boldly slipped
A manuscript.
Without me, when would Genius turn a rhyme?
It would be answering letters all the time.

CAROLINA AND DOCTOR.
The Poet dies, his glory does not end,
For commentators in a swarm descend
And, syllable by syllable, with learned fuss,
They edit, annotate, emend, discuss

Versification,
Punctuation,
Vowel enlacement,
Caesura placement,
The rôle he gives
To demonstratives,
His liking for
Bird-Metaphor,
And golden thimbles
As birth symbols;
While others plan
To explore the Man,
Learn what he drank,
The name of his bank,
And, of course, discover
How he was as a lover.
But no one thanks, in Essays or Reviews,
The Servants of the Servant of the Muse.

[*A train whistle is heard.* DOCTOR *looks at his watch.*]

DOCTOR. Our mountain trolley is on time.

III. A SCHEDULED ARRIVAL

DOCTOR.   Lina, when Toni comes
I want you to be patient with him. He's going through a phase,
Poor boy, and sulks a lot. I'm glad Elizabeth is here
For someone nearer his own age may laugh him out of it.
CAROLINA. I shouldn't trust Elizabeth too far if I were you.
DOCTOR. Now, really, Lina, what has she done now?
CAROLINA.   The other day
I caught her reading Hofmannsthal.
DOCTOR.   Well, I have read him too.
CAROLINA. That's different.

[TONI REISCHMANN *enters from outside, carrying a
small valise. He is almost tall, slender, and has thick
black hair combed straight back from his forehead.
Though he bears no physical resemblance to his father,
it would seem as though he has deliberately gone to
extremes to point up their differences further: he is
dressed in a severe black suit and his spotless white
shirt has a high stiff collar; but his sullen reticence*

> *encourages the suspicion that they make him uncom-*
> *fortable; just as his surliness has an air of natural*
> *good-humour suppressed in the service of some theo-*
> *retical discipline pertaining to "no-nonsense".—A*
> *servant enters and takes his valise away; also a maid*
> *who puts a large tray with a coffee-pot and six cups on*
> *a table near the back.*]

TONI.   Hello, father.

DOCTOR.   Aren't you going to say
    Good-morning to Aunt Lina?

TONI.   Good morning. Where's my room?

CAROLINA. I'm sorry. It's not ready yet. You know what inns are like.

DOCTOR. Did you enjoy your journey, son?

TONI.   Alright.

CAROLINA. How was the Orient Express?

TONI.   Alright.

DOCTOR. How did your viva voce go?

TONI.   Alright.

CAROLINA. You must be glad it's over.

TONI.   It's alright.

CAROLINA. Do you take cream and sugar?

TONI.   I don't mind.

DOCTOR. You'd like a rest this morning?

TONI.   I don't mind.

CAROLINA. Would you like trout for dinner?

TONI.   I don't mind.

DOCTOR. We might go fishing later.

TONI.   I don't mind.

DOCTOR. Did you see "Lohengrin" last Tuesday?

TONI.   No.

CAROLINA. Don't you young men approve of Wagner?

TONI.   No.

DOCTOR. I thought your great friend Hans admired him?

TONI.   Oh,
    For God's sake, Dad, why must you pester so?

                               [*Chime.*]

CAROLINA. Oh dear, what a morning! They'll be down in a moment
    And I'm not half done. If Hilda would only . . .

IV. APPEARANCES AND VISIONS

CAROLINA [*hurries out to* HILDA].
Frau Mack, if you'd sit with us a bit, the Master
Would be most pleased, I'm certain.
HILDA [*looks up vaguely from her knitting*]. The Master? Ah, so . . .

> [*She gives* CAROLINA *a sudden shrewd sideways glance.*]

To hear what I see and see what I've heard . . .

> [*Then, lapsing into winsome youthfulness.*]

If I may bring my knitting?
CAROLINA [*cheerfully*].   Why not?

> [HILDA *puts her knitting back into the reticule and comes in from the terrace with* CAROLINA *who seats her downstage and then goes to the* DOCTOR, *showing her fingers crossed. Nodding, she whispers optimistically.*]

CAROLINA.   To-day!

> [GREGOR MITTENHOFER, *his arm about* ELIZABETH ZIMMER, *enters briskly right back, and pauses with her on the landing.* MITTENHOFER *is a tall, well-built man of almost sixty, wearing a corduroy jacket and knickerbockers. His high forehead and Beethoven-like mane of snow-white hair are impressive, and he is apt to accentuate both by quite often shaking his head back.*]

> [ELIZABETH *is in her early twenties: beautiful, at her ease, both stronger and less logical than she realizes, and intelligent. She is dressed with simple, not over-youthful elegance. Their entrance, though a daily occurrence, is also a daily occasion, and* MITTENHOFER *makes the most of it. And* CAROLINA *and the* DOCTOR, *though they have already seen him that morning, play their rôles in the occasion by rushing back to the foot of the landing.* TONI *rises slowly;* HILDA *goes on knitting.*]

MITTENHOFER. Good morning!

CAROLINA AND DOCTOR. Good morning, Master.

TONI. Good morning, Sir.

MITTENHOFER. Toni, how nice to see you!
  Elizabeth, this is my godson, Toni.
  Toni *Gregor* Reischmann, Elizabeth Zimmer.
  Wonderful! Now you have someone young to talk to, no?
  Too much musty old past in this place—, —don't you think?
  So you two can brighten it up
  Prattling on about the future, eh?

> [TONI *has remained near the table, but when* ELIZA-
> BETH *holds out her hand to him, he walks over to the*
> *stairs.* ELIZABETH *comes down a step or two.*]

ELIZABETH. How do you do.

> [MITTENHOFER *places his hands on their shoul-*
> *ders.—When* TONI *takes her hand,* HILDA *drops her*
> *knitting and cries: Her expression takes on a visionary*
> *fixity. The others remain frozen.*]

HILDA.   Ah! Snow falls on blossoming
                      Woodland and meadow
                      Swiftly to-morrow.
                      What shall be hidden?
                      Under its fold

            Much that was meant to be
                      Shall know its meaning:
                      Near the cold heaven
                      Snow falls revealing
                      Earth to be cold.

            To the Immortal, high
                      On their white altar,
                      Mortal heat neither
                      Simple nor wicked
                      Lamb-like is fed.

            Paired in the sacrifice,
                      Do they die justly
                      Though it be fated?
                      Never forget the
                      Old gods are dead.

MITTENHOFER. Quiet. Quickly leave us alone.
CAROLINA. Quiet. Leave them quickly alone.
      The terrace. Come. We cannot disturb them.
      Walk softly. No talk. So.
DOCTOR. Toni, come. We cannot disturb them.
      Don't be difficult. Won't you go?
ELIZABETH. I'm going, Lina. I've learned.
TONI.   Oh God,
      What a shamelessly low variety show!

                                        [TONI *stamps off.*]

MITTENHOFER. Capital! Capital! The Gods are good!
ELIZABETH. I wish he wouldn't. What good is it, though?
HILDA. O lovers, what stars disturb you? Lo!
      Their footsteps go through the falling snow!

                        [*During the above,* CAROLINA *quietly shepherds the
                        others on to the terrace.* MITTENHOFER *takes paper
                        and pen from his desk and seats himself near* HILDA,
                        ever so often taking notes.]

MITTENHOFER. Read me runes I know I know.

HILDA.   I gave her laurel ever-green
                        She had no will to wear
                              My kiss was like fever,
                              She begged me to leave her
                              Ever in its care.
                        I gave to him a name to keep
                              That was not hers to bear.
                              Falala . . .

                        She gave me flowers holy-white
                        That were not his to wear.
                              His kiss was like fever,
                              He held her forever
                              Only, only there,
                        And gave to me a tear to weep
                              Not hers alone to bear.
                              Falala . . .

                        They gave each other roses wild
                        From vales they had not crossed.
                              Their kiss was two fevers,

In season the lovers
Found, alas, the cost:
When everything is lost for love,
Love too is also lost.
Falala . . .

[*She sits. Then she resumes as she began.*]

Winter and Spring have met
Now on the slope, where,
Worried, the glacier
Moves down, revealing
Spring come to woe.

Footsteps unfollowed go
On to the mountain;
Briefly their Eden
Blooms in the falling
Snow . . .

[HILDA *breaks off and rises.*]

The vision is ended for to-day.
The world must have and go its way.

V. WORLDLY BUSINESS

[HILDA *picks up her reticule and returns to the terrace.* CAROLINA *re-enters and moves hesitantly towards* MITTENHOFER, *who has seated himself at the desk.*]

MITTENHOFER. Good. Good. Exactly what I hoped for.
The note that I had vainly groped for,
Of magic, tenderness and warning.
Even the form is now in sight.
CAROLINA [*timidly*].
Master . . .
MITTENHOFER. Don't bother me! Alright.
What have you got for me this morning?
CAROLINA. Master, the first reviews have come:
I think you will be pleased with some.

[*She hands a bunch of the clippings, then pours him a
cup of coffee and places it near him on the desk.*]

MITTENHOFER. Critics . . . Scoundrels! Literary hacks!
Their praise is worse than their attacks.

"Among contemporary poets . . ." Oh!
Who are they, I should like to know?
To certain palates, prunes and peaches,
Water and wine, are just the same.
Whom do they rank this time with me?
I thought as much . . . The Old Stale Three!
George who so primly preaches
The love that dare not speak its name;
Rilke, so sensitive, so lonely,
Rolling on from Schloss to Schloss
Gathering precious little moss;
Hofmannsthal, the one and only
Well-bred, worldly-wise Duenna
To show jeunes filles round Old Vienna.

    Let those birds
    Drop their turds!
    THEY'RE NO GOOD!

[*To* CAROLINA.] Take this ridiculous trash away.
I'll look at it later in the day.
Is the typescript of that poem made?
CAROLINA. Yes, Master.
MITTENHOFER.   Where is it?
CAROLINA.   I'm afraid
    There may be some mistakes.
MITTENHOFER.   Indeed?
CAROLINA. Your handwriting was hard to read.
MITTENHOFER. Nonsense! My hand is perfectly clear.
    New glasses, that is what you need.
    Don't you get finicky with me, my dear.

                            [*Reading the typescript.*]

Di-dum, di-dum, diddy-dum, di-dum,
Dum-diddy, dum-diddy, dum, dum, dum,
Di-dum, diddy-dum, dum-diddy . . .
                          WHAT?
[*Screaming.*] POET? "And the gulls wave at the Poet . . ."
How dare you think I would write such rot!
PORT, PORT, you COW! rhyming with FORT.
Didn't that cross your tiny mind?
If you weren't deaf as well as blind,

I suppose you'd have thought the first too short
And altered it to "coastguard FOET".
Why not? It wouldn't be worse than the drivel
You used to write as a girl. Don't snivel!—
By all means scribble on your own,
But leave my poetry alone.
    Lina von K
    Types away:
    SHE'S NO GOOD!

CAROLINA [*in tears.*] Forgive me, Master.
MITTENHOFER.   Do sit still!
    Don't twitch like that.
CAROLINA.   I'm feeling ill.
    Oh please don't scold me!
MITTENHOFER.   Ill? You've never
    Been ill in your life. You're strong as a horse.
    What has come over you? Spring fever?
    [*Suddenly laughing.*] Spring fever! I should have guessed. Of course!
    My godson . . . May . . . the cow-bells . . . and the Alps!
    Poor Lina's heart! How it thumps and palps!

    How tempting is a handsome page
    To Gräfin of a certain age . . .
CAROLINA [*totters to her feet, sobbing hysterically*].
    You cruel beast! I can't bear it!

                          [*She falls in a dead faint.*]

MITTENHOFER. Get up! You're shamming! Get up at once!
    Lina! LINA! O God, what a bore!
    Where's our Wilhelm? Doctor! DOCTOR!

             [DOCTOR *comes running from the terrace.*]

    Look! Lina's fainted or had a fit.
    It can't be drink. What is it?
DOCTOR.   Flu.
    I told her she ought to go to bed.
MITTENHOFER. Then why didn't she? Get her there now.
    The maid will help you. I'm going to work.
    A *nice* way to start the morning!

                       [*He retires to his study.*]

VI. HELP

[DOCTOR *rings a bell to summon the maid, and between them, they help* CAROLINA *into an armchair left.* DOCTOR *pours* CAROLINA *coffee and holds it to her lips. The maid carries the coffee tray out.* CAROLINA *comes round gradually. During this, the study door opens slowly and* MITTENHOFER *peeps out. Seeing that the others have their backs to him and are safely busy, he tip-toes back to the chair he had been sitting on, humming softly to himself.*]

MITTENHOFER. Good Titania, show the way
 To thy hiding place to-day.

> [*He looks under the cushion of the chair.*]

 Bad Titania! Must I seek
 Till the middle of next week?

> [*He looks in the flower-pot.*]

 I spy with my little eye!

> [*He takes out the money, counts it, puts it in his pocket, and genuflects to the pot.*]

 Kind Titania! On bended knee
 I thank thee for thy gift to me.

> [*He returns to his study and shuts the door softly.*]

DOCTOR. I've warned you, Lina; you're not of steel,
 Whatever you think. How do you feel?
CAROLINA. Numb, Doctor. To-day I'm not
 Equal to cures of any kind.
 Death in fact looks dazzlingly attractive.

> [*Tolls begin to be heard from the valley.*]

VII. BEAUTY IN DEATH

CAROLINA. And the grave, lovely . . .
DOCTOR [*shocked*].   Lina!

> [JOSEF MAUER *enters hurriedly from outside.* MAUER *is an alpine guide, in every way typical; proud of his position, certain of his judgements, conscious of his effects and a part of his own costume.*]

MAUER [*excitedly*].   Gräfin . . .
 Doctor . . . on the Hammerhorn . . . a dead man's
 Been found!

CAROLINA.   It's in the air. That sound . . . ?
MAUER.

    From the valley? The tolls. They're taking him down to the village.
    O strange it was finding him. Face up he was, stranded
    By the glacier, with his cheeks cherry-red and aglow
    Like a young man's alive as he lay there dead for the years
    To come, and the ice in his hair still melting, a kid's face
    Big-eyeing the sky, and his skull cracked at the back.
CAROLINA. Pardon me, Mr Mauer, but I'm puzzled
    How *this* concerns *us*.
MAUER [*slightly resentful*]. I was almost to that.
CAROLINA [*resigned*]. Excuse me. I'm ill. Go on with your news.
MAUER. I'd vow his fate was falling into the crevasse.
    It must have been. For a body to come down the mountain
    From there, held in the ice-field, and given the thaw
    We've had this spring, it's pretty exactly as I can
    Figure, the lad's been locked in that glacier forty
    Years now!
CAROLINA [*whispering*].
             You can't mean . . . ?
MAUER.   Can't I ever though! Yes,
    Don't you see, it's certain I am, and Doctor
    Reischmann, Gräfin, you'll agree, the corpse is really
    Him—Mrs Mack's long-lost husband!

                                [*The tolls cease.*]

DOCTOR. Who is to tell her?

VII. WHO IS TO TELL HER?

DOCTOR.   And how? Will you?
CAROLINA. Tell her? It might not be tactful to do
    If her visions could not survive the telling.
DOCTOR. I'm certain the Master will consider the good
    It might work her as more than worth it. You should.
CAROLINA. Perhaps you're right. But I'm hardly feeling
    Well enough now.
DOCTOR.   A woman is best.
CAROLINA. Then ask Fräulein Zimmer, I suggest.
DOCTOR. Brilliant! I'll tell her and bring them here.
CAROLINA.   Leaving them
    Alone then . . .
DOCTOR.   Right! We'll leave them alone.

[*He hurries out to the terrace.*]

CAROLINA [*with a slight smile, to herself*].
   When the Master's visions must be his own,
   Let Fräulein Zimmer make peace by having them.

> [*Chime.* CAROLINA *automatically picks up some papers and starts to leave . . .* MAUER *steps forward.*]

MAUER. Tell Mr Mittenhofer the weather to-morrow
   Will be sunny. Good day.
CAROLINA.   Good day.

> [MAUER *leaves the inn.* CAROLINA *wanly exits to her room through the middle door right.* DOCTOR *leads* HILDA *and* ELIZABETH *in from the terrace and seats them downstage right.*]

DOCTOR.   Best sit inside now:
   Doctor knows how these nice days can turn out dangerous.

> [*He leaves them over-tactfully, and exits downstage right.*]

IX. TO-DAY'S WEATHER

HILDA. How lovely you are! And so anxious. Why?
ELIZABETH.   You must listen:
   Forty years you've been here.
HILDA.   Forty years? So you say;
      But I came only yesterday,
      And in to-morrow's whispering
         My long to-day renew.
ELIZABETH. You are too much alone.
HILDA.   You are too much alone:
      But O think not that some unknown
      To-morrow yet, my child, may bring
         Less solitude for you.
ELIZABETH. Can I explain . . .
HILDA.   Can I explain there is a love
      Far, far more dangerous than love?
      Flee here!
ELIZABETH.   You must listen to me!
HILDA [*with increasing intensity*].
                You must listen to me!
   The mountain beacons in the sun. Could you believe

A torch so cold? Learn and believe—
    Like death it looms between
    To-morrow and yesterday
    Its white eternity.
    Go where the world is green
        And go to-day!
        I beg you, flee,
My child!

> [ELIZABETH *kneels next to* HILDA *and puts her arm about her waist.*]

ELIZABETH. My child, I listen: you must listen too
    And listening, repeat, that you
    May learn, and learning, will believe,
        Repeat, that I may learn . . .

> [*Gradually, at first with single words and then with increasingly longer phrases, and after a bit completely,* HILDA *repeats like a lesson after her what* ELIZABETH *says.*]

ELIZABETH AND HILDA.
How I came here one yesterday, my wedding day,
    And how to-day, he went away,
    My bridegroom, and how long I grieve
        His long delayed return.
Forty years. Forty years of to-day. But time moves,
    The springs return, the glacier moves,
    In time relinquishing its prey.
        My bridegroom was its prey.
To-day, dear God, they found him where the glacier ends.
    My sworn to-day of waiting ends;
        And time unlocks the tears
        That in my crystal burned.
        There cold and dead he lay,
        There after forty years
            He has returned
            To-day, to-day . . .

> [*During the foregoing,* TONI *has entered quietly from the terrace. He is touched; more by* ELIZABETH's *unsuspected warmth, perhaps, than by the news she is breaking.* HILDA *buries her face in her hands a moment, then looks up, her expression emotionless.*]

HILDA. How late it is. I am grown old
   And must have time to think.
   Leave me, my child.

> [As ELIZABETH *gets to her feet, the chime sounds and*
> MITTENHOFER *enters from his study.* ELIZABETH
> *joins him.*]

MITTENHOFER. Eleven o'clock. Time for our walk.
   Well now, you mustn't spend too much time
   With the mad, my dear:
   Youth should develop its own follies pure-bred
   And not cross them with riper species.

> [*When they turn to leave, he catches sight of* TONI *in
> the doorway and, passing him, on their way to the ter-
> race, he slaps him jovially on the back and completes
> his remarks with:*]

   Eh Toni?

X. A VISIONARY INTERLUDE

[TONI *watches a moment in the direction they have gone, then turns slowly front
and passes his arm across his eyes. His expression is almost that of Hilda's earlier
visionary stare, but his journey from the present is backwards.*]

TONI.   O far and unforgotten May!
          My mother, dying, would each day
            Await a dear delight
              With me—
          We saw one blackbird sing the white
            Blooms from our cherry-tree.

          Her head would then in profile lie
          As though she sang a lullaby
            To one who had not grown
              Too tall,
          Too much himself to be her own
            Yet not his own at all.

          Then one day to the blackbird's cries,
          My vision clouded in her eyes
            And saw the blooms grow cold
              And fade

And die, and all that earth could hold
Invisible, dismayed.

> [TONI *turns back to stare at the last place he had seen*
> *Elizabeth.*]

XI. TO-MORROW: TWO FOLLIES CROSS

[HILDA's *expression gradually clears and becomes almost ecstatic. Suddenly she*
rises.]

HILDA. Conqueror, you have returned as you swore me,
Bringing your wife what is hers to become.
Long my wait, but to-morrow before me
Daily waits and shall ever be dumb.
Mine is the now you deliver me into,
Ours the vow you deliver me from!

TONI. In her love I would begin to
Live and would myself become;
No to-morrow yet before me
Wanting her has meaning now:
Long I waited, but the vow
Made to love our eyes have spoken,
Death cannot release me from!

HILDA. *Vale,* my hero! The crystal is broken!
What a nice day it is! More are to come!

> [HILDA, *leaving her reticule behind, deliriously exits*
> *right front.* TONI *remains, still gazing in the direc-*
> *tion Elizabeth has gone.*]

QUICK CURTAIN

Act II
The Emergence of the Bride

I. A PASSION

[*Der Schwarze Adler. Some days later. Mid-afternoon.* TONI *is standing where he*
was when the curtain fell on Act I. Now, however, he is dressed in a style more
appropriate to a mountain resort: chamois jacket, heavy trousers, open-collar shirt.

A moment after the curtain rises, ELIZABETH *enters from outside carrying flowers; she is dressed differently than she was in Act I, though in the same style. On entering the inn parlor, she puts down the flowers, glances quickly about the room . . . and then she and* TONI *rush into each other's arms. They embrace.*]

TONI. Elizabeth!
ELIZABETH.   Toni!
TONI. My dearest!
ELIZABETH.   My dear!
TONI AND ELIZABETH.
     Look at me! Tell me,
     Tell me it's true!
TONI. True that you
     Are in my arms.
ELIZABETH. True that I
     Am in your arms.

TONI. I dwelt in a world
     Of anonymous shadows
     Where none had faces
     Save me alone.
     I was myself
     But what were they
     But a dream of mine?
     But then you came
     And day broke.

ELIZABETH. I dwelt in a world,
     An anonymous shadow,
     For all had faces
     Save me alone.
     They were themselves
     But what was I
     But a dream of theirs?
     But then you came
     And day broke.

TONI AND ELIZABETH.
     Joy! Joy! At last
     To stand alive
     In a living world
     Where instead of silence
     The crying heart
     Hears another

Heart reply
And know that we
Are not alone.

TONI. Farewell the darkness, hail the shining day!
Our world awaits us and forbids delay.
Let us go now!
ELIZABETH.   Would that we could, but I
Owe him his right to hear me say good-bye.
TONI. Say it at once, then. I shall go and wake him.
ELIZABETH. Not yet. It would be cruelty to take him
So unawares. Be patient. Let me find
The moment. Love should teach us to be kind.

> [*The embrace.* CAROLINA *enters weakly middle right,
> sees them and screams.*]

CAROLINA. Doctor! Quickly! Come! Look there!

> [DOCTOR *enters hurriedly right front;* CAROLINA
> *points at the couple, who have moved quickly but un-
> abashedly away from each other.*]

[*To* TONI *and* ELIZABETH.] Aren't you ashamed? Surely the
Master . . .
TONI. Please let me explain. We love each other.
CAROLINA. Rubbish! Thank goodness I got up in time
To take steps to stop this nonsense.
[*To* DOCTOR.] You speak to him; I'll talk to her.
We'll settle this like sensible people
Quickly and quietly. At quarter past four.
He'll be coming down.
[*To* ELIZABETH.]   You come with me.

II. SENSIBLE TALK

[ELIZABETH *shrugs her shoulders lightly and goes out to the terrace followed by*
CAROLINA. *There she goes to the railing and stares out into space, keeping her
back to* CAROLINA. *The men remain in the parlor, downstage.*]

DOCTOR. You don't know what you're doing.
TONI.   I know this.
Love has filled my life with glory.
What else matters?
DOCTOR.   What of your future?

Toni. She is my future.

Carolina.   Fräulein, I'm waiting
      To hear whatever you have to say.

Doctor. It's no good, boy. Your Godfather . . .

Toni. The Master! The Master! It makes me sick!
      What the world needs are warmer hearts,
         Not older poets.

Carolina.   You have your place here
      As we all have.

Doctor.   How can you marry
      A woman whom the whole world knows
      Was your Godfather's mistress.

Carolina. You're untrue to your trust! You've betrayed the Master!

Doctor. You must face facts.

Toni.   And the fact is
      You hate Elizabeth. You hate love.
      I don't believe you loved Mother.
      Did you marry her for her money and breeding?

Doctor. Don't!

Toni.   Did you? She's dead now.
      You can tell me the truth.

Doctor.   Toni, how can you!

Carolina. Must I remind you that the Master has his work?

Toni. I shouldn't have said that. I'm sorry. Forgive me!

Carolina. He's not to be upset! He's not to be worried!

Doctor. When I lost her, Toni, I longed to die.
      All I want is to see you happy,
      The sort of son she would have hoped for.

Carolina. How often has this happened before?

Doctor. Elizabeth is nice, but she's not for you.

Carolina. The truth, please!

Doctor.   Toni, I know
      I'm a foolish and fussy old father at times,
      But you mean so much to me.

Carolina.   I command you to answer!

Doctor. God bless you, my boy.

                              [Exits slowly downstage right.]

Carolina.   Go on!
      Speak, you slut!

[ELIZABETH, *barely controlling her temper, turns around to face* CAROLINA *and, in a deliberately even tone of voice, finally answers her.*]

ELIZABETH. You spoke of my place.
    Aren't you, Gräfin, forgetting yours?
    Or did you hire me? Is it your job
    To procure for the Master? Excuse my asking.

[CAROLINA *looks her full in the face a moment and then turns and walks to the back of the terrace. Chime.*]

III. EACH IN HIS PLACE

ELIZABETH. False, father, false to you!
    Untrue! Insane!
    Falsely I made
    An idol of a vain
    Ignoble child,
    Falsely believed
    Your spirit dwelt in him,
    By lust, by vanity deceived.
    False to the bone. Defiled!
    How shall I atone
    For having so betrayed your love?

TONI. Cold, cold,
    The glittering ball of the world;
        Strong, strong,
    The rich, the righteous, the old:
        Blind, blind
    To what is lovely, true and kind;
        Deaf, deaf
    To the artless cry of the heart;
        All, all
    Conspire to quench the fire of love.

[CAROLINA *enters the parlor back right and approaches* TONI.]

CAROLINA. If you want Elizabeth, she's waiting for you.
    You'll find her on the terrace. You better both
    Make up your minds what you mean to do
    And fast. It's time for the Master's tea.

IV. THE MASTER'S TIME

[*Chime. During the foregoing, servants have brought in a tea table from downstage right, and exited.* CAROLINA *inspects it briefly, adjusts a few things on it, and withdraws backstage.* TONI *goes out to join* ELIZABETH. *A moment after the chime,* MITTENHOFER *enters from his rooms and quickly and quietly settles down to a substantial tea, ignoring everything but his food.*]

ELIZABETH [*furiously*]. You were right.
      Take me away,
      Somewhere, anywhere,
      I don't mind,
      But now, out of this place:
      I cannot face
      Another day.
      Let our Gräfin find
      Someone more suitable,
      Respectable, dutiful:
      There must be plenty
      Of nice wellbred girls under twenty
      Who would jump at her offer
      Of board and bed with Herr Mittenhofer.

                [MITTENHOFER *looks up from his tea for a moment, turns his head, and notices* CAROLINA.]

MITTENHOFER.
    Glad to see you up again. You ought to eat more and work less.

                [CAROLINA *comes forward and stands by the tea table.*]

ELIZABETH. Kiss me!
CAROLINA.   I'm not hungry.
TONI.   Careful!
MITTENHOFER.   Where is our ex-prophetess?
CAROLINA.
    In the Gasthaus, I imagine, drinking schnapps and playing skat.
    Naturally, the guides all cheat her, but she likes it.
MITTENHOFER.   So! That's that.
TONI. Aren't you going to tell him?
MITTENHOFER.   When I cannot write, I find
    Food the only consolation.
ELIZABETH.   Toni, what a filthy mind
    That old woman has. Let *her* give the information.
    I must not derange his schedule, *I* must not forget my station.

TONI. Still, I think we ought to tell him . . .

CAROLINA.   Master, don't you think you really need
    Peace and solitude? How can you work or concentrate or read
    Properly when certain people . . .

MITTENHOFER [*sharply*].   Certain people? I detest
    Sly insinuations! Who?

TONI.   And don't you think it would be best
    If you talked to father?

MITTENHOFER.   Elizabeth, of course, for one.
    Who else?

TONI.   He's so upset and worried. I'm, you see, his only son.

MITTENHOFER. Well?

CAROLINA.   I didn't want to tell you, but . . .

MITTENHOFER.   You're longing, I can see,
    To tell me about her and Toni. Well, that's hardly news to me.

CAROLINA. Kissing him in public places!

MITTENHOFER.   Better than behind locked doors!

CAROLINA. But what are we to do?

ELIZABETH.   Oh, Toni . . .

MITTENHOFER.   Let the children play, of course.

ELIZABETH. Must we talk so much?

CAROLINA.   But, Master . . .

MITTENHOFER.   Since you have no sense of taste,
    Ask Elizabeth to join me. These muffins are too good to waste.

TONI. Darling!

ELIZABETH.   No. You wouldn't kiss me when I asked you. Now I don't
    Feel like kissing anyone!

MITTENHOFER [*picking up crumbs from the table and popping them into his
    mouth*].
              She will . . . she won't . . . she will . . . she . . . won't . . .

> [CAROLINA, *at* MITTENHOFER's *request, has gone
> out to the terrace. There she approaches the couple
> with exaggerated cordiality.*]

CAROLINA. Excuse my interrupting what must be
    An important conversation. The Master says that he
    Would like Elizabeth to join him now at tea.
    I didn't tell him anything.

> [*She leaves them, re-enters the parlor, picks up some
> things from the desk, and exits into Mittenhofer's
> room.*]

TONI.   Let me
    Come with you.
ELIZABETH.   No! I've questions of my own
    To settle. I must handle them alone.

> [*Chime.* ELIZABETH *goes in to join* MITTEN-
> HOFER; TONI *sits on the terrace in a deckchair, his*
> *back to the audience.*]

V. PERSONAL QUESTIONS

MITTENHOFER. Sit down, dear child.
    Are you cross with me?
ELIZABETH. No. Not cross.
MITTENHOFER. But you were, weren't you, my dear,
    Angry with me for my anger at you
    When you told Hilda about her husband?
ELIZABETH. It wasn't your anger at me I minded:
    I thought you unjust to her.
MITTENHOFER. And you were right.
    I was unjust. And why?
ELIZABETH. Why? Because you only
    Thought of yourself
    As you always do.
MITTENHOFER. No, there you make a mistake.
    I was angry for the sake
    Of an unmade verse
    Crying out to be made.
ELIZABETH. But, surely you ought
    To have put her good
    Before any thought
    Of what she could give.
    You, of all people, should.
    Haven't you taught
    My whole generation
    That the deadly sin
    Is lack of imagination?
MITTENHOFER. You are right, of course.
    Once again I'm made to learn
    That in the end
    A poet must depend
    On no one but himself.
    For to-day, my dear,

My lovely Muse, I hear
Through the words in which you plead
For an old woman
The voice of your young need,
Your heart calling me:
"Let Elizabeth go free!"
ELIZABETH. No! No!
I wasn't thinking of myself.
MITTENHOFER. Weren't you, my dear?
ELIZABETH. But what should I want
To be free for,
To be free from?
MITTENHOFER. Free for?
Do we ever know that?
Free from?
From what would you be free?
Well, first of all, from me.
Let me do what you say
I ought to do,
Put myself in your place.
Now whom do I see
Facing me?
A booming old bore
Who repeats his stories,
A spoiled child
Who stamps and screams
When his will is crossed;
And then—oh dear!—
The atmosphere
Surrounding him,
The adoration, the fuss:
How ridiculous,
How humorless
It looks to you,
Doesn't it? Yes.
Nevertheless,
Believe it or not,
I need all this
To protect and save
The tiny store
Of what within
Is genuine.

You, dear, I know,
Read with perception
But you cannot know,
Have any conception
Of what it is like
To be a poet,
Of what it means
Never, never
To feel, to think, to see, to hear,
Without reflecting: "Now,
Could I use that somehow?
Would it translate
Into number and rhyme?"
Until in time
One no longer knows
What is true and false
Or right and wrong.
Only what goes
And won't go into song.
Now do you see
Why I so often
Fail other people,
Yes, even you?
But there I go
Performing again.
Shall I never learn to stop it?
Elizabeth, my dear,
Forgive me!

ELIZABETH.   It is I
Who need forgiveness,
How unjust I have been!

MITTENHOFER. Only promise me this:
If ever you wish to go away . . .

ELIZABETH. I don't!

MITTENHOFER.   Not now, perhaps.
But sooner or later
You will, and then
You must tell me. Promise?

ELIZABETH. I promise.

MITTENHOFER.   Then all is well.

[CAROLINA *re-enters from Mittenhofer's room.*]

CAROLINA. Your room has been aired and is ready for you.
There's clean foolscap. It's Five nearly.

> [MITTENHOFER *rises and kisses* ELIZABETH *on the
> forehead.*]

MITTENHOFER. Bless you, my child.

> [MITTENHOFER *exits to his room. Servants come in
> right front and remove the tea table.*]

ELIZABETH. Carolina, I'm sorry I upset you.
CAROLINA. *You*
Upset *me?* Kindly mind
Your own troubles, and don't try
To poke your nose into those of others.

> [CAROLINA *exits right center. Chime.*]

VI. THE TROUBLES OF OTHERS

ELIZABETH. My own, my own, the little planet flies,
The snow-flake falls through ever colder years:
My own, upon a human cheek it dies
Not in its own but in another's tears.

> [TONI *comes in timidly from the terrace.*]

TONI. Did you tell him?

VII. WHAT MUST BE TOLD

ELIZABETH. No.
TONI. But dear, why not?
One of us must, after all.
ELIZABETH. After all, perhaps there is nothing
To tell. What could I tell him?
Nothing he doesn't know already.
And what do we know, Toni,
About each other?
TONI. We know—we know
We love each other.
ELIZABETH. Do we?
I know I loved my father. Then I thought
I loved your Godfather, then . . .
TONI. Elizabeth, your voice is so strange. What
Has happened? You're not yourself.

ELIZABETH.   Perhaps not. Perhaps I never was.
                        Was I myself when I dreamed
                   Of becoming his mistress?
TONI.   Please don't!
ELIZABETH.   The dream came true, didn't it,
                   Like in the fairy tales. The goose-girl
                        Won her Prince. She was supposed
                   To live happily ever after.
                        But something happened.
TONI.   The spell
                   Of the old sorcerer was broken.
                        That's what happened.
ELIZABETH.   She was bored;
                   You came . . .
TONI.   The moment the shepherd boy
                   Beheld the Princess, he knew
                   He would love her forever . . .
ELIZABETH.   She thought
                   She heard him say he loved her.
                   Did you say that, or was she under
                        A new spell?
TONI.   Do you love me
                   Or don't you?
ELIZABETH.   Toni, dear, please listen.
                   I don't think I can leave him.
TONI [*whispering*]. What do you mean?
ELIZABETH.   Try to understand.
                   There are some women, perhaps,
                   Who can only feel what a wife should
                        For an older man.
TONI.   No! No!
                   You can't mean that. I don't believe it!
                   I won't! It's not you speaking!
                   That devil must have hypnotized you!
                        But I'll put a stop to that.

                        [*He turns angrily toward the door of Mittenhofer's
                        study.*]

          We must get this right!

                        [*As* TONI *strides towards the study door,* CAROLINA
                        *comes out of the middle door, takes in quickly what is
                        happening, and bars his way.*]

CAROLINA.   Mr Reischmann!
   You might know the Master is not to be
      Interrupted!
TONI [*shouting*]. The Mittenhofer
   Will damn well do as I wish!
CAROLINA [*screaming*]. It's the wrong time!

VIII. THE WRONG TIME

ELIZABETH.   Toni!
TONI.   It's right
   Enough for me. It's now. I'll see him!

> [*As* TONI *is about to push* CAROLINA *aside,* MIT-
> TENHOFER, *drawn by the noise, comes out of his
> study. He is quite self-possessed, a semi-humorous
> quizzical expression on his face. A few moments later
> the* DOCTOR, *also drawn by the disturbance, enters
> agitated downstage right.* ELIZABETH, *after her one
> attempt to stop* TONI, *sits downstage left facing front,
> her face set.*]

MITTENHOFER [*mildly*]. You may, Toni. You do. No need to fuss.
   It's alright, Lina. What's come over us?
   We're not in a palace here, or in a school:
   There's no need for rebellion or for protocol.
TONI. I love Elizabeth. She said she loved me;
   Then suddenly she said she didn't know.
   I want to know what's happened. Is she afraid
   To offend the Great White Bard or afraid of him?
   Well, now he knows! And no bolt's fallen yet.
   Elizabeth, tell them! Tell them!
DOCTOR. Forgive him, Master. He's a boy. And stop him, too!
   He'll be ruined! It's madness for him; it won't do.
TONI. Tell him you love me, Elizabeth. Tell him it's true!
   I can't do anymore now. Now it's up to you.
CAROLINA. Madness!

> [CAROLINA *retires upstage and watches the rest of
> the scene stonily.*]

MITTENHOFER [*emphatically*]. One moment, Toni. Wilhelm, please.

> [MITTENHOFER *comes down to* ELIZABETH.]

My dear, conventionalities
Don't suit us: tell me openly
Your feelings, as I asked you to,
And with no fear that I may be
Too selfish or too weak to hear.

DOCTOR. Forgive him, Master. It won't do!

MITTENHOFER. Have you forgotten Toni's my son, too?
He's fallen in love. I can't see why
That needs forgiving.
                    [*To* ELIZABETH *again.*] Or why, dear
Child if you love my son, knowing how near
My heart he is, you still are shy
          And cannot say
          Quite frankly to me—
          Yes, no, or which one,
          And have done.

TONI.   We'll leave to-day!
          Don't let his devilry
          Touch you! I should have known
          What he'd have done.

DOCTOR [*aside*]. If I could pray,
          I would that she
          Refute my son,
          And this have done.

ELIZABETH [*evenly, almost coldly*]. Why must I weigh
          My heart publicly
          To oblige anyone?
          Leave me alone!

MITTENHOFER. Forgive me, both. I should have known:
          I did think Toni self-deceived;
          The self-deception was my own.
          [*To* ELIZABETH.] I'd say no more if I believed
          You weak; the scene's intolerable:
          Still, you're not called upon to choose
          Between two beaux, but to fulfil
          The woman, or remain the Muse.

TONI [*anguished*]. Elizabeth, no! It's more than that to me!
          If you can't say you love me, when it's true,
          Then all the rest means nothing, nothing; then
          I'd soon believe your love for me was pity—

And how could I believe in myself again?
Yet even in pity, don't abandon me!
How could I live then? What could I do?
DOCTOR [*coming down to* ELIZABETH].
    If you can't say you love him, can't you see
    It can't be serious! He has his work to do.
    He's young. He'll recover. The briefest mercy
    Is telling him you don't love him, for it is true.
MITTENHOFER. If you didn't love him, you'd have told me.
    To think of sparing me is barren pity.
    I'm not that young, recover easily.
CAROLINA. It's a madhouse here! Mere idiocy!

IX. THE BRIDE

[ELIZABETH, *the conflicting arguments coming from all sides, finally puts her hands over her ears, shakes her head as though trying to negate them all, then bursts into tears and buries her face in her hands. Suddenly from backstage, a cowbell is rung loudly. This is followed by the sound of* HILDA *singing.* ELIZABETH *lifts her head. The others shift position in a strained effort to look casual.* HILDA *enters from below on* MAUER's *arm. She is slightly tipsy and holding the large bell in one hand and an enormous cigarette holder in the other.* MAUER *is holding her sunshade over her head. She is elaborately dressed in the height of 1910 fashion or at least in what approximation of the "height" would be available in a resort shop off-season, and is made up more suitably to her age than she was in Act One. When they reach the parlor entrance,* MAUER *closes the sunshade and* HILDA *stops singing and takes in the silent embarrassed group in the room.*]

HILDA.   Won't someone say: "This was
                        All that was needed?"
                        So. It's been discovered.
                        Old Dantey-wantey
                        Must be upset.
                    Did the headmistress here
                        Catch you out with your
                        Hand in the cooky-
                        Jar? Did you wake for
                        Latin Verse late?
                    Doubtless it's serious:
                        Still, you should know
                    From here you make a quite
                        Comic tableau.

MITTENHOFER. Then if Frau Mack will excuse us, we . . .

HILDA [*to* CAROLINA].   Duchess
    Queerstation, do be a sweetheart and get me
    One teensie Armagnac, won't you. I'm breathless.
    Climbing at my age, dear!
CAROLINA.   Really!
HILDA [*shrugging her shoulders*].   Oh hoity-
    Toity.
MITTENHOFER.
        Frau Mack . . .
HILDA [*waving him back*]. No, not you. You'd just spill it.
    Josef will go.

> [MAUER *exits downstage right, leaving Hilda's sun-
> shade against the wall near the door.*]

        He's a gentleman; which is
    More than I'd say about some of the ladies
    I could point out here. Put that in a sonnet,
    Ducky, it tops the old rot that you used to
    Steal from me once, but I better had warned you—
    This time I get ten percent or I sue!
TONI. Elizabeth, I beg you . . .   ⎤
DOCTOR. Master, you must prevent . . .   ⎥
CAROLINA. If you'd just let me take . . . ⎥
MITTENHOFER. This can't go on any . . . ⎦
HILDA [*angrily ringing her bell*].   Order here! Order! I
    Won't have this noise!

> [*Going to* ELIZABETH.]

        They've made you cry,
    My child. Don't let them anymore.
        Look at them as absurd
    And hardly worth your tears.

> [MAUER *returns with a drink on a tray, which he
> brings to* HILDA.]

        Thank you, Josef.

> [MAUER *retires to the terrace. Hilda gives her glass to*
> ELIZABETH.]

                                        I think,
    My dear, you'd better have this drink.

> [ELIZABETH *sips it briefly. She looks up.*]

ELIZABETH. Frau Mack, do you think I'm a whore?

HILDA.　　　　La! what a naughty word.
　　　　　　　Even so,
　　　　　I don't think you are one
　　　　　Of "our poor fallen sisters", dear, in fact quite definitely
　　　　　　No.

ELIZABETH [*rising*]. Toni, will you marry me?

TONI.　　　　Elizabeth! Yes! Didn't you know?

DOCTOR.　　　Don't do this to my son!

HILDA.　　You're making a mistake, my child, he's not your future.
　　　　　Leave here with me on holiday;
　　　　　We need it. To-morrow we'll go
　　　　　　And have a good time!

ELIZABETH [*to* TONI].
　　　　　We can't be married now, you know. You have your future.

TONI.　　　　I'd wait forever and a day
　　　　　If you are waiting too.

ELIZABETH [*to* HILDA].　　　　I'll go.
　　　　[*To* TONI.]
　　　　　　Then all in good time.

DOCTOR.　You're making a mistake, my son. She's not your future.
　　　　　Don't make me force you to obey.
　　　　　You can't get married now, you know,
　　　　　Nor for a long time.

MITTENHOFER [*aside*].
　　　　　The young, the lovers, theirs, I know, will be the future.
　　　　　They shall inherit yesterday
　　　　　Lightly, lightly as fallen snow,
　　　　　　Yes, and for all time.

ELIZABETH. Doctor, I realize that you,
　　　Much as you like me personally,
　　　Strongly object . . .

　　　　　　　　[MITTENHOFER *interrupts her by placing his hand
　　　　　　　　on her shoulder.*]

MITTENHOFER.　　　　My dear, if I may . . .
　　　Wilhelm, I can guess why you do;
　　　Surely it's more important we
　　　Both know there isn't anyone
　　　Who'd better nurse our son.
　　　Admit your reasons are passé,

My friend; and as my friend, have faith in me.
Bless them. You will, hearing that prophecy
Their love fulfils for us. I'll tell you of
The poem I'm working on, called "*The Young Lovers*".

X. THE YOUNG LOVERS

MITTENHOFER. Out of Eden, bringing Eden
    With them, the young lovers come
    Hand in hand to the cold lands.
    The snow falls. There is no welcome.
    Their singleness reproaches our mingled
    Isolations, their love our songless
    Ice-altars; we refuse the rose
    Of Heaven's children. Nevertheless,
    One who dare break the barrier . . .
    His own . . . who only will turn, will move to
    Reach for and bless their happiness,
    Shall heedlessly enter Eden too.
    They bring us a gift from afar:
    A fragile, an eternal flower.

ELIZABETH. *Hand in hand* . . . Is it so
    Simple as it would seem?
    I only know I know
    A love too like a dream.
    Hand in hand I went
    With one, a lonely Muse;
    And now the Muse is sent
    Away, and cannot choose
    But choose a happiness
    Her whole heart fears; while I
    With all my heart would bless
    The love he wins me by.

HILDA. *The snow falls* . . .Ah! The snow
    Drifts through a dangerous dream
    My whole heart fears, and I
    Must live no longer by.
    Happiness is the glow
    Of sunlight on a stream
    That dazzles from the eye
    All that abides below.
    No, No! I will not know!

TONI. *Their love* . . .Our love. Yet, O!
   My whole heart fears that he,
   In giving her to me,
   Keeps much of her I know
   That I shall never know,
   And I, when I should bless,
   Accept my happiness
   In love ungratefully.

DOCTOR. *The barrier* . . . is there.
   My whole heart fears to bless
   Their love, but does not dare
   Prevent me saying yes.

CAROLINA. They forget the soil, who forget the hour.
   Where nothing can root, nothing will flower.

[*Chime.*]

XI. THE FLOWER

[*After a brief pause, the* DOCTOR *takes* TONI'S *hand and places it in* ELIZABETH'S *hand. No one moves for a moment; the* DOCTOR *keeps his eyes down.*]

TONI. Thank you, father.
ELIZABETH.   Dare I thank you too?
DOCTOR. No more now, please.

[DOCTOR *walks away slowly.*]

ELIZABETH [*to* MITTENHOFER]. What can I say to you?
   Gregor, I'm ashamed . . .
MITTENHOFER.   Ah, you see,
   My dear, I meant you to be.
   I can be sly, you know, and at this stage,
   Having a boon to beg you, I
   Imagined shame would smooth the way
      To having you comply.
ELIZABETH. Ask anything!
MITTENHOFER.   For one more day?
ELIZABETH.   One day?

[MITTENHOFER *takes* TONI'S *and* ELIZABETH'S *hands in his.*]

MITTENHOFER. In some few days, my dears, I shall be sixty:
   Foolishly, perhaps, I had hoped by then to have finished

An opus . . . yours . . . *The Young Lovers*—in order
To have it ready to read on my birthday. Help me,
Both of you; from the flanks of the Hammerhorn brings me
Edelweiss, a visionary "aid"
I've often found effective when all else
Failed. Don't chide my childishness by refusing,
My dears, or mock me.
                              Remain here one more day . . .

TONI.   Remain here one more day,
                         One day alone with me
                         When neither secrecy
                         Nor guilt can touch our love.
ELIZABETH [*to herself*]. One day? How light a fee
                         To bribe Eternity!
MITTENHOFER.   One day alone for me.
                         Let my last memory.
                         Of you, my child, be of
                       A girl who brought me inspiration.
ELIZABETH.   I'll stay. That small consideration
                         Is due you both.
                         [*She laughs.*]   I hate
                       To sound so vain . . . what can I do?
                       You've spoiled me with flattery, you two.
                         Frau Hilda, will you wait?
HILDA.   I'll wait below. No more for me.
                       Thin air served up with poetry
                         Is not a proper diet.
                       My late lamented husband died
                       On that meal up a mountainside.
                         God rest him. I decry it!
MITTENHOFER.
Frau Hilda, you're so right . . . for yourself. But I must hope
Your visions, in these hands I hold, may be revived.

                                                    [*Chime.*]

XII. THE VISION OF TO-MORROW

ELIZABETH. To-morrow from the mountain may your vision be restored.
TONI. To-morrow may we gratefully repay you for our love.
HILDA. To-morrow, to a world that must be faster. I can't wait!

                                                    [*Chime.*]

DOCTOR. Master, it's time for your tonic. Shall I make it?
MITTENHOFER. No, no. These two are my tonic to-day. I don't need it.
TONI AND ELIZABETH.
     To-morrow is the frontier we shall cross to our reward!
MITTENHOFER AND DOCTOR [*separately, aside*].
     To-morrow is expectancy, but can it say enough?
HILDA. There's something called *The Merry Widow* on. It should be great!

[*Chime.*]

CAROLINA.
     Shall I bring out your manuscripts, Master? Your day's been broken.
MITTENHOFER.
     No, no. It's too late now. Just leave me to ponder my nonsense.
CAROLINA, MITTENHOFER AND DOCTOR [*separately, aside*].
     To-morrow, shall we pay To-day what we cannot afford?
TONI, ELIZABETH AND HILDA.
     To-morrow will begin what our to-morrows are to prove.
ALL. To-morrow shades our vision, for to-day is growing late.

[*Chime.*]

[*They disperse:* TONI *and* MITTENHOFER *shake
hands warmly;* ELIZABETH *kisses* MITTENHOFER
on the cheek. He pushes her gently away. She and
TONI *go on to the terrace arm in arm. The* DOCTOR,
his head bowed, goes off downstage right with HILDA,
who pats him on the shoulder to cheer him up.
CAROLINA, *stiff with disapproval, exits right center.
Twilight. Servants enter, draw curtains cutting off the
view of terrace and mountain, and light lamps.*
MAUER, *after* TONI *and* ELIZABETH *pass him on
the terrace, looks into the parlor, and when* MITTEN-
HOFER *is alone, addresses him.*]

MAUER. Herr Mittenhofer, I've had not time this month
     To find you some Hammerhorn edelweiss, but I forecast
     To-morrow's weather as warm enough . . .
MITTENHOFER [*dismissing him briefly but courteously*]. Never mind,
     I shan't need any. Thank you for your thoughtfulness.
MAUER.   Good night.
MITTENHOFER.   Good night.

XIII. THE END OF THE DAY

[MITTENHOFER *stands for a while with his back to the audience. Then, his shoulders rise, his fists clench. He turns round, his features distorted with rage. He stamps his feet and makes a noise like an enraged ram.*]

MITTENHOFER. *BAH!* What a bunch! What a scrubby bouquet!
　　The heart sinks. Look!

> [*Holding up a hand, he counts off on his fingers those he mentions.*]

　　　　　A lunatic witch
Who refuses to be mad; an aristocratic bore
Who wants to play Nanny to her private Emperor;
A doctor who needs a rhyming guinea-pig
To make him famous, and make newly-rich
His motherless whelp, that rutting little prig
Who imagines it's rebellion to disobey
His father once; *AND* a fatherless bitch
Who found a papa-dog from whom to run away!
Why don't they just blow up and disappear!
Why don't they all *DIE?*

> [*He picks up an inkwell and looks about for a suitable spot in which to hurl it. Suddenly he finds himself face to face with* HILDA, *who has entered a few moments earlier to retrieve her sunshade. His gesture suspended in mid-air, he stares at her.*]

HILDA [*wagging her sunshade at him*].
　　　　　Naughty, naughty, dear!

> [*With a bellow of rage,* MITTENHOFER *puts the inkwell down and stalks back to his study.* HILDA, *laughing uncontrollably, collapses into a chair.*]

QUICK CURTAIN

Act III
Man and Wife

1. ECHOES

[*The same scene. The next morning.* HILDA *is standing where she was at the close of Act Two, dressed discreetly for travelling and surrounded by luggage.* TONI *and* ELIZABETH, *dressed for mountain climbing, are on the terrace about to ascend left.* HILDA *waves to them; they wave back and, holding hands, exeunt up the stairs singing a folk-song, Wandervogel style, which gradually fades away during the following scene.*]

TONI AND ELIZABETH.
>On yonder lofty mountain
>A lofty castle stands
>Where dwell three lovely maidens,
>The fairest in the land.
>
>The eldest is called Susanna,
>The second Annamarie;
>I dare not name the youngest
>For my heart's love is She.
>
>A stream runs down the valley,
>A mill-wheel spins away,
>It grinds the precious flour
>Of love both night and day.
>
>But now the wheel is broken
>And love is at an end
>And two who walked together,
>By different roads will wend.
>
>Give me your hand; who ever
>Believed that we should part,
>Or summer change to winter
>And light to heavy heart?

>>[HILDA, *after she has waved to them, shakes her head sadly, and turns to come further downstage.*]

HILDA. Farewell. It is to-day. Farewell to-day
>To more than half my life:
>A fool's romantic hell
>Of always being interesting.

[DR REISCHMANN *has already entered front right,
dressed in a black suit.*]

DOCTOR [*to* HILDA *mechanically*]. Morning.
HILDA [*mechanically, like Doctor*]. Morning.

> [*He crosses, absently, to the terrace, putting a small
> doctor's bag down first.*]

DOCTOR. Thank God they're out of sight.
    Hilda's right . . .
    It's best to go.

> [*From his room,* MITTENHOFER *can be heard going
> over his notes for his poem.*]

MITTENHOFER. She begged me to leave her.
    Grieve her. Believe her.
    No. No. No.
    Then would she beg . . .
    Wooden leg . . . Mumbly Peg . . . Mad Meg
    Egg. Egg.

> [*Shouting and ringing a bell.*]

    Where's that egg!

> [*At the sound of the bell,* CAROLINA *enters distract-
> edly right center and takes a dish from a maid who has
> come in hurriedly right front.*]

CAROLINA. Oh dear, oh dear . . .

> [*She brings it to Mittenhofer's room, leaving the door
> open.*]

MITTENHOFER. Thanks, Lina.
    Thank you. You're welcome. Thank you.
    Here. Type these notes up, please.
CAROLINA [*exiting from his room*].
    Of course.
MITTENHOFER [*shouting to the* DOCTOR, *who has just returned from the
    terrace*].
    No jabs to-day. Skin's too thin.
DOCTOR. Of course.

> [CAROLINA *closes his door, then turns to* REISCH-
> MANN, *holding up the papers she is carrying.*]

CAROLINA [*vaguely*].
> So far behind. A few lines first.
> Be back in a minute.

>   [*Exits.*]

HILDA [*almost completely unaware of the others*].
> Morning . . .
> And yet he was the one
> Man I could ever have loved,
> A man who might have been great;
> Though, God knows, it hardly was
> Great honour to his memory
> To make him play at God.

DOCTOR [*almost as though he were addressing the whole outdoors*].
> Antonia! Antonia!
> What would you have done?
> That spring, after you died,
> I ate so much and lay
> In the sun, loving it,
> And felt my love for you had not been ample.
> What have I done to Toni? Am I vile?

MITTENHOFER [*as before*].
> They then would beg for roses. *With* roses.
> *Through* roses. Moses
> Proposes noses in modest medical doses . . .
> God! Nothing goes.
> Nothing, my dearest darling, goe-ses.

>   [*From Carolina's room, the sound of typing can be
>   heard, sometimes fast, sometimes hesitant, interspersed
>   with her reading from the manuscript aloud, and puz-
>   zling over the handwriting.*]

CAROLINA. Out of Eden . . . the young lovers . . .
> Hell? No.
> Hold hands? No.
> *Cold. Cold Lands.*
> The snow falls. There is . . . no?
> NO welcome. Yes.
> There. For now.

>   [CAROLINA *re-enters and goes to* DR REISCHMANN
>   *with some keys.*]

Here are the keys to the town house.

DOCTOR [*giving her the small bag*].
    Here are his medicines.
    Tell them I've gone.
CAROLINA. Of course.
DOCTOR.   Thank you.
CAROLINA.   You're welcome.
HILDA [*as before*].
    What can I really do?
    What prevent or delay?
    I'm too young to-day.
    I'm too old to-day.
MITTENHOFER. Elegy. Be. Fee. He. Me. Mimi.
    Young lovers.
    Plovers in dish covers.
    No. No. No.
    Prisoner's cell. Dingly Dell.
    Hell. Hell. Hell.
    Passing bell.
    Farewell. Farewell.

II. FAREWELLS

HILDA.   Gräfin . . .
CAROLINA. What, I wonder, can you have to say to me?
HILDA. Good-bye . . .
CAROLINA.   Good-bye, then.
HILDA.   An apology . . .
CAROLINA. Really, Frau Mack, there's no necessity.
HILDA. Come, Lina, we're too old to part this way.
    Yesterday I was foolish. Don't, I pray,
    Be foolish in return for that to-day.
    Let's look at ourselves and laugh—or we might weep—
    Two childless dreaming babies no one would keep,
    Who've kept our place and find it hard to sleep.

> [*She picks up her reticule and takes out part of the
> presumably enormous scarf she had been knitting for
> years.* MITTENHOFER *enters unobserved.*]

    Laugh at this monster baby I have knit
    For forty years, and as you laugh, admit
    Your own dear monster laughable a bit.
    We shall then say that laughter brought our tears

And part in friendship, or in what appears
Enough like friendship to beguile our years.
MITTENHOFER [*comes forward*].
    Come, Lina, laugh. Yes, even laugh at me.
    It's good for you.
HILDA [*aside to* MITTENHOFER, *almost pleadingly*].
                    Please. Do tread cautiously.
DOCTOR. Yes, Lina, smile at least.
MITTENHOFER [*to* HILDA, *lifting his eyebrows*].
                          Tread cautiously?

> [HILDA *shrugs her shoulders and turns away from him.*]

CAROLINA [*to* HILDA].
    It seems too late to laugh. Please take my hand.
HILDA [*doing so, warmly*].
    Of course, Lina. Thank you. I understand.
MITTENHOFER. Thanks, Wilhelm, for going ahead of us to get
    The house in order. I hope it's not too upset.
DOCTOR. Nothing . . .

> [*The warning whistle is heard from the station. The* DOCTOR *consults his watch.*]

    It's time.

III. SCHEDULED DEPARTURES

HILDA [*with a gesture embracing the inn and the landscape*].
    Farewell. Good-bye.
CAROLINA AND MITTENHOFER.
            Good-bye.
DOCTOR.   In a few days.

> [*Servants enter and take out the luggage, including a small valise of the Doctor's, except for the reticule which* HILDA *indicates with a gesture is to be left behind. At the door to the terrace, she and the* DOCTOR *stop;* CAROLINA *and* MITTENHOFER *remain downstage, facing front.*]

ALL FOUR.   The young in pairs, the old in twos
        Proceed, and more and more the old rely
           On seeming casual because

We never can tell
When any new good-bye
May prove to be farewell.

[HILDA *and the* DOCTOR *leave.* MITTENHOFER
sits near his desk; CAROLINA *stands behind him.*]

MITTENHOFER.   Well, that leaves two to go.

IV. TWO TO GO

MITTENHOFER.   I must work. I must see
If I can get my Elegy
Finished in time.
CAROLINA.   Your Elegy?
MITTENHOFER [*with weary impatience*].
            The poem. The poem.
            What else have I to be
                Concerned about. It seems to me
                You ought to know.
CAROLINA.   It seems to me
            You're concerned about her.
            And still, you set her free,
            You made the match and practically
            Made her ask him. Why?
MITTENHOFER.   Practically.

[*The whistle of the departing train is heard.*]

            Once it was out, I had no choice.
            It would always have been there—
            A damp emotional untidiness
                In the air
                Clinging to her
            That I would not have been able to bear.
                She had to go and choose to go
                Herself, I knew and know.
CAROLINA.   Permit me. It's much better so.
            I've said before, and say it once again:
                It's best for you to be alone.
MITTENHOFER [*with bitter satisfaction*].
                Alone. Well, they're up there alone,
                And much good may it do them, the

Young lovers: Will they find what love can mean
   Or should be?
   Just wait and see
How long they tease alive their ecstasy.
   A year? I don't imagine so.
   And then where will she go?

CAROLINA.   Permit me. I won't care to know.
What matters is—I'll say it once again—
   It's best for you to be alone.

MITTENHOFER [*with a childish self-pity disguised as elderly stoicism*].
   Perhaps you're right. You always know
   What's best for me. And I should not
Continue to depend the way I do—
   Or exploit—
   Yes, even what
Is freely offered one, perhaps one ought
   To, for the good of all, let go.
   You and Wilhelm are so—

CAROLINA [*interrupting*].
   That is not the same, you know!
It's only we who never intrude
   But help maintain your solitude.
We know well, and I'll say it once again:
   It's best for you to be alone.

MITTENHOFER. Alone. Whether I wish it or not, Lina.

   [MAUER *enters hurriedly from outside.*]

MAUER. Good day. I only have a moment. It's a dire
   Blizzard coming on quickly, and then we'll be blanketed
   In minutes. Is anyone from here out on the mountain?
   Because if a good guide went now, he could,
   With God's help, bring them back. Anyone gone?

MITTENHOFER [*rising slowly*].
   Why . . . not that I know of.

MAUER.   It's just as well!

   [At MITTENHOFER's *words,* CAROLINA *goes rigid,*
   shudders, and then, making a sudden movement turn-
   ing towards MAUER, *she knocks a heavy object off the*
   desk.]

Gräfin?

CAROLINA [*without looking at either of them*].
>   Nothing. Nerves. The flu. How grey
>   The air is getting.
MAUER.   I must go to the other inns
>   And ask.

>   [*He starts to hurry out, but pauses at the terrace door
>   and shrugs.*]

>   Weather has its way of madly happening.
>   Its own. It's wrong! I'm right usually.

>   [*Exit.*]

V. MAD HAPPENINGS

[CAROLINA *stands as she was, ever so often shivering slightly;* MITTENHOFER
goes to her.]

MITTENHOFER [*an easy emphasis underlining his sympathetic air*].
>   Lina, you look dreadful. You did
>   Get up too soon, you silly, to handle
>   These boring chores. A change of scene . . .
CAROLINA [*intensely*]. No Master, I need no rest. I've wanted none
>   For all these years; and I will not go away.
>   Where would you have me go? No place and no one
>   Wait me anymore. I am where I will stay.

>   [*During the following, the sky darkens rapidly and it
>   begins to snow.*]

MITTENHOFER. My dearest Lina, I meant no harm, you know.
CAROLINA [*at first accusingly suspicious, then self-assured*].
>   Didn't you, Master, didn't you? No, of course
>   You couldn't have. I'm certain. For if I go,
>   How could you manage things? Would you have the force
>   Both to work and to remember your routine?
>   You are so vague, my child, and as for change of scene,
>   Why look out there—the snow has begun to fall
>   And overnight all will be changed, Master, all. . . .

>   [*She hurries over to the stove, kneels by it, and begins
>   to make a fire.*]

>   I'll build a fire and tend it;
>   The cold I'll keep outside.

Sweet boy, you cannot hide
Heartbreak but shall mend it
        Near your bride,
Wisely weeping, end it,
Be again clear-eyed.

[*Taking part of the scarf from Hilda's reticule and holding it against her cheek.*]

Child, I dare not tell your
Father's name although
Like the falling snow
It cloaks the earth to quell your
        Every foe;
And that he loves you well your
Miracles will show.

[*Slowly rising to her feet.*]

Wait a bit. I have forgotten something. What
Can it be, I wonder? Nothing. All is well.
Why this is Eden nor were we ever out
Of it. How warm it is. I am with you still;
And still the roses bloom, I water each day.
Yet . . . yet . . . I forget . . . What has happened to me?

MITTENHOFER [*to himself, gazing at* CAROLINA *intently*].
        Everything must be paid for
                Eventually
        In time or in the service
                Of eternity:
        I do not ask the price for
                They shall pay for me.

[CAROLINA *presses her hand to her forehead and then suddenly bursts into hysterical laughter. Afterwards she shakes her head and smiles.*]

CAROLINA. What is disquieting? The quiet. The clock's not wound.
    Stopped. Think of that. Too astounding.

[*She takes the clock-key from her pocket and goes over to the clock. She and* MITTENHOFER *look steadily into each other's eyes. Her voice is expressionless.*]

A day has gone
Unmarked upon;
No telling chime
Divided time
In useful parts
To keep the heart's
Besetting sin,
Undiscipline,
In measured bounds.
The helpmate sounds
Of yesterday
Must have their say
That we may now
From Now watch how
The Fates convene
To change the scene.

[*She winds the clock and then moves the hands. At every quarter-hour there is a chime. The lights dim; the air seems filled with snow. The set divides in half and rolls off into the wings,* CAROLINA *and* MITTENHOFER *together on the right half. The chimes continue.*]

VI. CHANGE OF SCENE

[*On the Hammerhorn. Snowstorm.* TONI *appears, closely followed by* ELIZABETH, *their forms only vaguely visible through the driving snow. Both are in the last stages of exhaustion.*]

ELIZABETH. I can't go on.
TONI.   Come, here's a little
    Shelf of rock under which to shelter
    Against the storm. We'll stop here.
    [*With forced cheerfulness.*] Won't Gregor be cross when we come back
    Without his magic edelweiss?
ELIZABETH [*quietly*]. You needn't lie, dear. I know.
TONI.   I know.
    What a funny kind of fairy tale
    We've gotten into, where Godmother sends
    Wild weather on the wedding night.
ELIZABETH. Now that no choice can change what is,
    Without hope, in innocent play,
    We may dream of a world that won't be.

Toni. Come closer: clasp my hand
   Let us pretend we are looking back
   Over the years. You begin.

VII. MAN AND WIFE

Elizabeth. Who are we?
Toni.   An old couple
   With white hair.
Elizabeth.   What are we doing?
Toni. Sitting together by the fire.
   Now I'll ask. Have we been married
   A long time?
Elizabeth.   We two have lived
   As one flesh for forty years.
Toni. Did we have children?
Elizabeth.   Of course, we did.
   Bruno is the eldest of our three boys . . .
Toni. Then came Olga, our only daughter.
   Then Detlef . . .
Elizabeth.   Then Willi who died as a baby.
   I shall never forget how good and gentle
   You were to me then. That stopped me
   Later when I nearly left you.
Toni. Left me? But why? What had I done?
Elizabeth. Have you forgotten the girl in Munich?
Toni. So you knew all the time and said nothing!
   I took such care to be discreet.
Elizabeth. Do you still miss her?
Toni.   At moments, yes,
   Like a dream that is lost at daybreak.
   The bond that endured was our common burden.
   But we'll change the subject. Our children grew up.
Elizabeth. Bruno is now a Bank Director . . . ;
   Olga married an engineer
   And lives in Lima . . .
Toni.   And little Detlef?
Elizabeth. Was it our fault? Did we fail our darling?
   He's always in trouble and need of help:
   He'll never be able to earn his living . . .
Toni. It grows dark: we grow weary.
   But before sleep there's a final question
   We have to ask as husband and wife.

ELIZABETH. Toni?

TONI.   Yes, dear.

ELIZABETH.   Tell me the truth:
    Is the hand you hold Elizabeth's hand?

TONI [*tenderly*]. No, my dear, but the name will do.
    Elizabeth?

ELIZABETH.   Yes, dear.

TONI.   Tell me the truth:
    Is the hand you hold Toni's hand?

ELIZABETH [*tenderly*]. No, my dear, but the name will do.

BOTH. Now we know. Now we are free
    To die together and with good will
    Say farewell to a real world.

VIII. TONI AND ELIZABETH

Not for love were we led here.
But to unlearn our own lies,
Each through each, in our last hour,
And come to death with clean hearts.

What Grace gave, we gladly take,
Thankful although even this
Bond will break in a brief while,
And our souls fare forth alone.

God of Truth, forgive our sins,
All offences we fools made
Against thee. Grant us Thy peace.
Light with Thy Love our lives' end.

[*Total darkness envelops the scene. Tolls.*]

IX. ELEGY FOR YOUNG LOVERS

[*Behind the scrim, right, a spotlight reveals a dressing-table with mirror, brush and comb, etc.* MITTENHOFER, *in tails and white waistcoat, is putting the last touches to his toilet. Lying on the table is a manuscript book. During the following, two men bring a reading desk on stage and set it up center near the footlights.*]

MITTENHOFER [*looking at himself in the mirror*].
    One. Two. Three. Four.
    Whom do we adore?
    Gregor! Gregor! Gregor!

□

Five. Six. Seven. Eight.
Whom do we appreciate?
Gregor! Gregor! Gregor!

Happy Birthday, dear Gregor!

> [*During his second verse,* CAROLINA *has entered noiselessly behind him.*]

CAROLINA.   Gregor, it's time.
MITTENHOFER. And time, like Gregor, marches on,
While Lina lingers, wishing both were gone.

> [*He picks up his manuscript book and chucks* CARO-LINA *under the chin.*]

Don't you, dear?

> [*Chime.* CAROLINA *remains rigid. The light on the dressing room goes out and the stage lights come up. It is the stage of a Theatre in Vienna. The scrim, no longer transparent, is now an ornamental backdrop for* MITTENHOFER's *reading: Mount Parnassus, the Muses crowning a Poet, Apollo with lyre and cherubim.* MITTENHOFER *strides out to the reading desk, puts his manuscript book on it, bows left, right and center. Then he holds up his hand as if to ask for silence.*]

MITTENHOFER. Your Serene Highness, Your Excellency the Minister of Culture, Ladies and Gentlemen. I am going to open this reading with the last poem I have written, ELEGY FOR YOUNG LOVERS. It is dedicated to the memory of a brave and beautiful young couple, Toni Reischmann and Elizabeth Zimmer who, as some of you know, perished recently on the Hammerhorn. "In death they were not divided."

> [*He opens the manuscript book and begins to read, solemnly and with hardly any gestures. We do not actually hear any words, but from behind him come one by one until they are all together, the voices of all who contributed to the writing of the poem:*
>
> HILDA *with her visions,* CAROLINA *with her money and management,* DR REISCHMANN *with his medi-*

cines, TONI *and* ELIZABETH *with their illusory but rhymable love.*

The lights fade until there is nothing but a spotlight on MITTENHOFER. *His poem has been written. The opera is over.*]

SLOW CURTAIN

Genesis of a Libretto

Before he can begin to think about what he will write, a librettist must first learn from the composer the scale and style of the work as the composer envisages it musically. Before we knew anything else, for example, we knew from Mr Henze that he wanted to compose a "chamber" opera for a small cast with no chorus, and for a small subtle orchestra; he also wanted a subject and situation which would call for tender, beautiful noises. The notion that these conditions suggested to us was of five or six persons, each of whom suffered from a different obsession so that, while all inhabiting a common world, each would interpret that world and the actions of the others in a completely different way. The first obsession we thought of was the obsession with the past, embodied in a character like Miss Havisham in Dickens' *Great Expectations*. This idea survived all our trials and errors to become Hilda Mack, the old lady who has visions. Then, casting around for a young heroine, we toyed with the idea of a ladies-maid masquerading as a great lady. The interest in this situation was to have come from showing that, though she was, socially speaking, an imposter, by nature, in her sensibility and instinctive behavior, she was really the great lady she was impersonating. Needless to say, a young man of good family was to have fallen in love with her and she with him. Loving him, but knowing that he was under an illusion as to her true social status, after a brief period of mutual happiness, she was to have disappeared, and, to make this properly pathetic, we thought of giving her an incurable disease. She was not to be aware of this, but the audience would know. This called for a doctor as a character and, in that case, why shouldn't the young man be the doctor's son? The ladies-maid was presently scrapped, but the doctor and his romantically minded son stayed in. She was also responsible for the location of the libretto we finally wrote. Wanting a place where a ladies-maid could successfully masquerade as a great lady without fear of exposure, a mountain resort out of season seemed the most plausible, as well as providing romantic scenery for a romance.

Believing that the conventional triangle can always be made interesting, we decided that the naive and romantic young man should have a mature, worldly and cynical rival. In conformity with our general theme, he, too, would have to suffer from some obsession. How about a great actor—his professional talent pitted against the amateur talent of the heroine—whose supreme ambition in life is to play the lead in Byron's *Manfred*—hence his presence in the mountain inn for the sake of "getting" the authentic atmosphere?

This proved a false trail and soon we found ourselves completely stuck.

Whatever we made our actor do, we could never think of anything for him to *sing*.

Furthermore, though we had a few tentative relations between pairs (father-son, boy-girl, girl-actor), we had no pattern of relations, no plot. How, for example, was the doctor to be related to the actor, or the mad old lady to any of the others? And no pattern means no ensembles.

The break-through came when we realised that the older rival, whoever he might be, must be the principal character in the libretto, the figure to whom all the other characters would already be related before the curtain rose. We were now in a position to ask ourselves two crucial questions. "What kind of person can dominate an opera both dramatically and vocally?" and "What kind of mature man can be intimately and simultaneously involved with a mad old lady, a young girl and a doctor?"

There is an admirable aphorism by Hofmannsthal: "Singing is near miraculous because it is a mastering of what is otherwise a pure instrument of egotism—the human voice." This does not, of course, imply, either that singers are humble or that the ideal operatic character is a saint. It means that, when we listen to a character in an opera, he seems to be singing, not only on his own behalf as an individual in a particular situation at a particular time and place, but also on behalf of the whole human race, dead, living and unborn. That is why the most successful operatic characters, however individualised, are a local embodiment of some myth; both their persons and their situations express some aspect of the human condition which is the significant case at all times. It also means that singing, like ballet dancing, is a virtuoso art, a gift which few possess. In consequence, whatever catastrophes befall a operatic character, so long as he or she continues to sing, the effect is always of triumph, never of defeat. Whatever he does, even dying, seems to be what he means to do: the slave, the passive sufferer cannot sing.

Once we had asked ourselves the two questions mentioned above, we soon got our answer—the artist-genius of the nineteenth and early twentieth century.

This is a genuine myth because the lack of identity between Goodness and Beauty, between the character of man and the character of his creations, is a permanent aspect of the human condition. The Theme of *Elegy for Young Lovers* is summed up in two lines by Yeats:

> *The intellect of man is forced to choose*
> *Perfection of the life or of the work.*

Aesthetically speaking, the personal existence of the artist is accidental; the essential thing is his production. The artist-genius, as the nineteenth century conceived him, made this aesthetic presupposition an ethical absolute, that is to say, he claimed to represent the highest, most authentic, mode of human existence.

Accept this claim, and it follows that the artist-genius is morally bound as a sacred duty to exploit others whenever such exploitation will benefit his work and to sacrifice them whenever their existence is a hindrance to his production.

Once we had our artist-genius, it was possible to construct a plot: we had only to think of the various reasons he would have for needing others—to inspire him, to provide him with creature comforts, to keep him in good health, etc.—to arrive at a pattern of relationships. Our ambition in writing the libretto has been to see how much psychological drama and character interest we could make compatible with the conventions of the operatic medium, and the Great Ancestors whose blessing we continually found ourselves invoking were Ibsen and Hofmannsthal.

The dramatic portrayal of an artist-genius presents several difficulties. It is impossible, for example, to represent a great poet in a spoken verse drama because, even if the playwright is himself a great poet, the only poetry he can write is his own, so that it is impossible for the audience to distinguish between the verse he gives his hero to speak as a character in the play and the verse he gives him to recite as a specimen of his work as a poet. For the same reason, a great composer cannot be represented in an opera. Our hero, Gregor Mittenhofer, is a great poet. Throughout the opera he has been working on a poem; in order to complete it successfully, he (morally) murders two people and breaks the spirit of a third. Unless, at the end, the audience are convinced that the poem is a very good one, the whole dramatic and moral point of the opera is lost. We believe that this conviction can be secured by having the poem represented in another artistic medium—as a man, Mittenhofer sings words; as a poet he is dumb, and his poem is represented by orchestral sound and pure vocalisation.

The artist-genius is not only a nineteenth and early twentieth century myth but also a European myth, and the two centres of European culture during this period were Paris and Vienna. We felt, therefore, that our hero would have to be related to one of these two cities, and our personal preferences led us to choose Vienna. Needless to say, this does not mean that we think his outrageous behavior an Austrian characteristic. As a matter of fact, the only things about him which were suggested to us by historical incidents were drawn from the life of a poet—no matter whom—who wrote in English.

W. H. AUDEN
CHESTER KALLMAN

The Bassarids

*Opera Seria with
Intermezzo in One Act
based on "The Bacchae"
of Euripides*

BY W. H. AUDEN AND
CHESTER KALLMAN
FOR THE MUSIC OF
HANS WERNER HENZE

[*1963*]

Die Mythe log . . .
GOTTFRIED BENN

CHARACTERS IN THE OPERA

DIONYSUS, *also* VOICE *and* STRANGER

PENTHEUS, *King of Thebes*
CADMUS, *his grandfather, founder of Thebes*
TIRESIAS, *an old blind prophet*
CAPTAIN OF THE GUARD

AGAVE, *daughter to Cadmus and Pentheus' mother*
AUTONOE, *her sister*
BEROE, *an old slave, once nurse to Semele and Pentheus*

YOUNG WOMAN, *slave in Agave's household*
CHILD, *her daughter*

BASSARIDS (MAENADS *and* BACCHANTS); CITIZENS OF THEBES; GUARDS; SERVANTS

CHARACTERS IN "THE JUDGEMENT OF CALLIOPE"

VENUS (*Agave*)
PERSEPHONE (*Autonoe*)
CALLIOPE (*Tiresias*)

ADONIS (*Captain*)

SERVANTS; MUSICIANS

The action takes place in the Courtyard of the Royal Palace in Thebes, and on Mount Kithairon.

[THEBES: THE COURTYARD OF THE ROYAL PALACE. *Stage center, three sides and two half-sides of what would be an octagon were it completed, bound this principal arena. Three or four steps lead up from it on all sides, the apexes on the higher level having tall Ionic columns to further suggest its limits. Stage right, the entrance to the palace, its steps continuing, interrupted by a landing, the steps from the center arena. Stage left, the tomb of Semele, the ruins of her house in which a simple altar, a flame burning on it, has been set. The palace entrance is flanked by Guards, represented by statuary. Behind the central border of the arena, the sharply raked stage continues to a line, behind which steps lead downward out of sight: this provides a clear division between the fore-stage (Thebes) and the small amphitheatre which fills the back of the stage (Mount Kithairon), and will later seat the Chorus—presumably some distance from the city. Right and left towards the rear, statues of various gods and goddesses. At the rise of the curtain, it is midday: brilliant hard light.* CITIZENS *of Thebes are gathered in tribute to their new King; they are arranged in perfect, somewhat lifeless symmetry, wearing with a certain stiffness the traditional white draperies of a generalized classical Antiquity.*]

CITIZENS.   Pentheus is now our lord.
Cadmus, son of Agenor,
Who followed the moon-cow
Eastward from Delphi,
Founded our city,
Has given the throne
To his daughter's son.
Long life to our young Duke.
Under his rule
May Thebes prosper.

Pentheus is now our lord.
Cadmus, son of Argiope,
Who slew the Serpent,
Bid the Sown Ones
Build our citadel,
Has handed the sceptre
To a Sown Man's son.
Long life to our young Duke.
Under his sway
May Thebes prosper.

Pentheus is now our lord.
Son of Agave and Echion,
May he walk in the ways
Of wisdom and right

Like his fore-fathers,
Ever find favor
With the High Gods.
Long life to our young Duke.
Under his hand
May Thebes increase.

VOICE [*off*].   Ayayalya!
The God Dionysus
Has entered Boeotia!

CITIZENS [*with mounting excitement, after each phrase part of group then near-
est the back turning and running off*].
Ayayalya!
Long have we waited,
Long watched:
Ayayalya!
Dance, O Boeotia,
Clap hands, O Thebes,
Run, run, run to welcome
The God Dionysus
In the glens of Kithairon!

> [*The stage is empty for a moment, but even before one
> can be aware of this,* CADMUS, BEROE, AGAVE,
> *and* TIRESIAS *appear from right to left: the first three
> stepping from behind columns, the last entering in
> front of Semele's tomb.* CADMUS *is the embodiment of
> legendary age: long white beard, staff, blue cloak and
> draped costume suggesting a Minoan rather than
> Hellenic past. His forehead is girded by a thin gold
> band from which a ruby hangs over his brow. The fact
> that a definite feebleness has set in, cannot obscure an
> essential regality: his thoughts and speech may be dif-
> fuse, but they never go astray.* BEROE *also belongs to
> a remote past. She is dressed in the sort of anony-
> mously colored Amah's clothes that suggest the crone as
> much as they indicate the slave; and long but intimate
> servitude has given her the ability to crouch away into
> nothing, or to suddenly re-appear out of that nothing,
> with no apparent effort, and a swiftness that belies her
> years.* AGAVE *always moves and stands with imperi-
> ous feminine ease; she is still beautiful, obviously more*

a woman than a mother, inclined to mockery and, at her deepest level, much less frivolous and unfeeling than she could know. And more vulnerable. Her dress and hairdo are elaborate: in the style of the French Second Empire. She favors shades of rose and green, and manages to carry off what could be gaudiness in another woman, with grandeur and even subtlety. TIRESIAS *is dressed in the complete get-up of an Anglican Archdeacon. He also wears dark glasses and taps with a cane to find his way. More than slightly inclined to an androgynous corpulence, he tends to cover his consciousness of this slightly comic failing with a hurried and portentous self-importance. In addition to his usual costume, his cane has been hastily decorated with fennel, and he carries a fawn-skin thrown over one arm; as he taps his way slowly towards the back,* CADMUS *and* AGAVE *come forward.* BEROE *steps a little to the rear. The* CITIZENS *can still be heard growing ever more distant.*]

CITIZENS [*off*]. Ayayalya!
    Ay . . . ay . . . a . . . ly . . . a . . .
TIRESIAS. I too would join the dance.
    I too would wear a fawn-skin.
    Who will guide me to Kithairon?
    Dionysus, give me strength!

CADMUS.
    Wait. I need you. Tiresias. Return, friend.
AGAVE.
    Father . . .
CADMUS.   Tiresias!
TIRESIAS [*stopping and turning*].
               The God is come!
CADMUS.   God?
TIRESIAS.
    Come with me. You must. We'll dance there to honor
    Young Dionysus.
AGAVE [*laughing*].
    Dance?
CADMUS [*terrified*].
        Dionysus?

AGAVE [*to* TIRESIAS, *contemptuous*].
                You dance?
CADMUS.   Dionysus . . .
   [*To* TIRESIAS.]
   You believe?
AGAVE [*scornful*].
           Dionysus . . .

                                   [*She turns away.*]

CADMUS [*a frightened whisper*].
                   Then my people
   Followed him to Kithairon . . .
TIRESIAS.   Come and join them.
CADMUS [*a cry*].
   I?
BEROE [*to herself, awed*].
    Dionysus . . .
CADMUS.
   Wait. Are you certain of this God you follow?
   Have you ever considered that he may be
   Sent us to try our loyalty to Hera?
TIRESIAS.
   Who? Dionysus?
   He is the youngest of the Gods; soon Hera
   Also will befriend his might. On Olympus
   Now and Delphi his place waits amongst Gods, the
   God Dionysus!
CADMUS.
   Hera . . .
TIRESIAS.   Dionysus is here to claim Thebes
   His: O father of Thebes, if you reject him,
   Tremble for your children.
CADMUS.   Ares . . .
TIRESIAS.   But *he* is
   Here, Dionysus,
   Here!
CADMUS. You have known the anger of our Mother
   Hera and have paid with your eye-sight . . .
TIRESIAS.   That our Father
   Zeus could dower me with sight of the future . . .
CADMUS.
   Will Dionysus
   Guard you against her?

TIRESIAS.   Hera will permit . . .
CADMUS.   Will
    What? Permit? Have you forgotten Ares?
    Did he not *permit* me to kill his serpent?
    He . . .
TIRESIAS. Dionysus
    Waits for me.
CADMUS.   Wait. Discover me their purpose:
    Theirs. They war amongst themselves and faint ichor
    Bleeds from them, but blood falls on us! It stains my
    House!
TIRESIAS. Dionysus
    Kills and renews and can release you. Where is
    Pentheus our King? Bring Pentheus with you
    Quickly . . .
CADMUS [*reluctantly*].
        No one has seen him for a week. That
    Name, Dionysus,
    Angers him, I know. And know nothing more.
AGAVE [*turning and pointing to* BEROE].   *She*
    Sees him. Ask *her.*
BEROE.   He prays to the All-Father
    Zeus for guidance. He goes hungry. The loud cries
    "Hail Dionysus!"
    He did not hear. He is a pious man. His
    Reign will cast a new glory upon Thebes.
TIRESIAS.   You—
    Plead with him, Beroe. Beg him to placate
    Wild Dionysus:
    You were Semele's nurse and you were his . . .
BEROE [*anxious to withdraw, in a low voice*].   He
    Sent me to . . .
TIRESIAS.   He *must* believe his a blest House
    Bearing Semele, and to thank Semele,
    Greet Dionysus
    Born of her.
AGAVE.   My sister was *no* God's mother.
    She was punished. Her blasphemy was punished.
TIRESIAS.
    Yet Dionysus lives!
CADMUS.   Could I but *know*: Who
    Is Dionysus?

TIRESIAS.
>All he claims to be.

AGAVE [*coldly*].   Nothing. A wine-skin
>Emptied with its wine. Ask her. Was my sister
>Loved by Zeus?

BEROE [*turning her head away*].
>   I know nothing . . .

>   [*She exits hurriedly left.*]

AGAVE [*mimicking her sarcastically*].   I know nothing . . .
>*That's* Dionysus!

CADMUS.
>Nothing can be certain, daughter. I beg you,
>Think . . .

AGAVE.   I am certain.

CADMUS [*half to himself*].   Think . . .

TIRESIAS.   And I am certain
>I must worship him. I come, Dionysus!

>   [*He mounts the steps and turns.*]

>Fear Dionysus!

>   [*He taps his way slowly to the descending stairs.*]

CADMUS.
>Please! Tiresias! Come back! Advise me!
>Friend!

>   [TIRESIAS *descends out of sight. The Amphitheatre
>   begins to fill with the* BASSARIDS. *In the semi-
>   darkness at the back of the stage, one is only aware of a
>   subdued variety of bright colors.*]

AGAVE.   Let him go: the blindest of all women
>Thrust upon by Eros, and limpest man. Go.
>Blank Dionysus
>Calls, the Dionysus of girls, the boy-god.
>Hop to him, both your love-gods in a fever.
>Go.

CADMUS. Agave, I implore you: be silent.

AGAVE.
>Why?

CADMUS. Dionysus . . .

BASSARIDS.
>Praise Dionysus!

[*All during the following scene their hymn continues as background; it grows ever more solemn, exultant, sustained, deliberate and slow, in marked contrast to the nervous banter and obsessive questioning fear being played stage front.* CADMUS *comes slowly forward towards the left. The* CAPTAIN *of the Guard enters left followed, at a little distance, by* BEROE. *He is in the black armor of the Fourteenth Century Frankish Knights, the beaked visor up, a short sword—his sign of rank—at his side. He is a handsome man past his first youth, and what has kept him looking young is an unquestioning devotion to fixed standards like his duties and to simple objects like his dog. The candid childishness of his expression, combined with the matured strength of his physical poise, give him something of the sexual charm associated with "children of nature." As a highly competent police officer, he is of course no such thing. Entering he bows to* AGAVE, *who steps forward to intercept his path to the palace stairs. Pause. He is slightly embarrassed at the prospect of conversation with her. During this pause,* CADMUS *begins: the hymn has been going on through this brief pantomime.*]

BASSARIDS.　　Long have we waited
For the sound of his footsteps;
Long have we watched
For a glimpse of his presence.
Ayayalya.

Tales have come to us
Of his marvellous deeds,
His victorious progress
Through far-off lands.
Ayayalya.

The Nile paid homage
To the God of Joy;
The sea-board cities knelt
To the God of Feasts.
Ayayalya.

Sun-baked Persia submitted
When she heard his timbrels;
India dropped her spears

When she saw his thyrsus.
Ayayalya.

Glorious was his sojourn
In auriferous Phrygia;
Triumphant was his visit
To mountainous Thrace.
Ayayalya.

The Son of Zeus has returned
To the place of his begetting;
The Son of Semele has come back
To his mother's tomb.
Ayayalya.

CADMUS [*to himself*].
   Think . . . Are They close? How distantly clouds take
   Shape on Olympus, darkly descend: we
   Wait. Could a new young god be my grandson?
   They are the ageless forebears of ageing
   Man and were never children of man. No.
   Never. And can they change, can the Gods change?

                    [*Meanwhile,* CAPTAIN, *after his slight hesitation,
                    resumes walking towards the palace;* AGAVE,
                    *coming forward a bit, detains him by slightly raising
                    her hand. He keeps his head bowed.* BEROE *remains
                    at the back, ever so often giving* AGAVE *a swift
                    glance sharp with judgement and hatred.*]

AGAVE. You're here, Captain? Strange.
CAPTAIN.   Your Highness?
AGAVE.   I'm surprised.
   You're young, Captain: Why . . . when half Thebes escaped
   With fierce yelps of joy to Kithairon, that you
   Did not wreath your hair with vine-leaves, put on
   A fawn-skin and go, is strange.
CAPTAIN.   Strange? I had
   No orders to proceed to Kithairon, no word
   Commanding me save what Beroe . . .
AGAVE [*interrupting with a laugh*].   Save what she
   Commands? Captain, what a strange Maenad holds
   Your strength locked in Thebes. Or can sharpened youth
   At night-fall elude her watch?

CAPTAIN [*anxious to get away*].   Madam . . .

AGAVE.   And

Your dog's too? I trust he's well.

CAPTAIN [*in spite of his embarrassment, pleased, he lifts his head and smiles*].

You are kind

To ask, Madam. Yes, he's well. Thank you. Well.

AGAVE. How loyal you are.

CAPTAIN.   Please, my Lord Pentheus

Your son, Madam, bade me hurry . . .

AGAVE [*indifferently*].   You may go.

> [*He turns and exits hurriedly into the palace;* AGAVE *turns away.* AUTONOE, *in dress and manner a less commanding imitation of her sister, has entered Right earlier, and stood aside in order to observe the foregoing colloquy, now quietly approaches* AGAVE *who has not noticed her yet.*]

CADMUS [*continuing*]. Radiant Pallas, if thou art yet my

Patroness, tell me: have I offended

Them or neglected any? Remind them

How at my marriage humbly I served them

Wine and was grateful. Humbly. Remind them.

AUTONOE [*tapping* AGAVE *lightly on the shoulder*].

My sister is reproached.

AGAVE [*turning*].   Reproached?

AUTONOE.   Not by me.

I can't blame a wish so well justified.

AGAVE [*laughing*]. You're mad. But should I go mad thus, I'd not—

Like one sister—claim a god brought me low.

AUTONOE. A man might be thought a god were he loved

Enough.

AGAVE [*again laughing; the sisters punctuate all their remaining conversation with light cultivated laughter*].

Semele was in love then?

AUTONOE.   Oh, she

Believed any man who won *her* her charms

Transformed to a god.

AGAVE.   I've no use for Gods

Of my making nor if mine to command.

AUTONOE. It's true *he'd* obey you.

AGAVE.   He?

AUTONOE [*with a gesture indicating the palace entrance*].
                                        He; the young
And pure God who left—the shy Captain.
AGAVE.   He . . .
I fear, loves his dog, his dog only.
AUTONOE.   Ah!
How kind of him!
AGAVE.   Was there some kinder Captain here
When *kind* Semele . . . ?
CADMUS [*continuing*].
I can remember only their laughter
Now. Were they happy then? Have I blamed them
Ever or ever ventured ungrateful
Thoughts in my woe? Shine! Wait. They are laughing
Still; I can hear them.
BEROE [*respectfully approaching* CADMUS].
                        Sire, would you let me
Help you? Your grandson . . .
CADMUS [*startled*].   Grandson!
BEROE.   . . . the King has
Asked that his kinsmen gather to hear his
First proclamation. If I may . . .

[*Liveried* SLAVES *have earlier brought out heavy gilted fauteuils, upholstered in richly embroidered cloth, and placed them on the upper edges of the arena.* AGAVE *and* AUTONOE *have just seated themselves when, with a hint of fanfares in the music,* CAPTAIN *appears in the palace doorway holding a large scroll and begins, as befits the solemnity of an official occasion, to descend slowly and walk to the center of the stage. During this, the hymn ends. As* BEROE *leads* CADMUS *to his chair, he looks back towards the tomb with sad tenderness.*]

CADMUS.   Semele . . .

[*He sits;* BEROE *again withdraws towards the back.*]

CAPTAIN [*opening the scroll and reading: he intones*].

We, Pentheus, King of Thebes, do hereby declare:

Whereas certain idlers and babblers have deceived you with their ridiculous inventions, impiously asserting that the Immortal Gods do lust after mortals and strive jealously for their favors, let all such blasphemers henceforth be anathema.

As touching our House, whoever shall say or think that the Son of Chronos did abduct Europa from Tyre and ravish her in a Cretan grove, let him be anathema.

Whoever shall say or think that, in this very city, the Father of the Gods had carnal knowledge of Semele, daughter of Cadmus, and begot a child upon her, let him be anathema.

Whosoever, knowing of persons who, openly or in secret, continue in such wicked opinions, does not denounce them that they may swiftly be brought to judgement, whosoever shall harbor, comfort or protect them, let him be anathema.

We, Pentheus, the King, have spoken.

[*Silence.*]

CADMUS [*horrified*].
    No. no.
BEROE [*proud, frightened*].
        Child of my breast . . .
AUTONOE [*to* AGAVE].   Did he tell you?
AGAVE [*shrugging*].   He tells me nothing.
CADMUS. May no ill come of this.
AUTONOE.   Will they obey him?

    [*They speak to each other or exclaim in withdrawn whispers, and do not notice* PENTHEUS *appearing in the palace doorway. The* KING *is young, and very much at the mercy of his strong convictions. In appearance spare, athletic, scholarly. In dress, monastic and soldierly: a medieval king in the sort of dress he might wear on a pilgrimage. He also wears a long cloak. The color of his costume is that of undyed sackcloth. The seriousness of this, his first public appearance since assuming reign, gives his face an even greater intensity and maturity than usual, but he is older than his years in any case.*]

CAPTAIN [*springing to attention*].   The King!

    [*So astounded has been his family by the proclamation, and so further taken aback by the totally self-absorbed*

purpose in his expression, that there is absolute silence
as he descends, crosses the stage, and ascends the steps
to Semele's tomb. All eyes are on him. CAPTAIN,
when PENTHEUS *passes him, slowly retraces his steps*
and stands at attention at the foot of the palace steps.]

PENTHEUS. Too lax was the Law in permitting
　　Weak ignorant women to kindle
　　This flame on Semele's tomb: too
　　Long, relic-mad credulous pilgrims
　　Have made Thebes a ridiculous by-word.

[He removes his cloak and, after a slight pause hold-
ing it in front of himself, quickly throws it on the altar,
extinguishing the flame.]

　　Their fire I extinguish, will put to
　　Death any who dare to relight it.

[As PENTHEUS *descends from the tomb and walks*
back to the center of the stage, the sound of a guitar
being tuned can be heard off: during the ensuing
scene, this sound becomes more and more frequent.
PENTHEUS *stands with his back to the others on the*
spot Captain earlier stood.]

CADMUS. Pentheus! Pentheus! No!
AGAVE [*any awe she may have felt gone, triumphantly*].
　　　　　　　　　　　Excellent! Simple and proper!
　　King and son, I am proud. She lies alone now in peace:
　　You have omened us well.
PENTHEUS [*half turning to her with a slight ironic bow*].
　　　　　　　　　Mother, my thanks: though I could wish
　　Deeper modesty had shown fuller appraisal of my
　　Wishes here.
CADMUS.　　　　Pentheus!
PENTHEUS [*after answering* AGAVE *turns round fully to make a deep bow and*
　　finally notices that apart from his kin and BEROE, *the stage is empty;*
　　furiously].
　　　　　　　　　Captain!
　　Where are my people? Were there not orders
　　Bidding them gather?
CADMUS.　　　　　　　Pentheus, listen . . .
PENTHEUS [*completely ignoring* CADMUS].
　　Answer me!

CAPTAIN [*hesitant*].

     Sire, they were told. They were here . . .

PENTHEUS [*ominous*].

  Yes?

AGAVE [*stepping between them*].

    They danced off to Kithairon.

  Thebes lacks my deep immodesty.

CAPTAIN. Some oriental conjuror who claims that

  He's Dionysus . . .

PENTHEUS. Captain, follow me!

CAPTAIN.   Sire.

     [PENTHEUS *furiously re-enters the palace followed by*
     CAPTAIN. BEROE *furtively makes her way left front*
     where she is hidden from the others by the rise of the
     palace stairs. SLAVES *remove the chairs.* CADMUS
     reaches out his arm as though to detain PENTHEUS.]

CADMUS.   Pentheus, listen . . .

     [*He slowly turns and ascends the altar: there he sits,*
     head in hands.]

AUTONOE.   A tempest.

  A chaste fury. Turned on you, sister, too.

     [*During the following, the sounds of tuning grow*
     even more frequent: it is as though they were spurring
     AGAVE *on to an exaltation beyond her actual words.*]

AGAVE. He is raw still, but right

  To wish his will done

  In his way, not even

  As a mother imagines his way.

CADMUS. Daughter. Semele.

  Pardon his rashness.

BEROE. Daughter. Semele.

  Pardon his rashness.

AGAVE. He is a King, no

  Son but a father.

  How happy I am that

  He is not so bloodless as I had feared;

  He is young and strong:

  When his time comes to wed,

  May the tender communion

Be with strength. Echion,
Echion, may we know a reign then
Long, just, and yet more forceful!
AUTONOE. Well thought. Well . . .

> [*During the last three lines of* AGAVE's *arioso, the
> tuning is replaced by the unmistakable strumming
> introduction to a "gallant" serenade.* AUTONOE
> *breaks off as she becomes aware of the off-stage*
> VOICE (DIONYSUS) *that begins immediately after
> she does.*]

VOICE. How fair is wild Kithairon:
　　Lush and green in her scented glades
　　Grow ivy, vine, and bryony;
　　From her caverns of cool stone
　　Crystal-clear fountains flow.

> [AUTONOE, *on her silence, turns towards where she
> believes the* VOICE *comes from;* AGAVE *puts a re-
> straining hand on her, her own expression more puz-
> zled than rapt. Yet now:*]

AGAVE AND AUTONOE [*softly*].
　　O . . .
VOICE. Birds hold a tuneful parliament
　　And the honey-bee loudly hums,
　　Here the fawn and the wolf-cub
　　Sport and play in an amity:
　　Men and maids also dance.
AUTONOE [*clearly*]. Dance . . .

> [AGAVE *also turns and faces back-stage.*]

VOICE. How apt, to dulcet melodies
　　Of the flute, to the merry drum,
　　They turn, with what agility,
　　To the measure accordant,
　　Foot it slow, foot it quick.
AUTONOE. Quick.
AGAVE.　　　　　Quick.

> [*They slip their arms about each other's waists.* CADMUS
> *rises slowly and turns to observe them. A short time
> after,* BEROE *peers out from behind the balustrade to
> look on.*]

VOICE. O what a pleasant hermitage,
　　Far from Nemesis, the overjust.
　　Come. Come. Yourselves associate
　　With our glad unanimity:
　　Join the dance. Come away.

> [AGAVE *and* AUTONOE, *alternately together and apart, begin to turn like dancing dolls moving towards the back and finally descending out of sight. Their dance is slow and stately.*]

AGAVE AND AUTONOE. Come away. Join the dance.
　　Away. Away. Dance. Dance.
BASSARIDS. Dance O Boeotia.
　　Clap hands O Thebes.
　　Thebes, clap hands.
　　Boeotia, dance . . . .
BEROE [*fierce, pitiless*].
　　Go. Dance your little mockeries.
CADMUS [*helpless, tender*].
　　They go. Semele's flame is gone.
BEROE. Go.
CADMUS.　I must watch my blood go.
BEROE. Go.
CADMUS.　Go. Our doom hurries you.
　　We must fall, that your dance . . . .
BEROE. Dance . . . .
AGAVE AND AUTONOE [*off*].
　　　　　Dance . . . .
VOICE.　　　　Dance . . . .
CADMUS. . . . Raise Dionysus!

> [*Pause.* PENTHEUS *appears in the palace doorway,* CAPTAIN *behind him.* BEROE *hurriedly re-hides herself.* CADMUS, *the very certainty of his despair strengthening him and giving him again the absolute commanding dignity that befits the founder of a city and descendant of Gods, holds up his hand to stop* PENTHEUS.]

CADMUS. Wait, Pentheus, and say nothing. No, say nothing.
　　By my consent, you command in Thebes:
　　Remember well. Remembering, give no order
　　Until I have been heard. Bow your head.

Bow your head. Gods have stood before me and spoken.
Their words are gone. Our city stands yet
And the radiance of their speech robes our endeavors
Of stone and rich deed. And earth glows.

Semele was the loveliest of my daughters:
A joy that cried *Alas!* in full bloom.
A light slain by light, a flame dancing the hillside
Seen and gone and never understood.

And gone and seen again dancing there forever
When night falls back and for one full day
Our Mother wears the speaking of her perfection.
Young, I have looked into Her sad eyes.

You will say I am confused and have forgotten.
That is true, yes: but what will you see
When you disrobe the earth and silence the shining
On our temples? Great King, bow your head.

BASSARIDS [*under the following scene*].
We have come dancing through broad fields,
Fields newly awake lifted our
Light steps as a green quickening
At a tip touch overtook all
Unawareness.
                Dance, Boeotia!

Gaze down at our wealth laboring
In an earth sown with our steps, look
Where the wild orchis, our first wide
Pure gaze of the spring turns to us
With remembrance.
                Dance, Boeotia!

Can the spring fail us now, prime blood
Sink back to its roots fearfully?
Hold wine to the sun, pledge with it
To the great God of our blood's fire,
Dionysus.
                Dance, Boeotia!

PENTHEUS [*descending the steps*].
You have been heard. Head bowed, I have listened. But
One thing, one that I long waited to hear, you most

Carefully shunned: Do you in your wisdom think
Dionysus a God or no?

CADMUS. I believe him a God, the son
Semele bore Zeus miraculously, a God
Glorious, fearful, new to the Gods and, new
To himself and his strength, proving them both on man.

PENTHEUS. So. Why, then, have you stayed? You, who in fear of each
Of the Gods, a poor love of the Gods, have built
Shrines to them all, why now do you wait so long
When the youngest one, your kinsman as well, has called?
Go. Or have you exhausted fear?

CADMUS. No, King Pentheus, no. I fear:
For my King most. I am old,
And Kithairon's young joys cannot be mine. The God
Knows my place is in Thebes. Here I may honor him,
Here wait. He will respect such love.

PENTHEUS. For Thebes? Could you resign such love?
East winds brought you a new name: Dionysus. That
Name was the fear, *that* Cadmus resigned to me.
Fearing for Thebes? No. Spent and afraid of death.

CADMUS. Look! Was I wrong? Look well at your emptied streets!
Youth I believed best fit to receive the new;
No god crossed or neglected shadowed your past like mine:
But, King, have you no awe? No fear?

PENTHEUS. No fear, not of the Gods. I fear
Man, that sly chaos of need; the Gods
Do have my awe: would they, the Serenely Pure,
Ravish our blue-eyed children? Can you be awed
To have sired an Olympian slut?

CADMUS. You believe she was justly slain,
Semele, by the Thunderer for her lie?

PENTHEUS. Cadmus's Gods may punish, the Gods do not.
Chance rules *us* when we know them not:
Light unsullied, they beckon us
To perfect brief lives in Immortal Truth.
Thebes can. Not through your shrine to a lie.

CADMUS. Great Thebes prospered when I was her King.

PENTHEUS. Great Thebes would have remained home in Thebes.
When relic-mongers grew rich peddling their wisps of charred
Straw as True Strands of Semele's hair, how great
Thebes was—ploughed for the evil seed!
On Kithairon, Truth will root out that harvest: Him,

Your Dionysus, whosoever he be, we shall
Find, kill. As for his sworn votaries, they may choose
Which they prefer: To foreswear him at once, or die!
CADMUS. Also your mother?
PENTHEUS.   What!
CADMUS.   Also your mother?

> [*For a moment they face each other silently.*]

PENTHEUS [*calm*].   Yes.
Also my mother. Now, Captain. The Guard. At once!

> [*As the points of the* GUARD'S *spears appear ascend-
> ing at the back steps* CADMUS *turns away and hurls
> himself to the ground in terror.*]

CADMUS. Run. Run. Help me! The Sown Men have arisen. Quick.
Throw in a stone. Quick. Let them destroy themselves!

> [*The* GUARD, *visors down, is lined up at the top of the
> stairs.* PENTHEUS *indicates to* CAPTAIN *that he help
> CADMUS to his feet. Once standing, CADMUS
> pushes CAPTAIN's hand away and, ashamed, keeps
> his face averted.*]

PENTHEUS. Look. Look well. Let *King* Cadmus fear not. For Thebes.
His own quarters wait. Ease and seclusion wait.
Sire, go honorably, wearing old age in peace.

> [CADMUS *slowly ascends the palace stairs. At the en-
> trance he turns to the city and stretches his hands to-
> wards it.* PENTHEUS *has his back to him.*]

CADMUS. Take, Thebes, built by the seed of Gods,
One man's blessing. But O, he who has watched that seed
Spring forth armed, how shall he know peace?

> [*Exits into palace.*]

PENTHEUS. Captain, you have your orders: return with
All you can find, kill all who resist. Go.

> [*Exeunt* CAPTAIN *and* GUARD *to the rear.*]

BASSARIDS. Strange feet startle the road from Thebes.
March. Foe, nearing us, wound our soil.
And the seed of our soil would die,
Dionysus, should foe rule.

[During the above, PENTHEUS, *having watched the* GUARD *depart, turns thoughtfully and comes down stage.* BEROE *comes out of hiding and kneels before him. He lifts her to her feet and embraces her. Then he walks with her to the palace stairs and sits on them. She also sits, half-crouching, at his feet.]*

PENTHEUS. Faithful Beroe!
    Whom else can I trust
    Not to betray me?
    To you alone
    Can I open my heart.
    Listen, Beroe!
    For speak I must:
    The best in Thebes
    Do but worship shadows
    Of the True Good.

    They honor Its excellence
    Under many a name
    Of God and Goddess:
    But the Good is One,
    Not male or female,
    They acknowledge Its glory
    With statues and temples
    Fair to behold:
    But the Good is invisible
    And dwells nowhere.

    Well, let it be so,
    For so it must be
    With little children
    Until they have come
    To understanding.
    Truth and righteousness
    Glimmer through
    The ancient rites:
    But they shall not worship
    The Ungood!

BASSARIDS. Day. Hide. Robed in the bark of pine,
    Wait. Wear mien of the beast. Be still.
    And with night we shall rouse with you,
    Dionysus, the new moon.

[Lights fade slowly on the Amphitheatre. By the time
PENTHEUS *finishes his Aria, all the light is concen-*
trated on the arena.]

PENTHEUS [*with rising excitement*].
    Dionysus!
    Dionysus!
    Dionysus
    Is but a name
    For the nameless Nothing
    That hates the Light.
    Who has not heard
    Its lying whispers?
    "Come! Come!
    To me! To me!
    In my darkness
    Is no distinction;
    Here is neither
    Square nor circle,
    Even nor odd;
    Men are beasts
    And beasts are men.
    Down! Down!
    To me! To me!
    Forget! Forget!
    Honor and shame.
    Here all is possible,
    Wish is deed.
    Here you may do,
    Do, do,
    Do the forbidden
    Shameless thing."

Bear witness, Beroe,
To what I swear,
To this, my vow! [*He kneels.*]
I, Pentheus,
King of Thebes,
Henceforth will abstain
From wine, from meats
And from woman's bed,
Live sober and chaste
Till the day I die!

BEROE [*throughout* PENTHEUS' *Aria mutters some prayer to herself over and over again, like an old woman reciting the Rosary. Usually the words are inaudible, a sort of droning chant, but, every now and then, a fragment is heard*].

. . . Oldest One, have mercy upon us . . .

. . . there before the Sky-Gods came . . .

. . . Mother of all things . . .

. . . wisest, oldest . . .

. . . Queen of the Double Axe, have mercy upon us . . .

. . . have forgotten Thee . . .

. . . the cranes Thy messengers . . .

. . . blood of the innocent . . .

. . . in Thy holy groves . . .

. . . save the child of my breast . . .

. . . deliver him . . .

. . . be not angry . . .

. . . spare my dear Lord . . .

> [*The* GUARD *can be heard returning. On a platform that juts out from the higher level into the arena halfway back on the side behind the palace steps,* SLAVES *place a throne—in style similar to the fauteuils.* PENTHEUS *rises;* BEROE *goes more left front. The Prisoners, led by* CAPTAIN *and followed by the* GUARD, *come up from the back and are herded to the right of the Arena. The Prisoners consist of* AGAVE, AUTONOE, TIRESIAS *and a youthful* STRANGER (DIONYSUS). *Also four or five male* BACCHANTS, *bearded, barefoot and wearing dirty dungarees, and a* YOUNG WOMAN, *dressed like an ordinary housewife would to do her chores. By her hand she holds a* CHILD, *her daughter, who rather seems to be leading her. The* CHILD *is dressed in her Sunday best, her hair curled; she holds an enormous realistic doll, which she ever so often bends over to make it say: "Mamma, mamma." All wear and carry bits of the Bacchic paraphernalia;* AGAVE *and* AUTONOE *have let down their hair and are barefoot. The* STRANGER *looks like a rather affected adolescent, his affectation that of Byronic languor, and he is dressed in the sort of open-collared shirt and narrow pants that his model might have worn for a picnic on the Roman Campagna. He has elaborately waved long*

hair. A half-smile constantly seems to come and go over his whole expression. He uses his thyrsus as though it were a walking stick and leans on it when he has taken his place in the Arena. This further accents the languor which is more "nineties" than Byronic. With the exception of this STRANGER *and, to a certain degree,* TIRESIAS, *the Prisoners are completely entranced: they hum to themselves, once in a while softly singing "Ayayalya". The* GUARD *completely enclose the Arena, their backs to the audience.* PENTHEUS, *though forewarned, is obviously startled to see his mother, not to mention the others familiar to him, but he regains his composure quickly, though not deeply enough to enable him to address them as individuals. During this pantomime, the* BASSARIDS *can be more distinctly heard.*]

BASSARIDS. Blessed be Thebes, our city,
　　Nurse of the maiden Semele;
　　Blessed be Semele, the beautiful,
　　Whom Zeus loved and won;
　　Blessed be Zeus, the almighty
　　Lord of earth and sky.
PENTHEUS [*after he has seated himself on the throne*].
　　What? A poor handful, Captain?
CAPTAIN.　　　　　　　　　　　　A handful,
　　Sire, was as many as we could discover;
　　Though I could hear more, many more, they
　　Could not be seen.
PENTHEUS.　　　　　So be it. They serve. [*Rising.*] You
　　Hunters who dare Kithairon, the shepherds'
　　Haven, say: where is he who inspired such
　　Courage, who leads your singing and dancing.
　　Tell me, that I may bow to his wonder.
　　Tell me.

[*The humming grows louder.*]

　　Where is he?

[*Even louder humming. The doll's "Mamma. Mamma" as well.*]

　　Where is my younger,

Greater, more travelled kinsman, the scattered
God our All-Father wombed in his thigh, your
Love, Dionysus? Tell me!

> [*The* STRANGER *slowly lifts his thyrsus: the hum-
> ming and other noises reach a climax and cease.*
> TIRESIAS *steps importantly forward.*]

BASSARIDS. She conceived a child,
    And for six months
    It grew in her womb
    Till, deceived by the wiles
    Of jealous Hera,
    Guardian of wedlock,
    She commanded the God
    To reveal his glory,
    Denied him her bed.

TIRESIAS.   One moment . . .

> [*His "dissertation" is delivered with a speed that
> borders on incoherence.*]

My King will not be angered if I speak to him
Informally, I know. He knows Tiresias
And values his advice as Cadmus did, I know.

Now, Pentheus, you must not be too literal
About the Gods, but you know that, *you* understand
That Chronos, shall we say, is Time: Time, *but* . . . revered.

And so on. Well now, Pentheus, you surely see
That wine—just think of it as wine and nothing more—
If not in rude excess, is one of mankind's boons:

That you'd admit, I know. A boon? Where from? A God!
It must be. Well then, Pentheus, as wine is born
Each year from parched wry stems, like lightning shaped, so must

Its God be born. So people think. So tales begin.
So worship spreads: a good, when it is worship of
What's good, and wine is that, you did admit, you know.

Now, each can worship in his way. With Cadmus I
Pretend to take this harmless tale as true in all
Details; though you and he, the God himself, must know

Much better, yes. And I. We see the facts, we know
Our tongue, we know that anciently the words for "pledge"
And "thigh" were similar; so when the people say . . .

BASSARIDS. In untimely travail
　　She bore him a son
　　Ere the lightning flash
　　Of his love consumed her:
　　But Hermes, the swift,
　　Caught up the babe,
　　Sewed him into
　　His father's thigh
　　With golden pins.

PENTHEUS [*beckons* CAPTAIN *back to him, then with great deliberation, low*].
　　Captain, who is that youth? He does not seem
　　Tranced like the others.
CAPTAIN.　　　　　　　　　All of the others
　　Came when he bade them come. They would all have
　　Hidden themselves, I am sure, if he had not.
　　Maybe a priest of this Dionysus . . .
PENTHEUS. So.

　　　　　　　　[*He dismisses* CAPTAIN *with a wave of his hand.
　　　　　　　　Then, to himself:*]

　　　　Is he smiling? At me? At the Bassarids?
　　Perfumed. Aloof. Effeminate. Sly. Wait.

　　　　　　　　[*During the above, the humming—joined by the other
　　　　　　　　"noises"—has begun again, its reverent tone gradu-
　　　　　　　　ally changing to one with a hint of menace. As such it
　　　　　　　　continues under the following:*]

PENTHEUS [*rising and interrupting* TIRESIAS].
　　Have done, Tiresias.
　　The wine you'd have your King adore, has not,
　　I mark, improved your prowess as a seer.

BASSARIDS. Child of the double door,
　　Twice-born Dionysus,
　　Smite our lawless oppressor
　　Pentheus, sullen offspring
　　Of a serpent's tooth. Avenge us!
　　Slay this wicked man!

PENTHEUS. Captain, my kin remain. And this prophet.
Also that stranger. As for the others . . .
Who is that woman there who goes whoring
Led by her daughter?
CAPTAIN. A slave, Sire,
Of the Lady Agave's household.
PENTHEUS. So. Put them
Both to the Question. Do likewise with any
Aliens among this rabble till pain
Persuade them to tell where *he* is, this so-called
God, Dionysus. Take them away.
CAPTAIN. Sire.

[CAPTAIN *and some of the* GUARD *take the indicated Prisoners away. The doll's "Mamma, mamma" can be heard growing more distant off-stage.*]

PENTHEUS. So.

[*He steps down from the throne and approaches* AGAVE. *Although extremely overwrought, he yet manages, addressing her, not to raise his voice. His manner, in fact, is almost that of a loving, obedient son, even when he says "Obey me".*]

Mother. Agave. Speak.

[*Pause. The* STRANGER *again slowly raises his thyrsus:* AGAVE *turns and faces* PENTHEUS *directly.*]

You remember Echion my father?
AGAVE [*expressionless*]. Yes.
PENTHEUS. You loved him and bore me.
AGAVE. Yes.
PENTHEUS. And named me Pentheus.
AGAVE. Yes.
PENTHEUS. You have been to Kithairon.
AGAVE. Yes.
PENTHEUS. I am Pentheus, King of Thebes.
Answer. Obey me. What did you see there?

AGAVE [*rapt*]. On a forest footpath, round a far bend,
Time stopped, I stepped into
A world awaiting me as it ever was;
Surfaces hailed me, edges and apertures:
There they were and thus.

Boles, as their wont is, welcomed with their backs,
Verging fruits gave me vague regards,
Laughing leaves displayed their profiles,
And flowers opened their old mouths
In songs too slow for sound.

Hunter and hunted on those high hills
Whirled as one in a wild daedal,
Renewing life. Ichneumon's children
Fed on the paralysed flesh of Arachne,
So fell before to flies.

Savoury odors in the noon silence
Rose from the goat-herd's galloping pot;
A white cloud drifted; a cliff echoed
To the axe-chant of a charcoal burner:
Lost-happy were earth and I.

> [*After her last words, she pauses as though in hesitation;
> the* STRANGER *lifts his thyrsus and describes a circle
> in the air. While he is doing so,* BEROE *approaches*
> PENTHEUS, *her eyes full of fear.*]

BEROE [*urgently whispering*].
    Master. Pentheus. Listen. Listen.
PENTHEUS [*impatient*].
    Later, Beroe. You should not be here.

> [*To* AGAVE, *more aggressively than before.*]

I am Pentheus, King of Thebes,
Your son. Answer. Where
Is he, he who calls
Himself Dionysus? Where?
BEROE [*to* PENTHEUS *who is too occupied with* AGAVE *to hear*].
    You must listen. Must. I know.
    There he is, he who calls
    Himself Dionysus. There. The God.
    I know him. Pentheus!
    Pentheus! Master.
AGAVE. On a forest footpath, round a far bend *etc.*
AUTONOE. Ayayalya . . .
TIRESIAS [*a bit after the others, still at breakneck speed*].
    Now Pentheus, you must not be too literal

About the Gods. You surely see that wine, as wine,
Is one of mankind's boons. A boon? Where from? A God!
It must be! Well then, Pentheus, as wine is born
Each year . . .

STRANGER [*has slowly walked to just behind* TIRESIAS. *He whispers at him,
each word distinct, separate, and of equal weight. When he begins,*
TIRESIAS *stops immediately and does not move*].

Keep your sight upon tomorrow,
Seer, old, smooth, blind:
I was torn that I be gathered,
I fell who have arisen,
Died I. I live:
Know not, can you,
Hearing now what I have spoken?
Looking backward here tomorrow,
You cannot know:
Live I, I died—
Blind smooth old seer.

TIRESIAS [*the moment the* STRANGER *ceases and steps back, continues, the
whole "incident" obliterated from his mind*].
        . . . from parched wry stems, like lightning shaped, so must
Its God be born: so tales begin, so worship spreads.
With Cadmus I pretend to take this harmless tale
As true in all details. We see. We know our tongue.
We know that anciently the words for "pledge" and "thigh"
Were similar; so when the people say that Zeus . . .

PENTHEUS. I am Pentheus, King of Thebes *etc.*

BEROE. You must listen. Must. I know *etc.*

BASSARIDS [*semi-chorus*].
    In untimely travail *etc.*

BASSARIDS [*semi-chorus*].
    Child of the double door *etc.*

STRANGER. Died I, I live.
    Live I, I died. [*Da capo and da capo ad lib.*]

    [*The* STRANGER *taps the ground lightly with his
    thyrsus. Silence.* PENTHEUS *tightens his fist as though
    to keep control of himself, and stares with hopeless
    anger at* AGAVE.]

BASSARIDS [*loud and distinct*].
    Child of the double door *etc.*

PENTHEUS [*very measuredly*].
  I am Pentheus, King of Thebes.
  Obey. Answer. Where
  Is he, he who calls
  Himself Dionysus? Where?

  [*Pause.*]

  No answers? None? You'd force my hand?
CAPTAIN [*re-entering hurriedly*].   Sire . . .
PENTHEUS.   Captain, what
  New information have you?
CAPTAIN.   None, Sire. None.
PENTHEUS [*furious*].   You tried?
CAPTAIN. All, Sire. They felt no pain, it seemed. The daughter first
  And then the mother. Sire, they sang. The others too,
  The foreign ones. I did my best. One died, Sire. No one
  Said a word. Never have I seen . . .
PENTHEUS [*impatiently*].   Enough. We are
  Not finished yet. First, Captain, take my mother back
  To her quarters with her sister. Lock them in.
  Then . . . You, Tiresias. I set you free. Your trade
  In prophecy, however, has been Thebes' disgrace
  Too long. So. Captain, you will take four men. Your task:
  Pull down his house. Let no one take him in. Go.
CAPTAIN.   Sire.

          [CAPTAIN *goes and takes* AGAVE *and* AUTONOE,
          *each by the arm. As he leads them into the palace, they
          put their arms about his waist and lean against his
          shoulders, humming as before.* PENTHEUS *stares at
          this furiously, then turns away with a slight shudder of
          disgust.* BEROE *again tries to attract his attention,
          but he sees nothing. She goes to hide herself again, in
          the hope of speaking to him when he is alone. This
          time, she slips through the line of the* GUARD *to wait
          behind the palace steps, out of sight of the audience.*]

TIRESIAS [*portentously*].
  The scattered seed will come to harvest. Not the man.

          [PENTHEUS *contemptuously waves him away. As*
          TIRESIAS *slowly makes his exit,* CAPTAIN *re-enters
          from the palace, taps four of the* GUARD *on the shoul-*

der and takes them with himself in the same direction.
All during this, the STRANGER *has been facing front*
and smiling slightly with complete unconcern.
PENTHEUS *studies him carefully, as though to gauge*
what tactics might best succeed in eliciting informa-
tion from him. He decides on a casual, half-amused,
friendly condescension combined with—what he con-
siders a "shock" tactic—an abrupt, undevious form of
questioning. The STRANGER's *answers, like his re-*
marks to TIRESIAS *earlier, are soft, even-toned, with*
a slight pause between each word, sometimes even be-
tween each syllable.]

PENTHEUS. Dionysus—you have seen him? You are his priest?
STRANGER. I serve him, yes. And I have known his presence, yes.
PENTHEUS. I am also told you command his riotous throng here.
STRANGER. No riotous throng. And I obey. The God commands.
PENTHEUS. You have seen him, serve him, follow him then: where is *he?*
STRANGER. Beside myself, here with me, radiant. Are you blind?
PENTHEUS. Is that the presence you have known, the air, boy?
STRANGER. Many are *his* forms. [*With a soft laugh.*]
⠀⠀⠀⠀⠀⠀⠀⠀⠀⠀⠀⠀⠀Do *you* think the Gods are visible?
PANTHEUS. Silence! Or answer what I ask. With due respect.
STRANGER. Respect? The ungodly man who neither sees nor knows
⠀⠀⠀The deed he does, the God he seeks, the man he is?
PENTHEUS [*contemptuous*].
⠀⠀⠀Slave, bow to Pentheus, son of Echion, King of Thebes,
⠀⠀⠀Whose deeds obey the Truth he seeks. Answer as truly
⠀⠀⠀*Your* name, parentage, land, and how you found *your* . . . God.
STRANGER [*bowing his head and answering in a slow bashful whisper, like a*
⠀⠀⠀⠀⠀*little boy*].
⠀⠀⠀My name, King . . . Pentheus, . . . Acoetes: I
⠀⠀⠀Am Lydian, a merchant's son. For him I sailed
⠀⠀⠀To Delos, bought him cloth. Returning home
⠀⠀⠀We beached at Chios. There, the God . . . But you will laugh.
PENTHEUS. Oh no. Tell more. Narrate it well. Your death is near.

STRANGER [*lifting his head, exalted, smiling, visionary*].
⠀⠀⠀I found a child asleep, more beautiful
⠀⠀⠀Than any child I'd seen.
⠀⠀⠀*Naxos,* he cried awakening.
⠀⠀⠀*Naxos,* I told my crew, and we set sail.

Blue into white the sea split by the bow.
He watched the sea or slept.
The crew watched him. They saw a slave
Earning much gold for them. I saw a God.

He woke and wept: *Naxos is far astern!*
I was their prisoner.
Naxos is far ahead, they laughed.
The bow stood poised in the divided wave.

Vines clambered up the mast and roped the oars.
A leopard pawed the deck.
The maddened crew leapt in the sea,
Dolphins, not men. The God was everywhere.

I have lit a torch in the waves; the wind
Carries it singing here.
The oaks of Kithairon sway, sway.
I follow the God, Pentheus. You shall.

> [*He turns and faces* PENTHEUS. *Neither move.
> Slowly* PENTHEUS *gives way to his long suppressed
> rage.* CAPTAIN *returns and stands waiting orders
> at the foot of the stairs. During this interval the*
> BASSARIDS *are even more distinctly heard.*]

BASSARIDS. Closer to Delphi the sun
    Drops, drops, drops. God of the vine,
    Stronger and worthier we
    Grow, grow, grow into the night.
PENTHEUS [*building from measured rage to an exasperated scream*].
    Lies. Lies. Lies. Am I not King?
    Captain, take him away.
    Root out his perfumed hair.
    Break that smiling mouth of its lie.
    Lay whips to his pampered flesh.
    Out of my sight! Anathema!

> [*The* STRANGER *is taken off, unprotesting, by* CAP-
> TAIN *and some of the* GUARD. *The sky begins to
> darken quickly.*]

Lies! King Pentheus
Is answered with a lie
To his every question. Lies.

What shall he call on? Where
Is the One, the Good?
The heavens are dark with lies.
And who would help him there?
How will Perfection turn
Into the Thunderer he needs
If the King himself is not to become
A lie, a lie, a lie?

> [*Darkness. Earthquake. Sounds of falling masonry.*
> PENTHEUS' *cloak is lifted into the air and flies away
> from Semele's tomb. The flame shoots up to the full
> height of the stage and then subsides, burning as it did
> before it was smothered. The Prisoners can be heard as
> they escape to Kithairon, like an echo of* PENTHEUS'
> *last cry.*]

PRISONERS [*crescendo and decrescendo*].
    Aly . . aly . . aly . . ayayalya . . .
BASSARIDS. Ayayalya!

> [*The stage grows light, but not fully. Rear left some
> statues have fallen; the* GUARD *are huddled rear
> right; the* STRANGER *is standing between the altar
> flame and* PENTHEUS. *During his first words he
> moves closer to him. Throughout this scene his words
> are duplicated by the* BASSARIDS *in unison with
> him; as the scene progresses, their voices extend the
> final vowels of his last words, these "echoes" becoming
> increasingly prolonged.*]

PENTHEUS [*more bewildered than angry*].
    You! That you dare! Who set you free?
STRANGER. Dionysus. He whose arm across the dark
    Of our captivity blinded our captors.
    He moved the earth. Your prison stands no more. The thick
    Locked doors you set between Agave and her God,
    Her love has shattered. He has freed us, Iacchos, all.
PENTHEUS [*mechanically*].
    My guards were bribed. An earthquake is no miracle.
CAPTAIN [*entering breathlessly*].
    Sire . . .
PENTHEUS [*interrupting him sternly and going on to command him but with only*

*the externals of sternness and command in his voice and words: he is
deeply distracted by now, and tired*].

Yes. I know. I know. Take all your men. Pursue
Them to Kithairon. Root them out. Kill. Kill. Kill.
STRANGER [*before* CAPTAIN *can move, with absolute authority*].
                                                        Wait!

                    [PENTHEUS *is now too curious even to be surprised;
                    the* STRANGER *addresses him confidentially.*]

The God is in them. They are strong. Your spears will find
No entry, but their fennel-wands will find your blood.
PENTHEUS [*nodding*]. You are right. Yes, you are right. [*To the* CAPTAIN.]
                                                        Wait. He is right.
Yes. No more bloodshed. No. Wait. Go. Go lock the gate.
The Electran gate. Yes. Go. And then you must return.
Not here. Close by. To wait. We must think first. We are King.

                    [*Exeunt* CAPTAIN *and* GUARDS *rear. During the
                    following,* PENTHEUS *and the* STRANGER *move
                    gradually apart, always facing each other,* PENTHEUS
                    also facing the flame over the other's shoulder.]

You were right. Yes. We can see. Yes. You must know.
STRANGER. I know what he knows. He has made you see I know.
PENTHEUS. See. Yes. I would see. Yes. You know. Yes. Tell me: when
    Are these . . . rites . . . most . . . —you know, yes, *you* know—most
    . . . themselves?
STRANGER. At night. The dark blood best in darkness glows to woo
    The darkness to itself. We dance. Come, night! Mine! Me!
PENTHEUS. You dance. I know that step. Who cares with whom they
    dance?
    Penelope, drunk, drops her loom. The suitors leap!
    You are beautiful. No doubt you . . . dance . . . with much success.
STRANGER. What should my beauty matter were the rites what you
    Believe they are? The chaste are chaste, the unchaste unchaste
    There as elsewhere, but there aflame with what they are.
PENTHEUS. Ha! The flame. Who lit . . . ? Death. Wait. The chaste are
    chaste, you say,
    The unchaste . . . Which are you?
STRANGER.   I? I am I.
PENTHEUS.   My mother?
STRANGER. You know her. *She* told *you*, you know.
PENTHEUS.   I know.

STRANGER.   Then see.

PENTHEUS. See. I would see. Yes. Yes. I had forgotten. See.

STRANGER. He will help you as he helped before. To see. To know.

> [*He points behind the palace steps, where* BEROE *has been hiding.*]

STRANGER. You. Woman. Bring . . .

> [*He hesitates a moment.* PENTHEUS *looks even more intently, almost through him, at the flame, then turns and faces* BEROE.]

PENTHEUS AND STRANGER.   . . . my mother's mirror. Quickly.

> [BEROE *hurries into the palace.*]

STRANGER.   He
    From high . . .

PENTHEUS.   . . . comes far . . .

> [BEROE *re-enters holding the small hand mirror; she hesitates.*]

STRANGER.   . . . to me . . .

> [BEROE *hurries across and gives the* STRANGER *the mirror, never lifting her head; then goes behind the tomb.*]

PENTHEUS.   . . . here.

STRANGER [*holding the mirror so as to catch the reflection of the flame*].
                                       Go, flame, see!

PENTHEUS [*from the other side of the stage following each move of the mirror with his eyes*].   See!

PENTHEUS AND STRANGER [*as the stage begins to darken and the first bits of scenery begin to descend*].   Ha!

BASSARIDS. Ha-ha-ha-ha-ha-ha-ha . . . . . .

Intermezzo

[*The descending scenery closes off the arena, utilising its columns as corners. The set is a realistically painted representation of a Boucher-like garden, with statues of mythological groups like Leda and the Swan, Cupid and Psyche, etc. Amidst the shrubbery, Satyrs pursuing Nymphs can be seen. Also Silenus. At the rear center, and left and right front, are pergolas with wicker doors. Finally the scene is framed by the painted proscenium arch of a Roccoco theatre, with stage boxes on both sides. This cuts off our view of* PENTHEUS *and the* STRANGER, *but their shadows are depicted in the stage boxes. During this transition the laughter of the* BASSARIDS *has continued as a sort of a cappella Overture. The lights come on.* AGAVE *and* AUTONOE *enter center: they are dressed as "Marie Antoinette" Shepherdesses, their crooks twined with fennel leaves, little bunches of grapes decorating their tricorns, their bodices using a fawn-skin pattern, fans hanging at the sides of the skirts. Liveried* SERVANTS *enter left and right carrying couches appropriate to the period, which are placed near the front.* MUSICIANS, *dressed with rustic quaintness, enter after them carrying their own chairs, and seat themselves at the back.* AGAVE *and* AUTONOE *are screaming with laughter and collapse breathlessly on their couches, lolling about and fanning themselves.*]

AUTONOE. "On a forest footpath, round a far bend . . ."
    You *are* ingenious!
AGAVE.   My dear, I thought he'd *never* end.
    "I am Pentheus, King of Thebes. Obey me. Answer."
    He may be King. He'll never make a *dancer.*
AUTONOE. "Where is he who calls himself Sir Bacchus?"
    As if we *cared!*
AGAVE.   I thought he would attack us.
AUTONOE. My dear, he doesn't have the brawn to.
AGAVE. That, at the very least, one might be drawn to.
AUTONOE. You think the Captain will . . .
AGAVE.   I do.
AUTONOE. I'm burning for the rendezvous.
AGAVE. What? He isn't coming here for you!
AUTONOE. Poo!
    Thou sayest. Oh . . .
    He is so . . . so . . . so . . .
AGAVE. Godly . . .
AUTONOE.   Manly . . .
AGAVE.   Earthy . . .
AUTONOE.   So aloof . . .
AGAVE. A bull!
AUTONOE.   The most divine of beasts on cloven hoof!
AGAVE. *I* know how to attract him: Woof, woof, woof!

             [*Screams of laughter. Enter* CAPTAIN *center: in place of his helmet he is wearing vine-leaves, his armor is not complete, and a sheep-skin is slung across his shoulder; he carries a spear decorated like a thyrsus.*]

CAPTAIN. Ladies, I'm here as promised. I stole away.
AGAVE AND AUTONOE. Clever as well as handsome! Come, let's play!
CAPTAIN [*looking bewildered from one to the other*].
    Your Majesty?
    Your Royal Highness?
AGAVE AND AUTONOE. To me! To me!
    Make yourself free
    Of sheep-skin and of shyness!
CAPTAIN. I should return soon. The King may call me.
AGAVE. Oh him. You've time.
AUTONOE.   You've lots of time.
AGAVE AND AUTONOE.   Take *all* me!

> [*Enter* TIRESIAS *center. Over his usual dress, a very elaborate arrangement of draped fawn-skins has been set, and instead of his buckled shoes he wears gilted sandals. He carries a thyrsus and wears a wreath of ivy. His movements are much more nimble than usual. The ladies are not too pleased to see him. All during the fore-going they have been drinking wine from enormous gold goblets which the* SERVANTS *fill from pitchers.*]

TIRESIAS. Ayayalya. I heard voices. Ladies, you appall me!
AGAVE AND AUTONOE. La!
TIRESIAS.   *Not* your morals.
    But Royalty . . .
AGAVE AND AUTONOE.   Poo!
TIRESIAS.   . . . in *public* quarrels
    Over a guardsman's caresses!
AGAVE AND AUTONOE [*indicating the* CAPTAIN].
    We're shepherds here . . .
CAPTAIN [*indicating them*].   . . . and shepherdesses.
ALL [*mechanically*].
    Ayayalya.
TIRESIAS [*portentous*].
         Whom Bacchus blesses.
    So you might have offered me some wine.
    That, after all, is given as a sign
    Of our Secret Society.
AGAVE [*surly*]. Wine for you? We ladies tope
    To give ourselves a greater scope
    To profit from the gentlemen's sobriety.

AUTONOE. Or so we hope.
   But *she* . . .
TIRESIAS. Please, ladies, leave the final word to me.
   I understand what this is all about:
   We should do best to act it out.
AGAVE, AUTONOE, AND CAPTAIN [*shocked*].
   To *act* it out?
TIRESIAS. A charade, you know.
AGAVE, AUTONOE, AND CAPTAIN.
   Oh . . .
   Why should candor lack
   In our happy Bac-
   -chic family?
TIRESIAS. It would never do
   To divulge what's true
   Of kin and kith
   Too nakedly
   In Arcady:
   We must find a Myth
   To drape it with.
   Now let me see . . .
AGAVE, AUTONOE, AND CAPTAIN.
   The old blind seer
   Thinks young, sees clear,
   Because his dear
   New God is near.
TIRESIAS. Yes! I have it! Let's play "*The*
   Judgement of Calliope."
   [*To* AGAVE.] You shall be Venus, the sea-born, the fertile.
   Fetch the lady a branch of myrtle.
   [*To* AUTONOE.] You are Dame Proserpine, all mankind your due.
   Bring the lady a branch of yew.
   [*To* CAPTAIN.] You'll be Adonis, their sweeting, their star.
AGAVE AND AUTONOE [*pointing to* CAPTAIN].
   You are Adonis just as you are!
TIRESIAS. I'll be Calliope, judging you girls
   Find me a wig . . .
CAPTAIN.   With mountains of curls!
AGAVE, AUTONOE, AND CAPTAIN [*while* SERVANTS *remove the couches and
      bring back the required properties, including a gavel. When the wig is
      placed on* TIRESIAS' *head, he fluffs it up a bit as though acknowledging
      the compliments of the others*].

Hail to Tiresias,
Our future's looking-glass,
Let him the judgement pass
On what perplexes.
He dines at Wisdom's feast,
Prophecy's peerless priest,
Having lived as at least
Two of the sexes.

TIRESIAS [*standing before* PENTHEUS' *throne, which is still in place*].
    Give me the gavel. Take your positions.
    Dance your dance. Strike up, musicians.

THE JUDGEMENT OF CALLIOPE

> [AGAVE, AUTONOE, *and the* CAPTAIN *dance to a brief overture for guitars, then arrange themselves before the throne, their grouping suggesting the grouping of the trial scene,* CAPTAIN *taking the* STRANGER'S *place.*]

CALLIOPE [*recitative or ballad narration*].
    Calliope, I, by Jove on high
    Appointed to try this case,
    Bid all abide by what I decide
    And neither chide nor grimace.
    Two heavenly dames—you know their names—
    Have quarrelled as well known is:
    So first of all, as witness I call
    The cause of their quarrel. Adonis
    Shall duly, shall truly
    Concerning his birth report:
    Exact now, in fact now
    Before the Muse's Court.

ADONIS [*taking the stand*].
    King Cinryas of Cyprus,
    He had a daughter, Smyrna;
    In face and hue she was fair to view,
    Said all who did discern her.
    That King too proud, he boasted loud,
    Giving the board a thump, sirs:
    "Compared with her, I do aver

That Venus is a frump, sirs!"
Venus, hearing this arrogant swearing,
Was enraged past bearing, and cried:

CALLIOPE [*interrupting*].
   Let Venus appear: the Court will hear
   From her own lips what she cried.

ARIA

VENUS.   These two, I say,
                               Shall rue this day.
                               I will inspire
                               In the daughter a fire
                               To lie with her Sire:
                               Soon to a son
                               He shall be Father-
                               Grandfather in one.

CABALETTA

My curse shall fall
On one and all
Who hold me thus in scorn.

CALLIOPE. Adonis, proceed.
ADONIS.   It happened indeed
   As Venus did design:
   Smyrna sped to her father's bed
   When he was flown with wine,
   And in the dark he could not mark
   To whom he did incline.
   When the King beheld that her belly swelled
   And learned the reason why, sirs,
   He raved and roared and drew his sword
   And swore that she should die, sirs.
   Out through the gate to escape his hate
   In terror great she flew:
   [*Falsetto.*] "Venus," she cried, "forgive my pride,
   Forgive and save me! Do!"
VENUS [*interrupting*].
   I *did* intervene upon the scene,
   And not a moment too early:
   As his sword come down upon her crown
   I changed her into a myrrh-tree.

ADONIS. The trunk he split and out of it
    I fell. My tale is ended.
VENUS. The Court will agree he belongs to me
    By whom he was so befriended.
PROSERPINE. When Venus is kind, she has something in mind;
    Let her tell us what she intended.
VENUS. Proserpine dear, from what I hear,
    For one so chaste and godly,
    So primly just, so lacking in bust,
    You behaved, people say, rather oddly.
CALLIOPE [*banging her gavel on the arms of the throne*].
    Ladies, peace! Your wrangle cease,
    And show the respect that is due
    To me and the Law.
               [*To* VENUS.] When the child you saw,
    What did you think and do?
VENUS. The Queen of Love has nothing to hide:
    I took one look and cried:

ARIA

    Vulcan, the gaby, would kill this baby,
    And Mars too, maybe, would frown:
    They both might suspect—which is not incorrect—
    That I've certain plans of my own.
    This boy, I see, is likely to be
    A handsome lad when grown;
    And why should a Goddess as lovely as I
    Be faithful to two alone?

    I shall build a box with heavy locks
    And hide him inside, but then
    I must look for a spot where it will not
    Be opened by Gods or men.
    Among the shades in Pluto's glades
    The babe should be safe enough:
    Avernus dim is the place for him
    Until he's of age to love.

  I left what was mine with Dame Proserpine,
  But I was far too trusting:
  The Court will agree that she cheated me
  In a fashion most disgusting.
PROSERPINE. That is a lie! Her charge I deny!
    Let her tell the truth, not hide it.

I swear by the dead that she never said
I was not to look inside it.
CALLIOPE. You raised the lid?
PROSERPINE.   Of course I did.
Like any woman, I had to.
But Adonis here will witness bear
That he was very glad, too.
[*To* ADONIS.] Come, my sweeting, with me repeating
The song of our meeting, sing!

ARIA (*leading to* DUET)

Pluto the bold has now grown old
And far too cold for play,
But your white flesh is as clean and fresh
As roses or new-mown hay.
To delay would be waste, let us make haste,
Come, embrace me, dear boy!
Closely entwine your limbs with mine:
Together we'll die for joy.
ADONIS. Excuse me, Ma'am, but you see that I am
But an innocent lamb, a boy:
What is it that you expect me to do?
How can one die for joy?

PROSERPINE. I was the first. Let Venus burst
And be off to Olympus above.
The Court will agree he belongs to me
Who taught him the arts of Love.

ROUND

VENUS AND PROSERPINE.
For shame, Madam! Your claim, Madam,
You shall forthwith resign.
Lie not! Deny not!
The lad by rights is mine.
ADONIS. To please both, to ease both,
Would take more strength than mine.
CALLIOPE [*pounding her gavel*].
Give ear now and hear now
The judgement of the Court.

[*Finally* CALLIOPE *obtains silence and rises to her
feet.*]

Both Goddesses have equal claim,
So their rights shall be the same:
But a mortal also is
Entitled to some liberties.
When the Goat the year doth reign,
Adonis with Venus shall remain;
When the Serpent holds the sway,
He with Proserpine shall stay;
When the Lion is on the throne,
He is free to sleep alone.

[*She sits.*]

VENUS, PROSERPINE, AND ADONIS [*bowing with mock reverence*].
Hail to Calliope, hail to the Muse
So just in her dealings, so wise in her views!

[*All three,* ADONIS *in the middle, come down towards the footlights.*]

TRIO

VENUS. My girdle I'll wear throughout the year,
Wear it both night and day:
For when I put on my magic zone,
Adonis will have to obey.
He shall be mine both in summer shine
And under the winter stars:
My only fear is lest news of my dear
Should come to the ear of Mars.

PROSERPINE. Her girdle she'll wear and steal my share,
My third of the year, away:
For when she puts on her magic zone,
Adonis will have to stay,
Leave me alone to sigh and moan
Under the winter stars:
But both shall wail when I tell the tale,
As I certainly shall, to Mars.

ADONIS. It isn't fair. She'll take my share,
My third of the year, away.
Ladies in love can't get enough,
Let the men do what they may.

Would that I might, for just one night
Sleep alone under moon and stars!
When the truth comes out, as it will, no doubt,
I shall have to reckon with Mars.

ADONIS [*taking one step forward*].
    And it was so, as you all know:
    My fate could not be prevented:
    In the guise of a boar, Mars did me gore,
    And all the world lamented.

CHORALE

> [*The tune—Matthäuspassion?—or a variant of it, we
> shall hear again when* PENTHEUS' *body is brought in.*]

TUTTI.   On hearing of the slaughter
                 Upon Mount Lebanon's side,
                 (Their) Our eyes were filled with water:
                 (They) We cried and cried and cried.

> [*They discard their properties and become "them-
> selves" again.*]

Ha-ha, ha-ha, ha-ha, ha-ha-ha!
CAPTAIN [*coming forward while the others still laugh*].
    My prospects here are gross and grim:
    Those two will have me limb from limb.

> [*He tip-toes off center.*]

AGAVE. When once I have my hands on him,
    They'll never tear us limb from limb.

> [*She skips out center.*]

AUTONOE. I mean to satisfy my whim
    To feast on him from limb to limb.

> [*She dances out center.*]

TIRESIAS [*as the sounds of the others' laughter grows fainter and the* SERVANTS
    gather the props and leave, and the MUSICIANS *also go*].
    His chances of escape are dim:
    Those girls will tear him limb from limb.

> [*Using his thyrsus as a sort of pole-vault, he nimbly
> exits left by a series of hops and leaps. During his last*

bit, the lights begin to lower and the scenery to slowly ascend.]

END OF THE INTERMEZZO

[*The sounds of their realistic laughter fade into the* BASSARIDS' *musical laughter. The proscenium is the last of the scenery to rise.* PENTHEUS *and the* STRANGER *are where they were, the* STRANGER *still holding the mirror, which he then puts down near him. Twilight is just beginning. The scene is accompanied only by the sort of tuning noises that preceded the earlier serenade. Its tempo, still in the shadow of the foregoing "Scherzo," starts at a restrained Allegro and gets faster and faster, returning to its first tempo only towards the end,* PENTHEUS' *exit into the palace.*]

PENTHEUS [*in an agony of disgust*].
    Could I have only
    Seen the raw deed plainly
    Wished, wooed, done!
    The farmyard beasts
    Make no jests
    Of their sin—
    But this! Eyes cannot lie!
STRANGER. They saw what they would see.
PENTHEUS. The Truth! My loathing
    Would find all or nothing:
    I must go!
    Their darkness I
    Shall probe, see,
    Scatter, know!
    At once! I must! I shall!
STRANGER. They will see you and kill.
PENTHEUS. No. I am strong!
STRANGER. They are many.
PENTHEUS. But I shall hide.
STRANGER. They will find you.
PENTHEUS. But I must go.
STRANGER. Let me help you.
PENTHEUS. What must I do?
STRANGER. Dress as they dress.
PENTHEUS. The lawless men?

STRANGER. No, the women.

PENTHEUS. No. Not in woman's dress.

STRANGER. In man's they know you. Yes.

PENTHEUS. But they will see I am no woman; they will know.

STRANGER. Go now and dress. I will arrange it for you. Go.

PENTHEUS. It must be. Let it be.

STRANGER. You serve the God in me.

PENTHEUS. But if they see me here before I go, and laugh:
    I could not bear that laugh.

STRANGER. In secret, when you go,
    The God will lead you through the city.

PENTHEUS [*hurrying into the palace*].   I must go.

             [PENTHEUS *is not quite gone, when* BEROE *enters*
             from behind the tomb and falls at the STRANGER's
             feet.]

BEROE. Spare him, Dionysus.

DIONYSUS.   You know me, woman?

BEROE. He is a good man. Spare him.
    Give him time. He will worship.

DIONYSUS. What is his goodness to me?
    I have no need of his worship.
    I have no need of time.

BEROE. Spare him for my sake.

DIONYSUS.   Woman?

BEROE. Youngest of the Gods, I am Beroe:
    I was your mother's nurse, was his:
    I love him. I loved her.

DIONYSUS. You are Beroe who loved my mother
    With such love, you were not there
    To shield her, shield the God in her womb,
    When Hera, to destroy my mother
    And me, took your shape, yours,
    Beroe, and with your voice
    Convinced her to invite her doom.

BEROE. You live. You are a God.
    Could I withstand the will of Hera?

DIONYSUS. Pray Hera, woman. Not me.
    Go.

BEROE. Spare him, Dionysus.

DIONYSUS.   No.

[*As* BEROE *reluctantly, for all her terror, starts to exit left to behind the tomb,* PENTHEUS *re-appears in the palace doorway. For one horrified moment, she turns and sees him before she leaves: he is dressed in one of* AGAVE's *dresses—in style one appropriate for a drive in the Bois de Boulogne—and has obviously put it on hastily. It is also obviously a bad fit. From somewhere he has taken a fawn-skin and tied it about his waist; his head is covered with a scarf, a few leaves tied together into a loose wreath over it. He wears sandals, but they are more those of an anchorite than any woman's. His expression is dazed as he slowly descends the steps, his eyes always on* DIONYSUS. *The red of sunset grows more and more intense.*]

DIONYSUS. Can this be the King? I see there a true daughter of Cadmus.
PENTHEUS. I see two suns descending. Two Thebes glow in their long rays.
　We drive down the furrow; you lead: a bull. Yes, I can see you:
　A horned beast, beautiful. We bring two Earths to fruition.
DIONYSUS AND BASSARIDS. Praise Dionysus! He is here, his peace made.
PENTHEUS [*suddenly coy and feminine*].
　And I? Have I dressed myself well in truth? Yes? Like Agave?
DIONYSUS. Herself. [*Holding the mirror before him and helping him arrange the wreath.*]
　　　Look. Blood will tell. [*Handing him the thyrsus.*]
　　　　　　　Now take this. Hold it above you.
　Now dance, your right foot and right hand at the same time,
　Your head up. Now a cry of pure joy leaps from your throat: O
DIONYSUS, PENTHEUS, AND BASSARIDS.
　Praise Dionysus! He is here, his peace made.

　　　[*So completely is* PENTHEUS *possessed by the* GOD *that they sing as one.*]

PENTHEUS AND DIONYSUS. Captain! At once!

　　　[CAPTAIN *enters hurriedly right.* PENTHEUS *faces him,* DIONYSUS *is behind the King.*]

　　　　　　　　Captain, the way
Is no longer dark. Bring back all my Guard.
Let them see the King dares
Hunt in the glades of holy Kithairon

Though he would not let any of them go
To sure death. He wants them
To line his way to the West Gates
Destined for glory. Go. He knows the true way.

> [CAPTAIN *exits hastily center.*]

BASSARIDS. Praise Dionysus! He is here, his peace made.
PENTHEUS, DIONYSUS, AND BASSARIDS.
He sees all that he would. He will climb
High on the great pine
Overlooking what they had hoped to
Hide from him.
Who will know Pentheus?
He is Thebes. He will triumph. He could lift
Wooded Kithairon from its roots.
Oh! How Agave will smile and
Scold when she bears him
Home in her arms, her lost babe!
Hurry, cousin. Follow him!

> [CAPTAIN *and* GUARD *have returned center; they
> line both sides of a path to the back steps. The stage is
> bathed in a blood-red light.* PENTHEUS *hesitates a
> moment, then* DIONYSUS *takes his hand and leads
> him like bridegroom under an arch formed by the*
> GUARD's *spears, to the rear and out of sight.*]

BASSARIDS. Praise Dionysus! He is here, his peace made.

> [GUARD *remain where they are, their spears now at
> their sides. The light fades into evening. The atmo-
> sphere is desolate: the empty city, silence. Then*
> BEROE *is heard, still in hiding, giving a hopeless wail
> of wordless grief. She emerges to this wail and crosses
> to the palace stairs slowly.*]

BEROE.   Unaya!
              Unaya!
Night and again the night,
The great cold and the dark.
              Unaya!
The day with grief tomorrow,
The empty and naked day.
              Unaya!

For my King is no longer there;
I shall see my King no more.
              Unaya!

              [CADMUS *enters from the palace,* SERVANTS *behind*
              him.]

Lord Cadmus! Our King is gone!
CADMUS. The earth quaked when the Gods laughed.
    I heard. Come, Beroe.

              [BEROE *ascends the stairs and seats herself, crouch-*
              ing, at his feet.]

              Captain.
CAPTAIN [*stepping forward*]. Sire . . .
CADMUS.   The King has gone?
CAPTAIN.   To Kithairon
    With a Lydian priest.
BEROE.   The God . . .
CAPTAIN. I'll find him if you wish, my hound . . .
CADMUS. Would die. And you. No, no,
    Thebes must keep you, at least, for I fear
    That Thebes will soon be kingless, perhaps
    Already is.
              [*To the* SERVANTS.] Remove his throne.
    His needs are other. If ever we see
    Pentheus again, my heart forebodes
    We shall wish that we did not. Tonight
    There is nothing we can do but wait.
    Dismiss the Guard. Go now and rest.
    The old sleep little. I and Beroe
    Will keep watch. If, by morning,
    We have heard nothing, you and your men
    May search Kithairon. Good night, Captain.
CAPTAIN. Good night, Sire.

              [*Exeunt* CAPTAIN *and* GUARD *left. Night is falling*
              fast; almost the only light on CADMUS *and* BEROE
              comes from the flame on Semele's tomb.]

CADMUS.   Fall night,
    Fall Thebes, fall oblivion
    Upon all we know, my place is here

For what shall be, I pray, my last
Night upon Earth, and last of memory.

> [*During the following Chorus, a scrim rises slowly at
> the front of the stage. At the sides are depicted steep
> cliffs which cut off our view of the palace and tomb;
> then, left, we see jutting out from the cliff, the top
> branches of an enormous pine, one long branch of it
> stretching half-way across the stage, its level coincid-
> ing with the landing of the palace steps. Further back-
> stage, drops with foliage obscure the columns. The
> effect, in spite of the darkness, must be of looking
> down from a great height, the illusion must be realistic
> on the same level that the permanent set is realistic,
> and in no way resemble the style of the Intermezzo.*]

BASSARIDS.

Now night opens wide all day locks: our deep-skied consolations!
We woke made older, woke to toil's way, thoughtful and naked
In loud light, and watched the smooth maggot hatch hungry, who
        waits us.
Our close walls burn. They crumble. Come, night, whisper us how to
Praise Dionysus. He is near, his peace made.

His arms lift Kithairon, stars flock her streams, Everywhere waits at
Our hand, all now Kithairon, where one night of beginning
The great pines are summoned, rise full as now: look and
        remember:
Your light heart keeping time to no time's music, in silence
Praise Dionysus. He is near, his peace made.

> [*A procession of torches, as though lit at Semele's tomb,
> crosses the stage diagonally. After it passes, the back of
> the stage, through the foliage, seems alive with dancing
> fire-flies. In the faint light,* PENTHEUS, *his dress even
> more disordered than before, can be seen crouching on
> a branch of the pine.*]

PENTHEUS [*in a hurried whisper*]. Waiting. For what? Go to it! Go!
Your shadow watches, waits, knows and sees . . .
Nothing, nothing, lights, warm
Nothingness. King and God are not needed:
Shall we descend to comfort oblivion?
O dance, dance the due praise.
And waiting? Loveliness. Nothing?

Pentheus, is Agave near and peace made?
BASSARIDS. Praise Dionysus, He is near, his peace made.]
    With pure heart we out-dance joy in joys
    Wiser than wisdom,
    Each by each together expectant.
PENTHEUS. Each by each . . .
BASSARIDS. Juster than might, in our
    Mighty limbs more than justice, we await
    Him who is watching, waits and knows.
PENTHEUS. Him who is watching . . .
BASSARIDS.   Fulfill us!
    Bring us the deed of
    Courage and love that most will . . .
PENTHEUS [*half rising from his perch*].
    One is holy. He is here.
PENTHEUS AND BASSARIDS. Praise Dionysus. He is here, his peace made.

> [PENTHEUS *appears to descend the tree: the scrim rises
> further, a tangle of foliage through which* PENTHEUS
> *can be faintly seen, walking towards the back. Absolute
> silence. We lose sight of him. The front of the stage is
> an archway of trees. Fire-fly light only.*]

MAENADS [*Woman's Chorus only*].
    Diony-
    -sus appear
    As a bull,
    As a snake,
    As a lion,
    Snorting fire:
    In the night
    Come to us,
    God of joy!
    Diony-
    -sus appear!
VOICE. Wait, wait, my loyal Maenads,
    Soon I shall, but tonight there lurks
    Within these woods a trespasser
    Come to spy on our rituals:
    Seek him out, hunt him down.
MAENADS. Hunt him down!
VOICE. Up, up, my keen-eyed hunters:
    Smell him, track him, in hot pursuit

Run, run to seize, to punish,
All imbued with a frenzy.
Do with him what you will.
MAENADS. What you will.

> [*The fire-fly lights go out. Within a moment the glade
> begins to be criss-crossed by the rapid darts of light
> from electric torches as they hunt for* PENTHEUS.]

Ay. Ay. Al. Y. A. . . . .
Hide! Hide!
We shall find you.
Fly! Fly!
We shall overtake you.
We are before you,
We are behind you
And on either side.
We are drawing nearer,
Nearer, nearer:
We are closing in for the kill.
Ay. Ay. Al. Y. A.

> [*One ray of light, recalling the light reflected from*
> AGAVE's *mirror, falls on* PENTHEUS *from above: in
> a moment all the torches are turned on him, and he
> stands in a pool of light, the circle of which narrows
> during the following.* PENTHEUS *stands near the
> front of the stage: his hand is held across his eyes, his
> dress is slipping down from one shoulder, his shawl
> and wreath have already been lost. The hand across
> his eyes still clutches the thyrsus. As the others sing, he
> slowly falls to his knees.*]

VOICE. Meet each other at last:
    See what you longed to see.
MAENADS. Son of the Lion,
    Beast of the wood,
    Behold yourself
    In the circle of light
    We have drawn about you.
    Stand. Stand.
    There is time. There is time.
    You cannot break out of the trap.
    Wait. Wait.

Till we stretch out our hands to take you.
We have met at last.

PENTHEUS [*slowly removing his hand from his eyes, gazes upward, dazed*].
I looked into eyes that were my own.
A full red mouth was rounded on my music.
It slavered like a bull's.
I was a faceless God
And worshipped Pentheus.

There stood my grief. It smiled at me.
My lips were shaped on: "*You shall be forgotten.*"
My front knees dropped. He whispered in my ear:
"*Am I not pure? Say no.*"

Biting my nape, he drove my flesh away.

> [*Tearing open his clothes at his chest, with a fully conscious cry of desperate grief.*]

No! No! This flesh is me!
MAENADS [*a prolonged whisper*]. No.
PENTHEUS [*each line softer than the one before*].
Mother, remember . . .
MAENADS [*each line louder than the one before*].
                    No.
PENTHEUS. Echion, my father.
MAENADS.   No.
PENTHEUS. You loved him . . .
MAENADS.   No!
PENTHEUS. And bore me . . .
MAENADS.   No!
PENTHEUS. And named me . . .
MAENADS.   No!
PENTHEUS [*a soft whisper*].
Pentheus . . .
MAENADS I [*a prolonged scream*].
            NO!
MAENADS II [*crescendo*]. Ayayalya. . . .
PENTHEUS. Ah!

> [*At this last, torches were turned upward, PENTHEUS hidden by backs: then darkness. The scrim rises: dense foliage on it.*]

MAENADS [*at first fortissimo, then rapidly dying away into distance*].
     Ayayalya!
     Glory to Dionysus who has blessed our hunting:
     In the glens of Kithairon we had the Mastery.
AGAVE'S VOICE. Tell, maidens: what was our quarry?
MAENADS. A lion-cub in the pride of his youth,
     A noble son of the King of beasts.
AGAVE'S VOICE. Tell, maidens: who was keenest-eyed?
MAENADS. Agave. . . .

> [*The scrim has continued rising until it is a transparency: the faint red of dawn: Courtyard of the Palace:* CADMUS *and* BEROE *as before.*]

CADMUS. Long and cold has been our night-watch
     In silent Thebes, her dark streets
     Full of fear. Yet I dread still more
     What sights and sounds this dawn may bring.
     Listen!
MAENADS [*very faintly at first, then steadily getting louder and nearer*].
     Ayayalya!
     Glory to Dionysus who has blessed our hunting:
     In the glens of Kithairon we had the Mastery.
AGAVE'S VOICE. Tell, maidens: what was our quarry?
MAENADS. A lion-cub in the pride of his youth,
     A noble son of the King of beasts.
CADMUS. With a song of joy they approach, bearing
     Their ill-tidings. O mocking God!
AGAVE'S VOICE. Tell, maidens: who was keenest-eyed?
MAENADS. Agave, daughter of Cadmus,
     Was the first to cry Havoc.
AGAVE'S VOICE. Tell, maidens: who was swiftest?
MAENADS. Agave, daughter of Cadmus,
     Brought the beast to bay.
TIRESIAS [*entering right very excitedly, dressed as at the trial: at a gabble*].
     Cadmus! Cadmus! Do you hear the music?
     How glad it is. Pentheus must
     Have repented, and Dionysus
     Pardoned us all. Blessed be his name:
     Let us go to greet them!
CADMUS [*shaking his head with sad contempt*].
     We can do nothing
     But stand here and await the worst.

AGAVE'S AND AUTONOE'S VOICES.
Not with a net,
Not with a snare
Was the prey taken,
But with our bare fingers.
MAENADS. Ayayalya!
AGAVE'S AND AUTONOE'S VOICES [*now very close*].
Not with an arrow,
Not with a spear
Was he brought low,
But with our bare hands.
MAENADS [*pouring on stage from the back*].
Ayayalya!

> [*The* BACCHANTS *come in immediately after them
> from the right and left. All the* MAENADS *are dressed
> exactly alike: black short skirts, red wool stockings,
> ballet slippers, blouses in a fawn-skin pattern, hair à
> la Brigitte Bardot, their brows wreathed with ivy. The*
> BACCHANTS *are also uniform: sandals, dirty dun-
> garees, sports-shirts in a fawn-skin pattern, long hair
> and beards. All the* BASSARIDS *carry a thyrsus. The
> young female* SLAVE *is among the* MAENADS, *her
> daughter still with her and dressed exactly like her; she
> still has her doll.*]

MAENADS. The God gave women the strength of Gods:
We tore the strong-sinewed one limb from limb.

Praise Agave, daughter of Cadmus,
For her great deeds in the glens of Kithairon.

> [*The ranks of the* MAENADS *at the rear break open:*
> AGAVE *and* AUTONOE *ascend into view. They are
> dressed as they were during the trial scene, except that
> their long hair is tangled with leaves and twigs, and
> their dresses are spattered with blood and in shreds.
> Both are in a state of extreme excitement:* AGAVE
> *holds* PENTHEUS'S *head in her arms.*]

AGAVE. Behold the head of the young wild lion,
The cub I hunted and have brought home!
CADMUS. I fared, but I did not fear enough.
Dionysus, born of my blood,
Has destroyed my House.

BEROE. Unaya! Unaya!
TIRESIAS. How ill it is to be blind on a day
    Of great events. Where is Pentheus?
    Tell me, Cadmus: be my eyes.
MAENADS. Ayayalya!

[CADMUS *descends the stairs and approaches* AGAVE
who has come downstage.]

AGAVE.   Smile, father.
    Can old age never smile? What is it?
    Where is the King? A young man
    Should not study too much. Would he
    But learn from me the joys of the chase,
    The blood would return to his pale cheeks
    And Pentheus learn to laugh. Where is he?
    I wish to see him.
CADMUS.   If the Gods listened
    To mortal prayers, your mind would remain
    Forever dark, but the Gods are without
    Pity.
BEROE. Unaya! Unaya!
TIRESIAS. What has happened? Where is Pentheus?
    Tell me, Cadmus: be my eyes.
MAENADS. Ayayalya!
AGAVE.   Why do you all stare so?
    Have I not done well?

[*Pause.*]

CADMUS.   Daughter,
    Listen to me and do what I say.
    Raise your eyes and look at the sky.

[*Pause.*]

    Does it look the same?
AGAVE.   No . . . it seems
    Brighter, clearer.
CADMUS.   And in yourself,
    Do you feel a change?
AGAVE.   A cloud
    Seems to be lifting. There is something
    I have forgotten but ought to remember.
    Help me, father.

CADMUS. Tell me, daughter:
To whom did I give you in marriage?
AGAVE. To Echion,
The Sown Man.
CADMUS. Did you bear him a son?
AGAVE. I did.
CADMUS. He was named?
AGAVE. Pentheus.
CADMUS. Daughter,
What is the head you hold in your arms?
AGAVE. A . . . A . . . A li . . . A lion's.
I heard them say a lion's.
CADMUS. Daughter,
Look at it now. You must. Look.
AGAVE. Ah!
CADMUS. Look!
AGAVE. No!
CADMUS. Look!
AGAVE. No! No!
CADMUS. Is it a lion's?
AGAVE [*stunned, instinctively holding the head closer to herself and trying to cover it with shreds of her dress, half to cover it, half to protect it*].
Pentheus! Dead! Who did this? Who
Placed his head in my arms?
CADMUS. Daughter,
Now we are come to the hour of truth.
You and your sister did this deed.
You slew your son.
AUTONOE [*hysterical*]. It wasn't me.
I didn't mean to. She made me do it.
She clawed him first.

> [AUTONOE *rushes away to hide herself in the anonymity of the* BASSARIDS, *but they turn their backs upon her abruptly and will not let her join them.*]

AGAVE. How? Where?
CADMUS. In Kithairon.
AGAVE. Kithairon? Why were we there?
What did we do?

> [CAPTAIN *with two* GUARDS *enter back with a covered bier containing the body of* PENTHEUS. *The*

BASSARIDS, *backs to them, break open to let the pro-*
cession pass. The bier is set down stage front.]

CADMUS [*during the above*].
                    What you did,
    Alas, you will have to see. Why,
    Ask Dionysus. Captain. . .
CAPTAIN [*very matter-of-fact*]. Sire,
    As you commanded, we searched Kithairon
    For King Pentheus: we found his body
    Torn to pieces, the limbs scattered
    Among the rocks and under the trees.
    What we were able to recover, we composed
    As decently as we could.
CADMUS.   Daughter,
    Go to your son: your guilt is no
    Greater than his.

                    [*He lifts the cover of the bier:* AGAVE *shudderingly*
                    nears it.]

                    Look upon him
    For the last time.
AGAVE.   No! No!
    Father, have mercy!
                    [*Pointing to* CAPTAIN.] Take his sword
    And slay me, slay me now!

                              [*She totters and seems about to fall.*]

CADMUS [*as he re-covers the bier*].
                    Beroe!
    Help the Queen.

                    [BEROE *catches* AGAVE *about the waist and gently*
                    leads her to the palace steps and helps her to sit down.
                    As AGAVE *leans back against the stairs,* BEROE *takes*
                    the head from her and, tenderly holding it to herself,
                    she goes and kneels at the bier.]

AGAVE [*repeatedly*].   Unaya! Unaya!

CADMUS. Night and again the night.
    The great House has fallen,
    Never to be rebuilt.
    I who raised these walls

Am brought down to the dust.
Night and again the night.
Accursed in my old age,
Alone, outcast, dishonored.
Night and again the night.
Cadmus of Thebes, whose daughter
Murdered her own child.
Night and again the night.

BEROE [*lifting the cover and placing the head with its body; then re-covering it*].
Night and again the night.
Unaya!
The Oldest One has forgotten,
The Mother is grown weak.
Night and again the night.
Unaya!
The master I loved is fallen,
The child of my breast is dead.
Night and again the night.
The Double Axe could not save him,
The Mother no longer rules.
Night and again the night.
Unaya!

AUTONOE. I didn't want to do it.
Agave made me do it.
She always was the stronger.
I didn't want to do it.
Agave made me do it
And now we both must suffer.
I didn't want to do it.
Agave made me do it.
She wouldn't listen to me.
Agave, I always told her,
Be careful what you say:
The Gods alone are holy,
And what they will, they do.

TIRESIAS. I grieve for this young man:
But Fate, though cruel, is just.
He who was deaf to my warning
Can now hear nothing at all.
I grieve for this young man.
He who mocked the prophet

Is now unable to speak.
I grieve for this young man.
He who pulled down my dwelling
Must dwell now in a grave.
I grieve for this young man
And his unhappy mother.
But Fate, though cruel, is just.
The Gods alone are holy,
And what they will, they do.

BASSARIDS. We were far away on the lonely mountain
Dancing in innocent joy
To the pure sound of the flute,
Singing of Dionysus,
Twice-born God of the vine.
We heard nothing. We saw nothing.
We took no part in her lawless frenzy,
We had no share in his bloody death.
We heard nothing. We saw nothing.
We were far away on the lonely mountain
Dancing in innocent joy.
We heard nothing. We saw nothing.
We took no part in her lawless frenzy,
We had no share in his bloody death.

[*During the ensemble,* AGAVE *has slowly recovered dignity sufficient to feel her grief rather than to simply be numb with it. Towards the close she rises and, still weeping, crosses over to the bier.* BEROE, *seeing her approach, rises and goes away.*]

AGAVE. At your bier-side, my dead son,
I will not speak of a mother's care
Or a son's love that were not there.
Without choice we are made one:
A bond binds us for all time,
For your death is my crime.

We dream that, we dream this,
Of fair faces, of high walls,
But the doom gathers, the curse falls,
And we see the world as the world is:
The grass withered where the sun shone,
The lake dry, the birds gone.

To cry "Forgive me!", to weep, son,
Would change nothing. You lie dead,
Beyond blame, beyond dread
Of words spoken, of deeds done.
We both did what neither would:
The strong Gods are not good.

Bear him hence and give him burial
As befits a King. I must remain
To receive judgement.

> [*The two* GUARDS *carry the bier off left during the
> first lines of the following: tune: Chorale in the Inter-
> mezzo.*]

BASSARIDS. O let my ways be lowly
And all vain thoughts eschew:
The Gods alone are holy,
And what they will, they . . .

> [*The music is cut off in the middle of a bar. Pause.
> Enter* DIONYSUS *right, dressed up to the nines in
> Beau Brummel fashion: elaborate cravate, monocle,
> lorgnette, etc., whistling and twirling his thyrsus like a
> cane. He crosses the stage and mounts Semele's tomb.
> Pause.*]

DIONYSUS. I see that you know who I am now,
Though still in the guise of a mortal,
People of the City of Seven
Gates. Yes, I am Semele's son and
Zeus'; I *am* Dionysus. Had all shown
Wisdom and acknowledged my Godhead,
Thebes would now be happy. But some failed.
They insulted my mother, they mocked me.
The result you can see with your own eyes,
Will remember as long as you live. Soon,
You shall see me revealed in my glory,
All save those polluted with blood.
                    [*Turning to* CADMUS.] You,
Cadmus, Autonoe, Agave,
I doom to perpetual exile.
You are banished from Thebes. You will go now,
Go each in a different direction.

Prepare, then, to part. You will not meet
Each other again. You will not see
Boeotia again.
CADMUS.   An Immortal
God ought to forgive, not be angry
Forever like ignorant   ⌈ men.
DIONYSUS [*cutting him short*]. ⌊   Captain!

      [CAPTAIN *steps forward and stands at attention.*]

Light torches there. [*He points to the altar flame.*]
     Set fire to the palace.
Raze it to the ground.

      [CAPTAIN *salutes. Followed by the returned* GUARDS,
      he and they take brands from behind the tomb, light
      them at the altar and quickly cross the stage to the
      palace, leaving the doors open on entry.]

CADMUS.   O may kind death
Come soon, put an end to my sorrow!
DIONYSUS. The grandson of Ares will not die:
He will pass in the end to the Blessed
Isles.
CADMUS. Islands accursed to me! All
May find peace beyond Acheron. Not I.
DIONYSUS. I have spoken. No longer delay. Go.
BASSARIDS [*secco*]. Go, unclean ones. Go.

      [CAPTAIN *and* GUARDS *re-enter from the palace; a*
      red glow can be seen through the open doors; smoke
      slowly be-fogs the scene during the following.]

BEROE [*going to* AGAVE'*s side*].
There was an unspoken hate between us.
A greater grief has consumed it. We are two
Women without hope. Let me go with you
For Pentheus' sake, the King you bore,
The King I loved.
BASSARIDS. Go, unclean ones. Go.
TIRESIAS [*going to* CADMUS' *side*].
     I am sorry, Cadmus.
Very sorry indeed, more sorry
Than I can say. Let me at least
See my old friend on his way, come with you
As far as the gate.

BASSARIDS. Go, unclean ones. Go.
CADMUS, AGAVE, AND AUTONOE.
    By stony ways through uncouth lands
    We must wander till the end,
    Beg our bread from strangers' hands,
    Take what shelter chance may send.
    But, let them whisper what they may,
    Noble was the House that fell.
    Ill though all must fare, I say
AGAVE AND AUTONOE. Father, sister, Thebes, farewell.
CADMUS. Daughters dear, and Thebes, farewell.
BASSARIDS. Go. Go.

> [CADMUS and TIRESIAS *exeunt right,* AUTONOE
> *left:* AGAVE *and* BEROE *are about to exit back, when*
> AGAVE *turns to* DIONYSUS.]

AGAVE. You have done your worst, Dionysus:
    Now I need fear you no more.
    In this hour of your triumph, I say this,
    Say it not only to you
    But to Zeus and all on Olympus:
    Think of the altarless Fates.
    Where is gelded Uranus? Or Chronos,
    Once an invincible God?
    Rape, torture and kill while you can: one
    Tartarus waits for you all.

> [*She faces him defiantly for a moment. He ignores her.*
> *Smoke and flame—played on the scrim—have almost*
> *obscured the stage. Exeunt* AGAVE *and* BEROE.
> *During the first verse of the following, only*
> DIONYSUS *can be seen, his face exultant in the fire-*
> *glow: then he too disappears. The scrim is a sheet of*
> *flame.*]

DIONYSUS. I came to Thebes
    To take vengeance;
    Vengeance taken,
    Now I go.
    Down slaves,
    Kneel and adore.

BASSARIDS. Hail, Dionysus,
    Man-smasher,

Tearer, devourer
Of raw flesh!
Our Lord, our God!
We kneel and adore.

VOICE. Persephone! Persephone!
Persephone, Queen
Of the sunless realm,
Hear me, hear me!
I, Dionysus,
Command you now:
In the name of my father
Zeus the Almighty
Unbar your gates,
Release the shade
Of my mother, Semele.
In the name of Zeus.
Unbar, unbar!

BASSARIDS I. Ah! Ah!
The face of the God
Revealed in his glory,
Too dazzling for mortals!
We cover our faces:
We kneel and adore.

BASSARIDS II. Ah! Ah!
The voice of the God
Revealed in his power,
Too holy for mortals!
We stop our ears:
We kneel and adore.

VOICE. Rise, mother,
Rise from the dead
And join your son!
Zeus the Almighty
Has raised us up
Among the Immortals
To dwell forever
In the courts of Heaven.
Rise, mother,
Semele no longer:
Thyone I name you,
Goddess on high!

BASSARIDS. Ah! Ah!
Incomprehensible
Mysteries, not
For mortals to know
We see not, we hear not:
We kneel and adore!

> [*The flames sink. The scrim rises. Hiding the amphi-theatre is a sky of dazzling Mediterranean blue. Of the palace, only a jagged blackened wall is left. Upon Semele's tomb sit two enormous primitive fertility idols of an African or South Seas type: fetish masks, etc. The male is daubed with red paint. The* GUARD, *visors down, stand about the base of the tomb; the* BASSARIDS, *some prostrate, some kneeling, in semi-circle about it. The* CHILD, *holding her doll, gazes up at the idols, fascinated.*]

BASSARIDS [*prolonged ad lib*]. Knee . . . . l. A . . . . . . do . . . . . re.

> [*Suddenly the* CHILD *rushes forward to the foot of the tomb, her doll reiterating its: "Mamma, mamma, mamma."*]

BASSARIDS. A . . . . do . . . . . re.

> [TIRESIAS *re-appears right. He is outlined clearly against the sky as he stretches out both hands towards the idols and sinks to his knees. Vines descend and sprout everywhere, wreathing the columns, covering the blackened wall. The* CHILD *smashes her doll at the foot of the tomb and jumps up and down with joy.*]

CURTAIN

Love's Labour's Lost

*Operatic Pastoral in
Three Acts after
William Shakespeare*

BY W. H. AUDEN AND
CHESTER KALLMAN
FOR THE MUSIC OF
NICOLAS NABOKOV

[*1969*]

Act I Scene 1

[A pavilion in the royal park. A fine spring morning. Seated on chairs, the KING, BEROWNE *and* DUMAINE. *At a writing-table to one side,* DON ARMADO. *Facing them,* MOTH *stands, singing.]*

ARIA

MOTH.
When daisies pied and violets blue,
  And lady-smocks all silver-white,
And cuckoo-buds of yellow hue
  Do paint the meadows with delight,
The cuckoo then on every tree
Mocks married men; for thus sings he,
          Cuckoo;
Cuckoo, cuckoo: O word of fear,
Unpleasing to a married ear!

When shepherds pipe on oaten straws
  And merry larks are ploughmen's clocks,
When turtles tread, and rooks, and daws,
  And maidens bleach their summer smocks,
The cuckoo then on every tree
Mocks married men; for thus sings he
          Cuckoo;
Cuckoo, cuckoo: O word of fear,
Unpleasing to a married ear!

[Applause. MOTH *bows.]*

KING. Well sung, Master Moth. *[Turning to* ARMADO.*]*
    Now, is the paper writ?
ARMADO. Here, Lord, your fair words as you spoke them,
    In letters fair as I could make them. *[Hands* KING *a scroll.]*

[Exeunt MOTH *and* ARMADO. *The others rise and come forward.]*

SOLO, *leading to* TRIO

KING.
Dumaine, Berowne, you both have sworn
  To study here with me,
To hold the busy world in scorn,
  And serve Philosophy:
All earthly pleasures we'll eschew,
  All vain delights exclude,

In contemplation of the True,
  The Beautiful, the Good.

If still prepared your vows to keep,
  Subscribe to this decree.
DUMAINE [*signing*]. I'm still prepared my vows to keep:
  I'll sign it willingly.
BEROWNE.   To see no ladies, to fast not sleep,
  Are vows too hard for me.

KING AND DUMAINE.
          You swore to that, Berowne, and to the rest.
BEROWNE.   By yea and nay, sirs, then I swore in jest.
          What is the end of study? Let me know.
KING.   To know what else we should not know.

ARIA

BEROWNE.   The solemn plodder learns to quote
          As gospel what another wrote,
          And many, long before they find
          Where light in darkness lies, go blind.
                  No delight is more vain
                  Than one purchased with pain.

          The clerks who charter Heaven's lights
          And give a name to every star,
          Have no more pleasure of their nights
          Than those who know not what they are.
                  No delight is more vain
                  Than one purchased with pain.

TRIO

KING. How well he's read to reason against reading.
DUMAINE. Proceeded well to stop all good proceeding.
BEROWNE. The Spring is near when green geese are a-breeding.
DUMAINE. How follows that?
BEROWNE.   Fit in its place and time.
DUMAINE. In reason nothing.
BEROWNE.   Something, then, in rhyme.

KING.   Well, sit you out, Berowne: adieu.
BEROWNE.   No, I have sworn to stay with you.
          To your decree I'll write my name.
          But, firstly, let me read the same.

[Takes Scroll from the KING *and reads it.]*

"For three years we ban
All women from court,
From our tongue and our thought,
And during that time
It shall be a crime
In Navarre for a man
To speak with a maid.
This we decree."
If this be so,
Then, I'm afraid,
My liege, you'll be
The first offender.
For well you know
The French King's daughter
Is hastening hither
About the surrender
Of Aquitaine
To her old father.
This law you must break
For courtesy's sake,
Or she comes in vain.

KING. What say you, Lords, but this was quite forgot.
BEROWNE. So study evermore is overshot.
KING AND DUMAINE. We must of force dispense with this decree.
　　She must lie here on mere necessity.
BEROWNE. If I break faith, this word shall speak for me.
　　I am forsworn on mere necessity.
　　[Signing.] Yet I, although I seem so loth,
　　May be the last to keep his oath.

　　　　　　　　　　　　　　　　[Enter BOYET.]

BOYET. Her Highness, Daughter of the King of France
　　Craves audience of Your Grace.

　　　　　　　　　[Fanfare. Enter PRINCESS, ROSALINE *and* KATH-
　　　　　　　　　ERINE.]

KING. Fair Princess, welcome to our court.
PRINCESS. What welcome? I see none.
KING. Dear Lady—I have sworn an oath.
PRINCESS. We had been told
　　You shun our company

For study's sake,
And this is true, I see.
'Twere sinful both
To keep or break that oath.
But pardon me;
I am too bold. [*Hands* KING *a paper.*]
Read this to learn the purpose of our visitation
And give my suit your fair consideration.
KING. Madam, I will do all I may.
Take some refreshment, now, I pray,
While I peruse it.

> [KING *retires back-stage. The* LADIES *seat themselves.*
> SERVANTS *hand round refreshments.* BEROWNE *and*
> DUMAINE *approach* BOYET.]

BEROWNE. What's her name in the cap?
BOYET. Rosaline, by good hap.
BEROWNE. Is she wedded or no?
BOYET. To her will, sir, or so.
BEROWNE [*bowing*]. You are welcome, sir: adieu.
BOYET [*bowing*]. Farewell to me, sir, and welcome to you.

> [BEROWNE *goes to* ROSALINE's *side.*]

DUMAINE. Sir, I pray you: what lady is that same?
BOYET. The heir of Alençon, Katherine her name.
DUMAINE [*bowing*]. A gallant lady, Monsieur: fare you well.

> [DUMAINE *goes to* KATHERINE's *side.*]

BEROWNE. Did I not dance with you in Brabant once?
ROSALINE. Did I not dance with you in Brabant once?
BEROWNE. I know you did.
ROSALINE. How needless, then, to ask the question.
BEROWNE. Your wit's too hot. It speeds too fast. 'Twill tire.
ROSALINE. Not till it leaves the rider in the mire.
BOYET [*aside*]. You are well-matched, my merry lords:
Our wenches' tongues are sharp as swords.
DUMAINE. Lady, I commend you to my heart:
I would you heard it groan.
KATHERINE. Is the fool sick?
DUMAINE. Sick at the heart.
KATHERINE. Alack, let it blood.
DUMAINE. Would that do it good?

KATHERINE. My physic says aye.
DUMAINE. Will you prick my heart with your eye?
KATHERINE. No, with my knife.
DUMAINE. Now God save thy life.
KATHERINE. And yours from long living.
DUMAINE. I cannot stay thanksgiving. [*Bows and rejoins* BOYET.]
BEROWNE. What time of day?
ROSALINE. The hour that fools should ask.
BEROWNE. Now fair befall your mask.
ROSALINE. Fair fall the face it covers.
BEROWNE. And send you many lovers.
ROSALINE. Amen, so you be none.
BEROWNE. Nay, then, I will be gone. [*Bows and rejoins* BOYET.]

[*The* KING *comes forward.*]

SPOKEN. AGAINST MUSIC?

KING. Madam, your father here doth intimate
    The payment of a hundred thousand crowns
    Disbursèd by my father in his wars.
    I do protest I never heard of it;
    But, if you prove it, I will pay it back,
    Or yield up Aquitaine.
PRINCESS.   We arrest your word.
    Boyet, you can produce acquittances.
BOYET. So please Your Grace, the packet is not come.
    To-morrow you shall have a sight of them.

[*Singing resumes.*]

KING. Till to-morrow, then,
    At which interview
    All that is just
    I will grant to you.
    O fair Princess,
    Although you must
    Be lodged apart,
    You shall find no less
    A welcome there
    Than if you were
    Lodged in my heart.
    May you well-satisfied go hence.
    We will escort you to your tents.

TUTTI. May sweet content consort with you,
    And every wish you will come true:

Fair weather bless $\begin{Bmatrix} \text{your} \\ \text{our} \end{Bmatrix}$ sojourn here,

Mirth attend us and good cheer.

                                    [*Exeunt.*]

CURTAIN

Act I Scene 2

[*Garden with little summer-house: rustic table and chairs. Books, papers, etc.* ARMADO *and* MOTH.]

ARIA

ARMADO.   Love is a devil:
                            There is no evil
                            Angel but Love.
                            But Cupid's arrow
                            Is too much odds
                            For a Spaniard's rapier.
                            Passados he respects not,
                            Duellos he regards not,
                            His disgrace it is
                            To be called boy,
                            His glory it is
                            To subdue men.
                            Adieu, valor,
                            Rust, rapier,
                            Be still, drum,
                            For your manager,
                            Armado, is in love.

                      [ARMADO *looks up and sights* JAQUENETTA *approaching.*]

Protect me, Love! Sweet boy, retire!

                      [MOTH *goes behind a wall of the summer-house, from which he can look out.*]

O lend me trumpets, oboes, drums
To wing my dictions of desire
Into her heart. She comes! She comes! [*Steps back.*]

[*Enter* JAQUENETTA, *carrying a basket of linen.*]

JAQUENETTA.   If it be my doom to die
                    Still a maid, good-bye, good-bye;
                    Light a candle, heave a sigh—
                    No more, no more,
                    No more would I a maid be.

[ARMADO *steps forward.*]

ARMADO. Stay! Stay! Bright essence of obscurity:
   O humbly bred, humiliate the high!

                    For e'en as King Cophetua,
                    By base-born beauty flayed,
                    Raised her his heart obeyed,
                    So you by love may get you a
                    New station *in perpetua*,
                    O wounding beggar-maid!

JAQUENETTA.   You make me quite afraid, sir
                    My head is in a whirl, sir.
                    But I'm *not* a beggar-maid, sir,
                    I'm an honest serving-girl, sir.
                    So have a care!

ARMADO [*aside*].   Despair! Despair!
MOTH [*aside*].   O cru-el fair!

JAQUENETTA.   I cannot pass the day with you,
                    The ladies wait, you know,
                    For me to wash and sew.
                    I'm not a girl to play with, you
                    Had better keep away; with you
                    Life's idle. I must go!

ARMADO. Deny me not your glance . . .
JAQUENETTA.   Sir?
ARMADO. My heart is on its knee . . .
JAQUENETTA.   Sir?
ARMADO. To implore a gracious answer.

JAQUENETTA. But just how can that be, sir?
    Heart on its *knee?*
    Now I can see
    You mock at me!
ARMADO [*aside*]. O mockery!
    O scholarly
    Humility!
MOTH [*aside*]. Flee not thy flea,
    Be my Queen-Bee,
    Sheba-like She!

> [JAQUENETTA *abruptly picks up her basket and exits,*
> *singing jauntily.*]

JAQUENETTA.   I am heart-sick, heaven send
                    Me a true and loving friend,
                    Who will give my woes an end . . .
                    No more, no more,
                    No more would I a maid be.

> [ARMADO *signals to* MOTH, *who puts the objects*
> *requested on the table which he sets in front of*
> ARMADO.]

ARMADO. Quill. Paper. Ink. The love she could not hear
    May enter through the eye.
    Though love forswears me who forswore
    My oath to forswear love. I die!
    My heart was at her feet; she trod,
    O heartless maid, upon it!
    Assist me, some extemporal god
    Of Rhyme, for I am sure
    I shall turn sonnet.
    Devise wit, write pen, for I
    Am for whole volumes in folio!
MOTH [*aside*]. Here begins an imbroglio!

> [*Deep in thought,* ARMADO *makes several passes in*
> *the air with his quill, but always stops just short of*
> *putting it to the paper.*]

ARMADO. Poor wit! No phrase rings sublimely enough,
    No Spanish, Latin, English, Greek or French.
    Sing, boy: my spirit grows heavy with love.

MOTH [*aside*]. And that's a great marvel, loving a light wench,
　　Past conjuring or disappearing.
ARMADO. Warble, child,
　　Make passionate my sense of hearing.

ARIA

MOTH.　　　　　　　　　　*No more!* Heart-sick,
　　　　　　　　　　　　　No more!
　　　　　　　　　　You may not cry:
　　　　　　　　　More must be borne, and you
　　　　　　　　　　　　　Not die.
　　　　　　　　　More loves will be untrue,
　　　　　　　　　　Friends go before
　　　　　　　　Into the dark, and you must yet
　　　　　　Harbor light on a pinch of candle-wick
　　　　　　　　Years, years, and not forget
　　　　　　　　　　Each Good-Bye.

　　　　　　　　　[*During the aria,* ARMADO *has been scribbling furi-
　　　　　　　　　ously. Now he rolls up and ties his red scroll with a
　　　　　　　　　ribbon. He looks up.*]

ARMADO. Berowne! O shame, should he divine!

　　　　　　　　　[*Gives scroll to* MOTH, *and makes him hide it at once
　　　　　　　　　under his cloak.*]

　　Take this to her,
　　Dan Cupid, fly!
　　Alacrity
　　And secrecy!

　　　　　　　　　[*Enter* BEROWNE. ARMADO, *fearing that he may
　　　　　　　　　have seen him giving* MOTH *the scroll, picks up a
　　　　　　　　　large book from the table and hands it to* MOTH.]

　　Study your Latin. There's a good child!

　　　　　　　　　[*Exit* ARMADO *hurriedly.* BEROWNE *has hardly no-
　　　　　　　　　ticed him.* MOTH *starts to leave.* BEROWNE *suddenly
　　　　　　　　　looks up.*]

BEROWNE. Stay for a moment. There's a good child!

　　　　　　　　　[*He gives* MOTH *a green scroll and a large coin.*]

You know my Lady Rosaline?
Takes this to her,
Dan Cupid, fly!
Alacrity
And secrecy!

ARIA

MOTH [*aside*]. Too witless are they so to woo,
                Their vow so to belie,
                To hunt in hiding, to pursue
                What honor should deny:
                Who cheat for love will hear *Cuckoo!*
                Once they have won it. Fie!
                I know what men and women do,
                But can't imagine why.
                      To-whit! Tu-whoo!
                      Cuckoo! Cuckoo!
                      Good-Bye! Good-Bye! Good-Bye! [*Exit.*]

> [*During the aria,* BEROWNE *roves restlessly about, occasionally striking his forehead, and crying out to himself disjointed words, which echo words from* MOTH'*s aria.*]

BEROWNE. . . . witless . . . my vow . . . my honor . . .
    Love! . . . Fie! . . . Women! . . . Women!! . . .

> [*Seeing that* MOTH *is still there, he motions impatiently to him to depart. The last part of* MOTH'*s "Good-Bye" refrain is addressed to* BEROWNE.]

ARIA

          I in love!
          Fie! Fie!
          I who ever
          Mocked and flouted
          The wingèd boy,
          That wimpled-whining,
          Senior-junior,
          Giant-dwarf,
          Dan Cupid,
          Regent of love-rhymes,
          Liege of loiterers,

Prince of malcontents
And folded arms.
I to serve him!
I be his corporal!
I wear his colors
Like a tumbler's hoop!
Fie! Fie!

I to be perjured!
I forsworn!
For what? For what?
A whitely wanton
With a velvet brow,
And two pitch-balls
Stuck in her face
To serve as eyes.
I to sigh for her!
I to watch for her!
I to pray for her!
Fie! Fie!
It is a curse.
Yet I will love,
Yet I will sue,
Yet I will groan:
Some love my Lady
And some Joan.

CURTAIN

Act I Scene 3

[*Tents in the park.* PRINCESS, ROSALINE, KATHERINE *and* BOYET, *all dressed to go hunting.*]

PRINCESS. In so far as so brief an acquaintance affords
    An opinion, what do you think of our lords?
KATHERINE. Dumaine, I deem, in truth
    A well-accomplished youth;
    Graceful his walk,
    Courteous his talk,
    And how, how
    Noble his brow!

ROSALINE. Berowne has keener wit.
    A merrier man I never met.
    And yet . . . and yet . . .
    He fills me with fear.
PRINCESS. With fear? Why so?

ARIA

ROSALINE.   Well, O well his kind I know,
                   Well endowed with every grace,
                   Ready wit and handsome face,
                        Who, where'er they go,
                   Can expect to be admired,
                   And their company desired:
                        Life a play,
                   Where they always get their way.

                   True, at first they mean no harm,
                   Gladden all they move among,
                   True, so long as they are young,
                      Charmed by those they charm.
                   Ah! but easy charmers tend
                   To grow cruel in the end,
                      Turn when old
                   Lecherous, treacherous and cold.

PRINCESS. God bless you, ladies! Are you both in love?
BOYET. If so, you will have no occasion for sighs,
    For if my observation which, I think, seldom lies
    Deceive me not now, all three are infected.
KATHERINE. With what?
BOYET. With that which we lovers entitle affected.
ROSALINE. Your reason?

ARIA

BOYET.   Why, all their behaviours did make their retire
          To the court of their eyes, peeping thorough desire:
          Their tongues, all impatient to speak and not see,
          Did stumble with haste in their eyesight to be;
          All senses to that sense did make their repair,
          To feel only looking on fairest of fair.

PRINCESS. You are an old love-monger, who loves to surprise.
BOYET. I have only fashioned mouths of their eyes
    By adding a tongue which I know never lies.

[*Enter* MOTH *with a red scroll.*]

MOTH. God save Your Grace!

PRINCESS. What is it, boy?

MOTH. I have a letter from Monsieur Berowne
    To one Lady Rosaline.

BOYET. What did I tell you? Now you must own
    How just were those observations of mine.

ROSALINE. A surprise, but a pleasing surprise, I must own!

KATHERINE. I wish there was also a letter for me!

PRINCESS. Monsieur Berowne is a good friend of mine.
    Take it, Boyet. We will see what we see.

[MOTH *hands scroll to* BOYET.]

BOYET. This letter is mistook, it is meant for none here;
    It is writ to Jaquenetta.

PRINCESS.   We will read it, I swear.
    Break the neck of the wax. Now, ladies, give ear.

BOYET [*reading*]. By heaven, that thou art fair, is most infallible; true, that
    thou art beauteous; truth itself, that thou art lovely. More fairer than
    fair, beautiful than beauteous, truer than truth itself, have commiser-
    ation on thy heroical vassal! Thus, expecting thy reply, I profane my
    lips on thy foot, my eyes on thy picture, and my heart on thy every
    part. Thine, in the dearest design of industry, Don Adriano de
    Armado.

PRINCESS. What plume of feathers indited this letter?

KATHERINE. What weather-cock? Did you ever hear better?

ROSALINE [*aside*]. Is there another letter astray?
    Reason says No, but Heart says Yea.

PRINCESS [*to* MOTH]. Who gave you this letter?

MOTH.   I told you: my lord.

PRINCESS. To whom should you give it?

MOTH.   From my lord to my lady.

PRINCESS. From which lord to which lady?

MOTH. From my Lord Berowne, a good master of mine,
    To a lady of France that he called Rosaline.

PRINCESS. Cannot you read, boy?

ARIETTA

MOTH.   Of age too tender
                    To read, my part
                    Is played by heart;
                    To learning, to art,

> And matters of such kind,
> I am still blind.

PRINCESS. Boy, I see mischief in your eye.
　　What have you done? We shall see by-and-by.
BOYET. Sooner, perhaps than you think: for soon,
　　Ladies, I think, the lords will be here
　　To join with us in hunting the deer.
PRINCESS. I don't believe it!
KATHERINE.　　　　　　　　Impossible!
BOYET. Wait, then, and see. I'll wager they will.
　　And each, I say, will be hunting his dear,
　　As the stags go trotting after their does.
PRINCESS. You are teasing, Boyet: come, bring us our bows.
KATHERINE. If our suitors arrive and if suitors they be,
　　Hoping to shoot us: shall we stand, shall we flee?
ROSALINE. There's an old rhyme to fit: we will rhyme, three to three.

ROUND

PRINCESS, ROSALINE, KATHERINE, AND, TOWARDS THE END, BOYET.
> You cannot hit it, hit it, hit it,
> You cannot hit it, my good man.
> No, you cannot, cannot, cannot,
> But maybe another can.

　　　　　　　　　　　　　　　　[*Sound of horns.*]

BOYET. Horns! Do you hear?
　　I said they'd be here.

　　　　　　　[*Enter* KING, BEROWNE *and* DUMAINE *in hunting
　　　　　　　dress.*]

KING. The hunt is up! Fair Madam, rise!
PRINCESS. You lay your books down? Is that wise? ⎤
DUMAINE. The hunt is up! Fair lady, rise!　　　　⎦
KATHERINE. And the pursuit of learning dies.
KING AND DUMAINE. We aim at wisdom as it flies. ⎤
BEROWNE. The hunt is up! Dear lady, rise!　　　　⎦
　　One word.
ROSALINE.　　One word?
BOYET [*aside*].　　　　　About her eyes.
PRINCESS AND KATHERINE. With ladies.
KING AND DUMAINE.　　　　　　　　Fair . . .
PRINCESS AND KATHERINE.　　　　　　　　　A fair surprise! ⎦

BEROWNE. Did you receive . . .
ROSALINE. A scroll?
BEROWNE.   A scroll.
ROSALINE. I can't believe
   Such prankish droll
   Coxcombery,
   Pretending love,
   Was meant for me.

BOYET [*aside*]. Behind the weave
   Of folderol,
   Adam finds Eve
   And plays his role,
   Though gallantry
   Conceal the love
   That's clear to me.

KING AND DUMAINE. When springtime fair
   So moved the air
   With *Nonny, Nonny No,*
   Our diligence
   Lost every sense
   To *Trolilo Trololilo!*

PRINCESS AND KATHERINE. We thought you came
   In friendship's name
   But now you tell us *No!*
   We would not be
   Mere company
   To *Trolilo Trololilo!*

[*They turn their backs to* KING *and* DUMAINE.]

BEROWNE [*aside*].
   Can it be? Yes, it can. You have earned it,
   Berowne, by your playing the fool!
   You have held out your hand and have burned it.
   Ah! The lesson was hard. Have you learned it?
   Then go back, loving blockhead, to school.

ROSALINE [*aside*].
   Can it be? Yes, it can. I suspected
   Berowne had been straying from school.
   He has written me, as I expected.
   Let him think he is harshly rejected:
   Let the scourge of all fools play the fool.

KING AND DUMAINE [*aside*].
> How and why? That was hardly expected.
> Have I broken a heart or a rule?
> Has my unspoken love been suspected
> And, before I declare it, rejected?
> Can it be? Yes. And I play the fool!

PRINCESS AND KATHERINE [*aside*].
> They are shocked and amazed. They have earned it:
> If the tomes they would ponder at school
> Teach no gallantry, now they have learned it.
> As they gave us Good Day we returned it . . .
> Play lightly, but do *not* play the fool.

MOTH AND BOYET [*aside*].
> Agitation unexpected
> Blurs the surface of the pool.
> What has churned it? What has turned it
> From an aspect clear and cool.
>
> Tropic winds have roughed and burned it;
> And, below, a thrashing school
> Of neglected, half-suspected,
> Fierce emotions play the fool.

[*Pause.*]

KING. Construe my speeches better if you may.
BEROWNE [*aside*]. Farewell, my mad-cap care-free month of May!
PRINCESS. Gracious, we hear them on a gracious day.
> Your hand!
KING.   Sweet Madam.
PRINCESS.   Lead the way.
ROSALINE [*aside*]. What manly melancholy airs!
> He even plays at his despairs.
BEROWNE [*aside*]. Farewell, my brief and flowering holiday!

[*They start, in canon, the Hunting Song, in the following order:* KING, PRINCESS, DUMAINE, KATHERINE, BOYET. BEROWNE, *still distracted, at first sings instead:*]

BEROWNE.   The time is up, the time is up,
> Unmercifully the time is up.

[*He turns and sees* ROSALINE *holding out her hand to him. A moment's pause. She picks up the song from the others and then he, too, joins in.*]

TUTTI

The hunt is up, the hunt is up!*
Sing merrily we, the hunt is up.

    The birds they sing,
    The deer they fling;
        Hey nonny, nonny no!
    The hounds they cry;
    The hunters they fly.
        Hey trolilo, trololilo.

    The wood resounds
    To hear the hounds,
        Hey nonny, nonny no!
    The rocks report
    This merry sport.
        Hey trolilo, trololilo.

    Then hie apace
    Upon the chase.
        Hey nonny, nonny no!
    Whilst everything
    Doth sweetly sing
        Hey trolilo, trololilo.

The hunt is up, the hunt is up!
Sing merrily we, the hunt is up!

A CRY [*offstage*]. Halloo! Halloo!

    [*All turn their backs to the audience and stretch their bows.* MOTH *throws aside his cloak and reveals that he, too, is in hunting costume. With his bow he mimics shooting at the backs of them all, then turns and kneels on one knee.*]

CURTAIN

*The authorship of this hunting song is unknown. First printed in Thomas Ravenscroft's *A Briefe Discourse* (1614) and first set by John Bennet.

Act II Scene 1

[*A clearing in the park. Enter* BEROWNE *in a state of agitation.*]

ARIOSO

BEROWNE.   This love is as mad as Ajax.
                 It kills sheep: it kills me.
                 Ergo: I am a sheep.
                 Who but a sheep would make eyes
                 At one who scorns his love?
                 The fool wrote her the rhyme,
                 The boy brought her the rhyme,
                 She made mock of the rhyme
                 And sport of the fool.
                 O, but her eyes!
                 But for her eyes
                 I would not love her.
                 But by those eyes
                 And Heaven I do!
                 I do! I do!
                 O Rosaline, sweet cruelty!
                 Have mercy on thy votary!

KING [*off*]. Ah me!
BEROWNE [*moving aside*].
               The King. And with paper and pen!
KING [*entering*].
   Ah me!
BEROWNE. Shot, by Heaven! If he sighs again . . . [*Hides in tree.*]
KING. Ah me!
BEROWNE.   The secret is out, my fellow in crime.
KING. How shall I tell her of my love?
BEROWNE.   Not in rhyme.
KING [*composing verses*].
    O sweet Princess! No . . . no . . .
    O Queen of Queens . . . How high . . .
    No . . . *How far thou dost excel . . .*
BEROWNE. Another rhymester. So!
    Another traitor.   Fie!
    Another victim.   Well!
KING [*still writing*].
    Nor thought can think
    Nor tongue of mortal tell.

How to send her my song!
I'll drop it . . . Who appears?
Watch, eyes, and listen ears.   [*Hides in a tree. Enter*
BEROWNE. We try, dear God, we try!   DUMAINE.]

    Celestial as thou art,
    O, pardon, love, this wrong
    That praises Heaven
    In such an earthly tongue.
DUMAINE. Ah me! Queen of Heaven,
    Venus, thou art too strong!
KING. Dumaine! Hand upon heart!
BEROWNE. Ah me!
DUMAINE.   Ah me!
BEROWNE.   Dumaine!
KING. In love, I hope. Sweet fellowship in shame.
BEROWNE. One drunkard loves another of the name.
DUMAINE. O Katherine . . .
    O Kate . . . O most divine . . .
    O that I had my wish.
KING. And I had mine . . .
DUMAINE. Ah me!
BEROWNE.   Amen
    To that, so I had mine.
KING [*reading from his scroll*].
    So sweet a kiss the Golden Sun gives not
    To those fresh morning drops upon the rose,
    As thy eye beams when their fresh rays have smote
    The night of dew that on my cheeks down flows.
    Nor shines the silver Moon one half so bright
    Through the transparent bosom of the deep
    As doth thy face through tears of mine give light!
    Thou shinest in each tear that I do weep,
    No drop, but as a coach doth carry thee:
    So ridest thou triumphing in my woe.
    Do but behold the tears that swell in me
    And they thy glory through my grief will show:
    But do not love thyself, then thou wilt keep
    My tears for glasses, and still make me weep.
    O Queen of Queens, how far thou dost excel,
    No thought can think, nor tongue of mortal tell.
DUMAINE. Am I the first that have been perjured so?

BEROWNE. I could put thee in comfort—
    Not by two that I know.
DUMAINE. Would that Berowne and King were lovers too.
    When all are false, then who can say—"Untrue!"?
    [*Reads from his scroll.*]
        Do not call it sin in me
        That I am forsworn for thee,
        Thou for whom great Jove would swear
        Juno but an Ethiop were.
BEROWNE. This is the liver vein, which makes flesh a deity,
    A green goose, a goddess, pure idolatry.
    God amend us, God amend us.
    We are much out of the way.
DUMAINE. By whom shall I send this?
    Company? Stay . . . [*Hides in tree.*]

                [*Enter* ARMADO *and* MOTH.]

BEROWNE. All hid, all hid, an old infant play.
    Like a demi-god sit I in the sky
    And wretched fools' secrets heedfully o'er-eye.
ARMADO. Ah me, the very grove
    Seems melodious with love.
BEROWNE. More sacks to the mill.
    O heavens, I have my wish—
    All are transformed:
    Four woodcocks in a dish.
DUMAINE. Our Spaniard looks distraught.
KING. I'll wager he is caught.
ARMADO. Sweet Dan Cupid, ingenious boy,
    Did you give her the letter?
MOTH. Which letter?
ARMADO.   My letter.
MOTH. Which her?
ARMADO.   Jaquenetta.
MOTH. I was given a letter,
    I bore a letter,
    I delivered a letter.
ARMADO. When she had read it, what did she say?
KING AND DUMAINE. When she has read it, what will she say?
BEROWNE. Could she have read it? O my dismay!
MOTH. I cannot say.

ARMADO. Torture me not with your mischief!
    Mock not my grief!
    Did she read it?
MOTH. Patience, patience, Master: she had no time.
    I tell you the truth and you call it a crime.

          [He comes forward, sits under a tree and opens a book.]

THE OTHERS [*a capella*].
        To know that she said No
        Would cause less woe.
        O cruel fate—
        In agonies of doubt to wait,
        To make my moan
        To my own self alone,
        To indulge the flame I cannot quench.
KING.   O Goddess . . .
ARMADO.   Goddess . . .
DUMAINE.   Goddess . . .
BEROWNE.   Wench!

               QUINTET

KING.   The silver moon shines not one half so bright
        Through the transparent bosom of the deep,
        As doth thy face through tears of mine give light;
        Thou shinest in each tear that I do weep.

BEROWNE. Ah, never faith could hold, if not to beauty vowed!
        Though to myself forsworn, to thee I'll faithful prove.
        Celestial as thou art, O pardon, love, this wrong,
        That sings heaven's praise with such an earthly tongue.

DUMAINE.   Do not call it sin in me
        That I am forsworn for thee;
        Thou for whom great Jove would swear
        Juno but an Ethiop were;
        And deny himself for Jove,
        Turning mortal for thy love.

ARMADO. Shall I command thy love? I may. Shall I enforce thy love? I
    could. Shall I entreat thy love? I will. What shalt thou exchange for
    rags? Robes? For thyself? Me.

MOTH [*ad lib, occasionally hesitating and consulting his book*].
     Amo
     Amas
     Amat
     Amamus
     Amatis
     Amant.

> [DUMAINE *steps down from his tree and addresses* ARMADO.]

DUMAINE. I arraign you for High Treason
     Against the King's decree
     That in his court should be
     No dalliance with womenkind
     Lest Passion should subvert the Mind
     To plot against Pure Reason.

> [KING *steps down and addresses* DUMAINE.]

KING. Your case is also such,
     Who have offended twice as much.
     I heard your rhymes, observed your passion,
     And noted well your fashion.

> [BEROWNE *steps down and addresses the* KING.]

BEROWNE. What grace have you thus to reprove
     Who are the most in love?
     O with what patience have I sat
     To see a king become a gnat.
KING. Were we betrayed, then, to your view?
BEROWNE. 'Tis I who was betrayed by you.
     I that am honest, hold it sin
     To break what I'm engaged in.
     When shall you hear that I
     Will praise a hand, a foot, an eye?

> [JAQUENETTA, *carrying a blue scroll, rushes in and flings herself at the* KING'S *feet.*]

JAQUENETTA. O Sire, believe an innocent soul!
     As I was ironing, Moth brought me this scroll.
     I can't understand why he brought it to me.
     I cannot read, Sire, but I could see
     From the shape of the lines that it must be in rhyme,
     And verses are always, I know, about love.

O Sire, Sire, I'm so frightened because
I heard it proclaimed that love is a crime.
O Sire, I swear by the heavens above
I've done nothing, nothing, have broken no laws.
I have brought it as soon as I possibly could.
O Sire, I swear I have always been good.

> [KING *takes the scroll and opens it.* BEROWNE *sees that it is his,* ARMADO *that it is not his.*]

KING. Have no fear, Jaquenetta.
   What you have done
   Is well. But now leave us.
BEROWNE [*aside*]. I can't believe it. It's my letter.
   Cockscombery, said Rosaline.
   Well, at least it was not mine.
ARMADO [*furiously to* MOTH]. You treacherous deceiver!
BEROWNE [*with amusement to* MOTH]. You little rogue!
   Don't you see what you've done?

MOTH.   Of age too tender
                  To read, my part
                  Is played by heart;
                  To learning, to art
                  And matters of such kind
                  I am still blind.

KING [*reading letter aloud*].
   If love make me forsworn, how shall I swear to love?
   Ah, never faith could hold, if not to beauty vowed . . .
   But this is written in your hand, Berowne.

> [BEROWNE *snatches the scroll away and tries to tear it up.*]

BEROWNE. A mere literary exercise, my liege.
   An imitation of Petrarch.
   I can't imagine how the wench obtained it.
ARMADO [*in a whisper to* MOTH].
   Where is my scroll, you wicked Machiavel?

> [MOTH *produces it. The* KING *snatches the scroll back from* BEROWNE.]

KING. Now, on your honor, is that true?
BEROWNE. Guilty, my lords, guilty. I confess. I confess.
KING. What?

BEROWNE. That three fools lacked one fool to make up the mess.
KING. So we are four, and all in love.
BEROWNE. And thereby all untrue.
DUMAINE AND ARMADO. What follows? What are we to do?

ROUND

KING, BEROWNE, DUMAINE AND ARMADO [*capering with hands on hearts*].
      By one soft glance we were undone,
      And have undone our binding vow.
      We blush to feel no shame. What plan
      Could best advance our folly now?

          [*During the Round* BOYET *enters unnoticed and, seeing them behaving so oddly, quickly hides behind a tree.*]

KING. I have a plan. Come close. I'll whisper it.
    This wood has ears as we know all too well.

SCHERZO: INSTRUMENTAL QUINTET

          [*All but* MOTH *huddle together. The Instruments portray the animated character of the words we cannot hear. As* BOYET *leans out from his hiding-place to listen, the fifth instrument (bass-tuba?) underlines the others rather clumsily on sustained notes. When the scherzo is over,* KING, BEROWNE, DUMAINE *and* ARMADO *give their scrolls and favors to* MOTH.]

BEROWNE. The whole truth's known, sweet liar, thanks to you.
    But this time let the road you take lie true.
ARMADO. I'll see to that.
    No tricks this time, Master Robin Goodfellow. Adieu.
MOTH. Tu-whit! Tu-whoo!

          [*Exeunt* ARMADO *and* MOTH.]

KING. Now use your wits, Berowne, to prove
    It lawful in Navarre to love.

SOLO *leading to* TRIO

BEROWNE.   Learning, my lords, requires a ground
         Excellence its cause and base.
         Where, my lords, can these be found
         But in a woman's face.

□

> Let no poet write whose ink
> Is untempered by love's sighs:
> Let no scholar dare to think.
> Cold to love's ecstasies.

KING, BEROWNE AND DUMAINE.

> Love the lowest sound can hear,
> Love's attention never fails:
> Love's touch is finer, tenderer,
> Finer, tenderer, softer, more sensible
> Than are the horns of snails,
> The horns of cockled snails.

> Love's voice can tame the savage brute,
> His tongue more musical, more fair,
> More moving than Apollo's lute,
> More moving, ravishing, delectable than Apollo's lute,
> Strung with his golden hair,
> Immortal golden hair.

> Where, then, the Truth that we require?
> Where shall we study to be wise?
> Where is the right Promethean fire,
> The life-giving, thought-inspiring, right Promethean fire?
> Where? Where? Where?
> Where but in women's eyes?

> Where lie the answers to our dreams?
> Where the Eternal Verities?
> Where are the books, the academes,
> That teach, that show, that contain, that nourish the whole
>   world?
> Where? Where? Where?

BEROWNE. Yes, where, my lords?

TUTTI. In women's eyes!

> > > > > > > *[Exeunt, with arms linked, singing.]*

> Tra-la-la! Tra-la-la!

> > > > > *[As this fades out in the distance,* BOYET *steps out rubbing his hands.]*

BOYET. Aha!

CURTAIN

Act II Scene 2

[*The ladies' tents. Seated* PRINCESS, ROSALINE *and* KATHERINE *with their scrolls. To one side, standing,* JAQUENETTA, *peering suspiciously at hers.*]

PRINCESS. Look what I have from the King!
    This diamond chain!
KATHERINE. These gloves were sent me from Dumaine.
ROSALINE. These pearls were Berowne's offering.
PRINCESS. But something else came with them?
ROSALINE.   Yes.
PRINCESS. Don't tell us. We can guess.
    We all have had them. Rhymes!
KATHERINE. Rhymes!

                                      [*They unroll their scrolls.*]

PRINCESS, ROSALINE AND KATHERINE.
    Rhymes! Rhymes!
    Wretched rhymes,
    Exclaiming their woe
    With O after O:
    Each of them hopes
    To win our graces
    With ridiculous tropes
    About our faces.
PRINCESS. I'm the Moon, says the King.
    What are you, Rosaline?
ROSALINE. A goddess divine.
PRINCESS. Untrue! Untrue!
    We're as mortal as they.
KATHERINE. Dumaine seems to say
    He is wed to a shrew
    And would leave her for me.
PRINCESS, ROSALINE AND KATHERINE.
    What fools they be!
JAQUENETTA. I don't understand.
    I thought love was banned.
    Does he ask for my hand?
    Or, as I guess,
    For somewhat less
    And something more.
PRINCESS, ROSALINE AND KATHERINE.
    What wasted ingenuity
    Of huge hypocrisy!

[Enter BOYET, *doubled up with laughter.]*

BOYET. O Your Grace! O Your Grace!

PRINCESS. What news, Boyet? I see mirth in your face.

BOYET. Arm, wenches and prepare!
 Encounters mounted are.
 Love will appear disguised
 That you may be surprised.
 Stand in your own defence,
 Or fly, like cowards, hence!

PRINCESS. By Cupid, who are they
 Whom you have scouted? Say!

BOYET *[presto].* This noon I sought the shade
 Of a leafy glade
 To rest, but all in vain.
 I'd hardly closed my eye
 When I was wakened by
 Men's voices that I knew.
 The King came into view,
 Berowne, then, with Dumaine
 And Don Armado too,
 Chanting a merry round,
 And dancing on the ground,
 A sight so odd to see,
 I hid behind a tree,
 The King said, "I've a plan,
 But closer come, for no
 Eavesdropping ear must know."
 And then they all began
 To whisper, hoping so,
 Not to be overheard,
 But I caught every word.
 Believe it, believe it not,
 The four have laid a plot
 To call upon you here,
 Dressed in outlandish gear,
 Pretending that they be
 Travellers from Muscovy.

PRINCESS. Come they to visit us?

BOYET. They do, apparelled thus,
 To parle, to court, to dance.
 And each his suit advance
 With her whom he will know
 By the favor he did bestow.

PRINCESS. O will they? Will they? No!
    Those gallants shall be tasked,
    For we will all be masked,
    And none shall have the grace
    To see a lady's face.
    We'll change our favors too,
    So each shall falsely woo.
    I will be Rosaline,
    Rosaline me,
    Jaquenetta Katherine:
    Confused they all shall be.
KATHERINE. What is your purpose, then?
PRINCESS. To mock these mocking men.
    If they intend deceit,
    We'll answer, cheat for cheat.
JAQUENETTA. O Madam, I'm afraid:
    I'm but a country maid,
    And speak no gentle's tongue.
PRINCESS. Enough that you are young!
    Say nothing: he'll believe
    You are Milady Eve.

[*Exit* JAQUENETTA.]

TRIO

[*All aside and very amoroso, belying the tartness of their words.*]

PRINCESS.   A Royal Highness
            To woo disguised!
            How ill-advised:
            I find it worse
            Than wooing in verse.
            More folly is revealed,
            More uncomely slyness,
            Than any shyness
            Or flaw concealed.
            O why must you
            Think intrigue and art
            Needful to subdue
            My conquered heart?

ROSALINE.   My dear Berowne,
            Although I own

You have my heart,
You shall never know it,
Intriguing creature,
If you willfully woo it
With such a light nature
And burdensome art.

KATHERINE.   Dumaine thinks me quarry
To hunt and to harry
With odes and with masks,
But I will evade him
Until I have made him
Do harder tasks:
That is the one art
That captures my heart.

BOYET.   Burning they come from Muscovy afar
Only to find it icy in Navarre.
PRINCESS, ROSALINE AND KATHERINE.
We women know what cozeners men are!

PRINCESS.   Love us, ladies, they all cry,
Love us, love us, or we die:
Murder, ladies, is a crime.
        Enough!
Men have died from time to time,
And the worms have eaten them,
        But not for love.

ROSALINE.   Men are April when they woo,
Vowing ever to be true,
But December when they wed.
        Enough!
Silly 'twere to be misled:
Great their show, but in the deed
        Little their love.

KATHERINE.   Maidens fair and maidens young,
Never trust a honeyed tongue,
Nor a sugar-coated pen.
        Enough!
Service they will swear, but when
We have served them, often then
        They scorn our love.

BOYET.   Ladies, not so fierce, I beg.
                         Men it were who fathered you,
                         Men your mothers answered to
                              With *Yes.*
                         Carriage bold, a well-turned leg,
                         Burning glances, words of praise,
                         Do they totally displease?
                              Now! Confess!

PRINCESS, ROSALINE AND KATHERINE.
                         There speaks the Man!

                         [Contrapuntal reprise of the above as a quartet.]

TUTTI.   Burning, burning, burning,
                         They come from Muscovy afar,
                         Only to find it icy, icy, icy,
                         Icy in Navarre.

                              CURTAIN

                              ## Act III

[Late afternoon. Autumn. KING, DUMAINE, BEROWNE *masked and disguised as "noble" Russians.* ARMADO, *masked and disguised in attendance. They face the ladies,* ROSALINE, *masked and wearing the Princess' favor,* PRINCESS, *masked and wearing Rosaline's favor,* JAQUENETTA, *masked and wearing Katherine's favor.* KATHERINE, *to one side, partially shielded from the others by a tree, masked and dressed as Jaquenetta.* MOTH, *masked as a blackamoor, between the ranks of the ladies and gentlemen.* BOYET, *unmasked, to one side. "Russian" musicians, rear.]*

MOTH. All hail, the richest beauties on the earth!
     A holy parcel of the fairest dames
     That ever turned their backs to mortal views . . .

                         [The ladies turn their backs to him.]

BEROWNE. "Their eyes," villain, "their eyes."
MOTH. That ever turned their eyes to mortal views!
     Out—
BOYET. True. Out, indeed.
MOTH. Out of your favors, heavenly spirits, vouchsafe
     Not to behold—

BEROWNE. "Once to behold," rogue!
MOTH. Once to behold with your sun-beamèd eyes . . .
    With your sun-beamèd eyes . . .
BOYET. They will not answer to that epithet.
    You had best call it "daughter-beamèd eyes."
MOTH [*bursting into tears*].
    I cannot sing to such indifference! [*He runs out.*]
BOYET. Poor wanton babe befuddled with drink—
    A Muscovite weakness.
BEROWNE.   Damned impertinence.
    They put love out of countenance.
ROSALINE [*aside*]. Out of false countenance, I think.
KING. You try, Dumaine. Ask them to dance.

DUMAINE.   From the ice-clogged Arctic waters
            Where whales wallow
       On through steppes where slant-eyed Tartars
            Chew on tallow
  Down the murky Volga to the glittering Black Sea
            Rich with caviar
            Here at length we are—
       Here to learn more subtle graces
       From your fair society,
            Gracious ladies,
       And your lively, lovely faces:
       Please allow one speaking glance! [*Pause.*]
            Will you not dance?

ROSALINE [*slightly turning her head*].
    Surely you are weary from travelling long.
    To amuse ourselves, tiring you, would be wrong.

DUMAINE.   Though we knew that wolves and bears might
            Track us and rend us,
       Though the swift Siberian airs' might
            Could well end us,
  Though our friends were weeping when we parted Muscovy
            Barbarous with gold,
            Our hope kept us bold—
DUMAINE, BEROWNE AND KING.
       Here to learn more subtle graces
       From your fair society,
            Gracious ladies,

And your lively, lovely faces:
Please allow one speaking glance. [*Pause.*]
Will you not dance?

ROSALINE. Courtesy permits us no absolute *No*:
We shall dance. One dance. And then you shall go!

DUMAINE, BEROWNE AND KING.
Our thanks.
KING [*with a gesture*].
Music.

[*The Musicians start a Sarabande. The* KING *goes to* ROSALINE, BEROWNE *to the* PRINCESS, DUMAINE *to* JAQUENETTA.]

DUMAINE, BEROWNE AND KING.
And shall I dance with you?
BOYET [*aside*]. In disguise well-armored they will dance and will woo,
But sharp-tongued wenches will quickly run them through.

[*The couples dance.* ARMADO *takes advantage of this to make his way towards the tree behind which* KATHERINE *is standing. The* KING *and* ROSALINE *come forward dancing.*]

KING.   Madam, upon my soul I swear
                            To win your love or, failing,
                                With my love, to die!
ROSALINE.   A love so mortally ailing—
                            I want it not, I!
KING.   Here more-than-mortal and mortal pair:
                            For I above this world do prize
                            Your beauty, yet hold you as my
                                Own eyesight dear.
ROSALINE.   Alas, I fear
                            You cannot use your eyes!

[*They retire towards the back.*]

ARMADO. Psst, psst! 'Tis I, 'tis Don Armado
Wounded near death by Cupid's *passado*.

[*Noticing* BEROWNE *and the* PRINCESS *coming forward, he desists.*]

BEROWNE.   Lady, with all my heart I swear

<table>
<tr><td></td><td>My nesting heart already
Has to your heart flown!</td></tr>
</table>

PRINCESS.	My nesting heart already
	Has to your heart flown!
PRINCESS.	Retrieve it. I grow unsteady.
	They beat not as one.
BEROWNE.	No, no! I know them as meant to pair
	In endless harmonies of love
	As we with foot and hand have done
	In sarabande.
PRINCESS.	But hand-to-hand
	Does not mean hand-in-glove. [*They retire.*]

ARMADO. Jaquenetta, turn and look, look and see!

KATHERINE. Excuse me, sir, I speak no Muscovy.

DUMAINE [*coming forward with* JAQUENETTA *as* ARMADO *once more turns
       away*].   Mistress, upon my life I swear
                   Beyond all vain bravado,
                       I would serve but you!

ARMADO.	Beloved, it's Don Armado,	[*Repeat ad lib until*
	No Muscovite.	*"Reply! Reply!"*]
KATHERINE.	Who?	

DUMAINE.   You will not answer? O my despair!

DUMAINE AND BEROWNE.
             Submit my love to any test,

DUMAINE, BEROWNE AND KING.
             O say what you would have me do!

DUMAINE, BEROWNE, KING AND ARMADO.
             Reply! Reply!

KATHERINE.   Armado! Why,
             I never would have guessed!

ROSALINE AND PRINCESS. Your brief "Good-bye"
             Is all that I request.

DUMAINE [*helping* JAQUENETTA, *who has stumbled while dancing*].
             Your pardon, I
             Have made you feel distressed.

BOYET [*aside*].   Ha! Ha! I love a lovely jest.
             Ha! Ha! The lovers have their due.

   [*Parodying them.*]   Reply! Reply!
             Ha! Ha! But I
             Must keep my laugh suppressed.

KATHERINE [*pointing to the others, in an ornate vivace*].
    O *splendide mendax!*
    O intrigue *par excellence!*
    How *sub divo* they advance
    Con amore in a dance
    Pari passu their romance!
    O natura naturans!

    A delightful ostentation, a show,
    A pageant, an antic, *video et gaudeo,*
    Laus Deo, bene intelligo
    The spur, the ground, the very *fons et origo*
    O troppo troppo troppo
    Of its why and wherefor—
    Omnia vincit amor!

ARMADO [*ecstatically recovering from his dumbfoundedness*].
    O Muse-possessed. O glory!
ARMADO AND KATHERINE. *Et nos cedamos amori!*
DUMAINE, BEROWNE AND KING. Submit my love, *etc. ad lib.*
ROSALINE AND PRINCESS. Your brief, *etc. ad lib.*
BOYET.   Ha! Ha! I love, *etc. ad lib.*
ARMADO AND KATHERINE. *Omnia vincit amor*
    Et nos cedamos amori, ad lib.

    [*Just as the dance and the ensemble are approaching
    their climax,* MOTH *interrupts by hurriedly entering
    and running directly to the* PRINCESS. *After the in-
    terruption the Musicians continue for a while and
    then, one by one, cease playing and then leave.*]

MOTH. Princess, Highness,
    A messenger for you
    Has arrived at the palace.
PRINCESS [*removing her mask*].
    The papers. Boyet, be so kind.

    [BOYET *hurries out, unable to suppress his laughter
    which can be heard for a while after his exit. The other
    ladies remove their masks and exchange their favors.
    Consternation of the men.* BEROWNE *furiously turns
    towards where* BOYET *exited.*]

BEROWNE. Hop, dotard, hop! Hop laughing to your grave!
    I see it now—

Some carry-tale, some please-man, some slight zany,
Some mumble-news, some trencher-knight, some Dick,
Told our intents before. Yes, Boyet, I mean you.
And I know why: because we still are young
And you are old despite your honeyed tongue.

[*He turns back towards the others in a sulky rage.*]

KATHERINE.   Blame not Boyet. Indict
Instead your fickle eye-sight
That saw us in the light
    Of your favors merely.
All fantasy withstood,
Love's unwavering eye should
See, as you saw a child could,
    Who we are quite clearly.

[*Pause.* MOTH *bows in acknowledgement and exits.
After a moment* BEROWNE *shrugs his shoulders.*]

BEROWNE.   Our silly game
Has been disclosed,
And red with shame
We stand exposed.
What can we do
But make confession
Of our vanity
And beg your mercy?
Yes, ladies, you
Have taught us a lesson.

Having learned in school
To be clever by rule,
When he falls in love
A boy supposes,
And what could be crazier,
That words are enough,
That epanorthosis
And paranomasia
Are magic arts
That unlock all hearts.

[*Turns to the men.*] Now our folly we see:
Recite, lords, with me,
A litany.

KING, BEROWNE, DUMAINE AND ARMADO.
>From what boys call
Poesy, all
That merely verbal is,
>From filling a canticle
With figures pedantical,
Three-piled hyperboles,
Tropes metaphorical,
Conceits rhetorical
And phrases hollow,
Save us, Apollo!

Hear, ladies, hear!
Henceforth we forswear
All spruce affectation,
All vain ostentation:
Henceforth we will praise
In terms that are true,
Henceforth we will woo
In honest prose
With russet yeas
And kersey noes.

PRINCESS. Swear to forswear! No, no! More oaths to scorn!
You are, good sirs, already oversworn.
Rosaline, the King swore . . . ? Let us hear.
ROSALINE. Madam, he swore that he did hold me dear
As precious eyesight; adding thereto moreover
That he would wed me, or else die my lover.
PRINCESS. God give you joy of him. Berowne to me
Swore we should love in endless harmony.
Must I believe it all was sworn in vain?
And Jaquenetta, tell us of Dumaine.
JAQUENETTA. Faith, Madam, I had such trouble with dancing,
I did not hear one word of his romancing.

[The women laugh.]

PRINCESS. Faith, Jaquenetta, we give not their professions.

*[*JAQUENETTA *exits giggling. After a bit* ARMADO
quietly follows her.]

KING. This is not kind. We have made our confessions.
We came to amuse you. You have had your sport.
We propose now to lead you to our court.

PRINCESS. This field shall hold us. You forswear again:
  Nor God nor I delight in perjured men.
KING [*with exasperation*].
  What can we do or say to please you, then?
  Our perjuries we owe to you,
  Your beauty broke our will.
BEROWNE. No matter what we show to you,
  You always take it ill.
DUMAINE. The first time we attended you,
  You spoke up and pretended you
  All felt that we'd offended you,
  And now you mock us still.
PRINCESS. We thought it all a game with you
  Of courtesy and wit.
ROSALINE. And thought to play the same with you,
  As being only fit.
KATHERINE. To sonnetise and dance for us,
  From Russia trek to France for us,
  Are not to give a chance for us
  To credit love a bit.
KING. Our eyes said more than rhyme can say.
PRINCESS. Who on an eye would fix?
ROSALINE. Of true love only time can say.
BEROWNE. Can but the agèd mix?
DUMAINE. You would not pay attention, no!
KATHERINE. How could we your intention know?

> [BEROWNE *suddenly bursts out into uncontrollable laughter. The others cease their bickering stances to look at him in incomprehending amazement.*]

BEROWNE. Pretension to pretension, O
  We are well matched, we six!

> [*Pause. Then all begin laughing hilariously.* BOYET *enters solemnly and kneels before the* PRINCESS.]

BOYET. Madam, the King your father. . .
PRINCESS. Dead!
BOYET.   My tale is told.

> [*The* PRINCESS *turns away and bows her head in grief.* ROSALINE *and* KATHERINE *hurry to her side, but she indicates that she would like to be alone. Twilight. Falling leaves.*]

KING, BEROWNE, DUMAINE, BOYET, ROSALINE, KATHERINE.
                    A cloud has crossed the sun.
                    In our familiar park
                            The shafts of dark
                            Oblivion
                    Invade and find their mark.

KING.   How fares your Majesty?
PRINCESS.   Boyet, prepare. The day
                            Goes on its way
                            And so must we. [*Exit* BOYET.]
KING.   Madam, I beg you stay.

                    You know my love: remain
                    To learn all it would give
                            To ease your grief,
                            To still your pain.
PRINCESS.   We thank you, but must leave.

KING.   If must, one deed we must
                    Accomplish ere you leave:
                            To pledge our love
                            Now in the last
                    Brief moments that we have.

PRINCESS.   A time too short, my lord,
                    To pledge eternity;
                            And how should I
                            Build on your word,
                    Knowing your dear perjury?

                    To show my love your care,
                    Repent your vows forsworn:
                            Let some forlorn
                            Retreat of prayer
                    Receive you whilst I mourn.

                    Then, my dear lord, more dear
                    In my secured belief
                            In you, should grief
                            After a year
                    Grant me again my life,

                    Come from your hermitage
                    To find me . . .

KING.   At your feet!
PRINCESS.   Equal to meet . . .
KING.   My love!
PRINCESS.   . . . And pledge
                    The love now sued with heat

                    If such a trial it bear
                    And not be cooled, nor die.
KING.   Sweet Madam, I—
PRINCESS.   No, do not swear!
                    Ponder and then reply.

BEROWNE AND DUMAINE.
                    And I, my love, and I?
KATHERINE.   Follow the King and sue
                        When he comes too.
DUMAINE.   And your reply? ⎤
BEROWNE.   Reply? ⎦
KATHERINE.   Yes. . . .
BEROWNE.   Studies my lady?
KATHERINE.   If I still love you.

ROSALINE.   Your wit is known,
                    But wants new fields to conquer,
                        Your wit is keen
                    But wants a deeper touch:
                        Therefore, Berowne,
                    Visit the sick and dying,
                        See if you can,
                        Hale in your brawn
                        And your fruitful brain,
                    Day after day this twelvemonth,
                        Make wretched men
                    Less wretched by your fancy.
                        Go seek to win
                    Answering smiles from pain.

BEROWNE. To move wild laughter in the throat of death?
    It is impossible. It cannot be.
    Mirth cannot move a soul in agony.

ROSALINE.   That's the way, then,
                    To choke a gibing spirit
                        Born of the vain

Unthinking laughter clowns
         Accord a clown!
Abandon it: believe me,
         I'll not complain
         Were Antic's reign
         To be overthrown;
But if the suffering hear you
         Without disdain,
I'll take your flaw forgiven.
         This way alone,
I swear, will I be won!

[*Enter* ARMADO, *followed at a little distance by*
JAQUENETTA. MOTH *enters from the other side,
once more in attendance.* ARMADO *kneels before the*
KING.]

ARMADO. Sire, with your permission
      I would marry Jaquenetta:
      To this end and for her love
      I have solemnly undertaken
      To hold the plough a term of
      A twelvemonth and a day.
KING. We grant, admiringly, your petition.
      My thoughtful lords, we are overtaken.
      What do we have to say?
KING, BEROWNE AND DUMAINE.
      Taken to task
      By what you ask . . .
ARMADO.   Maid.
KING, BEROWNE AND DUMAINE.
      We mean to prove
      Worthy of love . . .
JAQUENETTA.   Man.
KING, BEROWNE AND DUMAINE.
      Without an oath
      To find our troth . . .
ARMADO.   I do love thee . . .
KING, BEROWNE AND DUMAINE.
      Our deeds to be
      Oaths wordlessly . . .
JAQUENETTA.   So I have heard you say.

KING, BEROWNE, DUMAINE AND ARMADO.
  A twelvemonth and a day.
BOYET [*entering*]. All is in readiness, Madam.
PRINCESS. Ah, sweet my lord, and so we take our leave.

> [*By now the "costumes" of all lie in a heap on the
> ground. Evening. Servants dress the ladies in black
> cloaks. All but* BEROWNE *turn to each other to make
> their adieux.* BEROWNE *stands thoughtful stage
> front. After a moment all come down near him.*]

BEROWNE [*at first half to himself, then gradually more and more to the others*].
               Jack has not Jill—
  Like an old play our wooing does not end.
         Your courtesy,
     Dear ladies, might have still
  Made of our sport a comedy: I say,
    And say no more. So must it be;
    So be it. We have reached an end,
    No end, and yet an end of play.

OMNES [*except* MOTH].   Spring, summer, fall
   The leaves have turned that but a day ago
         Broke into leaf,
     And in a moment all
  Our little world with such a little span
    Between frivolity and grief,
    Sleeping will turn beneath the snow
    And dream the destinies of man.

       But we instead
  Have wakened from a light and youthful dream
       To find a day
    Resembling night, where dead
  And living in a long communion dwell,
    Where all things go and all things stay,
    And are and are not what they seem,
    And time and death are real. Farewell.

> [*The men, without* ARMADO *or* MOTH, *and the
> women, attended by* BOYET, *begin leaving slowly in
> different directions.* JAQUENETTA *remains a little
> way from* ARMADO, *looking towards the ladies.
> Night. Wintry landscape. Snow.*]

MOTH.   When icicles hang by the wall,
And Dick the shepherd blows his nail;
And Tom bears logs into the hall,
And milk comes frozen home in pail:
When blood is nipped, and ways be foul,
Then nightly sings the staring Owl
Tu-whit, to-who.
    A merry note,
    While greasy Joan doth keel the pot.

When all aloud the wind doth blow,
And coughing drowns the Parson's saw:
And birds sit brooding in the snow,
And Marian's nose looks red and raw:
When roasted crabs hiss in the bowl,
Then nightly sings the staring Owl
Tu-whit, to-who.
    A merry note,
    While greasy Joan doth keel the pot.

ARMADO. The words of Mercury
Are harsh after the songs of Apollo:
[*To* JAQUENETTA.] You that way; we this way.

> [ARMADO *and* JAQUENETTA *start in different directions.* MOTH, *a half-frozen Cupid now, draws his cloak about tightly and shivers. He slowly turns as though to follow* ARMADO.]

SLOW CURTAIN

The Entertainment of the Senses

[An Anti-Masque for
James Shirley's
Cupid and Death]

BY W. H. AUDEN AND
CHESTER KALLMAN
MUSIC BY
JOHN GARDNER

[*1973*]

CHAMBERLAIN [*spoken*].
    Ladies and gents,
    Our troupe now presents:
    THE ENTERTAINMENT OF THE SENSES

FIRST APE. I'm Touch.
    Touch me, touch me
    If you'd smoothly learn much
    How I've gone roughly free.

    First of all, don't be touchy and take my advice:
    Be intimate but not too nice.
    Fidelity and all that
    Has become old hat;
    Today it's not done
    To sleep with only one
    And chastity's non-U.
    Merely grab what is your due
    And stroke it enough
    With no prattle of love;
    For Cupid, as Eros, you surely must know
    If you're not old and silly,
    Now presides over the Touch-and-Go
    Of busy Piccadilly.
    When you see a fair form, chase it
    And if possible embrace it,
    Be it a girl or a boy.
    Don't be bashful: be brash, be fresh.
    Life is short, so enjoy
    Whatever contact your flesh
    May at the moment crave:
    There's no sex-life in the grave.

    But when you hands make their sex tours
    They may run into peculiar textures
    Nature never quite thought of,
    Wrought of
    Coal-tar and spit
    By brilliant hags
    For keeping one fit
    Without bumps, concavities, bulges or sags,
    Much plastic, elastic and chilly
    What-nots about willy-nilly;

And reaching for loot with a thief's
Dactyl dexterity you may steal upon briefs
Of genuine simulated seal-skin
And be flummuxed when chancing on real skin.
But if you're not sure
If they're meant to allure
Or only divert and protect,
For heaven's sake, do not object,
Since the Mode may be such,
And you mustn't lose touch:
No one cares what you think, but how you behave:
Lack of feeling is nothing, lack of touch very grave.

And there are many more new
Tactile sensations
Available to you
In developed nations,
And unknown to the peasant,
Not all of them pleasant:
If you handle a faulty switch
Your fingers may violently twitch
At the unexpected shock;
But we can't put back the clock.
On the whole we should clap
At the way things are going:
For comfort there's no competing
With Central Heating
And the joy of knowing
There's always hot water on tap.
Then on warm days now
You can cool your brow
With the breeze from an
Electric fan.
On Cupid's face there's a sensual grin
Because foam-baths have come in;
No cake of soap
Can ever hope
To provide so soft a lave:
It's a shame there'll be none in the grave.

ALL FIVE. *Mild und leise*
You'd be wiser
Not to be defenceless:

Nor walls nor fences
Can guard your senses—
Why not just be senseless?

SECOND APE. I'm Taste.
Taste me, taste me
In nutritional haste
For my new A.B.C.

Realize, since there is no disputing with Taste
That though oft violated, I always am chaste.
Nowadays you may carp that I'm not what I should be:
I am what I am when I am what I would be:
e.g. If I were a herb I'd be evenly branched,
Born crispy and gold, I'd be powdered and blanched,
As a wine I'd be water and wolf's blood, and if
I were tropical fish I'd arrive frozen stiff,
If I were a chick I'd be battery-fed,
And if I were a sponge I'd be sliced up as bread.
If I were a meal that was meant to seduce
A male into marriage, I'd moan "What's the use?"
Feed the Beast, I have heard, but what slips to his belly
Doesn't matter too much when he's glued to the Telly;
And if I had intentions more directly erotic,
I'd remember that Cupid's gone macrobiotic;
Though his too-divine packaging rouse appetite,
It won't show that his palate has gone with his sight.
But were I just myself, I'd meet woe in this Hall,
For how could I sing being nothing at all?
So I'll be a burnt roast, and if my guests are meanies
Who dote on their food, they'll get *six* Dry Martinis;
And I'll don heavy clogs and dance several jigs on
Dear Elizabeth David and darling Jane Grigson:
Oh they're wonderful ladies, but will make a fuss
About opening tins, not at all, girls, like us.
The poor cranks may complain I'm a nerveless dull bitch—
They're just jealous because I'm so vitamin-rich:
And if *you* think me insipid, unnatural and coy,
You can dowse me in ketchup or souse me with soy.
As for *her,* hungry Nature, that well-seasoned tart
Who arrives uninvited and consumes A-La-Carte,
Let her bring her own Glutinate with if she's smart:
After all she's just there to corrupt and deprave
When she dines upon gamey old you in the grave.

ALL FIVE. *Mild und leise*, etc.

THIRD APE. I'm Smell.
Smell me, smell me
To be sure you can tell
What a chic smell should be.

Let's say you're a woman, going out for the best:
First of all, I suggest
That Pro-Lib or Anti, you should and you can
Start with your arm-pits and shave like a man.
Then douche, dab and diddle because, dear, you know
That *Bachelor's-Offer* isn't short for B.O.
And the gent who awaits you, never mind what it costs
Will have taken precaution against fumes and exhausts;
Though he forgets the aroma of wine would
Be drowned by his smokes, that is not your affair:
He will reek like an acre of pine-wood
To show you and Cupid how much he could care.
Well,
Swell—
But what now of you, and how should you smell?
There's fragrance of course in the blooms of the wood,
But for Nature to give you the aroma she should
For you to get on and get off in,
You'll need more bouquets than they put on a coffin:
So be well-advised
Now you're de-odorised
And reach for a scent that you chose
Because, though worn out by assault, your own nose
Twitched at it because it was well-synthesised.
And with the vernal voice of the turtle *I* sing
When I pray
You—now spray
Yourself as though you were fertilising
The passive eggs of a fish;
And the creature you hatch
Can now swish
To make a fine catch
Safely downstream,
The exotic,
Narcotic,
Whiff of a dream,

A for-the-few, not-the-many thing,
A pound, not a penny thing,
Oh!
So
If you want power, affection and pelf,
Sweet, smell like anything
Except yourself.
But if you're mad to be natural and personal, save
Your money and be Mother Nature's unspoilable slave:
She'll see that you stink like us all in the grave.

ALL FIVE. *Mild und leise*, etc.

FOURTH APE. I'm hearing.
   Hear me, hear me
   Prove you pure noise endearing
   As it now is to me.

   When Life seems dreary, Oh
   Switch on your Stereo
   And turn the volume to high:
   Soft music makes us cry.
   The songs of birds may be seraphic
   But, however sweet, they can't compete
   With the roar of city traffic
   Or the stentorian sound
   Of a Jet-plane leaving the ground.
   So when you motor-bike
   Down the M.1. or its like,
   Imagine you're late—
   Accelerate, accelerate,
   Show your decibel power
   At a hundred an hour.
   It's no longer a sin
   To make a din
   Since that, until lately
   Unknown, unstately
   God, Cacophony
   Made his Theophany;
   And Cupid, bored by peace and quiet,
   Only aims to cause a riot.
   So, lovers, fill your lungs
   And let go with your tongues

To talk, talk, talk, talk
With your Transistors on as you walk.
For the prissy minority
Who prefer a low sonority
There's only one thing to be done:
Become a Trappist or a Nun.
Let them. Come, girls and boys,
More noise, more noise!
Yell while you can and save
Your silence for the grave.

ALL FIVE. *Mild und leise,* etc.

FIFTH APE. I'm Sight.
See me, see me
Make the scene a delight
In life optically.

A mountain, we must confess, is
No longer a surprise;
What really impresses
Contemporary eyes
Are the vertical escarpments
Of High-rise Apartments:
Each rectangular block
Makes Gothic or Baroque
Look over-complicated,
Their cathedrals out-dated.
Then already the printed word
Is beginning to seem absurd;
It's so easy to misconstrue,
And far too many do.
Now only a snob
Would take on the job
Of scanning a book
When he could look
At life up close and so real on
Telly from San Francisco to Ceylon.
But, if his fancy leans
To Fiction, Movies tell
The tallest stories well,
And there are Fashion Ads
In glossy magazines—

Long-haired lassies and lads
All shot in shocking color—
Black and white was so much duller.
It's a new world, so make sure
Should you go on tour
To Greece or New York or the Fens,
To be in the swing:
Never look at a thing
Except through a camera lens.
Yes, we're lucky: whereas
As soon as the sun withdrew
Our forebears had to make do
With candles or with gas,
We have the felicity
To possess electricity,
Can lighten our rooms
And dispel the Glooms
With lots and lots
Of bulbs of at least a hundred watts.
And Cupid, called blind,
You will find
Is only short-sighted
And likes life well-lighted,
Preferring to know
At just whom he is aiming his bow:
Candles that splutter
And very soon gutter
Remind him of Plato's cave
And the blindness of the grave.

ALL FIVE [*stretto*].
      Though our views be reprehensible
      To you and indefensible,
      Please admit they're comprehensible
      And, naturally, sensible.
                  Good-bye!
      When you get a little older
      You'll discover like Isolde:
   "We must love one another *and* die!"

> [*Enter* DEATH *from behind, unseen by the others. He folds his arms and looks on.*]

CHAMBERLAIN. Dear listeners, you have heard tonight
    What my five apes have had to say
    About our senses five,
    Through which we know we are alive:
    Touch and Taste and Smell
    As well as Hearing and Sight,
    And the different roles they play
    Now as compared with yesterday.
    Cupid, the god, would certainly nod,
    And you'll all agree, I'm sure, with me
    That they are perfectly right.
    The moral is, as they have said:
    Be with-it, with-it, with-it till you're dead.

RADIO PLAYS

The Dark Valley

[*1940*]

[*Music: halting and eerie. A goose honks in the distance. Music up and down. Goose honks again. Music up and down.*]

WOMAN [*calling*]. Na-na. Na-na!

[*Goose honks. Music out. Feet breaking twigs as the old woman walks.*]

Na-na. Na-na. The ungrateful creature. If I turn my back for a moment she takes off somewhere. She does it on purpose. Just because I'm old and can't catch her by running. She revels in it. Oh, I know very well why she waddles away. She's ashamed to be looked after by an old hag, a poor old woman alone in the mountains, with not a neighbor near to help her, someone whom the women whisper about in the village, and the dogs growl at if she goes near them, and the men spit as she passes by, and the children are dragged indoors by their mothers, in case she should frighten them into a fever.

[*Wind.*]

Once this valley was full of voices, effort and action, engines and men. For where a vein pointed promising the golden metal went miners like moles after, hewing into the hill their hopeful way. They sank a shaft from the surface of the earth, they drove through darkness, drifts with a purpose; in sombre stopes they scooped out ore, gold-speckled quartz with their quick hammers. They managed much, those many miners. But father was foremost, first of them all with drill and dynamite and daring hands at deeds deep down where no daylight was, and equally noble was no man living; Father moved like a river, riding the world.

[*Pause.*]

When father spoke the monsters grew mild in the sea, and the roses opened and the eagle hung spellbound over the spellbound lamb. When he smiled it was the shining spaces of summer, but when he frowned it was ages of ice, his anger ended the earth. O but *he* is ended, ended his life, lost, away, a no one, a nothing as if he never were. He perished in an explosion, his body was broken by a blast in the earth. He was drunk, they lied, the low and evil; he was killed by his lack of care, the mine-owners wrote, and their mean hearts were glad he was a ghost, for his greatness galled them. He was a stag among sheep, a star among tapers, alone with fools in a foul field.

[*Goose off.*]

Na-na. There you are, you slut. Come here at once. Alright. Stay there if you want. Go on, stare at yourself in the water and starve. I don't mind. Nor will the foxes, I'm sure. You'll find them *most* flattering. Na-na. Come here at once. Wait till I find a stone. [*She throws.*] You little fool, I'll bash your head in.

[*Stone striking in water off.*]

That frightened you, didn't it? A bit too close to be quite comfortable, eh? A narrow escape from—well, from it, the nasty thing that's always just round the corner but a lady doesn't mention in public. You're quite right. One shouldn't speak of such things. Let's forget about it.

[*Pause.*]

Let's think of something nice like food. Yes, come along, Nana, it's supper time, time for greedy little geese to stuff their guts and then bed-time. [*She is stalking the goose.*] Hushaby, sleep, sleep and such lovely dreams, flying away away away over the tree-tops, not even bothering to look back down at the poor old woman waving goodbye but just going on and on above the forest, over the tops of the mountains, and then there it is, the fairy castle. The gate stands open. There's not a soul to be seen. Into the courtyard, through the door, up the winding stair to the little room at the very top of the tower. Ah, how your heart beats. At last I shall meet him, my wonderful gander, husband, my fairy prince. Knock. Knock. Who's there? Queen Nana? Come in, my dear. I've been expecting you for a thousand years. In you rush with a flutter of feathers . . . [*She grabs the goose.*]

[*Goose squawks angrily.*]

Got you, now we'll go my way for a change. Something funny has happened, eh? There's no handsome rich young gander standing there, but only the poor old woman you left behind.

[*Goose squawks angrily.*]

Squawking won't mend matters. There's a nice little coop of wire netting waiting for you while I get things ready.

[Goose being put in coop.]

In you go, now, and stay quiet till I need you. [*Door fastened.*] Not bad is it? Plenty of air? Plenty of room between the wire to look at the view. Food and water and no worries. What more do you want. Now, you're a good respectable goose at last. What's freedom anyway? Ask the boys and girls in the city, ask any of them, ask the typists and the teletypists, ask the chiropractors or the air-conditioning contractors, ask the brokers and the bell-hops and the beerpump makers and the baby carriage makers and the solicitors and the soapboilers and the public caterers and the public messengers and the housewives and the midwives and the masseurs and the restaurateurs and the retail stationers and the probationers and the librarians and the Rotarians and the beauticians and the morticians and the electricians and the physicians and the politicians and the pediatricians—Go on, ask them, ring them up and ask for a statement and what will they tell you? "Dear Goose, aren't you a lucky girl, to have a kind old woman to look after you and feed you and give you a nice coop to live in. Think of all the poor underprivileged wild geese with no roof over their heads, having to lay their eggs just anywhere, and liable to be gobbled up any moment by some horrid fox. We're lucky too. We can read and write and do sums. Our coops have four walls and a roof and light and heat and hot and cold running water. And all we have to do in return is address envelopes or take dictation or pull levers; which is ever so easy and we only have to do it for eight hours a day. The rest of our time we're absolutely free. No one interferes. We can relax and romp as much as we like. We have such fun. Mustn't it have been awful in the old days before there was any progress, before there was any science to make people safe?" Yes, Nana, you're safe. . . . For the time being, anyway. . . . Safe until . . .

[Goose honks.]

Until what, you'd like to know, eh? Ah, who knows the answer to that? Do you? What an idea. Shall we say, until the unexpected happens, whatever and whenever that may be. And until then, we might as well go on happily with our daily routine. You shall stay here in your coop and enjoy your supper and I'll go and get fresh water. We must have water, Nana, you know. Water's needed for everything. We die without it. We die *in* it. But there are worse ways. Think of all the babies suffocated in their sleep by large black cats, of all the skaters drowned in millponds when the ice breaks, of all the hilarious parties returning from dances whose cars skid and plunge them shrieking over cliffs. Think of all the geese, Nana.

[Goose noise.]

You'd be surprised at all the possibilities of hungry hawks and fam-
ished foxes, and stealthy stoats and lurking lynxes and bold bad
bears, at all the varieties of clutch and claw and teeth and talon and
snap and snatch.

[Ravens croaking overhead.]

Cry your curse from the crags, cry it again; black ravens over this
ruined place. *[Sighs.]* I must get water.

[Footsteps on twigs.]

[Sings.]   Eyes look into the well
                    Tears run down from the eye
                    The tower cracked and fell
                    From the quiet winter sky

[Fade in stream and waterfall.]

The shaft is full of water and the wind whistles through the broken
buildings of an abandoned mine. For after father died, the lode
vanished—in vain they searched.

[Feet on steps continuing. Waterfall up.]

The gold was gone; they got nothing; they lost heart; gave up their
drilling; it paid no longer; they departed poor. And none remained
but mother and I on this stony farm in a stony silence. She never
loved me. I knew it from the first. She was prim and pious and pray-
ing always for father's soul, and shuddered at his songs and thought
him wicked and wept much. For she wanted a dummy who would
drive her to church, in a blue suit; bowing to the neighbors, holy and
hollow and half alive. And she could not *bear* me because I was like
him and he knew it and loved me and would lift me up in his great
hands as he imitated a lion roaring or a rutting stag.

[Bucket in stream. Waterfall fades and stream fades.]

Water—at least we have water.

[Sings.]   Under the midnight stone
                    Love was buried by thieves
                    The robbed hearts weep alone
                    The damned rustle like leaves

[Distant avalanche.]

The avalanches have been falling all afternoon for the sun is still shining in the white snow peaks and the useless wastes of that world are full of useless light and heat that can do nothing. But this deep dale is dark always. Here summer has no success and short the distance of noon from night and near ever are the cold crags to this crevice where roars the glacier torrent in a gloomy twilight, wild waters in a winter dusk. Let the day break its heart on the hard heights for what it can do, the dark returns, and even up there it is autumn already.

[*Goose fades in.*]

Did you think I'd forgotten about you, Nana? Why do you look at me like that? I know what you're thinking. The old woman is going mad. Only mad people talk to themselves. You wouldn't do such a thing, would you, not a fat sensible tame goose like yourself. Aren't you glad you're not old and mad like me? Old women die, but a sensible goose lives on forever, getting fatter and fatter, while old women have to work, getting everything ready, putting the water on the stove, shelling the peas, sharpening the . . . There now, I nearly said it. You must try to excuse an old woman whose tongue is always running away with her. Stuff yourself till you burst. I'll be back in a moment.

[*Sings.*]   Eyes look into the well
Tears run down from the eye
The tower cracked and fell
From the quiet winter sky

[*Door opens and shuts off.* WOMAN *fades out.*]

Under the midnight stone
Love was buried by thieves
The robbed hearts weep alone
The damned rustle like leaves

[WOMAN *fades in. Door opens and shuts off.*]

The palace servants sing
The ships put out to sea
The form that pleased a king
Swings on the elder tree.

[*Goose scolds.*]

Well, what are you fussing about now. You can't still be hungry. What do you want this time. Some new excitement. What shall it be. A bus trip to the national park? A cruise in the South Seas? The new novel everybody's talking about? A new boy friend? After all, you belong to the younger generation and I'm only a silly old woman with old-fashioned ideas. One must keep up with the times, Nana, unless one wants to become just a back number. Still unsatisfied? What about some fresh green peas, then. [*Goose grunts.*] Oh,—sulky! Then, a pretty little mountain primrose? [*Goose grunts.*] It's a shame that you're kept shut up in a wire coop when every girl nowadays has a latchkey and goes to college and knows how babies are born. The young have a right to a good time. Are you jealous? Would you like to go down to the village hall one evening and play with all the other boys and girls. I'm sure they'd be delighted, and they wouldn't mind your being a goose a bit. The young are so tolerant. They'd think you just too cute. You'd be the belle of the evening. And what would you think of them, Nana? Would you think them wonderful, the heroes of a new age, the brilliant free thinkers, the great lovers? No, even a goose wouldn't take long to see through the noise and nonsense to their frightened barren little hearts and heads. Even you would soon discover that for all their pretence, they think love disgusting. To read about it and photograph it, to talk and titter is one thing, but to touch a real live person. Ugh. Only soap and bathsalts and Epsom salts and scrubbing brushes and toothbrushes, and depilatories and perfumes and powders, and shaving creams and face creams, and skin tonics and hair tonics and breath sweeteners and perspiration removers and nail files and eyebrow tweezers can make it bearable. And even then it must be just the right hour and the right room and the right clothes and the right sofa and the right temperature and the right moon and the right music and the right liquor and the right words. O but it was otherwise, Nana, when I was born. Then love was a God who drove men mad. Girls kept it secret for it was danger and death and many died, drowned in streams or stoned or burnt or buried alive. No one spoke of freedom then on this farm. There was no radio, or magazines, or movies or romantic novels or picnics or drives or dances. And mother watched every movement I made, afraid that father's passionate blood would appear in his daughter. For the god of love was father's friend—yes and mine. Mine also. It was the god that helped me defeat my mother and made her blind, and never betrayed me. For he came to me in secret on soft feet, like the wind through the keyhole he came to my chamber; he came at his will through windows and walls and the watching eyes were ignorant of his presence. In the yard or the kitchen, cooking or washing, or feeding the hens or helping in the field, he was suddenly at my side and I shook with joy—for his arms were about me and my beauty his.

He never spoke nor said "I love you" nor told me his name but I knew
he was noble, with the blood of a prince and a prince's favour, clear-
eyed as an eagle though he hid his face. And when he went away the
world was empty. He kissed me farewell. I watched him stride up the
mountain valley and vanish forever, and all the clocks stopped as
the clouds hid him.

[*Goose grunts. Airplane fades in overhead.*]

Look up, Nana, look up. There he goes. Do you see him? The new
man in his new machine. Applaud him, Nana.

[*Claps hands. Goose honking derisively.*]

If you're lucky he might even wave at you. Yes, sure enough he is
waving.

[*Goose noise.*]

Shout yourself hoarse. Show him that even the geese know he's the
lord of creation, the master of matter whom the winds and waves
obey. Think of it, Nana. Every evening at six o'clock, week in and
week out, winter or summer, storm or sunshine, that plane with its
mail and its millionaires passes over this spot, punctual to the second.
Think of that. What a triumph of organization. What a brain he must
have, stuffed with wonderful plans for the future of humanity, for
you and for me. For nothing's so small as to be beneath his notice,
you know. He thinks of everybody. We're all free and equal, he says.
We all have a right to do our share in the government by answering
questions and filling up forms. All of us, even geese. Even your exis-
tence, Nana, is recognized in the capitol. Some official has you down
on a file under Geese, Domestic, along with gelatine, geldings, gems,
gentians, gentlemen, geraniums, gerfalcons, Germans, germs, ger-
micides, and geysers. As a statistic you exert immense influence.
Professors use you in university courses, you help columnists and
economists and political prophets, you win debates and defeat gov-
ernments, you turn the scale for peace or war. Aren't you proud of
yourself.

[*A distant sound of hunting—horns and hounds.*]

But you mustn't think he's only a brain, a dreary bookworm weedy,
weary and wan who reads all day and never goes out of doors or takes
any exercise. O dear no: he's not like that at all. Can't you hear him
down there in the forest, hunting the wild boar, with horns and
hounds. And if he isn't hunting he's fishing or riding or rowing or

swimming or jumping or boxing or playing baseball or football or netball or hockey or lacrosse. No one is more particular than he about his figure and his complexion, his chest-expansion and his biceps. And if he does love books and theatres, he loves great Nature more. Nothing delights him so much as sleeping in log cabins or under canvas, or cooking canned food on a camp fire, or saying woodgy-woodgy to his wife in a stony wilderness.

[*Horns again.*]

But what do these hunters hope for, Nana; these sensitive lives from lighted cities. What shall the wilderness whisper in their ears; what secret do they seek in the shadows of the fir-tree; what is it they ask of animals and stones, of the cold streams in the calm hills? Why do they come here like an army with their apparatus, with their rucksacks and field glasses and fishing rods and rifles and campstoves and corkscrews and cowboy clothes, waterproof waders and windbreaker jackets, the masters of Nature who know all?

[*Horns again.*]

They lie, Nana; they know nothing. They are only tame geese on a wild goose chase. Listen to the lifeless longing for life, the lost and learned looking for their home. But nothing they run after shall they ever find. The lions leap aside in the valleys evading their vision; quickly into a quiet their quarry escapes; the unicorn wanders away; the treasure lies hidden under the stone; the precious gold is at peace in the rock; and echo will not answer when they ask for help. The clouds are gathering round the granite peaks; and the black storm broods above preparing to loose its rain on a ruined race.

[*Horns again.*]

For those horns are the howls of hunted creatures, the trumpets of a regiment retreating in rout, fleeing in panic through a perilous landscape with sinister shadows in pursuit behind them as they stumble through the darkness of a dreadful dream. But why am I telling you all this, Nana? What can it matter to you what happens to the human race? What good can it do you if it lives or dies? You will die first.

[*Goose noise.*]

There now, don't get alarmed. Of course, I don't mean anything personal. After all, you won't be the only one. I shall die too. Whatever happens to us there will still be tame geese and old women for a long time to come. At least we have to hope so.

[*Patter of raindrops.*]

O dear, here comes the rain and I'm afraid we shall have to interrupt our little chat. Old women aren't like geese you know. If they get wet, they catch cold and die and then, who would look after poor Nana? So I must go indoors. Never mind. It's only going to be a shower this time. I'll be back as soon as it's over. By then I ought to be about ready. Yes, Nana, soon it will be your turn.

> *[During the song she goes indoors and busies herself in the kitchen as she sings.]*

SONG

Lady weeping at the crossroads
Would you meet your love
In the twilight with his greyhounds
And the hawk on his glove?

> *[Door opens and shuts on microphone. Steps on wooden floor.]*

Bribe the birds then on the branches
Bribe them to be dumb
Stare the hot sun out of heaven
That the night may come

> *[Kitchen clock, utensils, etc., etc.]*

Starless are the nights of travel
Bleak the winter wind
Run with terror all before you
And regret behind

Run until you hear the ocean's
Everlasting cry
Deep though it may be and bitter
You must drink it dry

Wear out patience in the lowest
Dungeons of the sea
Searching through the stranded shipwrecks
For the golden key

Push onto the world's end, pay the
Dread guard with a kiss
Cross the rotten bridge that totters
Over the abyss.

There stands the ruined castle
Ready to explore

Enter, climb the marble staircase
Open the locked door

Cross the silent empty ballroom
Doubt and danger past
Blow the cobwebs from the mirror
See yourself at last

[*Steps on wooden floor.*]

Put your hand behind the wainscot
You have done your part
Find the penknife there and plunge it
Into your false heart

[*Door opening and shutting. Goose fades in.*]

Yes, Nana, I'm coming. And how did my dear Nana enjoy the shower.
Freshened you up a bit, eh. Still, it's nice to have got it over. Look, the
sun's coming out over the valley. We shall have a fine evening after all.
The day is going to end well for all of us. But now I warn you, Nana,
this grindstone is going to make a horrid noise.

[*Grindstone.*]

I'm sorry but it has to be done. Life can't always be pleasant, can it?
Geese have to hatch eggs, and grow fat. And old women have to
sharpen knives. What for? Why? You may well ask, but who knows?
Why are we alive? Why don't we die?

[*Distant church bells.*]

It's Sunday evening, Nana. Time for all respectable people to take
their prayerbooks and go to church with their charming children,
kneel in pews and murmur responses, sing hymns to the organ and
hear a sermon, and be gently assured that somehow or other, all
things for the righteous shall come right in the end. The minister is
modern and well-mannered and mild, and well-read in evolution and
the latest theories of physics and astronomy and is tolerance itself.
The flames of hell are an old-fashioned idea, for his God is a mathe-
matician and much like a man, and understands perfectly and ex-
pects little. For business is business, and lust is a natural need like
eating, and the search for the gold of grace is a grueling voyage. And
he will forgive them if they go astray or are lazy and look for light no
longer. For the All-Father is proud of his pretty world, and takes her
on his knees, Nana, as I take you now, and strokes her back smiling

till she squirms with pleasure, and feels with his fingers in her feathery neck, and calls her his daughter and his dear darling, his treasure, his princess, his precious goose, and she looks into his eyes and is ever so happy, for the sunset is beautiful and the bells are ringing, though she wonders a little why his loving hands are gripping so tightly that she gasps for air. "Father, why—what is the matter? What have I done? Father, why are you looking so fierce? Father, don't you remember, I'm the world you made. Father, I'm so young and white, I don't want to die. Father . . . "

[*Church bells up and fade.*]

The Rocking Horse Winner

BY D. H. LAWRENCE

ADAPTED FOR RADIO BY W. H. AUDEN

AND JAMES STERN

[*1941*]

[*Scene 1.* MOTHER *and* PAUL *at breakfast.*]

MOTHER. One spoonful is quite enough, Paul. Sugar isn't good for you.

PAUL. Mother, why don't we have a car of our own, instead of always using Uncle Oscar's?

MOTHER. Because we're poor, dear.

PAUL. But why are we poor, mother?

MOTHER. Well—I suppose—I suppose because daddy had no luck.

[*Pause.*]

PAUL. Is luck money, mother?

MOTHER. No, dear. Not exactly.

PAUL. Oh. . . . I thought when Uncle Oscar said *filthy lucker,* it meant money.

MOTHER. It does mean money, but it's *lucre,* not *lucker.*

PAUL. Then what *is* luck, mother?

MOTHER. It's what causes you to have money. If you're lucky, you have money. If you aren't, you don't.

[*Pause.*]

PAUL. Is father unlucky, mother?

MOTHER. Most unlucky, I should say.

PAUL. Are you unlucky, mother?

MOTHER [*snapping*]. Don't talk so much. Eat up your porridge.

[*Pause.*]

PAUL [*stoutly*]. Well, anyway, I'm lucky.

MOTHER. What makes you think so?

PAUL. God told me.

[*Enter* UNCLE OSCAR.]

OSCAR. Morning Joan. Morning Paul. What's the Almighty been telling you this time?

MOTHER. Paul has decided to differ from the rest of our family, and be lucky.

OSCAR. Well, perhaps he's not so far wrong; come to think of it, I have a little present for him.

PAUL. Oh!

MOTHER. Really, Oscar, you spoil the child. Ten shillings is much too much at his age. Paul, where are your manners. Say thank you, Uncle Oscar, at once. [*Fade.*]

[*Scene 2. Fade in. The garage.* PAUL *and* BASSETT. BASSETT *is racing the engine.*]

PAUL. Bassett. Bassett. Do stop that beastly engine and listen.

[BASSETT stops engine.]

BASSETT. 'Ullo, Master Paul . . .

PAUL. Look!

BASSETT. Well, I never. Where did you get that ten bob from, eh?

PAUL. Uncle Oscar. Now I can pay you back the five shillings you lent me to put on Blush of Dawn.

BASSETT. Forget about that perishin' 'orse, Master Paul. That was my mistake.

PAUL. Oh no, I've got to pay you back. I'll win next time. I want you to put this on a horse today.

BASSETT. Well, I never! Talkin' like a born gambler as the sayin' is. What would your mother say if she knew about them five shillings? You keep your money. Gamblin' don't pay. It's all a matter o' luck, and not many's lucky.

PAUL. I'm lucky, Bassett. I know I am. What races are there tomorrow?

BASSETT [*on his favorite topic*]. Well, forgetting about gamblin', Master Paul, there's a h'interestin' race tomorrow at Sandown, the Brandon Plate. I 'ear this three year old of Abie Taylor's, Strident Fire . . .

PAUL. Couldn't I have something on him?

BASSETT. If you did, you'd be balmy, 'cos he's carryin' a ten pound penalty for winnin' last time out. An', anyway, listen to me as knows. What about Ginger Cross? What about Rock of Erin? A corker to gallop over a mile. And Singhalese and Bective, for that matter . . . Then, there's Somerville what won the Manmouth 'ouse stakes.

PAUL. Well, just this ten shillings on one of them. Please, Bassett, I've got to make some money.

BASSETT. See 'ere, Master Paul. It ain't no use. Your mother wouldn't like it now, would she . . . Blimey. Ten o'clock and nothin' h'achieved but 'orse talk. Now then, Master Paul, you run along or I'll never have this car ready. [*Starts engine. Fade.*]

[*Scene 3.*]

1ST VOICE. There must be more money. It means so much.
2ND VOICE. It isn't nice if there's not enough.
1ST VOICE. If you once need money, there's never enough.
2ND VOICE. If you have money there's always hot water
  And long cool rooms with lawns outside
  And polished silver and a peaceful feeling.
1ST VOICE. If you've no money you can't have a garden.
  You must play with rough boys near the station
  Where the streets are dirty and the drains are so bad.
2ND VOICE. Lucky people have a lovely smell.
1ST VOICE. If you're unlucky, you often have headaches.
  Unlucky people look old in the morning.
  Unlucky eyes stare into their plate.
  Unlucky hands hate opening letters.
  Unlucky mouths turn down at the corners.
  Unlucky people don't love you much.
2ND VOICE. Lucky people are never laughed at,
  And get good marks when they go to school,
  And a truthful answer when they ask a question,
  And a ready smile when they make a joke.
  Lucky people are always loved.
PAUL. Am I lucky?
1ST VOICE. Perhaps you are and perhaps you aren't.
  Who knows about luck?
PAUL. Does anyone know?
2ND VOICE. Ask the things you have known the longest.
  Ask the things that are next to your heart.
  Ask the table—ask the chair.
  Ask the rocking horse over there.
  Perhaps they know and perhaps they don't.
1ST VOICE. Who knows? Who knows? Perhaps one of them knows.
  If you're lucky you'll know who to ask.
  If you're lucky you'll ask the right question.
  If you're lucky you'll get the right answer.
  If you're lucky *you can't* go wrong.

PAUL. Rocking horse I've known you longest,
    Rocking horse, you are next to my heart
    Help me, Rocking horse, find my luck.
2ND VOICE. Perhaps he will and perhaps he won't.
PAUL. You must. You must. I've got to have luck.
2ND VOICE. Perhaps you have and perhaps you haven't.
1ST VOICE. You will get what you want if you want it enough.
PAUL. Of course I want it. I want luck more than anything else in the
    world.
2ND VOICE. Perhaps you do and perhaps you don't.
1ST VOICE. If you want it enough, you must love it enough.
PAUL. But I do love it.
1ST VOICE. More than father?
PAUL. Yes.
1ST VOICE. More than Uncle Oscar?
PAUL. Yes.
1ST VOICE. More than Bassett—[*Pause.*] More than Bassett?
PAUL. Y. . . es.
1ST VOICE. More than mother?
PAUL. Don't.
1ST VOICE. More than mother?
PAUL. Please. Please don't make me say it.
1ST VOICE. If you want luck enough you must love luck enough.
2ND VOICE. Lucky people are always loved.
PAUL. Very well. Yes.
1ST VOICE. Will you love luck forever?
PAUL. I will.
1ST VOICE. Swear?
2ND VOICE. Swear!
PAUL. I swear by the Filthy Lucre to Love Luck for ever and ever. Amen.
1ST VOICE. We witness your vow.
2ND VOICE. Now mount your horse and ride.

[PAUL *begins riding the horse. As the pace increases
the voices die away behind him.*]

2ND VOICE. The child of this house has chosen his fate,
    He's riding forth to find his luck.
1ST VOICE. Did his father or mother manage to find it?
2ND VOICE. No, they never found it.
1ST VOICE. Will Paul find it?
2ND VOICE. Perhaps he will and perhaps he won't.

[*High note of a whistling wind.*]

PAUL. Faster! Faster! Take me to where there is luck. I've got to get there. Now take me.

> [*Under the whistle, the sound of galloping horses. Underneath the hooves the sound of voices in rhythm gradually getting louder:*]

Strident Fire
Ginger Cross
Singhalese   [*Twice.*]
Somerville
Bective

Strident Fire
Somerville   [*Three times.*]
Ginger Cross
Singhalese

Somerville
Singhalese   [*Three times.*]
Ginger Cross

Somerville
Singhalese   [*Four times.*]
Singhalese
Somerville

Singhalese
Singhalese   [*Much louder on cheering.*]
Singhalese   [*Crescendo.*]
Singhalese

> [*Complete silence.*]

PAUL [*in a whisper*]. I knew I could do it. I knew I was lucky. [*Loudly.*] Bassett. Bassett!

> [*Music.*]

[*Scene 4. Out in a garden. Background of birds and a lawn mower.*]

1ST VOICE. What is Paul doing?
2ND VOICE. Paul is riding.
1ST VOICE. Riding again? Why he's always riding.
2ND VOICE. If you once love luck you must go on loving.
1ST VOICE. Does he find this luck that he loves so much?

2ND VOICE. Sometimes he does and sometimes he doesn't.
> Luck doesn't stay still like a silver spoon
> Luck isn't certain like six o'clock
> Luck isn't a mark on a map like London
> Luck isn't there whenever you look
> As the world is there when you wake in the morning
> Luck can't be trained to come to your whistle
> Luck is hard to catch and harder to keep.
> If you catch luck once you must go on catching
> No matter whether it's wet or fine
> If the leaves are brown or the buds are bursting
> The apples dropping or the daffodils out,
> If father's in the city or asleep in his chair,
> If mother's out calling or coming upstairs
> If you love luck once you must go on loving.

1ST VOICE. Paul loves his riding.

2ND VOICE. No Paul loves luck.
> If you once love luck, that's all you love.

1ST VOICE. It sounds so lonely.

2ND VOICE.   You bet it's lonely
> If you ride after luck, you ride alone.

[Fade music.]

[*Scene 5.* MOTHER *and* UNCLE OSCAR *coming upstairs to Paul's room.*]

MOTHER. He's so strange nowadays—so distant. I don't know what to make of him. Fancy riding a rocking horse at his age.

OSCAR. About time he had a real pony.

MOTHER. I know, Oscar, but where's the money? You know what Harry is. Always just about to get on to a good thing. What am I going to do? I got another writ yesterday. And Paul will be having to go to Eton before we know where we are.

OSCAR. Perhaps Harry will have a sudden stroke of luck.

MOTHER [*scornfully*]. Harry . . . luck . . .

[*They open the door into Paul's room. Sound of* PAUL *riding.*]

MOTHER. Paul . . . [*No answer.*] You see, I told you. He doesn't notice anybody. Paul.

PAUL. Well, I got there.

MOTHER. Got where?

PAUL. Where I wanted to go.

OSCAR. That's a nice horse you've got there. What's his name?

PAUL. Well, he has different names. Last week he was called Sansovino. Today he's called Daffodil.

OSCAR. Well I never. Do you hear that Joan? Sansovino won the Ascot. Since when have you read the racing news?

MOTHER. He's always talking about racing to Bassett.

OSCAR. Is he indeed. So Bassett told you Daffodil is going to win the Lincoln tomorrow, did he?

PAUL. No. Bassett didn't tell me anything.

OSCAR. Say, son, ever been to a race?

PAUL. No.

OSCAR. Well, how about you and I going to the Lincoln together.

PAUL. Oh wonderful, Uncle Oscar.

MOTHER. Oscar, I really don't think you ought to take him. There's been enough gambling in our family already, you know.

OSCAR. Nonsense, my dear. The fresh air'll do him good. [*Fade.*]

[*Scene 6.* OSCAR *and* PAUL *in car driving to race.*]

PAUL. . . . Bassett bet me five shillings and I lost. Then you gave me ten shillings and I started winning.

OSCAR. And you've been at it ever since, eh. But what makes you think Daffodil's going to win today? The Times doesn't fancy him this morning. Mirza's the favorite you know.

PAUL. I just know, that's all.

OSCAR. Got something on him?

PAUL. All except twenty pounds. I keep that in reserve.

OSCAR [*laughing*]. All except twenty pounds. And what are you betting then, you young romancer?

PAUL. Three hundred. You won't tell anyone, will you, Uncle Oscar? I promised Bassett. We're partners, you see. You won't, will you?

OSCAR. I'll keep your secret, you young Nat Gould. But where's the three hundred?

PAUL. Bassett keeps it for me.

OSCAR. And what's *he* putting on Daffodil?

PAUL. He won't go as high as I do, I expect. Perhaps a hundred and fifty.

OSCAR [*laughing*]. What, pennies? . . . Well, we're nearly there now. I'm putting twenty on Mirza—I'll put five for you on any horse you fancy. What's your price?

PAUL. Daffodil.

OSCAR. Surely not the whole fiver on Daffodil?

PAUL. I should if it was my own fiver.

OSCAR. That's fair enough. Right you are. A fiver on Daffodil. [*Fade.*]

[*Scene 7. Race Course. Crowd noises. Voices overlap.*]

1st Bookie. I'll take three-to-one on the field. Ikey Moran lays yer three-to-one.

2nd Bookie. Tommy Reilly's the one to lay yer lovely prices. Six-to-one. General h'Allenby.

Oscar. What price Daffodil?

1st Bookie. Daffydill? Seven-to-two—oh, ore right. Four-to-one to you, Mr Rockyfeller. 'Ow much, eh? Two fivers on Daffydill, forty quid to ten. Numbers four hundred forty-eight and nine. Good luck to you, young fellah; got a lucky fice, you 'ave. . . . Yes ma'am wot's your little heart yearnin' after? Mirza the favorite—'alf crown to win number four 'undred and forty-for-er.

2nd Bookie. Ten-to-one on Bold Herbert. Three-to-one the field. Seven-to-one-bar-two, four-to-one Lancelot, sevens bar.

Tipster [*at the top of his lungs*]. Ah've—gaht—a horse.

Paul. Uncle Oscar, look at that enormous black man with feathers in his head.

Oscar. Oh, that's the famous tipster Monolulu. Listen.

Tipster. Ladies—genlemen—li'l childer. Hear yuh ma words. Ah come not from Heaven and not from de odder place. No sir, lak an arrow from A-frica ah come from de cradle ob de turf to bring all oh yah da good tidin's. For Monolulu, de lucky, he [*roars*] HAS—GAHT—A—HORSE. Nah, yuh 'member last tahme we was togedder ah told you ah had a horse. But what yuh do? Yah jis turn a deaf ear—a deaf ear, as de Lord Hisself said. So now. Ladies, genlemen, lil chillen—jis yuh lend me dose ears once mo'—while ah pernounce da Participators in dis great ee-vent. Heah, numbah Fahve on de card, de favor-ryte— Mirza de Magnify-cat, de winnah ob fo' Beeg Races. Heah, numbah Seven, Lancy-lot, two ells in his famous name—two ells in Lincoln— and [*louder*] two ells in Lucky—Mon-o-lu-lu. [*Cheers.*] Den dere's Daf-fodeel, de po'tender ob Spring—tah me: but da ain't no spring to-day.

Oscar. That's a nasty one for us, old man. My goodness, come on, son, or we won't see the race. [*Fade out.*]

[*Scene 8. The race. Fade in.*]

Oscar [*excited*]. Here, give me the glasses. Where's my infernal card. Here we are. Daffodil. White and blue hoops, scarlet cap. My God, he's not in the lead. There he is, son. He's on the rail, though. If he gets shut in there, we're . . .

FRENCH VOICE [*French pronunciation*]. Mais vite, alors. Eet ees eempossy-
    bil. Lon-slow! Lon-slow!
OSCAR. My dear man, do stop waving that hat about, we can't see a thing.
    Who the devil cares about Lancelot anyway.
FRENCH VOICE. Ah mon Dieu. Lon-slow. Le chockee, ee does not eat ze
    'orse.
OSCAR. Here they come, Paul. They're in the straight now. By Jove, Daf-
    fodil's up in front. He's got through.
CROWD. Mirza, come on Mirza.
BOOKIE [*Irish*]. The fav'rite's bate! Lancylot walks it. I'll take ten to one
    bar Lancylot.
FRENCH VOICE [*screams*]. Lon-slow weens!
OSCAR [*shouting*]. He doesn't. Daffodil's at him. They're neck and neck.
    He's passed him. Daffodil's won it. Daffodil's race by half-a-length.
    Paul, my boy, you're a lucky devil. [*Fade out.*]

[*Scene 9. Car on the way back.* UNCLE OSCAR *and* PAUL.]

OSCAR. Look here, son—What am I to do with these, eh? Four fat fivers?
PAUL [*quite unmoved*]. Oh, I'll see what Bassett says. Let me think, I should
    have fifteen hundred, twenty in reserve—and now this twenty.
OSCAR. Look here. You're not *serious* about Bassett and this fifteen hun-
    dred business, are you.
PAUL. Of course, I am. But you promised it should be between you and
    me, Uncle Oscar, didn't you?
OSCAR. But . . .
PAUL. Honor bright?
OSCAR. Honor bright all right, son; but I don't understand.
PAUL. Why don't you become a partner with Bassett and me? You could
    become a partner if you wish, but you'd have to promise not to let it
    go beyond us three. Bassett and I are lucky you see, and you must be
    lucky too, because it was your ten shillings I started winning with.
OSCAR. Perhaps I'd better. [*Car draws up.*] Well, here we are back at the old
    home and there's Bassett with his nose in a flowerbed. Shall we have a
    talk with him now?
PAUL. Let's.
OSCAR [*calling*]. Bassett. If you've a moment to spare we'd like to have a
    word with you.
BASSETT [*calling back.*] Just coming, sir.
    [*Fade in.*] It's like this, you see, sir. Master Paul, 'e would get me
    talkin' about racin' events—spinnin' yarns you know, sir. And he was
    always keen on knowin' if I'd made a little something or lost. After I'd

put that five shillings on Blush O' Dawn for 'im, and that went down
the drain, as they say, I didn't want 'im to go on, but he wanted so bad
to put that ten bob 'e 'ad from you on Singhalese, I 'adn't the 'eart to
refuse, and blimey, 'e won.

PAUL. We're all right when we're sure. It's when we're not quite *sure* that
we go down.

BASSETT. Oh but we're careful then.

OSCAR [*chuckling*]. But when are you *sure?*

BASSETT [*in a religiously solemn voice*]. It's Master Paul, sir. It's as if 'e 'ad it
from 'Eaven. Like Daffodil today.

PAUL. That was sure as eggs.

OSCAR. Did you put anything on Daffodil?

BASSETT. Yes, sir, I made a bit.

OSCAR. It's amazing.

PAUL. Sometimes I'm *absolutely* sure, like about Daffodil and sometimes I
have an idea, and sometimes I haven't even an idea, have I, Bassett?
Then we're careful, because we mostly go down.

OSCAR. You do, do you? And when you're sure, what makes you sure,
Sonny?

PAUL [*evasively*]. Oh, I don't know. I'm sure, that's all. [*Changing subject.*]
Will you become a partner, then, Uncle Oscar, with Bassett and me,
just us three?

BASSETT. If Master Paul offers you to be partners, sir, I would if I were
you; if you'll excuse me.

[*Scene 10.* PAUL *and* OSCAR.]

OSCAR. Let's see now, at ten to one, that's ten thousand for you, Paul—five
thousand for Bassett—and two thousand is mine. I don't like it, son.
This sort of thing makes me nervous.

PAUL. You needn't be, Uncle. I was sure about Lively Spark but perhaps I
shan't be sure again for a long time.

OSCAR. But what are you going to do with your money?

PAUL. I started it for mother, because she says father is so unlucky and
doesn't make any money. She gets writs, you know.

OSCAR. I know, son.

PAUL. And then the house whispers at me and I can't bear it. It's awful. I
thought if I was lucky . . .

OSCAR. Well you certainly seem to be. What do you want me to do then?

PAUL. I want mother to have the money, but she mustn't know where it
comes from. I shouldn't like her to know I was lucky. She'd stop me.

OSCAR. Very well. I'll manage that for you. But I don't feel comfortable
about all this. It isn't natural. [*Fade.*]

[*Scene 11. Voices in the house.*]

1ST VOICE. The house looks more like it used to look
    Once again there are bowls of great red roses
    On the drawing room piano, new dining room curtains,
    Two cars in the garage, an extra gardener.
    A pretty parlourmaid.
2ND VOICE. Paul has been riding.
1ST VOICE. He must have been lucky.
2ND VOICE. You bet he's been lucky
    But lucky once is not always lucky.
    He wasn't sure about the Grand National,
    He was wrong on the Leger.
1ST VOICE. Luck always changes.
2ND VOICE. Sometimes it does and sometimes it doesn't.
    Sometimes isn't enough for some.
1ST VOICE. There's still the Derby.
2ND VOICE.   Yes, there's the Derby.
1ST VOICE. If he doesn't know what will happen then
    Where is the money to keep him at Eton,
    Where will the gardener's wages come from
    How will his mother afford new furs
    Who'll pay the parlourmaid, who'll buy the roses
    What will the servants say about Father?
    He's got to be lucky about the Derby
    He's got to have luck now, more than ever.
    There must be more money now, more than ever,
    Paul's got to ride or there won't be enough.
2ND VOICE. Once you need money, you've never enough,
    Once you need luck, you'll always need it,
    Once you start riding, you cannot stop. [*Fade.*]

[*Scene 12. A party. Dance music.*]

VOICE OF A FRIEND. Hullo Joan, didn't Harry come up to town with you
    today?
MOTHER. Yes, but he has to dine with a man who has a scheme for extrac-
    ting radium from beer bottles. Harry says it's wonderful.
FRIEND. You poor darling. It was a portable refrigerator last time, wasn't
    it? Dear Harry is always so enthusiastic. Here's Oscar. I've got to
    dance now with the Irish attaché. My dear, he's divine. See you later.
OSCAR. Here's your drink. I managed to pick my way to the bar at last.
    Heavens, what a crowd.

MOTHER. Oscar, I'm terribly worried about Paul.

OSCAR. Why, my dear? What's the matter?

MOTHER. There's something seriously wrong with him. He'll hardly taste his food and just sits staring into space. When I suggested this morning going away to the sea-side, he got quite hysterical and said he couldn't go away before the Derby. A normal child doesn't behave like that about a horse race. I don't like leaving him alone. I wish I hadn't come this evening.

OSCAR. Steady, my dear. Your nerves are all on edge. Paul's all right. Just a little highly-strung, that's all.

MOTHER. Oscar, you know something. I know you do. What's happening behind my back? Where did that ten thousand pounds come from?

OSCAR. Didn't the lawyer . . . ?

MOTHER. You're lying. You're hiding something. I'm going home. At once. I *know* there's something wrong. [*Fade.*]

[*Scene 13. Paul's room.* PAUL *already riding.*]

1ST VOICE. Paul looks tired.

2ND VOICE.   You bet he's tired.
    If you love luck you are always tired.

1ST VOICE. There must be more money now, more than ever
    He's got to be lucky about the Derby
    He's got to have luck or there won't be enough.

2ND VOICE. Once you need money, there's never enough.

[*Voices fade away. Wind.*]

PAUL. Faster. Faster. You've got to tell me about the Derby.

[*Voices fade in crescendo and diminuendo.*]

VOICES. Pounds, shillings, and pence,
    The horse jumped over the fence.
    And what do you think he was after?
    Pounds, shillings and pence. [*Voices fade.*]

PAUL. Faster. Faster, do you hear?

[*Voices fade in as before.*]

VOICES. Paul's out of his wits
    He won't go to school
    His mother gets writs
    His father's a fool. [*Voices fade.*]

PAUL. Why are you so slow? Please go faster. Please don't fail me now.

[*Voice of* MONOLULU *fades in.*]

MONOLULU. Ma voice rang over de hills
   You jis turn a deaf ear
   You jis turn a deaf ear.
PAUL [*screaming*]. Be quiet. Go away, do you hear.
   O God, you told me I was lucky.
   Let me be sure, just once more
   And I promise I'll never ride again.
   Never. Never.

[*Sound of galloping horses.*]

They're coming. They're coming. I knew it would be all right.

[*Voices under galloping.*]

VOICES. Surprising
   Cummerbund
   Malabar   [*Twice.*]
   Numskull

   Surprising
   Malabar   [*Three times.*]
   Cummerbund

   Malabar
   Cummerbund
   Cummerbund   [*Four times.*]
   Malabar

[*Roars of the crowd.*]

   Malabar
   Malabar
   Malabar.

MOTHER [*loudly*]. Paul!

[*Riding stops. Then* PAUL *crashes to the ground.*]

Darling, what's the matter? Speak to me, Paul. Oscar, help me lift him
into bed. O God. I *knew* something was wrong.
PAUL [*in delirium*]. Malabar. I *know*, Bassett. Do you hear, Bassett? It's
Malabar.
MOTHER. It's not Bassett, darling, it's Mother.

PAUL. Malabar. Malabar. I knew I could get there.
OSCAR. I'll go and phone Dr Williams. [*Aside.*] Malabar. Poor devil. I wonder if he really knows this time. [*Fade.*]

[*Scene 14. Paul's room.*]

BASSETT. Good afternoon, Ma'am. 'Ow is 'e?
MOTHER. He is very, very sick, Bassett. You must only stay a moment.
BASSETT. I won't stay long, Ma'am. but I got some noos as ought to make 'im feel better. Master Paul. Master Paul. Can you 'ear me, Master Paul? You were right. Malabar came in first a clean win at fourteen-to-one. You've made seventy thousand pounds, Master Paul, you 'ave.
MOTHER. What are you talking about, Bassett? What's Paul been doing?
BASSETT. 'E 'ad it from 'Eaven, Ma'am, all the winners.
PAUL. I knew Malabar, didn't I, Mother? Seventy thousand pounds. I call that lucky, don't you, Mother? When I'm sure, Bassett can go as high as he likes. I never told you, Mother, did I, that if I can ride my horse and get there, then I'm sure, quite sure. You see, I'm lucky. [*Fade.*]

[*Scene 15. The garden.*]

1ST VOICE. What is Paul doing?
2ND VOICE.   Paul is dying.
1ST VOICE. How is his mother?
2ND VOICE.   She watches and weeps.
1ST VOICE. Does she blame her luck?
2ND VOICE.   Not any more.
  Those who blame luck are bound to an image
  That has many names—Money, Prestige,
  Originality, Family Pride,
  But in fact is simply the fear of Death.
  Those who love luck are in love with themselves.
  Those who weep know images useless
  Those who mourn know all images vain
  Now at last, she weeps, she weeps and watches
  Now at last she knows she loves her son.
1ST VOICE. Does Paul know this?
2ND VOICE.   Yes, Paul knows now.
  That's why he needn't ride any longer
  The world of Perhaps has become the Certain,
  Paul is no longer afraid of his fear
  Paul is no longer in love with luck.

1st Voice. The image that made this house unlucky
    The envy of which we were the unwilling voices
    Is fading now. We need not whisper
    Out of the rose-bush or under the stairs.
    Now a real death replaces its unreal image
    And sorrow silences envy for ever,
    Silences us. We are glad to be silent.
    Grief understood is a form of freedom
    Love is born from the death of this child.

LITURGICAL DRAMA

The Play of Daniel

[1957]

I

Welcome, good people, watch and listen
To a play in praise of the prophet Daniel,
Beloved of the Lord. Long has he dwelt
In brick Babylon, built by a river,
Far from Jerusalem, his real home,
A son of Judah, suffering exile
Since Jehoakim turned from the true God
To worship idols in high places.
Painful was the price to be paid for that:
For the cruel king of the Chaldees,
Nebuchadnezzar with a numberless host
Besieged Jerusalem and soon prevailed.
He broke her gates, burned her with fire,
Her men and women he made captive,
Her temple treasures he took away.
Shut them in the house of Shinah, his ungod,
A brass thing in which no breath was.
But Daniel, the pious, from the days of his youth,
Worshipped the One and walked humbly,
So God gave him gifts of vision
That found him favor in this foreign land.
He alone was ready to read the dreams
That Nebuchadnezzar in the night had,
And the fate he foretold befell that king,
Whole senses forsook him for seven years;
Like a witless ox he ate grass,
Nameless, naked, his nails like claws.
Those days are done. He died, and now
His son Belshazzar sits on the throne.
See, he approaches, his princes with him.

II

Mighty Belshazzar commands a feast;
A thousand lords give him thanks and glory.

Flushed and foolish, flown with pride,
He bids his servants to bring hither
The goodly goblets of gold and silver,
The consecrated cups and vessels
Set aside for sacred use
In Jehovah's temple, but taken thence
When Nebuchadnezzar annexed Judah.
His wanton wives drank wine therefrom.
With lustful lips and looks profane,
Their shouts grow shameless at Belshazzar's table
In honor of idols of their own devising
Forgetting God from whom all greatness comes.
In this heedless hour a hand appears,
Phantom fingers come forth and write
Words on the wall, a wonder to behold.
The sight silences; they cease laughing;
Full of fear is the face of the king,
Belshazzar of Babylon; his bowels quake,
His knees knock. In his need he cries:
"Summon my soothsayers, the sages of my kingdom
My wise men. Wealth shall he have,
Garments of scarlet and gold chains,
Who reads what is written, unriddles these words."
The loremasters, the learned of Babylon,
Are brought to the palace; they peer, they frown,
They stare astonished at the strange words;
They know them not; their knowledge is vain;
The truth is not in them to interpret rightly
What is said there. Sad at heart
Are the king and his court; care fills them.

III

News of this hap is noised abroad:
In her quiet quarters the Queen hears it,
And in loving haste leaves her chamber
To counsel the king. Comely her form,
Gracious to gaze on like the green cedar,
Blithe in bearing like a blossoming rose,
As she enters the hall with her handmaidens.
"My lord," she says, "Live for ever,
May thy days endure. There dwells in thy kingdom

A holy man, mighty in wisdom,
His speech inspired by the spirit of God,
Whom thy father favored for he found none
So apt to expound a hard sentence,
Unriddle visions and read the meaning
Of dark dreams. Daniel is his name.
Show him this writing, for surely he will
Interpret it truly. Be troubled no more!"
Hearkening to her counsel, the king says:
"Find me this man and fetch him hither!"
Searching the city, the satraps come
To Daniel's dwelling. "Come down," they call,
"And hasten with us to the High King,
He wishes for thy wisdom, great reward shall be thine
If thou canst tell him the true meaning
Of the secret signs, and assuage his fear."
"Princes," says the prophet, "if it please God,
The Lord of truth, to enlighten my spirit,
I will read these runes; direct me thither."

IV

He is come to the court and the king says:
"Art thou that child of churlish Judah
Who is deemed wise? Is Daniel thy name?
My soothsayers, the sages of Babylon
Cannot understand the strange writing:
If thou canst make its meaning clear,
Glory and gold shall be given thee."
And Daniel answers: "Hail, O King!
When Nebuchadnezzar, as thou knowest well,
Forgot the God from whom his glory came
In the lust of his pride, the light of reason
Fled from him, he fed on grass
Like a brute beast. Thy boast is worse.
Thou has lifted thyself against the Lord of Heaven,
Profaning what was sacred, the vessels of His house,
Made obeisance to idols of brass and stone:
For this thou art judged. Thus I interpret
The words on the wall, a warning of doom.
Mene saith the Lord: thy might is finished.
Tekel saith the Lord: tested in the balance,

Thou art found wanting, thy weight is less.
Pheres saith the Lord: thy fall is certain,
Thy crown shall leave thee, thy kingdom be divided
Thy power apportioned to Persians and Medes."
Then Belshazzar is ashamed, he shakes with fear.
"I have sinned," he says, "Let the sacred vessels,
God's treasure, be returned to Judah
To own for ever. Let honor be shown
To this wise man in whose mouth is truth."
With merry music and mirthful song
The princes praise the prophet Daniel
The Queen also for her quickness of heart
And his lieges leave their lord alone.

[*Pause.*]

Now Belshazzar shivers as shades of night
Fall upon fields and fortified cities:
In solitude and silence his soul is delivered
To wanhope and weakness. "Ah, woe!", he sighs,
"My doom is upon me, death is near,
The fate foretold, what I fear will be.
Once God gave me glory and power,
Triumph for a time; now He takes them back;
Nor strength nor cunning can stay His hand.
The might of kings is in their many warriors,
Bowmen, spearmen and burnished chariots,
But His power is in Himself to impose His will;
He issues no orders, His heart intends
'Let this happen!' and, Lo!, it does.
Men trust in towers, in turreted keeps
And high walls, but who can point
Upward or downward or out yonder,
This way or that, saying 'There He dwells'?
With a man one can bargain;—'Be my friend
And I will give you gold or cattle,
Horses or women', but who can say
Of the Lord Almighty 'He lacks this.
I perceive the desire that will sway His judgment'?
Nor valor nor vanity avail me now.
I go to my grave, my glory is brought
To dust and darkness: but, as death takes me,
Let me turn to the Truth, entrust my soul

To the Lord of Light, the Living God!"
And now in the night there is noise of battle:
Darius the Great who rules the Medes,
Comes forth as a victor, invades the land,
Slays Belshazzar, sits on his throne.

V

Now Darius rules: he raises Daniel
To high office for his excellent spirit,
Favors, befriends, prefers him over
Presidents and princes, plans to make him
Ruler of the realm. Wroth are the lords,
Jealous of this Jew. They join together,
Watch and wait for his ways to err,
But find no fault; he is faithful in all.
"We cannot," they say, "find occasion against him
Unless it relate to the Law of His God."

VI

The plotting princes approach the king.
"Darius," they say, "may your reign be long!
The captains of your court have counselled together
To establish a statute, a stern decree.
This have we thought. For thirty days
Whosoever shall ask a petition
Of any save thee shall be thrown straightway,
Alive to the lions. Long live Darius!
Wilt thou sign, great King, and seal the writing,
That none may annul this new law?"
Then Darius, thinking no evil,
Signs and seals it. The sinful men
Hurry hence to the house of Daniel
Where, at a window, towards Jerusalem,
The prophet is praying with pure heart
To the true God. They return to Darius.
"O King," they cry, "thy decree went forth
That whosoever should ask a petition
Of any save thee should be thrown to the lions,
But this man Daniel has dared disobey thee;
Openly he asks for help from his God."

Darius is sad, he sees their envy;
He labors long to deliver Daniel.
But the accusers cry: "The decree was thine.
Didst thou not sign and seal the writing
That none should annul it? It shall not be changed."
"Alas," says the king, "the law is thus."
Grieving greatly, he gives orders
That Daniel be cast in the den of lions.
"Daniel," he cries, "I can do no other.
Forgive thy friend! May God save thee!"

VII

So Daniel is down in the deep pit,
Alone among lions. But the Lord of Heaven
Sends an angel with a sword to keep
Those beasts at bay that they bite him not.
And a second angel He sends in the night
To Habakkuk, a holy prophet,
Saying: "Arise! The road is long.
I am bid to bring you to Babylon town
And the dark den where Daniel lies."
"That is full far," says that faithful man,
"And I know not the way; nevertheless
I will go to greet him." God's angel
Takes him by the hair; in a trice they come
To the perilous pit; he appears to Daniel,
Refreshes with food his fainting spirit.

VIII

Day dawns; to the den of lions
The king is come. He calls aloud:
"Daniel, O Daniel, my dear friend,
Dost thou live yet? Hath the Lord thy God
Saved His servant from sudden death?"
And Daniel answers: "Hail, O King!
I am safe and sound. God sent me an angel
With a shining sword to shut the mouths
Of the hungry lions. They lie asleep."
Glad is Darius at this great wonder,
Bids his bodyguard bring up Daniel,

Set him free, and in fury commands:
"Let his accusers be cast in the pit!"
The princes and presidents who plotted evil
Rue their wrong. Ere they reach the bottom
Their bones are broken, their bodies rent,
Torn in pieces by the teeth of the lions.
So Daniel was restored to his state of honor
And dwelt in peace until his days' end.
Visions revealed to him events to come;
Truly he foretold the return of Judah
To its own home, and the end of Jerusalem,
Her final fall when, in fullness of time,
The wise Word that was from the beginning,
Maker of all things, should be made flesh
And suffer death to redeem mankind.

IX

And now, good people, our play is done.
But, to grace our going, let God's angel
Tell you tidings of eternal joy.
To the maiden Mary, the immaculate Virgin,
A baby is born in Bethlehem City
Who is called Christ, our King and Savior.
Sing glory to God and good-will,
Peace to all peoples! Praise the Lord!

FILM NARRATIVES

Runner

[1962]

FIRST VOICE. Excellence is a gift: among mankind
      To one is assigned a ready wit,
      To another swiftness of eye or foot.

      Art which raises Nature to perfection
      Itself demands the passion of the elect
      Who expect to win.

      As Pindar long ago in Greece was proud to hail
      Thessalian Hippokleas, even so
      It is meet we praise in our days fleet-footed
      Bruce Kidd from Toronto.

ANNOUNCER. The Place of Training: The East York Track Club
    The Trainer: Fred Foote
    The Training Schedule: Two hours a day, six days a week.
    Average distance run per week: One hundred miles.

SECOND VOICE.   All visible, visibly
                Moving things
                Spin or swing,
                One of the two,
                Move as the limbs
                Of a runner do,
                To and fro,
                Forward and back,
                Or, as they swiftly
                Carry him,
                In orbit go
                Round an endless track:
                So, everywhere, every
                Creature disporting
                Itself according
                To the Law of its making,
                In the rivals' dance
                Of a balanced pair
                Or the ring-dance
                Round a common centre,

Delights the eye
By its symmetry
As it changes place,
Blessing the unchangeable
Absolute rest
Of the space they share.

FIRST VOICE.   Speed is inborn in sprinter's muscle
But long learning alone can build
Stamina and strength
SECOND VOICE.   By instruction only
Can limbs learn to live their movement
Without thinking
FIRST VOICE.   All-important
Is leg-action
SECOND VOICE.   Arms are for balance
Of more moment is mileage run
Than time taken.

ANNOUNCER. Now for the main event of this Dominion Day Celebration
in East York—the two-mile invitation race.

We have three international track stars here this afternoon:
Lt Max Truex of the United States Navy, in the dark trunks:
Lazlo Tabori, late of Hungary, in the light trunks; and of course,
Toronto's own Bruce Kidd.

The runners are lining up at the start mark—the officials are ready.

They're off!

They're jockeying for position around the first bend,
Tabori's taking a strong lead. Kidd's right after him.
Now! Truex is moving out in front. Tabori's coming up strong
behind him.
Coming down the straightaway now, it's Tabori, Truex, and Kidd.

FIRST VOICE.   Trusting each other
Rivals shall ride to race together
Be firm friends.
SECOND VOICE.   Foolish is he
Who, greedy for victory, grits his teeth
Frowns fiercely before contests,
And no neighbour

FIRST VOICE.   It is nice to win
                    But sport shall be loved by losers also
                    Foul is envy
SECOND VOICE.   False are those
                    With warm words for the winner after
                    A poor race
FIRST VOICE.   Pleasing to the ear
                    Are clapping crowds
SECOND VOICE.   But the cold stop-watch
                    Tells the truth
FIRST VOICE.   There is time and place
                    For a fine performance
SECOND VOICE.   Fate forbids
                    Mortals to be at their best always
                    God-given is the great day.

ANNOUNCER.

Truex is spurting ahead but Tabori and Kidd are hot on his heels.
One mile to go and the runners are maintaining a grueling pace.

Now we have the official standing in the two-mile event—
Kidd first, Tabori second and Truex third.

SECOND VOICE.   The camera's eye
                    Does not lie,
                    But it cannot show
                    The life within,
                    The life of a runner
                    Or yours or mine,
                    That race which is neither
                    Fast nor slow
                    For nothing can ever
                    Happen twice,
                    That story which moves
                    Like music when
                    Begotten notes
                    New notes beget,
                    Making the flowing
                    Of Time a growing,
                    Till what it could be
                    At last it is
                    Where Fate is Freedom,
                    Grace and Surprise.

US

[*1967?*]

The waiting land

Was this the Vineland the Vikings' legend
Said they saw? If so, the glimpse
Was soon forgotten. Centuries passed.
The map was blank till Iberians looking
For a less expensive passage, a quicker
Route to the Indias, rich in spices,
Stumbled instead on a strange continent.

Vast, unhumanized, a virgin wilderness,
The land lay in her long sleep,
Waiting to be woken by western man.

Quite empty? No. There were noble savages,
Indian tribes, tillers and hunters,
Roaming freely through the forests and plains,
Well content with their way of life.

Early settlement

When we came to these shores and encountered the Indians,
There was good-will at first: gifts were exchanged
And treaties sworn. Presently though . . .

Each year the coast became more civil,
Till we broke with England to be our own masters,
And founded a republic, the first on earth
Where all men should be equal and free.
Immigrants were needed. Immigrants came.

Immigration

Most were poor, peasants and such
From the underlayers of the old world's
Stratified heap. They streamed to join us,
Men and women, a million a year.
These came by choice: as they crossed the Atlantic
They looked forward with hope. . . .

□

. . . . Unlike those earlier
Luckless millions who were made to come
Torn from their African homes by force.

No rejoicing, though, for Indians:
We wanted their land,
With war and whiskey we worsted them.

Scenes of American achievement

America: A land of great plenty with promises to keep.

The highway sequence

Our frontier lands are fully settled;
Overcrowding is our headache now.

So we have built superhighways and automobiles
To give us freedom of movement.

We have pinned our hopes on our machines.

Yes, we have pinned our hopes on our machines.

The wild landscapes

However, for our rare moments of escape, we have managed to preserve a
few landscapes that are still wild. Here, we still may wander by ourselves
and fall again under the spell of nature, and re-enter her magic circle
where we lived when we were children.

These precious places are few and far between.

The beach sequence

Solitude and privacy are not easy to come by in a mechanized world.

Devastation of our natural resources

The marvelous machines we have made obey us,
And couldn't care less for the consequences:
Nothing good or evil can happen to them.
If we want it that way, they will lay waste the earth,
Loot the land and leave behind them
An irredeemable desolation.

□

Yes, we are free in our greed to let poisons
Befoul the streams till the fish die,
Discommodate cities, turning smiling fields
Into junk graveyards and garbage dumps,
Let noxious effluvia fill the air, polluting our lungs.

The American neighborhood

Pleasant places exist, of course, comfortable retreats
Where the air smells good, the nights are quiet, and
One can forget about all the problems of the world outside.

The American poor

For the unskilled, the unschooled, there is now no place in this world,
neither on the land, nor in the city.

Nobody needs them, and they know it.

Finale

The eyes of the world are upon us
And wonder what we're worth,
For much they see dishonors
The richest country on earth.

Shamefully we betray
Our noble dead if we,
After two hundred years,
Cannot or will not see,
Behind their conscious ideas,
More clearly what is meant
By certain truths that they
Believed self-evident.

On each of us depends
What sort of judgment waits
For you, for me, our friends,
And these United States.

APPENDICES

"The Life of an American": A Scenario by W. H. Auden and Christopher Isherwood

EARLY in 1939 Auden and Christopher Isherwood prepared a scenario for a film to be titled *The Life of an American*. Nothing came of this project, and Isherwood, when asked near the end of his life, could remember nothing about it, although he believed (plausibly) that most of the scenario was his own work.

Isherwood typed the scenario and preserved it in his collection (now in the possession of Don Bachardy). He tentatively dated the typescript "1938–39?" Because it is typed on standard American typing paper it was almost certainly prepared during the months when he and Auden lived together in New York, between late January and early May 1939. It is conceivable, however, that they wrote it during their first brief visit to New York in July 1938.

The text below corrects trivial spelling errors in Isherwood's typescript, but leaves unchanged Isherwood's practice of typing "e.g." in lowercase immediately after the end of a sentence. In the typescript the description of the scene beginning "Scene during the slump" ends "a few months to life"; I have emended the last word to "live".

THE LIFE OF AN AMERICAN

An interesting and cheap four-reeler could be made in which the part of the central character was taken by the camera. The hero sees life through the lens of the camera, so that the audience identifies itself with him. To make this possible, the story must be as ordinary and universal as possible. We suggest the life of an average American.

All the other characters speak and act as in any other film, but the hero's voice is represented by a commentator speaking in the first person, as if telling the story of his life. When necessary, he describes his feelings. e.g. "I turned away because I didn't want her to see how much I cared."

The telling of the story by reminiscence enables the film to be kept short, by confining it to selected significant incidents and, above all, to viewpoints (?) in which the peculiar role of the camera as an actor can be fully exploited. These are:

1. Anything involving the hero's physical growth. In the opening scenes the camera is near the ground, and rises steadily through the hero's boyhood and youth.

2. Anything involving the hero's physical movements—crawling, toddling, running, stooping, turning around.

3. Anything involving the hero's face, or his own perception of his body. (A fight, visiting the oculist or the dentist, weeping, kissing.)

It is possible that occasionally the subjective feelings of the hero could be allowed to destroy the visual image. e.g. When he is suffering from his first calf love, he visits the girl in her home. Her family are sitting around as usual, but instead of the girl, there is a pillar of blazing light and he says, "I thought she looked like a goddess." Or again, when walking through the city streets, very unhappy, they could appear absolutely dead and deserted.

SOME POSSIBLE INCIDENTS

Childhood (Hero is born in a small Middle-West town about 1887)	Being frightened by a large dog and rescued by his mother. Getting his father to tell him a story. A picnic where he falls in the water.
Boyhood	Falling asleep in a dull lesson and catching it from the teacher. Fighting the school bully. Learning to ride a bicycle. Beginning to take an interest in his clothes and to wash his hands.
Youth	His first romance (she never knows). Being interviewed for his first job. The first time he gets drunk.
Early Manhood (marries around 1909)	Courtship (first chance meeting, and country walk during which he proposes). Marriage and honeymoon trip to Niagara Falls. Birth of a daughter.
War (1917)	Recruiting meeting at which he volunteers. Saying goodbye to his wife. A bayonet charge.
Post War (Inherits some money from his parents and starts a business in N.Y. on his own.)	The new house. Getting the news of a fortunate speculation in Real Estate. Flirtation with his typist (wife discovers). Scene showing estrangement and embarrassment. Scene during the slump when money is lost. Reconciliation in misfortune with his wife. Marriage of

daughter. Visit to the doctor who tells him he has only a few months to live.

(1938)   Walk home after the news.

Then there is a black-out and in the darkness voices are heard saying.
"He's going."
"Hush, he may be able to hear you." etc.
The camera opens again, and there is a bedroom. Enter his wife and daughter, nurse, etc. His wife takes his hand and says, "Speak to me." There is no answer. Only a roar increasing in volume as the screen image breaks up, whirls round, and fades.

W. H. AUDEN

CHRISTOPHER ISHERWOOD

When Auden visited Los Angeles in the first week of August 1940, he spent some time in Hollywood, where, as Britten reported a few weeks later to Ralph Hawkes, he "made some excellent contacts for him & me (& Christopher Isherwood who is on contract there now) to do a musical film. . . . the man he is in contact with is Mr McKenna, M.G.M. Story department" (Britten, *Letters from a Life*, 1991, vol. 2, p. 855). Nothing came of these contacts. A proposal for stage work that arose during the same visit similarly came to nothing. On 14 August 1940, a week after Auden returned east, Aldous Huxley wrote to Frieda Lawrence, who had asked Huxley to revamp a dramatization by Melchior Lengyel of *Lady Chatterley's Lover*. Huxley wrote that he had neither the time nor the ability to do the job, "However, I think we have the right man on the spot in the person of Christopher Isherwood, who would probably collaborate with W. H. Auden, the poet . . . They are interested in the problem and would like to attempt it. The idea is that as soon as Isherwood has finished his present stint of movie work and as soon as Lengyel has finished cutting and revising the script along the lines we have suggested to date, he (Isherwood) should get down to the job, with assistance from Auden, who is in New York, and of myself" (*Letters of Aldous Huxley*, 1969, pp. 456–57). The plan evaporated in October when nothing had been heard from Auden. Possibly he never heard about the proposal, which Isherwood and Huxley may have made on his behalf.

"The Queen's Masque"

Auden wrote *The Queen's Masque* to honor Chester Kallman's twenty-second birthday on 7 January 1943. It was performed privately by Kallman's friends in Ann Arbor, where he was taking courses toward an M.A. in English at the University of Michigan. Auden did not attend the performance. He was teaching in Swarthmore at the time and had sent the script to its director, Strowan Robertson, at whose apartment it apparently was performed.

The manuscript of the masque, consisting of the main text and a set of later additions, is now in the Berg Collection of the New York Public Library. The main text that Auden first sent Robertson, probably in the last days of December 1942, lacked the three Ghosts. He then added three pages containing dialogue and songs for the Ghosts, which he sent with an undated letter to Kallman (now in a private collection) that ends: "P.P.S. Enclosed. An erratum for Strowan." The text below follows Auden's instructions in these additional pages by incorporating the added material. In the first version, after Mabel's line "God help the poor old buffer in his pain" (p. 425), Ella's speech reads:

> No more of that. All must be laughter here
> And youth and song. Queen Anastasia this year
> Completes the twenty-second of Her reign.

And this speech is followed immediately by the recitative "Come hither, nymphs of Angel Hall". The speech is replaced by Auden's "First Insertion" from the additional pages, which contain the revised version of Ella's line and the entrance and dialogue for the first Ghost. The "Second Insertion" begins with the entrance of the second Ghost (p. 427) and continues through "Does Anastasia rule the People?"—"Yes." The surrounding text was unchanged. The "Third Insertion" begins with Ella's "Let us pray now for Her to whom we owe" (p. 429) and continues through the exit of the third Ghost. The surrounding text was unchanged. An unknown hand marked one possibly authorial change in the text, replacing the second line of Queen of Dullness's recitative (p. 428) with "Ur-Mutter calls you in Ur-Despair."

The manuscript is marked by another unknown hand with abbreviated names of musical works; they were probably chosen by the director, although they may have been specified by Auden in a letter now lost. These musical cues generally name only the larger work from which a brief selection was chosen. The music that accompanies the opening text, down to Ella's "Assez", is "Tch[aikovsky] 4th [Symphony]". The music for the first Ghost's Blues is noted as "Im Guter Stimmel [*sic*]", perhaps an error for "In guter Stimmung". The recitative "Come hither, nymphs of Angel Hall" is spoken over "Die Walküre", and the duet "Heil Anastasia, the Queen of Hearts" is spoken over "Parsifal". The music for the second Ghost's Blues is marked as "Les Boules de Neiges [*sic*]". The entrance of the Queen of Dullness is marked "Donizetti"; her Recitative is marked "D of SPF [i.e., Dance of the Sugarplum Fairy]"; and her Aria is marked "Ov MSND [i.e., Overture to A Midsummer Night's Dream]". The music for the third Ghost is "L for TO [i.e., The Love for Three Oranges]". The Litany is spoken over "Coriolan O[verture]", and the concluding Grand Chorus over "Roman Carnival". Auden may have hinted at the musical styles required by alluding in his stage directions to the repertories of Lotte Lenya, Marlene Dietrich, and Marianne Oswald.

Many of the names in the masque are local or private references. Nelson Bentley, favorite son of the masque's Queen of Dullness, was an undergraduate poet who had dropped out of Auden's class at Michigan in 1941 with a complaint to the effect that Auden was evil and cynical about the classics (see Charles H. Miller, *Auden, an American Friendship*, 1983, p. 29). Bentley's later indignation at one of Kallman's music reviews for the student newspaper, the *Michigan Daily*, gave Auden a name for the group of friends that performed the masque. In response to Kallman's dismissive review of Shostakovich's Seventh Symphony, on 11 December 1942, Bentley wrote (in one of many letters from offended students printed the next day): "The truth of the matter is that almost everyone excepting Kallman and his Klever Kompanions realized that they were witnessing a magnificent performance of the work that tells most fully the unconquerable spirit of the Soviet people, their intense suffering, [etc.]" In an undated letter shortly afterward Auden reported to Kallman that a friend in Ann Arbor had told him that "one of the abusive letters was from our dear old friend Nelson Bentley" (letter in a private collection).

Other local references include Angel (properly Angell) Hall, the ponderous building in Mussolini-modern style that housed the Department of English. W. Lloyd Berridge was a kind but conventional psychological counselor (not an M.D.) at the university; the masque evidently alludes to an instance of his misunderstanding or disapproval of homosexuality. The Abbess was probably Kallman's student friend Dorothy Farnan. Willy (William Rodgers) and Jack (Jack Barker) were two of Kallman's paramours. "Eury's dish" perhaps echoes someone's mispronunciation of Eurydice. Most of the other names in the work are those of public and literary figures of the period, although "Percy" is evidently Shelley.

The text below does not attempt to correct Auden's German and French.

The Queen's Masque

BY

BOJO, THE HOMO

---

*To be
Presented at 803 South State Street
on
January 7ᵗʰ 1943
by
Kallman's Klever Kompanions
under
the direction of
Mʳ Strowan Robertson*

DRAMATIS PERSONAE

MABEL
ELLA
FIRST ECHO
SECOND ECHO
THE QUEEN OF DULLNESS
THREE GHOSTS

[THE QUEEN OF DULLNESS can be doubled with one of the ECHOES.
The other can manage the phonograph.]

MABEL [*solus*]. Has Hitler died? Is coffee to be had?
    What's going on here? Everyone's gone mad.

                                             [*Enter* ELLA.]

    Pardon.
ELLA.   You're welcome, stranger. Have you come?
    —I mean—to date our revels frolicsome
    In gay Ann Arbor where it's great to be
    At all times, but to-night especially.
MABEL. Ann Arbor? Not Queen Anastasia's seat?
ELLA. The same.
MABEL.   O Wonne and occasion sweet.
    From coast to coast at mention of Her name,
    Cold faggots kindle to a genial flame,
    Excited fairies down their steeples slide,
    And savage wolves are glad to give a ride.
ELLA. For Her the burly driver stops his truck
    And goes down on his knees to beg—for luck.
MABEL. Trunkless, the agitated coastguard stands
    To do Her service.
ELLA.   She alone commands
    The uniquely moulded, and the common stamp
    And rules the courthouse,
MABEL.   And the campus
ELLA.   And the camp.
MABEL. 'Tis even whispered that Her beauty's spell
    Bewitched self-loving Merlin in his well.
    He weeps, they say.
ELLA.   His wisdom was in vain.
MABEL. God help the poor old buffer in his pain.
ELLA. Assez. Vénus s'ennuie de cette affaire.
    Kopf hoh. Queen Anastasia this year
    Completes the twenty-second of Her reign.

                                    [*Enter* GHOST.]

MABEL. What youth is this who, pale as sauerkraut,
    Gate-crashes on our party.
ELLA.   The ghost, no doubt,
    Of some poor strich whom Anastasia sank
    As he was cruising.
MABEL.   That girl could stop a tank.

BLUES [*halbmal Lotte, halbmal Marlene*]

GHOST. Im Frühlingstage wann die Winterschnupfen
       Setzen sich nass noch in Taschentuch,
    Und laute Schwänze wachsen im Hosen,
       Der Bub von Frau Minne ist bei mir am Besuch.

    Wie geht's, du olle Sack? Gibt es 'was neues,
       Eine Liebe, zum Beispiel, ohne Not und Rache?
    Weiss die Welt was los ist, oder sagt man schon wieder
       "Es hat kein Zweck; so ist die Sache"?

    Er hat 'was, der Dicker, der schwul Cupido, nicht?
       Obwohl er ein Bischen dof ist. Na ja,
    Man hat Dir als kleines Kind zu heiss gebadet,
       Du frecher Luder, was machst Du denn da?

    Pass auf, Mensch; dass ist mein Herz den Du frisst.
       Das kommt nicht im Frage: es schmeckt nicht gut.
    Die Anastasia hat es vergiftet. Es is allerhand,
       Und geht nie vorbei, das Leid sie mir tut.

                            [*Exit* GHOST.]

ELLA. His grief has killed his grammar.
MABEL.   Impatience bites
    My bottom, sister: call the vassal knights.

RECITATIVE

MABEL.
    Come hither, nymphs of Angel Hall,
    Of tea-room and of coffee-stall,
       Come hither to get laid;
    Hither, ye shepherds of defense
    Who in unpractised innocence
       Among the cows have strayed.
FIRST ECHO.   . . . Have strayed.
SECOND ECHO.   . . . trade.

ELLA.
    And hither, ye much-married men:
    Wise husbands will, just now and then,
       Their normal habits vary:
    Queen Anastasia bids you do,
    Upon Her birthday, what, to you,
       May not be customary.

FIRST ECHO.   . . . Customary.
SECOND ECHO.   . . . O Mary!

DUET

MABEL AND ELLA. Heil Anastasia, the Queen of Hearts.
MABEL. O Belle of Brooklyn.
ELLA.   Maid of Michigan.
MABEL AND ELLA. The members of the Homintern arise
    And beg permission just to kiss your fan.
MABEL. O gay and giddy girl.
ELLA.   O girl of parts.
MABEL. What lips.
ELLA.   What eyes.
MABEL.   What curls.
ELLA.   What size.
MABEL. Sing, soldier.
ELLA.   Sailor.
MABEL.   Pilot.
ELLA.   And Marine.
MABEL AND ELLA. Heil Anastasia. LONG LIVE THE QUEEN.

[*Enter* GHOST.]

MABEL. *Another* ghost.
ELLA.   There're hundreds on Her list.
MABEL. I don't approve, dear; I'm a pragmatist.

BLUES [*à la Marianne Oswald*]

GHOST.   La reine de belles fesses,
                        Anastase, m'a fait
                    Beaucoup, beaucoup de promesses
                        Au lit là-bas;
                    Vraiment, c'est un type, mais
                        Elle ne les garde PAS.

                    Anastase a promis au corps
                        Qu'elle lui montrerait
                    Ces jolies anges encore
                        Qui, tu sais, sont comme ça:
                    Le salop l'a oubliée;
                        Les p'tits n'arrivent PAS.

                    Anastase a promis au coeur
                        Qu'elle lui donnerait
                    Un coup, Dimanche, à sept heures.

Minuit s'en va:
La ventre attend son *hullo*, mais
Elle ne téléphone PAS.

Pour Anastase j'ai perdu mon âme,
Elle m'a tué.
J'ai léché le cul de Madame;
Hélas, hélas.
Je veux lui dire Merde, Merde, mais
Je ne peux *PAS*.

[*Exit* GHOST.]

MABEL. *Most* unamerican.
ELLA.   Free French, I guess.
MABEL. Does Anastasia rule the People?
ELLA.   Yes.

[*The toilet flushes.*]

MABEL. I hear a roar of waters.
ELLA.   Look, who's here.
    The Deadly Queen of Dullness.
MABEL.   *Well.* My *dear*,
    Get her before the moths do.
ELLA.   Stand aside
    And let her render her last number. Hide.

[*Enter* THE QUEEN OF DULLNESS.]

RECITATIVE

QUEEN OF DULLNESS.
    Revenge. Revenge. O Great Boyg, hear my prayer
    The Queen of Dullness calls you in despair.
    Come, Nelson Bentley, dearest son; take thou
    This copy of *Look Homeward Angel* now
    And let it drop on Anastasia's head
            To smite Her dead.
    Where is my Bentley. Ow.

ARIA

What terror grips me by the balls.
My power fails, my kingdom falls.
Sibelius, Shostakovich, Brahms,
Percy and Edna, Archie and Benét,

> O where are they?
> Queen Anastasia's ray
> Dissolves their charms.
> My reign is done.
> I'm sunk. She's won.
> O Weh. O Weh.

> [*Exit* QUEEN OF DULLNESS.]

ELLA.   Dullness, farewell. Come back ten years ago.
              Let us pray now for Her to whom we owe
              Lucidity and joy. On with the show.

> [*Enter* GHOST *who flops down at once on his knees.*]

GHOST.   Bojo gaga Anastasia
                Gigli homo clu Aphasia
                Ainu, Meestair Rhansom, crasia.

ELLA. There must be some mistake. [*To* GHOST.] I say, you know
     This is a birthday masque not F 6.
GHOST.   O. [*Retires in confusion.*]

LITANY

MABEL.   From the Dean's disapproval, and from Eury's dish,
ELLA.   From the professor's blue pencil and piss-elegant swish,
MABEL.   From Dr Berridge, the Abbess, dykes and fish,
CHORUS.   GOD SAVE QUEEN ANASTASIA.

ELLA.   From breaking out and from breaking wind,
MABEL.   From social diseases before or behind,
ELLA.   From the unsympathetic, the small, and the blind,
CHORUS.   GOD SAVE QUEEN ANASTASIA.

MABEL.   From Dorothy Thompson, author of *Listen Hans*,
ELLA.   From the anti-semite, the Zionist, the Y.C.L., and the dunce,
MABEL.   And from Willy and Jack arriving both at once,
CHORUS.   GOD SAVE QUEEN ANASTASIA.

GRAND CHORUS

> O loyal subjects, girl and boy,
> Your carnal motions now employ;
>   Dance as the Muses bid,
> In chains like daisies, hand in hand;
> Do as you would be done by, and
>   Be done by as you did.

Auden and Brecht's Versions of "The Duchess of Malfi"

EDITED BY A. R. BRAUNMULLER

§1 A BRIEF HISTORY OF THE COLLABORATION

FROM 1944 through 1946 Auden collaborated with Bertolt Brecht in an attempt to create an adaptation of John Webster's *The Duchess of Malfi* suitable for Broadway. The fruits of their collaboration included at least two heavily rewritten typescripts of the play, although the version that finally appeared on stage included little of the work of either collaborator.

Auden joined the project only after Brecht had worked intermittently on it for almost a year. In the spring of 1943 the Viennese actress Elisabeth Bergner, then living in America, asked Brecht for a vehicle. Bergner's husband, the producer Paul Czinner, suggested an adaptation of *The Duchess of Malfi*. Brecht found the proposal attractive. He had a detailed knowledge of Renaissance English drama, and had already written several adaptations and reworkings; in November 1941 he had proposed *A Woman Killed with Kindness* by Thomas Heywood as a "classic" vehicle for Bergner.

Brecht had little difficulty writing plausible, rough-hewn English verse, but preferred to work with a native speaker on a project designed for an English-speaking audience. Assisted by one of his earliest American translators, H. R. Hays, he began work on *The Duchess* around April or May 1943. Probably at Bergner and Czinner's suggestion, he incorporated material from Webster's other tragedy *The White Devil* while modifying and amplifying the text of *The Duchess*. Brecht and Hays copyrighted a version of the play on 26 June. A revised text of this version, with notes by A. R. Braunmuller, appears in the British edition of Brecht's *Collected Plays*, vol. 7 (London, 1976). Sheets from the first typescript became the basis for much of Brecht's later work on the play.

At the beginning of December 1943 Brecht wrote Auden to ask if he might be interested in collaborating with him on new scenes and verses for Webster's play: "I have told Miss Bergner that no one could do this as well as you." (Brecht's letter, written in German, appears in his *Briefe*, 1981, vol. 1, p. 486; an English translation appears in Brecht's *Letters*, 1990, p. 375.) Brecht did not mention Hays in his letter. Hays, evidently recognizing a fait accompli, quit the collaboration when he learned that Auden had been invited to join.

Brecht stayed in New York during the winter of 1943–44 and apparently worked with Auden during Auden's occasional visits from Swarthmore in January or February. Probably at this time Auden wrote a rhymed epilogue (also used in their 1946 version) incorporating some lines from Webster's tragicomedy *The Devil's Law Case*. Auden seems to have done little work on the play at this time, but Brecht pursued the project intermittently during the next year and a half. A reconstruction of "the version over which he [Brecht] seems to have exercised the most influence and on which he expended the most care" appears, with notes by A. R. Braunmuller, in the American edition of Brecht's *Collected Plays*, vol. 7 (New York, 1974).

During the summer of 1945, after leaving Swarthmore, Auden worked in Germany for the United States Strategic Bombing Survey. When he settled in New York in September he apparently resumed work on the play at Czinner's request, and prepared a version with two substantially new scenes and extensive cuts and rearrangements of Webster's original. This version does not derive directly from Auden's or Brecht's earlier texts, although it probably reflects their early plans and discussions. On 24 October the typescript was copyrighted by Auden alone. The title page identifies the play only by title, without naming an author or adapter. Excerpts from this version are printed in §2.

In early November 1945 Auden made a ten-day visit to Bergner and Czinner in Chicago, where he continued to rework the play. He apparently completed a revised draft (now lost) by the end of 1945 or January 1946. Then, from February until April 1946, when Brecht and Auden lived near each other on 57th Street in New York, the two reworked Auden's draft, and worked together more closely and frequently than at any other time in their collaboration. On 4 April 1946 they copyrighted a version of the play that was identified on the title page of the typescript as "*The Duchess of Malfi* by W. H. Auden and Bertold Brecht". The misspelling of Brecht's name is characteristic of Auden, who presumably hired the typist and whose agent probably made the application for copyright. Excerpts from this text are printed in §3. Brecht's friend Ruth Berlau recalled that during this phase of the collaboration Brecht prepared drafts of the adaptation and took them to Auden for discussion and further changes, but that, in her experience, Auden did not create new drafts. If Berlau's recollection is correct, it may imply that Brecht accepted the work that Auden had done earlier and that Auden now had little to add. (Berlau's account, which does not mention that she was in a hospital during much of this phase of the collaboration, appears in her memoir, *Brechts Lai-Tu*, 1985, pp. 171–75, translated as *Living for Brecht*, 1987, pp. 132–37.) Brecht, after finishing work on the copyright text, continued to revise the play, again independently of Auden. A version prepared entirely by Brecht in 1945–46 is printed in Brecht's *Werke: Stücke 7*, 1991, with an extensive commentary by Michael Voges; this edition also includes some fragments of the texts printed below that were prepared by Auden alone and by Auden and Brecht in collaboration.

Until he moved to California in early May 1946, Brecht worked with Czinner and Bergner on plans for a production. Probably during the spring of 1946, Benjamin Britten was commissioned to write incidental music. During the summer of 1946, Czinner hired George Rylands as the director of the projected Broadway production. Rylands had directed a commercially successful version of Webster's play in London a year earlier; Czinner hired him at the urging of his financial backers, but he consulted with neither Brecht nor (in all probability) Auden. When Rylands arrived in New York in late August, he learned for the first time that Auden and Brecht had massively altered the play, and he insisted on performing Webster's original text. Bergner accepted Rylands's conditions and effectively abandoned her commission to Brecht, although Rylands agreed to accept a few of Brecht and Auden's changes.

Rylands's production was tried out first at the Metropolitan Theatre in Providence, Rhode Island (20 September), then in Boston (week of 23 September), Hartford (30 September and 1 October), New Haven (2–4 October), and Princeton (7–8 October). Brecht, when he arrived in Boston to see the tryouts, was outraged to find that the adapted version had been abandoned, and withdrew his name from the production. The programs for the tryouts credit Brecht and Auden for the adaptation; the program for the Broadway opening at the Ethel Barrymore Theatre on 15 October 1946 names Auden only. The production was a critical and commercial fiasco and closed on 16 November.

Brecht made no attempt to publish the work in his later collections. Auden was equally unenthusiastic. He wrote to John Willett, Brecht's translator and editor, on 18 August 1958: "God forbid that anybody should get hold of that Duchess of Malfi: I cannot recall the incident without a shudder. I have the impression that most of the additions were mine, but repression has done its merciful work."

This appendix reprints the scenes from the versions copyrighted in 1945 and 1946 that contain substantially new verse by Auden and Brecht. Scenes largely adapted from Webster are summarized. The Bertolt-Brecht-Archiv in Berlin contains more typescripts and manuscripts of *The Duchess* than of any other work by Brecht, but the only material that can be positively associated with Auden are copies and partial copies of the two copyright typescripts. The few surviving manuscript drafts of Auden's work are mentioned in the notes below. Britten's incidental music for the production is lost.

A song tentatively attributed to Auden in the American edition of Brecht's *Collected Plays*, vol. 7, p. 433, was in fact the work of Brecht and Hays. The only text in the English-language editions of Brecht's *Collected Plays* that can be positively identified as Auden's are the lines he wrote for the epilogue printed in the notes to the American edition (pp. 416–17) and used in the 1946 version printed below (p. 477).

§2 Auden's 1945 Version

The typescript copyrighted on 24 October 1945 was registered in Auden's name alone; no author or adapter is named on the title page. Most of the newly written verse in the play is probably Auden's, and the structure of this version appears to be largely independent of earlier versions by Brecht and Hays. The absence of Brecht's name on the copyright page does not necessarily imply that Brecht had no part in the writing, but the version as a whole seems to show little of Brecht's handiwork.

Auden's adaptation has many fewer strictly new lines than the other surviving versions. Auden drops or rearranges Webster's original text; he adds lines from Webster's *White Devil*; occasionally he inserts entirely new material. The principal excision is the Julia subplot, which Webster used to justify the Cardinal's death morally and to accomplish it practically; the omission of the Cardinal's mistress required revisions in motivation and character relations, especially in the final scene. Auden also excises much of the mumbo-jumbo surrounding the Duchess's secret family (here reduced from three children to one), its discovery, and its destruction. The roles of both Antonio and Bosola are reduced, the former losing his devotion to the Duchess, the latter much of his moral ambivalence and psychological interest. Webster's startling decision to have the heroine die three-quarters of the way through the play meant that his long final act could combine obvious melodramatic peripeties with a leisurely and ironic presentation of the remaining characters' deaths. All this Auden reduces to Act 3, Scene 2, where his rapid-fire near-Grand Guignol threatens to induce laughter rather than pity or fear.

Brecht and his collaborators all distrusted, and hence rewrote or at least rearranged, Webster's first act. Auden drops many subsidiary characters and both changes and heightens the two brothers' sexual and political manipulation of the Duchess. In the second act, Auden reduces the torture of Webster's Duchess and moves her murder offstage, probably because Elisabeth Bergner had already had one bad experience with a classic death scene—her 1925 performance in an adaptation of Dumas's *La Dame aux camélias* (on which Brecht had also worked). Just as Auden introduced Ferdinand's determination not to marry in I.1, in III.1 he omits Ferdinand's economic excuses for murdering his sister. In Webster's play Bosola kills both Ferdinand and his brother, but Auden develops two peripheral Websterian metaphors—"shadow" and "echo"—into an effective episode where the insane Ferdinand kills the Cardinal. Bosola's suicide is also new with Auden's version. Several of the characters' dying speeches in III.2 are lifted from *The White Devil*, and Auden gives one detachable passage from that play a surprising and ominous new context at the beginning of I.2 (see notes below).

The excerpts printed below are taken from the copyright typescript, now in the Manuscript Division of the Library of Congress (copyright registration D 95637). Another copy in the Bertolt-Brecht-Archiv in Berlin (BBA 1767) has a manuscript revision by Auden (see the note to I.1 below). Rough pencil drafts of some of the speeches in I.1 and III.2 are in a notebook now at the University of Texas; this notebook also contains a fair copy of *The Age of Anxiety*, which Auden had substantially completed shortly before he began work on this version of *The Duchess*.

Auden and Brecht worked from the texts of *The Duchess of Malfi* and *The White Devil* in the Mermaid edition of Webster and Tourneur (1887; reprinted 1903).* Auden evidently marked up this edition for the typist, and the typescript reproduces some of the Mermaid's mechanical errors in layout. He also added stage directions at the opening of scenes. Auden's drafts at the University of Texas show that he was careful to indent the second part of a verse line shared by two or more speakers. The typist treated the indentions casually; the text below restores them.

*References to Webster's text in the present edition follow the act and scene numbering of the editions by John Russell Brown (The Revels Plays).

This text also corrects errors where the typist evidently miscopied from the printed original that had been marked up by Auden. Other errors evidently resulted from misreadings of Auden's hand in new or revised passages: such errors as "candle" for Webster's "caudle" (pp. 437, 455), or "know" for Webster's "burns" (in "The fire know well", pp. 445, 473), result from Auden's characteristic scrawl. In these and similar cases where the typescript is incoherent or manifestly ungrammatical, the reading of the Mermaid text has been adopted. Text added by Auden often has his characteristically light punctuation, with a notable absence of question marks; in unambiguous cases the punctuation has not been changed, but terminal punctuation has been added at the end of speeches that lack it in the typescript.

Act I, Scene 1

The full text of this scene is printed below. Much of it is adapted and rearranged from Webster's I.1. The Cardinal's opening speech is from Webster's V.5; his dialogue with Bosola is largely from Webster's I.1, where it occurs between Bosola and Antonio's confidant Delio, a character omitted by Auden. Bosola's sentence "When knaves . . ." at the end of the dialogue is from *The White Devil*, II.1.

The episode starting with the Page's announcement of Ferdinand and continuing through the dialogue of Ferdinand and the Cardinal is new, although it incorporates about a dozen lines from Webster's I.1 and from *The White Devil*, I.2 (the winter's snake), IV.2 (cut her into atomies), and, heavily adapted, III.1 (the claw of a blackbird). In this episode Ferdinand determines to stay unmarried and the Cardinal takes responsibility for his sister's first marriage, and, as in the earlier Brecht-Hays versions, the voyage of Webster's Lord Silvio is given to Ferdinand. The end of the scene, between Bosola and Ferdinand, is based on Webster's I.1. In the text below I have incorporated a revision made in Auden's hand in the copy of the typescript in the Bertolt-Brecht-Archiv (BBA 1767); the lines "Of his physician who hath sworn / The late duke was incapable and left" (p. 437) replace the original "That Malfi was incapable and left".

Act I Scene 1

[In the Cardinal's Palace.]

[Enter CARDINAL *L. reading.]*

CARDINAL. I am puzzled in a question about hell:
　　He says, in hell there's one material fire,
　　And yet it shall not burn all men alike.
　　Lay him by. How tedious is a guilty conscience!
　　When I look into the fish-ponds in my gardens,
　　Methinks I see a thing armed with a rake,
　　That seems to strike at me.

[*Enter* BOSOLA *L.*]

BOSOLA. I do haunt you still.

CARDINAL. So.

BOSOLA. I have done you better service than to be slighted thus. Miserable age where only the reward of doing well is the doing of it.

CARDINAL. You enforce your merit too much.

BOSOLA. I fell into the galleys in your service; where, for two years together, I wore two towels instead of a shirt, with a knot on the shoulder, after the fashion of a Roman mantle.

CARDINAL. Would you could become honest.

BOSOLA. With all your divinity do but direct me the way to it. I have known many travel far for it and yet return as errant knaves as they went forth because they carried themselves always along with them. Slighted thus—there are rewards for hawks and dogs when they have done us service; but for a soldier that hazards his limbs in a battle, nothing but a kind of geometry is his best transportation.

CARDINAL. Geometry?

BOSOLA. Ay, to hang in a fair pair of slings, take his latter swing in the world upon an honorable pair of crutches from hospital to hospital. I will thrive some way: blackbirds fatten best in hard weather; why not I in these dog days? Fare you well!

CARDINAL. Stay. Your pleading touches me. Bosola, I confess you have been much neglected. I know you're valiant. I would not have this melancholy poison your goodness. I'll seek preferment for you. Here's my hand on it.

BOSOLA. What cunning is afoot? When knaves come to preferment, they rise as gallowses are raised in the low countries, one upon another's shoulders.

[*Enter* PAGE *R.*]

PAGE. The Duke of Calabria is without, my Lord. He would speak with you.

CARDINAL. Let him approach.
[*To* BOSOLA.] Leave us, but wait for me without
I would speak with you further.

[*Exit* BOSOLA *L.*]

We are engaged to mischief and must on:
The way ascends not straight, but imitates
The subtle windings of a winter snake.

[Enter FERDINAND *R.]*

Welcome, good brother Ferdinand. How looks your voyage?

FERDINAND. Alas, too instant.
 All is equipped. The wind stands fair. Our ship
 Sails with the evening tide.

CARDINAL.   What. Is adventure
 So leaden to your spirit.

FERDINAND.   Who would exchange
 The Italian paradise for England's cold
 And heretic shore.

CARDINAL.   Necessities of state
 Require your passage. Come, dear brother,
 Forsake your doleful dump. The English court
 Is famed for splendor; nor shall you lack
 Gallant acquaintance. Here is a letter
 For my Lord of Norfolk, a noble Lord
 With a most fair daughter.

FERDINAND.   Were she Helen
 She should not make me blink. I'll never marry.

CARDINAL. So have you oft protested. But beware.
 Cupid can lay his engines in the dark.
 He's in his element there. Not once nor twice
 Have storied and forbidding vows
 Roared flaming skyward that a moment since
 Had frowned eternal. Who can tell what miles
 That pioneer can tunnel in a twelvemonth
 Or under whom? Shall we next summer see you
 Returning with a bride or greeted smiling
 By a re-wedded sister.

FERDINAND.   Ud's death, brother,
 Your jest's unwholesome. Our sister jig it
 Like loose and perishable beasts
 It is not to be thought on. No dedicate nun
 E'er practised days of chaster virtue. Why,
 Her nights, nay more, her very sleeps
 Are more in heaven than other ladies' shrifts.

CARDINAL. Yet did she marry.

FERDINAND. At your persuasion and despite her tears
 To wed a dukedom she wore Malfi's ring.
 And partnered with a mummy, one that looked
 Like the claw of a blackbird, first salted,

Then broiled in a caudle. I have inquired
Of his physician who hath sworn
The late duke was incapable and left
His duchess virgin.

CARDINAL.   Greater her danger then.
She's young. She's fair. Her state of widowhood
Gives liberal opportunities if youth
Should hotly hanker. Mistress of her house,
No father to command her. You, who were by,
Afar in England and myself perforce
Often in Rome. If she should fondly wink
Whose eye will write it down? Whose ear remark
If her door creak at midnight? She is fair,
Fair, Ferdinand, and rich. How many gallants,
E'en as we talk are dreaming they possess
Her body and her treasure.

FERDINAND.   She must be watched
Close as a dying infant by its mother.
Antonio is the great master of her household
I'll speak him presently.

CARDINAL.   You are deceived in him
His nature is too honest for this business
I know a fellow excellently fitted
To be your instrument. Daniel de Bosola.

FERDINAND. The Court gall. One that spent for murder
Years in the galleys and now rails at courts
And princely vices.

CARDINAL.   He rails at what he wants,

[*Church bells begin to ring.*]

Would be as lecherous, cruel and proud
Bloody and envious as any man
If he had means to be so. He's your creature.
I must attend now to my priestly offices.
I'll send him to you. Let us renew right hands.

[*Exit* CARDINAL *R.*]

FERDINAND. I could swear she's honest. If she be not, then modesty is
devilish. A naked man in bed with her. I'd cut her into atomies and
let the irregular north wind sweep her up and blow her into his nos-
trils. O sweet sister. I have swallowed a choke-pear. My fears are fal-
len upon me.

[*Enter* BOSOLA *L.*]

BOSOLA. I was lured to you.

FERDINAND.   There's gold.

BOSOLA.   So:
    What follows? Never rained such showers as these
    Without thunderbolts i' the tail of them: whose throat must I cut?

FERDINAND. Your inclination to shed blood rides post
    Before my occasion to use you. I give you that
    To live i' the court here, and observe the duchess;
    To note all the particulars of her behavior,
    What suitors do solicit her for marriage,
    And whom she best affects. She's a young widow,
    I would not have her marry again.

BOSOLA.   No sir?

FERDINAND. Do not you ask the reason; but be satisfied
    I say I would not.

BOSOLA.   It seems you would create me
    One of your familiars.

FERDINAND.   Familiar! What's that?

BOSOLA. Why, a very quaint invisible devil in flesh,
    An intelligencer.

FERDINAND.   Such a kind of thriving thing
    I would wish thee; and ere long thou mayest arrive
    At a higher place by 't.

BOSOLA.   Take your devils,
    Which hell calls angels; these cursed gifts would make
    You a corrupter, me an impudent traitor;
    And should I take these, they'd take me to hell.

FERDINAND. Sir, I'll take nothing from you that I have given;
    There is a place I shall procure for you
    This morning, the provisorship o' the horse;
    Is 't not worth thanks?

BOSOLA. I would have you curse yourself now, that your bounty
    (Which makes men truly noble) e'er should make me
    A villain. O, that to avoid ingratitude
    For the good deed you have done me, I must do
    All the ill man can invent! Thus the devil
    Candies all sins o'er; and what Heaven terms vile
    That names he complimental.

FERDINAND.   Be yourself;
    Keep your old garb of melancholy; 'twill express

You envy those that stand above your reach,
Yet strive not to come near 'em: this will gain
Access to private lodgings, where yourself
May, like a politic dormouse—
BOSOLA.   As I have seen some
Feed in a lord's dish, half asleep, not seeming
To listen to any talk; and yet these rogues
Have cut his throat in a dream. What's my place?
The provisorship o' the horse? Say, then, my corruption
Grew out of horse-dung: I am your creature.
FERDINAND. Away!

CURTAIN

Act I, Scene 2

The Duchess and Cariola. The Page sings Cornelia's dirge for her dead son from *The White Devil*, V.4 ("Call for the robin red-breast and the wren"). A few new lines of dialogue bring in Ferdinand, the Cardinal, Bosola, and others, and the Duchess says to Ferdinand: "All the best fortunes of a sister's wish / Bring you a shipboard." Ferdinand commends Bosola to the Duchess. As in Webster's I.1, the Cardinal and Ferdinand warn the Duchess against remarriage (but Auden has Cariola exit so that she hears neither this dialogue nor the Duchess's soliloquy after her brother's departure in which she resolves to marry); the Duchess, alone with Cariola, admits Antonio and then performs a ceremony of marriage witnessed by the concealed Cariola. The Cardinal's last speech before he exits with Ferdinand is a sententia on earthquakes taken from *The White Devil*, I.2, and used again in Auden and Brecht's 1946 version (p. 460).

Act I, Scene 3

The first half is based on Webster's II.1, omitting two satiric dialogues at the start and Antonio's serious conversation with Delio at the end. Bosola has detected the Duchess's pregnancy. The Duchess enters with Antonio, pretends that her illness is the effect of green fruit, and exits in a cold sweat. Bosola, left alone, speaks his opening soliloquy from Webster's II.2, with the aphorism "A quiet woman . . ." added from *The White Devil*, IV.2:

BOSOLA. So, so, there's no question but her techiness and most vulturous eating of the apricots are apparent signs of breeding. So quiet-looking a lady. Who would have thought it? Yet it hath often been noted so. A quiet woman is a still water under a great bridge. A man may shoot her safely.

The remainder of the scene conflates Webster's II.2 and II.3. Antonio enters with servants and orders the gates locked; Auden omits the comic dialogue of the Officers in Webster's II.2. A shriek is heard; Bosola enters, convinced it is the Duchess in childbirth, and is deflected by Antonio. After Antonio's exit, Bosola finds a horoscope, left accidentally by Antonio, of the birth of the Duchess's son.

Act II, Scene 1

Reproduces Webster's II.5. Ferdinand rages to the Cardinal against their sister.

Act II, Scene 2

Closely follows Webster's III.1, with Cariola substituted for Delio as the recipient of Antonio's news, and omitting Antonio's revelation that the Duchess has had two more children. Antonio tells Cariola of the dangerous behavior of Ferdinand, newly arrived at court. Ferdinand enters with the Duchess and promises her a husband. Ferdinand tells his spy Bosola of his intent to force a confession from the Duchess.

Act II, Scene 3

Based closely on Webster's III.2. Antonio, the Duchess, and Cariola in happy domesticity. Unlike Webster, who (followed by Brecht and Hays) has Antonio and Cariola playfully slip off the stage to trick the Duchess into talking to herself, Auden has the Duchess explicitly dismiss them in the speech printed below; the lines from "You have oft" to "yet much withered" are from *The White Devil*, II.2.

DUCHESS. O, that's soon answered.
>   Did you ever in your life know an ill painter
>   Desire to have his dwelling next door to the shop
>   Of an excellent picture-maker? 'Twould disgrace
>   His face-making, and undo him. I prithee,
>   When were we so merry?—My hair tangles.
>   Leave me for a while.

>   [*Exeunt* ANTONIO *and* CARIOLA.]

>   [DUCHESS *looking in her mirror.*]

>   You have oft for these two lips
>   Neglected Cassia or the natural sweets
>   Of the spring violet. They are not yet much withered.
>   Doth not the colour of my hair 'gin to change?
>   When I wax gray, I shall have all the court
>   Powder their hair with arras, to be like me.
>   You have cause to love me; I entered you into my heart
>   Before you would vouchsafe to call for the keys. . . .

As in Webster, Ferdinand enters at this point in her soliloquy, gives her a poniard, accuses her, and angrily leaves her. Antonio and Cariola return. Bosola enters; the Duchess attempts to explain the disturbance by pretending to accuse Antonio of false financial dealings. When Bosola exits, the Duchess tells Antonio to flee, and when Bosola returns, pretends to banish Antonio. Mistakenly trusting Bosola, the Duchess reveals to him that she has married Antonio and borne his child. Bosola advises the Duchess to feign a pilgrimage to a spot near Antonio's place of exile.

Act II, Scene 4

Auden's version omits the scene in which Bosola reveals to Ferdinand his sister's remaining secrets (Webster's III.3) and a scene of silent pageantry in which the Cardinal formally pronounces banishment upon the Duchess, Antonio, and their children (Webster's III.4). Auden's II.4 follows Webster's III.5 closely, changing references to the Duchess's children from plural to singular and omitting most of the Duchess's dialogue with Bosola. The Duchess reports an ominous dream to Antonio; Bosola enters, disguised, with a guard, and commands the Duchess to return to her palace. Auden, like Brecht and Hays earlier, omits Bosola's earlier entrance in the scene when he bears an equivocal letter from Ferdinand.

Act III, Scene 1

Conflates, with omissions and slight reorderings, Webster's IV.1 and IV.2. Printed below is the opening of the scene, based on Webster's IV.1; Auden simplifies Webster's complex action by substituting Antonio's body for a waxwork of it; Webster has Bosola mistakenly kill Antonio in V.4. Notes on the remainder of the scene follow the text of the opening section.

Act III Scene 1

[*The Duchess' bedchamber. A diagonal curtain makes it possible to shut off the bed and half the room. This curtain is drawn to as the scene opens.*]

[*Enter* BOSOLA *and* SERVANTS *carrying a chest.*]

BOSOLA. All comfort to your grace.
DUCHESS.   I will have none.
    Pray thee, why dost thou wrap thy poisoned pills
    In gold and sugar.
BOSOLA. Here is a present from your princely brother
    And may it arrive welcome for it brings
    Rare benefit.
CARIOLA.   A costly gift.
BOSOLA. There's more within. Here is the key, pray open it.

        [*The* DUCHESS *unlocks it.* ANTONIO's *body falls out.*]

    Now you may know directly he is dead
    Hereafter you may wisely cease to grieve
    For that which cannot be recovered.
DUCHESS. O horrible. I could curse the stars
    And those three smiling seasons of the year
    Into a Russian winter: nay the world
    To its first chaos. I am full of daggers.
    Puff, let me blow these vipers from me. [*Faints.*]
CARIOLA. My lady faints. Help me carry her.

> [BOSOLA *and* CARIOLA *carry* DUCHESS *through Curtain L.* FERDINAND *enters R.* BOSOLA *re-enters L.*]

FERDINAND. Excellent as I would wish.
BOSOLA.   Why do you do this?
FERDINAND. To bring her to despair.
BOSOLA.   Faith, end here,
    And go no farther in your cruelty:
    Send her a penitential garment to put on
    Next to her delicate skin, and furnish her
    With beads and prayer books.
FERDINAND. Damn her! That body of hers
    While that my blood ran pure in 't was more worth
    Than that which thou wouldst comfort, called a soul.
    Remove this ruined relic of her lust. Come with me
    Your work is not yet ended.
BOSOLA.   Must I see her again?
FERDINAND. Yes, and soon.
BOSOLA.   Never.
FERDINAND.   You must.

> [*Exeunt* FERDINAND *and* BOSOLA *carrying* AN-TONIO's *body.*]

> [CARIOLA *draws curtains back.*]

> [DUCHESS *is seated in a chair near her dressing table.*]

CARIOLA. Pray, dry your eyes.
    What think you of, Madam?
DUCHESS.   Of nothing;
    When I muse thus, I sleep.

The remainder of the scene, following the dialogue between Cariola and the Duchess immediately above, abridges Webster's IV.2. Bosola, disguised as an old man, tortures the Duchess with threats of her death (Auden omits Webster's mocking dance of madmen); executioners enter (Auden omits Webster's dirge "Hark, now everything is still"), Cariola is forced off the stage, and Bosola draws a curtain to hide the execution. Ferdinand enters, is shown the murdered Duchess by Bosola, and accuses Bosola of villainy. Auden omits the lines in which Ferdinand recalls his hope "to have gained / An infinite mass of treasure" by the Duchess's death. Bosola's concluding speech, based on his final speech in Webster's scene (but omitting the Duchess's brief return to life), incorporates from *The White Devil*, V.3, the lines from "The dull owl" to "waits on princes":

BOSOLA. He's much distracted. Off, my painted honour!
    While with vain hopes our faculties we tire,
    We seem to sweat in ice and freeze in fire.
    What would I do, were this to do again?
    I would not change my peace of conscience
    For all the wealth of Europe.— [*Looks through curtain.*]
    O sacred innocence, that sweetly sleeps
    On turtles' feathers. The dull owl
    Beats not against thy casement; the hoarse wolf
    Scents not thy carrion: pity winds thy corse
    Whilst horror waits on princes. My estate is sunk
    Below the degree of fear: where were
    These penitent fountains while she was living?
    O, they were frozen up! Here is a sight
    As direful to my soul as is the sword
    Unto a wretch hath slain his father. Come,
    I'll bear thee hence,
    And execute thy last will; that's deliver
    Thy body to the reverend dispose
    Of some good women: that the cruel tyrant
    Shall not deny me. Then I'll post to Milan,
    Where somewhat I will speedily enact
    Worth my dejection. [*Exit.*]

Act III, Scene 2

Printed in full below. This scene is even more heavily rewritten than I.1. Auden's version mingles passages from Webster's V.2 (Ferdinand's lycanthropy, Bosola's demand for compensation), IV.3 (a vestige of Webster's echo scene), I.1 (the spring in your face is but the engendering of toads), IV.4 (the warning not to interfere should Ferdinand cry out in the night, Bosola's decision to kill both Duke and

Cardinal), and V.5 (the killings). The Cardinal's speech from "Listen. / The Lord Ferdinand . . ." is new, as is Bosola's decision to make the Cardinal "sweat / For his cold wickedness". Ferdinand's description of his brother as "shadow" is inspired by the episode in Webster's V.2, where a lycanthropic Ferdinand insanely attempts to throttle his shadow, and the echo scene is rationalized and better integrated than in Webster. Ferdinand's last two speeches are borrowed from speeches given to two different characters in *The White Devil*, V.6, combined with one line from Webster's last speech for Ferdinand. The Cardinal's final speech also mixes lines from *The White Devil*, V.6, and Webster's *Duchess*, V.5. Bosola's penultimate speech and suicide are new; all but the last two sentences of his final speech are from *The White Devil*, V.6; the last two sentences come from separate speeches in Webster's *Duchess*, V.5. The uneven line lengths near the end are reproduced from the typescript and probably misrepresent Auden's intentions.

Act III Scene 2

[*A corridor in the Cardinal's Palace.*]

[*Enter* BOSOLA, DOCTOR *and* COURTIERS.]

1ST COURTIER. 'Twas a foul storm tonight.
2ND COURTIER. The Lord Ferdinand's chamber shook like an osier.
BOSOLA. I pray thee, Doctor, what is his disease?
DOCTOR. A very pestilent disease,
    They call lycanthropia.
BOSOLA.   What's that?
    I need a dictionary to 't.
DOCTOR.   I'll tell you.
    In those that are possessed with 't there o'erflows
    Such melancholy humour they imagine
    Themselves to be transformed into wolves;
    Steal forth to churchyards in the dead of night,
    And dig dead bodies up; as two nights since
    One met the duke 'bout midnight in a lane
    Behind Saint Mark's church, with the leg of a man
    Upon his shoulder; and he howled fearfully;
    Said he was a wolf, only the difference
    Was, a wolf's skin was hairy on the outside,
    His on the inside; bade them take their swords,
    Rip up his flesh, and try: straight I was sent for,
    And, having ministered to him, found his grace
    Very well recovered.

BOSOLA.   I am glad on 't.
DOCTOR. Yet not without some fear
    Of a relapse.

                        [*Enter* CARDINAL.]

CARDINAL. You shall not watch tonight by the sick prince;
    His grace is very well recovered.
1ST COURTIER. Good my lord, suffer us.
CARDINAL.   O, by no means;
    The noise, and change of object in his eye,
    Doth more distract him: I pray, all to bed;
    And though you hear him in his violent fit,
    Do not rise, I entreat you.
2ND COURTIER. So, sir; we shall not.
BOSOLA.   Sir, I would speak with you.
1ST COURTIER. We'll leave your grace
    Wishing to the sick prince, our noble lord
    All health of mind and body.
CARDINAL.   You are most welcome.

                [*Exeunt* DOCTOR *and* COURTIERS.]

    Now, sir, why do you look so wildly
    Wherefore cam'st thou hither.
BOSOLA. That I might find a great man like yourself
    Not out of his wits as the Lord Ferdinand
    To remember my service.
CARDINAL.   So you shall
    If you'll do one thing for me, I'll entreat,
    I'd make you what you would be. There is
    A fortune attends thee.
BOSOLA. Shall I go sue to Fortune any longer?
    'Tis the fool's pilgrimage.
CARDINAL.   I have honors in store for thee.
BOSOLA. There are many ways that conduct to seeming honor
    And some of them very dirty ones.
CARDINAL. Throw to the devil
    Thy melancholy. The fire burns well;
    What need we keep a stirring of 't and make
    A greater smother. Listen.
    The Lord Ferdinand's sickness is likely to prove mortal
    To others than himself. 'Tis to be feared

That in his guilty madness he'll confess
The Duchess' murder. We are both in danger
You for its execution, I because
Her death hath brought me profit. Our safety says
He can't live long. Be secret here.
I'll fetch him. At my signal strike.
Our witness shall be proof his own hand slew him.

[*Exit* CARDINAL.]

BOSOLA. O my fate moves swift
I have this cardinal in the forge already
Now I'll bring him to the hammer. He shall sweat
For his cold wickedness, more loved in hell
Than any boiling lust.
That must be paid for too. Then after
I'll be mine own example. O this court
Shall see a terrible cleansing. [*Hides in closet.*]

[*Enter* CARDINAL *with* FERDINAND.]

FERDINAND. Leave me. Is the chaos become
General that a man is faced by his shadow.
CARDINAL. Calm yourself.
FERDINAND. Away, shadow.
　　　The spring in your face is but the engendering of toads. Away, I
say. I am studying the art of patience. Strangling is a very quiet death.
Whisper softly; do you agree to it? So: it must be done i' the dark. I
prithee remember: Millions are now in graves that at last day like
mandrakes shall rise shrieking. What I have done, I have done: I'll
confess nothing. Hush. Disturb her not. She is asleep now. O heavens,
shall I never see her more.
BOSOLA [*as an echo*]. Never see her more.
FERDINAND. There, thou black spider. Didst hear her
'Twas my sister's voice.
BOSOLA. Ay, sister's voice.
CARDINAL. You fancy merely. This ancient palace
Has a famed echo.
FERDINAND.　　　　Then is Echo my good angel.
Shadow my familiar devil who leads me on
To my eternal ruin but she calls me back
To lost repentance. O sweet Echo, save me
From my foul shadow. Use thy heavenly skill.
BOSOLA. Kill.

FERDINAND [*drawing his sword*]. Echo hath judged thee, shadow. Pray and
    be sudden.
CARDINAL. Help. I am betrayed. Bosola. Help me. I'll faithfully divide
    Revenues with thee. Shall I die like a leveret
    Without any resistance? Help. Help. Help. I am slain. [*Falls.*]
FERDINAND. I have done thy bidding, Echo. Say 'twas well
    In thy clear voice of comfort. They lie that say
    Thou art a dead thing.
BOSOLA [*emerging*]. Thou art a dead thing. [*Stabs* FERDINAND.]
    Sink thou main cause of my undoing.
FERDINAND.   O I smell soot
    Most stinking soot. The chimney is afire
    There's a plumber laying pipes in my guts. It scalds.
CARDINAL. Bosola, why hast thou done this?
BOSOLA. For justice and revenge. For the Duchess of Malfi
    And Antonio murdered. For myself corrupted
    Then neglected. All Italy shall glory
    That thou which stoodst like a huge pyramid
    Begun upon a large and ample base
    Shalt end in a little point, a kind of nothing.
FERDINAND. My soul like to a ship in a black storm
    Is driven I know not whither.
    My sister, O my sister. There's the cause on 't. [*Dies.*]
CARDINAL. I recover like a spent taper for a flash
    And instantly go out. O Justice
    I suffer now for what hath former been.
    Let me be laid by and never thought of. [*Dies.*]
VOICES WITHOUT. This way, this way, break open the doors.
    This way.
BOSOLA. Still there remains one prisoner to punish
    The executioner must lead himself by the hand
    To his own gallows. [*Stabs himself.*]
                    Now my revenge is perfect.

            [*Enter* DOCTOR *and* COURTIERS.]

1ST COURTIER. How now, my lord.
DOCTOR. O sad disaster.
2ND COURTIER. How comes this.
1ST COURTIER. Thou wretched thing of blood.
BOSOLA. Leave thy idle questions
    I am i' the way to study the long silence:
    To prate were idle. I remember nothing.

There is nothing of so infinite vexation
As man's own thoughts. Fare you well.
Mine is another voyage. [*Dies.*]

CURTAIN

§3 AUDEN AND BRECHT'S 1946 VERSION

Shortly after completing the version he had copyrighted on 24 October 1945, Auden worked with the Czinners in Chicago on further changes to *The Duchess*. As he reported to the literary scholar Theodore Spencer on 17 November, a day after his return to New York: "I was in Chicago for 10 days rehashing *The Duchess of Malfi* for Elizabeth [*sic*] Bergner. Scholars will be *appalled*." (Auden's letters to Spencer are in the Harvard University Archives.) Probably around the end of the year or early in 1946, Auden completed a draft of a new version and sent it to Spencer for comments, as he did with much of his work during this period. The new draft evidently included matter that Auden and Brecht retained in the version copyrighted in April 1946, matter that Auden defended in a letter to Spencer on 21 January 1946. In Auden's letter "chopcherry" refers to the song by George Peele used in Auden and Brecht's II.4 (p. 465), and "the dream" is Ferdinand's dream in I.2 (p. 456):

Many thanks for your letters, the return of the Duchess, and the Sidney [i.e., Spencer's essay on Sidney].

Chopcherry is a bit whimsey, I know, but can you suggest a better song which will meet the conditions

a) It must be Elizabethan
b) It must be slightly sexy
c) It must be light and "merry"
d) It must give the characters an excuse to laugh.

The dream is not very Webster, alas, but the best I can do. W uses dreams a good deal, and I must somehow explain Ferdinand's motives. I must just trust to the actor to smooth over the gaping parts by "wonderful" behaviour.

In February 1946 Brecht, who was now living a few blocks away from Auden in New York, resumed work with him on the adaptation. They apparently used Auden's most recent draft as the basis for further revisions. (In later years Auden seems to have forgotten that he had done some earlier work on the play with Brecht. He gave a summary account of his work on *The Duchess* in a letter to John Willett on 2 March 1957: "Elisabeth Bergner got it into her tiny head that she wanted to play the Duchess because she wanted to play a respectable woman. She decided that some extra speeches were needed and asked me to write them. Exactly what previous commitments she had with Brecht I don't know, but suddenly there he was as a collaborator.")

On 16 February Brecht wrote to Bergner:

Here's a brief report on the results so far of 2 conversations between Auden and me.

In the discussion about the character of Antonio, the first problem was that Auden sees the piece as completely decadent, Malfi's "affair" with Antonio as something she allows herself out of a sort of presumptuousness and which sets her will against the will of her brothers, etc. So Antonio can certainly be a sort of gigolo; the silk stockings and bombast fit in with it, as well as his displays of cowardice and selfishness.

Provisional agreement: since it is not represented in the text, I held on to the idea (which is firm in Auden) of the "perversity" of Malfi's entering into this sort of a marriage, and suggested looking at her civil marriage (in this case completely normal, as we had it) as an adventure, which then also turns out to be fatal. In this way Antonio can also become stronger, more reasonable, and in his way more important; and the family, which in the gigolo-perspective would be almost impossible to explain, once again gets its poetic and pure normality. (It won't be necessary, however, to keep the additions to the courtship scene which we had, a few cuts would be enough.)

We considered making a single scene out of the first two scenes, as we had them. Keeping Auden's new lines but so that it's hinted at that the brothers' reasons for opposing the marriage are different, that of the Cardinal more or less financial, that of the Duke mysterious.

Bosola becomes a *librarian*, a *frustrated scholar* [italicized words in English]. We'll keep the midwife, who enters after the love scene and catches Bosola's eye.

The brief exchange between Antonio and Delio during the uproar is cut, Cariola takes over some of it (Delio can't be sent from Antonio to the Cardinal, unless, as in Webster, the outcome of his mission is reported).

We will discuss whether Ferdinand ought to get the letter with the news before—which is what I think—or after he's taken prisoner. [Apparently Auden and Brecht decided against Brecht's preference; see p. 462.]

In the scene where Ferdinand surprises Malfi in the bedroom, Antonio should figure more forcefully and insist on his right to defend his wife.

In the ban scene, as a compromise, only the first sentences of the Cardinal are to be in Latin. The third section, in which the Church forbids every Christian to help Malfi, etc. stays in English. [This refers to the variant of II.5 described on p. 467.]

This is how far we've got. The discussion is interesting, Auden very agreeable and open-minded.

Let me know if you have any objections. I'm hoping that the core tragic love story, really one of the most beautiful in literature, slowly emerges. . . . (Brecht, *Briefe*, 1981, vol. 1, pp. 519–20; another translation, with one phrase omitted, appears in Brecht's *Letters*, 1990, pp. 401–2)

Not all of these decisions appeared in the finished text that resulted from Auden and Brecht's further work on the play, and that was copyrighted by them on 4

April 1946. The midwife (or Old Lady of Webster's II.2) does not appear in the copyrighted text, and Bosola is not a frustrated scholar. Typescript fragments of speeches apparently prepared by Brecht as trials for these and other abandoned ideas from this stage of the collaboration are in the Bertolt-Brecht-Archiv.

The finished text of the 1946 copyright version alters and supplements Webster's text far more drastically than that of 1945. Some of the structural changes resemble those made in Brecht and Hays's versions from the early years of the project, and were probably reintroduced by Brecht.

In the 1946 version Delio is restored after his disappearance in 1945 (although he exchanges many of his lines with Webster's Antonio), and the Duchess again has more than one child. Ferdinand now goes off to the wars, and two new scenes are added, one of them reporting Ferdinand's capture by the Turks, the other a Brechtian episode in which citizens comment on their rulers. As in 1945 the Julia subplot is excised, and the deaths in the final scene occur at a pace that seems rapid even for Jacobean tragedy.

The excerpts printed below are taken from the copyright typescript, now in the Manuscript Division of the Library of Congress (copyright registration DU 2445).

The epilogue is perhaps the earliest stage of the 1946 text. Auden wrote a pencil draft of the opening lines of the epilogue (the closing lines are from *The Devil's Law Case*) perhaps around January or February 1944 in a notebook (now in the Poetry Collection at the State University of New York at Buffalo) that he used for writing *The Sea and the Mirror* at around the same time. On the other hand, it is at least possible that Auden took up the notebook again in 1946 in order to sketch the epilogue while preparing the rest of the 1946 version.

Act I, Scene 1

The full text of this scene is printed below. Much of it is based on excerpts from Webster's I.1, but with the roles of Antonio and Delio reversed. Antonio's second speech and his report of Ferdinand's departure for the wars are new, as is Delio's comparison of Bosola to a ghost.

Act I Scene 1

ANTONIO. Dear Delio, you are welcome to your country;
    You have been long in France and you return
    A very formal Frenchman in your habit:
    How do you like the French court?
DELIO.   I admire it.
    In seeking to reduce both state and people
    To a fixed order, their judicious king
    Begins at home; quits first his royal palace
    Of flattering sycophants, of dissolute
    And infamous persons, considering the court

Is like a common fountain whence should flow
Pure silver drops.

ANTONIO.   Would it were so with us.
Intelligencers, pandars, malcontents
And a thousand such political monsters make
Our air unwholesome.

DELIO.   You did promise me
To make me the partaker of the natures
Of some of your great courtiers. The Cardinal now,
How is his temper? They say he's a brave fellow.
Will play his five thousand crowns at tennis, dance,
Court ladies, and one that hath fought single combats.

ANTONIO. Some such flashes superficially hang on him for form; but observe his inward character: he is a melancholy churchman; the spring in his face is nothing but the engendering of toads; where he is jealous of any man, he lays worse plots for them than ever was imposed on Hercules. He should have been Pope; but instead of coming to it by the primitive decency of the church, he did bestow bribes so largely and so impudently as if he would have carried it away without Heaven's knowledge. Some good he hath done—

DELIO. You have given too much of him.
What's his brother?

ANTONIO. The duke there? A most perverse and turbulent nature;
What appears in him mirth is merely outside;
If he laugh heartily, it is to laugh
All honesty out of fashion.

DELIO.   Twins?

ANTONIO.   In quality.
He speaks with others' tongues, and hears men's suits
With others' ears; will seem to sleep o' the bench
Only to entrap offenders in their answers;
Dooms men to death by information;
Rewards by hearsay.

DELIO.   Then the law to him
Is like a foul black cobweb to a spider,—
He makes it his dwelling and a prison
To entangle those shall feed him.

ANTONIO.   Most true:
The Italian sky already
Brightens at his foreseen departure to the wars.
But for their sister, the right noble duchess
You never fixed your eye on three fair medals

Cast in one figure, of so different temper.
For her discourse, it is so full of rapture,
You only will begin then to be sorry
When she doth end her speech, and wish, in wonder,
She held it less vain-glory to talk much,
Then your penance to hear her: whilst she speaks,
She throws upon a man so sweet a look,
That it were able to raise one to a galliard
That lay in a dead palsy, and to dote
On that sweet countenance; but in that look
There speaketh so divine a continence
As cuts off all lascivious and vain hope.
Her days are practiced in such noble virtue,
That sure her nights, nay, more, her very sleeps,
Are more in Heaven than other ladies' shrifts.
Let all sweet ladies break their flattering glasses,
And dress themselves in her.
DELIO.   Fie, Antonio,
You play the wire-drawer with her commendations.
ANTONIO. I'll case the picture up: only thus much;
All her particular worth grows to this sum,—
She stains the time past, lights the time to come.
DELIO. Look, the Cardinal approaches; but who is he
That harries to o'ertake him, as the thin ghost
Comes up on the lone traveller.
ANTONIO.   'Tis Bosola,
The only court gall. Yet I observe his railing
Is not for simple love of piety
Indeed, he rails at those things which he wants;
Would be as lecherous, covetous, or proud,
Bloody, or envious, as any man,
If he had means to be so.

                    [*Enter the* CARDINAL *and* BOSOLA.]

BOSOLA. I do haunt you still.
CARDINAL. So.
BOSOLA. I have done you better service than to be slighted thus. Miserable age, where only the reward of doing well is the doing of it!
CARDINAL. You enforce your merit too much.
BOSOLA. I fell into the galleys in your service; where, for two years together, I wore two towels instead of a shirt, with a knot on the shoulder, after the fashion of a Roman mantle. Slighted thus! I will thrive

some way: blackbirds fatten best in hard weather; why not I in these dog-days?

CARDINAL. Would you could become honest!

BOSOLA. With all your divinity do but direct me the way to it. I have known many travel far for it, and yet return as arrant knaves as they went forth, because they carried themselves always along with them.

[*Exit* CARDINAL.]

Are you gone? Some fellows, they say, are possessed with the devil, but this great fellow were able to possess the greatest devil, and make him worse.

ANTONIO. He hath denied thee some suit?

BOSOLA. He and his brother are like plum-trees that grow crooked over standing-pools; they are rich and o'er-laden with fruit, but none but crows, pies, and caterpillars feed on them. Could I be one of their flattering panders, I would hang on their ears like a horseleech, till I were full, and then drop off. Fare ye well, sir: and yet do not you scorn us; for places in the court are but like beds in the hospital, where this man's head lies at that man's foot, and so lower and lower. [*Exits.*]

DELIO. I knew this fellow seven years in the galleys
For a notorious murder; and 'twas thought
The cardinal suborned it:

ANTONIO.   'Tis great pity
He should be thus neglected: I have heard
He's very valiant. This foul melancholy
Will poison all his goodness.

[*Enter* CARIOLA.]

CARIOLA. You must attend my lady in the gallery
Some half an hour hence.

ANTONIO.   Good Cariola, I shall.

[*Exeunt.*]

Act I, Scene 2

This scene consists of excerpts rearranged from Webster's I.1 interspersed with much new material. The opening dialogue between Ferdinand and the Cardinal is new (with a few lines from Webster, including the blackbird's claw from *The White Devil*, III.1), as is Ferdinand's incestuous dream about his sister. The dialogue between Bosola and Ferdinand has been altered from Webster's I.1 to reflect the reordering of events in the scene. The brief exchange of the Cardinal and the

Duchess with Ferdinand about his voyage is also new. The rest of the scene is mostly adapted from I.1, with some additions by Auden and Brecht. The Cardinal's final speech is from *The White Devil*, I.2.

In the opening pages of this scene, until Bosola's entrance, the typist was evidently struggling with Auden's handwriting; some of the typist's errors, like "when" for "where", are frequent occurrences in typescripts made from Auden's holograph. The text below makes obvious corrections, such as "heirs" for "hairs", and makes other emendations based on Webster or the 1945 version. I have followed the typist in leaving a blank space, here between square brackets, where the typist found Auden's hand unreadable. In the Cardinal's first speech the line "Be vexed by might-be till we know it may" verges on the edge of incoherence but makes enough sense to let it stand; the typescript has a hyphen surrounded by spaces, suggesting that the typist misread "might-be" as "might—be". In the Cardinal's fourth speech, the line "If she should truth / Of marriage" I have reluctantly emended "truth" to "troth" in the vain hope of rendering this phrase slightly less nonsensical, but the lost original may have been quite different. In the Cardinal's speech beginning "You are deceived in him", the typist may have dropped a few words between "By needless fears, I know" and "your instrument" ("you instrument" in the typescript). However, the words that may be missing, "a fellow / Excellently fitted to be" (see p. 437 for the corresponding speech in the 1945 version), are paraphrased a few lines later. Some punctuation has been added at the ends of lines to clarify the ends of sentences or parenthetical phrases.

Act I Scene 2

FERDINAND. She must be watched, I say.

CARDINAL.   Be patient, brother
    Rage is a sorry actor. We're agreed
    'Tis better that our sister should continue
    A widow without heirs that at her death—
    May God preserve her long—her whole estate
    Shall then revert to ours. But let us not
    Be vexed by might-be till we know it may.
    Sum your suspicions up and you shall find
    That beauty and gay clothes, a merry heart
    And a good stomach to feast, are all
    The crimes that you can charge her with.
    Hath any come to suit her?

FERDINAND.   I would have slain
    The first that dared.

CARDINAL.   Hath Giovanna
    Herself inclined to any?

FERDINAND.   She married once.
    O frailty of woman!

CARDINAL.   In policy,
    To wed a dukedom she wore Malfi's ring
    And partnered with a mummy. One that looked
    Like the claw of a blackbird first salted
    Then broiled in a caudle. Was that frail?
    Come, Ferdinand.
FERDINAND.   'Tis true. I have inquired
    Of the late duke's physician who hath sworn
    That Malfi was incapable and left
    His duchess virgin. But greater her danger then.
    She's young. She's fair. Her state of widowhood
    Gives liberal opportunity if youth
    Should hotly hanker. Mistress of her own house,
    No father to command her, and myself
    Departed to the wars, an ignoramus
    If she should loudly wink.
CARDINAL.   'Tis womanish
    So to be creature of your moonling fancies.
    It is our sister that we speak of, not
    Some chandler's daughter. Our Arragonian blood
    Runs [   ] in her. She would not fix
    Her choice on some mean oysterman nor wed
    Where's she ashamed to own. If she should troth
    Of marriage, it will be with some great lord,
    And we shall be acquainted in good time
    To put it off.
FERDINAND.   Best natures do commit
    The grossest faults.
CARDINAL.   If it will ease your mind
    Ere you depart, we'll counsel her together
    Against the very thought.
FERDINAND.   We will, we will.
    But counsel is not enough. For you return
    To distant Rome where, if she disregard
    Our solemn warnings, you may hear too late.
    No, I must find another pair of eyes
    To do the duty of my own, to note
    If she should glance or sigh or whisper.
    Antonio is the great master of her household,
    I'll speak to him presently.
CARDINAL.   You are deceived in him.
    His nature is too honest for such business.

If you are thus determined to be ruled
By needless fears, I know your instrument.
Daniel de Bosola. He is now without
Craving employment. One excellently fitted
For your intelligence. I'll send him to you. [*Exit* CARDINAL.]
FERDINAND. Shall I desert, whom Nature hath appointed
   To be the sentry of my sister's honor?
   We had one father, in one womb took life,
   Were brought up twins together, yet must live
   At distance now like strangers. O I could wish
   That the first pillow whereon we were cradled
   Had proved to both a grave. Last night I dreamed,
   Methought I walked with Giovanna hand in hand
   About a frolic garden situate
   Within a barbarous forest. Suddenly
   Out of a gloomy grove there came a music
   Of lascivious flutes whereat straightway
   Her face began to simper, she outwrenched her hand
   And flew to her damnation. When I pursued,
   Brambles sprang up like sword points in my path,
   And when I called "Come back", that music, changed
   To hideous dissonance, drowned out my cries
   And mocked my bleeding hands. If dreams indeed
   Prefigure truth, how featly will she run
   To jig it like the loose and perishing beast.
   O my sweet sister. I have swallowed a choke-pear
   My fears are fallen upon me.

                                        [*Enter* BOSOLA.]

BOSOLA. I was lured to you.
FERDINAND. My brother, here, the cardinal, could never
   Abide you.
BOSOLA.   Never since he was in my debt.
FERDINAND. May be some oblique character in your face,
   Made him suspect you.
BOSOLA.   Doth he study physiognomy?
   There's no more credit to be given to the face
   Than to a sick man's urine, which some call
   The physician's whore because she cozens him.
   He did suspect me wrongfully.

FERDINAND.   For that
    You must give great men leave to take their times.
    Distrust doth cause us seldom be deceived:
    You see the oft shaking of the cedar-tree
    Fastens it more at root.
BOSOLA.   Yet, take heed:
    For to suspect a friend unworthily
    Instructs him the next way to suspect you,
    And prompts him to deceive you.
FERDINAND.   There's gold.
BOSOLA.   So:
    What follows? never rained such showers as these
    Without thunderbolts i' the tail of them: whose throat must I cut?
FERDINAND. Your inclination to shed blood rides post
    Before my occasion to use you. I give you that
    To live i' the court here, and observe the duchess;
    To note all the particulars of her behavior,
    What suitors do solicit her for marriage,
    And whom she best affects. She's a young widow:
    I would not have her marry again.
BOSOLA.   No, sir?
FERDINAND. Do not you ask the reason; but be satisfied
    I say I would not.
BOSOLA.   It seems you would create me
    One of your familiars.
FERDINAND.   Familiar! what's that?
BOSOLA. Why, a very quaint invisible devil in flesh,
    An intelligencer.
FERDINAND.   Such a kind of thriving thing
    I would wish thee; and ere long thou mayest arrive
    At a higher place by 't.
BOSOLA.   Take your devils,
    Which hell calls angels; these cursed gifts would make
    You a corrupter, me an impudent traitor;
    And should I take these, they'd take me to hell.
FERDINAND. Sir, I'll take nothing from you that I have given.
    There is a place I shall procure for you
    This morning, the provisorship of the horse
    Is 't not worth thanks.
BOSOLA. I would have you curse yourself now, that your bounty
    (Which makes men truly noble) e'er should make me

A villain. O, that to avoid ingratitude
For the good deed you have done me, I must do
All the ill man can invent! Thus the devil
Candies all sins o'er; and what Heaven terms vile,
That names he complimental.

FERDINAND.   Be yourself;
Keep your old garb of melancholy; 'twill express
You envy those that stand above your reach,
Yet strive not to come near 'em: this will gain
Access to private lodgings, where yourself
May, like a politic dormouse—

BOSOLA.   As I have seen some
Feed in a lord's dish, half asleep, not seeming
To listen to any talk; and yet those rogues
Have cut his throat in a dream. What's my place?
The provisorship o' the horse? Say, then, my corruption
Grew out of horse-dung: I am your creature.

FERDINAND. The Duchess comes. Stand aside till I call for you.

[*Enter* CARDINAL, DUCHESS, *etc.*]

CARDINAL. Are the caroches come to bring you down to the haven.

FERDINAND. Yes, The wind stands fair. Our ship
Sails with the turning tide.

DUCHESS. All the best fortunes of a sister's wish
Bring you shipboard. May your lance
Flashing with terror on the Saracen
Unghost his heretic flesh, and victory soon
Fetch you with blazon home.

FERDINAND.   Amen. Dear sister,
I have a parting suit to you.

DUCHESS.   To me, sir.

FERDINAND [*motioning* BOSOLA *forward, who bows.*]
A gentleman here, Daniel de Bosola
One that was in the galleys.

DUCHESS.   Yes, I know him.

FERDINAND. A worthy fellow he is: pray let me entreat for
The provisorship of your horse.

DUCHESS.   Your knowledge of him
Commends him and prefers him.

[BOSOLA *kisses the* DUCHESS' *hand.*]

CARDINAL. Bid these withdraw. We would speak with you in private.

[ALL *exit.* CARIOLA *L. The rest R.*]

We are to part from you; and your own discretion
Must now be your director.
FERDINAND.   You are a widow;
You know already what man is; and therefore
Let not youth, high promotion, eloquence—
CARDINAL.   No,
Nor any thing without the addition, honour,
Sway your high blood.
FERDINAND.   Marry! They are most luxurious
Will wed twice.
CARDINAL.   O, fie!
FERDINAND.   Their livers are more spotted
Than Laban's sheep.
DUCHESS.   Diamonds are of most value,
They say, that have passed through most jewellers' hands.
FERDINAND. Whores by that rule are precious.
DUCHESS.   Will you hear me?
I'll never marry.
CARDINAL.   So most widows say;
But commonly that motion lasts no longer
Than the turning of an hour-glass; the funeral sermon
And it end both together.
FERDINAND.   Now hear me:
You live in a rank pasture, here, i' the court;
There is a kind of honey-dew that's deadly;
'Twill poison your fame; look to 't: be not cunning;
For they whose faces do belie their hearts
Are witches ere they arrive at twenty years,
Ay, and give the devil suck.
DUCHESS. This is terrible good counsel.
FERDINAND. Hypocrisy is woven of a fine small thread,
Subtler than Vulcan's engine, yet, believe 't
Your darkest actions, nay, your privat'st thoughts,
Will come to light.
CARDINAL.   You may flatter yourself,
And take your own choice; privately be married
Under the eyes of night—
FERDINAND.   Think 't the best voyage
That e'er you made; like the irregular crab,
Which, though 't goes backward, thinks that it goes right

Because it goes its own way; but observe,
Such weddings may more properly be said
To be executed than celebrated.

CARDINAL. The marriage night
Is the entrance into some prison.

FERDINAND.   And those joys,
Those lustful pleasures, are like heavy sleeps
Which do fore-run man's mischief.

CARDINAL. Wisdom begins at the end; remember it.

DUCHESS. I think this speech between you both was studied,
It came so roundly off.

FERDINAND.   You are my sister;
This was my father's poniard, do you see?
I'd be loth to see 't look rusty, 'cause 'twas his.
I would have you give o'er these chargeable revels:
A visor and a mask are whispering rooms
That were never built for goodness—fare ye well—
And women like that part which, like the lamprey,
Hath never a bone in 't.

DUCHESS.   Fie, sir!

FERDINAND.   Nay,
I mean the tongue; variety of courtship:
What cannot a neat knave with a smooth tale
Make a woman believe? Farewell, lusty widow.

CARDINAL.   Earthquakes leave behind
When they have tyrannized, iron, lead and stone,
But, woe to ruin, violent lust leaves none.

                                                    [*Exeunt.*]

DUCHESS. Shall this move me? If all my royal kindred
Lay in my way unto this marriage,
I'd make them my low footsteps: and even now,
Even in this hate, as men in some great battles,
By apprehending danger, have achieved
Almost impossible actions (I have heard soldiers say so)
So I through frights and threatenings will assay
This dangerous venture. O Heaven assist me now
For I am going into a wilderness
Where I shall find nor path nor friendly clue
To be my guide.

                        CURTAIN

Act I, Scene 3

The final section of Webster's I.1. The Duchess, alone with Cariola, admits Antonio and then performs a ceremony of marriage witnessed by the concealed Cariola.

Interlude

Cornelia's dirge for her dead son from *The White Devil* ("Call for the robin redbreast and the wren"), sung by Cariola.

Act I, Scene 4

Like the first half of I.3 in the 1945 version, the first third of this scene is abridged from Webster's II.1, omitting two satiric dialogues at the start, but retaining Antonio's serious conversation with Delio at the end of Webster's scene. Bosola has detected the Duchess's pregnancy. After Antonio and Delio exit, Bosola re-enters and speaks a prose soliloquy cobbled together from his opening lines in Webster's II.2, a passage about a quiet woman from *The White Devil*, IV.2, a recollection of Webster's "The devil / Candies all sins o'er" from *The Duchess*, I.1, and new material. Bosola's soliloquy continues in verse with the first sixteen lines of his "meditation" to Castruchio and the Old Lady near the start of Webster's II.1 (only the first line and a half are reprinted below):

BOSOLA. So, so, there's no question but her techiness and most vulturous eating of the apricots are apparent signs of breeding. So quiet-looking a lady. Yet it hath oft been noted so. A quiet woman is a still water under a great bridge. A man may shoot her safely. 'Tis an old tale. Since Adam first knew Eve, no second has passed but some pair of their lost children went frenziedly to it. Fie. Fie. What are all the smooth endearments with which man o'er candies his lust but spells against self-loathing.
What thing is in this outward form of man
To be beloved? [*etc.*]

As in Webster's II.2, Antonio enters with Delio and two "Head Servants" (replacing Webster's Roderigo and Grisolan), and, following Webster's comic dialogue among the Officers (here transformed into Servants), Antonio orders the gates locked. After the Servants exit, Delio wishes Antonio "all the joys of a blessed father" and they exit. The rest of the scene follows Webster's II.3: Bosola enters on hearing the Duchess shriek, is confronted by Antonio, and, after Antonio's exit, finds a report, left accidentally by Antonio, of the birth of the Duchess's son.

Act I, Scene 5

New to this version; printed below. In Bosola's first speech the three sentences beginning "He lifts up his nose" are adapted from verse in Webster's III.3, and the long sentence beginning "Some would think" is from Webster's II.1.

Act I Scene 5

[*Enter* BOSOLA *with a letter.*]

BOSOLA. To be a familiar of great statesmen is surely to grow learned in the grammar of deceit. I'm in the way to become a fantastical scholar of faces. The Cardinal now. He lifts up his nose like a foul porpoise before a storm. And my lord Ferdinand. He laughs like a deadly canon that lightens ere it smokes. This letter shall make his gall o'erflow his liver.

Some would think the souls of princes were brought forth by some more weighty cause than those of meaner persons: they are deceived, there's the same hand to them; the like passions sway them; the same reason that makes a vicar go to law for a tithe-pig, and undo his neighbors, makes them spoil a whole province, and batter down goodly cities with a cannon.

But who could leave in such haste as if he had ridden all night to find sanctuary from the wolves.

[*Enter* MESSENGER.]

How, sir. What brings you so abruptly?

MESSENGER. A ship is arrived at Venice with messages of disaster. As they lay encamped near Tyre, our regiments were surprised in the night—by some treachery 'tis feared. The Lord Sylvio and the Marquis of Pescara are slain and the Lord Duke Ferdinand, taken captive, is removed to Damascus till the price of his ransom shall be determined. I must immediately inform the Duchess.

BOSOLA. You had best speak with her steward, Antonio.

MESSENGER. I pray you, sir, see to the stabling of my horse. I'll within.

[*Exit* MESSENGER.]

BOSOLA [*tearing up letter*].
    To air with this before its ink is dry
    So unforeseen occasion interrupts
    Our fair or foul designs; but Fate,
    Being eternal, has nor soon nor late
    Though foolish men imagine that her laws
    Have been suspended when they seem to pause.

Act II, Scene 1

New to this version; printed below.

Act II Scene 1

1ST CITIZEN. The coach passed by like a whirlwind.

2ND CITIZEN. Whither was it headed?

1ST CITIZEN. For the Cardinal's palace.

[*Enter* 3RD CITIZEN.]

2ND CITIZEN. Did you see him?

3RD CITIZEN. Ay. I caught a glimpse of his face ere a hand pulled down the shutter. 'Twas the Calabrian duke.

2ND CITIZEN. God be praised. He hath endured a long captivity.

1ST CITIZEN. 'Tis said the Lord Cardinal was loath to part with so great a sum for his brother's ransom. It hath cost him two fair manors.

3RD CITIZEN. His sudden homecoming is like to prove the undoing of some. When he hears that his sister hath turned whore, we may expect an earthquake.

1ST CITIZEN. 'Tis reported she hath littered three bastards.

3RD CITIZEN. Five.

1ST CITIZEN. With a dozen fathers to claim a share in the begetting of each.

3RD CITIZEN. You can tell her ladyship's footmen on the street by their sizeable noses.

2ND CITIZEN. Shame on you both to glorify such rumors in which a conspicuous mountain of falsehood overwhelms some poor atomy of truth.

Those who blame others do themselves accuse
And envy most where they do most abuse.

Act II, Scene 2

Ferdinand rages to the Cardinal against their sister. This scene closely follows Webster's II.5 except for a few minor cuts and two substitutions of new material that make the Cardinal more conciliatory than in the original version. After Ferdinand wishes that he could be a tempest that he might lay waste to the Duchess's territory, Webster has the Cardinal reply: "Shall our blood, / The royal blood of Arragon and Castile / Be thus attainted?" Auden and Brecht substitute:

CARDINAL. Sooth, generally for women,
    A man might strive to make glass malleable,
    Ere he should make them fixed.

After Ferdinand imagines making soft lint for the Duchess's wounds when he has hewed her to pieces, Webster has three speeches beginning with the Cardinal's

"Cursèd creature" and ending with his "It cannot wield it"; Auden and Brecht give the Cardinal a single speech:

CARDINAL. We need go borrow that fantastic glass
    Invented by Galileo the Florentine
    To view another spacious world i' the moon,
    And look to find a constant woman there.

After the Cardinal's speech in Webster that ends "Come, put yourself / In tune", Auden and Brecht add five further lines for the Cardinal and three new lines for Ferdinand, all of which replace the opening sentence of Ferdinand's speech, "So I will only study to seem the thing I am not:"

CARDINAL. [*As in Webster, through:*] Come, put yourself
    In tune.
    There is no evidence
    That she be married. Say that she hath
    Taken her pleasure unwisely, hath she not
    Some privilege? Great ladies before this
    Have done likewise.
FERDINAND. How! Wouldst make her shame a trifle?
    By this hand
    Beware, brother.
    I could kill her now [*etc., as in Webster*].

Act II, Scene 3

Abridged from Webster's III.1. Antonio tells Delio of the dangerous behavior of Ferdinand, newly arrived at court. Ferdinand enters with the Duchess and promises her a husband. Ferdinand tells his spy Bosola of his intent to force a confession from the Duchess.

Act II, Scene 4

Based on Webster's III.2. Antonio, the Duchess, and Cariola in happy domesticity. At the point where Antonio describes the judgement of Paris as a motion "able to benight the apprehension of the severest counsellor of Europe", Auden and Brecht insert two new speeches and a song from George Peele's *The Old Wives' Tale*. (The second and third lines should perhaps be repunctuated "absolute; wise, fair, and rich / His".) The proverb about apes in hell is recalled from *Much Ado About Nothing*.

DUCHESS. Then is such a counsellor in his dotage.
    Love is a monarch absolute, wise, fair, and rich,
    His prostrate subjects.

ANTONIO.   There, Cariola,
   Your riddle's answered. Is your resolve yet fixed
   To lead apes in hell? Come, a song, but none
   Of your sad plaints of constancy betrayed,
   Or maidens drowned in wells. Let hope and gladness
   Move you to music now.

SONG

CARIOLA.   When as the rye reach to the chin,
              And chopcherry, chopcherry ripe within,
              Strawberries swimming in the cream,
              And schoolboys playing in the stream;
              Then O, then O, then O my true love said
              Till that time come again,
              She could not live a maid.

The scene continues, as in Webster, with the Duchess' "I prithee, / When were we so merry? My hair tangles." The rest of the scene follows Webster. Antonio and Cariola steal away, and the Duchess begins a soliloquy. Ferdinand enters, gives her a poniard, accuses her, and angrily leaves her. Antonio and Cariola return. Auden and Brecht expand Webster's dialogue in which the Duchess shows Antonio the poinard. The first sentence below is from Webster; the rest until "How now!" is added:

ANTONIO.   This hath a handle to 't,
   As well as a point. Fetch me my horse.
   I'll gallop after, turn his gift towards him
   And so fasten the keen edge in his rank gall.
DUCHESS. Stay. Do you hate me so to let yourself be slain
   That I may die of grief?
ANTONIO.   No, let me go.
   Better fall once than be forever falling.

                             [*Knocking within.*]

How now! who knocks? more earthquakes? [*etc., as in Webster*]

As in Webster, Bosola enters; the Duchess attempts to explain the disturbance by pretending to accuse Antonio of false financial dealings. When Bosola exits, the Duchess tells Antonio to flee, and when Bosola returns, pretends to banish Antonio. Mistakenly trusting Bosola, the Duchess reveals to him that she has married Antonio and borne his child. Bosola advises the Duchess to feign a pilgrimage to a spot near Antonio's exile.

Act II, Scene 5

The first half of the scene (printed below) is new, except for the first three speeches, which are from Webster's III.4. The new speeches substitute the form of excommunication for the dumb show in Webster's scene. The typist probably worked from Auden or Brecht's lightly punctuated manuscript; I have inserted an occasional comma where its presence is positively required. The remainder of the scene, not printed here, reproduces the final section of Webster's III.4, where the two pilgrims discuss the legal basis of the Duchess's banishment.

Act II Scene 5

1ST PILGRIM. I have not seen a goodlier shrine than this
    Yet I have visited many.
2ND PILGRIM. The Cardinal of Arragon is arrived
    To conduct the services, and his sister duchess likewise
    To pay her vow of pilgrimage. I expect
    A noble ceremony.
1ST PILGRIM.   No question—They come.
VOICE OF CARDINAL. Herefore, through the authority of the Almighty
    God, Father of Heaven and His Son, Our Savior, I, Cardinal of An-
    cona, denounce, Proclaim and declare Giovanna Theresa Duchess of
    Malfi and her paramour, Antonio Bologna, together with their chil-
    dren, Anathema by the avise and assistance of our Holy Father, the
    Pope, and all bishops, abbots, priors and other prelates and ministers
    of our Holy Church, for her open lechery and sins of the flesh.
1ST PILGRIM. He hath excommunicated her!
VOICE OF CARDINAL. I curse her head and the hairs of her head, her eyes,
    her mouth, her nose, her tongue, her teeth, her neck, her shoulders,
    her breast, her heart, her arms, her legs, her back, her stomach, her
    womb, and every part of her body from the top of her head to the
    soles of her feet.
2ND PILGRIM.   There hath been no rumor
    She was to be judged.
1ST PILGRIM.   And to think 'twas said
    She came here for sanctuary!
CARDINAL'S VOICE. I dissever and part them from the Church of God
    and likewise from contracts and oaths of law. I forbid all Christian
    men to have any company with them and all her earthly goods I seize
    in the name of the Holy Church. And as their candles go from our
    sight so may their souls go from the visage of God and their good
    fame from the world.
1ST PILGRIM. Here's a strange turn of state! [*etc., as in Webster*]

This scene evidently corresponds to the "third section" of the "ban scene" mentioned in Brecht's letter to Bergner (p. 449). A version of the scene with all three sections survives in a typescript in the Bertolt-Brecht-Archiv, printed in the notes to both editions of Brecht's *Collected Works*, vol. 7 (American edition, pp. 436–44; British edition, pp. 432–39) and in the notes in Brecht's *Werke: Stücke 7*, pp. 342–50. The few newly written lines in this scene appear to be Brecht's work, not Auden's, although the scene almost certainly dates from the period of their collaboration. The first section of the longer version consists of a dialogue of the French and English ambassadors about the proceedings against the Duchess. Their lines are borrowed from *The White Devil*, III.1, with a few new lines of verse added. In the second section, Ferdinand and the Cardinal enter as guards bring in the Duchess, Antonio, and their children, and then a lawyer, the Cardinal, and Ferdinand make their accusations against the Duchess and Antonio. Much of this section is taken from *The White Devil*, III.2, again with some new lines of verse. In the final section of the scene, as in the 1946 copyright version, the Cardinal pronounces his ban on the Duchess, then, in a brief episode dropped in the copyright version, pulls her wedding ring from her finger.

Act II, Scene 6

Reproduces Webster's III.5. The Duchess reports an ominous dream to Antonio. Bosola enters briefly with an equivocal letter from Ferdinand asking for Antonio to come to him. Bosola enters again, disguised, with a guard, and commands the Duchess to return to her palace. The Duchess tells Antonio to flee with their eldest son.

Act II, Scene 7

Printed below. Mostly new, but the Echo and some other lines are based on Webster's V.3.

Act II Scene 7

SON. Father, when shall we rest?
ANTONIO. Courage, dear son,
    'Tis but an hour's journey to the inn
    Where we may eat and sleep.
SON.   My legs refuse
    To bear me longer. Let me sit a while
    A little while.
ANTONIO.   Poor child! One moment then.
    Longer we dare not. We must haste. The day
    Already wears its hunted twilight look
    Come, dry your tears and listen. This fortification
    Grown from the ruins of an ancient abbey

Gives the best echo you have ever heard
As plain in the distinction of the words
As if a spirit answered. You may make it
A huntsman or a falconer, a musician
Or a thing of sorrow.

ECHO. A thing of sorrow.

ANTONIO. There, did you hear it, son? So soon asleep!
Sweet innocent who playest in thy dream
With tops and spangles not those deadly toys
That princes skirmish with and canst not spell
The puzzle of these ruins. Here in this court
Which now lies naked to the injuries
Of stormy weather, some men be interred
Loved the church so well and gave so largely to 't
They thought it should have canopied their bones
Till doomsday; but all things have their end:
Churches and cities which have diseases like to men,
That have like death that we have.

ECHO. Like Death that we have.

ANTONIO. O fearful echo that accuses my life
Of its long weakness; that has not made its path
By definite steps but sought its shelter
In the strong wills of others. Now
I am caught between their fighting stars, a clerk
Unpractised in the sword. O my soul,
Is 't still impossible to fly your fate?

ECHO. O, fly your fate.

ANTONIO. Unmoving stones, would you give such counsel
To a bold nature. Echo, I'll not talk with thee
For thou art a dead thing.

ECHO. Thou art a dead thing.

ANTONIO. My duchess is asleep now
And her little ones, I hope sweetly: O Heaven
Shall I never see her more?

ECHO. Never see her more.

ANTONIO. O dreadful repetition.
Methought that on the sudden a clear light
Presented me a face folded in sorrow.
Come, boy, awake. We have delayed too long.

SON. Let me sleep, mother. Kiss me once more.

ANTONIO. Dost thou dream of her
Forgetting where thou art? I'll carry thee.

Sleep on, beloved child, believing 'tis her arms
Not thy poor father's.

[Echo of galloping hooves is heard.]

       O hark, the walls
Echo to baying hooves. Where shall the quarry
Turn for salvation now. The hunt is up
And we are gone forever.

[Exeunt.]

Act III, Scene 1

Printed below. With a few new lines, and a few lines taken from Webster's IV.2, this scene is constructed from passages that appear in a different sequence in Webster's IV.1. In the opening section of the scene Auden and Brecht give Cariola lines that Webster assigned to Bosola.

Act III Scene 1

DUCHESS. I'll go pray;—No, I'll go curse.
CARIOLA. O, fie.
DUCHESS.   I could curse the stars.
CARIOLA.   Oh, fearful.
DUCHESS. And those three smiling seasons of the year
    Into a Russian winter; nay, the world
    To its first chaos.
CARIOLA. Look you, the stars shine still.
DUCHESS.   O, but you must
    Remember my curse hath a great way to go
    Plagues, that make lanes through largest families
    Consume them.
CARIOLA.   Fie, lady.
DUCHESS.   Let them, like tyrants,
    Never be remembered but for the ill they have done.
    Let all the zealous prayers of mortified
    Churchmen forget them.
    Let Heaven a little while cease crowning martyrs
    To punish them. I am full of daggers.
    Puff, let me blow these vipers from me.

[Enter BOSOLA.]

BOSOLA. All comfort to Your Grace.

DUCHESS. Good comfortable fellow,
   Persuade a wretch that's broke upon the wheel
   To have all his bones new set, entreat him live
   To be executed again. Comfort, comfort.
   Pray thee, why dost thou wrap thy poisoned pills
   In gold and sugar. Who must dispatch me?
   I account this world a tedious theatre
   For I do play a part in 't 'gainst my will.
   Why art thou come?

> [SERVANTS *bring in a chest.*]

BOSOLA. Here is a present from your princely brothers
   And may it arrive welcome, for it brings
   Rare benefit: Here is the key. They bid you
   Open it.

CARIOLA. 'Tis a costly gift.

> [DUCHESS *unlocks the chest. The bodies of* ANTO-
> NIO *and the* ELDEST CHILD *fall out.* CARIOLA
> *screams.* DUCHESS *faints.*]

BOSOLA. Now you may know directly they are dead
   Hereafter you may wisely cease to grieve
   For that which cannot be recovered.

CARIOLA. Thy lady faints. Help me carry her to bed.

BOSOLA [*to the fainting* DUCHESS *as they carry her out*]. O, fie! despair? Re-
member you are a Christian. Leave this vain sorrow. Things being at
the worst begin to mend: the bee when he hath shot his sting into
your hand may then play with your eyelid.

> [*Exeunt* CARIOLA *and* BOSOLA. *Enter* FERDI-
> NAND. *Re-enter* BOSOLA.]

FERDINAND. Excellent, as I would wish.

BOSOLA. Why do you do this?

FERDINAND.   To bring her to despair.

BOSOLA. Faith, end here,
   And go no farther in your cruelty:
   Send her a penitential garment to put on
   Next to her delicate skin, and furnish her
   With beads and prayer-books.

FERDINAND. Damn her! that body of hers,
   While that my blood ran pure in 't, was more worth

Than that which thou wouldst comfort, called a soul.
Curse upon her!
I will no longer study in the book
Of another's heart.
Your work is almost ended.
BOSOLA. Must I see her again?
FERDINAND.   Yes.
BOSOLA.   Never.
FERDINAND.   You must.

[*Exeunt.*]

Interlude

Bosola, alone, speaks his rhymed speech from Webster's IV.2 beginning "Hark, now everything is still".

Act III, Scene 2

Based on Webster's IV.2, with many cuts and rearrangements. The Duchess and Cariola speak together sadly. Bosola enters (apparently, as in Webster, in disguise), tells the Duchess he is come to make her tomb, and discourses to her about her mortality. Executioners enter; Cariola is forced out; the Duchess is strangled by the Executioners, who exit. Ferdinand enters, mourns the Duchess, disputes with Bosola, and exits. Bosola soliloquizes over his sunk estate and exits.

Act III, Scene 3, and Epilogue

Printed below. As in 1945, this concluding scene is heavily rearranged from passages in Webster's V.2 and V.5, with a few lines from IV.2 and from *The White Devil*, V.6. For some of the sources of this scene, see the notes to the concluding scene of the 1945 version (pp. 443–44). The text below includes emendations based on the 1945 text.

The opening of the scene, until the exit of the Doctor and Courtiers, matches the opening of III.2 in the 1945 version, except that the 1946 text does not have Bosola enter at first and either omits his lines or gives them to the 1st Courtier. The Cardinal's question about hell is restored to its original place near the end of the play, instead of opening the play as in 1945. In the dialogue between the Cardinal and Bosola and in Bosola's soliloquy, the 1946 text modifies the new lines written in 1945 by emphasizing Ferdinand's anger at the Cardinal. The dialogue between Ferdinand and the Cardinal is loosely based on Webster's V.2. The Cardinal's urging Bosola to strike Ferdinand is new, and the rapid succession of deaths, as in the 1945 text, borrows speeches from *The White Devil*, V.6.

About half the epilogue is new; lines 12–16 and 19–22 are taken from a song in *The Devil's Law Case*, V.4, and line 11 is adapted from the same song.

Act III Scene 3

1st COURTIER. 'Twas a foul storm tonight.

2nd COURTIER. The Lord Ferdinand's chamber shook like an osier.

1st COURTIER. I pray thee, Doctor, what is his disease?

DOCTOR. A very pestilent disease,
    They call lycanthropia.

1st COURTIER.   What's that?
    I need a dictionary to 't.

DOCTOR.   I'll tell you.
    In those that are possessed with 't there o'erflows
    Such melancholy humour they imagine
    Themselves to be transformed into wolves;
    Steal forth to churchyards in the dead of night,
    And dig dead bodies up; as two nights since
    One met the duke 'bout midnight in a lane
    Behind Saint Mark's church, with the leg of a man
    Upon his shoulder; and he howled fearfully;
    Said he was a wolf, only the difference
    Was, a wolf's skin was hairy on the outside,
    His on the inside; bade them take their swords,
    Rip up his flesh, and try: straight I was sent for,
    And, having ministered to him, found his grace
    Very well recovered.

1st COURTIER.   I am glad on 't.

DOCTOR. Yet not without some fear
    Of a relapse.

                                      [Enter CARDINAL.]

CARDINAL. You shall not watch tonight by the sick prince;
    His grace is very well recovered.

1st COURTIER. Good my lord, suffer us.

CARDINAL.   O, by no means;
    The noise, and change of object in his eye,
    Doth more distract him: I pray, all to bed;
    And though you hear him in his violent fit,
    Do not rise, I entreat you.

2nd COURTIER. So, sir; we shall not.

1st COURTIER.   We'll leave your grace
    Wishing to the sick prince, our noble lord
    All health of mind and body.

CARDINAL.   You are most welcome.

[*Exeunt* DOCTOR *and* COURTIERS.]

I am puzzled in a question about hell:
He says, in hell there's one material fire,
And yet it shall not burn all men alike.
Lay him by. How tedious is a guilty conscience!
When I look into the fish-ponds in my garden,
Methinks I see a thing armed with a rake,
That seems to strike at me.

[*Enter* BOSOLA.]

Now, sir, why do you look so wildly
Wherefore cam'st thou hither.
BOSOLA. That I might find a great man like yourself
    Not out of his wits as the Lord Ferdinand
    To remember my service.
CARDINAL.   So you shall
    If you'll do one thing for me, I'll entreat,
    I'd make you what you would be. There is
    A fortune attends thee.
BOSOLA. Shall I go sue to Fortune any longer?
    'Tis the fool's pilgrimage.
CARDINAL.   I have honors in store for thee.
BOSOLA. There are many ways that conduct to seeming honor
    And some of them very dirty ones.
CARDINAL. Throw to the devil
    Thy melancholy. The fire burns well;
    What need we keep a stirring of 't and make
    A greater smother. Listen.
    The Lord Ferdinand's sickness is likely to prove mortal
    To others than himself. His frenzy has strange turns
    Now railing against me his brother
    Till I fear for my life, now thinking
    To confess the Duchess' murder. Our safety says
    He cannot live long. Be secret here.
    I'll fetch him in. Then at my signal strike.
    Our witness shall be proof his own hand slew him.
BOSOLA. You shall find me ready.

[*Exit* CARDINAL.]

BOSOLA.   O my fate moves swift.
    I have this cardinal in the forge already

Now I'll bring him to the hammer. He shall sweat
For his cold avarice more loved in hell
Than any boiling lust although
That must be paid for too. Then after
I'll be my own example. O this court
Shall see a thorough cleansing.
The weakest arm is strong enough that strikes
With the sword of justice. Still methinks the Duchess
Haunts me: then, then! 'Tis nothing but my melancholy
They cure. Be resolute, my soul.

[*Enter* CARDINAL *with* FERDINAND.]

CARDINAL. Calm yourself, brother.
FERDINAND.   Indeed I am to blame
    For did you ever hear the dusky raven
    Chide blackness? or was 't ever known the devil
    Railed against cloven creatures? Look, look!
    What's that follows me?
CARDINAL. Nothing.
FERDINAND. Yes.
CARDINAL. 'Tis your shadow.
FERDINAND. Stay it: let it not haunt me.
CARDINAL. Impossible, if you move and the light shine.
FERDINAND. I will throttle it. [*Throws himself down on his shadow.*]
CARDINAL. O brother, you are angry with nothing.
FERDINAND. You are a fool. How is it possible I should catch my shadow
    unless I fall upon 't. [CARDINAL *attempts to raise him.*] Leave me. I am
    studying the art of patience.
CARDINAL. 'Tis a noble virtue.
FERDINAND. To drive six snails before me from this town to Moscow;
    neither use goad nor whip to them, but let them take their own time;
    the patient'st man i' the world match me for an experiment and I'll
    crawl after like a sheepbiter.
CARDINAL [*raising him up*]. Come, sit in this chair. I'll fetch you your phy-
    sician. [*Signs to* BOSOLA *who does not move.*]
FERDINAND. Hide me from him. What I have done, I have done. I'll con-
    fess nothing. Strangling is a very quiet death. Whisper softly; do you
    agree to 't? So: it must be done in the dark. Hush! Disturb her not.
    Sweet Giovanna, how lovely art thou now! Had I infinite worlds, they
    were too little for thee. My loose thoughts scatter like quicksilver. I
    was bewitched.
CARDINAL [*to* BOSOLA]. 'Tis time. Strike while he's in his fit.
FERDINAND. Why do you whisper? Do I not know you?

CARDINAL. Yes. 'Tis your brother who loves you.
[*Aside.*] Be swift. He grows dangerous.
FERDINAND. You lie. 'Tis the devil who whispers that my sister was a strumpet. I'll change your speeches. [*Draws his sword.*]
CARDINAL. Bosola. Help.
BOSOLA. Now thou art caught in thine own engine.
FERDINAND. Let me turn rat-catcher. I'll do a miracle and free the court from all foul vermin. [*Attacks* CARDINAL.]
CARDINAL. Ha! Help. Our guard.
BOSOLA. Thou art deceived. They are out of thy howling.
FERDINAND. Who would have thought the devil could skip so nimbly with his lame leg. When I have slain their master his black jury shall recant and pronounce her honest.
CARDINAL [*to* BOSOLA]. Help; and I will faithfully divide revenues with thee.
BOSOLA. Thy prayers and pratters are both unreasonable.
FERDINAND. Yield, yield! I give you the honor of arms
Shake my sword over you. Will you yield?
I'll not waste longer time; there. [*Stabs* CARDINAL.]
CARDINAL. You have hurt me.
BOSOLA. Again!

[FERDINAND *stabs again.*]

CARDINAL. Shall I die like a leveret without any resistance? Help. Help. Help. I am slain. [*Falls.*]
FERDINAND. What. Is the devil dead and doomsday not yet come. I'll draw it nearer by a perspective and make a glass that shall set all the world on fire upon an instant.

[BOSOLA *appears.*]

Ha! art thou the physician. Give me a posset to procure sleep. My pillow is stuffed with a litter of porcupines.
BOSOLA. My medicine is swift and certain. [*Stabs* FERDINAND.]
Sink thou main cause of my undoing.
FERDINAND. O I smell soot
Most stinking soot. The chimney's afire
There's a plumber laying pipes in my guts. It scalds.
CARDINAL. Why hast thou done this.
BOSOLA. For the Duchess of Malfi and Antonio murdered
With all their children. For myself corrupted
Then neglected. All Italy shall glory
That thou which stoodst like a huge pyramid
Begun upon a large and ample base
Shalt end in a little point, a kind of nothing.

FERDINAND. Give me some wet hay; I am broken-winded.
    I do account this world but a dog-kennel.
    I will vault credit and affect high pleasures
    Beyond death.
BOSOLA.   He seems to come to himself
    Now he's so near the bottom.
CARDINAL. I recover like a spent taper
    And instantly go out. O Justice
    I suffer now for what hath former been
    Let me be laid by and never thought of. [*Dies.*]
FERDINAND. My soul like to a ship in a black storm
    Is driven I know not whither.
    My sister, O my sister. There's the cause on 't.
    Whether we fall by ambition, blood or lust
    Like diamonds, we are cut with our own dust. [*Dies.*]
VOICES [*without*]. This way, this way. Break open the doors.
    This way.
BOSOLA. The last part of my life
    Hath done me best service. Now there remains
    One prisoner more to punish. The executioner
    Must lead himself at the last to his own gallows.

                          [BOSOLA *stabs himself*.]

    Now my revenge is perfect.

                    [*Enter* DELIO *and* COURTIERS.]

DELIO. How now, my lord.
1ST COURTIER. O sad disaster.
2ND COURTIER. How comes this.
DELIO. Thou wretched thing of blood.
BOSOLA. Leave thy idle questions
    I am i' the way to study the long silence.
    To prate were idle. I remember nothing.
    There's nothing of so infinite vexation
    As man's own thoughts. Fare you well
    Mine is another voyage. [*Dies.*]

            [DELIO *steps forward and the* CURTAIN FALLS
            behind him.]

                       CURTAIN

Epilogue

DELIO.   May these deaths enacted here
              Purge by pity and by fear
              Till each chastened conscience be
              From all fatal passions free.
              Hidden hatreds, loves obscure
              Fevers living could not cure
              Pride and jealousy and lust
              Ruined these to squandered dust.
              Here their greatness ended: May
              This portent teach us to survey
              Our progression from our birth
              We are set, we grow, we turn to earth
              Courts adieu and all delights
              All bewitching appetites!
              Sweetest breath and clearest eye
              Like perfumes go out and die,
              Praise and conversation
              Fall silent as we die alone.
              Vain the ambition of kings
              Who seek by trophies and dead things
              To leave a living name behind
              And weave but nets to catch the wind.

§4 THE VERSION PRODUCED IN 1946

George Rylands arrived in New York to direct *The Duchess of Malfi* late in August 1946, and learned during his first meeting with Bergner and Czinner that he was expected to produce a radically revised version of the play. He recalled later:

> I objected strongly to directing any other text than the original Auden's version made a great many changes—and after a great deal of argument I reluctantly agreed to a compromise in two respects. The first was that I agreed to a soliloquy for Ferdinand of about ten lines towards the end of the first Act in which he indicated that he had an incestuous passion for his sister [p. 456]. Elisabeth assured me that the American public would not accept the character without an expressed motive. This didn't do much harm. More vexing and (in my opinion) unnecessary was her belief that the public wouldn't be able to swallow the WAXWORKS [in Webster's IV.1]. And so in that scene we had a small boy and girl who tumbled out of a cupboard dead. You doubtless know that there are regulations about the employment of children in the American theatre and (again if my memory is correct) we had to employ the offspring of

police officials—different ones in each place. There may have been some slight re-writing with cutting in the last Act but these TWO were the major changes. (Letter to Mendelson, 1 May 1967)

Although Brecht's objections to Rylands's production led him to withdraw his name from the Broadway opening on 15 October 1946, he apparently helped rehearse the actors and rearranged the text after Rylands returned to England at the end of the first week of performances in New York.

After the production closed Brecht initiated legal action against Czinner for violating his contractual agreement to produce the version prepared by Brecht and Auden. Details of this and Brecht's other activities connected with the collaboration are reported by James K. Lyon in *Bertolt Brecht in America*, 1980, pp. 142–50.

"On the Way": A Scenario for an Unwritten Libretto

WHILE summering in Italy in 1949, Auden and Kallman wrote a scenario for a libretto, their next collaborative work after *The Rake's Progress*. Kallman recalled that they wrote the scenario in Florence, probably during a week's visit in the middle of June. Auden told Stravinsky, in a postcard of 2 July [1949]: "Mr Kallman and I are writing a comic libretto about the Muse and her relations with Berlioz, Mendelssohn and Rossini." On 15 October 1949 Auden reported to Isherwood:

> We've worked out a new libretto which we hope to sell to some composer about the relations of the Muse to three bards who resemble Berlioz, Mendelssohn (a mezzo-soprano) and Rossini, and to a police chief. Berlioz has a mad-scene in drag, and Rossini and a cook a big aria about how to cook Tournedos-à-la-Rossini. And the *intrigues*, my dear. We went nearly dotty working them out.

After writing the scenario, Auden and Kallman never wrote any of the libretto itself, but Auden may have had some interest in working on it late in 1949; on 8 November he wrote from New York to Kallman, who was still in Italy, "have you sent off my copy of *On the Way* because it hasn't arrived" (letter in the Berg Collection). Perhaps around the time of the premiere of *The Rake's Progress* in 1951, they discussed the project with Stravinsky, who apparently expressed little interest. Robert Craft twice published a recollection of these discussions. He wrote first that the protagonists were to have been "Rossini (the man of stomach), Berlioz (the man of heart), and Mendelssohn (the man of sensiblity)" ("The Poet and the Rake", *W. H. Auden: A Tribute*, ed. Stephen Spender, 1975, p. 154); then, perhaps more plausibly, that they were to have been "Rossini (the man of heart), Berlioz (the man of intellect), and Mendelssohn (the man of sensibility)" (Vera Stravinsky and Robert Craft, *Stravinsky in Pictures and Documents*, 1978, p. 415).

Much of the scenario seems to be Kallman's work. On the title page of the manuscript Auden listed the authors as "Chester Kallman and W. H. Auden", although Kallman then reversed the order by crossing out Auden's name and writing it in again before his own. The manuscript (now in the Berg Collection) is an untitled scenario in Kallman's hand; a title page, dramatis personae, list of scenes, and preliminary note in Auden's hand were prepared slightly later. The first typescript, probably prepared by one of the authors' friends in Ischia, is based closely on the manuscript except for some omissions and errors. It survives in a complete top copy (at Texas) and a partial carbon copy (in the Berg Collection). The top copy has corrections in Kallman's hand, but the list of entrances and exits in the left-hand column and the list of musical numbers in the right-hand column is in Auden's hand, with small additions by Kallman. The incomplete carbon copy has the same corrections (with the accidental omission of one or two) in Auden's hand, and the lists in the left-hand and right-hand columns, also in Auden's hand. A second typescript, possibly prepared by Alan Ansen for the convenience of the authors, is an inaccurate transcript of one of the copies of the first typescript; a carbon copy is in the Berg Collection.

In Kallman's manuscript scenario, five characters who are renamed in the typescript are given either their real names (Berlioz, Mendelssohn, Rossini) or the names of their roles (Police-Commissioner, Cook). In the typescript (and in Auden's manuscript dramatis personae, prepared after Kallman wrote the manuscript scenario), the three composers are renamed Mousson, Schöngeist, and Pollicini, and the Police-Commissioner and Cook are renamed Sbuffone and Saltimbocca.

The text below is based on the manuscript, but uses the final forms of the characters' names and includes the revisions and additions made by the authors while correcting the first typescript. The manuscript and typescript both abbreviate the characters' names; this edition expands the abbreviations in the summary of the action, but retains them (slightly regularized) in the left-hand and right-hand columns. The text also corrects Kallman's trivial spelling errors, and slightly rationalizes his wayward punctuation.

On the Way

A romantic adventure
in three acts with a prologue and
an epilogue

LIBRETTO BY

W. H. AUDEN AND

CHESTER KALLMAN

DRAMATIS PERSONAE

GIORGIO SBUFFONE, 40,	*Tenor*
alias Lord Tantalus, *a chief of police*	
VERGILE MOUSSON, 25 ⎫	*Baritone*
GREGOR SCHÖNGEIST, 18 ⎬ *Bards*	*Mezzo-soprano*
GIOCONDO POLLICINI, 40 ⎭	*Bass*
AN INNKEEPER	
GISELLA SALTIMBOCCA, 30,	*Contralto*
alias Lady Tantalus, *a cook*	
STELLA ⎫	
MARIA ⎬ *The Muse*	*Soprano*
LAURA ⎭	

SCENES

Prologue.	Vergile Mousson's room in Rome.
Act I.	An Inn in the Alps.
Act II.	Same as Act I.
Act III.	Same as Act I.
Epilogue.	Outside the Inn.

Time: the 1830's.

NOTE

The subject of this libretto is the romantic sensibility of the post-Napoleonic period in Europe as exhibited by its artists, in particular by its musicians. Thus in appearance, costume and make-up the three bards, Mousson, Schöngeist and Pollicini should remind the audience of Berlioz, Mendelssohn and Rossini respectively.

In style and treatment the libretto is intended for an opera stemming from the tradition of the *Opéra Comique* as exemplified, for instance, by a work like *Manon;* i.e., unlike classical opera, it does not employ formal recitative but the non-lyrical passages are spoken or sung against a continuous orchestral background; on the other hand, unlike music drama, it retains formal "numbers", arias, ensembles, etc.

PROLOGUE: *Mousson's apartment in Rome. (Window with view, two doors, large full-length mirror back-center.) Night.*

SALT & SBUF	SALTIMBOCCA is reporting to SBUFFONE that MOUSSON, after receiving a letter, stalked out in a rage and has been gone for almost two days. SBUFFONE remarks that he is certain this letter contains news of a "conspiracy" which is probably not going well for the moment.—Has she found the letter?—No.—SBUFFONE complains that she is not very efficient. She retaliates that the pay is insufficient, that he had promised her a more "glamorous" career as an agent and that it gets on her nerves, at any rate, to work for a man who doesn't notice what he's eating.—Has she succeeded in opening the locked chest? Again No.—(Further exchange as before.)—They hear someone at the door. SBUFFONE hides behind window curtain.	Duet
		Dialogue
		Duet
		(interrupte
Enter MOUS	MOUSSON is carrying two parcels which he places on a table near where SBUFFONE is hiding.	
SALT & SBUF	SALTIMBOCCA asks if he wishes anything.—No, no, leave me alone.—She gains his attention long enough for SBUFFONE to feel one parcel and identify it as pistols,—but not long enough for him to even touch the other. And when MOUSSON gets the locked chest and places it on the table, SBUFFONE, aided by SALTIMBOCCA, manages to slip out.—Noticing that SALTIMBOCCA is still around (she has been trying to see what he's got in the other parcel—and trying to keep herself inconspicuous) he orders her angrily out and shuts the door.	Dialogue
		interspersir
		a
		Trio
Exit SBUF		
Exit SALT		

MOUS alone

MOUSSON carefully draws the curtains and takes a letter out of his pocket: "Betrayed, betrayed again, for the last time betrayed. To marry another, marry for money. No—death alone—the death of *all* of us (unwraps pistols) is the only answer." Opening the box with a key he takes out his notebooks and MSS. of unfinished work and bids them a sad farewell. Then opening the other parcel he takes out a dress—"Unknown I'll go and unsuspected find them.—Strike like a storm,—unless she see her error and come with me.—Let all art be disguise—oh spirit of falsehood—aid thou my true cause." Holds the dress in front of him and walks back to the mirror. As he is "modelling" the dress he hears a burst of laughter from the mirror. Startled he steps back as

Recit.

Aria

Recit.
Stretto with
    rubati }
Invocation

Enter MUSE

the MUSE steps out of the mirror in the same dress into the room. MOUSSON: Who are you?— My disguise?—MUSE: Disguise. (Takes the dress from him and tosses it into the mirror.)— MOUSSON: Will you do as I will? MUSE: I will, etc. "Let us be off." Gives her the pistols to carry, closes

MOUS: speaks
MUSE: sings
    (echo)
Duet in canon
    (MUSE

Exeunt MOUS & MUSE

the box, puts out all the lights and leaves with her in darkness.

following
MOUS)

After a short pause, the inner door flies open, the curtains are drawn back from the outside and

Orchestral
scherzo

Enter POLICE
Enter SBUF & SALT & ASSISTANTS
Exit ASSISTANTS

from both places Carabinieri appear carrying lights. Then the outer door opens and SBUFFONE enters flanked by two assistants and SALTIMBOCCA. He briefly orders his assistants—"Find his destination." Walks briskly to the table, seats himself at a chair held for him, goes through the empty parcel, expertly opens the locked box with some tool or other, and begins going through the notebook. Just before going through it he holds it triumphantly up. As though this were a signal the Carabinieri begin sacking the room with no apparent purpose but destruction. They are doing this as he carefully examines the notes and the

Spoken
    dialogue

CURTAIN FALLS

ACT ONE: *The Main Room of an Inn in Switzerland. Entrance L, large glass doors and windows rear with view of Alps. Gallery with four or five doors R to center*

and staircase leading down at either end. Beneath Gal-
lery entrance to dining-room of inn. Clock, porcelain
stove, potted plants for hiding behind—same for stairs—
as angular as possible. Morning, a few days later.

MOUS & SCHÖN   MOUSSON and SCHÖNGEIST at window sharing an   Duet
enthusiasm for alpine scenery—but each time
MOUSSON opens the window for the "bracing air",
SCHÖNGEIST begs him to close it because of the   and
draft. In recognition of this immediate "great
friendship" MOUSSON half-confides what he is up
to, produces the revolvers and invites SCHÖNGEIST   Dialogue
to come out for a walk and "target practice".
SCHÖNGEIST shudderingly declines. MOUSSON
Exit MOUS L.   leaves.

     Alone, SCHÖNGEIST reflects that, lovely as it is   Recit.
here, he longs for the home he left many years ago
at the death of his mother. Childhood memories.

Enter MUSE   The MUSE, behind him, steps through the pane
of the closed window, and—as it were—continues   Aria
his "musings" by singing—"If you remember you
are always near.—Recall the lawn. Recall the
summer-arbor, etc." He is entranced and turning
to her continues the "recalling" with her. After this   Duet
they agree to correspond. They will leave the
"communications" that day in the clock. As he
starts up to his room (stairs C),

Enter POLL   POLLICINI appears on the gallery (entering
from his room: door furthest L), and screams for
the INNKEEPER and his lunch. SCHÖNGEIST, at the
noise, claps his hands over his ears—"How can I
Exit SCHÖN   compose with this din?" and hurries into his room.

POLL & MUSE   POLLICINI: "You again." MUSE: "Yes."—"Why   Rapid Duet
don't you leave me alone—Rome, Vienna, Paris,—
you always turn up."—"I always shall"—"I don't
like you."—"I like *you.*"—"This time I won't
yield."—"We shall see."—etc. POLLICINI goes hur-
Exit POLL   riedly back to room and slams door.

Enter MOUS   MUSE stands entranced, and is found thus by
MOUSSON who enters L, rather in a hurry.
MOUSSON: "Don't stand there staring—the coach   Duet (MOUS
is coming soon. We must be getting ready to go."   agité, MUSE
MUSE: "I'm not going. I like it here."—"You must   quiet but
come. You said you'ld help. I can't manage without   firm)
you."—"Too bad."—"I insist."—etc. MOUSSON
tries to catch hold of her, but she evades him and

Exit MUSE

passes through the pane of the C window. He, on the other hand, has trouble opening the window to get out, and exclaims desperately—"And, oh my God, here comes the coach"—as he finally opens it

Exit MOUS
Enter SBUF &
SALT & INNK

and rushes after her.

SBUFFONE and SALTIMBOCCA, who enter now with the INNKEEPER and a servant who carries their bags up to their room (which the INNKEEPER points out to them as the servant enters it) are "disguised" as an English Lord and his Italian wife. Both are a bit overdressed for their parts. SBUFFONE asks who is staying and is told proudly: "Three artists, but MOUSSON is departing with the coach they have just left." Indeed, he continues, he must find him at once. The INNKEEPER goes upstairs C to knock on his door.

Running Ensemble interspersed with spoken comments, small trios, duets, arias

	UPSTAIRS ACTION	DOWNSTAIRS ACTION
Enter POLL	At which POLLICINI appears on the gallery and sees SALTIMBOCCA: "Now that's more what I like."	SBUFFONE remarks to SALTIMBOCCA: "Very suspicious." INNKEEPER comes down C. SALTIMBOCCA starts up L to change for lunch. INNKEEPER and
Exeunt SBUF & INNK		SBUFFONE go out to see if MOUSSON is in the coach.
	SALTIMBOCCA and POLLICINI indulge in mild flirtation which is interrupt-	
Enter SBUF & INNK	ed when she says, "Oh— here's my husband again,"	INNKEEPER and SBUFFONE re-enter L. "He's not
Exit SALT	and goes into her room.	in coach." MOUSSON enters
Enter MOUS	POLLICINI comes down L.	C window distressed looking for MUSE—wildly, abstract[ed]ly (SBUFFONE has aside—INNKEEPER goes
Exit INNK		into Dining-Room), and
Exit MOUS		goes up to look for her in his room. POLLICINI and SBUFFONE bow to each other, SBUFFONE starts upstairs, looks to see if
Enter SALT	SALTIMBOCCA comes out	POLLICINI is watching, and
Enter INNK	of room and descends stairs L.	hides behind plant. INNKEEPER announces *Lunch*. He, POLLICINI, and SALTIMBOCCA have brief "To eat, to eat—joy of creation"

Exeunt INNK,
POLL, SALT
Enter MOUS

Enter SCHÖN

Exit MOUS

Enter MOUS

MOUSSON peeks out of his door, and after seeing that the others have gone in to lunch, comes out of his room and starts tapping walls, stooping at keyholes and calling for the MUSE. Is embarrassed to be caught at this by SCHÖNGEIST, who comes from his room upstairs carrying a note and hurriedly re-enters his room. SCHÖNGEIST, more shocked than annoyed at this behavior, comes down C.—MOUSSON again sneaks out of his room and tiptoes part way down stairs L and hides to watch. He is curious but not over-suspicious of SCHÖNGEIST's actions— "Does he know where she is"—Comes down to get the note.

exclamation and go into the Dining-Room.

(Comments by SBUFFONE from hiding-place.)

At the clock he reads over the "note" or composition—"Oh thou comforter, daughter of memory" sort-of-thing, and after putting the note in the clock, goes into the Dining-Room.—
SBUFFONE comes down to get the note.

SBUFFONE and MOUSSON, thus meeting, bow elaborately and try, both, to get at the clock. SBUFFONE pretends to be a passionate admirer of MOUSSON's work and catches hold of his hand when he can exclaiming—"And oh the honor to *Duet with asi* touch the hand that so much beauty to the world has brought." MOUSSON is both flattered and annoyed at not being able to get at the note.—He is not at all suspicious that SBUFFONE is trying to get it. At an opportune moment, however, SBUFFONE

Exeunt MOUS &
SBUF
Enter MUSE

does retrieve it and then drags MOUSSON out to "take a walk and talk about art—I *am* so honored."
As they go out the MUSE enters from POLLICINI's room and descending the stair sings of the tranquil *Aria* joy and the excitement just to be in "his" room even when he isn't there.—How everything—the male disorder, the work-desk, etc.—all speak of him. As she reaches the window C, she carves his initial "G" (also the initial of SCHÖNGEIST and

Exit MUSE
Enter SCHÖN,
SALT, POLL

SBUFFONE) on it and then passes through it again.
The party in the dining-room enter,—SCHÖNGEIST going to the clock to see if the note has been taken, SALTIMBOCCA and POLLICINI strolling to the window making conversation—POLLICINI

being gallante (talk about the view).—SALTIM-
BOCCA notices the initial and exclaims loudly over

Enter INNK,
MOUS, SBUF

it. The INNKEEPER, hearing the exclamation, en-
ters. SCHÖNGEIST turns. SBUFFONE and MOUSSON
appear at the outside and come in.

SBUFFONE: "Who carved it? Who is G?"   Sextet

MOUSSON: "He *does* know where she is. She loves
him. (Checks at the clock) The note was for
her. O fury."

SCHÖNGEIST: "She received my letter. O joy."

POLLICINI: "I wish she wouldn't write my name
in public places. I hope this lady doesn't re-
alise it's me."

SALTIMBOCCA: "Well, I never. Someone is be-
having very strangely."

INNKEEPER: "Very peculiar things seem to be
happening in my Inn. I suppose they always
do."

CURTAIN

ACT TWO: *Same scene as Act One; Later the same
afternoon.*

SBUF

SBUFFONE alone, pacing the room, tells that he be- Recit.
lieves that all three of the artists are a revolution- monologue
ary committee—but exactly what their plot is and quasi-aria
who the fourth (who carved the initial) is or is up
to—though probably the secret "head"—he is not
sure. It must be worked out systematically.—
Discipline, discipline.—

Enter SALT

SALTIMBOCCA enters carrying coffee for him— Solo with
and he upbraids her for taking so long,—there is spoken
work to do. She merely shrugs her shoulders and dialogue in
sits down. He continues, therefore, his former response
monologue, in effect—"There seems to be this
girl—or man—I have a partial description in
this, SCHÖNGEIST's letter, and some strange nota-
tions from MOUSSON's notebook. We must expand
our data. Where is POLLICINI?"—SALTIMBOCCA:
"Asleep after eating."—SBUFFONE: "Well, then, we
can let him go for a while and concentrate on
MOUSSON, who's out walking with SCHÖNGEIST.
We've got to separate them somehow."—SALTIM-
BOCCA: "Oh all the fuss you make, just over some-
one's practical joke." SBUFFONE: "It's no use trying

to explain to a woman. And here they come now."

Exit SBUF He goes up hurriedly to his room as

Enter SCHÖN & SCHÖNGEIST and MOUSSON enter from outside.
MOUS MOUSSON is trying to question SCHÖNGEIST on the Trio
MUSE's whereabouts indirectly by talking to him
about Love—"I'll bet you young men nowadays
know *lots* of things. Devilish little things you are.
Come now confess,—we *are* great friends aren't
we?" SCHÖNGEIST, tired and wishing to be alone,
keeps deprecating MOUSSON's remarks vaguely
and saying aside: "Oh the vulgarity of the man."
SALTIMBOCCA, seeing her opportunity, presents
herself to MOUSSON: "Don't you recognize me,
dear Master?" MOUSSON, surprised, wishes of
course to know more about what she's doing here
"all dressed up"—but is also loth to leave
SCHÖNGEIST lest he miss locating the MUSE.
SCHÖNGEIST pleading a slight faintness keeps try-
ing to get away. SALTIMBOCCA to MOUSSON: "Can't
we be alone. I have so much to tell you." Finally she
turns to SCHÖNGEIST and says "You poor thing,
you do look unwell. I remember a man I knew,
looked just the way you do (gives a list of alarming
symptoms)—and he died like *that*, right after
lunch. When the surgeons opened him after out of
sheer curiosity, they found that his liver was *green*."
SCHÖNGEIST makes a choking noise and faints.

Enter SBUF,   Drawn by the noise, SBUFFONE comes out on the
INNK & MUSE Gallery, and seeing what has happened, comes
down. The INNKEEPER also enters. And in a hiding
place stage front, near the clock, the MUSE (rising
from the ground) appears. SBUFFONE and
Exeunt SCHÖN INNKEEPER carry SCHÖNGEIST upstairs, the
& SBUF INNKEEPER descending immediately to get some
Exit INNK broth for him.

Left alone with MOUSSON, SALTIMBOCCA tells Duo
him that when she worked for him she was a run-
away wife of this English lord and came to work
for him because she nourished a grand-passion for
him. In fact she adores all artists. Husbands are so
prosaic. But now he's found her and they're re-
turning to England. However, she adds proudly,
she did manage it so that they would return in
such a way as to overtake MOUSSON.—MOUSSON is
embarrassed by her advances, and even more so by
her enthusiastic praise of the beneficial effects of

adultery:—"It cleans the soul and elevates the Aria
mind. Adultery, adultery, the only reason to be
married,—my heart is free when I take wing into
the heavenly Empyrean of adultery." Rejected a bit
by him she says it obviously isn't moral compunc-
ture that's stopping him—"Everyone knows that Trio
artists are gloriously liberal and wicked—not to
say Revolutionary"—it must be a rival—probably
another married woman. MOUSSON says no, but
spurred on, confesses that he is in love—and sings Aria
his description of the MUSE (who, SALTIMBOCCA
also ascertains, is in the vicinity). He describes her
as "difficult, temperamental, unfaithful, proud,
terrible, etc." He also says he just has come to love
her and not the girl who betrayed him in Paris by
getting married to money.—All through this scene Trio
the MUSE, amused, makes comments from her
hiding place. (SALTIMBOCCA has been taking notes
while MOUSSON describes.)

Enter INNK   The INNKEEPER enters with the Broth, which
MOUSSON volunteers to take up to SCHÖNGEIST.
Exit INNK   As the INNKEEPER returns to the Dining-Room
and MOUSSON goes up to SCHÖNGEIST's room,
Enter SBUF   SBUFFONE comes out of SCHÖNGEIST's room and is
told, by SALTIMBOCCA, in gestures, that she has
gotten the Information. SBUFFONE thanks
MOUSSON on the Gallery for bringing the broth
Exeunt MOUS &   and relieving him of his vigil and goes into his
SBUF   room when MOUSSON goes into SCHÖNGEIST's.
Alone (except for the watching MUSE) SALTIM-
BOCCA congratulates herself on having behaved so
well and convincingly as a "lady of the world," and
wonders whether POLLICINI would admire her for
it. The MUSE, during this, starts her letter to
SCHÖNGEIST, but both stop their activity and ex-
claim in pleasure when
Enter POLL   POLLICINI comes out of his room, ascertains that Duet
SALTIMBOCCA, *not* the MUSE, is in sight, and
quickly descends the stairs. He makes conversation
with her on the miserable food at the Inn, and
what a contrast it is to such delicacies as he has had
as, let us say, Tournedos Rossini. Caught up in his
own enthusiasm he begins to describe how to make
the dish. But at various points, where he forgets
some little—and very important—ingredient or
cooking process, SALTIMBOCCA interrupts and

prompts him. They end together with a burst of enthusiasm for the dish and each other. POLLICINI confesses his wish to continue on a more intimate basis—and she, likewise, confesses her attraction to him.—"But your husband"—at this SALTIMBOCCA tells him the truth, that she is a Police Agent, *hates* the work—and that, however, owing to the nature of SBUFFONE's suspicions, she can direct him falsely and get him out of the way in order for them to have a Rendezvous. POLLICINI amused, though in an aside he admits that her being un-married may complicate things for him, agrees to the intrigue and says that he will await her in his room between eleven and twelve that night. During the above the MUSE has been silently listening but as the final assignation is being reached, she puts her head in her hands for a moment, and then, raising one hand in their direction   Trio repeats the words of the SALTIMBOCCA's soliloquy (see above), "A lady, a lady, a lady of the world," with great emphasis and concentration; and then

Exit MUSE   sinks out of sight as SBUFFONE appears and
Enter SBUF   comes down and POLLICINI excuses himself to him
Exit POLL   and SALTIMBOCCA on the grounds that he has work to do.

To SBUFFONE, SALTIMBOCCA gives her notes on   Quasi-duet MOUSSON and when asked about POLLICINI, she says that POLLICINI has a rendezvous with the mysterious one some distance from the Inn near a cave, at eleven-thirty. She advises him to be there waiting and to get rid of the others somehow if he wishes to catch the "chief" and not be overpowered by the others. He congratulates her on her cleverness in getting the information and the acumen of her advice. "Evidently," he observes, "this profession has really captured your imagination. It always does in the end. It is the highest calling. The world must be protected from itself—and most of all its artists. It leads to chaos and unhappiness. I know." She excuses herself—"After all my work, I

Exit SALT   am so tired"—and goes up to her room.

SBUFFONE, alone, arranges the evidence before   Aria him. "I have them now—despite their mystifications.—She's all things to all—and false to all at once. And they—vain in their souls—will, when they're shown her falsehood, tell on each other, be-

tray her and themselves. They thought themselves
so clever, but counted without me. One against
the other—and then, all caught and punished.—
First, an answer to SCHÖNGEIST from his ideal."—
He sits down and writes a cruel rejection to
SCHÖNGEIST purporting to come from the MUSE,
—reading the content as he writes it. Then he puts
it in the clock and says "That will do for him—and
now" he adds as

Enter MOUS   MOUSSON emerges from SCHÖNGEIST's room   Duet finale
and comes down. SBUFFONE inquires about the pa-
tient and, when told he seems to be resting quietly,
says, "That's very convenient for me because, I
don't mind telling you, that silly boy was getting in
my way as concerns a certain young lady who's
around. The poor boy thinks she loves him—
Heaven knows what she told him, she's like that,
she's (quotes MOUSSON's aria on the MUSE); but
she does take to me. In fact we have a date at
eleven-fifteen down the road in a little summer-
house.—As one man of the world to another,
could you see that he keeps to his room. Young
men are so silly." MOUSSON nods grimly. Then
both, aside, have a raging duet of revenge and re-
sentment using the same words: "Revenge for
every slight, for unkind words and subtle smiles,
revenge. Destroy, destroy their silly private bliss
and one bland order rule the world." MOUSSON
picks up a glass and smashes the "carved" window-
Exit MOUS   pane and rushes out. SBUFFONE laughs sar-
donically. As though it were an echo the MUSE is
heard laughing from off-stage. Puzzled, but not
quite believing his ears, SBUFFONE pauses and
looks about him as

THE CURTAIN FALLS

ACT THREE: *Same scene, late the same evening,*
Candlelight,—thunder storm beginning during act.

SALT   SALTIMBOCCA, alone, enjoys the pleasures of an-
ticipation: "The hour will soon be here, will soon   Recit. & Aria
be ours. And I shall go to him, the moment won."
(The clock strikes Ten.) She starts up in excite-

ment. "Soon O soon." A moment she reflects.
"And over just as quickly." No, she goes on, if only
she were something more than what she is—a lady,
a real lady, an inspiration, a companion, with *real*
position, not the pretence, then it need never end.
"Oh to be more and all the world to know it." As
she finishes

Enter MUSE   the MUSE steps out from behind the clock and
speaks to her directly—"Is that what you *really*   Dialogue
wish?" SALTIMBOCCA, not showing any surprise,
replies definitely in the affirmative. "You won't like
it" she's warned. "That's a risk I'll take. Anyway
(with a sigh) it's hardly likely to happen."—"It shall   &
happen if you wish. Come to your room. We'll ex-
change our clothes and you shall appear a lady to
all who see you." They ascend the stairs C together
singing, "How sweet to change and none but us the   Duet
wiser, change in a moment and change our lives

Exeunt SALT &   forever." As they enter the room the clock strikes
MUSE   again and

Enter SCHÖN   SCHÖNGEIST appears, comes down the other
stair L and hurries over to the clock. He finds the   Recit.
note left by SBUFFONE, broken-heartedly reads
aloud some of the crueller phrases, and then,
dazed and upset, sits down at the table and begins   &

Enter POLL   to weep. POLLICINI, entering from the Dining-
Room, finds him there and attempts to cheer him
up. "Really, you know, you shouldn't get so   Dialogue
upset."—"Oh you don't understand" —"Of course
I do, it's probably over some girl. Now it seems to
me you don't take the right attitude. You're too shy   Aria
and anxious and alone. You should be aggressive
and indifferent at the same time. Tremendously
social, tremendously intimate. Subtle and bold at
once. Come, you must cheer up, I'll summon all
the others and we'll have a drinking party in your
honor. So try to be a man of the world and act and
think on my advice."

POLLICINI rings for the INNKEEPER, orders wine
for all, and shouts up for everyone to come down.

Enter MOUS   Suspiciously, MOUSSON comes out of his room and
Enter SBUF   comes down. SBUFFONE, thinking some new mis-
chief afoot, hurries down too. And finally the
MUSE, dressed as SALTIMBOCCA (and seeming to
be her to all) comes down. POLLICINI explains he is
giving a little party in SCHÖNGEIST's honor—"The   Drinking-song

youngest of our bards." Drinks are poured round and POLLICINI proposes a toast to SCHÖNGEIST. All join in. In asides, MOUSSON expresses his determination to (1) catch the MUSE with SBUFFONE, and (2) try, in the mean-time, to annoy SBUFFONE by flirting openly with his wife; SCHÖNGEIST expresses his "misery"; the MUSE admires POLLICINI; and SBUFFONE, quietly pouring his drink into a potted plant, remarks that if they all get drunk, his work "will be so much the easier." When POLLICINI "forces" SCHÖNGEIST to lead the toast (SCHÖNGEIST has already, on one glass, become a bit tipsy), he (POLLICINI) confirms his rendezvous with the disguised MUSE. This, however, is difficult to do because of MOUSSON's ostentatious attentions to her. His chances are made whenever MOUSSON turns to see how SBUFFONE is taking the flirtation. POLLICINI says to the MUSE that if they all get drunk, the rendezvous "will be so much the easier" (see SBUFFONE above). SBUFFONE is indifferent and mildly amused.

& Ensemble

Exit MOUS

The clock strikes Eleven. MOUSSON excuses himself and goes out. SBUFFONE laughs to himself over this. After a moment SBUFFONE excuses himself and goes out. POLLICINI laughs to himself and bows briefly to the MUSE over this. SCHÖNGEIST continues, drunkenly, the drinking song, and pointing out to POLLICINI that he's acting on his advice, keeps trying to pinch and kiss the MUSE. POLLICINI and the MUSE agree that SCHÖNGEIST will probably pass out soon, and they kiss when he isn't looking. POLLICINI says he will await her in his room. She'd better see, as a woman can, that SCHÖNGEIST isn't ill. He goes up to his room. Alone with SCHÖNGEIST, the MUSE simply looks for a moment directly at him and he falls asleep in a chair.

Dwindling Ensemble

Exit SBUF

Exit POLL

Briefly the MUSE unburdens herself on the humiliations a Goddess must perforce suffer when she deals with the world of men: the disguises, the deceptions, the intrigues, the cruelty, the pinches! And art itself: how they disguise, distort, falsify what she gives them. And yet—so long as they need her she will need them to need her and the disguise, deception, etc., will go on and on.— Lightning flashes begin distantly.

Aria

The clock strikes again and the MUSE blows out
her candle (the only remaining light) and hides at

Enter SALT

the foot of the stairs L as SALTIMBOCCA, dressed as
the MUSE, comes quietly out of her room holding,
and shielding, a candle. Congratulating herself on
having become a lady and how pleased POLLICINI
is certain to be she tip-toes across the Gallery to his
room and knocks softly on the door. When

Enter POLL

POLLICINI opens it and sees her he exclaims: "Oh
my God, *you* again. Don't you know when you're

Exit POLL

not wanted," and shuts the door in her face.
Shocked and horrified SALTIMBOCCA staggers
back towards her room. Then, crying, "Where is
she? What has she done? Where is everyone?" she
comes quickly down C as the MUSE slips up the
stairs L, blows a kiss down to SALTIMBOCCA and

Exit MUSE

goes into POLLICINI's room. The storm has been
getting louder and brighter.

SALTIMBOCCA, in her extremely agitated state,
violently awakens SCHÖNGEIST demanding—
"Where is she? What has happened."—SCHÖN-
GEIST immediately begins reproaching her lachry-
mosely for her cruel letter. Further exasperated,
she exclaims—"Am I so changed?"—to which he,
reproachfully, answers "To me you are." At about

Enter SBUF

this point SBUFFONE enters. Seeing him SAL-
TIMBOCCA turns on him hysterically and blames
him for ruining her life. "So I should hope, ma-
dame," he replies coolly—"you are under arrest as
an enemy of the state. None of your little tricks
have worked." As he places his hand on her arm

Enter MOUS

and she is struggling, MOUSSON, revealed first in a
lightning flash at the window, mistaking the strug-
gle for an embrace, comes in holding his two
pistols, and cries "Cease immediately." General
surprise. "Thank you, dear master" says SALTIM-
BOCCA. MOUSSON laughs, "Dear master now. It is
too late. If you can die, you shall, you and your
cavalier." SALTIMBOCCA (desperately): "Don't you
recognize me?" MOUSSON: "I do, and finally for
what you truly are." The recriminations continue.
Unseen by MOUSSON, SCHÖNGEIST, who has been
somewhat in the background, comes up behind
him and knocks the pistols from his hands.
Quickly, as MOUSSON exclaims in rage, SBUFFONE
picks them up.—"A short-lived triumph sir and (to

Right margin annotations:

Spoken and
sung against
Storm-Music

Running
Ensemble

and

Growing
Storm

SCHÖNGEIST) thank you kindly. You may get off easier than the rest for that. I knew I could set your ridiculous lot one against the other." He pauses for a moment to take account of all present and noticing POLLICINI's absence cries—"Has one escaped?" In that instant SALTIMBOCCA also cries out—"POLLICINI's room, *that*'s where she is." All turn involuntarily and look up at the door to POLLICINI's room. At that instant every light is blown out, there is a loud crash of thunder, and when it dies out

MUSE (off)   the voice of the MUSE is heard in a sustained note over the ensuing silence. All stand hypnotised in their places. The MUSE sings then a simple com- Berceuse forting lullabye. As though acting as her manifest agent SALTIMBOCCA puts her arm about SCHÖNGEIST's shoulders and, his head leaning on
Exeunt SCHÖN   her shoulder, leads him gently and motherly to his
& SALT   room.

"A good trick—for a while" says SBUFFONE "but Spoken over if I blast you out of that room with these pistols,   Storm disguise and music won't help much."—"You big Vocal March booby," replies the voice "in your ridiculous dis- guise. Tomorrow you're going to apologize—or else. Or else everyone will know what's in the center-drawer of the big desk in your mother's house. And they'll know about that long conversa- tion you had at the Café Greco. And they'll know about the—apples! And remember to apologize in your proper clothes." His head hanging in shame, SBUFFONE marches to his room as though under
Exit SBUF   orders.

Silence. Then, in a desperate voice MOUSSON cries out—"And what am I do to?" Silence. "Com- mand me." Silence. "What is your wish?" Silence. With a cry of rage he rushes up the stairs. As he lifts his fist to pound on the door, the whole room is illuminated by a blinding flash of lighting and there is a deafening clap of thunder. Giving a ter- rible cry of despair, MOUSSON falls to the ground. The clock strikes Midnight as

THE CURTAIN FALLS SLOWLY.

EPILOGUE: *Scene: Courtyard in front of the Inn (repre-*
sented by a practical "flat"). The next morning. (Note:
the only solid prop on the stage is a staircase leading on
the outside of the Inn to a small balcony.)

POLL

POLLICINI, alone when the curtain rises, is holding Recit.
a large sheet of manuscript.—"Well, it happened
again and she is gone. And when I woke at
once this work came to me—which I don't quite
understand the meaning of. Always this puzzle, al-
ways this bewilderment. Why do I always yield?"

Enter SALT

At this point SALTIMBOCCA enters in her travelling
clothes. POLLICINI anxiously bids her Good Morn-
ing. She turns away. Pause. POLLICINI glances
again at the large sheet of manuscript. His face
brightens and, occasionally consulting the sheet,
he sings to her what is written on it. The "work" Aria (Turn)
asks her pardon for his weaknesses—but will she
accept them? It may happen again.—Can she pro-
tect him? Taking both past and future into
account—could she forgive him now? And as a
sign of all of these, will she join her life with his?

A short pause. Then she turns and, placing both Aria (Counter
her hands in his, asks if he, in his turn, can forgive   Turn)
her disgraceful past career and her attempt to be
something other than herself—which led to all the
trouble. Can he trust his weaknesses to be curbed
by hers? And his strengths not to be dissipated in
combatting hers? Can he bear to be protected by
someone who needs protection? To be jealously
loved by someone he possibly won't have the op-
portunity to be jealous of?—Again a pause. He
kisses her. They join in a brief thanksgiving to God Duo (Stand)
for having brought them together.

Enter SCHÖN

SCHÖNGEIST, all bundled up for travelling,
rather hung-over and sad, comes on, and bids
them a morose Good-Morning. The other two try Trio
to console him—"You mustn't think happiness im-
possible. Look at us. Have faith. It will come when
you least expect it. In the meantime be of good
heart." SCHÖNGEIST: "No, no. For you perhaps,
for *others*,—but not for me, not ever."—Just then

Enter INNK

the INNKEEPER enters carrying an absolutely enor- Dialogue
mous letter which he presents to SCHÖNGEIST,
saying—"This seems to be for you, sir. Judging by
the length I should advise you to read it in the

Exit INNK	coach which will be going any minute." Looking at the handwriting—"From her!" SCHÖNGEIST cries with joy and joins happily with the others in their optimistic viewpoint.	Trio (Concluded)
Enter SBUF	SBUFFONE then appears in his full regalia. They all regard him rather coldly. "I have an announcement to make," he says—"this is the last time you shall see me in this uniform. I have decided to retire on my return to Rome."—General surprise— "Yes—and to devote the rest of my days to finishing a work begun in my youth—an epic in twenty, perhaps thirty, books, on the famous Queens of history whose names do not contain the letter E. And I shall show it to no-one." POLLICINI pats him on the back. "But first I have a formal work to do. To you (turning to SCHÖNGEIST and giving him the MUSE's first note) I apologize for saddening you with a false letter and frightening you with a false accusation. To you (turning to POLLICINI) for allowing an intrigue to develop that might have destroyed your chances for married happiness before it even began. And to you my dear (turning to SALTIMBOCCA) for underpaying you for your work in a profession neither honorable nor fit for your talents, and for the same reason I have already apologized to Pollicini for." All in turn accept his apologies and conclude briefly on forgiveness. "Each in his heart knows much to be forgiven and from his heart must readily forgive."	March Theme (see Act Three) under spoken announcement
Enter INNK	But as SBUFFONE, producing MOUSSON's notebook, expresses his wish to return it to him and make the profoundest of apologies, the INN-KEEPER comes out in great agitation and tells them that MOUSSON has gone mad and seems to think that he is a Goddess—or something. At any rate, it is very strange.	Rondo Quartet
Enter MOUS	When the INNKEEPER finishes his "announcement", MOUSSON appears on the balcony dressed in the MUSE's dress and carrying a large hand-mirror.—Surprised comments of others.—"Your future, all of you", MOUSSON announces in great high-spirits, "I see it in this mirror. Festival continuous and rare sustained pleasure,—bursting coffers, wine of eternal youth,—never have fear, *I* shall not break my promise and it is *I* who tell you."—SBUFFONE steps towards him holding the	Aria (Mad scene)—I Cabaletta

notebook. MOUSSON lifts his hand: "Great shade, Napoleon,—you bring me, then, my future—a wealthy widow, high diplomacy, the fear and homage of all Europe. The ranks of Generals, the mobs of glittering ladies, fall back, divide,—and I pass on between them. Loved, feared, and hated— Vergile the man, Vergile the power." This is in a florid burst of exaltation while the others make comments. (POLLICINI: "Really, he takes himself too seriously." SCHÖNGEIST: "He must have drunk ten gallons." SALTIMBOCCA: "How like the man to think himself important." SBUFFONE: "How nouveau riche—one should be more self-effacing." INNKEEPER: "If this keeps up they'll never get their coach.") MOUSSON ends alone: "Now go. Remember *I* have spoken."—The INNKEEPER takes this opportunity to remind them of the coach. They depart hastily, only bidding farewell to the Inn that had changed their fates. MOUSSON has turned away from them and is looking steadily into the mirror.

Exeunt POLL, SALT, SCHÖN, SBUF, INNK

Alone, MOUSSON slowly descends the stairs: "Deserted, deserted—it is always so," he laments, "one married, one died, one wept and said she wished me for a friend. So it has been and all my life is buried. And I stand alone weeping at my grave." He tears off the dress. "Oh rend your garments, cover your head with ashes—and if nothing can weep for the death of less than nothing, weep for the child you never, never should have outgrown—and weep like the child you are. There in the mist of tears my mother waits rocking an empty cradle. It shall not be empty long." He sits on the ground and buries his face in his hands.

Enter MUSE

As he sits there the MUSE appears on the balcony clothed in white—and calls him by name. He sits up, facing forward. "What luxury," she says sternly, "when there is so much to be done. Reflect a moment—too much remains unfinished."—On his knees, still facing away from her, he begs her forgiveness: "I have not known you as you are, I followed others thinking they were you; I sought to use you following them—False paths I took pursuing falser fires. Star of my life—distant and cold and virginal and true—forgive me and remain." —The MUSE: "Work, work, alone. Look at your-

II Cabaletta
over ensem[

Interlude
(Quintet)

III Andante

Theme

self as you are, as you are *now,* not as you were or shall be. The play is over." Mousson picks up the mirror and looks into it. The Muse steps backward and "disappears." Putting down the mirror and picking up the notebook that Sbuffone has left, he rises. The "flat" drop is lifted into the flies leaving, except for the staircase—now leading into the air—, the stage bare back to the cyclorama.

Exit Muse

Mousson: "Oh Stella, Stella, how I have loved thee."

CURTAIN

Auden's Contributions to
Dramatic Works by Others

THREE times during 1953 Auden contributed to dramatic works written by others. In the spring he wrote a few lines of light verse for a comic play put together by faculty members at Smith College while he was a visiting research professor. In the summer, when Chester Kallman was writing *The Tuscan Players,* a libretto for Carlos Chávez, Auden provided six lines. In the autumn, at the request of William Walton, who was composing his opera *Troilus and Cressida* to a libretto by Christopher Hassall, Auden wrote a quintet as a sketch that Hassall might use as a model when resolving problems in the libretto. The texts of Auden's contributions to these three works appear below.

Auden may have made similar contributions to other dramatic works. Sir John Betjeman recalled that Auden "rapidly wrote in some parts for a village play" produced by Penelope Betjeman at Uffington, Berkshire, probably in 1934 or shortly afterward ("Oxford," *W. H. Auden: A Tribute,* ed. Stephen Spender, 1975, p. 45). The Poetry Collection at the State University of New York at Buffalo has two brief drafts of what appears to be a fragmentary narration for a play about Marie Antoinette. The style and handwriting suggest that these were perhaps written in the early 1940s for a play performed by children.

AUDEN'S CONTRIBUTION TO KALLMAN'S
THE TUSCAN PLAYERS

When the Mexican composer Carlos Chávez commissioned a libretto from Kallman in 1953, Auden suggested that Kallman use themes and incidents from Boccaccio instead of the Mexican themes that Kallman had first considered. Kallman began working on *The Tuscan Players* by late June 1953. On 15 September, after completing the second of three acts, he wrote to Lincoln Kirstein: "Six lines of act are Wystan's. A puzzle for the scholars." The puzzle cannot be solved beyond question, but five of Auden's six lines may be this exchange between Adam and Eve about the apple:

ADAM. Eve, as I love, so would I understand.
EVE.   Love is a word, a word is not enough.
ADAM. What are you holding in your hand?
EVE.   Share this and prove you share my love.
ADAM. Eve! You have broken the divine command!

The opera was first performed in New York in 1957 as *Panfilo and Lauretta,* and later performed under the titles *Love Propitiated* and *The Visitors.* Both the score and the libretto are unpublished. The text above is from two substantially identical typescripts of the libretto at the University of Texas.

AUDEN'S CONTRIBUTION TO THE 1953
SMITH COLLEGE FACULTY PLAY

In the spring of 1953 a group from the faculty of Smith College wrote and produced a topical comic extravaganza titled *Rosina, The White Rose of Northampton, or, She's More to be Tutored than Censured, or, From Pumpkin Patch to Paradise.* The play was performed once, on 17 April 1953, in John M. Greene Hall. The program listed the authors as Martha England, Elizabeth Gallaher, Marlies Kallmann, James Durbin, Wendell Johnson, and Robert Petersson. Auden played the role of the eponymous heroine's father, "Pa Greenseed, an innocent victim of ignorance". In Act I Pa Greenseed is a living person, in Acts II and II a ghost. Auden suggested that the father should appear in the later acts as a ghost, and performed in those acts wearing a white sheet and with his teeth out. Having agreed to perform on the condition that he would not have to contribute anything to the script, he did not participate in the sessions in which the authors hammered out the play, but he later turned in the lines he wished to speak when playing the Ghost. The program reports among its attributions of the play's lyrics that "the recitative of the Ghost was composed by the song team of W. H. Auden and W. A. Mozart." Incomplete mimeographed copies of the script are in the Berg Collection and the Smith College Archives. The production was reportedly enlivened by Auden's helpfulness in offering what appeared to be a glass of water to the actors as they came off the stage, without telling them that the glass contained gin.

Rosina is an innocent young student exposed to the temptations of Smith College. Her father's dialogue as a living person in Act I is clearly not Auden's work, but the speeches of the Ghost in Acts II and III are plausibly his. In Act II the Ghost appears before his daughter during a séance conducted by Flotsam the Fortuneteller. The Ghost warns Rosina against her would-be seducer, C. Wolfington Lupine:

[*Enter the* GHOST *of Rosina's father.*]

ROSINA [*jumping up*]. Paw! And without your overshoes!

GHOST [*in sepulchral tones*]. Mark me, Rosina.

ROSINA. Oh yes, paw.

GHOST. I am your father's ghost;
    Permitted for a time to walk this stage
    In order to prevent a foul outrage.

FLOTSAM [*to* ROSINA]. Don't be afraid, sweet—ghosts always talk like that.

GHOST. Now, Rosina, hear:
    'Tis given out by that designing lout

That he has you here to draw your talent out.
Oh most pernicious lie—most evil myth;
He'd have you think that this vile place is Smith.
But daughter, just take note of where you've been;
Has this the look of Sage or John M. Greene.
Arise—take wing—nor let them bar your pass,
Until you've reached the safety of a Basic Motors class.

ROSINA. I was beginning to suspect as much. Mr Lupine, you have deceived me, sir! [*To* GHOST.] But paw, what can I do?

GHOST. A white-robed choir is waiting in the wings;
Pay close attention to the song it sings.
And when it leaves with vestal garments flowing,
Stand not upon the order of your going.

> [*The* GHOST *raises its arm in a commanding gesture;*
> *enter from either side of the stage the celestial choir*
> *singing the Smith song. . . . etc.*]

In Act III, the Ghost returns to force Flotsam to reveal that she has forged a will:

> [GHOST *appears stage right.*]

FLOTSAM [*shrieks*]. *Do* go away—the next thing I know, you'll be giving away trade secrets on the street corner.

GHOST. Confess! Repent! Declare! Atone!
Or be victimized by my spectral moan!
Ubiquitous, I shall pursue
Until I've forced the truth from you.
[*To* ROSINA.] By dastard scheme be not beguiled—
Your father's back to save his child.

FLOTSAM. That's done it—I can stand *anything* but lame verse. Will you *really* go away if I tell them what I know?

GHOST [*amiably*]. I shall depart in the most pedestrian prose imaginable.

Auden apparently wrote another brief verse of warning. Earlier in Act II, before the first appearance of the Ghost, a Sobriety Corps appears onstage to remind Rosina:

> Sobriety, sobriety,
> A Heavenly cause—
> You'll never know anxiety
> Following Nature's laws.

This quatrain is not in the mimeographed text, but is recalled by Wendell Johnson in his memoir "Auden in Order" (*Confrontation*, Winter 1985, p. 70).

AUDEN'S QUINTET FOR WILLIAM WALTON'S
TROILUS AND CRESSIDA

Auden wrote his sketch of a quintet for Walton's *Troilus and Cressida* in the autumn of 1953, but he began suggesting revisions for the libretto a year earlier. In the summer of 1952 Walton was working on the opera in Ischia, still troubled by problems in the final act that had not been resolved since Christopher Hassall began writing the libretto in 1947. Auden offered over dinner to listen to the parts Walton had completed. Walton played them for him, probably in June, and described Auden's suggestions in a letter to Hassall:

> From my point of view, it is to say the least a bit of a bore to have to start the Act all over again but I think it may be worth it. . . . Unfortunately as W. had to go we were unable to discuss fully the last scene. But he said these things stuck out to his mind: that he felt Pand[arus]. who after all is a very important character should not be lost sight of too easily, that Cress. should not fall on Tro.'s body. At all costs must we avoid any resemblance to Tris[tan]. & Is[olde]. That Tro. should roundly curse her with his dying breath. That Cress. could as part of her dress have a dagger on her belt so as to avoid risk of it dropping if handed to her by Calk[as]., anyhow a far less clumsy way. That her last words are not right. Having been shunned and cursed all round by all, she would be almost mad with terror and hysteria—in fact a sort of Lucia. . . . I do hope, in fact I know, you won't take it all the wrong way as he was really fearfully amiable about the libretto but thought it useless to just make vague uneasy compliments. (Quoted in Michael Kennedy, *Portrait of Walton*, 1989, pp. 161–62)

After a visit to London in July, Walton reported Auden's further thoughts:

> He has a lot to say about Act III. But more of this anon when he's put down his ideas on paper. His main idea is that there should be a grand quintet so that everyone has a look in. (Quoted in Kennedy, p. 162)

In Ischia late the following year, 1953, Auden and Walton returned to the problems of the third act. Auden again suggested adding a quintet (or sextet). Walton asked him to write one. Auden at first refused to intrude on Hassall's work, but Walton finally convinced him to make the attempt. Just before Auden left Ischia for New York at the end of November 1953 he gave Walton a sketch of a quintet followed by some brief rhymed dialogue. Walton sent it to Hassall in December with these comments:

> The thing with Wystan was not too satisfactory as I didn't like to pester him too much as he was working. But the enclosed turned up just before he

left. . . . Whether we decide to have a sextet or not, I'm not at all sure, but if we do, this is a model of how it should be worked out, the parallel rhymes in each part etc. (Quoted in Kennedy, p. 168)

In January, responding to Hassall's anger at Auden's intrusion, Walton gave further details:

I see now from my letter of Dec. 8th that I was singularly inexplicit. That he did anything is entirely due to my asking him to look at Act III as I wasn't entirely happy about it. He took it and when next I saw him he said that both he and Chester had separately reached the conclusion that a quintet or sextet or some concerted piece was needed. After some discussion I said granted that a sextet is the thing, how and what is the proper way to lay it out because I don't know how it should be and am not at all sure that Chris H. (that's you) knows either (perhaps presumptuously assuming that you didn't though you remember we failed miserably when we tried to lay out a quartet towards the end of Act II?). I continued—can't you do it now—just sketch out how the rhymes etc. should balance etc. and C. H. will catch on in a trice. No, he said, he wouldn't do that and that in any case he would not dare to presume on somebody else's territory and that he had a high regard for you and wouldn't risk hurting his relations with you.

Anyhow in the end I persuaded him that it would be a great assistance to us both if he would just do an outline of how he thought this sextet could come about and he reluctantly in the end said he'd try but that it was to be considered nothing else but what is known in the film world as a guide-track and that is how and what I hoped you would take it for. He never meant that I should set it and I never for an instant have ever thought of doing so and even less so now. (Quoted in Kennedy, pp. 168–69)

Hassall eventually wrote a sextet using a more complex version of Auden's stanza, with ten lines instead of eight. One brief line of dialogue, Troilus's "On guard I say", occurs both in Auden's sketch and in Hassall's libretto. Walton finished the opera in 1954, and it was first performed later that year.

Auden's quintet survives in the form of a typescript page that he apparently retained when he gave another copy to Walton. It is now in the Berg Collection. The typescript contains some carefully written revisions (incorporated in the text below), and some hastily written additions to the heading and the names of the characters (not included below). The hastily written changes are these: to the typed title "Quintet" Auden added "(or Sextet)"; below the speech heading "Evadne & Calchas" he wrote "(+ Pandarus?)"; and he wrote the same parenthetical query next to the speech heading to Cressida's line, "Troilus!" At the foot of the page Auden wrote "(Then Chester's MSS)"; "Chester" is presumably a slip of the pen for "Christopher".

QUINTET

CRESSIDA.   Among fierce foes, a maid
                Weak, lonely and afraid;
                No succour ever came,
                No hope was to be seen.
                O what was she to do?
                When Diomede, she knew,
                Would take her for his Queen
                And save her from worse shame.

TROILUS.   How lightly you betrayed
                The tender vows we made
                For ever in Love's name,
                False, faithless, and unclean.
                And, while I dreamed of you
                Beside me, were untrue
                As though I had not been.
                O Cressida! The shame!

DIOMEDE.   How skillfully you played
                The coy and blushing maid
                Though hot from his bed you came,
                False, faithless and unclean
                That I might see in you
                A virgin fit to woo,
                And Argos hail as Queen
                A daughter of the game.

EVADNE & CALCHAS.
                The Fates must be obeyed,
                All strength, all beauty fade,
                Love quenches his quick flame,
                And withered is the green.
                Faithful and faithless do
                What they are doomed to do;
                So has it always been.
                Then who dare praise or blame?

TROILUS. One deed remains that can assuage my pain,
     To slay my rival or myself be slain.
     [*To* DIOMEDE.] Brave Diomede, to battle thee I call,
     For one of us, as Zeus decree, must fall.

DIOMEDE. Put up thy sword, thou fond and foolish boy;
    Shall there be bloodshed for this whore of Troy?
TROILUS [*attacking*]. On guard I say.
CALCHAS.   No!
CRESSIDA.   Troilus!

                    [DIOMEDE *runs him through.*]

EVADNE.   Alas!
DIOMEDE. Rash fool, but noble.

Auden's Lyrics for
"Man of La Mancha"

In 1963 Dale Wasserman commissioned Auden and Kallman to write the lyrics for *Man of La Mancha*, a staged version of Wasserman's 1959 television play, *I, Don Quixote*. In November and December 1963 Auden wrote about fifteen lyrics, mostly for the characters of Don Quixote and Sancho Panza. He wrote to Monroe K. Spears on 9 December 1963: "Have been trying to turn out lyrics for the Don Quixote Musical. The world of Show-Biz is, for me, very odd." Rex Harrison recalled an audition in New York where "Auden actually sang his lyrics" (*Observer*, 24 January 1965). Wasserman later rejected Auden's lyrics as unsuitable to the spirit of his play, and the collaboration ended in February 1964. The play was produced in 1965 with lyrics by Joe Darion.

Wasserman described the collaboration in "Tilting with 'Man of La Mancha'", *Los Angeles Times*, Calendar section, 5 March 1978. "Auden insisted upon fidelity to the novel; I had little love for *Don Quixote* nor interest in dramatizing it." Wasserman had shown Auden the speech from the television play in which Don Quixote says his goal is "To dream the impossible dream"; Auden "rejected it out of hand" and wrote in its place the "Song of the Quest" printed below. Wasserman recalled this exchange with Auden:

"Your words are existentialist," I argued. "They are also fatalistic."
"They are proper words for Don Quixote."
"They are not for Dale Wasserman."
Still we might have reconciled our differences but for the play's finale. Here Auden was adamant: Quixote must repudiate his quest and warn others against like folly. . . .
I said no, in thunder.
"Wasserman, the man was mad."
"It's a madness we happen to need."
"That is arrant romanticism."
"I know. But it happens to be my thesis."

Public announcements of plans for the musical named Auden and Kallman as collaborators (*New York Times*, 4 August 1963, section 2), but Wasserman reports that Auden wrote all the surviving lyrics: "In fact, I recall asking Auden why Kallman was to receive co-credit and he said 'That's simply our arrangement'" (letter to Mendelson, 3 October 1989). It is conceivable that Kallman may have planned to write the lyrics for Dulcinea and other characters who are not represented in Auden's contributions. A draft of a poem addressed to Dulcinea appears in one of Kallman's notebooks now at the University of Texas (the same notebook that contains the draft of Kallman's 1968 prologue to *The Bassarids*), but the poem seems to have been written some years after Auden's lyrics.

Auden later revised two of the lyrics, "Song of the Enchanters" (retitled "Song of the Ogres") and the Song of Sin in the Interlude (titled "Song of the Devil", with a new opening stanza to replace the recitative preceding the song), and published them in a privately printed pamphlet, *Two Songs* (The Phoenix Book Shop, 1968). He reprinted them in his book *City Without Walls* (1969). A somewhat earlier revised version of "Song of the Devil" appeared in *Isis*, 25 October 1967; the revised version of "Song of the Ogres" appeared in *New Statesman*, 1 August 1969. Among the poems that Auden gathered during the summer of 1973 for *Thank You, Fog* (published posthumously in 1974) were "The Golden Age" and a revised version of "Recitative by Death"; the typescripts of these seem to date from his work on the lyrics in 1963. Also among Auden's papers at the time of his death were typescripts of "Don Quixote's Credo" (retitled "D. Q.'s Credo"), Folly's song from the Interlude (titled "Song of Folly"), "Sancho Panza's Dream" (under the title "Highway to Glory: Sancho's Version [1-30]"), and the second page of a two-page typescript of the Interlude. All these typescripts are now in the Berg Collection. Dale Wasserman's files contain two sets of secretarial typescripts of Auden's lost originals of all the lyrics except "Don Quixote's Credo" and "The Golden Age". In the Wasserman typescripts Folly's song from the Interlude is on a separate sheet titled "Song of the Clown (2-7)", and the Recitative and Song of Sin are on separate sheets titled "Song of the Devil (2-6)". Their positions in the Interlude are indicated by stage directions. The full set of lyrics was published posthumously in *Antaeus*, Winter–Spring 1981.

The texts below are based on Auden's typescripts where available, otherwise on Wasserman's typescripts. The version of "Sancho Panza's Dream" in Wasserman's typescripts has the following variant readings: lines 3–4, "surveyed were fertile and prosperous, / And everyone paid their rents to me"; lines 9–10, "So, back to Chivalry and being / Sancho Panza again,"; line 13, "Behind a master who is mad,". In one of the two Wasserman typescripts the two final couplets of "Song of the Quest" appear in the reverse order of that printed below. Probably Auden's lost typescript of the song had marks indicating that the two couplets were to be transposed but only one of Wasserman's typists noticed the markings; it is impossible to say which version is Auden's final one, so I have chosen the one that seems to have the greater emotional logic, although the other may be more metrically satisfying. In Auden's typescript of Folly's song in the Interlude the last line reads "Don't stop! Smash on!" with the first two words deleted. In Death's recitative the Wasserman typescript capitalizes a few nouns that are not capitalized in Auden's typescript, but I have used these capitals on the assumption that they are consistent with Auden's usual practice and reflect the typescript he gave Wasserman.

In the Song of Sin in the Interlude (p. 519), Wasserman's secretarial typescripts place only the words "You're sick!" within quotation marks. When Auden revised the poem for *Isis* in 1967 and *Two Songs* in 1968, the quotation extended to the end of the penultimate stanza, and I have followed this clearly preferable reading. *City Without Walls* extends the quotation to the end of the poem, probably in error.

The numbers following the titles refer to the book and chapter numbers of the corresponding scenes in *Don Quixote*. One of the Wasserman typescripts of "Highway to Glory Song" has the number I.14, but nothing in that chapter corresponds to the lyric. Auden's typescript of "The Golden Age" has the number I.29, but the lyric is based on a speech in book I, chapter 11. Wasserman's typescripts indicate that below "Song of the Clown" Auden wrote this note: "(He should be equipped, I think, with various kinds of noise-makers, with which he ad-libs)". In Wasserman's typescripts, "Sancho Panza's Dream" and "Finale" both have the subhead "(tune: *Highway to Glory*)", and "Song of the Knight of the Mirrors" has the subhead "(tune: *The Enchanters*)". Auden's typescript of "The Golden Age" has two revisions in ink, both followed here: "an age of love, of plenty" replaces "an age of beauty, plenty", and "nymphs of seventy and more were lovely still and glamorous" replaces "nymphs of seventy and over still were gay and glamorous". Wasserman's typescripts are arranged in no particular order; the sequence of the lyrics as printed below reflects as closely as possible the sequence of events in *Don Quixote*.

[LYRICS FOR "MAN OF LA MANCHA"]

Highway to Glory Song

(I-14)

DON QUIXOTE.
> Out of a dream of ease and indolence
> > Woken at last, I hear the call
> Of the road to adventure, awaiting me, beckoning
> > Beyond the gate in my garden wall.
> See, how it runs, now straight, now sinuous,
> > Uphill and down! The world is wide.
> Onward it leads to noble deeds:
> > Saddle our steeds, and forth let us ride.

> > > Forth we'll ride together,
> > > > A Knight and his Esquire,
> > > To the world's end if need be
> > > > To find our heart's desire,
> > > To raise the weak and fallen up
> > > > To knock the tyrant down:
> > > On, on, on, to glory,
> > > > Valor and renown.

SANCHO PANZA.
> I, too, could do with a change of scenery:
> > There comes a day in a married man's life

When he needs a break, to take a long holiday
 From the noise of his kids and the voice of his wife.
When my master comes to an inn at sundown,
 Having done his noble deed for the day,
After we've dined, I shall not mind
 If the maid looks kind and ready for play.

Don Quixote and Sancho Panza.
   Forth we'll ride together,
    A Knight and his Esquire,
   To the world's end if need be
    To find our heart's desire,
   To raise the weak and fallen up
    To knock the tyrant down:
   On, on, on, to glory,
    Valor and renown.

Don Quixote.
  That wrongs may be righted, as a Knight I am plighted
   To beard the dragon in his loathsome den,
  To challenge the giant in his fortification
   Whose dungeons are crowded with tortured men,
  To enter the sorcerer's tower and liberate
   Hapless princesses entrapped within:
  Let me obey now my vow and away now
   Without delay now, the quest to begin.

Don Quixote and Sancho Panza.
   Forth we'll ride together,
    A Knight and his Esquire,
   To the world's end if need be
    To find our heart's desire,
   To raise the weak and fallen up
    To knock the tyrant down:
   On, on, on, to glory,
    Valor and renown.

Sancho Panza.
  My master's a Knight: I'm not, and a fight
   Fills me with fright, however, I'm told
  All dragons and giants and wizards, et cetera,
   Have buried hoards of silver and gold.
  Let him brandish the sword, I'll brandish the shovel,
   So that when at last we homeward ride

To a well-earned leisure, I may hear with pleasure
Fat bags of treasure clink at my side.

DON QUIXOTE AND SANCHO PANZA.
   Forth we'll ride together,
    A Knight and his Esquire,
   To the world's end if need be
    To find our heart's desire,
   To raise the weak and fallen up
    To knock the tyrant down:
   On, on, on, to glory,
    Valor and renown.

Don Quixote's Credo

A true Knight, worthy of the name,
Guards his honor from all shame,
Never turns his back to flee,
However strong the enemy,
Fierce in combat, but will show
Mercy to a fallen foe,
In victory without conceit,
Nor faint-hearted in defeat,
Chaste in body and in mind,
To his Lady ever true,
Courteous in speech and kind,
Giving everyman his due,
Generous to the needy, quick
To aid the wounded or the sick,
And, whatever may befall,
Whatever quest he undertake,
Doing and enduring all
For God and for his Lady's sake.

Song of the Barber

(I-19)

There's some magic influential
  About a barber's chair
Which makes men confidential
  While I'm cutting down their hair.

Their reasoning, their mores,
　　Are singular and weird:
I've heard some funny stories
　　While shaving off a beard.

For men tell things to barbers
　　About their private lives
They seldom tell their partners
　　And never tell their wives.

I've learned how to be pliant,
　　Without a moment's doubt
Size up what any client
　　Would like to talk about.

With some it's weather, others
　　Off-color limericks;
Some care about their mothers,
　　Some about politics.

At times I'm Democratic,
　　At times Republican,
Now cynic, now fanatic,
　　Depending on my man.

I'm perfect to the letter,
　　For I know, as I clip,
That if I slip, I'd better
　　Forget about the tip.

Song of the Enchanters

Little Knight, you are amusing;
Stop before you end by losing
　　Your shirt.
Run along to Mother, Gus;
Those who interfere with us
　　Get hurt.

Truth and Goodness, old maids prattle,
Always win the final battle.
　　They don't.
Life is rougher than it looks;
Love may triumph in the books.
　　You won't.

We're not joking, we assure you;
Those who tried your game before you
    Died hard.
What! Still spoiling for a fight?
Well, you've asked for it all right.
    On guard!

Brave and hopeful, aren't you? Don't be.
Night is falling and it won't be
    Long now.
You will never see the dawn,
Wish you never had been born.
    And how!

The Golden Age

(I-29)

DON QUIXOTE.
The poets tell us of an age of unalloyed felicity,
The Age of Gold, an age of love, of plenty and simplicity,
When summer lasted all the year and a perpetual greenery
Of lawns and woods and orchards made an eye-delighting scenery.

There was no pain or sickness then, no famine or calamity,
And men and beasts were not afraid but lived in perfect amity,
And every evening when the rooks were cawing from their rookery,
From every chimney rose the smell of some delicious cookery.

Then flowers bloomed and fruits grew ripe with effortless fertility,
And nymphs and shepherds danced all day in circles with agility;
Then every shepherd to his dear was ever true and amorous,
And nymphs of seventy and more were lovely still and glamorous.

    O but alas!
    Then it came to pass
    The Enchanters came
    Cold and old,
    Making day gray
    And the age of gold
    Passed away,
    For men fell
    Under their spell,
    Were doomed to gloom.

Joy fled,
There came instead
Grief, unbelief,
Lies, sighs,
Lust, mistrust,
Guile, bile,
Hearts grew unkind,
Minds blind,
Glum and numb,
Without hope or scope.
There was hate between states,
A life of strife,
Gaols and wails,
Donts, wonts,
Cants, shants,
No face with grace,
None glad, all sad.

It shall not be! Enchanters, flee! I challenge you to battle me!
Your powers I with scorn defy, your spells shall never rattle me.
Don Quixote de la Mancha is coming to attend to you,
To smash you into smithereens and put a final end to you.

Sancho Panza's Dream

(I-30)

I dreamed of an island where I was the Governor,
I sat on a throne with a beaut on my knee;
The fields I surveyed were rich and populous
And the farmers paid their taxes to me.
I was rich and lecherous, but dreams are treacherous,
For I woke as the fun was about to begin,
Just when my honey had gotten her clothes off,
Just as the money began to roll in.

Well, life is life and I am
    Old Sancho Panza again,
Riding a mangy donkey
    Along the roads of Spain
Behind a crazy master
    While a scorching sun looks down:
On, on, on,—I don't think—
    To valor and renown.

Song of the Quest

(I-57)

DON QUIXOTE.
   Once the voice has quietly spoken, every Knight must ride alone
   On the quest appointed him into the unknown
   One to seek the Healing Waters, one the Dark Tower to assail,
   One to find the Lost Princess, one to find the Grail.

   Through the Wood of Evil Counsel, through the Desert of Dismay,
   Past the Pools of Pestilence he must find the Way,
   Hemmed between the Haunted Marshes and the Mountains of the
      Dead,
   To the Valley of Regret and the Bridge of Dread.

   Falsehood greets him at the cross-roads, begs him stay with her
      awhile,
   Offers him a poisoned cup with a charming smile;
   Vizor down, in sable armor, Malice waits him at the ford;
   Cold and mocking are his eyes, pitiless his sword.

   No man can command his future; maybe, I am doomed to fail;
   Others will come after me till the Right prevail.
   Though I miss my goal and perish, unmarked in the wilderness,
   May my courage be the more, as my hope grows less.

Song of Dejection

(II-3)

DON QUIXOTE.
      There's a buzz in my ears crying: "Is there a point in these
         Romantic antics of yours at all?
      Is it quite sane to attempt in this century
         To act like Gawain or Amadis of Gaul?
      You a Knight Errant? Don't be ridiculous!
         You're much too poor and too old for a start."
      Sancho, my squire, am I a lunatic?
         Should I retire? I'm sick at heart.

SANCHO PANZA [*aside*].
      Truth would require that I say he's a lunatic,
         But I'd rather turn liar than break his heart.

DON QUIXOTE. The world is so much vaster,
   More indifferent than I thought;
  It has no use for glory
   Or knights of any sort.
  The road is endless and the hills
   Are waterless and brown;
  Why, why, why, they ask me,
   Seek valor and renown?

SANCHO PANZA. Give the world time, dear Master:
   It will praise you as it ought,
  And poets tell in story,
   How gallantly you fought.
  The road's a little long, but still
   Don't let that get you down:
  Fie, fie, fie, remember
   Your valor and renown!

DON QUIXOTE AND SANCHO PANZA.
   Forth we'll ride together
   A Knight and his Esquire,
  To the world's end if need be
   To find our heart's desire,
  To raise the weak and fallen up
   To knock the tyrant down:
  On, on, on, to glory,
   Valor and renown.

Interlude

(II-6 after the Blackout)

VOICE OF SIN [*shouting*]. One moment! Hold everything! I have an announcement to make! Lights please!

> [*The lights (house lights?) come on.* SIN, DEATH *and* FOLLY *are standing on stage with their masks off, that is to say, wearing fresh masks of a modern kind.* SIN *steps forward and addresses the audience.*]

SIN. Ladies and Gentlemen:
 I and my two friends here are most grateful to Mr Cervantes for having given us this opportunity to meet you all, and we hope he won't mind if we interrupt his story for a few minutes.

You see, we aren't really a bit interested in imaginary characters like his silly old Don Quixote; we only care about real people, like yourselves. Oddly enough, though, our real names are the same as those in your programme. I am Sin, and my colleagues are, on my left, Folly, on my right, Death. As soon as we heard we were to have the pleasure of meeting you, each of us composed something special for the occasion without telling the others, so that what you will hear will be as much a surprise to us as to you.

Well, Folly, you're always the impatient one. Suppose you start the ball rolling.

FOLLY.   Let's get together, folks!
                Let's hear a laugh from you,
                Swallow a benzedrine,
                Put on your Party Smile,
                    Join the Gang!
                To be reserved is gauche, all
                Privacy anti-social:
                    Life's a Bang.

                Take off your silencers,
                Turn up your radios,
                Pile on the decibels,
                Drown the unbearable
                    Silence within.
                Who knows life's why or wherefore?
                Who knows what we are here for?
                    Make a din!

                Let's have some action, folks!
                Swing from the chandeliers,
                Break up the furniture,
                Crazy as particles
                    In a cyclotron!
                What is all the fun for?
                Don't ask, or you'll be done for.
                    Smash on!

SIN. Bravo, Folly. Now, Death, let's hear from you. What have you got for us?
DEATH. A sermon.
SIN. Are you out of your mind? This isn't Spiritual Emphasis Week. People come to the theater to hear songs, not sermons.
DEATH. I can't sing, I'm tone deaf.
SIN. Dear, oh dear! What *are* we to do? At least we must have a musical

background. [*To the orchestra.*] Would you mind playing some music while my friend gives his address; something soft and very beautiful. Thank you so much.

DEATH [*reciting against music*].

> The progress you have made is very remarkable,
>   And Progress, I grant you, is always a boon:
> You have built more automobiles than are parkable,
>   Crashed the sound barrier, and may very soon
>   Be setting up juke-boxes on the silent Moon.
> Let me remind you, however, despite all that,
> I, Death, am still and will always be Cosmocrat.
>
> Still I sport with the young and the daring; at my whim
>   The climber steps upon the rotten boulder,
> The undertow catches boys as they swim,
>   The speeder swerves onto the slippery shoulder;
>   With others I wait until they get older
> Before assigning, according to my humor,
> To one a coronary, to one a tumor.
>
> Liberal are my views about Religion and Race;
>   Tax-posture, credit-rating, social ambition,
> Cut no ice with me. We shall meet face to face
>   For all the drugs and lies of your physician,
>   The costly euphemisms of the mortician:
> Westchester Matron or Bowery Bum,
> All shall dance with me when I rattle my drum.

SIN. Thank you, Death. I'm sure we've all been most edified. [*To audience.*] I'm sorry, ladies and gentlemen, but he's always been like this, and you can't teach an old dog new tricks, you know. And now it's my turn. I hope you'll enjoy my little song; at least it's cheerful.

[*Recitative.*]

> In my game of winning
> Mankind to sinning,
> To vice and to crime,
> From the very beginning,
> When men murdered each other with stone axes
> And paid no income taxes,
> Down to the present time
> When any taxpayer can see

Live murders on TV,
In every age,
At every stage,
In spinning my fiction,
I've always tried
To adapt my diction
To the contemporary -ism of pride.
At this point, I should like to remark
How grateful I am for your help.
In leading you all by the nose
Down the path which gradually goes
From the Light to the yelping Dark,
Having no, thanks to you, existence,
Has been of enormous assistance.

[*Song.*]
  Since Social Psychology replaced Theology,
  The process is twice as quick.
  When a conscience is tender and loth to surrender,
  I have only to whisper: "You're sick!
        Puritanical morality
           Is old-fogey, non-U:
        Enhance your Personality
           With a romance, with two.

"If you pass up a dame, you've yourself to blame,
  Shame is neurotic, so snatch:
All rules are too formal, in fact, they're abnormal
  For every desire is natch.
        So take your proper share, man, of
           Dope, or drink:
        Aren't you the Chairman of
           Ego Inc.?

"Truth is a mystical myth as statistical
  Methods have objectively shown,
A fad of the Churches: since the latest researches
  Into Motivation, it's known
        That Virtue is Hypocrisy,
           Honesty a joke.
        You live in a Democracy:
           Lie like other folk.

"Since men are like goods, what are shouldn'ts or shoulds
When you are the Leading Brand?
Let the others drop dead, you're way ahead,
Beat 'em up if they dare to demand
     What might your intention be,
        Or what could ensue:
     There's a difference of dimension be-
        tween the rest and you.

"If in the scrimmage of business your image
Should ever tarnish or stale,
Public Relations can take it and make it
Shine like a Knight of the Grail.
     You can mark up the price you sell at if
        Your package has glamor and show:
     Values are relative,
        Dough is dough."

So believe while you may that you're more O.K.,
More important than anyone else,
Till you find that you're hooked, your goose is cooked,
And you're only a cypher of Hell's.
     Till then, imagine that I'm proud of you:
        Enjoy your dream.
     I'm so bored with the whole fucking crowd of you
        I could scream.

Thank you. You've been a wonderful audience. But it's time for us to
say good-bye now and let you get back to Don Quixote. So off we'll go
with a farewell chorus. [*To* DEATH.] If you can't sing, croak.

TRIO.   We must go now,
             On with the show now,
             Ever so nice to have met you all,
             Look forward to meeting again,
             For, in the end, we shall get you all
             And won't *that* be jolly!
             Till then, we beg to remain
             Yours sincerely
             (Or very nearly)
             Death, Sin and Folly.

Song of the Knight of the Mirrors

Look! Unlearn your bookish lore.
Look! And learn the motives for
    Your acts.
Look again! Don't shut your eyes!
Look! It's time to recognize
    Some facts.

Look! Those noble knights of old
Were, when the whole truth is told,
    All crooks.
Look at Dulcinea! Mutt!
She's the common kitchen slut
    She looks.

[*After their duel.*]

Look! Have I not laid you low?
Look! Confess that you are no
    True Knight,
Only crazy in the head.
Look! Admit that all I've said
    Is right.

Don Quixote's Farewell

[*To* SANCHO PANZA.]
Humor me no longer, Sancho; faithful Squire, all that is past:
Do not look for this year's bird in the nest of last.
Don Quixote de la Mancha was a phantom of my brain;
I, Quijano, your Alonso, am myself again.

[*To* DOCTOR, *etc.*]
Pardon me, dear friends, the trouble all my follies made for you;
What I thought I thought was false; what I felt was true:
Every day's a new beginning, life's a quest for you and me,
Seeking to become the man each was meant to be.

[*To* ALDONZA.]
Child, come hither and forgive me; I am glad we met that night:
Though a princess you are not, what I saw was right,
You as your Creator sees you, in whose image you were made.
Dear Aldonza of the Inn, do not be afraid.

Take my hand and take my blessing; it is time to say good-bye;
For my quest is over now, and I have to die.
Child, have faith and hope and courage; I, your unworthy Knight
     foretell
You will find your happiness: Thank you, and farewell!

Finale

(II-30)

Good-bye, now, and good luck! Enjoy your liberty!
     We shall never forget you, however we end:
With your genial vision of man's condition
     You lit up our prison and made us your friend.
Prisoners know that only in comedy
     Can we really show what we seriously think:
A laugh makes endurable what is incurable,
     And the deepest truths are told with a wink.

          Through lands you'll never visit,
               In centuries ahead,
          Your Knight will still be riding
               Long after you are dead,
          And readers, some in palaces,
               And some, like us, in gaol,
          Hail, hail, hail Cervantes,
               The author of the tale.

          Forth they'll ride together,
               Your Knight and your Esquire,
          To the world's end, and further,
               To find our heart's desire,
          To raise the weak and fallen up,
               To knock the tyrant down,
          On, on, on, to glory,
               Valor and renown.

Auden's Dramatic Translations

AUDEN and Kallman published their translation of *The Magic Flute* as an "English version" complete with introduction, additional verse, and notes, and in effect, treated it as their own work as much as the work of the original authors. They published their translations of dramatic works with far more diffidence about their own contribution. This volume includes *The Magic Flute*, but leaves the other translated dramatic works, most of which are readily accessible, to a projected volume of Auden's translations. A brief list of the remaining translations follows.

ERNST TOLLER, *No More Peace!* (1936)

Auden first met Toller in Cintra in the spring of 1936; Auden and Isherwood were there working on *The Ascent of F 6* when Toller chanced to make a brief visit. Auden translated the lyrics, and Edward Crankshaw the dialogue, for the English version of Toller's *Nie wieder Friede!*, first performed at the Gate Theatre, London, 11 June 1936, and published in 1937 by Farrar & Rinehart, in New York, and by John Lane The Bodley Head, in London. Some of the lyrics also appeared separately: "Noah's Song", *New Statesman & Nation,* 13 June 1936; "Socrates' Song", "Rachel's Song", and "Duet", *London Mercury,* October 1936; and "Financier's Song" (as "Song for the Lost"), *Common Sense,* February 1937. The music for these songs was composed by Herbert Murrill, who also set Auden's lyrics for *The Dance of Death* and *The Dog Beneath the Skin.*

ERIKA MANN, *Pepper Mill* (1936)

Auden married Erika Mann in 1935 in order to provide her with a British passport. The English version of her revue *Die Pfeffermühle,* prepared late in 1936, included some of Auden's work. It was first performed at the Chanin Auditorium in New York, 5 January 1937, and stayed on the boards six nights. It was then revived at the New School Auditorium in New York, 22–24 January 1937. The program of the New School performances lists two items "by Ernst Toller and W. H. Auden": "Demagogue" and "Spies" (the "Dictator's Song" and "Spy Song" from Toller's *No More Peace!*). Erika Mann's concluding piece, "Cold," was evidently also translated by Auden, although he is not acknowledged in the New School program; as Erika Mann reported in a letter to her sister Katia, 24 October 1936, Auden had translated "Warum ist es so kalt?" as part of *Die Pfeffermühle* (Erika Mann, *Briefe und Antworten,* 1984, p. 99). Auden's cabaret sketch *Alfred* (see this edition's volume of *Plays,* pp. 437–39) was reportedly included in some performances of *Pepper Mill,* although it is not listed in the program of the New School performances. Other items in the revue were written by Erika and Klaus Mann and by Erich Mühsam, and adapted into English by John LaTouche and Edwin Denby.

Hallie Flanagan reported that in late 1936 "Erika Mann said that she and her husband, W. H. Auden, were collaborating on a play which they would like to have Federal Theatre consider" (Flanagan, *Arena,* 1940, p. 125). The play was probably *Pepper Mill.*

ERNST TOLLER, *Pastor Hall* (1938?)

Auden translated one of the songs in this play, published in 1939 (with Toller's *Blind Man's Buff*) by Random House in New York and by John Lane The Bodley Head in London. The translation of the rest of the play is attributed in the New York edition to Stephen Spender and Hugh Hunt, and in the London edition to Spender alone. The play was not performed in English around the time of publication, although a film version was made in England in 1940.

BERTOLT BRECHT, *The Caucasian Circle of Chalk* (1944)

Early in 1944 the Austrian actress Luise Rainer arranged to have two backers, Jules J. Leventhal and Robert Reud, commission *Der kaukasische Kreidekreis* from Brecht as a vehicle for her. (Rainer eventually withdrew, but the backers kept the project alive.) In June 1944 Brecht proposed Auden as a translator after Isherwood pleaded prior commitments. Leventhal and Reud arranged for Auden's friends James and Tania Stern to prepare a rough translation that would be adapted by Auden. The Sterns finished their translation in December and sent copies to Brecht and Auden. Auden wrote to James Stern on 18 December 1944: "Don't worry; I've really done some work on the Brecht. Truth to tell, there [is] not *so* much to do." In the end, Auden apparently did little more than retranslate Brecht's lyrics; when Brecht received a copy of the revised translation, probably in March 1945, he complained to Ruth Berlau that Auden had made no changes at all to the Sterns' prose. Berlau apparently asked Auden to rework the play, but Auden, who was about to leave for service in Germany with the United States Strategic Bombing Survey, refused. In November 1945 Stern sent a copy of the typescript to John Crowe Ransom, who published Act V of *The Caucasian Circle of Chalk* in the *Kenyon Review,* Spring 1946.

Ruth Berlau made a microfilm of Brecht's copy of the typescript and deposited it in the New York Public Library, where it was rediscovered in 1959 by John Willett, who hoped to include it in a volume of Brecht's plays in translation to be published by Methuen. Auden and the Sterns agreed to revise the translation, and Auden wrote to Stern on 13 October 1959:

Methuens sent me pages from the Chalky Caucasus, which I have revised as best I could. It's terrifying when a fifteen year old corpse which one has completely forgotten suddenly comes out of its grave. The only places where I have been deaf to your question-marks are the Azdak lyrics and the Mrs Plushbottom limerick. When the words are to be sung, the translator has either to do a version which will correspond exactly to the music (I have never seen the music for this play. I suppose it exists) or assume that new music will be written for the English version: in either case, the suitability of the words to setting is much more important than being literal, I believe: my practice is to read the original first for its meaning (my German is better now) and then put the original out of my head, and re-create.

In a postscript he added:

There is one line, I have left to you since I am very uncertain what it means
Schrecklich ist die Verführung zur Güte [Terrible is the temptation to goodness]

On 22 October, having been reminded by Stern that Brecht had added two stanzas to the Singer's praise of Azdak, he sent the stanzas beginning "No more did the Lower Orders". The revised translation, "by James and Tania Stern, with W. H. Auden", appeared as *The Caucasian Chalk Circle* in Methuen's edition of Brecht's *Plays*, vol. 1, 1960. Methuen's separate paperback edition, which appeared in 1963, contains revisions apparently made in consultation with Auden; this text was often reprinted. Later editions of the translation include further revisions made in 1984 by James Stern.

JEAN COCTEAU, *The Knights of the Round Table* (1951)

The London-based Group Theatre, for which Auden wrote most of his plays during the 1930s, was revived in 1950 as Group Theatre Productions Limited, and was headed, like the earlier Group, by Rupert Doone. Doone discussed with the BBC Third Programme the possibility of a joint commission to Auden for translations of Brecht's *Mutter Courage* and Cocteau's *Les Chevaliers de la Table Ronde*. In August 1950 Doone (probably during a visit to Italy) handed Auden an invitation from Harman Grisewood, Controller of the Third Programme, to consider the two plays. In his reply to Grisewood, dated 16 August, Auden wrote: "I imagine you have already heard from him [Doone] that I don't think *Mutter Courage* will quite do on aesthetic grounds and in addition I think it would be politically indiscreet to do it. On the other hand, I would be very interested in having a shot at translating Jean Cocteau's *Les Chevaliers de la Table ronde,* if it is available." (Auden's letter, hand-delivered by Doone, is in the BBC Written Archives Centre.) The BBC asked Auden to proceed.

In a letter of 11 October 1950 Auden told Doone: "As soon as I have really got my teaching here [Mount Holyoke College] into order, I shall start on the translation, i.e. I hope next week." (Auden's letters to Doone are in the Berg Collection.) On November 28 he told Grisewood: "The translation has been held up by pressure of teaching and lectures" and "I think I can promise it by the end of March." On 14 March 1951 he wrote Grisewood:

I took the script of *The Knights of the Round Table* to the N.Y. office of Curtis Brown [his agent] to-day, so it should be in London next week.

I have not included Cocteau's own notes on the production as I assume you can get hold of a copy of the French text if you need them. I've included his suggestions for music but, of course, in the Radio version there will have to be some more.

In one or two places, you will find that I have altered or introduced lines when they seemed necessary for clarity in the radio version. These are all marked.

He wrote similar terms to Doone on the same day, and on 18 April 1951 sent postcards to both Doone and Grisewood with a minor textual change.

A production planned for the 1951 Edinburgh Festival fell through, and the translation was first performed in an adaptation by Peter Watts in the BBC Third Programme on 22 May 1951. The first staged production was by the repertory company of the Playhouse Theatre, Salisbury, on 3 May 1954.

The translation was first published in 1964 by New Directions, New York, in *The Infernal Machine and Other Plays* by Cocteau. This edition includes a new introductory note by Auden and minor changes in the text; the correction Auden sent Doone appears in modified form. The typescript that Auden sent Doone, with corrections in Auden's hand, is in the Berg Collection. A microfiche copy of the 80-page BBC typescript prepared for the 1950 production is in the BBC Written Archives Centre. Five later typescript copies, all containing 115 pages but with numerous variations, are also in the Berg Collection; microfilm copies of a 90-page agency typescript are at Columbia University and the University of California, Berkeley.

LORENZO DA PONTE, *Don Giovanni* (1957)

After its performance of Auden and Kallman's version of *The Magic Flute*, the National Broadcasting Company Opera Theatre commissioned Auden and Kallman to translate *Don Giovanni*. They copyrighted their translation on 19 November 1957, but it was not broadcast until 10 April 1960.

The translation was published in 1961 as a libretto booklet by G. Schirmer in New York, and reprinted in *The Great Operas of Mozart*, published by Schirmer and Grosset & Dunlap in 1962. The copyright typescript is in the Manuscript Division of the Library of Congress (DU 45898) and a microfilm of the typescript used for the broadcast is in the archives of NBC.

BERTOLT BRECHT, *The Seven Deadly Sins* (1958)

Lincoln Kirstein and the New York City Ballet commissioned this translation of *Die sieben Todsünden der Kleinbürger* from Auden and Kallman in 1958. They completed it in late July or early August. Auden wrote John Willett on 18 August 1958: "In collaboration with Mr Chester Kallman, I have just done a version of *Die*

Sieben Todsünden. This, D.V., will be performed in November at the N.Y. City Center, with Lotte Lenya as the singing Anna and choreography by Balanchine." The translation was copyrighted on 19 September 1958, and was first produced on 4 December 1958.

The text appears in a mimeographed leaflet prepared for the New York City Ballet rehearsals, and was published in *Tulane Drama Review*, September 1961, apparently after Eric Bentley requested it on the magazine's behalf. Probably in late 1964 Bentley asked Auden if he could use Auden and Kallman's translations of *The Seven Deadly Sins* and *Mahagonny* in a projected volume of translations. Auden gave permission in an undated letter, but added: "I do hope someone has a correct and complete copy of the first. The second, as printed in Tulane Drama, has several typos." A corrected text appeared in the British edition of Brecht's *Collected Plays*, vol. 2, part 3, 1979, published by Methuen.

A typescript with corrections by Auden and Kallman is in the Berg Collection, with the title *The Seven Deadly Sins, A Song-Ballet*. The copyright typescript is now in the Manuscript Division of the Library of Congress (DU 47661).

BERTOLT BRECHT, *The Rise and Fall of the City of Mahagonny* (1960)

Around March 1960, Lotte Lenya began planning a new production of *Aufstieg und Fall der Stadt Mahagonny* with Auden and Kallman as translators. Her lawyer submitted an agreement on translation rights to their agent in April, and they may have discussed the project with her during a visit to Berlin in June. They finished the typescript at the end of July, and registered it for copyright on 1 September. What happened next is unclear. Lenya had told her lawyer at the end of March that Brecht changed his mind many times after agreeing to her plans for the production (letter to Charles B. Seton in the Kurt Weill Foundation for Music, New York); possibly Brecht continued to create difficulties. On 10 October 1960 Auden wrote Lincoln Kirstein, "We have translated *Mahagonny* but God knows if anything will ever come of it." On 30 January 1961 he wrote Isherwood that a producer was ready to stage the work that autumn, but "we can't get a straight Yes or No out of Madame. The truth is, I suspect, that she knows she is no longer capable of singing her old role, but can't bear to think of anyone else singing it."

No production took place during Auden's lifetime, but scenes 18 through the end were published in *Delos* 4, 1970. The complete text was published posthumously in 1976 by David R. Godine in Boston and by the Canadian branch of the Oxford University Press in Toronto the same year (title page misdated 1975). It was reset and reprinted in the British edition of Brecht's *Collected Plays*, vol. 2, part 3, 1979, published by Methuen.

The copyright typescript is now in the Manuscript Division of the Library of Congress (DU 51627). Two incomplete carbon copies, with corrections by Auden and Kallman, are in the Berg Collection. One page of a carbon copy, with revisions by Auden, is in the collection of Robert A. Wilson. A mimeographed typescript prepared for Lenya is in the Kurt Weill Foundation for Music.

CARLO GOLDONI, *Archifanfaro, King of Fools;*
or, It's Always Too Late to Learn (1962)

In May 1962 Newell Jenkins commissioned Auden and Kallman to translate Goldoni's libretto *Arcifanfano Re dei Matti* (first set by Baldassare Galuppi in 1749–50) for a Clarion Concerts production of Karl Ditters von Dittersdorf's 1776 resetting. Auden wrote to Elizabeth Mayer on 6 October 1962:

> The Goldoni-Dittsersdorf goes well. We've done about three-quarters of it. It's more fun than I expected and finding all the comic double rhymes is a nice test of one's virtuosity.

The typescript was copyrighted on 8 January 1963, and the translation was performed at Town Hall, New York, on 11 November 1965, and at Carnegie Hall on 5 January 1966. The translation was partly printed in the programs of both performances, and fourteen lines were quoted by Raymond Ericson in "Dittersdorf's Six 'Mad' Ones", *New York Times*, 24 October 1965, section 2. An incomplete text appears in the booklet that accompanies a recording made of the original performances and released in 1992 (VAI Audio 1010-2).

The copyright typescript, with corrections in Auden's hand, is now in the Manuscript Division of the Library of Congress (DU 56852). An incomplete copy, also with Auden's corrections, is in the Berg Collection. Six pages of a draft typescript, with revisions by Auden, are in the collection of Robert A. Wilson.

Archifanfaro, in the title given above, is the spelling used in the typescript. When the translation was produced, the program used the proper spelling, *Arcifanfano*.

BERTOLT BRECHT, Lyrics for *Mother Courage* (1965)

Auden was first asked to translate Brecht's *Mutter Courage und ihre Kinder* by the BBC and Group Theatre Productions Limited in 1950, but declined (see p. 525). In 1953 Eric Bentley, who was translating the play, asked Auden to help with the lyrics. Auden agreed, and Bentley sent him a set of preliminary versions. On receiving them, Auden wrote Bentley in a letter of 31 October 1953:

> The first thing to decide is whether we should try to make the translations fit the Dessau music, or ignore the latter entirely. Personally, seeing that they are chants, not operatic song, i.e. the music is subordinate to the words, I am strongly in favour of the latter course, since it makes it infinitely easier to make a translation that is readable. However you are the translator and must decide. If you want to keep the original music, there are one or two spots where your words don't fit, e.g. "Lucky all mortals who have none" has the first accent in the wrong place.

Auden and Bentley worked together on the translations after Auden returned to New York from Ischia in December 1953, but Auden's contributions can no longer be identified. In the acknowledgements to his translation (in his series *The Modern Theatre*, vol. 2, 1955) Bentley wrote that "W. H. Auden suggested a number of lines for the songs that would fit Dessau's music better."

During 1963–64, the National Theatre, under Laurence Olivier and William Gaskill, struggled to gain rights to perform Bentley's version of the play in London, but Stefan Brecht, the playwright's son, refused until he could be assured that new lyrics would be written. Bentley agreed that Auden should be invited to supply new versions, and in November 1964 Gaskill asked Auden if he would be willing to do so. Stefan Brecht accepted Auden as translator, and Auden completed his draft of the lyrics on 17 January 1965.

The production, with the lyrics set by Darius Milhaud, opened at the Old Vic on 12 May 1965, and the translations appeared in *Delos* 1, 1968, as "Songs from *Mutter Courage*" and were reprinted in *City Without Walls*, 1969, as "Eight Songs from *Mother Courage*".

In August 1971 John Willett asked Auden to translate the full text for the English edition of Brecht's *Collected Plays*. Auden replied on 6 September:

> On thinking it over, I have decided I cannot do *Mutter Courage*. The truth is that I think Brecht was a great lyric poet, but a second-rate dramatist. His natural poetic sensibility was pessimistic, even Christian, and he tried to harness this to an optimistic philosophy, e.g., he apparently wants us to take *M.C.* as a picture of what life is like under Capitalism, but I can only interpret the play as "That is what, since Adam fell, life is like—period."

OTHER PROJECTS

In April 1950 Auden was summoned by telegram from Ischia to Naples by the film director G. W. Pabst to prepare a synopsis of a German film script of the *Odyssey* that Pabst hoped to film with Ingmar Bergman. Auden was apparently enthusiastic enough to write a forty-page synopsis (now lost), but plans for him to prepare a full adaptation of the screenplay fell through. Auden wrote to E. R. Dodds on 26 May: "I nearly got involved in a movie on The Odyssey,—german script (not nearly as bad as I expected) and director, Italian money, American actors—but to my relief my agent asked too much money, so I am left in peace to write" (letter in the Bodleian Library).

Auden frequently expressed interest in translating further works by Brecht. On 18 August 1958 he wrote John Willett: "No, I never did a translation of the *Dreigroschenoper*, though I should have liked to very much. . . . I have toyed and still toy with the thought of some day translating *Baal* and *Das ertrunkenes Mädschen*."

Auden wrote Elizabeth Mayer on 9 June 65: "Chester and I are thinking of translating [Ferdinand] Raimund's *Der Alpenkönig und der Menschenfeind*, a beautiful play, don't you think? We're going to a performance of it this evening at the Burg Theater" (letter in the Berg Collection).

Auden said he knew nothing about *La Gran Tenda Verde,* listed as a planned collaboration (perhaps a translation?) with Kallman in *Contemporary Authors* 9–10, 1964. He also said that a newspaper report that he was translating Wagner's *Ring* had no basis in reality (*Evening Standard,* 14 December 1966).

TEXTUAL NOTES

Paul Bunyan

§1 History and Texts

From 1935 through 1938 Auden had collaborated with Benjamin Britten on documentary films, radio scripts, cabaret songs, and song cycles, and Britten had set the verse of *The Ascent of F 6* and *On the Frontier*. A hint of Britten's hopes for further collaborations appears in a letter to his friend John Pounder on 2 January 1937: "I have lots of work planned with him—I'm doing music for his new play F 6; discussing an opera & also talking about a review for a Cambridge theatre with him" (Britten, *Letters from a Life*, 1991, vol. 1, p. 465). Neither the opera nor the revue came to anything, and it is unclear whether the discussions were initiated by Britten or Auden.

Britten, accompanied by Peter Pears, left England for Canada in late April 1939. When they arrived in New York two months later, Auden was travelling across the continent with Chester Kallman. On 29 June Britten wrote to Ralph Hawkes, his publisher in London, to report a conversation with Hans W. Heinsheimer, who worked for Hawkes in New York: "He has told me that the opportunities are immense . . . for an operetta for children (for which I also have ideas & will write to Wystan Auden)" (letter at Boosey & Hawkes). Auden also had plans for a collaboration with Britten. On 14 August 1939 he wrote Britten from Santa Monica: "Shall get back to N.Y. (George Washington [Hotel]) at the beginning of Sept. Must see you then as I have several propositions to discuss with you beside longing to see you" (Berg Collection). Britten's ideas and Auden's propositions evidently converged in a stage work on the *Paul Bunyan* theme, and Britten's American publisher, Boosey, Hawkes, Belwin, obligingly commissioned it.

Auden recalled later: "The choice of subject was dictated by the demands of Boosey & Hawkes for something suitable for high schools. The sources were the New York Public Library" (letter to Daniel G. Hoffman, 17 January 1949, quoted in Hoffman's *Paul Bunyan: Last of the Frontier Demigods*, 1952, p. 144). Auden was writing the text by the middle of October 1939. On 27 October he wrote to Mrs A. E. Dodds: "I am also working on the libretto of an opera with Britten who is here" (letter in the Bodleian Library). On 22 November he discussed with Britten the completed first act (probably the equivalent of I.1 in the finished version) and four days later wrote to Mrs Dodds: "At the moment I am hard at work on my Operetta which is rather fun; Gilbertian rhymes etc". Before 16 December he mailed Britten the text of the songs for the cats and dog, and later in the month he worked with Britten for a week at the home of their friend Elizabeth Mayer in Amityville, Long Island. In these early stages the libretto was divided into a prologue and four acts, later renumbered as a prologue and two acts of two scenes each. A typescript of the substantially finished work was ready by the middle of January 1940.

As late as December 1939 Britten and Auden expected the work to be produced on Broadway at the end of January by Ballet Caravan, the company headed by

George Balanchine and Lincoln Kirstein. These plans fell through, and Auden began to explore other possibilities. On 7 January 1940 he wrote Archibald Mac-Leish that he hoped to see him during a trip to Washington later that month, "as there are several things I'd like to talk to you about, in the main an operetta which Britten and I have almost finished which *might* have radio possibilities, I think, and I'd like your advice" (letter in the Manuscript Division of the Library of Congress). The meeting did not take place. In the spring the Columbia University Department of Music agreed to stage the work, apparently after first finding it "too difficult" (Auden to Elizabeth Mayer, Britten, and others, 22 February 1940; letter in the Berg Collection). But the production was again delayed, partly because Britten had suspended work on the score after falling ill. In the autumn of 1940 Auden and Britten made further changes, and Britten seems to have finished much of the score around this time.

Casting and rehearsals began in early 1941. When Britten played the score to the cast in February he still had four numbers to compose. During rehearsals, the director, Milton Smith, suggested that Auden and Britten write a solo for Tiny, the lead soprano, who in the original text sang only in the choruses. They provided an aria overnight. They also made other extensive cuts and changes in the period shortly before the production.

On 4 May 1941 *Paul Bunyan* was performed at Brander Matthews Hall at Columbia University, in a production by the Columbia Theater Associates, with the cooperation of the university's Department of Music and a chorus from the New York Schola Cantorum. The conductor was Hugh Ross. The first performance was a preview for members of the League of Composers. A week of public performances began on 5 May.

After the lukewarm reception of the premiere, Auden and Britten prepared a shortened and rewritten text, but Britten did not compose the additional music required by the new text, and the work was abandoned. Auden reprinted some of the songs in his collected editions but took no further interest in the libretto. After Auden's death Britten returned to the version they prepared before the 1941 production and made minor revisions and additions to the music. Excerpts were performed in concert at the 1974 Aldeburgh Festival, and the complete operetta was broadcast by the BBC and staged at Aldeburgh two years later. The libretto of this revised version was published as a pamphlet by Faber Music in 1976, and republished in 1988 by Faber & Faber in book form with reproductions of a few pages of Auden's and Britten's manuscripts and a critical and historical essay by Donald Mitchell. Faber Music published a vocal score in 1978. When Britten began revising the work in 1974 he assigned it an opus number formerly assigned to another work composed in 1939, and the operetta was performed and published as his Opus 17.

The text of this edition is the text that Auden presented to Britten. Auden did not present the entire text at one time, so this edition includes additions and changes Auden made after preparing a virtually complete text, but it does not reflect cuts and changes made for musical purposes by Britten with Auden's consent, not does it reflect cuts and reordering introduced during rehearsals and production.

The following sources have been used. All, unless noted, are in the Britten-Pears Library at Aldeburgh:

MSS Fragmentary manuscripts and typescripts of scenes, dialogues, and songs written or typed by Auden; now in the Berg Collection, New York Public Library. Two or more versions of some scenes and songs are present, but the surviving fragments do not make up a complete text. Some of these fragments, together with other material now lost, were apparently the source of:

TSA An almost complete typescript of the libretto, probably prepared by Beata Mayer (the daughter of Elizabeth Mayer) in early January 1940, and based directly or indirectly on Auden's manuscripts and typescripts; Slim's and Tiny's songs were inserted later on separate pages evidently typed by Auden. Britten used this text for most of his musical composition, although a small portion of the music seems to have been composed before this typescript was prepared (the text of the Quartet of the Defeated is evidently based on Britten's setting rather than directly on any manuscript by Auden). Auden marked this typescript with further revisions during rehearsals. (Britten made further markings on this typescript when revising the work in 1974–75.) A carbon copy of pages on which the Interludes appear, with an additional page that includes further stanzas for the Interlude in Act II (stanzas not found in other typescripts), belongs to Mordecai Baumann, who sang the part of the Narrator in 1941.

TSB A typescript made by a typing agency probably just before rehearsals in 1941. This is very similar to TSA, but with detailed scene descriptions and stage directions, probably not written by Auden. Some trivial changes are marked in an unknown hand. No new material by Auden appears in this typescript. (Britten made some marks on this typescript in 1974–75.)

ML A mimeographed libretto used by the cast, evidently based on TSB but with slightly different stage directions and with more titles (probably added by Britten) for musical numbers. Some dialogue marked for deletion in TSA and TSB is absent. This text contains no new material by Auden. Another copy is in the Columbia University Music Library.

RTE A revised and abridged text prepared after the production (probably in June 1941) consisting of pages taken from ML, with additional pages and fragments typed by Auden.

RTF A cleaner typescript based on RTE with trivial corrections; not typed or marked by Auden, although marked with some deletions and transpositions in Britten's hand.

The text has also been collated with Britten's manuscript score in the Britten-Pears Library (and with incomplete reproduction copies of a piano-vocal score in the Library of Congress and the Columbia University Music Library), and with a recording made during one of the performances of the May 1941 production, now in the Columbia University Music Library.

The libretto was copyrighted as an unpublished text on 26 April 1941. The copyright copy deposited in Washington has not survived, but it was probably a copy of ML.

Some drafts and sketches of dialogues and songs that Auden added after writing the first drafts of the libretto appear in a notebook that he used in 1940–41, now in the Berg Collection.

Auden extracted four songs from the libretto for separate publication. The chorus of Lame Shadows and Animas ("You've no idea how dull it is") appeared in the *New Yorker*, 24 August 1940, under the title "The Glamour Boys and Girls Have Grievances Too". "The single creature leads a partial life" was reprinted in *Harper's Bazaar*, April 1945, and in three of Auden's collected editions: *Collected Poetry* (1945), its British counterpart *Collected Shorter Poems, 1930–1944* (1950), and *Collected Shorter Poems, 1927–1957* (1966). "Gold in the North came the blizzard to say" appeared in the 1945 and 1950 collected editions. "Carry her over the water" appeared in the 1945, 1950, and 1966 collected editions.

The main source of this edition's text is TSA, the text nearest to Auden's original manuscripts and typescripts. In portions of the work where the fragmentary MSS texts are evidently the direct (or almost direct) source of TSA, this edition is based on the MSS texts, and restores capitalization and spelling that were regularized by the typist of TSA. Passages added to TSA in Auden's hand are incorporated into the text of this edition, as are additional passages added in typescript after TSA was first prepared. The point at which these added passages should be inserted in TSA was generally indicated in Auden's hand; for example, he wrote "*Song*" at the point in the TSA text where Slim sings the lyric that appears on a separate sheet.

This edition's text includes titles for many of the musical numbers. A few of these titles appear in the typed text of TSA, but most were written into TSA in Britten's hand. Some of the titles appear in Auden's preliminary MSS and are clearly his own work. Of the remaining titles, which appear first in TSA, Auden probably devised many of them in conversation with Britten, but some may conceivably have been devised by Britten alone. The titles that *may* have been devised by Britten (they appear neither in Auden's preliminary MSS nor in the original TSA typescript before Britten marked it) are: "Chorus of Old Trees", "Quartet of Swedes", "Food Chorus (with Inkslinger)" [originally "Trio"], "The Love Song", "Tiny's Song", "Johnny's Regret", "Fido's Sympathy", "The Cats' Creed", "The Fight", "Hymn," "Christmas Party", and "Litany".

In his preliminary MSS Auden crossed out the title "Lame Shadows and Animas" and replaced it with "Film stars and Models"; in Britten's hand in TSA this is changed to "Dream Shadows."

ML introduced new or modified titles probably taken from Britten's score, and not included in this edition. The more significant new titles are: in I.1, "Bunyan's Greeting" (his opening speech), "Bunyan's Welcome" (his first speech to the lumberjacks), "Cooks' Duet" (Sam Sharkey and Ben Benny); in I.2, "Bunyan's Return" ("Look, look, the chief is back"); in II.1, "Bunyan's Warning" (his speech to the farmers beginning "If there isn't a flood"); and in II.1, "Bunyan's Farewell" (his speech in couplets). Further titles appear in the list of musical numbers that precedes the text. For the 1976 version Britten added a title at the opening of II.1, "Bunyan's Good Morning", and incorporated other simple titles descriptive of the music (e.g., "Western Union Boy's Song") and taken from the list of musical numbers in ML.

The subtitle "An Operetta in Two Acts" is taken from the typescripts. No subtitle appeared in the program for the first production. The published texts of Britten's 1976 version use the subtitle "An operetta in two acts and a prologue".

§2 AN EARLY VERSION OF THE PROLOGUE

Among Auden's early drafts (MSS) is a longer version of the Prologue than the version in the final text. The typescript was evidently prepared by Auden. A complete carbon copy survives, together with a partial top copy on which Auden marked extensive cuts. The complete text of the carbon follows, including some minor revisions that Auden marked on the top copy before making his cuts. Conjectural emendations appear within square brackets with an opening question mark. This prologue apparently survived in the libretto at least until early 1940; a note in *Tempo*, March 1940, briefly describes Britten's plans for the operetta and quotes from the opening lines of the prologue: "Paul Bunyan, says Auden, 'is an American myth.'"

Prologue

A MAN AND A WOMAN.

To begin with
Paul Bunyan is an American myth.
A myth is a collective dream
Where all our nights and lives
Are not as lonely as they seem,
For each one adds a bit
And shares in it.

And every dream deserves attention:
Dreams are a way of saying
Everything we know
At one go
So that in one moment we
Are all we were and are going to be:
Dream[s] are the meeting place
Of memory and intention
[?Where] We and our fate come face to face.

And America? Well,
Only our dreams can tell.
They say that every day
America's destroyed and recreated

By what we are and what we do:
America is I and you;
Like dreams, America is what we make it.

SEMI-CHORUS I.

Since the birth
Of the earth
Time has gone
On and on:
Rivers saunter,
Rivers run,
Till they enter
The enormous level sea
Where they prefer to be.

SEMI-CHORUS II.

But the sun
Is too hot
And will not
Let alone
Waves glad-handed
Lazy crowd,
Educates them
Till they change into a cloud,
But can't control them long.

SEMI-CHORUS I.

For the will
Just to fall
Is too strong
In them all;
Revolution
Turns to rain
Whence more solid
Sensible earth-creatures gain:
In falling they serve life.

CHORUS.   Here are we
Flower and tree,
Green, alive,
Glad to be,
And our proper
Places know:
Winds and waters

> Travel; we remain and grow;
> We like life to be slow.

3 Young Trees. No. No. No.

Chorus. O.

Young Tree. I'm sorry if it shocks you, but I, for one,
> Do *Not* want life to be slow.

1st Old Tree.   Bolshevism.

2nd Old Tree. If the East Wind catches you talking like that
> He'll pull you up by the roots.

3rd Old Tree.   It's only a phase.

1st Young Tree. Nor, I may say, am I the only one:
> Ask any of the younger generation.
> Some of us have been holding informal discussions
> To try and find out what we think about things,
> And the time has come now, I think, for one of us to make some
> > public statement.
> Frankly, we can't accept everything we were brought up to believe;
> For instance we are taught that all good trees love their homes:
> Well, we don't.
> That there is no face like an old face;
> Well, we don't think so.
> Nor do we believe that the only respectable career for any honest
> > vegetable
> Is to grow bigger and bigger every day.
> We're *bored* with standing still,
> We're *bored* with the whole idea of bigness.
> We want to go places and see things.

1st Old Tree. I never heard such nonsense.

3rd Old Tree. He's sick.

2nd Old Tree. I'm afraid it's something more serious than sickness.
> As you all know, philosophical speculation
> Has always been a little hobby of mine;
> What we have just listened to is not new,
> But a heresy with a very long history,
> And a very sad one, the Heresy of the Beasts.

1st Old Tree. It must be stamped out.

Trio of Old Trees.

> Long, long, long ago,
> In the epoch of the waters
> Green were all earth's sons and daughters,
> Ignorant of woe.

Alas, alas, among them one
Jealous of the moving sun,
Asked for liberty—
Foolish, foolish, foolishly—
In that moment of dissent,
Instantly she had her will
And became an animal,
That was all her punishment:
All that run or fly or creep,
Her unlucky issue, weep,
Fallen, fallen, fallen,
Into movement, death and fear.

1st Young Tree. That is *our* version of the story,
   To prove the innate superiority of plants;
   I suppose it's never struck you that perhaps
   The animals themselves feel differently about it?
   Have you ever thought of asking one?
3rd Old Tree. Me. Speak to an animal? I'd rather be blackmailed for
   the rest of my life by a fungus. They're unclean.
1st Old Tree. Ridiculous. It's common sense. You've only got to look
   at an animal to know it's unhappy.
3rd Old Tree. Haven't the experts proved conclusively that every
   animal dreams he's a tree.
2nd Old Tree. You mean, the Chlorophyll Complex.
3rd Old Tree. I always try to look the other way when one passes.
   I never *could* bear having anything near me that wasn't beautiful.
   O dear.

[*Enter* Three Wild Geese.]

Trio of Geese.   — * — Not really —
                        Do you mean that — * —
                        That was why she went so red
                        When you—I always said
                           — * — *
                           At the wedding
                        — * — * —
                        So *he* says * — * —
                        — * — don't tell a *soul.*

3rd Old Tree. I never listen to gossip. It's so plebeian.

1st OLD TREE. What can you expect from geese. All this travel
  Must be bad for the nerves, and as I've often noticed,
  Bad nerves mean bad manners
  And bad manners mean bad morals.
  Going abroad is bound to ruin the character.

TRIO.   O how terrible to be
                  As old-fashioned as a tree:
                  A dull stick that won't go out;
                  What on earth do they talk about?
                        An unexpressive
                        An unprogressive
                  Unsophisticated lout.
                  How can pines or grass or sage
                  Understand the Modern Age?

                              [*Enter* 4TH WILD GOOSE.]

QUARTET.   Tell us. What's the latest news,
                  What do you think, my dear, ∗ −
                  − ∗ − ∗ − ∗ −
                  − ∗ − ∗ − ∗ −
                        − ∗ − ∗
                  That's the most a-
                  mazing thing I've ever heard
                  Shall we tell them − ∗ But
                  You ought to − ∗ Shall I −

1st GOOSE. I know what you trees think of us birds,
  And that [?you] will probably be insulted at my speaking to you
      at all.
  Under normal circumstances I shouldn't dream of doing so
  But what my friend has just told me
  Concerns you so directly
  That I think you ought to know about it.
  I don't imagine you will like it much
  But liking or not liking won't make any difference
  To what is going to happen. So be prepared for a shock.
  You are all going to leave here.
OLD TREE. What.
OLD TREE.   It's a lie.
YOUNG TREE.   Hurrah.

OLD TREE.   Don't listen.
YOUNG TREE.   How.
1ST GOOSE. Far away from here
    A mission is going to find a performer.
OLD TREE. What mission?
GOOSE.   To bring you into another life.
YOUNG TREE. What kind of performer?
GOOSE.   A man.
YOUNG TREE. What is a man?
GOOSE.   A man is a form of life
    That dreams in order to act
    And acts in order to dream
    And has a name of his own.
OLD TREE. How neurotic. Any normal thing keeps dreams in their
        proper place.
1ST OLD TREE. What does anyone want a name of his own for
    As if his family name weren't good enough.
    It's indecent to want to be different from one's parents.
YOUNG TREE. Do tell us, what's his name?
GOOSE. Paul Bunyan.
OLD TREE.   How silly.
YOUNG TREE.   I think it sounds rather nice.
OLD TREE. And when, may I ask, are we to have the exquisite pleasure
        Of meeting this Paul Bunyan of yours?
GOOSE. He will be born at the next Blue Moon.
OLD TREE. She's lying isn't she, dear. It isn't true,
    O I'm so frightened.
OLD TREE.   O don't worry
    There won't be a Blue Moon in our lifetime
    In fact I doubt if such a phenomenon exists.
    Of course one is said to have occurred ten thousand years ago,
    But legends are never historically accurate.
OLD TREE. Don't say that. It's unlucky.

                              [*The Moon begins to turn Blue.*]

YOUNG TREE. Look at the moon. It's turning blue.
OLD TREE. I don't believe it.

QUARTET OF GEESE.
            It isn't very often the Conservatives are wrong
            To-morrow normally is only yesterday again
            Society is right in saying nine times out of ten
            Respectability's enough to carry one along.

> But once in a while the odd thing happens
> Once in a while the dream comes true
> And the whole pattern of life is altered
> Once in a while the moon turns blue.

TRIO OF YOUNG TREES.

> I want to be a ship's mast sailing on the sea
> I want to be a roof with a house under me
> I've always longed for edges—I'd love to be square—
> How swell to be a dado—swell to be a chair.

TRIO OF OLD TREES.

> We can't pretend we like it, that it's what we'd choose,
> But what's the point of fussing when one can't refuse
> And nothing is as bad as one thinks it will be
> The children look so happy—Well, well, we shall see.

QUARTET OF GEESE.

> Attempts at revolution are a failure as a rule,
> The eccentric or unusual isn't likely to succeed,
> Successful new experiments are very rare indeed,
> And nearly every rebel is a silly little fool.

TUTTI CHORUS.

> But once in a while the odd thing happens
> Once in a while the dream comes true
> And the whole pattern of life is altered
> Once in a while the Moon turns Blue.

CURTAIN

§3 THE EARLY TYPESCRIPTS AND THE PRE-PRODUCTION TEXT (1939–1941)

The first complete typescript (TSA) was apparently prepared in January 1940. In a postcard mailed on 16 January Auden thanked Beata Mayer, who had typed the script, for "a swell job." The text of TSA was evidently compiled from a variety of sources. These included some of the surviving fragmentary authorial manuscripts and typescripts (MSS); other sources were intermediate texts now lost. At least one source seems either to have been derived from Britten's sketch for the Quartet of the Defeated or was the sketch itself; Britten was living in the Mayer household when Beata Mayer typed the work, so she had access to texts that Britten had modified for musical reasons. In the 1970s Peter Pears wrote on the cover of the typescript: "This is the libretto used by BB for the actual musical composition, with corrections made by BB and WHA at (and ?before) rehearsals."

The text of TSA (including two pages inserted after the rest had been typed) represents almost the complete libretto. Slim's and Tiny's songs in I.2 are inserted on the two separately typed pages; Bunyan's closing speech in the same scene is added to the typescript in Auden's hand, as are a few minor additions and revisions elsewhere. The only section of the libretto absent from TSA is a group of stanzas in the Interlude in Act II (see note to p. 41, below).

Minor changes marked in TSA in Auden's hand have been incorporated silently into this edition. Many other cuts and changes in TSA are marked in Britten's hand, but most of these were evidently made in order to accommodate the music. These changes are not noted below except where they conceivably may have been made by Auden. Other changes in Britten's hand include many assignments of speeches or stanzas to named characters where Auden had assigned these only to a Semi-Chorus or to characters identified by numbers. Auden's original assignments are retained in this edition, but the more important changes are indicated in the notes.

Britten's 1976 version is largely similar to the text of this edition, except that the 1976 text incorporates the small cuts and changes he had made earlier to TSA, and omits the Love Song for Inkslinger and Chorus in I.2 and the number with the Lame Shadows and Animas in the same scene. Britten revised the score between 1974 and 1976, adding a new orchestral prologue and a setting for Paul Bunyan's speech at the end of I.2. The original scores for the ballad interludes had not survived, but Britten reconstructed them with the help of Peter Pears's memory of the 1941 version.

Page 4.

The list of characters is based on the somewhat incomplete original list in TSA, probably prepared by Britten. This edition restores "Lame Shadows and Animas" in place of the "Dream-shadows" in the TSA character list (see note to p. 29, below). The original list also included "Bill Booster, a boaster, Bass" among the characters from the Chorus (see note to p. 21, below). Auden and Britten first intended to divide the ballad Interludes between two singers identified in the list as Contralto and Baritone, but finally assigned them to a Baritone only.

Pages 5–8.

Britten, in setting the Prologue, assigned all the opening stanzas for the Semi-Choruses and Chorus to a single Chorus of Old Trees. On p. 7, in the final stanza for the Trio of Young Trees, he altered "ship's mast" to "vessel", "a house" to "houses", and "square" to "a square".

Auden used asterisks and dashes in his preliminary MSS to represents squawking sounds in the Trio of Wild Geese, and the same symbols appear in all later typescripts.

Near the end of the Prologue Auden used initial capitals in the phrase "the Moon turns Blue" in the stage direction and the final chorus; in this edition the same initial capitals are added in the first chorus of the Trio of Geese.

Page 10.

In TSA the opening stage direction ends: "Voice of Paul Bunyan off. Quiet and meditative." I have converted this into a speech heading.

The assignment to the Chorus of the line beginning "Timber-rrr" is an editorial emendation.

Page 12.

The telegram from the King of Sweden is based on the draft typescript among Auden's preliminary MSS. The text in TSA omits "Hel Helson. He is".

Page 13.

The duet for Sam Sharkey and Ben Benny is taken from Auden's preliminary MSS, which were slightly misread by the typist of TSA.

Page 14.

In the Trio an unknown hand inverted the first two and last two lines of the final stanza in TSA. Britten set the new sequence, but Auden retained the original when he reprinted the poem.

Page 15.

Bunyan's soliloquy that precedes the Blues is the shortened text on a late handwritten page among Auden's MSS and in TSA. A longer version appears in an early draft typescript among Auden's MSS:

Now at the beginning.

To those who pause on the borders of an untravelled empire, to those standing in empty sunlight on the eve of a tremendous task, to you all a word of welcome and warning.

Husbands of a shore jewelled with cities, roués of an antique garden, versed from childhood in the arts of compliment and caress, no wonder you are confident in your power to charm.

Nature the matriarch of the château, Nature the expensive harlot, Nature the drunken old concierge with a repertoire of song, Nature the refined governess, Nature the smiling goddess of gift, with all disguises of the Eternal Feminine your wit and aptitude for mimicry have never failed.

But with the virgin to whom you are about to be introduced, all etiquettes will be worse than useless.

This terrifying adolescent dislikes the whole idea of the gods, and has made up her mind to destroy all suitors. A solitary childhood has given her time to devise the most ingenious snares.

For the sturdy and stupid, physical battle with all the elaborate weapons of climate.

For the outward-looking a treacherous passivity, an apparently frank
revelation of endless vistas that, dazed by the riches of possibility,
they may quickly lose themselves in a philosophy of work and be-
come impotent professors of an aim they have forgotten.

And for the inward-regarding, the silence of distaste, the bored echo
that destroys faith.

[*Music.*]

Now as you fall asleep let a dream testify to the strength of her
reluctance.

The text of the Blues (Quartet of the Defeated) in TSA evidently derives from
Britten's setting of one of Auden's drafts. Some words that Britten omitted
when setting the piece are replaced by dashes in TSA; these words are restored
here from an early typescript draft among Auden's MSS. In TSA and later texts
the line printed here as "I cursed myself and lay down to die" appears as a series
of dashes followed by "I lay down to die". And in TSA the line "On the mountain-
top or right in town" does not appear at all, and a series of dashes appears in its
place. In the fourth stanza "young and swell" is the reading of Auden's draft
typescript and of the text of this song as published in his 1945 *Collected Poetry;* all
full texts of *Paul Bunyan* read "young and well".

Page 16.
    "Babe cocked her head" is an emendation (confirmed by the recording) for
"his head" in all typescripts.

Page 18.
    In TSA the final couplet of the interlude originally read "So they got ready to
come back / Which brings us to the Second Act." Auden wrote the revised ver-
sion into TSA when the operetta was divided into two acts and four scenes in-
stead of four acts.

Page 20.
    In the Food Chorus TSB and ML assign the stanza beginning "Iron, they say, is
healthy" to "Inkslinger [*haranguing the mob*]." In the final stanza, "rusty" is added
from the recording and score.

Page 21.
    In TSA, in a passage deleted in pencil, Slim enters with a character named Bill
Booster who has a few lines of dialogue and a song before he exits. When Boost-
er's scene was cut, probably some time before the start of rehearsals, Auden
made some revisions in TSA to the dialogue between Johnny and Slim that fol-
lowed Booster's exit, and indicated that Slim's song should be inserted within
this revised dialogue. Slim's song itself is inserted in TSA on a separate page
apparently typed by Auden. (In Britten's hand the first line of Slim's song is
altered to: "In foul and in fair days".) The original TSA text of Booster's scene

and the dialogue after Booster's exit appears below; it immediately follows the Chorus's "So you'd better get us out". This original version also appears in TSB, but it is not in ML, which uses the revised dialogue that Auden wrote into TSA.

[*Voice of* BILL BOOSTER *off.*]

BILL BOOSTER.

O I shot out a mosquito's eye
While practising with my six shooter in the Park
And I rode a kicking bronco round
Columbus Circle in the rush hour after dark.

[*Enter* BILL BOOSTER *and* HOT BISCUIT SLIM.]

BILL BOOSTER. Hello folks. My name's Bill Booster, but back home they call me the Tiger.

1. And your great-great-grandfather was a relative of the King of England.

2. Your grandfather was a frequent visitor at the White House.

3. Your mother received a secret proposal of marriage from a director of General Motors.

1. And your uncle was president of Harvard.

BILL BOOSTER. Say, how did you guess.

JOHNNY. It's obvious to the meanest intelligence.

BILL BOOSTER. Well, have you got a job going for a regular fellow like that?

JOHNNY. Sure, if you can pass the test.

BILL BOOSTER. What do I have to do? Eat a horse-shoe or swim Niagara Falls in a fur coat?

JOHNNY. No, nothing like that. It's ridiculously easy really. Just a formality. Here is a mirror. Take it in both hands and hold it straight in front of you at arm's length.

BILL BOOSTER [*looking at himself in the mirror*]. Say folks, are there any girls around here?

JOHNNY. Ssh. You're not allowed to talk while you are taking the test. Bring the mirror slowly towards you until the tip of your nose touches the centre of the mirror. Now stand quite still while I count ten. [*Count ten.*] Now try and take the mirror away from your face. Go on, take it away. Pull harder. [BILL BOOSTER *is hypnotized.*] Well, well, well. Who would have thought it.

MIRROR SONG

FIDO, MOPPET AND POPPET [*laughing*].
>Ha. Ha. Ha. Ha. Ha. Ha.
>Left is right, and right is wrong
>In the magic mirror song.
>
>In the mirror's magic light
>To is fro, and black is white.
>
>Paradoxes are undone
>Of the Many and the One.
>
>Eternity a moment's track
>Round infinity and back.
>
>Number and division brought
>To the circle of a nought.
>
>Motions, Forms, Entelechies
>With their Essences at peace.
>
>All existence in a sigh
>I. I. I. I. I. I. I.

[*Exeunt* MOPPET, POPPET AND BOOSTER.]

JOHNNY. Hullo stranger. I forgot all about you. What's your name?

SLIM. Slim.

JOHNNY. You don't look like a logger.

SLIM. I met Mr Bunyan the other day, and he told me he thought he might be wanting another cook soon.

CHORUS. Can you cook flapjacks? [*etc., as on p. 22.*]

Page 23.

In a handwritten draft of I.2 among Auden's MSS, Inkslinger's song is preceded by a brief scene with a Salesman that interrupts Inkslinger's speech to Fido. Stage directions that call for Fido to bite the Salesman may be inferred.

JOHNNY. Hello Fido. You staying here to keep me company. That's mighty nice of you. Fido, I want to ask you something and tell me the truth. Are you—

[SALESMAN *enters R.*]

SALESMAN. Good-afternoon, sir. Do you know the truth about Death? Death comes to all said the poet but he was old fashioned. Science has proved conclusively that there is no such thing as certainty. Progress has unsealed the secrets of Probability. For twenty-five cents you can become the possessor of this amazing brochure entitled "It's Modern to Be Immortal" where you will learn how suffering is already vulgar and out-of-date.

JOHNNY. Fido, just see if he's modern or just an old-fashioned poet.

FIDO [*song*]. O won't you tell us once again
SALESMAN. Ouch
FIDO. How Science has abolished pain
SALESMAN. Ouch
FIDO. Repeat that bit about the State
Where suffering is out-of-date
SALESMAN. Ouch.
FIDO. Dear me
SALESMAN. Ouch Ouch.
FIDO. You seem put out.
SALESMAN. Ouch Ouch Ouch Ouch
FIDO. You know I doubt
If you're as modern as you look
And not a plain old-fashioned crook.
SALESMAN. Ouch. [*Exit* SALESMAN.]

JOHNNY. It smells a bit fresher now. As I was saying when we were interrupted, I was just going to ask you a question. Tell me, Fido, in strict confidence, Are you happy. [*etc., as on p. 23.*]

Page 24.

The text of Inkslinger's song follows TSA except in the last four lines, which follow a separate typescript of the song among the preliminary MSS. Britten evidently asked Auden for a more swelling conclusion. Auden obliged; Britten copied the new version onto the separate typescript, from which it was copied into TSA and all later texts. The revised version reads:

> O but where are those beautiful places
> Where what you begin you complete
> Where the joy shines out of men's faces
> And all get sufficient to eat?

Page 25.

In the third stanza of the Love Song, all texts read "limb's", but the sense perhaps requires "limbs'".

Page 27.

Tiny's song was written during rehearsals for the opera in 1941. Auden made some sketches for her dialogue and song on the first page and rear endpaper of a notebook (now in the Berg Collection) that he had otherwise filled earlier in 1940–41. The finished text is inserted into TSA on a separate page typed by

Auden. Auden marked in TSA the point where the song was to be added and wrote in Inkslinger's line preceding the song; a facsimile of this page from TSA appears in Donald Mitchell's 1988 edition of the libretto, p. 124. The page on which the song itself was written seems to have been typed when Auden and Britten were working together; Auden used a virgule to indicate a caesura in each of Tiny's lines (e.g., "Whether the sun shine / Upon children playing") and typed out the full text of the ensemble of Tiny and the Chorus after her solo. The layout of the text in the present edition is a simplified version of Auden's typescript. The original form of the ensemble section follows:

CHORUS. The white bone
TINY. Mother, O Mother, tears arise in me.
CHORUS. Lies alone ⎤
TINY. Ah . . . ⎦
CHORUS. Like the limestone
TINY. Mother, O Mother, too soon you were dead.
CHORUS. Under the green grass ⎤
TINY. Ah . . . ⎦
CHORUS. All time goes by
TINY. Mother, O Mother, look down on me now.
CHORUS. We, too, shall lie ⎤
TINY. Ah . . . ⎦
CHORUS. Under death's eye
TINY. Mother, O Mother, till the day I die,
CHORUS. Alas. Alas. ⎤
TINY. Ah . . . ⎦

Page 29.

The Lame Shadows and Animas were Auden's Jungian names for these figures of dream. In one of the draft typescripts among Auden's preliminary MSS he crossed out "Lame Shadows and Animas" as a heading for their chorus and replaced it with "Film stars and Models". In TSA their entrance is called for in a stage direction that reads *Enter Dream Shadows* (Film Stars and Models)"; and Britten changed their speech headings from "1st Lame Shadow," "2nd Anima", etc., to "1st Dream Shadow", "2nd Dream Shadow", etc. Except in the TSA cast list, the name "Dream Shadow" is not used in any of Auden's drafts or in the typed text of TSA itself.

Page 31.

Bunyan's final speech was added in Auden's hand to TSA, apparently at a late stage of preparations for the production; a facsimile of the TSA page appears in Donald Mitchell's 1988 edition of the libretto, p. 142. In TSB the stage direction after the end of the final Chorus reads: "Chorus offstage singing lullaby in their sleep. Paul Bunyan's voice—to be written." Bunyan's speech does not appear in ML or any other early text.

Page 35.

In the Mocking of Hel Helson, Britten assigned Q's speeches to a 1st and 2nd

Questioner who speak in turn. The answers are assigned to the voices named in the questions: Heron, Moon, Wind, etc. The text here, taken primarily from a typescript among the preliminary MSS, omits minor changes evidently made by Britten for musical purposes.

Page 38.

The three duet stanzas sung by Slim and Tiny during the fight between Bunyan and Helson were added to the libretto, probably around the spring of 1940. Auden wrote out the stanzas on a separate page under the heading "Love duet"; a facsimile appears in Donald Mitchell's 1988 edition of the libretto, p. 101. At some earlier stage of planning, Auden and Britten evidently intended to use a different duet for Tiny and Slim, probably at another point in the libretto. This earlier duet survives as a separate typescript among Auden's preliminary MSS:

SLIM.   If a baby
            In a tram
       Only makes you mutter: "Precious
          Little lamb";
   Or if your dinner partner gives you an appraising look
    Then starts to tell the story of her life,
    And far from merely fiddling with your knife,
      Your body squirms and wriggles
      And you gasp between your giggles
  "How perfectly amazing but you ought to write a book".
     If when bitten
       By an ant,
    You're about to kill it and then
      Find you can't:
      That's Love.

TINY.   If the sunset
       Turns you queer,
     If you see a fairy in your
       Glass of beer;
  If you begin to get a thrill from simple little things,
    If as you dust the hat-stand in the hall
   You're struck dumb by the beauty of it all
     If the sausage that you're cooking
     Seems extraordinarily good-looking
  And expresses on the subway have the majesty of kings;
     If you feel a
      Sudden wish
    To embrace a tree or to ca-
      -ress a fish:
      That's Love.

SLIM.   There're as many
                     Loves as wines,
                 All sorts, though, exhibit certain
                    Common signs.

TINY.   For example if you're in a railway accident, or if
            You're on a liner when it strikes a reef,
            Or if your taxi skids and comes to grief,
               In that agonising swaying,
               If you find that you are praying:
       "I'm not afraid to die, but, dear O dear, I want to live";

BOTH.   When you don't think
                 Any more
              About love or money, then you
                 May be sure
                 That's Love.

Page 41.

The last nine couplets of the Interlude after II.1 are taken from the separate typescript of the three Interludes owned by Mordecai Baumann, who sang the role in 1941. The remaining text of the Interludes in this separate typescript is a carbon copy of the equivalent pages in TSA; the page with these last nine couplets was typed on a different machine. The text is emended here from the recording and score (the typescript text has "So let us feast" where all other texts have "So let's have a feast"). The nine couplets replace the following text in TSA:

> He summoned them all, said: "It breaks my heart
> But my work is done and I must depart.
>
> I must depart but it's Christmas Eve
> Let's have a feast before I leave."
>
> That is all I have to tell,
> The curtain rises; friends, farewell.

(In Britten's 1976 revision "The curtain rises" was replaced with "The party's starting".)

Page 42.

The text of the stanza beginning "But Miss Tiny here" is revised in TSA in Britten's hand; the second line is altered to read "I understand has now consented", and the fourth line to "They both look contented." In the score and recording this is corrected to "They both look very contented"—which is also the reading in Auden's preliminary MSS.

Page 43.

Each of the three stanzas of the song "Carry her over the water" is separately assigned in Britten's hand in TSA. The first stanza is assigned to 3 Solos; the second to Fido, Moppet, Poppet; and third to the Chorus.

Slim's stanza following the song is assigned in Britten's hand in TSA to Slim and Tiny.

Page 44.

In TSA, probably as a result of a skip of the eye, in place of the stanza beginning "We always knew that one day you", the Chorus repeats Johnny's stanza beginning "A lucky break". Britten wrote the replacement stanza into TSA, but apparently did not have a text for the third line at the time, as he wrote a squiggly line in its place. The text of the third line comes from the score and the recording.

Page 45.

In the second stanza of the Litany, "inertia and disillusion" is the text in Auden's preliminary MSS and in Britten's setting. The typescript texts read "inertia and delusion", probably as the result of a typist's misreading of Auden's hand.

Page 46.

The sequence of speeches in the final parts of the Litany follows Auden's pencilled revisions to his preliminary MSS, which indicated a rearrangement of his original sequence. The original sequence concluded:

From entertainments . . .
Paul, who are you? . . .
No longer the logger . . .
From children brought up . . .
Don't leave me, Paul . . .

Auden then wrote the numeral 1 next to the exchange beginning "Don't leave me, Paul"; 2 next to the stanza "From children brought up"; and 3 next to the lines from "Paul, who are you" through "No longer the logger" to "Good-bye, Paul." An arrow indicates that the section marked 3 should follow the section marked 2.

These rather obscure pencil markings were misunderstood or ignored by the typist of TSA (or rather by the typist of a lost intermediate and slightly revised text of this scene that was used as the basis of TSA). As a result, the sequence in TSA is the same as the sequence in Auden's preliminary MSS before he added the pencil markings indicating his desired rearrangement.

Britten later inserted markings in TSA that altered the sequence to the following, the sequence also used in the score:

From entertainments . . .
Don't leave me, Paul . . .
No longer the logger . . .
From children brought up . . .
Paul, who are you? . . .

In Britten's revised sequence, therefore, the curtain falls on Bunyan's "I am Act." This edition restores the sequence marked by Auden in his MSS, and closes with the exchange of farewells.

In the score, Helson's "Don't leave me, Paul. Where am I? What's to become . . ." is replaced by "Don't leave us, Paul. What's to become . . ."

§4 THE PRODUCTION VERSION (1941)

The TSB typescript prepared from a revised copy of TSA includes extensive stage directions probably not prepared by Auden. In the Prologue the directions specify that the scene is a clearing in the forest (the typist misread "forest" as "west"), and that the light changes from night to day and back to night during the course of the scene. In I.1 the scene is the same clearing, the time is spring, and early morning changes to night in the course of the scene. The Western Union Boy enters "riding a bicycle, singing, and crossing stage." In I.2 the time is summer, the trees are partially gone, the light moves from noon to night; the corner of a cook shack takes the place of some of the trees. In II.1 the same clearing is further cleared, with the cook shack at left and barracks at right; the light again changes from noon to sunset. Pioneer women are now part of the Chorus. In II.2 the time is winter, starting with sunset and moving on to night. The scene includes a full-size pine tree lit up as a Christmas tree in the background, and in the foreground a big table with candles. As the scene opens the Chorus is eating dinner; there are funny hats, streamers, noises.

The program of the first production described the scene as "A Grove in a Western Forest". The time of the Prologue is given as "Night", and for the four scenes, "A spring morning", "Summer", "Autumn", and "Christmas".

During rehearsals (and possibly shortly earlier) the operetta was heavily cut and rearranged. Slim and Tiny's arias were added, as was Bunyan's speech that concludes I.2. After the preview performance on 4 May 1941, however, the entire scene of Film Stars and Models (with Bunyan's final speech) was apparently dropped, and a scene from early in II.1 became the closing scene of I.2. These and other major changes detailed below can be identified from the recording made during the public production run:

I.1. After the Lumberjacks and others exit (p. 15), Inkslinger enters and accepts Bunyan's offer of a job (as on p. 16); in the middle of his dialogue with Bunyan, Inkslinger sings his song (p. 23). Then Bunyan introduces the Quartet of the Defeated (p. 15), which is followed by the Interlude.

I.2. After the Chorus exits to see Tiny (p. 23), Inkslinger sings his Regret (p. 28); then the Chorus returns, talking about Tiny. Bunyan's dialogue with Johnny does not end with their exchange of goodnights, but instead Bunyan tells Johnny to call the men, who enter as in this edition's II.1 (p. 32). The Lame Shadows and Animas do not appear at all; Bunyan's "The songs of dawn" (p. 32) is omitted. Act I ends with the exit of the Farmers (p. 34).

II.1. The scene opens with a dialogue for Helson and the four Cronies similar to that on p. 34. When the Cronies exit, Fido, Moppet, and Poppet enter (as on p. 36). After all three have exited again, the Mocking of Hel Helson occurs (pp. 34–35). Bunyan then summons Helson (as on p. 37), and the fight and the rest of the scene follow.

II.2. The recorded text of this scene corresponds to the text of this edition, with the final stanzas rearranged as described in the note to p. 46 above.

§5 THE POST-PRODUCTION TEXT (1941)

After the production in May 1941, the Berkshire Music Center informally suggested that the work might be produced at the Berkshire Festival during the summer. Auden began work on a radically revised and abridged version of the libretto. Probably early in June he typed the new and rewritten sections, and combined them with pages from a copy of the ML libretto to make the RTE text (see §1). But on 18 June, Hans W. Heinsheimer (acting for Britten's publisher) wrote to Britten, who was then in California, that the performance probably would not take place, "so do not bother to rewrite the music just now." He added, "You will receive a new script within a week or so" (letter in the Britten-Pears Library). This new script was presumably the RTF typescript, prepared from Auden's RTE text. Britten wrote to the composer Douglas Moore on 24 June "that the old piece is now undergoing thorough revision, which I shall be delighted to show you when I return to New York in the Fall", but he apparently never composed the music that the text would have required, and the revised libretto was never performed.

Milton Smith, the director of the first production, recalled that during the preparations he and Britten had "talked about the possibility of trying to make a more simplified version that might be useful in schools" (letter to Mendelson, 2 August 1967). Possibly the revised text was a product of these early discussions.

Auden and Britten probably planned the revisions before Britten left for California. In the new version they dropped Sam Sharkey and Ben Benny along with the dog and cats; they cut the subplot about the inadequate food, and in doing so dropped such showstoppers as the Western Union Boy's first entrance; and they removed the ballad Interludes. Helson and his cronies now occupied the center of the action, and Auden wrote extensive new dialogue for them. The two acts and four scenes of the earlier version were renumbered as four acts.

The post-production text survives in the two typescripts, RTE and RTF, both in the Britten-Pears Library. The text below is taken from RTE and presents all the passages newly typed by Auden, along with a few brief fragments pasted in from a copy of ML; brief descriptions of other sections taken over without change from ML are printed in italics in smaller type. References to titles of musical numbers in these brief descriptions sometimes cite titles added in ML (see p. 536). RTF is a retyped copy of RTE, not prepared by Auden; Britten marked some cuts and rearrangements in RTF, the most significant of which is the deletion of the dialogue and duet for Tiny and Slim in the midst of Helson's fight with Paul Bunyan.

Prologue

As on pp. 5–8.

Act I

Act I begins with Bunyan's Greeting, as on p. 10; the opening stage direction specifies that "Inkslinger is seated asleep against a tree." After Bunyan's Greeting:

> [INKSLINGER *who is snoring gives an extra loud snort and wakes up.*]

INKSLINGER. Who's there?

BUNYAN. Good-morning stranger.

INKSLINGER. You're rather large, aren't you? What are *you* doing here?

BUNYAN. My name's Paul Bunyan. I'm looking for men to help me turn this forest into lumber.

INKSLINGER. Really. Interesting things trees. I've been counting them, only the big ones of course. [*Consulting a notebook.*] Yesterday the total was 3674851.

BUNYAN. You can handle figures, then?

INKSLINGER. Think of an irrational number and I'll double it.

BUNYAN. Know any foreign languages?

INKSLINGER. Think of one and I'll write you its dictionary.

BUNYAN. You're just the person I'm looking for. I want a book-keeper to look after my accounts.

INKSLINGER. Sorry. I'm busy.

BUNYAN. Who do you work for?

INKSLINGER. Myself, silly. This is a free country.

BUNYAN. How much money have you got?

INKSLINGER [*looking in his pocket*]. Eleven cents.

BUNYAN. How are you going to eat?

INKSLINGER. Dunno. You wouldn't care to lend me a dollar, would you?

BUNYAN. If you work for me, you shall get a number of dollars. But I won't lend you one.

INKSLINGER. No, thank you. [*Sound of* LUMBERJACKS *off.*] Here come a whole crowd. Looking for you, I suppose. So I'll be moving. I don't like crowds. So long. [*Exit* INKSLINGER.]

Lumberjack's entrance and song, followed by Bunyan's Welcome and Quartet of Swedes, as on p. 11; then, after the fight of the four Swedes over which of them should be foreman:

> [HELSON *rises from the chorus and separates the fighters.*]

HELSON. That will do.

BUNYAN. Who are you?

HELSON. Hel Helson, formerly foreman to Nel Nelson, King of Sweden.

BUNYAN. Do you think you could manage these boys?

HELSON. I tank so.

BUNYAN. Why?

HELSON. I weigh 200 pounds and I've never lost a fight yet.

BUNYAN. Very well, you're in charge. You arrange things while I take a little walk.

HELSON. Can any of you cook?

CHORUS [*in turns*] 1. I think I could boil an egg.

2.   With a little practice, I might be able to fry bacon.

3.   I can open a can, if there's a can opener.

4.   I made coffee once when I was a kid, but the percolator broke.

5.   My aunt told me a recipe for making candy, but I never tried it.

HELSON. Can any of you *cook*?

[*Silence.*]

ONE OF THE CHORUS. I'm hungry.

[SLIM *heard off.*]

SLIM'S SONG

As on pp. 21–22.

HELSON. What's your name, stranger?

SLIM. Slim.

HELSON. You don't look like a logger.

SLIM. I'm not. The last job I had was as a cook.

HELSON. Can you cook flapjacks?

SLIM. Sure.

HELSON. Cookies.

SLIM. Sure.

HELSON. Steaks.

SLIM. Sure.

HELSON. Then, you're hired. Come on, boys, we must get the camp ready. We'll arrange the work in the morning. [*Giving directions.*] You go and chop wood. You get some water. You unpack the stores. Let's go.

[*Exeunt, all but the* FOUR SWEDES *who henceforward become the* FOUR CRONIES. *One of them whistles, bringing the next to his side. He whistles bringing the third. The third the fourth, down to the centre of the stage.*]

CRONIES 1. It's incredible.

2.   It's scandalous.

3.   Helson as foreman.
4.   Why not us?

CRONIES' SONG

CRONIES.
> Is this the free country
> We thought we had found?
> Why should Helson
> Boss us around?
> What right has Bunyan, we should like to ask
> To put a brute like that in authority
> Passing over men like us whose intelligence and force of
>   character makes them naturally fitted to such a task,
> And in total disregard of the clearly expressed wishes of the
>   popular majority.

[*Recitative.*]
1.   What shall we do?
2.   Wait for a dark night.
3.   But he is so strong.
1.   Put a snake in his boots.
2.   It might bite us.
3.   Poison ivy in his bunk.
1.   He might guess who did it.
2.   Powdered glass in his stew.
3.   We haven't any glass.
4.   No, no, that's crude. We shall never achieve our ends
> So long as Bunyan and Helson continue to be friends.
> We must be more subtle. The thing for us to do
> Is to find a way to cause trouble between the two.
> Appear to be very contented and flatter
> Both of these gentlemen, especially the latter.
> Because as any psychologist would tell us,
> Nothing is easier than to make a person jealous
> When, like Helson, they're strong but ugly and stupid.
> We must tell him he's as wise as Solomon and as charming as Cupid,
> And that his only fault is a certain lack of ambition,
> Otherwise he would not be contented with an inferior position
> As a foreman. That as long as he submits to Bunyan's dictation,
> He is being the foolish victim of a shameful exploitation.
> That as long as Bunyan is there, the logging business will be a
>   disaster.
> That the only thing that will save it is for him to become master.

And that if he will throw Bunyan out and assume control,
There isn't a man in the camp who won't be behind him, body and
    soul.
1. That's smart.
2. That's scientific.
3. Very good.
4. Are we agreed, then, on the idea?
1, 2, 3. We are indeed.
4. Then let us swear a pact of brotherhood.
1. I swear.
2. I swear.
3. I swear.
4. I swear.
CRONIES. We stand united
    The tyrants shall fall.
    Down with Helson.
    Down with Paul.

[INKSLINGER *enters in the distance with a lantern.*]

Someone is coming. Let us go in
And carefully work out in detail our plan.
That the decisive moment may arrive at last when prehistory ends
    and real history may begin,
For we shall throw off our chains, and found a society dedicated, of
    course, to Liberty, Equality, Fraternity, and the Rights of Man.

[*Exeunt* CRONIES.]

INKSLINGER. Mr Bunyan. Mr Bunyan.
BUNYAN. Hello, Mr Inkslinger. I was just coming to meet you. I saw a
    lantern in the distance and guessed it might be you. What's the mat-
    ter? Lost anything?
INKSLINGER. I want my supper.
BUNYAN. What about my little proposition?
INKSLINGER. You win. I'll take it.
BUNYAN. I'm glad. Ask for Hel Helson. He's my foreman, now, and tell
    him I sent you.
INKSLINGER. Another moron, I suppose. Good night, Mr Bunyan.
BUNYAN. Call me Paul.
INKSLINGER. You're stronger than I, but I'm not going to pretend to like
    you. Good-night. [*Exit.*]
BUNYAN. Good-night, Johnny. And good-luck.

Bunyan's introduction to the Quartet of the Defeated, followed by the quartet, as on pp. 15–
16; this concludes Act I.

Act II

[*The camp. Summer—trees partially gone—light moves from noon to night. Corner of a cook shack—takes place of some of the trees.*]

[*Everyone is working.* INKSLINGER *is seated outside the door of his office doing accounts.* SLIM *is going in and out of his cook-house with wood, etc. Others are hauling lumber, sawing, etc.*]

WORK SONG

[*The solo lines are taken by different people.*]

SOLO.	The logger works a twelve hour day.
CHORUS	*Timber. Timber.*
SOLO.	It's a hard life, brother, for little pay.
CHORUS.	*While the hawk flies over the mountain.*
SOLO.	If you think it's easy, take my place.
CHORUS.	*Timber. Timber.*
SOLO.	And I watch the sweat run down your face.
CHORUS.	*While the hawk flies over the mountain.*
HELSON.	Don't stand there mooning. Haul those logs.
A CRONY.	At times I envy the cats and dogs.
SOLO.	I've an ache in my arms and a crick in my back
	One day I'll drop dead of a heart-attack.
SLIM.	The cook-house is full of bluebottle flies.
	The wood is damp; the smoke gets in your eyes.
SOLOS.	My sister married a rich tycoon
	So now she doesn't get up till noon.

If no one had invented the circular saw
I'd be helping my Dad in his candy store.

In a hundred years, I may save enough
To buy a ring for the one I love.

Last night I dreamed I was twelve feet high
And it rained neat whiskey out of the sky.

I want to lie down; I don't want to roam.
    Timber. Timber.
When this tree falls I'm going home.
    While the hawk flies over the mountain.

[*Towards the end of the song, the men move off stage to jobs in various directions, leaving* INKSLINGER *alone.*]

INKSLINGER [*doing accounts*]. Four times nine is thirty-six, carry three, four fives are twenty, twenty-three, four threes are twelve and two makes fourteen, four sevens are, four sevens are, four sevens . . . [*throws down the book*]. O hell. I wish I were dead. I can't account for several hundred dollars, I have a headache, and to-morrow I shall be twenty-five.

INKSLINGER'S SONG

As on pp. 23–24.

[*Enter* SLIM.]

SLIM. They've been at it again.

INKSLINGER. What this time?

SLIM. Three loaves of bread, a can of meat-loaf, and a bottle of tomato ketchup.

INKSLINGER. You're positive it was them?

SLIM. Quite. I saw them leaving just as I came in, and I was only out of the store for a moment. Here's Helson now. You really must speak to him about it. This is the fourth time it's happened.

INKSLINGER. He won't be pleased. They're as thick as thieves.

[*Enter* HELSON *and* CRONIES.]

1ST CRONY. Have some of my baccy, Hels.

2ND CRONY. A match.

3RD CRONY. You look tired. And I don't wonder, when you have to work so hard.

4TH CRONY. Not like some people I could mention [*with a glance at* INKSLINGER].

1ST CRONY. It must be very difficult for you when the chief keeps going away without explaining properly what he wants done.

INKSLINGER [*clearing his throat*]. O . . . er . . . Helson . . . could I speak to you for a minute?

HELSON. Can't you see I'm busy?

INKSLINGER. But it's important.

HELSON. Well, what is it?

INKSLINGER. Slim here complains that some of the men are stealing food from the store.

SLIM. I saw them.

HELSON. Who?

SLIM [*pointing to the* CRONIES]. Them.

HELSON. I don't believe it. [*To the* CRONIES.] What do you say, boys?

1ST CRONY. I wouldn't demean myself by answering such a preposterous accusation.

2ND CRONY. The very suggestion fills me with indignation.

3RD CRONY. Unjust suspicions are a well-known symptom of nerves.

4TH CRONY. Or an uneasy conscience. Let us meet the charge with the silence it deserves.

1ST CRONY. Come, Cross.

3RD CRONY. Come, Andy.

[*Exeunt.*]

HELSON [*to* SLIM]. Well, I hope you're satisfied. Perhaps clever Mr Inkslinger made a mistake in his invoice.

INKSLINGER. If you weren't dumb as a fish, you'd see through those guys.

HELSON. You leave my friends alone, see.

INKSLINGER. Don't shout. I'm not deaf.

SLIM. O for goodness sake, don't start fighting. The trouble with this camp is that there isn't a girl around for miles. No wonder we get bad-tempered. Sometimes I think I shall go crazy. We can't go on like this.

[*Enter* SHEARS.]

SHEARS. I can't go on like this. I don't want to be a logger. I never did and I never shall. My father was a farmer, so was his father, and so was his father before that. Why I ever came here, I don't know. I must have been drunk. And now, how the hell shall I ever get away?

QUARTET

ALL.   I can't go on without the things I need.

SLIM.   There're more mouths than a single cook can feed.

SHEARS.   I'm homesick for the sheepfold and the byre.

HELSON.   Loggers are only human and they tire.

INKSLINGER.

              It's been months since I had anything to read.

SHEARS.   I want a field that I can plough and seed.

SLIM.   I want a woman very much indeed.

INKSLINGER.

              I want some books.

HELSON.   I want more hands to hire.

ALL.   I can't go on.

INKSLINGER.
    I rack my brains.
SLIM.   I sigh.
SHEARS.   I pray.
HELSON.   I plead.
ALL.   But Bunyan only smiles and takes no heed.
SHEARS.   Where is the farm?
HELSON.   The men?
INKSLINGER.   The money I require?
SLIM.   Where is the beauty of the heart's desire?
ALL.   I can't go on.

[*Enter one of the* CHORUS.]

ONE OF THE CHORUS. O there you are, Shears. I've been looking every-
    where for you. The chief is back. He wants to see you.
SHEARS. Me? What should he want to see *me* for, I wonder. [*Exit* SHEARS.]

[*Enter the rest of the* CHORUS.]

CHORUS. I never knew he had a daughter.
    She's much lovelier than I thought her.
    Tiny. What a pretty name.
    I am delighted that she came.
    Her eyes.
            Her cheeks.
                    Her lips.
                        Her nose.
    Why, she's a peach.
                    A dove.
                    A rose.

[*Enter* TINY.]

TINY. How do you do? I'm Tiny, Mr Bunyan's daughter.
CHORUS. Pleased to meet you, Miss Tiny.
    Look at me, Miss Tiny, I'm six feet tall.
    Look at me, Miss Tiny, I've the bluest eyes you ever saw.
    Feel my biceps, Miss Tiny.
    I can ride a bicycle.
    I can spell parallelogram.
    I've got fifty dollars salted away in an old sock.
    I'll run errands for you.
    I'll bring you breakfast in bed.

I'll tell you stories before you go to sleep.
I'll make you laugh by pulling faces.
I'm husky; you need someone to look after you.
You need someone to look after; I'm sick.
TINY. Excuse me. But which of you is the cook?
SLIM. Here I am, mam. Hot Biscuit Slim is my name.

[*Pause. Music. They look at each other.*]

DUET

SLIM.	O crystal fountain, shining ever clear.
TINY.	O magic mirror where my thoughts appear.
BOTH.	What world of secrets is reflected there.

SLIM.	I see a garden guarded by a high wall
	With many flowers, very beautiful,
	But the rose in the centre is the queen of them all.

TINY.	The green banks of a river greet my look,
	A young fisherman stands there casting his hook;
	As handsome as a prince in a story book.

SLIM.	Desire cries Pluck that rose; Fear cries Refrain.
TINY.	Heart whispers Welcome; but Shame bids Disdain.
SLIM.	O well.
TINY.	O mirror.
BOTH.	Tell me true.
	What should I do?

[*Slight pause.*]

TINY. Er . . . Father said I was to help you in the kitchen.
SLIM. I'm sure you'll be a great help, Miss Tiny. This way please.

[*Exeunt* TINY *and* SLIM.]

CHORUS. Did you see how he looked at her?
     Did you see how she looked at him?
     I shall take cooking lessons.

[*Enter* SHEARS.]

SHEARS. Boys, I've wonderful news for any of you who are tired of log-
     ging and would like to settle down. I've been talking to Mr Bunyan,
     and he says he has found the very place. A land where the wheat

grows as tall as church steeples and the potatoes are as big as airships.
And he wants to take us there just as soon as we can get ready. Let's
hurry.

CHORUS [*going off, some singing*].
>   It has always been my dream
>   Since I was only so high
>   To live upon a farm and watch
>   The wheat and barley grow high.

>   [INKSLINGER *is left alone on the stage. He sits down*
>   *on the steps of his office.*]

INKSLINGER'S LAMENT

JOHNNY [*alone*].   All the little brooks of love
>   Run down towards each other
>   Somewhere every valley ends
>   And loneliness is over
>   Some meet early, some meet late,
>   Some, like me, have long to wait.

>   [*Re-enter* CHORUS.]

CHORUS.   The shanty boy invades the wood
>   Upon his cruel mission;
>   To slay the tallest trees he can,
>   The height of his ambition.

SHEARS. We're quite ready, Mr Bunyan.
BUNYAN. Hel Helson.
HELSON. Yes.
BUNYAN. You're in charge here while I take our friends to the land of
Heart's Desire. As soon as the special machinery I've ordered arrives,
I want you to start clearing the Topsey-Turvey Mountain. Now those
of you who are coming with me must start at once as we have a thou-
sand miles to go before dark. But if you think farming is a soft job,
you'd better stay right here.

BUNYAN'S WARNING

>   If there isn't a flood, there's a drought,
>   If there isn't a frost, there's a heatwave,
>   If it isn't the insects, it's the banks.
>   You'll howl more than you'll sing,
>   You'll frown more than you'll smile,

You'll cry more than you'll laugh.
But some people seem to like it.
Let's get going.

              [*Exeunt the* FARMERS *singing. All but* HELSON *and the* CRONIES *go out to see them off.*]

FARMERS' SONG

CHORUS.   The farmer heeds wild Nature's cry
                  For Higher Education,
          And is a trusted friend to all
                  The best in vegetation.

          The shanty-boy sleeps in a bunk
                  With none to call him Dad, sir,
          And so you cannot wonder much
                  If he goes to the bad, sir.

          The farmer sees his little ones
                  Grow up like the green willow
          At night he has his Better Half
                  Beside him on the pillow.

              [*The others watch them go and all except* HELSON, SAM, BEN, CROSS *and* JEN *exeunt. Farmers' Chorus off.*]

RECITATIVE

1ST CRONY. The Topsey-Turvey Mountain. Why, that's the one that
    stands on its peak.
2ND CRONY. And the trees wave their roots in the air.
3RD CRONY.   And the flowers
    can speak.
4TH CRONY. Suppose the machinery never arrives.
1ST CRONY. It's going to cost some men their lives.
2ND CRONY. Bunyan goes off and you will be to blame
    When his crazy ideas don't work.
3RD CRONY.   It's a shame.
4TH CRONY. You're not going to take this order seriously, are you, Hels?
1ST CRONY. You could always say you didn't understand him and
    thought he meant something else.
2ND CRONY. Have you no will of your own?
HELSON. O leave me alone. [*Exits.*]

CRONIES. Everything is working out just right [*dancing with joy*]
    He's swallowed the bait,
    We shan't have to wait
    So very much longer before there's a fight.

CURTAIN

Act III

[*As before. On stage* HELSON *and* CRONIES.]

1ST CRONY. Why do you go on taking orders from him?
2ND CRONY. Personally, if you ask me, he isn't coming back.
3RD CRONY. Why don't you run this joint yourself? We'd support you.
4TH CRONY. Sure we would.
1ST CRONY. Hel for Boss.
2ND CRONY. Tell him where he gets off.
3RD CRONY. And that stooge of his, Johnny Inkslinger.
4TH CRONY. Stand up for your rights, Hel. You're the only boss around
    here.
HELSON. GET OUT.
1ST CRONY. Of course, Hels.
2ND CRONY. Anything you say, boss.
3RD CRONY. We were just going anyway.
4TH CRONY. Don't forget what we think of you.

[*Exeunt* CRONIES.]

[*Enter* SLIM *and* TINY.]

DUET

SLIM AND TINY.   Move, move from the trysting stone;
    White sun of summer depart.
    That I may be left alone
    With my true love close to my heart.

    The head that I love the best
    Shall lie all night on my breast.

HELSON. Must you make those lovey-dovey noises right in my ear? For
    God's sake go somewhere else. You make me sick.
SLIM. Don't be frightened, darling; he can't help it.

SLIM AND TINY [*duet*].

> Lost, lost is the world I knew,
> And I have lost myself too;
> Dear heart, since I found you.

[*Exeunt* TINY AND SLIM.]

THE MOCKING OF HEL HELSON

As on pp. 34–35.

[*Enter* CRONIES *followed by* INKSLINGER.]

1ST CRONY. He's back.

2ND CRONY. He's mad at you.

3RD CRONY. Now's your chance.

4TH CRONY. Remember.

INKSLINGER. Helson, Mr Bunyan wants to see you.

4TH CRONY. Don't pay any attention.

INKSLINGER. Helson, how can you be such as fool as to think these people are your friends. You're making trouble for yourself.

HELSON. I'm a fool am I? Making trouble for myself, eh? Well, I'm certainly going to make big trouble for you. I've been waiting for this for a long time. You're going to be sorry you were ever born. [*Starts slowly towards* INKSLINGER *who retreats.*]

1ST CRONY. Go on. Settle with him.

2ND CRONY. Give him the works.

3RD CRONY. The cissy.

4TH CRONY. O good.

BUNYAN [*very loud*]. Helson. Stop it.

HELSON. Stop for you? I'll kill you. [*Rushes out.*]

THE FIGHT

As on pp. 37–40 (slightly abridged), through the Cronies' exit.

BUNYAN. Have you forgiven me, Hels?

HELSON. I've been a fool, I'm sorry.

BUNYAN. You needn't be. I understand just what you must have felt. You think some of my schemes crazy. Well, so they are. But this country is so big, that it can't be built up without a little craziness. I'm really rather glad that this has happened. Sometimes a fight clears the air. For it's not till people get completely mad at each other, mad enough to come to blows, that they dare to tell the truth. And then they find that as a matter of fact they want pretty much the same things, that there are as many ways of wanting the same thing as there are people and that it takes all sorts to make a world. For instance this camp couldn't exist without Hels' muscles, and you were wrong, Johnny, to despise them. But you were wrong, too, Hels, in despising Johnny's brains because we can't do without them either. A job as big as this needs you all, and when there is no more logging to do, this country will need you even more. Come, let bygones be bygones. Here comes Slim and my daughter and it looks to me as if she won't be living with her father very much longer. That's a good omen. Let's shake hands and forget the past.

[*Enter* TINY AND SLIM.]

CHORUS HYMN. Often thoughts of hate conceal
            Love we are ashamed to feel;
            In the climax of a fight
            Lost affection comes to light.
            And the prisoners are set free,
            O great day of discovery.

> [*Final love song*—TINY AND SLIM *wandering across stage.*]
>
> [*Fade out on* CHORUS *(which is now both men and women) in place.*]

CURTAIN

Act IV

As Act II, Scene 2, pp. 41–46.

§6 AUDEN ON THE OPERETTA

Auden wrote a brief statement on *Paul Bunyan* for the use of the director, Hugh Ross, who quoted from it in the program note:

> The authors describe their work as a choral operetta, ". . . with many small parts rather than a few star roles." They explain that they conceive of Paul Bunyan, the giant hero of the Lumbermen, and one of the many mythical figures who appeared in American folklore during the Pioneer period, as ". . . a projection of the collective state of mind of a people whose tasks were primarily the physical mastery of nature.

This operetta presents in a compressed fairy-story form the develop-
ment of the continent from a virgin forest before the birth of Paul
Bunyan to settlement and cultivation when Paul Bunyan says good-
bye because he is no longer needed, i.e., the human task is now a
different one, of how to live well in a country that the pioneers have
made it possible to live in."

Auden also wrote a longer essay on the work which appeared in the theatre sec-
tion of *The New York Times*, 4 May 1941. The title Auden used in his typescript
(now in the possession of William Meredith) was simply "Paul Bunyan"; the news-
paper retitled the essay "Opera on an American Legend. Problem of Putting the
Story of Paul Bunyan on the Stage." The text that follows is taken from the type-
script with trivial emendations; it ignores the regularizations imposed by the news-
paper's house style on the printed version.

PAUL BUNYAN

Most myths are poetical history, that is to say, they are not pure phantasy,
but have a basis in actual events. Even in its dreams, the human mind does
not create out of nothing. The anthropomorphic gods of folk-legends
may, for example, in many instances, represent memories of invaders
with a superior culture; these, in their turn, should a further invasion
occur, may be demoted into giants and dragons. The phantastic elabora-
tions are an expression of the psychological attitudes of men towards real
events over which they have no control. Further, myths are collective cre-
ations; they cease to appear when a society has become sufficiently differ-
entiated for its individual members to have individual conceptions of
their tasks.

America is unique in being the only country to create myths after the
occurrence of the Industrial Revolution. Because it was an undeveloped
continent with an open frontier and a savage climate, conditions favour-
able to myth-making still existed. These were not, as in most previous
civilisations, primarily political, the reflection of a cultural struggle be-
tween two races (though Bunyan does fight the Indians), but geographi-
cal. In the New World, the struggle between Man and Nature was again
severe enough to obliterate individual differences in the face of a collec-
tive danger.

Appearing so late in history, Paul Bunyan has no magical powers; what
he does is what any man could do if he were as big and as inventive; in
fact, what Bunyan accomplishes as an individual, is precisely what the
lumbermen managed to accomplish as a team with the help of machinery.
Moreover he is like them as a character; his dreams have all the naive

swaggering optimism of the nineteenth century; he is as Victorian as New York.

Babe, the blue ox who gives him advice, remains a puzzle; I conceive of her quite arbitrarily, as a symbol of his anima, but, so far as I know, one explanation is as valid as another. Nor have I really the slightest idea why he should fail to get on with his wife, unless it signify that those who, like lumbermen, are often away from home, rarely develop the domestic virtues.

Associated with Bunyan are a number of satellite human figures, of which the most interesting are Hel Helson, his Swedish foreman, and Johnny Inkslinger, his book-keeper. These are eternal human types: Helson, the man of brawn but no brains, invaluable as long as he has somebody to give him orders whom he trusts, but dangerous when his consciousness of lacking intelligence turns into suspicion and hatred of those who possess it; and Inkslinger, the man of speculative and critical intelligence, whose temptation is to despise those who do the manual work that makes the life of thought possible. Both of them learn a lesson in their relations with Paul Bunyan; Helson through a physical fight in which he is the loser, Inkslinger through his stomach.

In writing an operetta about Bunyan, three difficulties arose. In the first place, his size and general mythical characteristics prevent his physical appearance on the stage—he is presented as a voice and, in order to differentiate him from the human characters, as a speaking voice. In consequence some one else had to be found to play the chief dramatic role, and Inkslinger seemed the most suitable, as satisfying Henry James' plea for a fine lucid intelligence as a compositional centre. Inkslinger, in fact, is the only person capable of understanding who Paul Bunyan really is, and, in a sense, the operetta is an account of his process of discovery. In the second place, the theatrical presentation of the majority of Bunyan's exploits would require the resources of Bayreuth, but not to refer to them at all would leave his character all too vaguely in the air. To get round this difficulty we have interposed simple narrative ballads between the scenes, as it were as solo Greek chorus. Lastly an opera with no female voices would be hard to produce and harder to listen to, yet, in its earlier stages at least, the conversion of forests into lumber is an exclusively male occupation. Accordingly we have introduced a camp dog and two camp cats, sung by a coloratura soprano and two mezzo-sopranos respectively.

The principal interest of the Bunyan legend to-day is as a reflection of the cultural problems that occur during the first stage of every civilisation, the stage of colonisation of the land and the conquest of Nature. The operetta, therefore, begins with a prologue in which America is still a virgin forest and Paul Bunyan has not yet been born, and ends with a Christmas party at which he bids farewell to his men because now he is no longer needed. External physical nature has been mastered, and for this very reason, can no longer dictate to men what they should do. Now their task is one of their human relations with each other and, for this, a collective mythical figure is no use, because the requirements of each relation are unique. Faith is essentially invisible.

At first sight it may seem presumptuous for a foreigner to take an American folk-tale as his subject, but in fact the implications of the Bunyan legend are not only American but universal.

Until the advent of the machine, the conquest of nature was still incomplete, and as users of the machine all countries share a common history. All countries are now faced at the same and for the first time with the same problem; now that, in a material sense, we can do anything almost that we like, how are we to know what is the right thing to do, and what is the wrong thing to avoid, for Nature is no longer a nurse with her swift punishments and rewards. Of what happens when men refuse to accept this necessity of choosing, and are terrified of or careless about their freedom, we have now only too clear a proof.

The Rake's Progress

§1 History, Authorship, Text, and Editions

Stravinsky saw Hogarth's engravings of "The Rake's Progress" at an exhibition at the Art Institute of Chicago in May 1947. When he returned home to Hollywood he asked his neighbor Aldous Huxley to suggest a librettist for an opera based on Hogarth's series. Huxley suggested Auden. On 26 September 1947 Stravinsky asked his American publisher Ralph Hawkes (of Boosey & Hawkes) to approach Auden on his behalf. Hawkes and Auden met in New York on 30 September, and Auden declared himself ready to begin work immediately. Stravinsky wrote to Auden on 6 October to confirm their agreement. Auden replied on 12 October with a request for Stravinsky's suggestions, adding, "I have one idea, which may be ridiculous, that between the two acts, there should be a choric parabasis as in Aristophanes" (an idea that came to partial fruition in *The Bassarids*). At Stravinsky's invitation, Auden flew to Hollywood on 11 November. When he left a week later, he and Stravinsky had completed a detailed scenario of the opera (see p. 581).

On 16 January 1948 Auden sent to Stravinsky a typescript of the first act, and revealed that he had invited Kallman to collaborate on the libretto; Stravinsky was privately annoyed to learn that his opera had a co-librettist who was unknown to him. Auden sent the second act on 26 January, and the third (with an addendum to the first act) on 9 February. He and Stravinsky met again in Washington on 31 March, when Auden presented a retyped and slightly revised version of the libretto and made some minor revisions at Stravinsky's request. In New York, on 5 April, Stravinsky met Kallman and was pleased to find that he liked him. Stravinsky played the first act for Auden in New York on 3 February 1949 and he and Auden made a slight change in the final lines. He and Auden again worked together later in the same month. In November 1948 and again in October and November 1949, Stravinsky requested and received from Auden some additional lines of verse. He and Auden met again in New York at the beginning of March 1950, when Stravinsky asked Auden to specify "the exact figures for the bidding in the Auctioneer's song" (Auden to Kallman, 7 March 1950; letter in the Berg Collection).

The premiere took place in Venice on 11 September 1951 at the Teatro la Fenice, as part of the Fourteenth International Festival of Contemporary Music of the Biennale di Venezia. Stravinsky was the conductor, with the chorus and orchestra from the Teatro alla Scala, Milan. The producer was Carl Ebert. Auden helped coach the chorus in English pronunciation. Shortly after the first performance, the librettists made a few small changes in the wording of the libretto. The American premiere took place at the Metropolitan Opera House in New York on 14 February 1953.*

---

*Auden reprinted Anne's aria in III.3 as a separate poem ("Barcarolle") in *The Shield of Achilles* (1955).

On returning to their summer home in Ischia after the Venice premiere, Auden and Kallman sketched an additional scene for the opera, evidently for their own amusement and Stravinsky's. As Kallman wrote to Igor and Vera Stravinsky on 19 September 1951 (letter in the Paul Sacher Foundation in Basel):

> Wystan and I have also been passing a little time working up an extra scene for the opera,—a scene that could only be printed or performed very very privately. It's to open the Third Act and be between Mother Goose, Trulove and Sellem. Details later: but we can reveal that M.G. and T. go off together at the end.

Possibly none of this scene was ever written down; no trace of it survives. (Kallman recalled this scene in a note written for the 1964 recording; see p. 628.) Kallman reported in the same letter that he and Auden had been "preparing production notes for 'The Rake'", but these notes have not survived.

Auden and Kallman probably contributed a few details to each other's work on the opera—and it was Kallman who suggested that Tom Rakewell should make three wishes—but their contributions are on the whole distinct and easily distinguishable. Writing either in fact or in effect from Auden's dictation, Alan Ansen offered this account of the work's authorship in a letter to the *Hudson Review*, Summer 1956:

> Dear Sirs:
>
> It is only recently that George McFadden's "*The Rake's Progress:* A Note on the Libretto," published in the Spring 1955 issue of *The Hudson Review*, has come to my attention. Having had the privilege of preparing a typescript of the libretto for Mr Stravinsky's attention, I feel peculiarly authorized to make a protest against the unscholarly carelessness with which the author has failed to take note of Mr Chester Kallman's contribution to the text.
>
> Though the scheme of the work was largely Mr. Auden's, its execution was in equal measure his responsibility and that of Mr Kallman.
>
> I am authorized to state the actual responsibility for the composition of the various scenes runs as follows:

Act I	Scene i	first half	Auden
		second half	Kallman
	Scene ii		Auden
	Scene iii		Kallman
Act II	Scene i	first half	Kallman
		second half	Auden
	Scene ii		Kallman
	Scene iii		Auden

Act III	Scene i		Kallman
	Scene ii	beginning & end	Auden
		recitativo secco	Kallman
	Scene iii		Auden

Particularly painful was the citation and analysis as the work of Mr Auden of lines written exclusively by Mr Kallman. These are the passages beginning "O Nature, green unnatural mother," "The simpler the trick," and "Always the quarry," that is, more than half of the specific quotations from the *Rake* in the article.

Mr McFadden's judgment that "the lyrics" are "of a simple and classic beauty which it would be hard to match in modern English verse" must redound as much to the credit of Mr Kallman as to that of Mr Auden.

In a periodical of your standing the appearance of so radically careless (though critically acute) an article is especially shocking and can serve only to mislead. I trust that the publication of this letter will undo the damage.

Yours truly,
Alan Ansen

Venice

Auden sent a more detailed but otherwise identical account to Robert Craft on 10 February 1959, when Craft was preparing to describe the history of the opera in his and Stravinsky's *Memories and Commentaries* (1960):

As there is a double question of interest about collaboration

    a)   Composer–Librettist

$$\text{b)}\quad \frac{\text{Librettist}}{2} - \frac{\text{Librettist}}{2}$$

it might be worthwhile introducing some of the discussions between Chester and myself. For instance, though of course two librettists are not two people but a composite personality, I have been amused at the way in which critics, trying to decide who wrote what, have guessed wrong. The actual facts are.

Act I

Scene 1. Down to the end of Tom's aria . . . "This beggar shall ride." W.H.A.

       from there to the end of the scene. C.K.

Scene 2. W.H.A.

Scene 3. C.K.

Act II

Scene 1. Down to the end of Tom's aria . . . "in my heart the dark." C.K.

from there to the end of scene. W.H.A.

Scene 2. C.K.

Scene 3. W.H.A.

Act III

Scene 1. C.K. (except for lyrics sung off-stage by Tom and Shadow).

Scene 2. Baba's [i.e., Shadow's] verses at beginning and end of scene. W.H.A.

middle (card-guessing game). C.K.

Scene 3 and Epilogue. W.H.A.

The notes below specify some instances where Auden wrote additional lines for scenes otherwise written by Kallman.

This text of this edition is based on the first typescript, which Auden sent to Stravinsky in three parts early in 1948, but the text includes the revisions made by the librettists when preparing the second typescript shortly afterward. The text also incorporates the changes and additions made by the librettists while Stravinsky was composing the opera, as well as further changes made shortly after the premiere in 1951.

The following sources have been used:

TSA   The first typescript, sent to Stravinsky in three parts in January and February 1948, now in the Paul Sacher Foundation in Basel. The first and third acts are top copies; the second act is a carbon. The first act may have been prepared by Kallman or an equally unprofessional typist; the second and third acts are slightly more skillfully typed. Both authors made minor changes and additions by hand, and noted next to a few stanzas, "omit if too much". Stravinsky marked further changes while composing the score.

TSB   The second typescript, prepared from a corrected copy of the first by a moderately skilled typist probably working for Boosey & Hawkes. On 31 March 1948 Auden presented Stravinsky with a carbon copy, with corrections in Auden's hand; Stravinsky (and an unknown hand) added other corrections while Stravinsky composed the score. This carbon copy is now in the Paul Sacher Foundation. A second carbon was submitted to the Copyright Office with Stravinsky's score and is now in the Library of Congress.

One page of a further typescript is reproduced in plate 13 of *Stravinsky in Pictures and Documents*, by Vera Stravinsky and Robert Craft (1978); this typescript is not authorial and was evidently prepared for Stravinsky's use in planning the opera. Alan Ansen also typed for Auden's use a further copy of the libretto, in which he noted some abandoned lines from drafts earlier than TSA; Ansen's carbon copy of this typescript is now in the Berg Collection, and the abandoned passages are noted below.

The libretto was published as a booklet by Boosey & Hawkes, London, on 17 August 1951, and reprinted with revisions and corrections by the New York office of the firm in February 1953. Later British impressions in 1959 and afterward contain many of the same revisions and corrections, as does a reset edition published in London in May 1966 (but dated on the last page "Dec./Jan. 64/65"). The libretto was evidently set from a heavily marked copy of TSB; the libretto reproduces one of its typing errors. The 1953 American impression adds an unsigned synopsis, probably by Kallman or Auden (see p. 611).

The text in the orchestral score, of which a few copies were printed on 17 August 1951 for use in performance, and in the vocal score, published 4 September 1951, is taken from Stravinsky's full manuscript score, but includes corrections made at Kallman's request when he read proof of the vocal score. Further corrections were made in the second printing of the vocal score in 1952, and were incorporated in the later printings of the libretto and in the miniature score published in 1962. These corrections are described in §3. The scores were edited in Boosey & Hawkes's London office and, unlike the typescripts, use British spelling throughout the text.

Some of Auden's early drafts of I.2 are in a notebook now in the British Library (Add. MS 53772). Two further pages of Auden's draft of I.2 and the opening page of Kallman's draft of II.1 are in the collection of Robert A. Wilson. Stravinsky's manuscript score and summary sketches are in the University of Southern California; further sketches are in Basel. A published report that Stravinsky gave Auden a manuscript sketch of Act I is incorrect; Stravinsky gave Auden only an ozalid copy, now lost.

In effect, this edition attempts to reproduce the text that the librettists offered the composer, which was not always the text that the composer set to music. Stravinsky used the first typescript when composing the opera, and neglected to copy into the first typescript all the revisions the librettists had made in the second. In some instances Stravinsky combined readings from the two typescripts, and in other instances he had already begun setting one version of the text when Auden sent a further revision.

The most obvious difference between the text in this edition (based on the typescripts) and the text in the printed libretto is the absence from the printed libretto of all headings like "Aria" and "Orchestral Recitative" that the authors included in their typescripts as suggestions to the composer. The stage directions in the printed libretto vary considerably from those in the typescripts, apparently partly because of changes introduced by Stravinsky or by Boosey & Hawkes's editor. After Kallman noticed the worst of these changes while reading proof of the vocal score (see the note to p. 61 below), he and Auden protested to Stravinsky and succeeded in restoring the general idea of the original stage direction. This edition reproduces the stage directions from the typescripts and ignores all revisions to the stage directions in the printed libretto and score that cannot be traced to the librettists.

Auden and Kallman gave some of their friends copies of the first printing of the libretto with revisions and corrections written in; not all copies contain the same changes. Two such marked copies are at the University of Texas; others remain in private hands. The authors' corrections of obvious typographical errors have been incorporated silently into the text of this edition; their revisions to the text are incorporated and noted below. All these corrections and revisions were incorporated in later printings of the libretto. The notes below refer to marked copies of the first printing collectively as "friends' copies" without specifying the revisions found in any one copy or which of the two librettists marked specific corrections in individual copies.

I have consulted the three published recordings conducted by Stravinsky. The 1951 premiere was recorded by RAI but released by Fonit Cetra (DOC 29) only in 1982. Stravinsky's first studio recording of the opera was released in 1953 by Columbia (SL-125) in the United States and by Philips elsewhere. The second studio recording was released in 1964 by Columbia (M3L 310 and M3S 710) in the United States and under the CBS label elsewhere. The revisions made to the text after the 1951 premiere are first heard in the 1953 recording.

Auden's correspondence with Stravinsky is in the Paul Sacher Foundation; a selection was printed in Stravinsky and Craft's *Memories and Commentaries* (1960), and a larger selection appears in *Stravinsky: Selected Correspondence*, vol. 1, edited by Craft (1982).

Robert Craft published two versions of a brief historical account of the libretto. The first version appeared as "A Note on the [musical] Sketches and the Two Versions of the Libretto" in *Igor Stravinsky: The Rake's Progress*, by Paul Griffiths (1982); the second version of this history, with one section omitted, appeared as "*The Rake's Progress:* The Evolution of the Libretto and the Sketches" in *Stravinsky: Selected Correspondence*, vol. 3, edited by Craft (1985). The notes below correct minor errors in Craft's account, but the errors are mentioned explicitly only where conflicts between Craft's account and this edition might be misleading. Robert Craft has generously confirmed the history of the text offered in this edition.

§2 AUDEN AND STRAVINSKY'S SCENARIO

Stravinsky's first letter to Auden, on 6 October 1947, proposed (in part) that Auden

> prepare a general outline of *The Rake's Progress*. I think at the moment of two acts, maybe five scenes (five [i.e., three] for the first act and two for the second act). . . .
>
> After the outline is completed, I suggest you prepare a free verse preliminary for the characters (arias, duets, trios, etc.), also for small chorus. . . . Of course, there is a sort of limitation as to form in view of Hogarth's style and period. Yet make it as contemporary as I treated Pergolesi in my *Pulcinella*. As the end of any work is of importance, I think that the hero's end in an asylum scratching a fiddle would make a meritorious conclusion to his stormy life. Don't you think so?

Auden replied on 12 October:

> Dear Mr Stravinsky,
> Thank you very much for your letter of Oct 6th which arrived this morning.
> As you say, it is a terrible nuisance being thousands of miles apart, but we must do the best we can.
> As a) you have thought about the Rake's Progress for some time and b) it is the librettist's job to satisfy the composer not the other way round, I should be most grateful if you could let me have any ideas you may have formed about characters, plot, etc.
> I think the Asylum finale sounds excellent, but, for instance, if he is to play the fiddle then, do you want the fiddle to run through the story?
> You speak of a "free verse preliminary". Do you want the arias and ensembles to be finally written in free verse or only as a basis for discussing the actual form they should take? If they were spoken, the eighteenth century style would of course demand rhyme but I know how different this is when the words are set.
> I have an idea, which may be ridiculous, that between the two acts, there should be a choric parabasis as in Aristophanes.
> I need hardly say that the chance of working with you is the greatest honor of my life.
> In addition to Aldous Huxley, I think we have another mutual friend, Nicholas Nabakov [sic].
>
> Yours very sincerely
Wystan Auden.
>
> P.S. I hope you can read my writing. Unfortunately I do not know how to type.

Stravinsky responded with an invitation to his home.

Alan Ansen recorded that Auden told him in conversation on 20 October 1947:

> There are to be seven characters—three men and three women, in addition to the hero. I think I'd like to connect it with the Seven Deadly Sins. The hero, of course, will represent Pride, the young girl Lust, I think. The rich old woman will be Avarice, the false friend Anger, the servant Envy and so on. Instead of the gambling scene I'd like to have a cockfight, but I don't know whether I can get away with it. Perhaps the crowd could be standing round concealing the cocks from view and the orchestra could imitate the noises they would make in fighting. Or perhaps we could use marionettes. I don't know. The final scene in the madhouse where the hero is crowned as Lucifer I'd like to treat as a coronation service. He ought to be anointed with a chamber pot, but I don't know whether people would stand for that. But piss is the only proper chrism. It has to be done in eighteenth century style.

Oh yes, there will be prose passages. The standard meter will have to be
heroic couplets. In the choruses, where the words aren't so important, I can
fool around with fancier meters. The girl turns up in the final scenes. I don't
know what I'm going to do with her. The duets ought to be got out of the way
earlier. In the last scene I want the hero to stand alone. But what *am* I going to
do with the plot? . . . (Ansen, *The Table Talk of W. H. Auden,* 1989, pp. 76–77)

None of this survived in the scenario that Auden and Stravinsky prepared dur-
ing Auden's visit on 11–18 November 1947. The typescript, transcribed below and
now in the Paul Sacher Foundation, was made by Auden and includes changes and
additions in his hand; a few minor corrections occur in Stravinsky's hand. The
only major change made to the typescript while it was being prepared was the
addition in Auden's hand of the directions that the villain whistles in I.1, II.1, and
II.3; these additions were evidently made around the time Auden and Stravinsky
were preparing III.1, where the hero's command to the villain, "Siffle!" is typed,
not written. On the foot of the last page Stravinsky dated the top copy: "Holly-
wood Nov 18 / 1947".

This transcript slightly regularizes the page layout and punctuation of the origi-
nal, and corrects minor spelling and typing errors, but it does not correct errors in
French grammar and vocabulary (*l'Adone; Elle ne la guardera pas; Vous l'avez envolé;*
etc.). Stravinsky, however, made a few corrections to other errors in Auden's
French, probably while they worked together, and these are silently incorporated.
The Paul Sacher Foundation has the top copy and carbon copy of the typescript;
Auden's corrections are slightly sparser on the carbon copy, so the corrections to
the top copy are transcribed here. In one instance Stravinsky wrote a correction
on the top copy, spelling out "Soprano", but Auden abbreviated this to "Sop."
when making the same correction on the carbon; here I have followed the carbon.
Robert Craft's account of the libretto incorrectly reports that a page is missing
from the transcript of the scenario that he printed in *Memories and Commentaries;*
the page in question is Chester Kallman's diagram of the trio in II.2, which
Stravinsky mistakenly filed with the scenario.

On 20 November 1947, two days after leaving Hollywood, Auden wrote to
Stravinsky with this suggested change in the scenario:

Cher Igor Stravinsky,
Memo. Act I, sc. 1.

Je crois que ça sera mieux si c'est un oncle inconnu de l'hero au lieu
de son père qui meurt, parce que comme ça, la richesse est tout à fait
imprévu, et la note pastorale n'est pas interrompue par le douleur,
seulement par la présence sinistre du villain. En ce cas, le girl pos-
sédera un père, pas un oncle.

Etes-vous en accord? je tiendrai silence pour Oui.

                                                        Wystan Auden

PLACE	CHARACTERS	ACTION	NUMBER
Act I, scene 1.			
Garden of Uncle's cottage in the country. Fine Spring afternoon.	Hero and Girl seated.	Pastoral comme Theocritus of love youth country etc. (Perhaps mention Adonis here?)	Duet, ten. & sop.
		Blesses (to himself) the pair and looks forward to their marriage.	Trio, ten., sop., bass.
	Girl & Unc. enter cottage leaving Hero solus.	Uncle summons Girl into house.	Piano recitative.
		Hero walks about garden humming melody of duo. His voice trails off into silence. Pause. He yawns.	
	Villain appears at garden gate. He whistles. Uncle and Girl reappear from the house.	Hero turns round. An exchange of questions and enigmatic answers.	Orch. recit., ten. & bass cantate.
		Villain explains how his coach has stuck in mud of lane. Uncle invites him in. Girl goes to fetch wine. They drink. Villain proposes toast to the Future and says he can foretell it. Girl asks him to tell hers.	Piano recit.
		He does so in the manner of a Baroque Delphic Oracle. Egged on by girl reluctant Hero asks his future.	Bass aria with soli comments.
	Servant enters with letter for Hero.	A brief silence. Villain whistles. (Villain: "Read it.") Hero reads Letter announcing illness of Father. "I must get to London." Villain offers services.	Orch. recit., ten.

PLACE	CHARACTERS	ACTION	NUMBER
	Curtain.	Ensemble in which Hero speaks of Father, Villain of inheritance, Girl and Uncle with foreboding of the future.	Quartet, sop., ten., bass cantate, & bass.
		Orchestral interlude?	

Act I, scene 2.

PLACE	CHARACTERS	ACTION	NUMBER
A Brothel. One table with three chairs. Centre back a cuckoo grandfather clock with an inscription TEMPUS FUGIT.	Madam. Whores & Roaring Boys.	They sing of the Love of War and the War of Love.	Chorus. Marche Militaire.
	Enter Hero & Villain. Greeted with great deference by Madam who escorts them to table.	Villain: "Ne vous dérangez pas, mes amis. Amusez-vous. Dansez."	Piano recit.
		They dance. Madam.	
	C. clock cries One.	Hero (frightened): "It's late, I want to go home."	
	C. clock cries Twelve.	Villain: "Late? That is easy to change. Look!"	
		Villain to Hero: "Let us see if you know your lesson." He takes him through the Catechism of Pleasure.	Gigue. Duet, ten. & bass. Comments by contralto.
		"Now you are ready for confirmation. Your attention Ladies and Gentlemen."	Orch. recit.
		Villain introduces Hero as Virgin and rich.	Orch. recit.
		Hero sings Serenade of the conventional gallant.	Ten. aria.
		All applaud and make a rush for Hero. Madam: "Va-t'en. Ce Gosse est à moi."	Bruits choriques.
		She leads Hero slowly out singing him a nursery rhyme.	Contralto aria.
	Curtain.	Villain whistles.	

Act I, scene 3.

Setting	Stage direction	Action	Music
Same as Scene 1. Winter Night. Full Moon.	Girl comes out of house dressed in travelling clothes.	She speaks of getting no letters, fears Hero has forgotten her and announces her intention to run away from home to London to find him.	Orch. recit. & sop. aria.

Act II, scene 1.

Setting	Stage direction	Action	Music
Hero's dining room. Morning. Same as Act II, 3, 4.	Hero en déshabillé at breakfast.	Hero speaks of his debts, his boredom with the bachelor life he has been leading and wonders what to do next. He yawns.	Orch. recit. & tenor aria.
	Enter Villain whistling.	Villain: "I have a present for you." He produces a miniature. Hero: "Who is this Medusa?" Villain: "Your wife-to-be." Hero: "I'd rather marry a hedgehog."	Piano recit.
		Villain: "You will change your mind when I tell you who she is." He gives a list of her titles.	Orch. recit.
		Hero: "Let me look again. No, I don't think I could."	Piano recit.
		Villain: "You know nothing about Marriage. Let me tell you, while you dress." Gives a lesson in the choice of a wife. Hero gets more and more excited and joins in. When he is ready, Villain cries "To Hymen's altar." Exeunt with bravura.	Bass aria turning into tenor & bass duet.
	Curtain.		

PLACE	CHARACTERS	ACTION	NUMBER
Act II, scene 2.			
Street outside Hero's front door.	Enter Girl.	She expresses her fear at her daring at being alone in the city.	Orch. sop. recit.
Dusk.	Footman at door.	She knocks at door. Footman tells her hero is not at home but expected soon. She comes down stage to a corner.	Piano recit., bass, sop.
	Procession of Tradesmen.	Procession of Tradesmen arrive with packages. She wonders fearfully what it means and expresses her love.	Sop. aria.
	Hero and Ugly Duchess in sedan chair.	Hero and Ugly D arrive.	Marche comique.
	Servants with torches.	With a cry the girl rushes forward, confronts hero and the fight is on.	Trio, sop., mezzo & ten
	Girl, Hero, Ugly Duchess.	Girl: "False one, what of your vows to me?" Hero: "Let me explain. What shall I say?" U.D.: "Who is this person?"	
	Curtain.		
Act II, scene 3.			
Dining room of hero's house.	Hero and Ugly Duchess at breakfast.	Wife chatters about nothing, Hero answers with absent-minded grunts.	Mezzo aria with tenor monosyllables.
Morning.		Wife complains that he doesn't listen or care for her and bursts into hysterics. Hero gets up and puts tea-cosy over her head. Sudden silence. He returns to his chair. He yawns.	

Enter Villain whistling.	Enter Villain wheeling fantastic apparatus for making gold out of sea water. Hero: "What on earth is that?" Villain: "Your fortune. Watch." Villain pours water into machine and turns handle explaining process. A nugget of gold drops out. He hands it to Hero. "There you are."	Piano recit. Comic orch. recit.
	He begins to suggest what can be done with absolute wealth. Hero joins in.	Ten. & bass duet.
	Villain: "Well, will you go into business with me?" Hero: "Yes." They shake hands. Villain: "Will you tell your wife." Hero: "It's not necessary." Points to her. "I have buried her." They exit with machine.	Piano recit.
Curtain.	Orchestral interlude.	

Act II, scene 4.

Same as previous scene except that furniture etc is stacked as for an auction & covered with cobwebs. Ugly Duchess has not moved.		
Afternoon.		
Chorus of respectable citizens come to bid. Girl.	Chorus sing a moral, while they examine the things.	Chorus.
	Enter Girl who runs from one group to another asking for news of the Hero. They reply, "He has disappeared, he ruined himself in a speculation etc."	Mezzo & chorus en chuchotant.
Auctioneer & assistants.	Auctioneer enters, mounts dais, starts selling Lots of fantastic objects. Voices in chorus bid	Ten. aria.
	Lot I Lot II	Chorus bids.

PLACE	CHARACTERS	ACTION	NUMBER
		Lot III is the Ugly Duchess herself labelled Chose Inconnue. Auctioneer plucks tea cosy off her head. She recognises Girl and breaks into a tirade blaming her for everything because the Hero only loved her.	Mezzo aria leading to mezzo and sop. duet.
	Hero and Villain off stage.	Hero & Villain are heard off singing a street cry Old Wives for Sale.	Ten. & bass in unison.
		Ugly Duchess (to girl): "Go to him if you want him. I don't." Girl runs out. Chorus: "Quelle histoire."	Ensemble.
	Curtain.		

Act III

Scene 1.

PLACE	CHARACTERS	ACTION	NUMBER
		Orchestral prelude.	
Cemetery. Starless night.	Hero & Villain playing dice on a grave.	Hero: "Je m'ennuie." Villain: "Qu'est-ce que vous désirez maintenant? La Plaisir?" H.: "Non." V.: "La gloire?" V.: "La puissance" H.: "Non." V.: "Quoi donc?" H.: "Le passé."	Orch. recit.
		Hero sings of lost innocence and love. V.: "Joue, alors." They play. Hero loses. V.: "Alors, mon vieux, c'est fini." He whistles.	Ten. aria.

Girl (off).

The voice of the Girl is heard in the distance expressing her undying love for the Hero.   Sop. aria (off).

H.: (in great excitement) "Non. Il reste encore une chose. Le futur. Joue."

V.: "Je refuse."

H.: "Vous ne pouvez pas. Je le commande. Joue."

A clock begins to strike Twelve.

V.: "C'est trop tard."

H.: "J'arrête le temps. Ecoute."

The clock stops in the middle of its striking.

Villain sings with defiant despair of the future of   Bass aria.
love that he can never have.

H.: "Assez. Joue."

They play. The Villain loses.   Orch. recit.

H.: "Eh bien. Siffle!"

Silence.

"Siffle!!"

Silence.

"Siffle!!!"

The Villain sinks into the grave. The clock finishes its striking.

H.: "Let it strike. Le temps ne m'effraie plus. Pour   Bass [i.e., ten.] arioso.
l'amour il n'y a pas du passé ou de futur, il n'y a que le présent. Amant et aimé, je suis l'Adone [*sic*], le toujours jeune."

Curtain.

PLACE	CHARACTERS	ACTION	NUMBER
Scene 2.			
Bedlam.	Hero. Chorus.	H.: "Lavez-vous, mes amis, couronnez-vous de fleurs, Vénus, reine de l'amour, me visitera." C.: "Elle n'arrivera jamais." H.: "Elle m'a fait sa promesse." C.: "Elle ne la guardera [*sic*] pas."	Ten., solo & chorus.
	Hero and Chorus of madmen.	They dance, mocking him. Hero sinks his face in his hands.	Danse choquante.
	Enter Keeper & Girl.	Keeper (to Chorus): "Allez-vous en." (Chorus retire.) (To Girl.) "Le voilà. N'ayez pas peur. Il n'est pas dangereux. Seulement, il s'imagine l'Adone. Entrez dans son jeu et il sera satisfait." Girl s'approche à l'Hero et l'appelle par son nom. Il leve la tête.	Piano recit.
		H.: "At last, Vénus, tu est arrivée. Je t'ai attendue pour si longtemps. Ces types-là m'ont dit que tu m'as oublié. Monte à ta [*sic*] trône." (He leads her to his chair and kneels at her feet.)	Orch recit., tenor.
		"O, Vénus, ma vraie déesse, pardonnez-moi mes péchés. J'ai dédaigné ton amour en chassant les ombres stupides. Mais maintenant le sanglier est mort et tout est changé. Je sais que je t'aime comme tu m'aimes. Pardonnes-moi, je t'implore." Girl: "Si tu m'aimes il n'y a rien à pardonner."	Tenor aria then ten. & sop. duet.

	Both: "L'amour change chaque enfers particulier à l'Elysée mutuel [sic]."	
	Hero. "Laisse-moi placer la tête sur tes genoux. Je suis fatigué et veux dormir. Chante, Vénus, chante à ton enfant."	Orch. recit.
	Girl sings a lullaby. Hero falls asleep.	Sop. aria.
Enter Keeper with Uncle.	Uncle (to Girl tout simplement): "The tale is ended, I have come to take you home."	Piano recit.
	Girl (to Hero, aussi très simplement): "Adieu. Dors tranquillement."	
	L'Hero s'éveille brusquement.	
Exeunt Keeper, Uncle & Girl.	H.: "Où es-tu, Vénus? Où es-tu. Les oiseaux chantent, les fleurs s'ouvrent. C'est le printemps. Viens. Vite. Je veux coucher avec toi.	
Re-enter Chorus.	"Holla, Achille, Hélène, Orphée, Platon, Eurydice, Perséphone. Où est ma Vénus. Vous l'avez envolé [sic] pendant que je dormais. Où l'avez vous cachée."	
	Chorus: "Il n'y avait personne ici."	
	H.: "Mon coeur se brise. La mort approche. Pleurez, mes chers amis, pleurez pour moi, l'Adone le toujours jeune, l'Adone que Vénus a aimé."	
Curtain.	Chorus: "Nous pleurons pour Adone, le jeune, le beau, que Vénus a aimé."	Fugal chorus.
Epilogue.		
Before the curtain.	Hero, Girl, Villain, Wife & Uncle sing a moral	Quintet.
	THE DEVIL FINDS WORK FOR IDLE HANDS TO DO.	

FIN

§3 Revisions to the Typescripts and Printed Texts

Auden sent the three acts of the first typescript (TSA) to Stravinsky on 16 January, 26 January, and 9 February 1948, and presented the second typescript to Stravinsky on 31 March. The typescripts made significant changes to the scenario; Auden noted them briefly in his letter of 26 January 1948, which accompanied the second act:

> Dear Igor Stravinsky,
>   Voici Acte II. It seemed best to transfer the Auction Scene to Act III, as that is where the time interval occurs. Have made a few slight alterations in our original plot in order to make each step of the Rake's Progress unique, i.e.
>
> | | |
> |---|---|
> | Bordel. | Le plaisir |
> | Baba. | L'Acte gratuite. |
> | La Machine. | Il desire devinir Dieu. |
>
> As I said in my wire [two days earlier], don't worry about length. Once you have the whole material to look at, you can form your own opinions and it won't be hard to make cuts and alterations.
>
> Yours ever
Wystan Auden

The following notes record the variants between TSA and TSB, and the revisions introduced by the librettists while Stravinsky was setting the text—revisions that did not in every instance appear in the libretto and vocal score published at the time of the premiere in 1951. Shortly after the premiere, the librettists made a few slight further revisions, most of which appeared in the second printing of the vocal score in 1952, in the American printing of the libretto prepared for the New York premiere in 1953, and in all later printings of the libretto.

The history of the text is complicated by the fact that Stravinsky used TSA when preparing his setting, although he marked in his copy of this first typescript most of the alterations that the librettists had introduced into the second.

After the premiere Stravinsky decided that he preferred to divide the opera into two acts of five and four scenes instead of the original three acts. Auden apparently agreed to the change at a meeting in New York in December 1951 to plan the 1953 Metropolitan Opera production. Kallman did not learn about the change until he returned to New York late in January 1952. On 27 January, probably with Auden's implicit concurrence, he sent Stravinsky lengthy arguments for retaining the original structure. Stravinsky replied on 31 January: "As you know, when I left all minds seemed quite set on the solution of 4 scenes in the Second Act." Kallman did not respond. Stravinsky favored the two-act structure in the opera house, but retained the three-act structure in published scores and recordings.

Page 48.

The list of characters and scenes is taken from TSB, with minor refinements taken from the printed libretto. Each act of TSA was preceded by a list of characters in the act; in the list in Act II Baba's name is followed by "(may be doubled if necessary with MOTHER GOOSE)". In conversation Auden and Kallman also suggested to Stravinsky that Trulove could be doubled with Sellem.

Page 50.

In Rakewell's Orchestral Recitative in TSA his frame is "not ill-formed" and he refuses to play the apprentice in "a copybook"; in TSB these read "not ill-favored" and "the copybook". Stravinsky copied these changes into TSA.

Page 51.

In Shadow's speech beginning "A lover's fancy" a comma is inserted in TSA, in Robert Craft's hand, after "let all who will". The comma does not appear in TSB, but is retained in later texts (although dropped, apparently by accident, in the orchestral score published by Boosey & Hawkes in 1962). Although the comma helps clarify the line, it is not authorial and is omitted in this edition.

Page 52.

In Shadow's Orchestral Recitative, both typescripts have "his thoughts were only England"; the printed libretto and scores have "his thoughts were but of England". The change seems authorial and is incorporated in this edition; it was perhaps made in a late stage of composition. In TSA the uncle "saw that you must be", but Auden corrected this in ink to "knew that you must be". The change was not reproduced in TSB.

Page 54.

The pact between Rakewell and Shadow was not part of the TSA version of Act I when Auden sent it to Stravinsky on 16 January 1948. Auden sent the lines from Rakewell's "Tell me, good Shadow" through his "A fair offer. 'Tis agreed." when he sent the TSA version of Act III on 9 February 1948.

In Rakewell's Orchestral Recitative, "father" is capitalized in the vocal score. The capital corresponds to Auden's normal usage and could conceivably have been added when Kallman read proof, but it does not occur in the typescripts or printed libretto.

Page 56.

The layout of both typescripts suggests that the librettists may have intended to indent Rakewell's italicized answers to Shadow's and Mother Goose's questions to a greater extent than they indented the questions. But the typescript layout is so inconsistent that the additional indentions are ignored in this edition.

Page 57.

At Stravinsky's request, Auden sent on 22 November 1948 an additional stanza for the Chorus, and specified that the new stanza ("Soon dawn will glitter") should precede the one in the typescripts. (Auden's letter is dated 23 November 1948, but the envelope is postmarked 22 November.)

In Shadow's speech "Sisters of Venus," Auden marked TSB to alter "a stranger to our rites" to "a stranger to our mysteries". Stravinsky preferred "rites" (the TSA reading) and used it in the opera.

Page 59.

In the opening stage direction for I.3, both typescripts originally read "Summer night", with "Summer" corrected to "Autumn" in Kallman's hand in TSA, in Auden's hand in TSB. The vocal score has the corrected reading, but all British printings of the libretto have "Summer", although the librettists marked the correction in friends' copies, and the correction was made in the printing made in America for the New York premiere in 1953.

In Anne's Recitative Secco, in TSA, the last phrase (added in Kallman's hand) reads "and wants the comfort of a helping hand." TSB, followed here, has "and needs the comfort of a faithful hand." The published scores follow TSA; the performance scores and printed libretto combine the two versions to make "and needs the comfort of a helping hand." Also in this speech, the vocal score capitalizes all three instances of "father"; although the capitals correspond to Auden's normal usage and could conceivably have been added when Kallman read proof, they do not occur in the typescripts or printed libretto.

Page 60.

In Anne's Cabaletta, TSA reads "Though it be bound / Or freed unwanted,". This is altered in Kallman's hand to "Though it be shunned / Or be forgotten,". TSB reads: "Though it be shunned / Or be rejected," with the last word altered in Auden's hand to "forgotten". (Robert Craft's published account of the text reports that this change was made when Auden and Stravinsky worked together in Washington on 31 March 1948, but the presence of the change in Kallman's hand in TSA suggests that Auden wrote out a change that had been made some time before TSA was sent to Stravinsky and that the librettists had then forgotten while preparing TSB.) When Stravinsky played the Cabaletta for Auden in New York on 3 February 1949, Auden asked that Anne's final note be changed to a high C. When Stravinsky replied that the final word was unsuitable for the upper octave, Auden provided a revised text. Later that day, Auden wrote Kallman, who was then in Italy (letter in the Berg Collection):

I'm afraid you'll have to swallow my couplet for the Cabaletta

> Time cannot alter
> My loving heart
> My ever-loving heart.

I was faced with fitting it into the music and it was the only thing I could think up that would fit.

Stravinsky may have altered these lines slightly; in the score, the Cabaletta concludes with this modified reprise of the opening lines, followed by Auden's addition:

> I go to him.
> Love cannot falter,
> Cannot desert,

> Time cannot alter
> A loving heart,
> An ever-loving heart.

Auden apparently never asked to have these new lines added to the printed libretto, but, in a slightly shorter form, they appear in the texts included with the 1964 recording and recordings released in later years. These texts were apparently prepared by the recording companies.

Page 60.

The stage direction in Rakewell's first speech heading in II.1 is added in Kallman's hand in TSA, but was omitted (probably by oversight) from TSB. It does not appear in the printed libretto or score.

Page 61.

Rakewell's response to Shadow's entrance line begins in both typescripts "Alone and sick at heart." Auden deleted "Alone" and capitalized "And" in TSB, probably while working with Stravinsky, and Stravinsky copied the deletion to TSA. The original reading survived into the printed libretto, but was corrected in the reset edition of 1966.

Page 62.

Shadow's "Consider her picture" reads in both typescripts "Regard her picture", but Stravinsky marked the change in TSA, presumably after Auden offered the change while they worked together in Washington on 31 March 1948.

Page 63.

When Kallman read proofs of the vocal score in late May or early June 1951, he found a change in the stage direction following Shadow's "Well?" and wrote about it to Auden. On 9 June 1951 Auden wrote to Stravinsky with the following argument, which Stravinsky accepted:

> Mr Kallman who has been proof reading the vocal score in New York writes me that in Act II, scene 1 (p. 85) [86 in the published edition] stage direction prior to No 48, the stage direction now indicates that the broadsheet of Baba should be visible to the audience—the face that is. Did you mean this, because there seem to me two serious objections.
>
> 1) It is physically impossible to show the broadsheet in such a way that it is equally visible in all parts of the house. Those of the audience who can't see it will be irritated.
>
> 2) More importantly, the revelation that Baba has a beard at this point will ruin the dramatic effect of the finale to Act II, scene 2.
>
> I know you must be frightfully busy, so don't bother to answer this, unless you violently disagree.

Page 64.

In the first line of Anne's aria, the 1966 reset edition of the libretto, following an error in the miniature score published in 1962, has "No steps in fear" for "No step in fear".

Page 66.

In Rakewell's speech to Anne, the quatrain from "Then, only let" to "in Virtue's name" is marked by Kallman in TSA "cut if too long". Stravinsky did cut it, and it is printed in brackets in the 1951 libretto booklet.

Page 67.

In the trio "Could it then have been known", Anne's line "See that you do not" is the text that Kallman wrote into TSA as a change from the original "See that you shall not"; this change was apparently neglected in preparing TSB, but the changed reading appears to be the librettists' final intention and was set by Stravinsky. Rakewell's stanza has "Obey thy exile" in both typescripts and in the first printing of the libretto, but shortly after the 1951 premiere this was altered, probably by Stravinsky, to "Obey your exile". As this change seems to parallel other changes made by Stravinsky from "thou" and "thy" to "you" and "your" (see notes to pp. 68 and 83 below), it is not incorporated in this edition, although the authors marked the change in at least one copy of the first printing of the libretto (now at the University of Texas), and it was made in the plates when the libretto was reprinted in America in 1953 and in all later printings of the first edition of the libretto. Unlike other changes made in the 1953 reprint of the libretto, this change was not made in the 1952 second printing of the vocal score, and it was overlooked in resetting the 1966 second British edition.

The version of Baba's stanza in the trio printed in this edition was the fourth version that the librettists offered to Stravinsky (who set a modified version of the third). Kallman wrote the first version, along with the rest of the scene; during Kallman's absence in Italy, Auden wrote the next three versions. Kallman's first version appears in both typescripts, as follows:

BABA [*poking her head out of the curtains for each remark; parlando*]. I *believe*
    I explained that I was waiting. . . . *Who* can this person be? . . . It
    could hardly be thought that wedded bliss entailed *such* manner of
    attention. . . . I confess that I do *not* understand. . . . When am I to
    be helped from this infernal box? . . . Should I expire, the world
    will know whom to blame. . . . Tell her to go, you have your duties
    as a spouse, you know, and I cannot but feel this is the least of
    them. . . . Allah! . . . I'm suffocating. . . . Hussy, begone, or I shall
    summon spirits and have you well haunted for your presump-
    tion. . . . A plague upon matrimony. . . . My love, if you do not
    wish Baba to be piqued, do see that she is not condemned to re-
    main immured in this conveyance forever.

Auden wrote a second version when Stravinsky told him that Baba's *parlando* interruptions interfered with his attempt "to hold the audience's attention focused on a single action". Stravinsky asked Auden "*to compose verses for Baba's grumbling*" that "should match those of Anne and Rake", and suggested that

Auden "reduce Baba's words to not more, and even rather less, than either Anne's or Rake's" (letter of 18 October 1949). Auden responded on 24 October 1949 by sending these new stanzas (on which he wrote scansion marks similar to those he had noted on some passages in TSA when he and Stravinsky reviewed it in Washington on 31 March 1948):

BABA. Why this delay? Away; or the crowd will . . . [*She sees Anne.*] O!
      And why, if I *may* be allowed to inquire, does my husband desire
      To converse with this person? Who is it, pray,
      He prefers to his Baba on their wedding-day?

      A family friend? An ancient flame?
      A bride has surely the prior claim
      On the bridal night! I'm quite perplexed
      And more, I confess, than a trifle vexed.

      Enough is enough! Baba is not used
      To be so abused. She is not amused.
      Come here, my love. I hate waiting.
      I'm suffocating. Heavens above!
      Will you permit me to sit in this conveyance
      For ever and ever?

In his accompanying letter, Auden wrote: "In order to distinguish Baba in character and emotion from the two lovers, it seems to me that her rhythm should be more irregular and her tempo of utterance faster. In writing her part, therefore, I have given any line of Baba's twice the number of accents as compared with the equivalent line of Anne or Tom's." His manuscript of Baba's part is laid out in two columns with lines from Anne's and Rakewell's stanzas on the left, to indicate which lines should be sung simultaneously. Corresponding to Baba's first quatrain are the following lines: "ANNE. Upon that foresworn ground / RAKEWELL. And on the frozen ground // ANNE. Should see love dead / RAKEWELL. The birds lie dead". Corresponding to Baba's second quatrain are: "RAKEWELL. Shall I awaken once again / ANNE. But should you vow to love, O then". And corresponding to Baba's six final lines are lines from Anne and Rakewell's stanzas broken into half-lines: "ANNE. Your promise keep / Walk the long aisle / And walking weep; // RAKEWELL. Obey thy exile, / Honor sleep // ANNE AND RAKEWELL. Forever". Their final word is written lower on the page than Baba's final line to indicate their unison should be sung after the line.

    In the same letter Auden offered a third version. He wrote: "If you find I have given her too many lines, cuts are easy to make," and suggested these shorter versions of Baba's first and second stanzas, adding that in her third stanza "Here there is a succession of short phrases, which can be used or not ad lib."

BABA.   Why this delay . . . Away . . . O. Who is it pray
             He prefers to his Baba on their wedding day.

             An ancient flame? I'm quite perplexed
             And more, I confess, than little vexed.

For these first two stanzas Stravinsky used a slightly cut version of this third
version, and appended the full final stanza from the second version.

Later, on 15 November 1949, Auden sent a fourth version (printed in this
edition), with a letter that seems to suggest a preference for it: "If you haven't
yet composed the Trio in Act II, scene 2, here is an alternative version of Baba's
part where the rhymes fit the others which you may prefer to what I sent you."

Page 68.

Both typescripts have the Crowd say to Baba, "Show thyself once"; the printed
libretto and scores have "Show yourself once". The change was probably made
by Stravinsky and is not followed here.

Page 69.

The stage direction for Baba's opening speech in II.3 is taken from TSB; Au-
den wrote a similar direction in TSA: "[*très vite, without a single break*]".

In the eighth line of the speech one of the librettists replaced the anachronis-
tic "alluvial gravels" of the typescripts with "fluminous gravels"; Stravinsky wrote
the change in TSA, an unknown hand in TSB. In the eleventh line "little statues"
similarly replaces "statuettes". The first change was made at the suggestion of
John Hayward. Auden had shown the typescript to Hayward and T. S. Eliot
(with whom Hayward shared a flat) some time after finishing it, perhaps in the
summer of 1948. In *Memories and Commentaries* Stravinsky reports that Auden
had shown a typescript of the libretto to Eliot shortly before Stravinsky and
Auden met in Washington on 31 March 1948, and that Eliot had noted "one
split infinitive [retained in III.3] and one anachronism—'alluvial,' I think; 'flu-
minous' would have been the word used in the Hogarth period" (U.S. ed.,
p. 151); but Auden did not meet Eliot at the time the libretto was being written,
and none of the corrections in the typescripts is in Eliot's or Hayward's hand.
(See also the note to p. 84, below.)

Page 71.

In the stage direction in which Rakewell cuts off Baba's aria, both typescripts
have "*seizes the tea cosy and plumps it down over her head, cutting*". Probably writing at
Auden's direction, Stravinsky modified this in TSA to "*seizes his* [?lightly altered to
a] *wig and plumps it down over her head* [*back to front* inserted], *cutting*"; this altered
version (which is followed in this edition) appeared in the printed libretto, with a
trivial transcription error. Robert Craft's published account of the text plausibly
reports that the change was made while Auden and Stravinsky worked together
in Washington on 31 March 1948. (Craft's account reports incorrectly that the
"tea cosy" of TSA was a "dust cover" in TSB, but "dust cover" appears nowhere in
any text of the opera; Craft reports privately that this was a proposed reading
that emerged in the discussions on 31 March 1948 when Stravinsky thought the

"tea cosy" would be too small.) In Rakewell's first line after this stage direction Stravinsky wrote in TSA "I can not laugh," in place of the typescript's "My heart is cold," but this change appears in no other English text. (The German translation in the vocal score, and the separately printed booklets with German, French, and Italian translations of the libretto, all have phrases equivalent to "I can not laugh," perhaps because the translators worked from copies of the non-authorial typescript prepared for Stravinsky's use while planning the opera.)

In the stage direction for Shadow's pantomime, both typescripts read "*he removes dust sheet: disclosed a phantastic baroque machine.*" Auden corrected TSB to "*sheet, disclosing*", which is the reading in this edition. The printed libretto has "*sheet: discloses*".

Page 72.

In Rakewell's vision of "an Eden of good-will" the hyphen appears in TSA and reflects Auden and Kallman's normal usage. All other texts omit it.

Page 73.

In TSA the first stanza of the Rakewell Shadow duet reads "secure from need"; TSB and the printed libretto, followed here, has "secure from want". Robert Craft reports privately that Stravinsky first set the text of TSB, then, in a change marked in the score he used for performances, restored the text of TSA, which appears in the printed score. The change in TSB seems to be authorial and is retained in this edition.

In Rakewell's second stanza, Auden wrote into TSA his revisions of "their infinite" and "This engine shall all men excite" to "his infinite" and "This engine Adam shall excite"; these are the readings of TSB, and are followed here. In Rakewell's third stanza, Auden similarly revised "Man shall ascend" to "He shall ascend".

Page 74.

Robert Craft reports privately that in Rakewell's speech beginning "Alas, good Shadow," the phrase "how am I" (the text of both typescripts) is altered in Stravinsky's performance scores to "who am I", the reading heard in the recording of the premiere performance. Because this seems to have been a late adjustment for the sake of the music, the text of the typescripts is preserved here.

In Shadow's speech beginning "Have no fear", Stravinsky marked in TSA a change from "outstanding citizens" to "notable citizens", and the same change is marked in an unknown hand on TSB. The change seems to be authorial.

Shadow's concluding speech in TSA simply reads "O master, should you not tell the good news to your wife?" An unknown hand has deleted "O master". In TSB, the phrase is retained and Rakewell's "What is it?" added, but Stravinsky set neither of these two phrases.

Page 75.

The two wide spaces within each line of the Crowd's chorus are present in both typescripts, and emphasized by carets inserted by the librettists. It seems likely that similar spacing is intended in the last line of the Chorus, although this is uncertain in the typescripts. The second line of the chorus in both typescripts reads "sober businessmen insane", corrected in Stravinsky's hand in each copy to "sober marchands [i.e., merchants] are insane". The correction of the anachronism is surely authorial.

Page 76.

Anne's last line before her exit reads "I'll search him in the house myself" in both typescripts and in the first printings of the libretto and the vocal score. Soon after the 1951 premiere, one of the librettists altered "search" to "seek". They marked the change in friends' copies of the libretto; it was made in the plates when the vocal score was reprinted in 1952 and when the libretto was reprinted for the New York premiere in 1953, as well as in all later printings of the libretto.

Page 77.

In Sellem's aria, the accents are marked in both typescripts; although the markings are much fewer in the second stanza, the difference is probably the result of inattention rather than an indication that the lines should be sung differently. The printed libretto, followed here, capitalizes "Wit" and "Profit"; neither word is capitalized in TSA, and only "Profit" is capitalized in TSB.

In the typescripts, the first of Sellem's three similar lines beginning "Bid, bid" appears in this form: "(whatever number it is decided to reach) bid, (   ) bid, going at (   ), going at (   ), going, going, gone." The second and third of the three lines are typed in a similar way, but with an empty open parenthesis in place of the explanatory parenthesis in the first of the three lines. The first two parentheses in each line evidently represent bids from the Crowd and the second two parentheses represent Sellem's repetition of the bid.

At Stravinsky's request Auden replaced the parentheses with detailed dialogue for the bidders and auctioneer. He sketched a first attempt, probably on 1 March 1950, on the notepaper of the Hotel Lombardy in New York when he and Stravinsky worked together. The first two sets of bids on this sketch are:

1) 7. 11. 17. 19. 20. 21./
2) 14, and ½, ¾, 15.

Above these, in smaller characters, is a sketch for the third set of bids:

50. 51. 52. 60. 80. 85. 89. 100.

(Written above each of these figures is the numeral "2" or "3", apparently representing the number of syllables in each figure, although a deleted figure replaced by "2" is written above "89". Probably Auden wrote the rhythmic pattern of syllables first, and then wrote the figures from 50 to 100 to flesh out the pattern.)

In a hand-delivered note to Stravinsky, written perhaps two days later, Auden sent a revised list of bids, as follows:

Act III scene 1

p. 3 [77]. after first verse of Sellem's song. (Aha! the what [*error for* pike])

Members of the crowd speak in turn the figure bid, which Sellem repeats.

    CROWD MEMBER. 7
    SELLEM. 7
    C.M.   11
    S.   11
    C.M.   14
    S.   14
    C.M.   19
    S.   19
    C.M.   20
    S.   20
    C.M.   23
    S.   23. going at 23, going, going, gone.

Verse II. p. 4 [*78*]. Aha! the palm.

    C.M.   15
    S.   15
    C.M.   And ½
    S.   And ½
    C.M.   ¾
    S.   ¾
    C.M.   16
    S.   16
    C.M.   17
    S.   17 going at 17, going, going, gone.

Verse III. p. 4 [*78*] Aha! the what.

    C.M.   50
    S.   50
    C.M.   55
    S.   55
    C.M.   60
    S.   60
    C.M.   61
    S.   61
    C.M.   62
    S.   62
    C.M.   70
    S.   70
    C.M.   90
    S.   90 going at 90, going at 90
    C.M.   100

S.   100 going at 100, going at 100, going, going,
          going, going GONE.

This edition generally follows the arrangement of the printed libretto in pre-
senting this material, but follows Auden's detailed version printed immediately
above in printing "going at seventeen" (or "twenty-three") once instead of twice
in the last line in each stanza. The printed libretto has dashes instead of commas
in Sellem's lines that begin "Bid"; the change was presumably the work of the
editor at Boosey & Hawkes.

Page 78.
  Sellem's line beginning "An unknown object" was followed in TSA by two de-
leted lines:

  They cannot face the future who have fear;
  Who dares, beyond the Almanack shall peer.

(Robert Craft's published account incorrectly reports that these lines were intro-
duced in TSB, where in fact they do not appear.) The line beginning "O you,
whose houses" is also deleted in TSA (and Stravinsky did not set it), but Auden
pencilled it in to TSB. In TSB the line beginning "A block of copal" is deleted by
an unknown hand, but Stravinsky set it, and there is no compelling reason to
omit it from this edition.

Page 79.
  In the typescripts, the cross-reference in the heading to Baba's aria refers to
the page in the typescript itself.
  The second line of Rakewell and Shadow's first street cry reads "Stale wives,
sharp wives," in the typescripts and first printing of the libretto. Shortly after
the 1951 premiere, the librettists changed "sharp" to "prim"; the change was
marked in friends' copies of the libretto, and was made in the plates of the
second printing of the vocal score in 1952, and when the libretto was reprinted
for the New York premiere in 1953, and in all later printings of the libretto. In a
copy given to Edith Sitwell in 1952 (now at the University of Texas) Auden wrote
the change as "trim"; the variation may have been intentional.

Page 80.
  In TSA Kallman appended a "Note on the suggested structure of the two-part
TRIO with CHORUS [p. 6. Act III, Sc. 1]" with a detailed outline of the musical
treatment. Another page on which Kallman outlined an even more detailed
diagram of the structure of the trio was mistakenly appended to the scenario of
the opera. This is the page that Craft's published account of the libretto reports
as missing from the transcript of the scenario printed in Stravinsky and Craft's
Memories and Commentaries (1960); in fact it does not belong with the scenario.

Page 81.
  In TSB, next to the speech heading of Rakewell and Shadow's "If boys had
wings", Auden pencilled "see III, 2", evidently a reference to the ballad tunes in
the opening of that scene.

Alan Ansen's typed copy of Act II (in the Berg Collection) includes in an endnote "Chester's cancelled version of RAKEWELL & SHADOW's song", a version that was presumably replaced by "If boys had wings":

> O dogs hunt cats and cats hunt mice
> And ladies hunt their hair for lice,
> But we, Ha! Ha! do better yet:
> We're hunting Zero with a net.
> And when we trap it in its lair,
> The world can have it,—we don't care!

And Ansen adds, under the heading "and last line:" a line that concluded the scene:

> We don't care. We don't care. We don't care.

Page 82.

The text of the concluding lines of the scene is taken from TSB, but with two changes in the last line, which in TSB reads "I've never been through such a thrilling day." Auden pencilled "We've" below "I've" in TSB (the revision appears in the vocal score but not the printed libretto), and Stravinsky replaced "thrilling" with "hectic" in TSA, probably at Auden's suggestion (the revision appears in all later texts). The text in TSA reads:

BABA [*to the* CROWD].   Out of my way! [*They fall back and she starts out, but at the door she pauses to remark:*]
          The next time *you* see Baba,—you will pay! [*grand exit—as the* CROWD, *amazed, murmurs:* "I've never been through such a thrilling day."]

Page 83.

The bracketed direction after "Duet" is taken from TSB, where Auden pencilled in the words beginning "in the traditional manner". In TSA, the direction ends "ballad tunes, see text Act III, Scene 2 [*for* 1], p. 7 [i.e., 81]".

In the typescripts (followed here) Shadow and Rakewell inconsistently use "thee" and "you" in the ballad stanzas at the beginning and end of the scene. Stravinsky altered "thee" and "thy" to "you" and "your" while working on TSA, and the changes were copied by an unknown hand to TSB. In the first printing of the vocal score "your" appears four times as "yuor", perhaps suggesting that the change was made in the score during the proofreading stage and was misread by the German compositor; the change was also made incompletely, and "thy" consistently became "your" in this scene only in the second printing of the score. (Robert Craft's published account reports that Stravinsky "insisted" on the changes when he and Auden worked together in New York in the spring of 1950; the evidence of the typescripts suggests that the changes were made when Auden and Stravinsky worked together in Washington on 31 March 1948.)

Page 84.

In Shadow's speech beginning "A game of chance" the typescripts and the first printings of the libretto and vocal score all read "to thoroughly decide". Shortly after the 1951 premiere the librettists (or the composer?) altered this to "to finally decide". The change was marked in friends' copies of the libretto and was made in the plates when the vocal score was reprinted in 1952 (with "to" omitted in error), when the libretto was reprinted for the New York premiere in 1953, and in all later printings. In the printed libretto (followed here) and in the second printing of the vocal score, Shadow asks Rakewell if he has a "pack of cards"; the earlier texts in the typescripts and the first printing of the vocal score read "deck of cards". The librettists changed "deck" to "pack" here and elsewhere in the scene, apparently shortly before the premiere, after John Hayward told them that "deck of cards" was an anachronism. (This correction seems to have been made at a different time from another correction by Hayward described in the note to p. 69, above).

In Shadow's speech beginning "You jest" Stravinsky altered "outcome" to "result" in TSA. The change appears in the vocal score and in the 1966 reset edition of the libretto, but is probably not authorial.

Page 86.

Robert Craft's 1982 published account of the libretto reports that "Auden had written the words, 'To crop the Spring's return', in the Lombardy Hotel, New York, at the beginning of April 1950 [i.e., when they worked together in March], on a sheet of hotel stationery that Stravinsky evidently misplaced"; as Craft reports privately, the words were discovered to be missing in the vocal and orchestral scores in Naples in August 1951. This report may be a confused recollection of a *setting* of these words that Stravinsky had written on stationery and then misplaced. The words themselves had always been present in both typescripts.

In the typescripts, the cross-reference following Anne's line "That is sworn before thee" refers to the page in the typescript itself.

Rakewell's "I wish for nothing else" is a replacement for the reading of the typescripts, "Wishful chance, farewell!" Auden pencilled the replacement in TSB (after first pencilling in and deleting "To wishing, then," as a replacement for "Wishful chance,"), probably when Auden and Stravinsky met in Washington on 31 March 1948. (Robert Craft's published account reports less plausibly, but conceivably, that the changes were made when Auden and Stravinsky worked together in New York in April [i.e., March] 1950.)

Auden pencilled the stage direction "Orchestra resumes" in TSB; Kallman had earlier written "Return of orchestra" in TSA.

Shadow's stage direction "Resuming the ballad." is followed in TSA by the deleted words "In utmost rage".

Page 87.

In the last stage direction of III.2, both typescripts read "now discovered", with "dis" deleted.

Page 89.

Alan Ansen's typed copy of Act III (in the Berg Collection) includes as an endnote the "original later cancelled" conclusion to the Keeper's final speech before leaving Anne with Tom: "So, as you desire, I'll leave you for a little while. But I shall be in earshot and, should you need me, you have but to call."

In both typescripts, three lines in Rakewell and Anne's duet are typed with the extra word-spacing reproduced here. The librettists added a caret in the extra word-spacing, presumably to indicate an unsung musical beat.

The last line of the duet reads "of Always or" in both typescripts. Auden altered this in TSB to "of Almost or", probably when he and Stravinsky worked on the libretto in Washington on 31 March 1948; Stravinsky copied the change into TSA, and it appears in all later texts.

Page 90.

In the second stanza of Anne's aria, both typescripts have "Discanting", an archaic variant spelling corrected in the printed texts (and here) to "Descanting".

In the Chorus's couplet after Anne's second stanza, Auden wrote into TSB a change from "Where are our" to "Where now our"; the change was probably made when he and Stravinsky worked together in Washington on 31 March 1948. Stravinsky copied the change into TSA, and although the revised reading did not appear in the first printing of the libretto, it appeared in all later printings.

Page 91.

In Anne's third line of her duet with Trulove, both typescripts have "the homesick spirit"; in TSA this is altered in an unknown hand to "the frantic spirit", a change that seems almost certainly authorial. The revised reading appears in the printed score, but the original reading appeared in the printed libretto until the reset second British edition of 1966.

In Rakewell's first speech after waking, Stravinsky did not include "Plato". The name appears in the printed libretto, although the authors crossed out the name in at least one copy, presumably merely in order to let that copy reflect the actual setting, and not to indicate that they had chosen to delete the name.

On a page accompanying TSA Auden wrote out different versions of the final chorus for Stravinsky to choose when setting (Stravinsky chose the last):

Act III, scene 3

Page 21 [*91*].

Fugal chorus

[4 syllables.   Mourn Adonis. Weep for Venus *deleted*]

5 syllables.   Mourn for Adonis
                 The dear of Venus

> Mourn (him) ever young
> Weep (beside) his bier.

6 syllables.

> Mourn for Adonis, mourn
> Mourn the dear of Venus
> Weep for him, ever young.
> Tread softly round his bier

7 syllables.

> Mourn Adonis ever young
> Weep for the dear of Venus
> Weep, tread softly round his bier

8 syllables

> Mourn for Adonis ever young
> Mourn for Adonis, Venus' dear
> Weep, weep, tread softly round his bier.
> Weep for the dear of Venus, weep.

Page 93.

In the third line from the end of the epilogue, Auden pencilled a change in TSB from "A work to do" to "His work to do", but this change was made in no other text.

§4 A PROLOGUE FOR A 1958 BROADCAST

For a BBC Television performance of the last five scenes of the 1958 Glyndebourne production of the opera, broadcast on 7 August 1958, Antony Craxton of the BBC asked Auden on 3 April 1958 to write an explanatory prologue, to be spoken in character by Trulove outside Tom's house. Auden replied on 19 April, "Do you think Trulove is the best person to describe the preceding events? The only person who knows them all really is Shadow (e.g. He was in the Brothel which Trulove was not)" (letter in the BBC Written Archives Centre). Although Glyndebourne preferred Trulove (perhaps because Shadow was played by Otakar Kraus, not a native speaker of English), Auden's proposal was accepted after a discussion with him in London on 16 June. Auden sent the prologue on 8 July.

The typescript that Auden sent is lost, but a transcript of it made by the BBC has "W. H. Auden & Chester Kallman" typed at the end, and Auden's cover letter describes the work as "a joint effort" (transcripts of the letter and typescript are in the Written Archives Centre). However, early drafts of the prologue appear in Auden's hand in a notebook now in the Berg Collection, and the work may largely have been his. The text below is taken from the BBC typescript. A few lines in the typescript are marked for deletion; these marks are ignored here, as is the insertion by an unknown hand of the word "of" between "but" and "pleasures" in line 19. In line 12 "heard" is an emendation for "hear". The text was first printed in *Oedipus Rex / The Rake's Progress / Igor Stravinsky,* ed. Nicholas John (Opera Guide 43, 1991).

PROLOGUE

(*spoken by* NICK SHADOW)

"I wish that I had money!" so Tom said.
 He'll wish he'd wished for nothing soon instead!
Tom is Tom Rakewell, my new master's name,
Who knows me as Nick Shadow since I came
To serve his wishes. Well, well, he will learn
I've other titles when I wish in turn.
Imagine him before my part began,
A handsome, lazy, penniless young man,
Engaged—how I detest her!—to his sweetheart, Anne.
He loved her but he loved himself still more,
Life without pain was what he asked me for.
I heard his prayer; immediately I flew
To tell him that his First Wish had come true;
An unknown uncle who had died of late
Had made him sole heir to a vast estate.
Lucky for Tom? Poor fool! The luck was mine.
I knew at once I had him on my line,
For in his heart I read his secret thought—
'Twas not of love, but pleasures to be bought.
To town I led him, there to introduce
My panting victim to kind Mother Goose.
What followed, you can guess: to my mind, whoring
And drunkenness and cards are vastly boring.
Tom's nature, though, I'm glad to say, proved such
That nature's pleasures did not please him much:
The noise and glitter soon began to pall,
The ruling senses made no sense at all,
Then, feeling nature but a foolish trap, he
Leaned back and sighed—"I wish that I were happy!",
And I, at once, was at his side once more,
His wish to grant and my wish to assure.
"The happy man," I said, "behaves in spite
Of custom, conscience, reason, appetite.
So, master, with your happiness in mind
Look on this portrait of strange womankind
—Baba the Turk—unrivalled anywhere,
 The present wonder of St Giles' Fair.
Marry her, Tom! Be happy and rejoice,
 Knowing you know no motive for your choice.

Think, Tom! Dare any marry her but you?"
He looked. He thought. He laughed. He went to woo.
Perhaps you ask, dear viewers, how this man
Could think of marriage and not think of Anne
Who is, I grant, a lovely loving She,
While Baba, to be candid, is—you'll see.
He thought of her and felt ashamed, but pride
Soon won his guilty conscience to my side;
The Tom of his reproaches is not weak
But wicked, unforgiveable, unique.
So to our play. The wedding-knot is tied,
And now you'll meet the bridegroom and the bride.
Too soon will Hymen's bed be full of lumps,
Baba in tears, and young Tom in the dumps.
What will his third wish be? All men are much the same;
Abused at home, they wish for public fame.
What road to ruin shall I then suggest?
Some business venture will, I think, be best.
Ruin . . . Despair . . . then . . . ah! one seeming-clever
Immortal soul called Tom is mine for ever.
But here the couple come . . . No? . . . It is Anne!
Praying that Heaven will defeat my plan.
So—damn her!—let her pray! Nick Shadow knows his man.

§5 Auden and Kallman on the Opera

The first press report on the opera was Albert Goldberg's "Igor Stravinsky Will
Write Another Opera, He Reveals", *Los Angeles Times,* 23 November 1947, based
on an interview with the composer and librettist while they worked on the scenario
a week earlier. Auden is not quoted, but is reported to plan to "follow such 18th
century models as Pope and Congreve." Auden and Stravinsky are both reported
to "profess an admiration for Handel's treatment of English texts".

Auden wrote a brief, apparently hasty account of the opera for the festival mag-
azine *La Biennale di Venezia,* October 1951. Auden wrote Lincoln Kirstein on 10
July, "I have to do a little piece on the libretto for *La Biennale* magazine." His essay
was translated anonymously into Italian before being printed and was evidently
garbled or cut in the process. The original English version is lost; the retranslation
printed beneath the Italian text has been prepared for this edition. The retransla-
tion includes a rough attempt to reconstruct a garbled passage in the Italian where
some of Auden's original text was apparently omitted; the argument that Auden
seems to have been making in this passage corresponds to a passage in the first
paragraph of his *Harper's Bazaar* article on the opera (p. 617). Auden or his transla-
tor misremembered the punctuation of Johnson's verses; a corrected version ap-
pears in the retranslation. I have omitted from the Italian text the Italian transla-

tion of Johnson's verses that in the magazine followed the English version. The Italian text is lightly emended: "fortunatamente" for "fortunamente" in the fifth paragraph; "soprano operistiche" for "soprano o operistiche" in the seventh.

COM'È NATO IL LIBRETTO DELL'OPERA "THE RAKE'S PROGRESS"*

DI W. H. AUDEN

Mi sono scoperto un po' tardi nella vita un interesse per la musica d'opera, poi, grazie sopratutto all'entusiasmo e all'erudizione del mio amico e collaboratore, Chester Kallman, e alle possibilità offerte dal Metropolitan Opera House di New York di sentire delle perfette esecuzioni, sono diventato un vero tifoso dell'opera.

L'invito fattomi nell'autunno del 1947 da Stravinsky di scrivergli un libretto, traendone il soggetto da "The Rake's Progress" mi giungeva perciò non soltanto come un onore inatteso, ma anche come la risposta divina ad una preghiera perchè de qualche anno nutrivo il desiderio di fare la mia prova come librettista.

Il tema delle serie di Hogarth—la storia cioè di un giovane uomo che si lascia distruggere dalle tentazioni che la sua buona fortuna gli offre—fu un tema preferito nel XVIII secolo in Inghilterra; anche il Dr Johnson scrisse dei versi su questo argomento.

> Long-expected one and twenty,
> Ling'ring year at last is flown,
> Pomp and Pleasure, Pride and Plenty,
> Great Sir John, are all your own . . .

*[Translation:]

HOW THE LIBRETTO OF THE OPERA "THE RAKE'S PROGRESS" WAS BORN
BY W. H. AUDEN

I came rather late in life to an interest in operatic music; then, thanks above all to the enthusiasm and erudition of my friend and collaborator, Chester Kallman, and to the opportunities provided by the Metropolitan Opera House in New York to hear perfect performances, I became a real opera fan.

Stravinsky's invitation to me in the autumn of 1947 to write a libretto for him on the subject of "The Rake's Progress" therefore struck me not only as an unexpected honor, but also as the divine answer to a prayer, because for some years I had been nurturing a desire to try my hand as a librettist.

The theme of Hogarth's sequence—the story, that is, of a young man who allows himself to be destroyed by the temptations which his good fortune offers him—was a favorite one in eighteenth-century England; even Dr Johnson wrote verses on the subject:

> Long-expected one and twenty
> Ling'ring year at last is flown,
> Pomp and Pleasure, Pride and Plenty
> Great Sir John, are all your own . . .

Call the Betty's, Kate's, and Jenny's,
Every name that laughs at Care,
Lavish of your Grandsire's guineas,
Show the spirit of an heir . . .

Altrettanto popolare era poi il rovescio di questa storia, quella cioè del
"Virtuoso Apprendista", il giovane che pur essendo privo di vantaggi fi-
nanziari e sociali, con l'esercizio della sua prudenza e della sua intel-
ligenza, finiva per sposare la figlia del padrone e diventava un ricco
signore.

Come soggetto per una Opera il "Rake's Progress" ha un grande van-
taggio; è un mito, stabilisce cioè una situazione nella quale tutti gli uomini,
almeno potenzialmente, si trovano proprio in quanto sono umani. Quel
tradizionale sentimento che un' "opera seria" non deve esser basata su un
tema contemporaneo è, secondo me giustificato dalla seguente ragione.
Tutti noi abbiamo imparato a parlare ma pochi di noi hanno potuto im-
parare a cantare. L'opera, come il Balletto Classico, è perciò nella sua
essenza, l'impresa di un virtuoso, ed una vittoria trionfante sulla sorte.
Ciò significa che quel paradosso che si ritrova in tutte le arti, per il quale
tutte le emozioni e le situazioni che nella vita reale sarebbero penose,
diventano nell'arte una sorgente di piacere, nell'arte operistica raggiunge
addirittura un vertice. Infatti mentre la cantante interpreta la parte di
una sposa abbandonata che sta per uccidersi, il pubblico sa e non può

Call the Bettys, Kates, and Jennys
Ev'ry name that laughs at Care,
Lavish of your Grandsire's guineas,
Show the Spirit of an heir . . .

But the twin of this story was just as popular, namely the tale of the "Virtuous Apprentice",
the youth who, although deprived of financial and social advantages, ended up, by the use
of his prudence and intelligence, marrying the master's daughter and becoming a rich
gentleman.

As a subject for an opera, the "Rake's Progress" has one great advantage: it is a myth; it
represents, that is, a situation in which all men, at least potentially, find themselves, in so far as
they are human beings. The traditional feeling that an *opera seria* should not be based on a
contemporary subject is, in my opinion, correct for the following reason. All of us have
learned to talk, but few of us have been able to learn to sing. Opera, like the classical ballet, is
therefore in essence the act of a virtuoso, and a triumphant victory over fate. This means that
the paradox implicit in all the arts, by which all the emotions and situations which in real life
would be painful become in art a source of pleasure, is quite explicit in the art of opera. In
fact, while the singer may be playing the role of a deserted bride who is about to kill herself,
the audience knows and cannot forget that she is actually doing what she loves most in life. If
the tragic situation were contemporary—were, that is, a situation which some people really
and unfortunately are in and others luckily are not—this paradox would disturb the audi-
ence. On the other hand, the story Hogarth depicts will not do for a libretto as it stands: in the
first place and above all, because Hogarth's rake has a passive character which simply yields to
temptation. A passive hero is impossible in opera because music is supremely an assertion of
volition and a passionate assertion. In spite of all my admiration for *La Bohème*, for example I

dimenticare che in verità essa sta facendo proprio ciò che nella vita ama di più. Se la tragica situazione fosse contemporanea, fosse cioè una situazione nella quale alcune persone effettivamente e disgraziatamente sono ed altre fortunatamente non sono, questo paradosso renderebbe inquieto il pubblico. D'altra parte, la storia che Hogarth dipinge, non va per un libretto così com'è. In primo luogo e sopratutto perchè il libertino di Hogarth ha un carattere passivo che semplicemente cede alla tentazione. Un eroe passivo è impossibile in un'Opera perchè la musica è preminentemente un'asserzione di volontà ed un'asserzione passionale. Malgrado tutta la mia ammirazione per la *Bohème,* per esempio, non riesco a rendermi ragione del contrasto fra l'incertezza con la quale si comportano i personaggi e la sicurezza con la quale la cantano. In secondo luogo tutte le tentazioni alle quali cede il personnaggio di Hogarth, vino, donne e carte, ecc. sono tutte quelle che in un'arte visuale non importano, ma contano invece molto in una trama drammatica.

Nel comporre il nostro libretto, il signor Kallman ed io abbiamo conservato gli elementi essenziali della versione di Hogarth come l'improvvisa eredità, lo sperpero della stessa, il matrimonio ad una brutta e vecchia donna, la vendita all'asta della proprietà dell'eroe e la sua fine in manicomio. Abbiamo poi aggiunto altri tre miti comuni: 1) la storia di Mefistofele—cioè il protagonista Tom Rakewell si prende un servo chiamato Ombra; 2) una partita di carte con il diavolo in cui il diavolo perde per soverchia fiducia in se stesso; 3) il mito dei tre desideri—nell'Opera il primo desiderio di Rakewell è di essere ricco, il secondo di essere felice e il terzo di essere buono. Questi tre desideri sono in relazione con le tre tentazioni e rispettivamente cioè con il desiderio del piacere, il desiderio dell'assoluta libertà spirituale in qualche atto gratuito, e il desiderio di diventare il salvatore del mondo. Il primo di questi desideri lo conduce

---

can never make any sense of the gap between the irresolution with which the characters act and the resolution with which they sing. In the second place, all the temptations which Hogarth's character yields to, wine, women and cards, etc., [*some text is apparently lacking in the Italian; the missing text perhaps was something to the effect of:* provide interesting subjects for visual art; but opera is the expression of passionate subjectivity, and these temptations are at best the secondary consequences, not the immediate expressions, of passionate subjectivity; subjective passions, such as the wish to be happy or good, etc.,] are all those which have no importance in visual art, but which, on the contrary, are very significant in a dramatic plot.

In composing our libretto, Mr Kallman and I have retained the essential elements of Hogarth's version, such as the unforeseen inheritance, the squandering of it, the marriage to an ugly old woman, the auction of the hero's property, and his end in Bedlam. Then we have added three other familiar myths: 1) the story of Mephistopheles—the protagonist Tom Rakewell engages a servant called Shadow; 2) a card game with the Devil which the Devil loses through overconfidence in himself; 3) the myth of the three wishes—in the opera Rakewell's first wish is to be rich, his second is to be happy, and his third is to be good. These three wishes are related to the three temptations, and so, respectively, to the wish for pleasure, the wish for absolute spiritual freedom through some gratuitous act, and the wish to become the savior of

naturalmente in una casa di piacare; quanto agli altri due non voglio divulgare dei segreti che voglio siano una sorpresa ma dirò soltanto che la seconda tentazione lo conduce al matrimonio con una donna che si chaima Baba la Turca; e la terza lo rende preoccupato di una curiosa macchina.

C'è naturalmente una giovane soprano virtuosa, Anna, una di quelle soprano operistiche, che sarebbe terribilmente noioso avere come compagna di tavola ad un pranzo ma alla quale sulla scena tutto si perdona. Nella scene del manicomio la pazzia del protagonista sta nel credersi lui Adone, e che Anna sia Venere, mentre i suoi colleghi di pazzia sono personaggi da leggenda greca.

Poichè l'opera come *Don Giovanni*, è un'Opera giocosa, la morte in manicomio, è seguita da un epilogo in cui i personaggi principali si presentano davanti al sipario, si tolgono le parrucche e cantano un'allegra morale.

E per concludere, due parole sullo stile del libretto. Ho appreso con molto piacere che Stravinsky voleva non un dramma musicale, ma l'opera tradizionale con recitativi, arie e cori e voleva perciò un libretto che desse molte possibilità di bel canto.

In quanto al soggetto, che è del XVIII secolo, abbiamo cercato di evitare i solecismi storici nella dizione senza essere noiosamente archeologici.

Nello scrivere i versi per le arie, chiunque come me, ha passato molti anni a scrivere versi, doveva trovarsi di fronte ad un problema affascinante, quello cioè di rovesciare completamente la sue solite abitudini di pensiero. Infatti la poesia è arte riflessiva, la sua esistenza è una prova che l'uomo non si soddisfa delle interiezioni della sensazione immediata e

---

the world. The first of these wishes naturally leads him into a brothel; as for the other two, I do not want to give away any secrets that I would like to be a surprise, but I will say only that the second temptation leads him into marriage with a woman called Baba the Turk; and the third makes him preoccupied with a curious machine.

There is of course a virtuous young soprano, Anne, one of those operatic sopranos who would be a terrible bore to have to sit next to at dinner, but to whom on stage all is forgiven. In the scene in Bedlam the protagonist's madness consists in believing that he is Adonis and that Anne is Venus, while his mad companions are characters from Greek myth.

Because, like *Don Giovanni*, this is an *opera giocosa*, the death in Bedlam is followed by an epilogue in which the main characters appear in front of the curtain, take off their wigs and sing a happy moral.

And to conclude, a few words on the style of the libretto. I learned with great pleasure that Stravinsky did not want a music-drama but a traditional opera with recitatives, arias, and choruses, and that he therefore wanted a libretto which provided lots of opportunities for beautiful singing.

As far as the subject, which is from the eighteenth century, is concerned, we have tried to avoid historical solecisms in the diction without being boringly archaeological.

In the composition of the verses for the arias, anyone who has, like me, spent many years writing poetry is bound to find himself confronted by a fascinating problem, namely that of reversing completely his normal habits of mind. As a matter of fact, poetry is a reflective art, its existence is proof that man cannot be content with the outbursts of immediate sensation

vuole capire ed organizzare ciò che sente. La musica, però, è la più imme-
diata delle arti e nello scrivere le parole per un'aria in cui, per distinguersi
dalla canzone e dall'aria popolare, le parole debbono essere completa-
mente subordinate alle note, il poeta deve ritornare all'immediato.

Il monologo di Marschellin nel *Rosenkavalier* è secondo me, troppo
buono come poesia; i dettagli del verso si impongono troppo all'atten-
zione di Strauss; le parole di "Ah non credea" nella *Sonnambula*, mentre
d'altra parte non sono troppo interessanti da leggere, fanno però proprio
quello che dovrebbero fare, provocano una delle più belle melodie del
mondo.

I versi che il librettista scrive, sono, per così dire, una lettera privata al
compositore; essi hanno il loro momento di gloria quando gli ispirano
una melodia; poi essi diventano spendibili come la fanteria per un gener-
ale cinese.

An American impression of the pamphlet edition of the libretto was prepared
for the Metropolitan Opera House premiere on 14 February 1953. An unsigned
synopsis that precedes the text was probably the work of Kallman or Auden. The
text reprinted below emends the description of place immediately below the title
by inserting the word "an". The text also incorporates a change marked in ink in
two of Auden's copies of the American edition (both copies in private collections):
the omission of the second "alone" from the third sentence of the synopsis of I.1,
which reads in the original printed text: "Left alone, Tom reveals that he believes
fortune alone the ruler of human destiny; . . ."

THE STORY OF THE OPERA

The Action Takes Place in an Eighteenth Century England

ACT ONE

Scene one: The garden of Trulove's country cottage. Spring afternoon. Tom
Rakewell and Anne are exchanging idyllic vows of love. Anne's father,

---

and that he wants to understand and organize what he feels. Music, however, is the most
immediate of the arts, and in writing the words for an aria in which, to distinguish it from
lyric and popular song, the words must be completely subordinate to the notes, the poet has
to return to the immediate.

The Marschallin's monologue in *Der Rosenkavalier* is, in my opinion, too good as poetry, the
details of the verse intrude too much on Strauss's attention; the words of "Ah non credea" in
La Sonnambula, on the other hand, though they are of little interest to read, do exactly what
they should, provoke one of the most beautiful melodies in the world.

The verses which the librettist writes are, so to speak, a private letter to the composer; they
have their moment of glory when they suggest a melody to him; then they become as expend-
able as infantry to a Chinese general.

Trulove, however, does not fully share their youthful optimism, and his doubts are increased by Tom's refusal to consider regular employment. Left alone, Tom reveals that he believes fortune the ruler of human destiny; and he makes his first wish: to have money. Immediately Shadow appears at the garden gate and tells Tom that he has important news for him about an unknown uncle. With Anne and her father, Tom hears that this uncle, who was Shadow's master, has recently died and left him all his money. Tom feels that this news justifies his belief in his own superior destiny, and shows his gratefulness to the bearer of good tidings by hiring him as his personal servant. They agree that Tom will pay him after a year and a day have elapsed. Tom promises Anne that he will send for her and marry her as soon as his affairs in London are settled. Together with his new servant, he sets out for the city.

Scene two: Mother Goose's, a London brothel. Summer. Now splendidly dressed and very much the heir, Tom abandons himself to the loose life of the city. In a mock catechism on Nature, Beauty and Pleasure, Tom's answers show how well he is learning Shadow's lessons. However, when asked to define Love, the memory of Anne brings him violently to himself. To prevent his leaving, Shadow, with a magic gesture, turns back the clock to show him that time is his to command. Repentance can come later. In a song of initiation into the "Temple of Delight", Tom sings of the love he has betrayed. The whores, attracted by his melancholy and his wealth, cluster around him, but Mother Goose claims him, by elder right, as hers.

Scene three: The garden of Trulove's cottage. Autumn night. Anne, who has not heard from Tom since he left, prays that he may be happy in spite of the sorrow she feels. After a moment's hesitation at the sound of her father's voice, she resolves to carry through her decision to leave immediately for London. She is certain Tom needs her help.

ACT TWO

Scene one: The morning room of Rakewell's house in London. Autumn morning. Tom is sated with the life of pleasure, and makes his second wish: to be happy. Shadow immediately enters carrying a circus handbill of the famous Baba the Turk, and urges Tom to marry this prodigy of nature. In answer to Tom's amazed "Have you taken leave of your senses?", Shadow argues that only freedom brings happiness, and that the only way freedom can be obtained is by ignoring both Passion and Reason. Since Tom is neither attracted by Baba nor obligated to her, he can therefore prove his freedom and obtain happiness by the completely unemotional and irrational act of marrying her. Caught by the idea, Tom impatiently dresses and sets out to woo Baba the Turk.

Scene two: The street before Rakewell's house. Autumn dusk. Anne hesitates before Tom's door. Finally, as she is about to knock, a procession of servants carrying strangely shaped parcels comes down the street and enters the house. Night falls; a sedan chair is carried in and Tom steps from it. Confused and agitated at seeing Anne, Tom urges her to forget him and return to the country. Anne gently refuses. In the midst of their exchange, Baba puts her head out of the sedan chair window to demand attention. She is heavily veiled in the Eastern fashion. Upon hearing that this is Tom's wife, Anne sadly leaves. Then, as Tom escorts his bride into the house, an admiring crowd throngs in, begging Baba to unveil herself. This she does graciously, revealing a full black beard.

Scene three: Morning room of Rakewell's house. Winter morning. The marriage has not brought Tom happiness. At breakfast, surrounded by the numerous incredible mementoes of his wife's travels, he sits glumly as Baba chatters away about her collection. When she tries to cheer him up, he violently repulses her. Baba, enraged, harangues him. She might never stop except that Tom cuts her short in the middle of a word by plumping an enormous wig over her face. After this he lies down to sleep, and Shadow enters, pushing a fantastic machine. With the aid of some bread from the table and a piece of the pottery that Baba has been breaking, Shadow demonstrates that the machine is an obvious false-bottom mechanism that seems to turn stones into bread. In his sleep, Tom utters his third wish: that his dream be true. When he wakens, he tells Shadow that he dreamed of a machine that could save the world from poverty. Then, when he actually sees the machine, he is overwhelmed, believing it authentic, his own invention and a means, by doing good, of again being worthy of Anne. As the two prepare to leave and sell stocks for the venture, Shadow inquires about Baba. Tom replies, "I've buried her." And indeed, Baba is still sitting with the wig over her face.

ACT THREE

Scene one: Morning room of Rakewell's house. Spring afternoon. Tom and all those who bought shares in his scheme are bankrupt. A crowd is gathered in the now dusty and dilapidated house for an auction. Anne enters, inquiring for Tom's whereabouts, but receives no sensible answer. The auction takes place, and the enthusiasm of the crowd reaches riot proportions at the sale of an "unknown object". This turns out to be Baba who, awakened from her trance, accuses the auctioneer and the crowd of theft.

Tom and Shadow are heard singing mockingly in the street. Anne re-enters and the two women recognize each other. Resigned to her financial ruin, Baba tenderly exhorts Anne to find Tom and save him, but to be-ware of Shadow. As for herself, she will return to the stage and again be a reigning favorite. Once more the voices are heard in the street and Anne hurries out. Baba, imperiously commanding her carriage, sweeps past the admiring crowd.

Scene two: A churchyard. The same night. The year and a day have elapsed and Shadow, revealing himself as an agent of Hell, demands Tom's soul as payment for his service: at midnight he must kill himself. A clock begins to chime twelve, and Tom is overcome with despair. After nine chimes, Shadow again demonstrates his power to tamper with time: the chiming ceases and he proposes a card game, with Tom's soul as the stake, to be played in this magic period of grace. Shadow will cut three cards and Tom must guess what they are. The first he guesses with the help of Shadow's hints. The tenth chime sounds. On the second card he makes a lucky guess, aided by fortune. The eleventh chime sounds. For the third card, which is the same as the first, it is the voice of Anne, in answer to his anguished cry of, "Return, O love", which makes him certain of his reply, "The Queen of Hearts." His wishing has come to an end. Midnight sounds and Tom faints. Defeated in the game, Shadow still has the power to deprive Tom of his reason. He sinks into the ground. Dawn comes. Tom, in his madness, thinks that he is Adonis.

Scene three: Bedlam. The madfolk torment Tom for his belief that Venus will come to visit him. As he lies despondently on his straw pallet, Anne enters. Told by the Keeper what form Tom's madness has taken, she as-sumes the role of the Goddess, consoling the repentant rake. As she sings him to sleep, the madfolk, also momentarily consoled by her voice, join in the song. Then, when her father comes to fetch her, Anne bids the sleep-ing Tom farewell and leaves. Tom, awakening with a start, wildly accuses the madfolk of having stolen her. They reply that no one has been there. Calling upon them to mourn Adonis, whom Venus loved, Tom sinks back lifelessly.

Epilogue

Before the curtain, the principals sing the moral: The Devil finds work for idle hands to do.

Auden and Kallman also wrote a program note for the American premiere. Simi-larities with Auden's other writings on the opera and a slip into the first-person singular in the final paragraph suggest that the entire note may be Auden's work. In the text below, the first dash in the final paragraph is an emendation for a comma.

THE MET AT WORK: WRITING A LIBRETTO

The first duty of the librettist is, needless to say, to write verses which excite the musical imagination of the composer; if these verses should also possess poetic merit in themselves, so much the better, but such merit is a secondary consideration. Many things, such as striking metaphors and images or subtle verbal ambiguities, which are highly prized in spoken poetry, have to be avoided; on the other hand, simple ejaculatory phrases, which look shy-making on the page, can be lifted into glory by notes.

In being given an eighteenth century subject to treat we were fortunate: the poetry of the Augustan age is commonly thought of as "unmusical" and prosy but, in fact, its very conventions, its insistence upon the lucid generality make it a style better suited to operatic treatment (*lieder* are another matter) than, say, the poetry of the Romantics.

In writing an aria or an ensemble, we always had two things in mind; firstly, an *idea* of a certain kind of music—not, of course, an actual piece of music, for that had yet to be written by Stravinsky—which would suggest a rhythmical or stanzaic pattern and, secondly, the poets of the period, for example, Pope, Gay, Swift and Christopher Smart.

Without confining ourselves to any exact date, we tried—harder, I fancy, than some translators of Mozart operas—to keep the diction of our characters in conformity with their costumes. In this attempt we are indebted to Mr John Hayward whose scholarship detected several errors: for instance, we had used the word *alluvial* which did not come into use till the nineteenth century (*fluminous* was the correct word for the period) and, while the phrase *a deck of cards* occurs in Shakespeare, by 1700 it had become an Americanism. Since we are talking of debts, this is a convenient occasion to thank Mr Geoffrey Gorer who, by suggesting a spade, enabled us to solve a problem which had had us completely stymied, namely, what on earth, in the card game scene between Rakewell and Shadow, was the second card to be?

W. H. AUDEN AND
CHESTER KALLMAN

Auden and Kallman gave a lecture recital on the opera on 28 January 1953 for the Metropolitan Opera Guild, in Town Hall, New York, about two weeks before the American premiere. The following unsigned report appeared in *Opera News*, 9 March 1953:

NOTES ON THE RAKE

In the lecture recital on Stravinsky's *Rake's Progress* presented under Guild auspices by the opera's librettists, W. H. Auden and Chester Kallman, several convictions were expressed which may lend interest to those attending the new opera in the future.

Mr Kallman was frank to mention his dissatisfaction with the Wagnerian system of music drama, by which the alternation of tension and relaxation necessitates long stretches of boredom to point up the emotional climaxes.

Wagner utilized his organizational techniques, announced Mr Kallman, to express unfulfilled longing and egotistic regret. His medium was too much his own to survive him.

Only two works since Wagner could be considered in their relation to modern opera, said Mr Kallman: *Falstaff* and *Boris*. The former, he felt, summed up Verdi's vocabulary, but like the hats of Dowager Queen Mary, should be left to its originator. Only Puccini successfully profited from Falstaff and in only one work, *Gianni Schicchi*. *Boris* he describes as a unique work, which should also be put aside as a model.

The *verismo* repertory depends for its effectiveness, on touching or violent occurrences, said Mr Kallman. Only four of its examples: *Cavalleria*, *Pagliacci*, *La Bohème* and *Tosca* have survived on the contemporary stage.

The Rake's Progress, conceived in the tradition of the late 18th and early 19th century, is based on operatic freedom, born of disciplined song. In this clear, formal discipline a moral order is implicit.

Mr Auden's contribution to the discussion was an exposition of the characters. Hogarth's interest lay in the social life of the England he knew. The hero of opera, on the other hand, varied widely from Hogarth's hero. He was actually a rake only between the first and second acts!

No composer can project himself completely in a past epoch, and write as if an intervening period had not existed, said Mr Auden. The demonic debauchee has been limned for all time in the Duke of Mantua and Don Giovanni.

Tom Rakewell, on the other hand, is a tragic figure, whose flaw is his inability to accept the present moment as valid, to whom the future is real as an anticipated possibility. Tom can only feel guilty; he cannot act. His first wish, for money, is in reality a desire for something to replace the responsibility of his parents for his welfare.

In the brothel, he returns to a world of rules and rituals, something between a church with its Anglican catechism and a nursery where his conscience is destroyed and he returns to the innocence of childhood.

Baba the Turk represents the world at its best, Mother Goose, the world at its worst. Anne, a descendant of Tatiana and Micaela, develops from a country girl to a vision of Venus herself. In the machine Tom seeks a mechanical means to replace the normal relations he seeks with other people. Shadow is a projection of Tom's self-destructive force and the final chorus of madmen may be taken as an angelic choir, indicating that the rake has gone to heaven!

Auden wrote the following brief article, timed to appear shortly before the American premiere, for *Harper's Bazaar*, February 1953:

THE RAKE'S PROGRESS

BY W. H. AUDEN

"The Rake's Progress," as depicted by Hogarth, is a bourgeois cautionary tale; its twin is the story of The Virtuous Apprentice who is never late for work, saves his pennies and finally marries the master's daughter. Wine, Women and Cards are to be avoided, not because debauchery is wrong in itself but because it lowers the bank balance; Chastity is the child of Economic Abstinence. Hogarth's Rake, that is, is not a demonically passionate man like Don Giovanni but a self-indulgent one who yields to the temptation of the immediate moment. Consequently in the engravings, the décor is more significant than the protagonist. In an opera this is impossible, for music is, par excellence, the expression of subjective activity; a character in opera can never appear the victim of circumstance; however unfortunate, he or she is bound to seem the architect of fate. When we look at a picture of a couple embracing, we know for certain that they are interested in each other, but are told very little about what each is feeling; when we listen to a love duet on the opera stage, it is just the other way round; we are certain that each is in love, but the cause of that love will seem to lie in each as subject not as an object. On the other hand, though a single picture defines the relations between its component figures, a story told in a succession of pictures is a succession of static tableaux in which the present supersedes the past; what is portrayed in one picture is not the cause of what is portrayed in the next but is merely previous to it.

In writing our libretto, therefore, Mr Kallman and I were faced with two problems: how to make Tom Rakewell a singing being, and how to make him a dramatic being with a coherent life story and a sustained involvement with others. Our Tom Rakewell is a man to whom the anticipation of experience is always exciting and its realization in actual fact always disappointing; temperamentally, therefore, he is a manic-depressive, elated by the prospect of the future and then disgusted by the remembrance of the recent past. To define and differentiate the stages of his flight from reality, we have employed the familiar fairy-story device of the three wishes (which are spoken not sung); these, in his case, are, successively, to be rich, to be happy and to make the world a utopia. The real world from which he flies but can never forget is represented by Anne Trulove (soprano) with whom, when the curtain rises, he is singing a love duet in an idyllic garden; the instigator and director of his flight is personified in Nick Shadow (baritone), whom his first wish causes to appear with the news that an unknown uncle has left him a fortune. Rakewell engages Shadow as his servant and, at the latter's suggestion, promises to pay whatever shall seem a just wage at the end of a year and a day. Shadow is, of course, a Mephisto disguised as a Leporello, who brings into Rakewell's consciousness what is already latent there. He leads him to a brothel where he loses his innocence. When Rakewell tires of pleasure and utters his second wish, Shadow suggests that he commit an absolutely gratuitous act, namely, marry Baba the Turk, a bearded lady from the circus. (In Hogarth, he marries an ugly old woman for her money.) When this joke palls and Rakewell utters his third wish, Shadow enters with a fake machine for turning stones into bread. (One Hogarth engraving is concerned with The Philosopher's Stone.) Ruined and hunted by those he has ruined, Rakewell is led by Shadow to a graveyard. The year and a day are up, Shadow reveals himself and forces Rakewell to play a card game with the latter's soul as the stake. Thanks to the Devil's traditional overconfidence and the Divine intervention of Anne, Shadow loses his prey but before disappearing strikes Rakewell insane. The last scene takes place (as in Hogarth) in Bedlam, Rakewell believes himself to be Adonis and Anne, who comes to see him, to be Venus. They sing a duet of forgiveness and he dies.

Kallman wrote a brief article on the opera, also timed to appear shortly before the American premiere, for the *New York Herald Tribune*, 8 February 1953. The text below omits the newspaper's subheadings; in the sixth paragraph "passive sufference" is the reading in the newspaper, and is plausibly what Kallman wrote.

NEW STRAVINSKY OPERA: "THE RAKE'S PROGRESS"
TO HAVE ITS AMERICAN PREMIERE
ON SATURDAY

BY CHESTER KALLMAN

Creating operatic characters and situations is, from the librettist's point of view, rather like writing a series of ground-basses. They must be intriguing and various and the words that serve them must be direct. To say

that they are successful as characters and situations is merely to say that
the composer has found them a convenient basis for convincing song.

The hundreds of little details that this statement ignores are in the last
analysis just that—details. They may finally make all the difference be-
tween a good and a bad text, but if the librettist cannot play his role as a
goad, he is bound to fail from the beginning as an operatic dramatist also.

Our plot and characters were suggested by Hogarth in the sense that
a friend might suggest a subject to be treated; it is how and where we be-
gan, not the ideal toward which we worked. Otherwise the greater our
success, the more unnecessary our work would have been; Hogarth's
"Rake's Progress" had been there before us. At best, we might have writ-
ten the script for a documentary film; and Stravinsky would have done
better by composing a tone poem. Since this was the last thing he wanted
to do, we were only too happy to write an "original" libretto.

The subject itself suggested a picaresque treatment: if a "progress"
does not pass many points, it can hardly describe itself as such. However,
if, with a variety of incident, there needed to be a corresponding change
in the principal character (the Rake), both that character and the inci-
dents in which he took part might, by the very fact of their moving to-
gether, cancel each other's effectiveness.

This meant that we had to place both against a fairly constant back-
ground. Our subject made this scenically impossible, so our constancy of
background had to be supplied by other characters. This led us, on one
side to Anne Trulove, the Rake's ever-faithful sweetheart and, on the other
side, to Shadow, his man-servant and evil familiar. And with two charac-
ters of such obviously symbolic nature on our hands, it became clear that
our picaresque was, further, to be a fable.

Moreover, as the Hogarth Rake merely slips pictorially down to Bedlam
through a series of weaknesses, different in decor but similar in nature, it
also became necessary for us to move our plot by additional means. Here,
as we already were dealing with a fable, the fairy-tale device of three
wishes suggested itself. First, it gave us an over-all design for a story that
might otherwise have lacked sequence, and second, it made it plain that
the Rake's adventures would be willed rather than simply undergone. Al-
though passive sufference might be possible in a pictorial medium, a sing-
ing character, and our protagonist at that, had to be more positive to hold
the center of the stage for three acts.

Thus our subject itself helped us to find a framework for its own char-
acters and situations. It remained then to know these characters well
enough to give them words; more than that, words that immediately re-
vealed their state. For a dramatist using the spoken word, this would not

be necessary. He can afford to build his characters slowly, gradually filling in their outlines as he shows them reacting to the present situations and as he unveils their pasts.

In an opera, a character unveiling his past would have one aria in which to do so, and would have to go on at once. Nor could a librettist linger over his situations with deft conversational strokes, a hint here and a hint there throwing light on the speakers. When a character sings, he reveals himself, and he reveals himself usually in emotional extremes. It therefore falls upon the librettist to make each such revelation complete in itself, to make each represent either a facet or a progress report. At the same time, each of these revelations must make music essential to its expression. In other words, a librettist must be a peculiar type of illusionist; his text must *seem* to tell all, and must be only providing the music with the opportunity of *really* telling all.

This does allow him to introduce characters that dramatists would assiduously avoid. In our case, there is the heroine, Anne. Such unrelieved virtue would be an unmitigated bore expressed by words alone; but we have the luxury of knowing that we had only to indicate her in lyrics and Stravinsky would make her both interesting and a dramatic necessity.

Music also allowed us to indulge the fantastic side of our fable. The elaborate preparations a dramatist must make before he dare assail the supernatural and fantastic convincingly, were not great worries for us. By the immediacy of music, these elements become real on being presented. There is, after all, no question of disbelieving a good tune. When Nick Shadow turns time back and stops it, or when the Rake marries a bearded lady, Baba the Turk, in order to prove his freedom from passion and reason, the audience may not be certain for the moment *why* it is happening, but music makes them quite certain that it *is*.

Auden recorded an extempore talk on *The Rake* for the BBC, probably during a visit to England in June 1953. The talk was broadcast in the Third Programme, 28 August 1953, the day before a broadcast of the opera from Edinburgh. The text of the talk printed below is taken from a transcript made by the BBC and now in the BBC Written Archives Centre. A few words have been added in brackets to make the spoken text clearer on the printed page, and the punctuation of the transcriber's version has been lightly emended. The capitalization of the transcript has been retained, as it is similar to that of Auden's own typescripts and may derive from a comparison of the broadcast text with Auden's notes.

The story of "The Rake's Progress" as depicted by Hogarth is a bourgeois parable (the other side of it is The Virtuous Apprentice), the moral of which is the virtue [of] and rewards for economic abstinence; wine, women, song, cards, are not so much wrong in themselves as wrong because they waste money. In that sense, the subject as it is in Hogarth is not really very interesting for a contemporary Opera, and you have to see what can be done with it.

Secondly, of course, any Visual Art is so different from music that you have almost to start again. Supposing I have a couple of lovers. In a picture it's very clear that each causes something in the other. It's not so clear that each for themselves makes a decision. In music, it's just the other way round. If I have couple singing a love duet, it's very clear that each one is insisting on feeling something; it's not nearly so clear that the other partner is responsible for it.

Hogarth, of course, is not really interested in a story as such but in using this as a peg on which to—round which to—put pictures of eighteenth century English life, so that when Mr Kallman and I were faced with the problem of treating this subject we had to think a good deal about what on earth could be done with it except the basic line—here is a young man who comes in for a lot of money and goes to the bad and ends in Bedlam. Also presumably, somewhere, he makes a marriage with— we'll see what we did with that in a moment.

Well, the first problem is the problem of the characterisation of the hero. Music is such—I think—a dynamic Art that you cannot really have a passive character in an opera. The mere fact that they sing at all is such an assertion of the will that you simply cannot deal with a passive character. The trouble in Hogarth when you look at it, is naturally, (a) that the Rake always yields, (b) basically all the temptations are the same.

The first thing then: what were we to do with the Rake—Tom Rakewell? Well, we began by splitting him in two—himself and his malevolent alter ego or shadow. The shadow could then propose various things, initiate actions to which he could respond. The Rake himself we made more or less into a manic-depressive— that allowed for certain obvious kinds of musical contrasts or moods. He is a person who does not live in the present. He is very excited about the possibilities for the future; the moment that they become real, he loses interest in them. With regard to the past he can feel only guilt and despair so that he cannot accept it into the present, and repent.

On the other side of the shadow is the Good Angel—Anne—the soprano, who is just a very good girl indeed—who would be an awful bore at dinner but she just has to sing very beautifully.

And then the question was, What were the different temptations to be?

Well, it's easy enough to start. He wishes for money. The idea of wishing—we then used an old fairy-story trick of the three wishes. The first wish he makes is for money. Shadow appears and tells him his uncle has died and brings him the money. Well, the first temptation is the obvious one: he goes to a brothel and he loses his innocence. His difficulty there: that he should in the middle of this suddenly remember his girl friend whom he has left behind in the country, and sing a kind of "I have been faithful to thee Cynara in my fashion" kind of aria, though as yet he hasn't done anything at all.

Right. He runs around, has a high old time, and then that becomes boring. He then has his second wish, which is to be happy, and at that point Shadow comes in and suggests that he marry a lady called Baba the Turk who has a beard. The point about this is, of course, that it is an act—you've got to eat. That is to say, Shadow says, "Now the way to be happy is to be free and you can only be free if you act irrespective either of pleasure, the demands of pleasure, or the demands of duty. You must do something absolutely gratuitous." So he does marry this bearded lady. Baba the Turk on her side—I might say that the beard, so to speak, represents her genius, something which makes her what she is and at the same time cuts her off from other people, so that her mistake in accepting this proposal is that she tries to fit into an ordinary family life, to be an ordinary person, and of course the whole thing breaks down.

Then that doesn't work. The third wish is he says he has a dream which he wishes were true and that—then Shadow brings in a kind of obviously absurd machine for turning stones into bread. Here the temptation is to do good by magic without having to change—good works without having to change yourself, and of course he gets further and further removed from reality.

To bring the whole thing to a conclusion—to land him in Bedlam—we used another thing from a fairy story, which is the Card Game with the Devil, where needless to say, in the end, because the Devil is so confident, and through the intervention of love and so on, Tom wins the match against the Devil, but the Devil, before he goes, says: "Well, there is something I can do. For the rest of your life you are going to be insane." Here we could have the Bedlam scene; the question is what kind of insanity are you going to have? So we thought: Well, if in a way Bedlam is going to represent Purgatory, what does he need? Well now, he must live, so to speak, in a world completely of the present, that has no future and no past. So, in the Asylum, in one sense he's mad because he thinks that he is Adonis and that his girl friend is Venus and will come to see him, which she finally does, and that all the mad people are various characters in the

Elysian Fields and so on. So, though in one sense he's completely out of touch with reality, on the other hand now he has to suffer the present which he's always refused.

Right. His girl friend comes to see him. She plays the part; they have an Aria—a Duet, I mean—about forgiveness. She sings him a lullaby. (Of course, that's a rather bare-faced crib from *Peer Gynt,* I'm afraid.) And he dies. And being an *opera giocosa,* all right—the house lights go up and the characters come forward and sing a plain little moral.

Perhaps it might be of some interest just to take one scene in detail. Take the second scene, which is the Brothel. Now we start by deciding what you want to avoid. Well, you don't want to do the *Dreigroschenoper* again, and you want, obviously, situations that are singable. So the first scene having been, if you like, a garden in the country, the Garden of Eden, now we move into a Brothel, where the inmates—so to speak— have gone so far downhill that they are now completely innocent because they've lost the faculty of conscience. So that in one sense, this Brothel is a nursery, where they sing nursery rhymes almost. The contrast, of course—the dramatic contrast—depends on how they look and the actual things they say. Further, from the Rake's point of view, this is going to be an initiation, a loss of innocence—so that it is also a Church—Church of this World. In fact it starts off when the Rake is catechised, as if it were a Confirmation Service by Shadow: "I vow and promise in your name", as if he were a Godfather and the Madame who runs the Brothel were a Bishop, and the Rake says,

> One aim in all things to pursue:—
> My duty to myself to do

SHADOW.   What is thy duty to thyself?
RAKEWELL.   To shut my ears to prude and preacher
> And follow Nature as my teacher.

And so on—to the point where Shadow asks him to define Love. Well presumably what he is supposed to do is what Alberich does in *Rheingold,* which is to renounce Love. Instead, at this point he tries to leave and here Shadow performs a magic act which he's able to do because of the Rake's particular attitude about time, which is to turn the clock back an hour and say: "Look, you see the hours obey your pleasure. You can repent in your own time." He then sits down and this idea of initiation is carried on—lots of the other kinds of things that you do in initiations. When little boys go to school, they often have to sing songs, so this is the point right now. Obviously, you think, in this scene now, you've got to have a very beautiful Aria for Tenor. Now, what is he to sing about? What are the kind of keywords you can use—what are they? Love, Weeping, and so on. So you work it out and you think, so this is actually what he sings:

> Love, too frequently betrayed
> For some plausible desire
> Or the world's enchanted fire,
> Still thy traitor in his sleep,
> Renews the vow he did not keep,
>   Weeping, weeping,
> He kneels before thy wounded shade.

> Love, my sorrow and my shame,
> Though thou daily be forgot,
> Goddess, O forget me not.
> Lest I perish, O be nigh
> [In my darkest hour that I,]
>   Dying, dying,
> May call upon thy sacred name.

Right. In a sense, you can see that this emotion is slightly false, because otherwise he should go home if he really felt this. Anyway, they crowd round and Madam says she claims him and they go off and the others, the Chorus, sing a kind of Nursery Rhyme, like a sort of "Ring a Ring of Roses" kind of game.

Finally, after they've gone off, they break up and Shadow comes forward with a glass and he simply says,

> Sweet dreams, my master. Dreams may lie,
> But dream. For when you wake, you die,

turns the glass upside down and the curtain falls. That's just an example of how we organised one scene.

Nobody, of course, ever remembers the names of librettists of operas, so that it's not a thing to do unless you really enjoy it. I was at a discussion in New York and some playwright got up and said, "Well, what is there in it for us?"

Well, of course, there isn't very much, if you don't like doing it. If you don't like this curious mad medium. I'm not thinking about things like Folk Song where the music organisation is subordinate to the verbal organisation. No, I'm thinking of Opera where the words must be completely at the composer's disposal. The real thing when one writes an Aria—the first thing one has to do is excite the composer into composing a beautiful tune. Presumably there should be some words which can be caught—they have to be very carefully placed. For that reason the question of diction in writing librettos is important. You cannot use elaborate metaphors, for example, because you probably won't hear them. There is no point in saying, "Sleep that knits up the ravelled sleeve of care" because you just would not hear and get the metaphor. So that in a curious way, I think, the eighteenth century, which is not thought of as being a century which produced musical verse, did produce some of the best kind of style—of verbal style—for setting to music. It's no accident so many of our hymns come from the eighteenth century and some of our most famous songs. Think of

> Where'er you walk cool winds [*for* gales] shall fan the glade;
> Trees, where you sit, shall crowd into a shade.
> Where'er you tread, the blushing flow'r[s] shall rise,
> And all things flourish where you turn your eyes.

or the Dryden-Purcell:

> Every Swain shall pay his duty;
> Grateful every Nymph shall prove.
> And as these are known for [*for* Excel in] Beauty,
> Those shall be Renowned for love

where this placing of a few key words which do get over allows a freedom to the composer to write as he chooses. That seems to me very important.

Here I would just like to say why really I like Opera and why I am interested in writing libretti more than, I think, in writing plays I would be. Because, first and foremost, it is the most un-*verismo* of all media. It is so strong that accidents, as a matter of fact, don't break the spell.

I remember seeing a performance in New York of *Norma* and there were Adalgisa and Norma singing away as Ancient Druids, and the Stage Manager, without realising he was being noticed, walked on behind in evening dress, and it simply didn't matter a bit.

Furthermore, I think, Opera is pre-eminently an assertion of freedom. That because it's a virtuoso—most of us can't sing—and however unfortunate the lives of the characters are—they may marry the wrong person, they may get murdered, all kinds of things—yet you always feel their lives are a triumph. I think one should feel that in all art, even a tragedy is nevertheless a triumph. And in a time when sometimes we feel that our freedom is very restricted, and we are inclined to believe that we are puppets of Fate, an art like opera is a very valuable counteractive, I think.

Think, even, of a person like Lucia. There, poor thing, she's parted from her boy friend, she's gone mad, she's stabbed her husband. And then you see her brought down; she's in the coffin; she's dead. But you're not really sorry for her. No, five minutes ago she was singing D above

High C. And I can only say that if that's not like what the world is like, it's what the world *ought* to be like.

The libretto booklet accompanying the Columbia recording issued in 1964 included the following note by Kallman. The booklet's error in printing Trulove as Truelove, and other minor editorial slips, are corrected here.

LOOKING AND THINKING BACK

To think back to the writing of the *Rake* libretto is, for me, to re-experience the euphoria in which we worked. I myself was drawn into the collaboration casually, almost accidentally. When Auden returned from California with the outline that he and Stravinsky had constructed for the opera, he showed it to me; and I made some slight criticisms: I found the placing of Shadow as a character too vague, and the yawn that summons him the first time too likely to resemble a soundless note in the remoter reaches of the typical opera house. Those at least are the two quibbles I recall and they were not well received. Auden's "Don't just point out little flaws if you have no idea what to put in their place," was said more in anger than sorrow. But it did impel me to more active thinking, and the days of discussion and argument that followed, during which stray lines for possible arias came to my mind unsummoned, led us into actually starting to work on the libretto together.

Not that the start itself was auspicious; my first contribution, Shadow's announcement of the inheritance, was mercilessly trimmed by my collaborator, and all I wrote for days afterward is tinged, even now, with a slight flush of "artistic" outrage. There is, however, very little indeed left of those days in the finished work. Auden, after looking over the long dialogue in couplets that I produced, said "Charmingly done. I think you can manage to do it in four lines, though." I did.

For the most part, we breezed along after that as the musicodramatic possibilities of our characters took more and more hold on us. To be sure, I can remember taking sixteen steady hours to write a three-line aria of Anne's, and the whole of Sellem's *scena* being thrown out after some days of work, and entirely rewritten. And Auden did all of his portions of Act Three in those brief parts of the day when he was not suffering acutely with trigeminal neuralgia. Yet our daily meetings at lunch to swap ideas were always excited and high-spirited; we would chant the new material in possible French, German or Italian *translationese*, and the day that Baba the Turk was born and named we both laughed until we could no longer stand up straight.

And now, after sixteen years, how does the libretto look to its authors?
A difficult question. The words are so irrevocably clothed in Stravinsky's
music for us, they are hard to approach as separate entities. Certainly we
are pleased and proud to have in some measure provoked that music;
absolute self-congratulation ends about there. Some weaknesses, which
our enthusiasm bridged without noticing, have become apparent to us:
the profusion of opening arias in Act Two (especially following Anne's big
number in the act before); the similarity in structure of Scenes One and
Three in that same act; the difficult costume changes that Baba in Act
Two and Tom in the last act have to make between scenes; the impossible
difficulty of putting the stones-into-bread machine across.

Our characters, naturally, appear as mere outlines without their music,
and none more so than Anne. Anne is a soprano. Period. Words can do
nothing but indicate her. I do remember that many times, distracted by
the sheer invariable goodness of her simple soul, I found verbalizing her
a task approaching penance. My solution was to imagine the most conven-
tional elementary soprano gesture that might serve in the situation, and
then to write words that could justify and perhaps illuminate that gesture.
That, despite the spiritual exasperation she inspired, she has become
quite real to me, is entirely due to Stravinsky. I even rather like her.

Tom gave us other troubles. As a Hogarth figure he is exclusively acted
upon, all the way from brothel to Bedlam. Modeling clay can't sing, and a
singing Rake was what we wanted; so we endowed him with his three
wishes, both to suggest that he had a little will of his own, and to accentu-
ate the sinister quality that the subject seemed to call for. That he does
sing, and convincingly, can be counted as a success for the librettists, too, I
think. It must be admitted, though, that placing our tenor between
Shadow, who rather triggers the wishes he too wickedly grants, and Anne,
the voice of Good Pursuant, neat as the pattern is, leaves this protagonist
almost as passive as his Hogarth original.

And our dear Baba. She is a well-traveled (perhaps) Turkish lady with a
beard who marries an English heir and, so far as the librettists know,
never shares a bed with him. To have our Rake, like Hogarth's, only
tempted by the acquisition of money (he marries a rich old woman in the
engravings) seemed to us dramatically monotonous. Tom marries Baba to
assert his freedom from both passion and reason (the explanation is in
the text); and Baba is a bearded lady because we thought this a theatrical
way of highlighting Tom's motiveless motives. Once she had acquired her
beard and her fantastic collection, however, she asserted herself as an
independent character, and kept the center of the stage by rights. So
much so, that we regretted her leaving it, and could only make that up to

her by giving her as grand an exit as possible. Making her a cartoon, even a cartoon of the *acte gratuit,* was no temptation of ours. What mezzo-sopranos and stage directors are tempted by is another matter.

So much for our part. Sometimes Auden and I amuse ourselves by inventing imaginary additions to the text. We had thought then to "economize" on the cast by having the roles of Mother Goose–Baba and Trulove–Sellem, doubled; and as a result neither Mother Goose nor Trulove has much chance to show off. Many things made these doublings impracticable (though Jean Madeira, in New York, did perform as Mother Goose and Baba one night), so our projected additions are 1) a duet for Anne and Trulove between her aria and stretta in Act One, and 2) an aria for Mother Goose between the opening chorus and the catechism in the Brothel Scene. We have also thought of a possible "Smoker" scene to open Act Three. Here Trulove, searching through London for Anne, would meet Mother Goose and be temporarily distracted from his search: duet and exeunt arm-in-arm, somewhat in the line of what book jackets call "lusty Eighteenth Century." Incidentally, an Anne-Trulove duet would remove one fairly comic feature of the text: the only remark that Anne now addresses to her father, and she does it twice, is, "Yes, Father." But then, of course, she is a *very* good girl.

There was, now that I think of it, one more thing we provided Stravinsky with—an index of vocal types. He had asked us, when the libretto was completed, whether any particular voices or timbres of voice had been in our minds during our writing of the various roles. There had been. And so we loaned him a record album with discs of Steber (Anne), Stignani (Baba), Bjoerling (Tom) and Domgraf-Fassbaender (Shadow). I have never asked him, but I am fairly certain that these voices figure in the timbres of the score. More certainly, Baba's coloratura, conceived in terms of Stignani's range and evenness of intonation, clearly characterizes her with the same uncaricaturized *brio* that we wished her words to convey. Also, and more important, the over-all vocal thinking on the part of all three collaborators makes *The Rake's Progress* something much more than the polemical anti-Music-Drama it is too often hailed or dismissed as: it is a tribute to opera in much the same way that *Apollon Musagète* is a tribute to the dance.

When I think back to the critiques of the *Rake,* I can only wonder. One example stays in mind: the anti-*Rake* Italian critics, after the première, all seized upon Anne's first act aria as an example of "pure pastiche"; then each gave the name of the composer who had been so "obviously" imitated. So obvious was the imitation that each cited another composer: Handel, Gluck, Mozart, Rossini, Weber and Verdi!

Here I stop. There is no looking or thinking back to the music of this opera, certainly not for me. It is with me. It is there.

CHESTER KALLMAN
JULY 1964

Auden also wrote briefly about the opera in one of his 1967 T. S. Eliot Memorial Lectures collected in *Secondary Worlds* (1968).

Delia

After the success of *The Rake's Progress* Stravinsky envisioned a second opera on historical models with a libretto by Auden and Kallman, and discussed his plans with Auden in New York during November and December 1951. On 11 December Auden wrote to James Stern: "Stravvy wants to do another opera with us." On 24 December, Auden wrote to Kallman, who was then in Italy (letter in the Berg Collection):

> His idea is as follows: a one-act opera lasting about 50 minutes, capable of being performed by amateurs (i.e. colleges) all over the states. Orchestra of 18, also amateur. After talking with him, I see that what he wants is a Jonsonian Masque, (I have lent him the Masques to read) and the subject I have suggested to him which he likes very much is the wedding of Art and Science performed by the Goddess of Wisdom. The comic antimasque will, of course, present some of our bugaboos like Twelve-Toners, Sociologists etc.

Stravinsky wrote to his publishers, Boosey & Hawkes, on 8 January 1952:

> I had time before leaving New York to fix with Auden the main lines of an opera in one act. . . . Auden is "blue-printing" the libretto, and he will complete it with Kallman when the latter (whose collaboration is very valuable) will be back. The theme is . . . a celebration of Wisdom in a manner comparable to Ben Jonson's Masques. Nevertheless, we will not stick to any set style musically or otherwise. The opera will require about six characters; a small chorus, a chamber ensemble of about 18; several tableaux. (Quoted in Vera Stravinsky and Robert Craft, *Stravinsky in Pictures and Documents*, 1978, pp. 204–5)

The finished libretto resembled this plan only slightly, and was not at all a celebration of Wisdom.

Kallman returned to New York around 22 January 1952 and immediately began discussing the work with Auden. Kallman wrote to Stravinsky on 27 January 1952: "Wystan and I have already started that terrible and ex[c]iting work of getting our ideas in order for the new libretto; but until things are much clearer in our minds, we're maintaining a mysterious and, we hope[,] intriguing silence" (letter in the Paul Sacher Foundation). Auden and Kallman telegraphed Stravinsky on 28 March, "Libretto finished this instant". Three days later Auden flew to Europe, leaving Alan Ansen, who worked as his secretary, and Kallman to send the libretto to Stravinsky. On 13 May 1952 Auden wrote his Oxford tutor Nevill Coghill, "we finished another libretto (one act) for Stravinsky called *Delia*. Style early Tudor: it was great fun doing all the things prosodically which will make Saintsbury turn in his grave" (letter in Edinburgh University Library).

On 17 April 1952 Auden wrote Ansen that he was "waiting anxiously . . . to hear what Stravvy's reactions to *Delia* are" (letter in the Berg Collection). Ansen, who had evidently received the news from Kallman, annotated the letter "Apparent refusal / No". Stravinsky seems to have given no specific reason for his reluctance, but he was then discussing other projects and his musical interests had begun to turn away from the classical recollections of *The Rake*. (However, as late as February 1953, Lincoln Kirstein was tentatively negotiating with Harold Taylor, president of Sarah Lawrence College, over funding for a possible premiere at the college, so Stravinsky may not yet have made his refusal definite or clear.)

With no immediate prospect of a musical setting for *Delia*, Auden decided to publish the text as a separate work. On 8 June 1953, he wrote to Alan Ansen from Ischia with a request to send a copy of *Delia* to the editor of the polyglot literary magazine *Botteghe Oscure*, published in Rome. The typescript that Ansen sent lacked one page, so an incomplete text appeared in the [Autumn] 1953 issue of the magazine (vol. 12). A few copies of the *Botteghe Oscure* setting, repaginated, were prepared as offprints and given to the librettists, who circulated them, sometimes with minor corrections, among their friends. The libretto was never reprinted, although Auden adapted the final chorus as the poem "Lauds" in *The Shield of Achilles* (1955) and later collections.

Auden and Kallman made no statement of the division of authorship of *Delia*. Many of Auden's contributions can be identified from his early drafts in a notebook now in the Harry Ransom Humanities Research Center at the University of Texas at Austin. The notebook includes sketches for the entire opening scene between Orlando and the Crone, to the point where the curtain rises; Bungay's rhymed invocations in his first scene with Xantippe; Sacrapant's speech that summons a feast for Delia, and the Three Owls' Round that follows; most of the text from the start of the Pageant through the end of the Crone's riddling instruction to Orlando; and the entire conclusion of the libretto starting with the Quartet "We are safe. We are sound." Auden probably wrote other parts of the work also. The Paul Sacher Foundation has a scrap of manuscript in Auden's hand (dated June 1952 in Stravinsky's hand) containing Sacrapant's quatrain, "In the name of No-name who" (p. 106); the four lines are an acrostic of Stravinsky's first name. The quatrain beginning "Vision, descend" (p. 124) is an acrostic of Vera Stravinsky's first name.

Three significant typescripts of *Delia* survive:

TSA   The working typescript, now in the Berg Collection, probably prepared by Kallman, with extensive revisions and corrections in his and Auden's hands. Some of these revisions seem to have been made after this typescript was used as the basis of:

TSB   A typescript prepared by Boosey & Hawkes, probably in early April 1952. Some pages were evidently typed twice to incorporate corrections. Stravinsky's carbon copy, now in the Paul Sacher Foundation, has the first version of these pages, with minor corrections marked in an unknown hand; the copyright copy, registered 18 April 1952 and now in the Manuscript Division of the Library of Congress, has the second version of these pages. An incomplete carbon is in the Berg Collection, and two other fragmentary carbons are in a private collection.

TSC   A typescript prepared professionally from TSA, apparently after further slight revisions not reflected in TSB; corrected and revised in Auden's hand. This was the typescript Ansen sent to *Botteghe Oscure*, and is heavily marked for the printer. The typescript (lacking three pages) is now at the University of Texas. The page omitted when the typescript was sent to the magazine is now in the Berg Collection.

Alan Ansen prepared a further typescript, copied from TSC, for his own use and the convenience of the librettists. Two carbon copies of this typescript are in the Berg Collection. Ansen also copied into TSA the revisions found in TSC.

The text in this edition is based on TSA, but includes revisions marked by the authors in TSC and in friends' copies of the offprint of the *Botteghe Oscure* text (now in private collections). The page layout of the *Botteghe Oscure* text obscures the stanza forms of the typescript, omits a line of verse (in addition to lacking the page omitted from the typescript), and is defective in other details. The page omitted from *Botteghe Oscure* begins with Sacrapant's "Now you have heard this knight admit the truth" and ends with Orlando's "You may ask but not demand" (pp. 117–18).

This edition does not reproduce the distinction between sung and spoken passages that appears in two of the typescripts (TSA and TSC) as a guide for the composer. The distinction is described in TSA in an instruction following the listing of Place, Time, and Period: "NOTE. Lines typed in *red* are intended to be sung, lines typed in *black* to be spoken, with or without a musical background." This instruction, curiously, does not apply to TSA itself, which is typed entirely in black but has the passages to be sung indicated by red lines written next to them; the instruction does apply to TSC, which has an almost identical note in Auden's hand, and has the sung passages typed with a red ribbon. Editorial markings in TSC indicate that the editor of *Botteghe Oscure* at first planned to reproduce the effect of two colors by using roman type for sung passages and italic type for spoken passages, but then gave up any attempt to represent the distinction on the printed page. It was probably Kallman's idea to use ribbon color to distinguish verse and prose, but when Hans Werner Henze asked about reproducing a similar distinction in the printed libretto of *Elegy for Young Lovers*, Kallman replied on 10 October 1960: "About printing the spoken parts in a different way in the librettino. I don't really think it's necessary or desirable. On a small page, different kinds of print look fussy and are distracting to the reader. Also, I always think that an element of surprise should be added by not indicating divisions to the reader that will be revealed to him when hears the work" (see p. 670).

In this edition most of the sung passages are immediately recognizable from their stanzaic form. As a general rule, all verses preceded by headings such as "Aria", "Recitative", or "Round" are sung, but some specific instances should be noted. The Echoes that repeat Delia's name are sung (pp. 108–9). Sacrapant's line at the end of Orlando and Delia's Duet is spoken, not sung (p. 113). Sacrapant's line immediately preceding the Pageant is sung, not spoken (p. 114). The Pageant itself is spoken. The torrent of echoes and more echoes is spoken (p. 119). In

Orlando, Xantippe, and Bungay's Trio (pp. 122–23), the couplets between the longer stanzas are spoken. The Crone's speech between the two parts of the concluding Chorus is spoken (pp. 125–26). In TSC some of the sections typed in red are marked in Auden's hand "or spoken". The sections so marked are Bungay's Arietta (p. 111); the Quintet for Sacrapant, Orlando, Delia, Bungay, and Xantippe (p. 114); the Trio for Delia, Sacrapant, and Orlando (p. 118); and the Duetto for Orlando and Delia, and the Recitative A Capella for Bungay and Xantippe (p. 124).

Before the last revisions to TSA, many of the spoken sections were headed "Recit.", and these headings were reproduced in TSB. Most of these headings were then deleted, and the spoken sections have no headings in TSC. The text in this edition omits the headings deleted from TSA. The heading "Prologue" at the start of the libretto does not correspond to any further heading that might indicate the end of the prologue and the start of the main text, but the librettists never deleted the heading.

Auden wrote one late revision in TSC, altering the last line of Toil's stanza from "Earneth with sweat and in tears eateth his bread" to "With sweat shall earn, in tears shall eat his bread" (p. 115). In friends' copies of the offprint from *Botteghe Oscure* Kallman noted the printer's omissions and made one change in the third stanza of Sacrapant and Delia's duet, altering "More would I give you" to "More would I save you" (p. 107). Both changes are incorporated in this edition. The capitalization in Sacrapant's quatrain "In the name of Noname who" follows the scrap of manuscript in the Paul Sacher Foundation, which adds capitals in the second and third lines.

The title page of TSB includes a subtitle "Opera Libretto in One Act" below "A Masque of Night"; this subtitle was perhaps added by Boosey & Hawkes's typist. The list of characters in TSB includes the voice parts for the six main characters: Sacrapant, bass; Orlando, tenor; Bungay, tenor buffo; Delia, soprano; Xantippe, contralto; The Crone, speaking voice (or mezzo-soprano). Instead of listing the "Chorus" and "Various woodland animals" as in TSA and TSC, TSB lists a "CHORUS of elves (invisible), owls and other animals." This was probably the work of the typist, who misread the deleted, original speech heading for the first chorus, "Invisible CHORUS of elves" (where the word "Chorus" was typed and the rest added in Auden's hand) as "CHORUS of Invisible Elves".

The Magic Flute

§1 HISTORY, AUTHORSHIP, TEXT, AND EDITIONS

In the spring of 1955 the National Broadcasting Company commissioned Auden and Kallman to translate *The Magic Flute* for a television production by the NBC Opera Theatre. The text that Auden and Kallman delivered in the autumn was less a translation than an adaptation; much of the spoken dialogue was entirely new and the course of the action was drastically altered from Emanuel Schikaneder's original. (Carl Ludwig Giesecke's claim to coauthorship is generally dismissed.)

Auden and Kallman worked on their version during the summer of 1955. On 16 September, Auden wrote to Lincoln Kirstein: "We have been madly busy with *The Magic Flute* which is all done except for one piece of dialogue. The order of the second act and the characterisation is completely changed. (God suddenly informed me that the 2nd Priest was a reformed drunk)." The work was finished within a few days of this letter, and a typescript was registered for copyright on 6 October 1955. The production, with slight revisions in the text, was broadcast on 15 January 1956. George Balanchine was the stage director and Lincoln Kirstein was "Special Production Consultant." Peter Herman Adler conducted. *The Magic Flute, An Opera in two acts, Music by W. A. Mozart, English version after the Libretto of Schikaneder and Giesecke by W. H. Auden and Chester Kallman* was published by Random House on 16 July 1956 (the copyright date was 14 June). Faber & Faber published a virtually identical British edition on 30 August 1957. *The Magic Flute* is the only one of Auden's translations that he published in book form under the imprint of his usual publishers.

For the book version Auden and Kallman added a lengthy Preface and Notes, and a Proem, Metalogue, and Postscript in verse. An article similar to the Preface, and signed by Auden alone, appeared as "Reflections on the 'Magic Flute'" in *Center,* the magazine of the New York City Center, in December 1955, with two brief excerpts from the translation in texts that resemble that of the copyright typescript. The "Metalogue to The Magic Flute" (by Auden) appeared separately in *Harper's Bazaar,* January 1956, and in *The Listener,* 26 January 1956; Auden reprinted the poem in *Homage to Clio* (1960) and *Collected Shorter Poems, 1927–1957* (1966). Act II of the translation, in a version with text and stage directions differing slightly from those of the typescript and the book, appeared in *The Score and I.M.A. Magazine,* March 1956.

Some of Auden's rough drafts for the translation and the Metalogue are in a notebook now in the Berg Collection. Typescripts of the Metalogue are in the Paul Sacher Foundation in Basel and in the Harry Ransom Humanities Research Center at the University of Texas at Austin.

Only a few sections of the translation can be assigned to one or the other of the librettists. Draft fragments in Auden's notebook in the Berg Collection indicate that he wrote all the spoken dialogue among Tamino, Papageno, and the Ladies in

I.1; the spoken dialogue and Sarastro's concluding monologue in II.2; and the spoken dialogue in II.3. He probably wrote considerably more that can no longer be identified, perhaps all the spoken dialogue. Most of the verse and prose added to the libretto for the book version is Auden's work. The Proem and Metalogue are his; the Postscript was begun by Kallman and completed by Auden and Kallman in collaboration. A fragment of Kallman's first draft of the Postscript, with Auden's additions, is in a private collection. Auden apparently wrote the Metalogue around October 1955, at the request of *Harper's Bazaar*. Around 19 October he sent Stravinsky a typescript of the poem (now in the Paul Sacher Foundation) with the title "Metalogue to The Magic Flute / (to be spoken by the singer taking the role of *Sarastro* upon the conclusion of his aria: *In diesen heilgen Hallen.*)" An almost identical subtitle appears over the texts in *Harper's Bazaar* and *The Listener*; the latter inserts between the title and subtitle: "In Memoriam, W. A. Mozart, b. January 27, 1756". The typescript of the Metalogue at the University of Texas has its pages numbered twice, once as pages 1–3, once as pages 37–39, and appears to have been part of a typescript for *Homage to Clio*. The subtitle in this typescript, and in *Homage to Clio,* reads ("Lines composed in commemoration of the Mozart Bicentenary. To be spoken by the singer playing the role of Sarastro)".

The text of this edition is the revised text used in the Random House edition, with some slight revisions taken from the text printed in *The Score and I.M.A. Magazine* in March 1956, and some slight corrections. The Random House text derives ultimately from the copyright typescript, now in the Manuscript Division of the Library of Congress. This typescript may have been prepared by Kallman, and it has extensive revisions in Auden's hand. A second typescript was prepared in November 1955 by a typist at NBC who may have worked from a second copy of the copyright typescript with some further revisions beyond those marked by Auden in the copyright copy; a microfilm copy of this typescript is held by NBC. Marked in pencil on the NBC copy are minor revisions and other changes evidently made during rehearsal. A few of these changes appear in the Random House edition, sometimes with slight modifications; others are abridgements made for the sake of the broadcast; one change marked in the NBC typescript is an early, incomplete version of the substitution offered in note *b* of the published text (p. 184). The copyright copy has a few stage directions; the NBC typescript has none.

The text of Act II published in *The Score and I.M.A. Magazine* in March 1956 seems to be taken from a separate typescript prepared at some point during or after the preparations for the broadcast performance, with many small differences of detail from the copyright and NBC typescripts and the Random House text. Some of the differences seem to be verbal revisions to the text that was printed in the book, perhaps changes made before the book was set in type but which the translators neglected or forgot at the time they prepared the text of the book or read the proofs. Most of the differences, however, are matters of punctuation and capitalization, where the variations are probably less the result of revision than of Auden's or Kallman's inconsistent practice when preparing another copy. The division into scenes in *The Score* differs slightly from that in the other versions; where the Random House text has two scenes, II.3 and II.4, *The Score* has a single scene with the heading "Finale" where II.4 begins in the Random House text. The descriptions at the heads of the scenes tend to be more detailed and slightly different in *The Score* than in the Random House version. II.1 is headed in *The Score* "A Council-Chamber in the temple-city of the Sun. SARASTRO and PRIESTS assembled"; in the Random House text, the heading is "A hall in the Temple City of the Sun." Stage directions in *The Score* tend to appear more frequently, although they are sometimes less careful and less literary in style; in II.4, for example, Pamina enters in *The Score* "with a dagger in her hand", in the Random House text "holding a dagger before her". *The Score*'s stage directions sometimes underline the obvious; in II.2, for example, Papageno is directed to fill the glass from which he drinks. The stage directions and speech headings in *The Score* generally abbreviate the characters' names; Monastatos, for example, usually appears as "MON", the First Priest as "1st PR". Like the copyright and NBC typescripts, the text in *The Score* repeats some of the lines that are repeated in the musical setting; these repetitions are generally omitted in the Random House text. (However, *The Score* has a footnote on the first page: "This new version was commissioned by N.B.C. for television. As printed here, it is for reading, i.e., the musical repetitions are not written out.") Abstract nouns such as Light, Truth, and Love are capitalized somewhat more frequently in *The Score,* but the Random House text capitalizes some instances of these nouns that *The Score* does not. The British style of *The Score* lets Papageno try to hang himself with a "halter"; the American text of the Random House edition gives him a "noose" (p. 178).

Although the text of Act II in *The Score* seems to represent at least in part a later stage of the translation than the text published in book form, I have not attempted to graft Act II from *The Score* onto Act I from the book. The style of the stage directions, the treatment of musical repeats, and other elements of the text vary too greatly to allow this solution, and most of the variants are slight. I have, however, taken the liberty of adopting some readings from the dialogue in *The Score* that seem to be clear improvements over other texts. These readings are:

II.2: page 158, line 16, comma after "Stole them"; page 158, line 20, italics in "Sarastro *says*"; page 160, line 2, "You hear, Tamino!" for "Then wifeless, lifeless?"; page 161, line 9, question mark after "without a wife"; page 163, line 30, comma after "Hearts may break"; page 165, line 24, "if Love has in it" for "If Love have in it" (*The Score* does not capitalize "Love"; the capital in Random House's "If" seems an editorial misreading); page 165, line 31, "Advice I know seems heartless:—Try to rest" for "Advice, I know, seems heartless. Try to rest"; page 167, line 31, "Die. Who shall die?" for "Dies. Who shall die?"; page 168, line 33, "Day and Night" for "Day and night"; page 169, line 1, "Yet, tamed by harmony" for "But tamed by harmony".

II.3: page 171, lines 5–6, "Truth" capitalized twice; page 172, line 14, "Money" for "money"; page 173, line 8, "he doesn't, but" for "he doesn't but"; page 173, line 19, italics in "I know you *think* you know"; page 173, line 20, italics removed from "Do you *think* you know"; page 173, line 35, "'Tis he, 'tis he" for "It's he, it's he"; page 174, lines 1–2, "*You,* but you don't . . . / You love *her*" for "You, but you don't . . . / *You* love *her*"; page 174, lines 5–6, "She loves *you.* / You're very stupid. *She* loves *you*" for "*She* loves *you.* / You're very stupid. She loves *you*"; page 174, line

28, "*I* know *how*" for "I know *how*"; page 175, line 8, "she gone to? Do I merit" for "she gone? O do I merit".

II.4: page 175, line 13, commas added in "dawn, on earth and ocean breaking,"; page 176, line 37, "Then Love" for "Then love".

II.5: page 177, lines 35–36, "Love" capitalized twice.

II.6: page 178, line 21, "O world so lovely" for "O world, so lovely"; page 178, lines 23–24, "Crown" and "Temple" capitalized.

II.7: page 179, line 25, "Yes" and "No" capitalized; page 180, line 2, "So, you wicked" for "So you wicked"; page 180, line 29, "I will be your faithful" for "I shall be your faithful".

II.8: page 181, lines 31–32, "Day" and "Midnight without" for "day" and "midnight with no"; page 182, line 2, "Night" capitalized.

I have corrected one obvious error in the Random House text ("class amongst" for "classed amongst" in the Metalogue, p. 153) and adjusted lineation and layout where the copyright typescript or the version in *The Score* is clearly correct. In II.2, the 2nd Priest's exit line before the Quintet (p. 159) reads "To be without me" in the Random House text, but reads "To do without me" in a pencil revision to the NBC typescript and in *The Score;* this reading is followed in this edition. (The NBC typescript, before the pencil revision was made, followed the copyright typescript's reading: "To stay alone here".) Later in II.2, in the last line of the trio of Tamino, Pamina, and Sarastro (p. 165), I have followed the copyright typescript and the text in *The Score* in placing the stage direction "[*Aside*]" in the middle of the line rather than at the beginning.

This edition follows the copyright typescript and the Random House text in their American spelling and punctuation. The typescript of the Metalogue that Auden sent to Stravinsky has British spellings, but when Auden published this poem in *The Listener* he acknowledged its American manner by appending a footnote to the line that names Bryn Mawr, Vassar, Bennington, and Smith: "The British reader should substitute the names of Newnham, Somerville, etc."

The Faber edition was evidently set directly from the Random House text and sometimes mistakenly adds spaces between lines at places corresponding to the Random House page breaks. The only notable difference between the two editions is typographical: the Random House edition uses letters for the endnotes, while the Faber edition uses numbers.

In the broadcast, immediately before the overture, while the television screen showed a bust of Mozart, the voice of the singer who took the role of the 2nd Priest was heard reading some lines of verse that Auden had evidently adapted from his Metalogue to introduce the televised opera. The text below is from the as-broadcast typescript held by NBC:

> Seldom may we recall the birth
> Of one who did no harm on earth.
> Today we come with grateful heart
> To pay our homage to Mozart
> Who has for nigh two hundred years
> Brought heavenly joy to mortal ears.

In honor, then, of this event
THE MAGIC FLUTE we now present,
Your minds and senses to regale
With music and with fairy-tale.

§2 AUDEN AND KALLMAN ON THE TRANSLATION

Each of the translators wrote a piece on the translation for a major New York newspaper. Auden's appeared in the *New York Times,* 8 January 1956, and Kallman's in the *New York Herald Tribune* on the day of the broadcast, 15 January 1956. The two pieces follow; the titles were evidently provided by the newspapers, and Auden's piece had the subtitle "A Translator Discusses the Problems of Changing an Opera's Language".

PUTTING IT IN ENGLISH

BY W. H. AUDEN

The task of the transliterator is simple enough to state. His version must convey the general sense of the original words and reproduce all points of emotional and dramatic intensity. It must conform to the musical prosody, be singable and, in addition, competent verse—not operese. And the literary style must be in keeping with the period in which the opera is set or felt.

In the case of the English language, his first difficulty is, of course, the scarcity of the pure open vowels required for a high tessitura. A translator of *The Magic Flute,* for instance, looks at a couplet that is easy to translate and scribbles down:

> *Now let my approach be courageous and sure:*
> *My purpose is honest and noble and pure*

only to find that he is expecting the poor tenor to sing "pure" on a sustained high G.

Fortunately for him, few librettos have the literary distinction of *Falstaff* or *Der Rosenkavalier.* Usually, in translating the arias, he has a free hand, provided he conveys the general emotion expressed. It is in dramatic interchanges, where the exact sense of a particular word may be the essential point, that the difficulties occur.

Thus, one of the most beautiful moments of *The Magic Flute* occurs in the finale of Act I, when, in reply to Papageno's frightened question as to what to say now, Pamina cries out: "Die Wahrheit!"

Dramatically, nothing will do here but the literal sense: "The Truth." But the prosody demands an extra syllable. It is impossible to spread truth over two notes and sing "troo-hooth" without sounding funny. "Truthful" has no intensity and any word added for the second syllable detracts something. I do not believe any satisfactory solution is possible; we, certainly, have not found it.

In his relation to the composer, the translator is in a different position from the original librettist. The latter writes his verses without any notion of the music to which they are going to be set, but the translator knows the music already and probably knows it better than the text.

If, as one assumes, he is a competent versifier, he can, without too much difficulty, copy the form of the original verses, their metres, rhymes, etc., and know that, if he does this accurately, his words will conform to the notes. It does not necessarily follow, however, that he should be content with this. The ideal goal he should set himself, whether attainable or not, is to make the audience believe, when his version is performed, that his are the words that the composer actually set.

Since every language has its unusual peculiarities, this can mean that a too faithful copy of the original may sometimes be a falsification. In comparison with German, for example, English has far fewer syllables upon which a run can be made or that sound well when spread over more than one note.

Because of this fact, we have, in a number of places, supplied more syllables than exist in the original. If it be asked: "Is the effect on the ear the same?", the answer is: "No. The English sounds more staccato than the German." It is our view—debatable, of course—that, if it is to sound natural and, incidentally, audible, in English, it should be more staccato.

Whatever liberties he may take with the text, the first principle of a conscientious transliterator is: No tampering with the notes.

He may, nevertheless, come to places where he feels that an exception ought to be made and that, could he summon the composer from the grave, the composer would approve of an alteration. If such an occasion does arise, it is always, I think, one in which the particular structure of the notes is, so to speak, an accident of the verbal prosody of the original libretto rather than an essential musical idea.

In the case of a work like *The Magic Flute,* it is very understandable if many ears are irritated by the slightest deviation from a score they have known and loved so well and for so long, just as my British ear is irritated when Americans pray, "Our Father, *who* art in Heaven" instead of "*which* art."

To such, one can only reply that one has every sympathy for them, but that *The Magic Flute* neither can nor ought to be identical with *Die Zauberflöte,* and that to judge the former, whether favorably or adversely, it should be listened to as if for the first time.

TEXT OF "MAGIC FLUTE" HAS
SPECIAL PROBLEMS

BY CHESTER KALLMAN

There is no opera I know of that asks for translation more than *The Magic Flute*, and for a translation that is also an interpretation. That is not to say that there would be any reason or excuse for transporting the action to the hospitable and mythical Dixie which has had to put up with guests as unlikely as *Carmen, Aida* and *The Cherry Orchard. The Magic Flute* must remain in its own Never-Never Land, of course; but that land itself cries out for sharper definition which a translator should attempt to provide.

The original libretto's reckless confusions of action and character are notorious; and those familiar with the German are also very aware of the linguistic difficulties abounding in the text. It would be difficult, in fact, to think of any opera that represents a greater musical triumph over its libretto.

Yet when all this has been said, another fact remains: the libretto is fascinating. Its very confusions give the opera an interest that it might lack had Schikaneder and Giesecke stuck by what was ostensibly their original intention: to write a straight fairy-tale about the rescue of a young girl from a wicked sorcerer. But the famous switch in purpose gave rise to a series of ambiguities. As the plot now stands, Tamino achieves his victory and helps to defeat the vengeful Queen of Night by using means provided him by the Queen herself. What we therefore have in *The Magic Flute* is a fable about Instinct and Reason, or Heart and Mind, their struggle, their purification by means of each other, and their reconciliation in the marriage of Tamino and Pamina.

Unfortunately this material has been obscured by two things. First, the inability of the original librettists to handle the subject they appear to have stumbled on unwittingly; second, the apparent willingness of the public to accept the story of *The Magic Flute* as merely a sublimely ridiculous scaffolding for Mozart's music. I need not enter here into all the contradictions of plot that no amount of allegoric interpretation can wish away. Perhaps the most obvious is Pamina's appearance in the Second Act Finale with a dagger that had been taken away from her earlier; and there are others. We have tried, in our version, to rearrange these matters in such a way that they will no longer bother those who have taken the trouble to notice them. Though not all of them, naturally, can be clarified this afternoon because of the cuts necessary to fit the opera into a two-hour telecast.

Rearrangement entailed other changes, and these were also based upon a wish to correct both the original bungling and the subsequent public "tolerance." Schikaneder, who created the role of Papageno, appears to have fancied himself as a comedian; and though there is historical evidence that Mozart found his horseplay excessive and irritating (there is practically none in the musical sections), it has remained "traditional." And audiences, obviously vexed by a lack of any clear narrative thread, have seized upon this one consistent wrong-note and helped, by their over-delighted reactions, keep the tradition alive.

We found, once the rest of the structure had been somewhat clarified, that a good part of the farce simply had to go. The basic conception of Papageno as a natural "child of Grace" remains; but his raids upon the more solemn affairs of the opera have been cut to a minimum and placed in the context of the English Pastoral tradition. That is, pastoral in the sophistication of its diction, and in the sense that the "natural" world serves here as a commentary on the more sophisticated world of its "betters," the world in which suffering is a necessary preliminary to salvation.

We believe that our arrangement restores the action to the intimate scale of Mozart's score, thus giving *The Magic Flute* greater unity and at the same time making it more appropriate to TV presentation.

A review by Joan Cross of the British edition of the libretto ("The Magic Flute: Auden v. Dent", *Tempo,* Winter 1958) compared Auden and Kallman's version unfavorably to the standard translation by Edward J. Dent. Auden and Kallman published a reply in the Spring 1958 issue of *Tempo:*

THE MAGIC FLUTE:
AUDEN-KALLMAN v. CROSS

"It is not easy," writes Miss Joan Cross in her review of our translation of *The Magic Flute,* "to be scrupulously fair to a new translation." For a singer who has studied and performed one version and neither studied nor heard the other, it may well be impossible. It is natural and proper that, out of personal affection for and loyalty to the Grand Old Man of Opera in English, Miss Cross should wish to defend the late Professor Dent against two American upstarts, but it might have occurred to her that, under the circumstances, a review were better left to a less partial judge.

Let us take a few points.

(1) "Time and again Auden errs musically." Professor Dent was a famous musicologist who knew a great deal more music than we do: It does not necessarily follow, however, that he knew the score of *Die Zauberflöte* any better. To the best of our knowledge, in every case where we have in any way departed from the musical metrics of the original, we have, in either the Introduction or the Appendix, noted the fact and stated our

reasons for so doing. Miss Cross has every right to take issue with any or all of them, but justice demands that she deal with our reasons and not leave the reader to suppose that the departures were due to an inability to read the score. For example, we provided two versions of *Bei Männern welche Liebe fühlen,* in one of which a syllable is set to every quaver, while in the other the syllabification of the original is preserved, not, as Miss Cross suggests, because we were uneasy about the first but because, if a translator does anything controversial, he should be prepared to submit his practice to an empirical test. Let a singer try out both and come to his or her conclusion as to which, in English, is nearest in spirit to Mozart's music. We ourselves have no doubt as to what, in the long run, the answer will be.

One finds it distasteful to criticise in public the work of a fellow-translator but, since Miss Cross quotes Professor Dent's version with the comment that "there can hardly be any *musical* doubt as to which is better," we are obliged to point out two details which bother us if they do not bother Miss Cross.

> The kindly voice of Mother Nature
> Wakes Love in bird and beast and flower.
> There's not on earth a single creature
> That can resist its tender power.

(a) Line Two begins with the words *wakes love, wakes* getting an unaccented quaver and *love* a two-quaver slur after the bar-line. At the tempo (Andantino) the relative weight of the two syllables, both as sound and meaning, make them awkward to sing without lengthening the first note or giving it an emphasis to which it has no *musical* right.

(b) The even-line rhymes in the German are *nicht-Pflicht,* pure monosyllables each set to a quaver. Professor Dent's rhymes *flower-power* are not true monosyllables so that, even if singers pucker their mouths to sing *flow'r-pow'r* or are willing to sound like stage Englishmen and sing *flah-pah,* they are going to find it difficult to be understood or musically at ease.

(2) Miss Cross quotes our version and Professor Dent's of the opening lines of Tamino's first aria. Of ours she says "Alas, these two lovely lines have a false musical accentuation": of his—"Though less beautiful, it is written with respect for the musical phrase."

Well, let's look.

Musical metre. (Larghetto).   ♩ | ♪. ♪♪♪♪♪ | ♩   *(bis)*

German   Dies Bildnis ist bezaubernd schön,
                                    Wie noch kein Auge je gesehn!

Dent   O loveliness beyond compare,
                                   Was ever maiden half so fair!

Auden-Kallman   True image of enchanting grace,
                                   O rare perfection's dwelling place!

We simply wish Miss Cross would explain "what we done wrong." At a
larghetto tempo *True* can be sung as metrically as *O*. Or is it the secondary
accent upon *of* which she objects to? But Dent similarly accents *-ness,* a
musical error of the same magnitude if error it be, for, in accenting *ist,*
Mozart has departed from the spoken rhythm of the German line in the
same way.

(3) "Time and again Auden's most 'readable' text is too obscure for
the direct and instantaneous understanding of the dramatic situation.
The beauty and invention in his use of words defeats its own end, and the
musicologist (Dent) who does not read half so splendidly, makes his points
more easily and clearly."

In support of this charge, Miss Cross cites nothing, unless she considers
obscure the two lines she quotes from Papageno's song

        The lark, the ruddock and the willow-wren,
        And the jolly nightingale I ken.

We should find this hard to believe did she not, after misquoting

        In vain do all the pretty little creatures fly
        When they the *tall* bird-catcher spy. (Her italics.)

complain: "This presents the already sorely-tried opera director with a
casting problem." The point, Miss Cross, is how Papageno looks to the
little birds. (Italics ours. Adjective omitted by Miss Cross.)

Without making any great claims for our translation, we can say that
the praise which, as Miss Cross admits, it received in the United States
after the television performance was not on the basis of its readability—it
was unpublished—but because listeners, rightly or wrongly, found it sing-
able and dramatically clear. And American Television, as we are sure Miss
Cross knows, is not Little Theatre or even Third Programme.

(4) Miss Cross thinks it was presumptuous of us to transpose some
scenes in the Second Act for the sake of dramatic clarity—"surely a task
for the musical director and *his* sense of the importance of the continuity
of the musical scheme." Maybe. But can she really believe that, in a Televi-
sion Studio, the translators would be permitted to make such transposi-
tions *without* the musical director's wholehearted support?

(5) "What is more interesting is his conversion of the rather dull dia-
logue into spoken verse. It is with a sigh that one discards it, but few

singers excel in the spoken word, and long hours would be spent in perfecting the use of this convention."

If singers were quite as poor speakers as Miss Cross seems to suggest, the only way to avoid embarrassment would be to cut the spoken dialogue altogether. In fact, however, she is unjust to her profession. Rehearsal time is even more limited in the Studio than it is in the Opera House, but, while coaching the singers in their spoken roles, we were pleased to have a theory of ours confirmed, namely, that, since they are trained to think in measures, singers are much better and quicker at learning to speak verse than actors from the spoken stage, most of whom to-day are metre-deaf.

One last point. Miss Cross subtitles her article *Auden v. Dent.* We ourselves, needless to say, never thought of our translation thus, not even as *Auden-Kallman v. Dent,* the subtitle to which, if Miss Cross had to insist on her thesis, caution as well as good-manners should have guided her. In this collaboration, as in *The Rake's Progress,* we aimed at a style "common" to both parties and, within that style, each worked at what he found most congenial. The result, we hope, has a wider range of expression than either could have achieved by himself. One would have thought that the title-page was sufficient evidence but, since Miss Cross ignores the fact of collaboration in reference to *The Rake's Progress* and forgets it in the second half of her comments on *The Magic Flute,* it would seem that, once some people have decided on their argument, what they read is not going to make them change it. For the record, it may interest Miss Cross to learn that, of the excerpts she quotes or refers to in the second half of her article, whether to praise or censure, only one was written by Auden.

New York, March 1958.   W. H. AUDEN
                                           CHESTER KALLMAN

Elegy for Young Lovers

§1 History, Authorship, Text, and Editions

Hans Werner Henze moved in 1953 to Forio d'Ischia, where he became friendly with Auden and Kallman. On 1 July 1954 Auden told Elizabeth Mayer, "I see a lot of Hans Haense and am very impressed with what I have seen of the Opera he is writing now [*König Hirsch*]" (letter in the Berg Collection). Henze moved to Naples in the winter of 1955–56, but he continued to see Auden and Kallman on Ischia. "In the late Autumn of 1958," Henze wrote in a program note for *Elegy for Young Lovers,* "I first asked my friends Auden and Kallman to write a libretto for me. We corresponded between Naples and New York, and met at last in the summer of 1959 in Auden's country house in Lower Austria. There followed lay-outs and rough sketches, and in December [in fact January 1960] the libretto was ready. Only small changes and revisions have later been necessary" (*Glyndebourne Festival Opera,* 1961, p. 40). Auden and Kallman's account of their initial plans for the opera appears in "Genesis of a Libretto" (p. 245).

The Süddeutscher Rundfunk had commissioned Henze to write a chamber opera for performance at its Schwetzinger Festspiele; *Elegy for Young Lovers* was accordingly first performed, in German, at Schloss Schwetzingen, on 20 May 1961 by an ensemble from the Bayerische Staatsoper. The performance was produced by Henze and conducted by Heinrich Bender. The first performance in English, with minor cuts, was at Glyndebourne, 13 July 1961, conducted by John Pritchard; Henze conducted the last three of the eight Glyndebourne performances. A more detailed history of the first outline of the libretto and evolution of the text appears in §2 and §3.

On 25 January 1960 Auden wrote Henze, "For your curiosity and the historical record, here is the list of whom wrote what", but the list itself is lost. (This letter and the rest of the surviving correspondence between Auden and Kallman and Henze is in the Paul Sacher Foundation in Basel.) Auden wrote Monroe K. Spears on 19 February 1962, "about 75% is by Mr Kallman." Kallman told a friend that he had written more than half the libretto. Fragmentary drafts in one of Auden's notebooks in the Berg Collection of the New York Public Library indicate that Auden wrote at least the following: in Act I, scene 2 (except possibly the positive reviews of Mittenhofer's works, which Kallman sent Henze separately), and scenes 3 and 5; in Act II, scenes 1–3, 5, 7 (perhaps also 4 and 6), and the dialogue between Hilda and Elizabeth in 9; and in Act III, scenes 6–8. (In *Secondary Worlds* Auden acknowledges authorship of these scenes from Act III.) This leaves about 65 percent of the text unattributed, and Auden's higher estimate in his letter to Spears suggests that Kallman may have written almost all the remaining scenes. Fragments of Kallman's typescript of an early draft of scenes 1, 4, and 7–11 of Act I, together with a fragment of Auden's typescript of I.5, are in the collection of Robert A. Wilson. Kallman's letters to Henze indicate that he also wrote II.12 and III.1, and suggest that he probably wrote II.8 (at least the second half), II.9 (first half), II.11, and II.13. In conversation with a friend Kallman claimed to have written the lines "Irregular stools, / Inspiration cools", in the duet in I.2, but these lines appear in Auden's rough draft. The complete typescript and most of the typescripts of later additions and revisions are apparently lost.

The libretto of *Elegy for Young Lovers* was published as a pamphlet by B. Schott's Söhne, in Mainz, on 5 June 1961. (The German version of the pamphlet libretto, translated by Prince Ludwig of Hesse in collaboration with Werner Schachteli and Henze, had been published earlier, on 15 May.) A similar English text appears in the miniature score published by Schott on 18 May 1961 and the piano score published on 10 July 1961; these texts lack some slight corrections and changes to the lost final typescript that Auden sent to Henze and that were incorporated in the pamphlet libretto. The text in the pamphlet libretto seems quite clean, but lacks titles like "Scherzo" and "Trio" to which Kallman referred in his letters to Henze. It probably also lacks some descriptions of musical numbers of the kind that Auden and Kallman usually included in the texts they presented to their composers, and it presents the text in the form that resulted from cuts and changes made by the librettists at Henze's request. This edition introduces some slight emendations in the text and layout of the pamphlet libretto and includes corrections that Auden and Kallman sent to Henze but which did not appear in the printed text.

As in the pamphlet libretto, the text of the opera is followed in this edition by Auden and Kallman's essay "Genesis of a Libretto". Henze wanted the essay to appear in the front of the booklet; Auden and Kallman preferred it to appear in the program. But Kallman wrote Henze on 10 October 1960: "If you really think the librettino must have it, though, then it should come as an after-piece. Placed before the text, it will make people look for things in the text it mentions, and thus get an unbalanced impression from their reading." It also appeared in German translation in the souvenir program book of the 1961 Schwetzinger Festspiele, and, in English, in the souvenir program book of the 1961 Glyndebourne season. Kallman also wrote a synopsis (see p. 670), which appeared, unsigned and in a German translation, in the booklet with the detailed program listings of the 1961 Schwetzinger Festspiele, and, signed by both librettists and in English, in the 1961 Glyndebourne souvenir program book.

§2 THE INITIAL PLANS

Henze first asked Auden and Kallman to collaborate on an opera in a letter, now lost, written late in 1958, to which Auden replied from New York on 6 January 1959:

> Delighted to get your letter. Chester & I would love to collaborate with you on an opera, provided we can earn some money thereby.
>
> What would you say to this idea? A re-incarnation of the Daphnis-Chloe story, set in an imaginary Forio in about 1910. One of them would have been brought up by grape-growing contadini, the other

by pescatori. Gnatho, the rich queen, would be a version of Norman Douglas, the anti-Christian romantic "Pagan". L[ycaenion] (Our copy of the novel is in Kirchstetten and I have forgotten her name), who teaches Daphnis the arts of love, a German Baronin from San Angelo, etc., etc. Though one wouldn't need a proper chorus, we think we should need a quartette of Forian Gossips at the side of the stage throughout, who would amorally comment upon the action and invariably get everything wrong, i.e., They would think that X & B, Y & A were having affairs when it fact it was X & Y, A & B, they would predict that N won't marry M when they do, or that K will marry L when he doesn't, etc. A straight romantic love story with a buffo background.

Henze's reply and any further correspondence early in 1959 has been lost. Auden recalled that his and Kallman's "original idea was that we would have four or five characters, each of whom was mad in a different way" (BBC discussion of the opera by Auden, Kallman, and Henze, broadcast in the Third Programme, 13 July 1961). They apparently decided during the spring to make their central character an artist-hero, but the details of the libretto were worked out only when Henze visited Auden and Kallman in Kirchstetten during the summer. Later that summer Auden and Kallman prepared a detailed draft outline of the first two acts before starting work on the text itself.

The typescript of the outline, now in the Harry Ransom Humanities Research Center at the University of Texas at Austin, was apparently typed by Auden and has notes and corrections in his and Kallman's hands, and comments in Henze's hand. Differences in layout and typing style between the outlines of first and second acts suggest that the second was prepared after a pause of days or weeks. The outline never included Act III; Auden said during the 1961 BBC discussion of the opera that he and Kallman had sent Henze "basic outlines [of] Act I and II", and he wrote in an undated letter to Henze late in 1959: "We are into the third Act (which will be quite short, I think)", a comment that he would not have made had Henze seen a scenario of Act III.

The text below slightly regularizes Auden's chaotic typing and silently incorporates the librettists' corrections and changes to the typescript of the outline. The initial letters used to identify the doctor's son are G.R. in Act I, T. in Act II. This change is reflected in a change marked in the dramatis personae after Act I was finished, but not incorporated in this text for the sake of clarity: the change alters the son's first name from "Gundolf (*Toni* to his friends)" to "Toni". Probably at the same time, the Doctor's first name was changed from Josef to Wilhelm. Some of the other characters' names were altered in the course of revisions to the libretto itself: Gundolf Hinterhofer became Gregor Mittenhofer (see p. 667); Egon Mauer became Josef Mauer; and Hulda Mack became Hilda Mack.

Elegy for Young Lovers

A SINGSPIEL

DRAMATIS PERSONAE

GUNDOLF HINTERHOFER (The Master), a famous poet
DR JOSEF REISCHMANN, a Physician
GUNDOLF (*Toni* to his friends) REISCHMANN, his son, godson
of the poet
EGON MAUER, a mountain guide

ELIZABETH ZIMMER, a young woman (c. 25)
HULDA MACK, an old lady
Die Gräfin CAROLINA VON KIRCHSTETTEN, patron of and unpaid
sec[retary] to poet

Outline of Act I (The Return of the Bridegroom)

Scene. The terrace of DER SCHWARZER ADLER, a mountain inn.
Time. A Spring morning in 1910.

1. Forty Years ago (Recit.)

> H.M. He left at dawn after our wedding night to conquer the
> HAMMERHORN for me. I dressed in this dress and came down to
> wait. He is still on the mountain. He speaks to me. He wishes me
> to wait until he returns. I live in that morning ever. All to-
> morrows are his words alone.

2. The morning chores (Scherzo)

> Secretary is going through mail. A train whistle is heard in the valley.
> Doctor comes in. Brief interchange (spoken?) about his son who is
> arriving on that train. (Son is studying to be a doctor, but wants to go
> in for Public Health. The R.'s are Jewish, by the way.) Sec resumes
> duties. Much rushing about. G.R. enters and is immediately put to
> work by his father (boiling syringe?) which he carries out good-
> humoredly. Doctor sings a *quatrain* about sacrifice to "Art". Scherzo
> resumes. Doctor notices that Secretary is not looking well and sug-
> gests taking her temperature. She refuses. The master hates illness
> around him and she has too much work to do. She sings the *quatrain*
> about sacrifice. She places the master's pocket-money for the day in
> the accustomed place. (A daily ritual. Nothing is ever said by either
> about finances.) In the last section of the trio, Sec reveals her slight
> distrust of Elizabeth. (She has caught her reading Hofmannsthal?).

The doctor's protests can complete the information needed about the Master and his latest "Muse".

> (*Note.* Elizabeth's background. Father a Lutheran Pastor in North Germany. Fine character and intellectual. Mother, really a passionate nature, but, because of it, very puritanical. E.g., Beethoven forbidden in the house as too emotional. We shall discover in the Second Art that, *sexually,* the poet is more attractive to her than the boy. What she is beginning to find impossible is his utter selfishness and his, to her, *boring* affectations.)

3. Entrances and Vision

Dr (spoken): Well, I'd better be getting ready to go fishing with the Master. Sec: O dear—I've got such a headache this morning I forget everything. The Master asked me to tell you that he means to stay in[,] he has had a "feeling" that H.M. is about to have one of her visions. (Her information about H.M.'s history and why the master comes to see her be planted.) Enter G.H. with E.Z. on his arm (introduction to *aria*). Ceremonial good-mornings. G.H. greets his godson and presents him to [E.Z.]. He has his hands on their shoulders as they shake hands. (A circuit is made. H.M. immediately goes off into a vision. All are "frozen" in their places as she sings her first verse.)

Aria. In the falling snow what was meant to be, shall find its meaning. Near the cold heavens the coldness of earth shall be revealed and what is mortal shall be fed to the immortal even as young lambs are sacrificed on an altar. What is fated is not what is just, for the old gods are dead.

The circuit breaks. The others leave G.H. and H.M. alone together and go to sit on the terrace, in sight, but officially out of earshot. While grouped and deaf in a convention, what they do are veristic acts, looking through telescope, reading, knitting, exchanging glances, etc. as H.M. continues

Aria. The meeting of youth and age is Spring on the mountain. The glacier moves and it is youth which is revealed dead. When all is lost for love that All includes love itself. An old man's passion is a warm day in winter. The passions of youth which cannot last because they are false are like a snowfall in Spring. In the unseasonable snow what should have ended in coolness will end in cold . . . etc.

Then suddenly H.M. stops and *speaks*. "The vision is ended" and goes out to sit on the terrace, taking the place of the Sec who comes in for

4. Worldly Affairs

The Sec hands G.H. carefully selected reviews. He reads from them, pleased but contemptuous of critics which leads him on to remarks, mock quotations etc. from his contemporaries which leads him again into reminiscences about his own life. (All this very buffa. He is feeling in fine form this morning.) He breaks off and asks the Sec for the typescript of some writing of his which she then hands him. He discovers some errors. This sets him off on a sarcastic tirade. (He is not *really* angry, but becomes intoxicated with his idea of being sarcastic and abusive.) He reminds her of her past, her attempts to be a writer, her rebellion against leading the useless life of a lady in Society, her decision to do something with her life by taking care of him. But what use is she? She can't spell, she can't cook . . . there follows a whole list of little mistakes that at one time or another she has made. She tries to apologise, on the edge of tears, and to explain that she is not feeling well. This makes matters worse. Nonsense. She's just hysterical. She has no business to be ill etc. Then a fancy strikes him and with a laugh he begins to tease her. It must be the spring and the arrival of a handsome young man that is affecting her. Young girls do fall in love with men as old as their fathers, but young men do not woo women old enough to be their mothers. Particularly if they are *plain,* my dear. The Sec starts to howl hysterically. G.H. shouts (spoken voice) for the doctor. For god's sake do something about Carolina. She's impossible this morning. I'm going to my room for my spiritual exercises now. In fifteen minutes I shall come down to take a walk with Elizabeth. Please see that she's ready and by the way, you might check her health too. There's no knowing what people will catch in this changeable weather. G.H. leaves. He has just got inside the door when he remembers something, comes back and takes his pocket money from the place where the Sec hid it.

5. Tidying Up (a buffa aria)

The Doctor recommends medicines to the Sec, and explains how even Genius depends upon physical chemistry, that soon, thanks to medicines, human beings will live to be two hundred. At this point the bell of the local church is heard tolling and Egon, the guide, enters to announce that the body of H.M.'s husband has at last come out of the glacier (forty years before he had fallen down a crevasse).

6. Who is to tell her?

Sec wonders first if H.M. should be told at all. Mightn't it upset her visionary powers? Doctor says that would be to her good. Sec then (being both annoyed with G.H. and not averse to making trouble for

Elizabeth should anything happen) suggests that Elizabeth would be the best person to break the news. She herself isn't well and anyway has never been good in dealing with women. The Doctor agrees and they call E over and explain what she has to do. The Doctor fetches H.M. and he and Carolina leave E and H.M. alone.

7. The Revelation

E. You've been here forty years.

H. Forty years? You say that. It was yesterday. And now there is nothing but to-morrow.

E. You must listen to me.

H. You must listen to me. The mountain is death. Death divides yesterday from to-morrow.

E. You have been alone too much.

H. You have been alone too much. Do not imagine you will not be alone to-morrow.

E. How can I tell you?

H. How can I tell you? O my child, you must learn that there is a love more dangerous than love.

E. (*Standing behind H and embracing her. H repeats her phrases in canon*). O my child, repeat my words after me carefully so that you may learn, that I may learn how yesterday, my wedding day, I came here with my bridegroom, and how to-day, to-day, to-day he went away and now to-day, to-day, to-day, where the glacier ends they found him. Time moves, the glacier moves, moves day by day. The glacier, time let go their prey, and to-day they found him where he lay, cold, my bridegroom conqueror cold and dead.

H. . . . cold and dead.

E. to-day, to-day, to-day . . .

H. to-day, to-day, to-day . . .

> (*Silence. G.R. has entered quietly and watched the above scene. He is moved, more perhaps by the unsuspected warmth and kindness of Elizabeth than by the news itself.*)

H (*spoken*). How late it is. I am tired. Leave me my child.

> (*G. H. enters noisily.*)

G.H. (*to E*). Eleven o'clock. Time for our walk my dear.

> (*As they leave, E catches G.R.'s eye. He gazes after her in rapt affection.*)

8. When follies cross

H (*cabaletta*). He has returned. It is day at last. After so long I am free from yesterday, free from to-morrow's whispering. Yes, it is to-day I sing. My bridegroom, what you promised and what I promised has been fulfilled. We are free from our vow.

G.R. (*cavatina—andantino*). To love at last. In her alone I find the love I have waited for so long. My yesterdays without her were nothing. Only to-morrow with her has meaning. My bride, in you shall the promise of love be fulfilled.

(*Curtain*)

Act II (The Emergence of the Bride)
(Early afternoon)

1. A Passion

Toni is standing where we left him when the curtain fell on Act I. It is some days later; he is differently dressed. Elizabeth enters and they rush into each other's arms. A duet:—ardent on T's side, tender and even slightly hesitant on E's. She insists on telling the Dichter. He reluctantly consents—he would rather they just ran away together—but is finally persuaded. They kiss to signify their accord. On the kiss Lina enters, screams and then calls for the Doctor so that there shall be

2. A Confrontation (Aria)

Carolina. Well, Doctor, what do you say to this? Haven't I enough to do keeping order here without having to keep your son under my eye as well? The Master has only to take his afternoon nap, for his Muse to start behaving like an alley-cat. A fine thing! It isn't enough that Hulda should have renounced having visions just when the Master has started a new poem based on her last one—he's having terrible trouble getting on with it—and, of course *I* have to bear the brunt of his *natural* ill-temper. Now he's to be further upset. Doctor, you speak to your son, and I'll take her in hand. The Master will be down for tea at 4.15 and everything must be tidied up by then. Come with me, Miss Zimmer.

Spoken

E. What a little comedy, Gräfin. What can we say to each other? It's the Master I have to speak to.

C. I know him better than you do. Let's talk this over like sensible *practical* people. (*E & C retire to the terrace, leaving Doctor and son down stage.*)

3. Practical Advice (Two separate duos, alternating with each other, so that now the audience hears the women and now the men.)

Woman to Woman

C. Well, Fräulein, just what do you think you're doing?—or who do think you are? (*Silence*) You have your place here as we have ours; if that place doesn't suit you, you'd better leave. (*Silence*) The Master's work must *not* be disturbed. Can you understand that? (*Silence*) Nor do I think you quite young enough to find your age an excuse for this shameless and unappetising behavior. (*Silence*) Well, Fräulein, what have you to say for yourself? Nothing? I am not surprised. Look at me!

E (*whose back has been turned on C during all this, turns round and faces her, and laughs*). And you, Gräfin, aren't you forgetting *your* place? After all, you didn't hire me, so you're hardly in a position to dismiss me.

Man to Man

D. My son, have you any idea of what you're doing?

T. I'm in love; that's better than any idea.

D. What about your future?

T. She is my future.

D. But what do you intend to do?

T. Live with her, live for her.

D. And your career?

T. Career? Where have you got with yours, Father?—Do you call it a life—looking after one old man? I don't. But at least it should make you understand why I am going to devote my life to one woman. And the love I shall give her is a finer thing than all those medicines you pump into the Master, as you call him. *Master*! The word makes me sick. What the world needs is more young lovers, not older poets.

D. We're not here to discuss my career, but your future. How will you live? You're just on the threshold of your chosen profession. Only your Final examinations and then your future opens. Don't tell me that, if you start having a love affair now, it won't interfere with your studies, because you know it will. And then, when you start your hospital work, it's not going to do you any good when people find out that you have a mistress as they certainly will. You can't marry her. First because marriage to a girl whose past is known to the world is out of the question from any point of view, mine, your friends', the world. Secondly, you haven't got the money to marry. And lastly, don't forget that you are a Jew and what that means in our society. To succeed a Jew has not only to work harder and be brighter than a Gentile; he has also to be more respectable.

T. We'll go away somewhere.

D. What will you live on?

T. We'll manage.

D. You won't, unless you are willing to live on her money. Are you?

T. No.

D. Well, hunger might make you change your mind, but if you do, you come to dislike all the sooner and regret your ruined career all the more sharply. You mustn't think that I have anything against Elizabeth as a person. I like her very much. But she's not for you. Speak to her, tell her what I've said, and ask her what *she* thinks. She seems to me a very sensible girl, and I believe she will realise that I am talking sense. You think my career has been a failure. Perhaps it has. Then, don't let your father go to his grave with the knowledge that his son is a failure too. (*He walks away*)

T. What does anything matter without love—success, reputation, all the world can offer—if love is lacking, they are meaningless.

(*The clock strikes*)

4. Clarifications (It is possible that all of this is spoken or in secco. As in the preceding section, there are two dialogues going on simultaneously. Lina and the poet down stage. Toni and Elizabeth on the terrace.)

C (*leaving E and coming down stage to T*). Elizabeth is waiting for you on the terrace: you'd better decide quickly what you are going to do. The Master is coming down for his tea.

> (*T joins E on the terrace. The Poet enters, sits down. C joins him. Tea is brought. The poet drinks his tea noisily and takes cake heartily. C refuses to eat or drink anything.*)

Secretary & Master

Poet (*wearily*). Where is our prophetess?

C. In the village drinking and playing cards.

P. So that's the end of that. It's all the more important that I get some edelweiss as soon as possible. I need it, badly.

C. What you need is peace and solitude. Certain people are obviously unwilling to respect your schedule and create disturbances. They take advantage of what they consider their special position in order to prevent a creative process they cannot understand and therefore resent. You should be alone.

P (*sharply*). Certain persons? I hate that sort of language. Who are you talking about? Elizabeth, of course. And who else?

C. I didn't want to tell you, but . . .

P. She and Toni are in love. That's no news to me. But it's quite meaningless.

C. Kissing in public places.

P. Less dangerous than behind locked doors. Ask Elizabeth to join me at tea.

Boy & Girl

E (*boiling with rage*). You were quite right, darling, and I was wrong. Let's go *now*. I can't stand this atmosphere another minute. Let's go and pack.

T (*who has been impressed by his father's argument in spite of himself*). But aren't you going to tell him what's happened?

E. At first I thought I ought to. But after being talked to by his bodyguard as if I were a call-girl, I see no reason why I should, really. Let her tell him. As she says, she is so *practical*. If I talked to him I might put his precious schedule out. I mustn't forget my station.

T. You shouldn't let Aunt Lina upset you. She's crazy and doesn't know what she says. I think you or I *must* tell him. And I want you to talk with Father. I know he can be awfully silly sometimes, but he's good and kind, and I can't bear to see him so worried and unhappy.

E. Talk. Talk. You're getting as bad as the others. I feel as if I didn't want to speak to a soul for a week.

T. Elizabeth, darling, don't.

E. I'm sorry.

C (*coming from the tea-table to the terrace*). Excuse me for interrupting, but the Master would like you, Elizabeth, to join him for tea. I didn't tell him anything.

> (*E goes to join the poet, leaving the others on the terrace. C in one chair, the Doctor in another and T looking out at the mountain.*)

5. *Further revelations*

P. Sit down, my child. You seem so thoughtful. Are you cross with me.

E. Not cross.

P. I thought that my anger with you for telling Hulda about her husband might have made you angry.

E. It did. I thought you were unjust.

P. And you were right. I was unjust. I had come to depend on Hulda so much. Too much, perhaps.

E. She has spent forty years of her life mourning. Surely, you won't grudge her a few years of sanity. She is enjoying herself for the first time in her life.

P.   I suppose she is. I didn't think of that.

E.   You only thought of yourself, as always. You never think of anyone else.

P.   No, there you're mistaken. I wasn't thinking about myself. I was thinking about a half-written poem, the blank half of a sheet of paper still to be filled. But I suppose that seems just as selfish to you.

E.   Surely you should have thought of her, of her right to *live*, before you thought of anything else, even a poem. Isn't that what you are always saying in your work. A whole generation is grateful to you for having taught them that.

P.   Then you might see that writing poems is what gives *me* the right to live. But let that go. I apologise—to you and to her. You are right. And I have learned—once again—that a poet must depend upon no one but himself—it is a lesson one learns many times in life and each time in a different and unexpected way. I see, also, my dear, my lovely Muse, that in pleading Hulda's case you were really pleading for your own right to live.

E.   I wasn't thinking of myself.

P.   Weren't you, my child? Perhaps you didn't think so. But when we plead another's case—unless we are paid advocates or professional debaters which you, my dear, are certainly not—the feeling we put into our words comes from our own hearts. You could never have spoken as you did if your desire for freedom had not been involved.

E (*meditatively*). But what should I wish to be free *for* . . . or *from*.

P.   For? Just to be free, perhaps. From? Many things. Me, first of all. Let me look at myself through your eyes. What do I see? A poseur and a windbag, with no spontaneous human feelings. And then my surroundings—the time schedule, the hero-worship, the whole atmosphere of "holy art". Ridiculous, isn't it? Yes, but I need it, I need all this mechanical unreality as a protection, to keep safe that which is really precious, that little store of real feelings which I dare not waste on externals. You enjoy reading poetry, I know, but you have no conception of what it's like to be a poet. Never to feel anything without wondering if it's poetically usable, never to sit on a chair or look at a mountain without testing the possibility of it as an image. And then, what *are* one's real feelings. Was it a real chair, or only a rhyme for despair? Do you wonder [if] this posing, this routine is necessary—just to keep going? Do you wonder if, as a person with other people, I am often a complete failure? But there I go again, you see. Making an interesting theatre of my weaknesses for your benefit. Forgive me again.

E (*moved*). Forgive me for ever reproaching you. I have nothing to forgive *you*.

P.   And promise me this. If you ever want to get away, tell me. It would be only natural if you did.

E.   I'll tell you. I promise.

(*P kisses her gently on the brow. C comes forward.*)

C (*to P*). Your room has been aired and you can work there now. It's just after five. (*P leaves after embracing E*)

E (*to C, impulsively*). I'm very sorry I upset you.

C (*coldly*). Upset *me*. You worry about your own problems, Fräulein, and don't try to imagine those of others. (*Exits*)

6. My Own Problems

E.   My own, my own, the little planet flies,
The snow-flake falls through ever colder years:
My own, upon a human cheek it dies,
Not in its own but in another's tears.

(*Toni enters timidly*)

7. Others

T.   Have you told him?

E.   No. Perhaps there's nothing to tell.

T.   Nothing to tell?

E.   Nothing he doesn't know already. He knows me better than I ever realised, just as he knows himself better than I could have imagined. But how much do we know about each other? What do I know of you or you of me? What can we tell him about us when we don't know it ourselves?

T.   But we know that we love each other.

E.   Love? I loved my father. (*Here some autobiographical stuff, rather flatly told as if about a third person and only half-believed.*) Well, now you know something about me.

T.   I know nothing. Do you love me or don't you? That's all I want to know.

E.   I think I do. I thought I loved your godfather. Then I was certain that I didn't. And now . . .

T.   What has happened to you?

E.   Toni, listen to me, listen carefully. I'm trying to explain to you and to myself what has happened to me.

T.   You're not yourself. Why all these riddles.

E. Perhaps you're right. No, I'm not myself. Was I myself when I took my little inheritance and sought him out, determined to become his mistress.

T. Don't. Don't.

E. O yes. I was going to live, live, live! Isn't that what we were going to do too, Toni?

T. We will, we will.

E. Everything happened as I planned it and then, I found myself trapped, bored, exasperated. Was I still myself? And then you came. He was always posing; you were yourself. He declaimed; you spoke. He knew all the meanings of the word love; you loved, loved me. You said you did, didn't you. Were you yourself then?

T. I did and I meant it. You said you loved me. Didn't *you* mean it?

E. Toni, I was wrong about him. I don't think I can leave him. Toni, listen . . . and please don't be hurt. The truth is that I'm one of those women who are attracted by older men.

T. You mean that you find *him* . . .

E. Yes, very. I should even if he were five times as impossible and a tenth of the poet he is.

T. I don't believe it. He's hypnotised you. It's not natural. I'm not going to have you tortured like this. We['re] going to have it out with him this minute.

(*He strides angrily towards the Poet's study [this might be a summer house]. C appears and intercepts him.*)

8. *The Wrong Time*

C. What do you think you're doing?

T. I must see the Master.

C. This is not the time. You know that quite well.

T. It's my time. (*Pushes past her and hammers on the door.*) Come out here. Something must be settled at once.

(*At the noise the Doctor comes forward and the Poet appears at the door, looking mildly curious and tolerantly amused. E buries her face in her hands.*)

T. So everybody's here. I'm glad. Because you've all got to know sooner or later. I love Elizabeth. She said she loved me. I want her to leave with me immediately. She said she would. Now something seems to have happened. Perhaps she is afraid of the Great Bard. Well, now that the Great Bard knows, she has nothing to be afraid of. Elizabeth, you have to make your choice now. And I want everyone to know what that choice is, so that they cannot accuse us later of having deceived them.

(*During this harangue, the Doctor and E try to interrupt him but without effect. C looks on stonily.*)

D (*to Poet*). Please forgive him. He doesn't know what he is saying. I've told him it was madness, I've told him that it was impossible. He'll be ruined. Forgive him. Stop him.

P. Please, Wilhelm, remember that someone else is involved as well as your son. (*Turns to E*) My child, you should have told me, as I asked you to. Has my love only made you afraid of me? Did you think me so selfish or so weak that I could not endure the truth? Then, the love you bear me—or bore me once—must have misled you. Come, my dear, tell me—that is, if you have anything to tell. (*Turns to Doctor*) Why do you ask me to forgive Toni? As if there was anything wrong about falling in love. And, after all, he's my son, too, in a sort of way. I have none of my own. (*Turns back to E*) You knew that, too, didn't you? We could all have been more open with each other. Well . . .

T. You devil!

D. Toni!

T. Elizabeth, I implore you. Tell him that you love me. Don't you see what he is doing?

E. Why should my heart be weighed in public like this? Leave me alone, all of you. (*Sits down and begins to cry*)

P (*to E*). I'm sorry. I should have known. I thought at first that it was Toni who was deceiving himself. Now I see that I was. You must both of you forgive me. This scene is intolerable, I know, but it has begun in public, so in public it must end. You're not choosing between two suitors, you know. What you and I have been to each other will remain with us both for ever. You are simply deciding whether you want to take the step now which, sooner or later, you must.

Trio

T. Don't leave me! Don't abandon me now. All I shall have to live with and feed on is bitterness. How could I work, how could I do anything? How could I believe in myself if you don't love me?

D. You can't love him seriously if you're not certain. He has his work to do. He's young. He'll get over it. Tell him the honest truth.

P. If you didn't love him, you would have told me so. Don't be afraid of hurting me. I'm not that young. Tell me the honest truth.

C (*spoken*). A madhouse!

(*Enter Hulda, accompanied by the guide. H is very smartly dressed and smoking a cigarette in a long holder. She is a little tiddly and makes a grand entrance. She pauses to take in the scene. All are silent and embarrassed.)*

9. The Bride

H. Won't someone say: This is all that was missing? So. It's all come out, has it? Goethe-woethe must be quite upset. (*To E*) Or didn't you report for duty on time? Or did our headmistress here catch you with your hand in the cookie-jar? I suppose it's all very serious but, from where I stand, you all look rather silly.

P. Frau Mack, be so good as to leave us alone.

H (*to P*). All in good time, Headmaster. If you will make scenes in railway stations, you can't get rid of the people who are waiting for trains. Very good that. Put it in a poem. Go on, back to the study and get it down before you forget it. At least, it's better than the woozy nonsense you used to steal from me. (*To C*) Duchess, bring me an Armagnac. I can't climb hills as well as I used to. O well, it doesn't matter. Egon will get it, won't you, duck. Egon's a gentleman which is more than I can say for some of the ladies present. You can use that, too, if you like, Virgiletto.

P. In that case, Frau Mack, we'll leave the station.

H (*ignoring him and going over to E*). What have they been doing to you, dearie. Don't cry. What you need is a drink. Here, have some of mine.

E (*after taking a sip*). (*Suddenly*) Frau Mack. Do you think I'm a whore?

H. O la-la, what a naughty word to use. No I don't think you're an "unfortunate woman" as we said in my day, and I think you're much nicer than what we used to call a nice girl.

E. Thank you. (*Rises*) Toni, will you marry me?

T. Elizabeth!

E. I don't mean immediately. But when you're in a position to.

T. Whenever you like. I'd wait years if you asked me to. I love you so.

D. It won't do. Stop them.

H (*to E*). You are making a mistake, my child. That isn't your future. And in any case, what you need at this moment is a holiday and a good time. I've taken a fancy to you. Why don't you come away with me and we'll both have a good time.

D. Don't do this to *my son*!

P. The young lovers . . .

E. Thank you, Frau Hulda. I will come with you, if you like. But I must settle this matter before I leave. Doctor, I know you don't like the thought of having me as a daughter-in-law . . .

P.   I can guess why not. Wilhelm, you're out of date. We've come a
     long way since La Dame aux Camellias. We've been good friends
     for a long time. For my sake, give them your blessing. The young
     lovers. Let me break a precedent and tell you about the poem
     I'm writing.

         Into an old cold world come two young lovers. It is not their
     intention to defy this world, but the Eden they create about them
     is a reproach to all, and many turn away. But if only one other
     person can be found who dares to befriend them, their mission
     will be fulfilled, and this person, too, will be admitted to Eden.
     Well, my poem seems to be coming to life.

         Here they are—the young lovers who have brought us a pre-
     cious gift from afar.

H.   Never heard such rot in all my life. You'd think they were selling
     a patent medicine.

D.   I see I've been behaving like a tyrannical father in a novel. I'm
     sorry. God bless you both!

H.   Now that's settled, the sooner we get off, the better. If you stay
     any longer you'll become as crazy as they are.
         (*They are about to disperse when the Poet stops them with a
         gesture*)

10. One More Thing

P.   Elizabeth, you know how dear you have been to me, how dear
     you still are. And you, too, Toni, though you may not know it; I
     love you almost as a son. Soon you will both go your ways and
     perhaps we shall never see each other again. But before you go, I
     have one request to make, the last thing I shall ever ask of you.
     In a few days, as you know, I shall be sixty. Well, I want you to
     give me a birthday present. I want you to go up the mountain
     and bring me back some edelweiss. I have always found that
     sleeping with some under my pillow inspired my dreams. I know,
     Elizabeth, that this would mean staying on one more day, but I
     should like my last memory of you to be of the young girl who
     was kind enough to bring an old man inspiration.

H.   *You* may stay another day, but *I'm* leaving by the morning train.

T.   Couldn't you stay this one more day. It's the least we can do for
     him. And, for my sake too, I should like you to stay. We've never
     had a single whole day alone together.

E (*to H*). Couldn't you wait for me?

H.   Not here. I cannot wait to get back to the world. It must have
     changed. Life is much faster, I expect. But join me there as soon

as you can. Don't dally. The air up here is too thin. Look what it
did to my lamented spouse. Sent him rushing off up a mountain
on his wedding morning. Thin air and poetry, my dear—a poor
diet. I shall go and pack (*To C*) Gräfin, I was very rude to you and
I apologise. Let's part as friends. It's so long since I did any pack-
ing that I've quite forgotten how. Please come and help me. No-
body could teach me better.

>   (*Exeunt H and C*)

P. and T.   Well? . . .

E.   Alright. I will. You both deserve it. Goodness gracious, that
sounds conceited, doesn't it. Between the two of you I must be
getting spoiled. (*To P*) Can I bring you some more tea.

P.   No more tea to-day.

D.   Besides, it's time for your tonic.

P.   No more tonic, to-day, either. I shall wait for the edelweiss. Now
all of you, go away and amuse yourselves. I want to sit and think.

>   (*They leave. Egon, the guide, who has tactfully withdrawn dur-
>   ing the preceding scenes, comes forward.*)

Egon.   Mr Hinterhofer: about that edelweiss you wanted me to get
you. I'm afraid you may have to wait a few days. The weather
report predicts bad storms.

P.   It doesn't matter. There's no hurry. I made a mistake. I find that
I have some left still.

>   (*Exit Eg.*)

11. *The Real Third Act Begins*

>   (*Gundolf make a noise like an enraged sheep and stamps his feet
>   like an angry child.*)

P.   BAA! What a bunch! A son who won't listen to his father. A
fatherless bitch looking for an old dog to run away from. A doc-
tor who wants a rhyming laboratory. A Countess who wants to be
the governess of her private Emperor. A lunatic who refuses to
be mad. Even an alpine guide who is afraid of a little bad
weather. BAA. Why don't they leave me alone? Why don't they
all DIE?

>   (*In his rage he picks up some piece of bric-a-brac and looks
>   around for a good place to throw it. Suddenly he finds himself
>   face to face with Hulda who has come to fetch her umbrella. Si-
>   lence. He puts the object down.*)

H (*wagging her umbrella at him*). Naughty! Naughty!

>   (*He roars like a bull and goes back into his study slamming the
>   door. Hulda collapses into a chair, laughing uncontrollably.*)

>   (*The Curtain Falls*)

§3 THE EVOLUTION OF THE TEXT

On 13 October 1959 Auden wrote to Lincoln Kirstein: "Are in the throes of a
libretto for Hans Haense—the main character is a cross between W. B. Yeats and
Stefan George: the setting, a mountain inn in Germany or Austria, the time c.
1910. The management of the action will owe something to Noh plays." On 22
October he wrote to James Stern:

> Chester and I are in the throes of a libretto for a German Composer
> Hans Haenze. Our main character is a cross between W. B. Yeats and
> Stefan Georg and is very libellous. (Setting, an Austrian mountain
> resort: time, c. 1910). Like W. B. Y., he gets ideas from a lady who has
> visions. She has been sitting in the inn for forty years waiting for her
> bridegroom to return from the mountain he went up on their wed-
> ding morning. Why I am telling you all this is that we want to steal
> from you your war-time muffler,* for her to have been knitting dur-
> ing this period. May we?

Late in October, probably shortly before they returned to New York, Auden
and Kallman sent Henze a typescript of the first act and the outline of the first and
second. The full text of the second act seems to have followed later in the autumn.
Henze's comments on the first act prompted Auden and Kallman to write revisions
that they sent before the end of the year; the revisions are only mentioned, not
described, in Auden's undated cover letter, but they evidently included a new text
of a "Doctor's aria" in I.6 that was omitted from the final text. The original text of
this aria appears on a fragmentary page of Kallman's draft typescript now in the
collection of Robert A. Wilson:

DOCTOR [taking little boxes and phials from various pockets and lining them upon
      the table].
  Well, well. Now, now.
  What have we here?

               My waistcoat and jacket
               Have pill-box and packet
               In every pocket—
               An orderly file
               Of what you will.
               It's worth your while
               To give it a try.
               Whatever befall you

*Stern, like many other British subjects, began to knit a scarf at the start of the First World
War. He could not bring himself to stop when the scarf reached a normal size, but continued
for several years until it reached a length of sixty feet. He kept it under his bed when he was
not working on it. On the day of the Armistice, he burst into tears and put the scarf away in
his closet. Auden told the story, without naming Stern, in an interview printed in the
Swarthmore College *Phoenix*, 14 December 1943.

Or too long ail you,
It cannot fail you.
The progress of medicine
Since Thomas Addison
Makes Thomas Edison
Seem very small fry.
In due season
I see no reason
For any person
Who is not willful
About being baleful,
And is properly pill-full
Ever to die.

This immediately preceded Carolina's line, "Numb, Doctor" (p. 204).

On 12 January 1960 Auden and Kallman sent the typescript of Act III, with revisions to Act II, a "Dramatis Personae with observations", and "Observations, prosodic and other, for the translator". (All these typescripts are now lost, but the cover letter is in the Sacher Foundation.) On 18 January Auden wrote James Stern: "Chester and I have finished our libretto—your muffler is in."

The revisions to Act II that Auden and Kallman sent on 12 January 1960 included at least one cut that can be tentatively identified from a long letter that Kallman sent Henze the next day. This letter contained detailed suggestions about the musical treatment of the work. (In my account of this and other letters, I have used the final versions of the characters' names, not the early versions in the typescript, although I have not altered quotations from the letters themselves; also, I identify scenes not by the page number of the typescript, as in Kallman's letters, but by the scene numbering in the published libretto, which evidently differs slightly from the numbering in the original typescript.) Kallman pointed out that in II.9, "Originally, the brief bit from Eliz's 'Doctor, I realize' down to Hint's 'Admit your reasons were inept [passé *in the final text*]' was in the same stanza form used by Hinty earlier in the scene. The cuts have altered that, but the stanzas are still sufficiently alike for this one to serve as a 'link' with the earlier material"— apparently a reference to "My dear, conventionalities" and "Forgive me, both" in II.8. Kallman also told Henze that if Toni's second speech in II.8 were too long, he could cut "the five lines after 'afraid of him' and go from there straight to the final 'Tell them! Tell them!'"; Henze apparently made a slightly smaller cut instead.

On 25 January 1960 Auden wrote Henze: "We will do the synopsis and a little piece on the conception of the libretto right away." On 8 April he sent "a little piece ['Genesis of a Libretto'] about the theme of the opera which I hope will soothe the shocked. Also another copy of the outline [synopsis]—can't imagine how the first went astray—and Act I with full stage directions. The others will follow in due course." Kallman noted in same letter that they had made "a few slight verbal revisions in the text".

Soon afterward Kallman sailed to Germany, arriving at Cuxhaven on 21 April.

Henze met him there and, during a stay in Hamburg, discussed revisions of the libretto. Auden, who had been in England, met Kallman in Berlin in late June, and they returned to Kirchstetten at the beginning of July. In a letter to Henze dated 6 July 1960 (but probably sent two or three days later) Kallman wrote that he was enclosing Toni's aria in I.10, and, in a handwritten addition, said he was also enclosing "yr 'reviews' for Hinty"—apparently a reference to Henze's request in a letter dated 7 July for lines in I.2 in which "Carolina would tell Dr Rei[s]chmann a bit more about important reviews" of the poet.

Henze's letter of 7 July asked for many other changes and cuts, most of which Kallman rejected in a letter of 15 July. But Auden and Kallman evidently did agree to other suggested changes. One was Henze's request that Hulda (later Hilda) not sing "the Lohengrin Wedding March" in II.9. Another was Henze's objection to a passage in which the poet asked for no applause in his speech to the audience in the final scene. As Henze said: "For various reasons, of which the most important is my superstition, fed by bad experiences, one should not ask for trouble so openly at the end of a play, and I beg you to change the text slightly there."

Henze visited Kirchstetten on 4–6 August 1960 to work on these and other changes. Auden wrote to Elizabeth Mayer on 8 August 1960: "Hans Henze was here for four [sic] days and played us some sketches from the Opera. They sounded exciting. The orchestra is going to be *very* odd."

On 31 August 1960 Auden sent a further note to Henze about the setting:

Act II Tea-quartet [II.4]

The important thing here is to treat Mittenhofer, Carolina, Toni and Elizabeth, not as individuals, but as the four elements which make up a single situation, i.e., the music should express the situation and ignore character. I see each couplet as a two-part musical phrase which goes on repeating itself, so that each character has to sing whatever bit of the tune happens to fall to him (or her) regardless of what he is saying.

With the same letter he and Kallman sent a revised opening of Act III. Henze then had the libretto retyped, together with the synopsis and "Genesis of a Libretto", and sent the new typescript to the librettists. Kallman thanked him for it on 10 October, but complained about the layout:

I don't know who did the typing, which has lots of easily findable and easily correctable misprints, BUT no sense of where verse lines should start on a page. Wystan always says I'm unnecessarily finicky on the point. Still, I typed all three acts and gave myself a lot of trouble keeping the alignments clear. Now they're all over the place and I can't see how to set them right without cluttering up the pages with probably incomprehensible markings or re-typing the whole damn thing.

Kallman added that the synopsis would be slightly revised to accommodate the changes in the libretto itself. Kallman mentioned one further change:

> I shall also write and send you this week a short insert for Act Two [II.12] to replace the original scene between Mittenhofer and Mauer that has now been cut. I think this is necessary for three reasons. ONE: Mauer entering with Hilda is not enough to justify his appearance on stage in the second act. TWO: He comes with weather reports in the first and third acts (and thus as a messenger of the gods) and should have the same function in the second. Wystan had the brilliant idea that his report in the second act should be wrong. That is, he should tell Mittenhofer that he expects the weather next day to be fine and that he may be able to get him his precious flowers the next day; and Mitty says, Never mind, I've made other arrangements. This exchange is what leads Mauer to make his closing remarks in Act Three about the weather "madly happening". In other words, the wanton fatefulness of the blizzard will be further underlined. See? The messenger of the gods, only human, has got the message incorrectly. . . .

Kallman's third reason was the need to provide a "brief rest before the climax".

After receiving the typescript of the first act in October 1959 Henze apparently had protested against the use of the names of George, Rilke, and Hofmannsthal in I.5. Auden, in the undated cover letter in which he sent a lost set of revisions, told Henze: "if you feel strongly against using their real names, substitute for *Georg[e]*, *Rilke, Hofmannsthal,* the names *Georgeous* [*sic*], *Milksop* and *Huff-and-Puff* respectively." Later Henze agreed to restore the real names, but his new typescript did not reflect the change and also made an unauthorized substitution in the same aria. Kallman asked about these matters in his letter of 10 October 1960:

> We see it's still "Huff-and-puff" *etc.* Is this a slip? I thought we'd agreed that keeping the real names 1) gave point to his remarks about them; and 2) placed Mittenhofer among his distinguished contemporaries without any ambiguity. Yes? And is there no chance of restoring "Let those birds drop their turds"? A good laugh never hurt any opera. Let us know.

The lines that Kallman asked to restore (and which are restored in this edition from the page of Auden's draft typescript in the collection of Robert A. Wilson) were replaced in Henze's typescript and the published texts by lines apparently written by Henze: "What a crew! / They won't do!"

Kallman raised other textual issues in this letter. He protested against some unauthorized cuts; Henze restored all the cuts Kallman specified, but Kallman's letter leaves open the possibility that there may have been others. Kallman promised to write the dedication that week, and added: "It had been part of our idea to include Huff-and-Puff's daughter in our share of the dedication, but since you don't know her, this must probably be eschewed."

On 18 October Kallman sent a further brief list of errata, apparently typed by Auden, of which only the first of (probably) two pages survives. On 8 February 1961 Kallman wrote to ask Henze to restore some of the dialogue between Toni and Elizabeth in III.7; apparently Henze agreed, and the libretto reached its final form. Henze finished the score later the same month.

In addition to revising the dialogue, Auden and Kallman had also revised the names of the characters. Early in 1960, in a letter now lost, Henze apparently asked Auden to change Hinterhofer's (later Mittenhofer's) first name from Gundolf, a name associated with Stefan George through George's disciple Friedrich Gundolf. Auden's reply, on 7 March 1960, apparently alludes to Henze's objection to the tone of the name:

Rebaptism.
I see your point about Gundolf, though our protagonist is someone to be respected, even as a monster. We suggest
GEROLD.
Please leave Hinterhofer [*inserted in the margin:* the name of our Austrian electrician] if you possibly can.

The change from Gundolf to Gerold was not final, and Henze discussed this and other changes in the characters' names when he met Kallman in Hamburg in late April. In his letter of 7 July 1960 Henze wrote: "You have not replied yet about the names but I trust that as soon as possible I will have the names already discussed with Chester in Hamburg." Possibly the final forms of the characters' names, including the metamorphosis of Gundolf Hinterhofer into Gregor Mittenhofer, were only settled during Henze's visit to Kirchstetten in early August. A letter from Auden and Kallman to Henze on 31 August uses the final forms of the names, with one exception: Kallman refers to Hilda (originally Hulda) as Hedwig. Henze had asked for a different name, and the final change to Hilda probably occurred some time after Auden and Kallman's letter.

Henze also asked Auden and Kallman to choose something other than edelweiss as the flower that the poet requires from the mountain (I.2, II.11, and II.12). In his letter of 7 July 1960 Henze wrote: "More and more the 'Edelweiss' appears to me as a little too bitty and unhappy a choice and I think this comes from what all Germans and Austrians have; we have grown up with tasteless songs and stories about this plant and it means something rather obvious and too much used in musical comedies and silly folk songs and stories." He hoped they "could think of a mysterious and very rare Alpine plant, flower or root which one could find in a book of biological sciences—this would give more magic and mystery to the whole subject." Auden, in a postscript to Kallman's reply to Henze of 15 July 1960, wrote: "It is[,] of course, possible to substitute a rare plant no one has heard of for Edelweiss, but why?" Henze proceeded to change edelweiss to Alvetern for the typescript that he sent to the librettists in September or early October. Kallman, in his letter of 10 October, rejected the change: "The 'symbol' has to be immediately comprehensible if it is to mean anything at all to the audience. . . . People, if they

get anything at all will think it [Alvetern] a reference to a Danish composer."
Henze restored Edelweiss (capitalized) for the published libretto, and for the En-
glish text in the piano score, but retained Alvetern in the German text of the piano
score, the English and German texts in the study score, and in the German version
of the pamphlet libretto.

After the Glyndebourne production, in which the scene on the mountain be-
tween Toni and Elizabeth was cut, Auden wrote on 8 August 1961 to Elizabeth
Mayer about a further change that Henze and the librettists planned but never
accomplished (letter in the Berg Collection):

> Glyndebourne could have been worse. . . . What was clear is that
> though, as it stood, it was better to cut the death scene, something
> important is lacking without it. We are going to re-write and recom-
> pose it and put it in *before* the orchestral storm instead of after.

With a few minor exceptions the text of this edition follows that of the published
libretto. "Schwarzer" is emended to "Schwarze" in the first sentence of the opening
stage direction and in the published synopsis; Auden and Kallman also used the
erroneous form in their outline and letters. In the last long stage direction in I.2
(p. 194), I have emended "her papers, she takes" to "her papers, takes". Follow-
ing the printed scores, I have emended "how inns are like" to "what inns are like"
(p. 197). In this libretto and in *The Bassarids,* Auden and Kallman use "ever so
often" for "every so often" (as on p. 200); I have let their usage stand. As noted
above, I have restored two lines in I.5 (p. 202). The published libretto mistakenly
gives both Toni and Elizabeth the same opening lines in their duet in II.1 (p. 210):
"I dwelt in a world / Of anonymous shadows,"; the list of errata and the printed
scores give Elizabeth the lines "I dwelt in a world, / An anonymous shadow,".
Following the printed scores, I have emended "It's not your speaking" to "It's not
you speaking" (p. 220). I have dropped a period after "aid" in Mittenhofer's line
"edelweiss, a visionary 'aid'" (p. 228).

The printed scores assign Carolina's lines "Would you like trout for dinner?"
and "Don't you young men approve of Wagner?" in I.3 (p. 197) to the Doctor. The
change gives more point to Toni's "For God's sake, Dad, why must you pester so?"
but the text in the published libretto is probably what Auden and Kallman wrote.

This edition makes a few slight corrections in lineation. In the published li-
bretto the last two lines of the Doctor's speech in I.2 beginning "Yes, and what
would poets do" (p. 194) are printed as prose; this edition restores the verse linea-
tion that was obviously intended. In I.3 (pp. 196–97) the published libretto treats
Carolina's "That's different" as a complete line of verse, followed by Toni's "Hello,
father" and the Doctor's "Aren't you going to say" treated as a single line of verse
divided between two speakers; this edition prints all three speeches as divisions of
a single line of verse. Two lines below, this edition prints Toni's "Where's my room"
as part of the same line of verse as the preceding phrase, rather than following the
published libretto, which prints it deeply indented on a line of its own. In III.1
(p. 232) the published libretto deeply indents the Doctor's and Hilda's "Morning";
this has no parallel elsewhere in the libretto, and the layout may have been a

confused attempt to render the lost typescript's treatment of the two lines as a single line of verse divided between two speakers.

Trivial typographical errors in the published libretto are corrected, but I have not altered the inconsistent capitalization of "he" and "him" in I.2. The published libretto prints the name of the flower as "Edelweiß"; the initial letter was probably capitalized when Henze restored Auden and Kallman's preferred flower in place of his choice of Alvetern, and the lowercase initial (and final "ss") used in this edition follows Auden's and Kallman's usage in their typed outlines and letters. Following German typographical convention, the published libretto sometimes indicates emphasis by letter-spacing; this edition restores the italics undoubtedly intended by the librettists.

The list of errata sent by the librettists to Henze on 18 October 1960 included a instruction to delete the heading "VII. Unworldly Weakness" from its position immediately above Carolina's line beginning "Numb, Doctor" (p. 204), and to re-number the remaining scenes of Act I. These instructions were followed in the published libretto, although not in the printed scores. The errata also noted: "The stage direction *Tolls begin to be heard from the valley* should come after . . . *Death in fact looks dazzlingly attractive*", a few lines below the deleted heading. This stage direction was not included in the published libretto, but appears in this edition. The printed scores lack this stage direction; instead they have a footnote by Henze that specifies that the sound of typical village church bells should be heard. The scene under the deleted heading had been truncated to three lines by the removal of the Doctor's aria, of which an early draft is printed on pp. 663–64.

The lost typescripts of Acts II and III used red ribbon to indicate dialogue that should be spoken, not sung, and Kallman specified the spoken lines of Act I in his letter to Henze on 13 January 1960 in which he offered suggestions on the musical treatment of the work. He also specified that all of Mauer's lines were to be "spoken . . . against music, as befits his role throughout the opera as a messenger of the Fates." Kallman identified the spoken lines in Act I thus: I.1, Hilda's final couplet; I.3, Carolina's final couplet and her opening lines in I.4 until "To-day!"; I.5, Mittenhofer's lines from "Get up!" to the end; I.6, the Doctor's couplet (which preceded "his Lullaby", apparently a later version of his deleted aria); I.7, all the lines from Mauer's first speech until the end of his last speech; I.9, Hilda's and Mittenhofer's final speeches. In Act II, where, Kallman wrote, the spoken speeches were typed in red in the lost typescript, "None of these bits, however, MUST be spoken (except for Mauer's)". The spoken passages may be identified tentatively from the score: II.1, from Carolina's "Aren't you ashamed" to "this nonsense"; II.5, perhaps Carolina's couplet "Your room has been aired" and her closing lines from "Kindly mind" (each set as recitative on a single note); II.8, Carolina's "Madness!"; II.9, Mittenhofer's last three words, *The Young Lovers*; II.10, Carolina's final couplet (marked "half spoken" in the score); II.11, Mittenhofer's final couplet; II.12, the Doctor's and Mittenhofer's first lines and Carolina's line "Shall I bring out your manuscripts", possibly Mittenhofer's "No, no. It's too late" (the only other line in the first part of this scene that, like the lines marked as spoken, does not rhyme), and Mauer's and Mittenhofer's dialogue at the end of the scene; II.13, Mittenhofer's first line and a half (marked "half sung" in the score), and Hilda's final line. In Act III, which evidently also used red markings to indicate spoken lines, the score suggests that these are: III.3, the opening line of verse, divided among four speakers (marked "half spoken" in the score); III.4, all of Mauer's speeches and Mittenhofer's reply to his question; III.5, Mittenhofer's opening sentence (marked "half spoken" in the score); III.9, Mittenhofer's concluding speech in the theatre.

In Kallman's letter to Henze of 10 October 1960 he responded to Henze's question about the possibility of indicating typographically the distinction between the sung and spoken portions of the text:

> About printing the spoken parts in a different way in the librettino. I don't really think it's necessary or desirable. On a small page, different kinds of print look fussy and are distracting to the reader. Also, I always think that an element of surprise should be added by not indicating divisions to the reader that will be revealed to him when he hears the work. Brackets indicating ensembles, however, should be included; if only in the simplest way.

§4 Auden and Kallman on the Opera

Kallman seems to have been the author of a synopsis of the opera first written apparently late in 1959 and slightly revised during 1960. The text first appeared, unsigned and in a German translation, in the booklet with the detailed program listings of the 1961 Schwetzinger Festspiele. The text below is the English version that appeared, signed by both librettists, in the 1961 Glyndebourne souvenir program book. On p. 673 "edelweiss" is an emendation for "the flower *Alvetern*", a phrase evidently introduced by Henze when he had the synopsis retyped late in 1960; in emending I have omitted the words "the flower", which are clearly Henze's clarifying addition.

SYNOPSIS

Forty years before the action of the opera begins, Hilda Mack and her bridegroom came to the Schwarze Adler, an inn in the Austrian Alps, for their honeymoon. The next morning he left the inn to climb the Hammerhorn, a nearby peak, "to conquer it for his bride", and was never seen again. Since then Hilda has remained at the inn, living in an eternal extension of that morning, waiting for his return. In this state she hears his voice from the mountain, and from his message has visions of the future.

For a number of years, Gregor Mittenhofer, a very prominent poet, has regularly arrived to consult her visions, the imagery of which he utilizes in his work; and in the early spring of 1910, he and his retinue have taken over the inn. With him are his personal physician, Dr Wilhelm Reischmann, his patroness and unpaid secretary, Carolina, Gräfin von Kirchstetten, and his young mistress, Elizabeth Zimmer.

ACT I   *The Emergence of the Bridegroom*

As the opera opens, Hilda tells of her bridegroom's fate. It is morning; the day, organized for the Master's convenience, has just begun. The Doctor goes to give him a rejuvenating injection; Carolina is sorting correspondence and reviews, and then reads her instructions for the day. The Master's chief concern is Hilda's distressing current lack of visions, and he insists that Carolina "do something" to make her perform that very day. But Carolina also has concerns of her own for the Master: his pocket money must not seem to come from her, for money has never been either openly discussed by them, or openly given by her. Also, whilst she admits that this affair with Elizabeth has given his poetry a new stimulus, she does not trust the girl; she has caught her reading other poets, and feels that in Muse-mistresses, divided tastes are as good as disloyalties.

From below, the daily train is heard arriving; and soon Toni, the Doctor's son, arrives at the inn. He is in his early twenties, studying medicine, and at the moment, inclined to be surly. Obviously, too, he finds the fuss and mystique surrounding the Master foolish and distasteful.

At the precisely scheduled hour, Mittenhofer and Elizabeth make their appearance. Elizabeth and Toni are introduced; and, as their hands touch, Hilda breaks out into one of her long-awaited visions.

Hilda and the poet are left alone together. The vision ends as suddenly as it had begun, and Hilda returns to the terrace to resume her knitting.

After Carolina comes back, Mittenhofer is at the top of his form, going raucously through his reviews—Carolina has weeded out any unfavourable ones—and scoring off his poetic "contemporaries" with extravagantly contemptuous good humour. When, however, he finds a mistake in a transcript made by Carolina, he turns on her; suddenly she faints. Disgustedly, he calls for the Doctor. Nor is he much more sympathetic when he hears she has come down with the 'flu. He retires to his study.

Josef Mauer, an Alpine guide, enters excitedly with news: a perfectly preserved body has emerged from the glacier, and according to his calculations, it must be that of Mr Mack, Hilda's long-missing bridegroom.

Carolina suggests that Elizabeth break the news to Hilda. She herself, she pleads, is not well. Josef gives his report on tomorrow's weather, and leaves.

Alone with Hilda, Elizabeth tries to make her understand what has happened. Toni, who has come in quietly from the terrace, is moved by the scene and impressed by Elizabeth's tenderness. Now it is time for Mittenhofer's morning stroll with her.

Hilda, suddenly roused from the blank state she had fallen into, joyously thanks her dead husband for once again releasing her into life and the anticipation of tomorrow by his re-appearance. Toni, staring devotedly after Elizabeth, declares that his tomorrow depends wholly upon loving her.

ACT II   *The Emergence of the Bride*

Some days have passed; Toni and Elizabeth are in love. They are caught embracing by Carolina. She is shocked, calls in the Doctor to speak to Toni, and takes Elizabeth out on the terrace, where she berates the silent girl for not knowing her place in the Master's community, nor being worthy of it. Dr Reischmann questions his son about what has happened. He is sure Toni cannot be serious, but Toni passionately avows his love for Elizabeth and his wish to marry her. To his father's objection that it would be unthinkable for him to marry his Godfather's mistress, Toni counters by accusing him of never having loved his dead wife, Toni's mother. At this, the Doctor weeps and asks Toni to imagine what his mother would feel to see her son ruining his life. The tears are effective; the boy is thoroughly ashamed of himself.

When he and Elizabeth meet again, their emotional positions are the reverse of what they were at the beginning of the scene: Elizabeth, furious at Carolina's insults and insinuations, is all for leaving at once; Toni feels that everything should be tactfully disclosed and discussed before they leave together.

During this conversation on the terrace, Mittenhofer has come out of his study to have tea. Carolina manages to exasperate him with her hints, but before she can explain more fully, he tells her he is quite aware of Toni and Elizabeth's "love", is certain it will pass, and intends to do or say nothing about it.

Carolina, on his instructions, asks Elizabeth to join him. Mittenhofer asks her if she has something to confide in him, and, seizing her momentary hesitation and emotional distance, confesses his own faults. His boring public pose, his inadequate personal responses, and his often childish wilfulness he says are all the protections of a talent that must always seek and preserve what is both genuine and exploitable for his poetry. He begs her, if she ever wishes to be free of all that, to tell him. He has persuaded her, she will not leave him or even tell him of Toni.

Elizabeth is ashamed. Together with a sense of isolation and uncertainty, this feeling prompts her to confess to Toni that her affection for him was aroused more by his sincerity, in contrast to Mittenhofer's seeming lack of it, than by any deep passion. In short, she now feels that she cannot leave the poet.

Outraged, Toni cries that she has been bewitched and, despite Carolina's intervention, calls Mittenhofer from his study to demand a showdown. Mittenhofer listens tolerantly, then takes charge of the situation by sympathetically asking the girl to tell him frankly whether or not she is in love with Toni and wishes to leave with him. Toni begs her to say yes, his father to say no; Elizabeth, at first stonily silent, finally bursts into tears.

At this moment, Hilda, slightly tipsy, returns to the inn, on Josef's arm. She takes in the situation at a glance, and makes outrageous comments, but advises Elizabeth to laugh at them all and leave with her. Elizabeth, exasperated by the attitudes of Carolina and the Doctor, is dimly aware that Mittenhofer's sympathy may easily be his method of dismissing her, and quietly asks Hilda if she thinks her a whore; then, after Hilda's definite negative, suddenly asks Toni if he will marry her.

Toni naturally says yes; Hilda tells her she is making a mistake; Dr Reischmann desperately objects. Mittenhofer takes charge once more. He tells them of the poem he is working on—*The Young Lovers*—which deals with the precious gift of Eden that young lovers bring to the old cold world, only to be envied and rejected, though all who would welcome them might enter Eden too.

All but Carolina, in spite of their personal reservations and premonitions, are moved to a seeming unanimity of consent. Sadly and silently, Dr Reischmann gives the youngsters his blessing. Everything appears settled. Elizabeth wishes to leave with Hilda the next day to think her problems out more clearly away from both Toni and Mittenhofer, but the poet has a last request. He asks her if she would remain one day more, and in that day climb the mountain with Toni and find edelweiss for him, since he needs it as a "visionary aid" to complete his poem, which he wishes to recite at his imminent sixtieth birthday celebration. Elizabeth consents.

Hilda, however, will not delay her departure: Elizabeth can join her in the city. All express their various anticipations of tomorrow, and disperse, leaving Mittenhofer alone.

He finally gives way to the resentment buried beneath the tolerance displayed earlier, and raves against each of the others, Elizabeth especially, ending "Why don't they all DIE!" But he has not been as alone as he thought: Hilda, coming back to retrieve her umbrella, has caught the end of his outburst. "Naughty, naughty, dear", she says; and he, with a bellow of rage, stalks out. Hilda collapses laughing into a chair.

ACT III *Man and Wife*

SCENE I

Dr Reischmann, unable to face the young couple again so soon, decides to leave with Hilda the next morning while the lovers are on the mountain.

Hilda, despite her eagerness to see the world again, feels she cannot leave without apologizing to Carolina. Carolina finally gives Hilda her hand. Mittenhofer comes out to say good-bye, and he and Carolina are left alone.

Under Carolina's sharp questioning, he admits that he had, in spite of himself, practically to push Elizabeth and Toni together. Even had Elizabeth remained with him afterwards, an "emotional untidiness" would have remained with her, and that would have made life uncomfortable and work difficult. As for Toni's and Elizabeth's love, he hardly believes it can last a year.

The sky darkens. Josef enters to tell them that a blizzard is coming up, and asks if anyone from the inn is on the mountain. After a moment's hesitation, Mittenhofer replies "Not that I know of". Carolina does not contradict him. Josef leaves.

There is a moment's silence; then Mittenhofer, seeing how pale and shaken Carolina has become, suggests that she ought to get away for a while. At this, Carolina panics: Where should she go? Her whole life is tied up with serving him. How could he manage without her?

The snow begins to fall, she lights a fire, and sings a lullaby. She recovers herself sufficiently to resume her obsessive guardianship. The clock hasn't been wound; in an almost expressionless ritual she winds and sets it. The snow falls more heavily, the lights fade.

SCENE II

On the mountain, Toni and Elizabeth, lost in the storm, admit the situation hopeless. Faced with imminent death, they romance about the married future they will never share: the children, the difficulties, all the domestic intimacies and differences they might have come to look back upon forty years from now. But neither can really foresee the future with the other. They have faced themselves honestly. They pray.

SCENE III

A dressing room and lecture platform. Mittenhofer is getting ready for his birthday celebration ceremony; Carolina, an automaton of service, helps him. He goes out to the reading-desk and announces that he will read his latest poem—the *Elegy for Young Lovers*—dedicated to the memories of Elizabeth Zimmer and Toni Reischmann who died on the Hammerhorn together.

We do not hear the poem itself; from behind the Master come the wordless voices of all who have contributed to his writing of it—Hilda with her visions, Carolina with her money and management, Dr Reisch-

mann with his medicines, Toni and Elizabeth with their illusory but usable
love. The poem has been finished. The opera is over.

W. H. AUDEN AND
CHESTER KALLMAN

Kallman wrote a brief note about the opera for the souvenir program of the 1961
Schwetzinger Festspiele; it appeared there in an unsigned German translation.
Confusions in the printed translation suggest that it was revised (without refer-
ence to the lost English original) from an earlier typescript translation (dated
Munich, 30 April 1961) now among Henze's papers at the Sacher Foundation. The
German text that follows is that of the typescript, which is obviously more com-
plete and coherent than the printed text. A retranslation into English, made for
this edition, is printed beneath the German.

EIN PERSÖNLICHER KOMMENTAR*

VON CHESTER KALLMAN

Außer in den Fällen, in denen ein Opernkomponist von seiner eigenen
künstlerischen Mission besessen ist, wie zum Beispiel Wagner, ist es wahr-
scheinlich unweise, seine Textbücher selbst zu schreiben. Natürlich wird
es unvermeidlich sein, daß, wenn das Libretto nicht von dem Kom-
ponisten selber stammt, eine Reibung zwischen dem Libretto und seiner
Vertonung entsteht. Aber, als erfolgreiche Zusammenarbeit betrachtet,
ist anzunehmen, daß durch diese Reibung ein Feuer entfacht wird, das
die Worte wie die Musik illuminiert. Nehmen wir ein klassisches Beispiel—
Don Giovanni. Es ist offensichtlich, daß da Ponte, wahrscheinlich mit
Molières Behandlung des Sujets im Kopf, beabsichtigt hat, eine leichte,
moralisierende Farce zu schreiben, während Mozart hingegen eine solche
Absicht nicht hatte. Durch die ganze Oper hindurch gibt seine dämo-
nische Musik selbst den farcenhaftesten Situationen einen Zweck und ein

*[Translation:]

A PERSONAL COMMENTARY

BY CHESTER KALLMAN

Except in those cases in which an opera composer is possessed by his own artistic mission—as,
for example, Wagner—it is probably unwise for him to write his own libretti. Of course when
the libretto does not come from the composer himself, it is inevitable that friction will arise
between the libretto and its musical setting. But where there is successful collaboration, it can
indeed be assumed that this friction sets a fire going, which illuminates the words as well as
the music. Consider a classic example—*Don Giovanni*. It is obvious that da Ponte, probably
with Molière's treatment of the subject in mind, intended to write a light moralistic farce,
while on the other hand Mozart had no such intent. Throughout the entire opera his de-

Gewicht, die oft in einem direkten Widerspruch zu den Absichten des Textes stehen. Das Ergebnis kann man wohl kaum als schlechte Vertonung bezeichnen; es ist eine tiefe und spontane Revelation des geballten Gefühls, das Don Giovannis äußerliche Frivolität heraushebt.

Natürlich soll dies nun auch nicht heißen, daß Librettist und Komponist unbedingt von Anfang an in zwei verschiedenen Richtungen laufen müssen. Wenn es keine künstlerische oder sonstige Sympathie zwischen da Ponte und Mozart gegeben hätte, würde ihre Zusammenarbeit wahrscheinlich zumindest schwierig, wenn nicht unmöglich gewesen sein. Gewiß würden Auden und ich niemals eine Zusammenarbeit mit Henze gewünscht haben, wenn wir ihn nicht persönlich schätzten und wenn wir nicht seine Begabung als Komponist bewunderten. Es ist keine Übertreibung zu sagen, daß diese Oper fast vollständig das Ergebnis dieser Sympathie darstellt. Vielleicht ist dies auch der Grund, daß wir eine Oper geschrieben haben, deren Hauptfigur ein kreativer Künstler ist.

Es ist vielleicht auch offensichtlich, daß das Fundament dieser Zusammenarbeit eine Übereinstimmung in gewissen Fragen des künstlerischen Geschmacks war, und daß gemeinsame künstlerische Überzeugungen vorhanden sind. Unter diesen Überzeugungen befindet sich auch der Glaube an die formalen Konventionen der Oper, gepaart mit dem Gesichtspunkt, daß jede dramatische Situation in der Oper ihre eigenen Formen bilden muß auf der Basis dieser Konventionen. Jedem, der über die Geschichte des Operntheaters nachgedacht hat, wird es deutlich werden,—ganz abgesehen davon, welche direkten Einflüsse für die Komposition von *Elegie für junge Liebende* wichtig geworden sind,—daß der Einfluß eines Komponisten, den wir alle drei verehren, nämlich Verdi,

---

monic music gives even the most farcical situations a purpose and a gravity that often stand in direct contradiction to the intentions of the text. The result could hardly be characterized as a bad musical setting; it is a deep and spontaneous revelation of the concentrated feeling that Don Giovanni's outward frivolousness throws into relief.

Of course, this is not to say that librettist and composer must necessarily go off in two different directions right from the start. If there had not been any artistic sympathy or sympathy of any kind between da Ponte and Mozart, their collaboration would probably have been at least difficult, if not indeed impossible. Auden and I would certainly never have wanted to collaborate with Henze if we had not personally respected him and admired his talent as a composer. It is no exaggeration to say that this opera is almost entirely the result of this sympathy. Perhaps this is also the reason that we have written an opera whose central figure is a creative artist.

It is also perhaps obvious that the foundation of our collaboration was an agreement about certain questions of artistic taste, and that common artistic convictions are present. Among these convictions is the belief, too, in the formal conventions of opera, joined with the point of view that every dramatic situation in the opera must create its own forms precisely on the basis of these conventions. It will be clear to anyone who has thought about the history of the operatic theater—quite apart from the question of the direct influences that became impor-

zwangsläufig der dominierende war. Während der Zusammenarbeit haben wir nie seinen Namen genannt; das war auch nicht notwendig, denn er war unablässig dabei.

Nun, da die Musik komponiert ist und da unsere eigenen Silben, Wörter, Phrasen, Verse und Situationen durch sie umgeformt wurden, ist dieser unausgesprochene Einfluß deutlich zu bemerken. Zu unseren Wortgestalten, in welchen die Charaktere dargestellt werden durch dem Einzelnen zugehörige prosodische Formen, hat Henze eine Musik gesetzt, in der jeder Charakter mindestens ein für ihn bestimmtes Instrument und ein für seine Welt gedachtes orchestrales Timbre zugeordnet bekam. Dadurch ist jede dramatische Begegnung der Charaktere untereinander dazu angetan, formale Spannungen zu erzeugen,—also rein musikalische,—ohne daß diese künstlich, gewissermaßen von außen herbeigeführt werden müssen. Die Vielfalt von Farben und Formen, die dadurch ermöglicht wird, sollte leicht hörbar und erkennbar sein, ohne daß weitere musikalische Analysen notwendig werden. Damit soll nicht gesagt sein, daß eine solche Analyse, wie auch ein häufigeres und vertieftes Hören, nicht weitere formale Einzelheiten an den Tag bringen würden, es soll nur heißen, daß solche Untersuchungen hier nicht am Platze sind und sogar unter Umständen das direkte Vergnügen verhindern könnten, das wir alle Drei zu bieten wünschten.

An dieser Stelle bleiben nur noch zwei Dinge zum Abschluß zu sagen oder zu klären, ohne weitschweifig werden zu wollen:—Erstens, daß die instrumentale Auslegung der Charaktere, wie ich sie oben andeutungsweise beschrieben habe, eine Technik ist, die Verdi schon im

---

tant for the composition of *Elegy for Young Lovers*—that the influence of one composer, whom all three of us admire, namely Verdi, was necessarily dominant. During our collaboration we never uttered his name; nor was that necessary, for he was constantly present.

Now, as music is composed and as our own syllables, words, phrases, verses and situations were reshaped by it, this unacknowledged influence is plain to see. To our word shapes, in which characters are represented by means of prosodic forms attached to each one individually, Henze composed a music in which each character is assigned at least one instrument destined for him and one orchestral timbre meant for his world. In this way each dramatic confrontation among the characters is designed to generate formal tensions—that is to say, purely musical ones—without their needing to be brought in by artificial means, as it were from the outside. The variety of colors and forms which in this way becomes possible should be easy to hear and to recognize without the necessity of further musical analyses. This is not to say that such an analysis, as well as a more frequent and more absorbed listening, would not bring to light additional formal details; it is only to say that such investigations are not appropriate here and in certain cases could even interfere with the direct pleasure that the three of us intended to give.

At this point there are only two things to say or to explain, without intending to go on and on: first, that the instrumental interpretation of the characters, which I alluded to above, is a technique that Verdi had already used in *Nabucco* and that, in the way that it has been studied and developed in the work before us here, has nothing to do with the technique of the

Nabucco benutzt hat, und die nichts zu tun hat mit der Technik des Leit-
motivs wie sie hier erforscht und entwickelt worden ist, das können Sie
selber in *Elegie für junge Liebende* hören. Zweitens ein Wort über den Kon-
flikt zwischen Libretto und Vertonung, von dem ich eingangs gesprochen
habe. Nun, Henzes Vertonung und Schwerpunktverteilung einiger un-
serer Szenen *waren* eine Überraschung für uns. Abgesehen von der uns
verbindenden Sympathie ist er weder Auden noch Kallman, Gott sei
Dank, sondern sehr viel Henze, und, wenn er uns überrascht hat und
eventuell sogar schockiert, so hat er doch Phasen unseres Werkes in
einem Maße erleuchtet, das auch für uns ebenso überraschend war, und
das, so hoffen wir, werden auch Sie hören.

Auden, Kallman, and Henze discussed the opera in an impromptu conversation
recorded for the BBC and broadcast 13 July 1961. A mimeographed transcript is
in the BBC Written Archives Centre, but is too garbled and disordered to be re-
printed in full. The notes above quote the most substantive comments on the
libretto.

Robert Craft quotes Auden's remark in conversation, 17 November 1962: "The
Elegy was our version of *Arabella*" (Craft, *Stravinsky: Chronicle of a Friendship, 1948–
1971* [1972], p. 211).

In Auden's lecture on his operas in *Secondary Worlds* (1968) he retold the story of
"Genesis of a Libretto" and provided a new synopsis. He wrote of the scene on the
mountaintop in Act III:

This scene, for which, incidentally, I was responsible, will not do at all,
and must some day be completely re-written. To my fond eye, it reads well
and might be effective in a spoken verse-play. But for opera it is far too
literary and complicated in the argument, far too dependent upon every
word being heard to get across when set to music.

The intended revision was never made.

---

leitmotif; the way that it has been studied and developed here is something you can hear
yourself in *Elegy for Young Lovers*. Secondly, a word about the conflict between libretto and
musical setting that I spoke about at the outset. Henze's musical setting and distribution of
crucial stresses in several of our scenes *were* a surprise for us. Apart from the sympathy that
unites us, it is neither Auden nor Kallman, thank God, but very much Henze. And if he has
surprised and sometimes perhaps even shocked us, he has also illuminated phases of our
work to an extent that was as surprising for us too; and that, we hope, is what you too will
hear.

The Bassarids

§1 History, Authorship, Text, and Editions

Auden and Kallman first proposed to Henze that they collaborate on a libretto based on *The Bacchae* during rehearsals for the Glyndebourne production of *Elegy for Young Lovers* in late June or early July 1961. "But unfortunately [as Henze recalled] they pronounced the Greek title in such a peculiar way that I did not understand it—and I was too embarrassed to ask them to repeat the word. When I was back in Rome again (almost a year had passed), I eventually flicked through an edition of the tragedies of Euripides and was immediately taken by the dramatic power of the work" ("*The Bassarids*, [1] Tradition and Cultural Heritage", in Henze's *Music and Politics*, translated by Peter Labanyi [1982], pp. 143–44; adapted from an interview with Klaus Geitel in *Die Welt*, 13 July 1966, which was reprinted in Henze's *Musik und Politik* [1976]).

Probably around May or June 1962 (as Henze wrote in the same essay),

> Auden and Kallman agreed to write the libretto for me on one harsh condition. Auden forced me to listen to *Götterdämmerung*, sent me to the Vienna State Opera for this purpose, and sent Kallman along too, to make sure I really sat through it right to the end. Just as Auden, that experienced old pedagogue, had led Stravinsky to the peak of classicism with the libretto for *The Rake's Progress*, so too he wanted to squeeze things out of me that he had already detected in other pieces of mine . . . such as the way the music "forgets itself" at certain moments, the stripping away of all stylistic apparel, the crude shamelessness of the musical statement. To make sure I got the point, Auden insisted I listen to *Götterdämmerung*.
>
> I had always avoided Wagner's work out of a certain antipathy. . . . But now Auden wanted me to overcome my dislike for Wagner, and just as a pupil passively bends to the will of his mentor I yielded to him and sat through *Götterdämmerung*—quite joylessly.

Auden discussed the idea of a libretto on *The Bacchae* with Igor Stravinsky and Robert Craft on 17 November 1962 (Craft, *Stravinsky: Chronicle of a Friendship, 1948–1971* [1972], p. 211). "After this," Henze recalled (again in the same essay), "in May 1963, we had a second meeting about *The Bassarids*." It may have been at this time that, as Henze remembered in an interview, "I asked Auden and Kallman to mould the opera to the form of a symphony" ("Henze's New Opera", interview with Alan Blyth, *Opera*, August 1966, p. 609).

Auden and Kallman began writing the libretto early in July 1963. Auden wrote to James Stern on 8 July: "we are in the throes of beginning our libretto for Henze on *The Bacchae*." He wrote to Lincoln Kirstein on 18 August: "Chester and I are deep in the *Bacchae* libretto which is turning out fiendishly difficult to do. To begin with, no singer *can* wear Greek costume. Dionysus will be dressed as a cross between Beau Brummel and Oscar Wilde." On 15 September he wrote Kirstein: "We finished the *Bacchae* last week and are now typing. At the moment I think it is the best libretto we have done so far. We are longing to show it you. It's a real shocker, I hope." Henze recalled, "At the end of August, completely unexpectedly, I received the finished libretto", but August is probably an error for September; Auden wrote Kirstein on 9 October: "*The Bassarids* is finished." Before this, Auden and Kallman apparently referred to the opera simply as *The Bacchae;* it may not have received its final title, which, unlike *The Bacchae,* refers to male as well as female followers of Dionysus, until Kallman typed the finished libretto. Another typescript, with slight cuts, was registered for copyright at the Library of Congress on 13 January 1964.

Auden and Kallman derived some of the details of their libretto from the commentary to E. R. Dodds's edition of the play. On 12 August 1963 Auden wrote to Dodds's wife, A. E. Dodds, who had been a friend for many years (Auden's letters to E. R. and A. E. Dodds are in the Bodleian Library):

> Chester and I are now deep in our *Bacchae* libretto, which presents some very difficult problems. To begin with, singers simply *cannot* wear Greek costume. Then, what at first sight looks like being fine for music, the big role Euripides gives the chorus, is a snare because, if one isn't careful, the thing turns into an oratorio which is boring as a stage-work. We plan to have in the middle—the opera will be one long act—a miniature satyr play which represents what Pentheus *thinks* Agave and Co are up to—a Boucher-like fête champêtre— elegant and whiffy—(it's the only part which will be rhymed). We are finding the Master's commentary a great help. We have given Agave only one sister (Autonoe) but have added two characters, Beroe, Pentheus' old nurse, the only person who really loves him, and a Captain of the guard, who is, like Eichmann, a Beamter who does whatever authority orders. Pentheus is presented as being, secretly, a believer in To Theon (perhaps he has been in Ionia). Like Plato, he knows that the people must have their myths and cults, but is determined to suppress those which represent the Olympians as immoral. In the end, of course, his emotional nature, for which an apathetic God cannot cater, overwhelms him. Agave believes in nothing and is bored. A young widow, she is in need of sex which, in her position, she cannot have. (Incidentally, how did Echion die? I cannot discover this from any of my reference books.) Cadmus is superstitious and terrified that there may be some god he has neglected and, in any case, all gods are easily offended. Tiresias, following the Master's suggestion, is a Broad Churchman. (Probably, he will be sung by a mezzo-soprano.) Beroe, the nurse, is a devotee of the Mother Goddess, and the only one who at once recognises that the stranger is

Dionysus. The palace will not be set on fire until the end (there is a little earthquake off-stage which releases the imprisoned Bacchae), and then it is the Captain who does it at the command of Dionysus.

Auden sent a copy of the finished libretto to Dodds, and responded on 8 October 1963 to Dodds's lost letter in reply:

> Am *so* delighted that you like *The Bassarids.* More than half the credit, though, goes to Chester, who wrote more than half of it.
>
> As you can see, the "poetry" has to be pretty bare in order to be able to be set to music.

In a later letter to Dodds, on 19 August 1966, Auden suggested one of his reasons for choosing *The Bacchae* as the subject of a libretto:

> It seems to me that while, like Aeschylus and Sophocles, insisting that the gods are great powers who must be worshipped, unlike them, at least in the *Bacchae, Hippolytus, Ion,* Euripides raises the ethical question: "Are they righteous?" From the point of view of orthodox polytheism, there is, surely, something rather subversive in his work.

Henze was working on another opera, *Der junge Lord,* when Auden and Kallman finished the libretto of *The Bassarids,* and he did not begin serious work on it until the summer of 1964. Although Auden and Kallman had apparently already sent him a few pages of minor cuts, some of them closely similar to the cuts made for the copyright typescript, Henze was still daunted by the length of the piece. Around this time a mimeographed typescript, based on the cut version, was prepared for Henze, probably by his publisher. One of Henze's assistants, working from this typescript, calculated that the libretto would require at least two hours of music, more than an audience could tolerate for a one-act opera—and Henze's musical plans for preludes, transformation music, entrances, and exits would make the complete opera require twice that amount of time. On 6 August he told Auden and Kallman: "You understand that you have to cut enormously", and sent them a copy (now lost) of the mimeographed text in which he marked suggested cuts. (The surviving correspondence between Auden and Kallman and Henze is in the Paul Sacher Foundation in Basel.) Kallman replied to Henze's letter on 11 August, before the marked copy of the libretto arrived: "About *Becky:* If cuts must be made, they must be made, but I think they had best be made by you with either or both of us together in the same place. . . . But, before you tear into the poor body of our lamb like a Bassarid, consider soberly the possibility of doing it in two acts, the curtain to fall into the precipice of stillness and distant laughter just before the Intermezzo. It is, I think, our *extensive* treatment of the story that distinguishes it; and cuts *could* (I don't say *must*) weaken the impact of the complete work by narrowing its vision."

On receiving the marked copy of the libretto, Auden wrote Henze on 16 August:

C and I are vain enough to believe that our text is worth reading
an-und-für-sich. That is to say, whatever cuts are made in the
setting—and, of course, we have always known that there would have
to be many—we want our text to be *printed* as is. It should be quite
easy to devise a way of indicating which bits have not been set. One of
our reasons for wanting this is a professional one which you will, I
know, appreciate. The libretto is strictly metered throughout—there
is no free verse. In listening to your opera, the ear cannot, of course,
detect this, but, when, as you have every right to do, you omit words
or parts of lines in your setting, if these are also omitted from the
printed text, the *reader's* ear will be vexed. Similarly, for a reader,
certain mythological and genealogical information is a help to under-
standing the work, even though, from a musical point of view, it can
and should be dispensed with.

The same letter included some corrections to the mimeographed typescript and
some further revisions that served to reduce the length of the work. At the same
time, they returned Henze's marked copy of the typescript with further com-
ments. They sent another two pages of cuts and revisions either with the typescript
or soon afterward.

On 31 August 1964 Auden wrote Henze: "On thinking it over, I don't believe it
will even be necessary in the printed libretto to indicate the bits unset. Nobody
reads a libretto by flashlight *during* the performance, and, if they follow in the
score, the unset bits will not be there to puzzle them."

In a letter now lost, Henze suggested changing the title. Auden replied on 19
October 1964: "No, *The Maenads* will not do: they are only women. Uncommon or
not, *The Bassarids* is a genuine word and sounds well both in English and German.
Also, slightly puzzling titles titivate public curiosity." (Auden later wrote to his
friend Elizabeth Mayer, on 18 July 1966: "The word *Bassarids* or *Bassariden* really
does exist, though to my astonishment it is not in the O.E.D. It means followers of
Dionysus of both sexes"; letter in the Berg Collection.)* On 23 November 1964, at
Henze's request, Auden sent a pronunciation guide for the Greek names.

Henze finished composing the opera around the beginning of October 1965. In
a letter of 6 October he asked Auden and Kallman for "a shortish, but complete
Inhaltsangabe, as would be printed in a program-note. There should also be an
explanation of what the fuck the 'Bassarids' mean." He asked also for "an Essay
like you did in the case of *Elegy*". On 20 October Auden replied:

> *An Article about the genesis of the Opera.* I am very much against try-
> ing to state a myth in abstract logical terms, which rob it of all its
> resonance, e.g., if one starts talking about recent history, one will
> have fools saying that Dionysus *is* Hitler. What can, I think, be writ-

---

*The word is in the second (1989) edition of the *Oxford English Dictionary*, with citations
from Swinburne, Robert Graves, and Ezra Pound.

ten, and Chester and I would gladly write, is a technical piece, ex-
plaining what had to be done in order to turn Euripides' tragedy into
an opera libretto, e.g., the uninstructed imagine that what makes his
play settable are the choruses, when in fact, it is precisely with the
chorus that one has to be sparing or else the thing turns into oratorio.
Then, the question of differentiating the characters, usw.

> *For the Programme.* I enclose what I think the audience should learn
> before the curtain rises.

The technical article Auden offered to write took shape as the two essays re-
printed in §4. The material that Auden enclosed with his letter apparently con-
sisted of the "Genealogical Tree", the notes on "Mythological Background", and
"Religious Attitudes of the Characters" that appeared in the program of the pre-
miere and in the vocal score, but not in the printed libretto. At Henze's request
Auden sent on 27 December 1965 a synopsis of the action to be printed in the
program; this too appeared in the vocal score.

In July 1966, a few weeks before the premiere, Henze seems to have proposed a
new collaboration. In a letter of 14 July Auden responded: "As for the Easter
Mysterium, it is difficult for us to have ideas till we can talk to you." Nothing came of
this proposal, although Auden's letter suggested as an alternative that they "might
be able to do something along the lines of a Mummer's play about the resurrection
of the New Year".

The Bassarids was first performed, in German, at the Salzburger Festspiele, on 6
August 1966, conducted by Christoph von Dohnányi; the production was by
Gustav Rudolf Sellner. The first performance in English was at the Santa Fe Opera
on 7 August 1968, conducted by Henze. For this production Kallman provided a
new Prologue (see §5) and the Intermezzo was cut. Auden wrote Elizabeth Mayer
on 9 August: "I am convinced that Hans has written a masterpiece, though we feel
that he overscored the Intermezzo" (letter in the Berg Collection).

The text of this edition is based on the typescript that Auden and Kallman sent
Henze, probably in September 1963, printed in full as Auden insisted in his letter
to Henze on 16 August 1964 (see above). This edition restores from the copyright
typescript one page lost from the original typescript. Details of this, and of other
changes and abridgements made by the librettists at Henze's request, are noted in
§2. I have silently incorporated corrections of typing errors noted by the librettists
in their letters to Henze. This edition emends "Boetia" to "Boeotia" and slightly
regularizes the layout of dialogue and stage directions. Apparently in response to
E. R. Dodds's comment on the printed libretto, Auden told Dodds in a letter of 19
August 1966, "*Cytheron* shall become *Kithairon.*" Because Auden never reprinted
The Bassarids he never had a chance to make this change, although he used Dodds's
preferred spelling when writing about the libretto in *Secondary Worlds* (1968; the
more familiar spelling was mistakenly restored by Faber & Faber in a 1984 paper-
back). I have made the change in the main text of this edition, but have left the
original spelling in passages quoted in these notes from the original typescripts.

Drafts of most of the libretto are in two notebooks now in the Berg Collection
containing Auden's contribution and one at the University of Texas containing

Kallman's share. These notebooks suggest that Auden wrote the following speeches in the first half of the libretto, preceding the Intermezzo: the opening chorus of Citizens (pp. 251–52); the first chorus of the Bassarids (pp. 257–58); Pentheus's proclamation (pp. 260–61); Pentheus's aria to Beroe beginning "Faithful Beroe!" (pp. 269–70); the stanza for the Bassarids beginning "Blessed be Thebes, our city" (p. 272), and probably the corresponding stanzas beginning "She conceived a child", "In untimely travail", and "Child of the double door" (pp. 273–74); and Agave's aria beginning "On a forest footpath" (pp. 275–76). In the Intermezzo, Kallman wrote the opening dialogue (pp. 284–87) and the four closing couplets (p. 292) after the characters "discard their properties"; no manuscript survives of "The Judgement of Calliope" but it is almost certainly Auden's work. In the text following the Intermezzo, Auden wrote the Maenads' chorus beginning "Diony- / -sus appear" (pp. 299–300), and probably everything after Pentheus's death—from the Maenads' "Ayayalya! / Glory to Dionysus who has blessed our hunting" (p. 302) to the end. Everything else, including the elaborate stage directions and the final preparation of the typescript, is probably Kallman's work. Auden and Kallman inserted a few words and lines in each other's sections during the course of revision.

In a notebook, now in the Berg Collection, that Auden used when writing drafts of *Elegy for Young Lovers* is a draft of a speech addressed by Pentheus to Cadmus. This speech does not correspond to anything in the finished text. Possibly this speech was written in 1959, if in fact Auden and Kallman thought of a *Bacchae* libretto then; it is equally possible that it dates from the first attempts to write the libretto in 1961.

The work was first published in the vocal score issued by B. Schott's Söhne, in Mainz, on 26 July 1966; the text included only the libretto as set by Henze, without the cut passages. Schott published the libretto booklet on 3 August 1966; this form of the text substantially reproduced the full libretto, with cuts and changes indicated by square brackets and footnotes.

§2 THE EVOLUTION OF THE TEXT

The earliest state of the text is the authorial typescript, which was typed by Kallman and sent to Henze probably in September 1963. It is now with Henze's papers in the Paul Sacher Foundation in Basel, and forms the basis of the text of this edition. The next state, sightly abridged, is the professionally typed carbon-copy typescript registered for copyright on 13 January 1964 and now in the Performing Arts Division of the Library of Congress.

Virtually all of the librettists' changes in the libretto were evidently made in response to Henze's requests for cuts. The earliest changes seem to be those made between the original typescript, completed in September 1963, and the copyright typescript, completed by January 1964; these changes, which the librettists evidently made to their own copy of the original, roughly correspond to changes apparently sent to Henze on two typed pages in the latter part of 1963, and affect the scenes of Pentheus's aria to Beroe (pp. 269–70) and Dionysus's final apotheosis and the lines that follow it (pp. 309–11). At some time after preparing the copyright typescript Auden and Kallman apparently sent Henze another revised passage, this one replacing the Captain's first dialogue with Agave (pp. 258–59). When Henze received this revised passage he discarded one page of the original; this edition restores the lost page from equivalent text in the copyright typescript.

All these revisions were incorporated in the mimeographed typescript prepared for Henze during the summer of 1964; a copy of this typescript is now in the Berg Collection. Perhaps around this time, before they saw this mimeographed version, Auden and Kallman sent Henze a revised version of the debate between Pentheus and Cadmus (pp. 265–68).

When Henze sent a marked copy of his mimeographed typescript to Auden and Kallman with notes suggesting cuts, the librettists responded with a further set of cuts and changes in a letter from Auden to Henze on 16 August; Auden's letter also rejected a few of Henze's suggested cuts but approved the rest. At some time after the middle of August 1964, Auden sent Henze two pages with a further set of cuts.

The title page of the mimeographed text corresponds to that of the authorial typescript as reproduced in this edition. The title of the copyright version is: "The Bassarids / Opera Seria, with Intermezzo, in One Act / by W. H. Auden and Chester Kallman / Music by Hans Werner Henze".

Auden and Kallman apparently added the epigraph (from Gottfried Benn's poem "Verlorenes Ich") during the early stages of revision; it appears in Henze's hand on the title page of the original typescript. Henze complained of the epigraph's obscurity in a letter to the librettists on 6 October 1965.

The list of characters in the mimeographed text identifies the voices of each of the characters; these identifications were evidently added by Henze. The list of characters in the printed text varies slightly from the text in the typescripts; the Captain leads "the Royal Guard" instead of "the Guard", and the heading "Characters in 'The Judgement of Calliope'" is expanded to read "Characters in the Intermezzo / 'The Judgement of Calliope'".

The mimeographed typescript adds the title "Introduction" above the beginning of the text; no further headings appear elsewhere in the text and the heading itself is absent from other texts. The printed libretto divides the text into four movements; the second begins when Pentheus appears in the palace doorway (p. 265); the third begins when the Stranger turns and faces Pentheus before Pentheus orders him removed (p. 280); the fourth begins with the Maenads' fortissimo shout immediately after Pentheus's death (p. 302). The third movement is divided into two parts by the Intermezzo.

The printed libretto incorporates the cuts and changes that Auden and Kallman had already sent Henze on separate sheets before August 1964. Further changes that Auden sent Henze with his letter of 16 August 1964 and on two pages sent later were indicated in the printed text by two methods: cuts were enclosed in square brackets; rewritten abridgements were printed in footnotes headed "text in the score".

Page 253.

The printed libretto adds the stage direction "*mysteriously*" between Tiresias's lines "Come with me . . ." and "Young Dionysus".

Page 257.

In his marked copy of the mimeographed typescript Henze evidently suggested cutting the stanza beginning "Sun-baked Persia"; Auden's letter of 16 August 1964 told him instead to cut the stanza beginning "The Nile paid homage".

Page 258.

The text from Agave's line beginning "You're young, Captain" through Autonoe's "It's true *he'd* obey you" and Agave's "He?" (p. 259) is taken from the copyright typescript, which evidently reproduces a page discarded from the first typescript when Auden and Kallman sent Henze two replacement pages at some time before August 1964. The replacement pages include substitutions for material crossed through on the page preceding and the page following the discarded page. The revised text, printed below, replaces everything in the original typescript from Cadmus's "Think . . . Are They close?" to the end of Beroe's speech beginning ". . . the King has / Asked that his kinsmen gather".

CADMUS [*to himself*].
    Think . . . Could a new young god be my grandson?
    They are the ageless forebears of ageing
    Man and were never children of man. No.
    Never. And can they change, can the gods change?

> [*Meanwhile, the* CAPTAIN, *after his slight hesitation, resumes walking towards the palace:* AGAVE, *coming forward a bit, detains him by slightly raising her hand. He keeps his head bowed.* BEROE *remains at the back, ever so often giving* AGAVE *a swift glance sharp with judgement and hatred.*]

AGAVE. You're here, Captain? Strange.
CAPTAIN.   Your Highness?
AGAVE.   I'm surprised.
    You're young, Captain: why, when half Thebes escaped
    To Cytheron, that you did not go, is strange.
CAPTAIN. I had not been told to go there. No word
    Commanding me save what Beroe . . .
AGAVE [*interrupting with a laugh*].   Save what she
    Commands you? Your Maenad? Must strong-armed youth
    At night-fall elude her watch?
CAPTAIN [*anxious to get away*].   Madam . . .
AGAVE.   And
    Your dog's too? I trust he's well.
CAPTAIN [*in spite of his embarrassment, pleased, he lifts his head and smiles*].
                        You are kind

To ask, Madam. Yes, he's well. [*A brief pause: then, hurriedly:*]
Please. The King
Your son, Madam, bade me hurry . . .

AGAVE [*indifferently*].   You may go.

> [*He bows and hurries into the palace;* AGAVE *turns
> away.* AUTONOE, *in dress and manner a less com-
> manding version of her sister, has entered R. earlier,
> and stood aside in order to observe the foregoing collo-
> quy: now she quietly approaches* AGAVE *who has not
> yet noticed her.*]

CADMUS [*continuing*]. Tell me, O Pallas, have I offended
Them or neglected any? Remind them:
Humbly I served them all at my marriage.

AUTONOE [*tapping* AGAVE *lightly on the shoulder*].
My sister is reproached.

AGAVE [*turning*].   Reproached?

AUTONOE.   Not by me.

AGAVE [*laughing*]. You're mad. But should I go mad thus, I'd not—
Like one sister—claim a god brought me low.

AUTONOE [*laughing archly: the sisters punctuate all their remaining
conversation with light cultivated laughter*].
A man might be thought a god were he loved
Enough. *She* believed who felled *her,* her charms
Transformed to a god.

AGAVE.   I've no use for gods
Of my making nor if mine to command.

AUTONOE [*indicating the palace entrance with a gesture*].
It's true *he'd* obey, the shy god there . . .

AGAVE.   He,
I fear, loves his dog, his dog only.

AUTONOE.   Ah!
How kind of him!

AGAVE.   Was there some kind Captain here,
As *kind* to Semele . . . ?

CADMUS [*continuing*].
I can remember only their laughter
Now. Were they happy? Wait! They are laughing
Still!

BEROE [*respectfully approaching* CADMUS].
     Sire, your grandson . . .

CADMUS [*startled*].   Grandson!

BEROE.   . . . the King has
    Asked that his kinsmen gather to hear his
    First proclamation. If I may . . .

Auden's letter of 16 August 1964 included further changes in this revised sequence; in place of the lines from the Captain's "I had not been told" through his "Please. The King", Auden offered:

CAPTAIN. I had not been told to go there, Madam.
AGAVE. Your brave dog, I trust, is well.
CAPTAIN. He's well, Madam. Please. The King *etc.*

Pages 265–66.
    In the second stanza of Cadmus's speech beginning "Wait, Pentheus" the printed libretto replaces the text of the first and copyright typescripts, "stone and of deed yet.", with "stone and rich deed." In the third stanza the printed libretto replaces "A brief *Alas* expired by its bloom.", with "A joy that cried *Alas!* in full bloom,". In the fourth stanza the printed libretto capitalizes "Her". The changes are not mentioned in Auden and Kallman's surviving letters to Henze, but are probably authorial revisions made for the printed text. Because this speech was never set, and the changes were made solely for reading, the revised text is used here.
    The entire passage in the first typescript from Cadmus's speech beginning "Wait, Pentheus" through the end of Pentheus's speech beginning "Great Thebes would have remained" (p. 267) was replaced by an abridged version on a typescript page that Auden and Kallman sent to Henze, probably in the summer of 1964. This revised page, which Henze labeled "Blatt A", reads:

CADMUS. Wait, Pentheus. Give no orders. Bow your head: you
    Rule by my consent. I spoke with gods.
    Their words, forgotten, were fire, it robed my daughters;
    And Semele was the loveliest:
    A light slain by light, a flame dancing the hillside
    Seen there and gone and never understood.

    And gone and seen again dancing there forever
    When night falls back and for one full day
    Our Mother wears the speaking of her perfection.
    Young, I have looked into her sad eyes.
    But what will you see when you disrobe their shining
    From earth and city? Great King, bow your head.

BASSARIDS. (*As before* [p. 266])

PENTHEUS [*descending the steps*].
    Royal head bowed, I have listened. But you did not say: is
    Dionysus a god or no?

CADMUS. I believe him a god and, new
  To himself and his strength, proving them both on man.
PENTHEUS. So. Why, then, have you stayed, you who in fear of each
  Of the gods have built shrines to all?
  Go. Or have you exhausted fear?
CADMUS. No, King Pentheus, no. I fear:
  Most for my King. Young joys are not mine. The god
  Knows what love I bear Thebes. Here I may honor him.
PENTHEUS. Could such love be resigned? No. Dionysus: that
  New name cancelled the love Cadmus resigned to me.
  Fearing for Thebes? No. Spent and afraid of death.
CADMUS. Youth I believed best fit to receive the new;
  No god crossed or neglected shadowed your past like mine;
  But, King, have you no awe? No fear?
PENTHEUS. No fear, not of the gods. I fear
  Man, that sly chaos of need; the gods
  Do have my awe. But can you be awed
  To have sired an Olympian slut?
CADMUS. You believe she was justly slain,
  Semele, by the Thunderer for a lie?
PENTHEUS. Cadmus's gods may punish, the gods do not.
  Chance rules us when we know them not:
  Thebes will. Not through your shrine to a lie!
CADMUS. Great Thebes prospered when I was King.
PENTHEUS. Great Thebes would have remained in Thebes!
  When relic-mongers grew rich peddling their wisps of charred
  Straw as True Strands of Semele's hair, how great
  Thebes was! We shall root out that greatness: him,
  Your new god, we shall find, kill. As for them, his sworn
  Votaries, let them forswear him at once, or die!

In attempting to incorporate this revised passage, the typist of the mimeo-
graphed text erroneously reproduced the phrase "as before" instead of retyping
the text to which it refers. After Pentheus's *"your* lie is dead", the printed libretto
adds a stage direction: *"pointing to the shrine."*.

In response to Henze's notes in the lost copy of the mimeographed text Au-
den further revised this passage in his letter of 16 August 1964. He replaced
some of the lines printed above with the following corresponding lines:

CADMUS. No, King Pentheus, no. I fear most for my king.
  But, King, have you no awe? No fear?
PENTHEUS. Cadmus' gods may punish; the gods do not.
  Chance rules us when we know them not. I fear

Man that sly chaos of need. The true gods
Have my awe. Your shrine was to a lie.
CADMUS. Great Thebes prospered when I was King.
PENTHEUS. How great Thebes was! We shall root out that greatness *etc.*

Then, in the two pages of cuts that Auden sent Henze some time after the middle of August 1964, he abridged the whole passage further:

CADMUS. Wait, Pentheus. Give no orders. Bow your head: you
Rule by my consent. I spoke with gods.
Their words, forgotten, were fire. It robed my daughters;
And Semele was the loveliest.
What will you see when you disrobe their shining
From earth and city? Great King, bow your head.
PENTHEUS. Royal head bowed, I have listened. But you did not
Say: is Dionysus a god or no?
CADMUS. I believe him a god.
PENTHEUS. So. Why, then, have you stayed, you who in fear of each
Of the gods have built shrines to all?
Go. Or have you exhausted fear?
CADMUS. I fear most for my King. Have you no awe? No fear?
PENTHEUS. Cadmus' gods may punish: the gods do not.
But Chance rules men who know them not.
CADMUS. Great Thebes prospered when I was King.
PENTHEUS. Thebes was great until this new god came,
Whom we shall find, kill. Captain! The Guard! At once!
CADMUS. Run. Run. Help me! The Sown Men have arisen.
PENTHEUS. Let *King* Cadmus fear not. For Thebes.
Sire, go honorably, wearing old age in peace.
Captain, you have your orders; return with
All you can find. Kill all who resist. Go. (*Cont. as in text*)

Page 267.
In the two lines that each begin "Great Thebes" the typescripts lack "her" and "home", both presumably added by the librettists for the printed libretto, as this dialogue was never set.

Page 269.
The typescript copyrighted 13 January 1964 has an abridged version of Pentheus's first speech to Beroe. This version omits the first five lines and begins at "Listen, Beroe". It also omits "For so it must be / . . . / To understanding."
The abridged version in the copyright text does not match the version that Auden and Kallman sent Henze probably in the latter part of 1963; this version alters both of Pentheus's speeches to Beroe, from "Faithful Beroe" to "Till the day I die!":

PENTHEUS. Faithful Beroe!
    To you alone
    Can I open my heart:
    The best in Thebes
    Do but worship shadows
    Of the True Good.
    They honor Its excellence
    Under many a name
    Of god and goddess,
    But the Good is one,
    Neither male nor female.
    They praise Its glory
    With statues and temples;
    But the Good is invisible,
    And dwells nowhere.
    Well, let it be so:
    Truth and righteousness
    Glimmer through
    The ancient rites:
    But they shall not worship
    The Ungood!

BASSARIDS. (*As before.*)

PENTHEUS. Dionysus *etc.* to
    Shameless thing." (*as before*)

    Bear witness, Beroe
    To this, my vow. [*He kneels.*]
    I, Pentheus,
    King of Thebes,
    Henceforth will abstain
    From wine, from meats,
    And from woman's bed
    Live sober and chaste
    Till the day I die!

In his letter of 16 August 1964 Auden further abridged the opening speech by sending a text that lacked "They honor Its excellence / . . . / Well, let it be so".

Page 271.

    In the long stage direction beginning "The Guard can be heard" the words "the Roman Campagna" are a correction marked by Kallman in friends' copies of the libretto. The printed text and all typescripts have "the Romagna" (i.e., Rome and its province), which Kallman probably misunderstood to mean the Roman Campagna.

Page 272.

In the two pages of cuts that Auden sent Henze after the middle of August 1964, the corresponding passage in the original text was abridged as follows:

PENTHEUS. What? A poor handful, Captain?
CAPTAIN. All, Sire, we could discover;
    Though we could hear more, many more.
PENTHEUS. So be it.
    Hunters who dare Cytheron,
    Who leads your singing and dancing?
    Tell me that I may bow to his wonder?
    Tell me. Where is he? My younger
    Greater, more travelled kinsman, your
    Love, Dionysus. Tell me.

[Pause.]

    [To CAPTAIN.] Captain, who is that youth? He does not seem
    Tranced like the others.
CAPTAIN.   All of the others
    Came when he bade them come.
    Maybe a priest of this Dionysus.
PENTHEUS. He shall remain. And my kin. And this prophet.
    As for the others . . .
    Who is that woman there who goes whoring
    Led by her daughter?
CAPTAIN.   A slave, Sire,
    Of the Lady Agave's household.
PENTHEUS.   So. Put them
    Both to the Question . . . *(Cont. as in text)*

In Pentheus's speech beginning "So be it." the typescripts and the corrections sent to Henze by Auden and Kallman all have "bow to his wonder". The printed libretto has "bow to this wonder", probably an error, but conceivably an authorial change.

Page 276.

In Agave's aria beginning "On a forest footpath" the last line of the third stanza reads in the first typescript "So fell before flies." The copyright typescript and printed libretto correct this to "So fell before to flies."

Page 278.

In the two pages of cuts and changes that Auden sent Henze after the middle of August 1964 was the following replacement for the corresponding lines in the original:

PENTHEUS. Enough. Captain, take my mother back
    To her quarters with her sister. Lock them in.
    Then send your men to this man's house
    And pull it down. Let no one take him in. Tiresias,
    You have disgraced Thebes with your trade in prophecy
    Too long. That trade is at an end. Go.
TIRESIAS. The scattered seed . . . etc. (Cont. as in text)

Page 279.

The Stranger's aria "I found a child asleep" was the subject of notes that Henze made in the lost copy of the mimeographed typescript that he sent to Auden and Kallman in August 1964. Auden's letter of 16 August refers to his own comments on those notes in the typescript, which Auden returned separately. In the letter Auden writes that the only possible cut in the aria is the stanza beginning "Blue into white". In the two pages of changes he sent after the middle of August he allowed this cut "If *absolutely* necessary" and added that the two lines "I have lit . . . singing here" could also be cut.

Page 281.

In the stage direction after the earthquake, the typescripts have "falling stones" where the printed libretto has "falling masonry". The change was probably authorial and is followed here.

Page 282.

Auden's letter to Henze on 16 August 1964 replaces the corresponding lines in the original text with the following:

PENTHEUS [*nodding*]. You are right. [*To* CAPTAIN.] No. Wait. Go. Go
    lock the gate.
    Yes. Go. And then you must return.
    Close by. We must think first. We are King.

Page 285.

In his letter of 16 August 1964 Auden authorized cutting the lines from Tiresias's "So you might have offered" to Agave's "from gentlemen's sobriety." In Agave's same speech, "tope" is misprinted "hope" in the printed libretto. The correct reading appears in the typescript, and was restored by Kallman in friends' copies of the printed text.

Page 286.

In Tiresias's speech beginning "Yes! I have it!" the typescript underlines only the first word in the title "*The* / Judgement of Calliope". While it is possible that Kallman intended but neglected to underline the remaining words of the title, which all appear on the following line, the emphasis of the first word alone probably emphasizes the rhyme. The full title appears in roman type in the printed libretto.

Page 287.

In the typescript the speeches of Calliope and Adonis, from "Calliope, I, by Jove on high" until the heading "Aria", were originally divided into four-line stanzas. Auden marked the typescript to indicate that the breaks dividing the first three stanzas (Calliope's first speech) should be closed, but evidently neglected to turn the page to close the breaks that divided the remaining three stanzas. Because the speeches that follow Venus's aria are in the same metre, I have also closed the breaks that in the typescript followed Adonis's lines "To whom he did incline." and "And swore that she should die, sirs." ("Sirs" is capitalized in the printed text.) In the printed libretto all the breaks are retained, despite Auden's markings.

Page 294.

The question mark at the end of Dionysus's "You know me, woman?" is marked, probably by Auden, in Stephen Spender's copy of the printed libretto.

Page 297.

In the stage direction beginning "Exeunt Captain and Guard left" the printed libretto inserts a sentence after the first: "Servants remove the throne." This is implied in the preceding dialogue and was probably added by Henze or the publisher.

Page 302.

In place of the Maenads' one-word opening of a speech, "Agave. . . . ", the printed libretto has "Agave, daughter of Cadmus, / Was the first to cry Havoc". In the original typescript the remainder of the speech occurs only when the opening word is repeated seven speeches later. The printed libretto also erroneously repeats the Maenads' stage direction, "*at first fortissimo* [etc.]", where the typescript has "*very faintly at first* [etc.]". The printed libretto adds the stage direction "*nearer*" to Agave's Voice's speech "Tell, maidens: who was swiftest", and to the Maenads' speech that immediately follows, beginning "Agave, daughter of Cadmus". The printed libretto also adds the stage direction "*very near*" to the speech of Agave's and Autonoe's Voices beginning "Not with a net".

Page 307.

In Tiresias's stanza the typescripts have "warnings" where the printed libretto and score have "warning". The change seems authorial and is followed here.

Page 309.

Among the abridgements on two pages of typescript that Auden and Kallman apparently sent to Henze in the latter part of 1963 was the instruction to cut Agave's three lines beginning "Bear him hence" and to expand the stage direction that followed those lines to read as follows:

> [AGAVE *bows her head. At a gesture from* CADMUS *the two* GUARDS *carry the bier off left during the first lines of the following: tune: Chorale in the Intermezzo.*]

Pages 309–11.

Among the abridgements on two pages of typescript that Auden and Kallman apparently sent to Henze in the latter part of 1963 was the following abridged version of the sequence from Dionysus's "I see that you know who I am now" to Agave's "Tartarus waits for you all." The spoken text matches that in the copyright typescript that had been prepared probably in January 1964, but the copyright typescript lacks almost all the stage directions in the version sent to Henze.

DIONYSUS. Yes, I am he: I *am* Dionysus.
    Soon you shall see me revealed in my glory,
    All save those polluted with blood. You,
    Cadmus, Autonoe, Agave,
    Are banished from Thebes. You will go now,
    Go each in a different direction.
    Prepare, then, to part. You will not meet
    Each other again. You will not see
    Boeotia again.
CADMUS.   An Immortal
    God ought to forgive, not be angry
    Forever like ignorant   ⌈ men.
DIONYSUS [*cutting him short*]. ⌊   Captain!

> [CAPTAIN *steps forward.* DIONYSUS *points to the altar flame.*]

    Light torches there. Set fire to the palace.
    Raze it to the ground.

> [CAPTAIN *salutes. Followed by the returned* GUARDS, *he and they take brands from behind the tomb, light them at the altar and quickly cross the stage to the palace, leaving the doors open on entry.*]

CADMUS.   O may kind death
    Come soon, put an end to my sorrow!
DIONYSUS. The grandson of Ares will not die:
    He will pass in the end to the Blessed
    Isles.
CADMUS. Islands accursed to me! All
    May find peace beyond Acheron. Not I.
DIONYSUS. I have spoken. No longer delay. Go.

> [CAPTAIN *and* GUARDS *re-enter from the palace: a red glow can be seen through its open doors. Smoke slowly befogs the scene during the following.*]

BEROE [*to* AGAVE]. Let me go with you. We are two
    Women without hope.
TIRESIAS [*to* CADMUS]. I am sorry, Cadmus. Let me at least
    See my old friend to the gate.
AGAVE AND AUTONOE. Father, sister, Thebes, farewell!
CADMUS. Daughters dear, and Thebes, farewell!
BASSARIDS. Go! Unclean ones! Go!

> [*To the continued dismissals of the* BASSARIDS,
> CADMUS *and* TIRESIAS *exeunt R.,* AUTONOE *L.*
> AGAVE *and* BEROE *are about to exit C. when*
> AGAVE *turns to* DIONYSUS.]

AGAVE. Dionysus, and all on Olympus:
    Think of the altarless Fates!
    Where is gelded Uranus? Or Chronos,
    Once an invincible god?
    Sport with us while you can: one
    Tartarus waits for you all!

§3 AUDEN AND KALLMAN'S PROGRAM NOTES

In response to Henze's request of 6 October 1965 for "a shortish, but complete Inhaltsangabe, as would be printed in a program-note", Auden and Kallman apparently provided on 20 October the following genealogical table and accounts of the "Mythological Background" and "Religious Attitudes of the Characters". Apparently in December 1965 Henze requested a synopsis for the program. Auden replied on 21 December, "Will write synopsis soon". On 27 December he sent the text with this comment: "I hope the enclosed is satisfactory and not madly too long. As you will see, I have avoided mentioning either the costumes of the characters or the appearance of the fertility idols in the final scene, as I think we want to surprise our audience with these."

    The following texts are taken from the vocal score, where they are signed by Auden and Kallman. Substantially similar texts appeared in the program of the Salzburg Festival premiere, where they are unsigned. The program has some minor errors in the genealogical tree and what appears to be an unauthorized editorial change: in the account of Agave's religious attitudes the text in the vocal score (followed here) has "a mask of cynical bitchiness, though"; the program has "a mask of cynical maliciousness though". The texts in the score use mostly American spellings; those in the program substitute some British spellings. The text of the synopsis in the vocal score, however, adds headings for the four movements (almost certainly not authorial, and omitted here), and omits the parenthetical cross-references found in the text in the program (almost certainly authorial, and included here). The abbreviations in these parenthetical cross-references are characteristic of Auden's typing.

GENEALOGICAL TREE

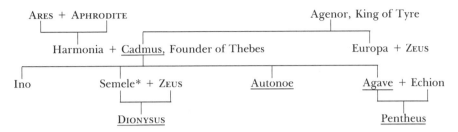

*Finally apotheosised as THYONE

MYTHOLOGICAL BACKGROUND

CADMUS

Zeus fell in love with Europa and, disguised as a bull, carried her off to Crete. At his father's bidding, Cadmus set out to find his sister, but was then told by the Delphic Oracle to abandon the search and, instead, to follow a cow he would presently meet, and found a city on the spot where the cow should first lie down. The cow led him to the site of the future city of Thebes. Cadmus sent his companions to a spring to fetch water for a sacrifice. The spring was guarded by a dragon which killed them all, but was then slain by Cadmus. The Goddess Athene told him to sow the dragon's teeth. From them sprang up armed warriors whom Cadmus set fighting with each other by casting a stone into their midst. They fought until there were only five survivors, who swore allegiance to Cadmus. These five, known as the Sown Men, helped him build the citadel of Thebes and became the ancestors of the city's noble families. One of them, Echion, married Cadmus' youngest daughter, Agave. Cadmus himself married Harmonia in a grand wedding at which all the Gods were present. When the opera opens he has just abdicated in favor of his grandson, Pentheus.

SEMELE

Cadmus' second daughter was courted by Zeus, disguised as a mortal. When his wife, the Goddess Hera, heard of the affair, she visited Semele, disguised as Semele's servant, Beroe, and persuaded her to demand that her lover disclose himself to her in all his divine splendor. Semele nagged at Zeus until he consented, and his lightning reduced her to ashes. Zeus, however, rescued her unborn child, Dionysus, and sewed him into his thigh from which, in due time, the boy was born. Hence, one of

Dionysus's titles is the Twice Born One. When the opera opens, Semele's tomb has already become a shrine of pilgrimage for devotees of the new cult of Dionysus. Some people, however, including her sisters, believe that Semele's lover was not Zeus but an ordinary mortal, and, consequently, view the cult with contempt.

ECHION

There is no mention in Greek mythology of when or how Echion died, but, when the opera opens, Agave has been a widow for some time.

BEROE

Greek mythology does not say what happened to Beroe after Semele's death. In the opera, Agave took her on to act as a nurse to Pentheus.

TIRESIAS

For a period in his life, Tiresias was transformed into a woman as punishment for killing the female of a pair of snakes. On account of his bisexual experience Zeus and Hera asked him to settle an argument they were having as to who derives most pleasure from the sexual act, the man or the woman. The woman, said Tiresias, at which Hera was so cross that she struck him with blindness. All Zeus could do in compensation was to grant him long life and the gift of prophecy. Neither in Euripides' tragedy nor in the opera, however, are his prophetic powers in evidence.

DIONYSUS

When the opera opens, Dionysus has already made a triumphant tour through Egypt and India and Phrygia. When he and Pentheus are first left alone together, he tells of an adventure which befell him in the Aegean. In the harbor of Icaria, he had hired a ship and crew to take him to the island of Naxos. The sailors proved to be pirates and steered for Asia, intending to sell him as a slave. Dionysus made a vine grow from the deck, enfolding the mast. Ivy twined about the rigging. The ship was filled with phantom beasts. The terrified pirates leaped overboard and were turned into dolphins.

THE JUDGEMENT OF CALLIOPE (*Intermezzo*)

Cinryas, King of Cyprus, boasted that his daughter Smyrna was more beautiful than Aphrodite. The goddess avenged this insult by making Smyrna fall in love with her father and sleep with him on a night when he was too drunk to know what he was doing. She became pregnant, and when Cinryas learned what had happened, he seized a sword and chased her from the palace. He finally overtook her, but Aphrodite changed her into a myrrh-tree which her father's sword split in two. Out fell the infant Adonis. Foreseeing that he would grow into a beautiful young man, Aphrodite hid the child in a chest which she entrusted to Persephone, Queen of the Dead. In course of time, Persephone, overcome by curiosity, opened the lid, fell in love with Adonis and took him off to her palace. Hearing of this, Aphrodite appealed to Zeus who delegated the case to the Muse Calliope. Calliope's verdict was that the two goddesses had equal claims upon Adonis—Aphrodite for saving his life when he was born, and Persephone for rescuing him from the chest—but that he was also entitled to an annual holiday from their insatiable demands. One third of the year he was to spend with Persephone, one third with Aphrodite, and one third by himself. Aphrodite, however, did not play fair; by wearing her magic girdle, she bewitched Adonis into spending all the year with her. The cheated Persephone thereupon went to Ares and told him that Aphrodite now had a mortal lover whom she preferred to him. The jealous god disguised himself as a boar and gored Adonis to death on Mount Lebanon.

RELIGIOUS ATTITUDES OF THE CHARACTERS

CADMUS

An old man, he has become the victim of superstitious terrors. He has learned by bitter experience that the gods are not only powerful but also jealous competitors for man's worship. It is difficult to pay reverence or to obey the orders of one without giving offence to another, and giving offence, however unintentionally, always brings misfortune. Unable to decide for himself whether Dionysus is or is not a god, the rise of his cult is one more occasion for dread. If Dionysus is divine and he, as king of Thebes, refuses to give the cult official sanction, divine vengeance will fall on the city. On the other hand, if Dionysus is only an ordinary mortal, sanction of the cult will outrage the existing gods. Rather than take a decision, he has abdicated and left to Pentheus the responsibility of choosing what course to take.

TIRESIAS

A vain, stupid, impotent old man, whose fear of death takes the form of trying to keep up with the young. He is enthusiastic about the cult of Dionysus simply because it is new, the latest thing in religious fashion.

AGAVE

She has lost all faith in the traditional polytheism in which she was brought up, and, when the opera opens, believes in nothing. She is lonely and unhappy, feelings she hides behind a mask of cynical bitchiness, though really a passionate nature. The obvious cause of her loneliness is that she has been left a widow while still fairly young, there is no man equal to her in rank whom she could take for a second husband, and she is too fastidious to take a lover whom she does not respect. She finds the Captain of the Royal Guard physically attractive, but she would never dream of having an affair with him.

However, her dissatisfaction goes much deeper than sexual frustration. Though not consciously aware of it, she is desperately looking for some faith which would give her life meaning and purpose.

PENTHEUS

One may suppose if one likes, that he has visited Ionia and studied under one of the philosophers there. At any rate, he has discarded polytheism, the gods of which have all the passions and vices of mortals. The god he has come to believe in is one, universal, and impersonal, the Good, to be apprehended by human reason. The source of human blindness and wrong-doing are the passions of the flesh. He knows that, if he were to tell the people of Thebes what he really believes, they would think him a blasphemer and an atheist. He must leave them their traditional cults and hope, by degrees, to purify them. But with this new cult of Dionysus, the deliberate worship, as it seems to him, of irrational passion, there can be no compromise. His attempt completely to suppress his instinctual life instead of integrating it with his rationality brings about his downfall. One might say that a similar fate would have befallen Sarastro, had there not been a Tamino and a Pamina to marry and so reconcile Day to Night.

BEROE

Descended from a people who once ruled Greece before they were conquered and enslaved by the Dorian invaders, she has remained faithful to the cult of the Mother Goddess and has never accepted the male-dominated Olympus of her masters.

THE CAPTAIN OF THE GUARD

As a policeman, a servant of the State, it is not, he believes, his business to have any opinion of his own, religious or political; his job is to carry out the orders of the legitimate authorities. While Cadmus reigned, he had obeyed Cadmus. So long as Pentheus is king, he obeys Pentheus. When Pentheus is dead and Cadmus declared an exile, authority has clearly passed to Dionysus, and he takes his orders from him.

SYNOPSIS OF THE ACTION

The chorus tell of Cadmus' abdication and wish happiness and wisdom to their new king and to the city of Thebes. Off-stage a voice suddenly cries:

"The God Dionysus has entered Boeotia." The chorus run off to welcome him.

The city of Thebes. On the right the royal palace. On the left the tomb of Semele upon which an altar-flame is burning. The city is almost empty since most of the citizens have gone off to Mount Cytheron to greet Dionysus. On stage are Cadmus, Tiresias, Agave and Beroe. They discuss Dionysus and reveal their various attitudes towards him. (See above. R[eligious] A[ttitudes].) Since his coronation, Pentheus has shut himself up alone in the palace where, according to Beroe, he has spent the time in fasting and prayer. Tiresias leaves to join the crowd on Mount Cytheron. The Captain of the Guard enters on his way to the palace to receive orders from Pentheus. Agave flirts with him but without exciting a response, and he goes into the palace. Her sister Autonoe joins her and they joke together about the Captain's good looks and earnestness. The Captain comes out of the palace and reads a royal proclamation, forbidding the citizens of Thebes to believe that Zeus had a son by Semele. Soon Pentheus appears himself, goes to Semele's tomb, extinguishes the altar-flame by casting his cloak over it, decrees death to any person who shall dare relight it and returns to the palace, followed by the Captain. Cadmus is horrified by Pentheus' action. Agave and Autonoe highly approve. Off-stage the sound of a string-instrument being tuned is heard, and presently a voice, which sings a serenade of invitation to go to Mount Cytheron and taste of its promised delights. Agave and Autonoe, hypnotised, dance away.

Cadmus warns Pentheus against rash action. Pentheus reiterates his determination to extirpate the cult of Dionysus, even if that involves punishing his mother. (See above. R. A.). He orders the Captain to go with his men to Mount Cytheron and take into custody all he can find there. Pentheus reveals to his old nurse what he really believes (see above. R. A.) and takes a vow to abstain from women and eating meat. Beroe prays to the Mother Goddess to protect him. (See above. R. A.).

The Judgement Hall in the Palace. The Captain brings in his prisoners, among them Tiresias, Autonoe, Agave, a woman slave of her household with a small daughter, and the Stranger. All are in a state of trance and hum continuously. Tiresias babbles hysterically about the relation of Dionysus to vineyards until Pentheus cuts him short. Pentheus orders the Captain to take away Agave's slave, her daughter and any of the prisoners who are not citizens of Thebes and put them to the torture. Pentheus attempts to wake his mother from her trance by asking her who she is, who her husband was and what his own name is. In answer Agave sings an aria, describing her experience on Mount Cytheron, a kind of Wordsworthian mystical vision of nature. Beroe, having recognised that the Stranger is Dionysus, tries to warn Pentheus but he will not listen to her. The Captain returns to say that torture had failed to extract any information from the prisoners. Pentheus orders him to confine Agave and Autonoe to their quarters, to set Tiresias free but to pull down his house. Pentheus, imagining the Stranger to be a priest of Dionysus, cross-questions him about the god, but receives riddling answers. Threatened with death, the Stranger sings an aria about Dionysus's voyage to Naxos (see above, M[ythological] B[ackground]).

The Captain returns and Pentheus orders him to put the Stranger to the torture. Left alone, Pentheus expresses his rage and fear at what has taken place. The stage darkens. There is an earthquake and the sound of falling masonry. Pentheus' cloak is plucked from Semele's tomb by invisible forces, and the altar-flame shoots up once more. The glad shouts of the prisoners are heard as they escape and flee back to Mount Cytheron. The Stranger re-enters and offers to grant Pentheus a vision of what his mother and the others are really doing on Mount Cytheron. Repelled and fascinated, Pentheus orders Beroe to bring them his mother's mirror. The Stranger holds it up, and Pentheus gazes into it.

Intermezzo

What the audience see are Pentheus' repressed phantasies, an over-refined, decadent world where sex is the subject of giggles. Agave, Autonoe, Tiresias, the Captain, are dressed like actors in some pastoral play at an eighteenth century French court. The charade they perform is the Judgement of Calliope (see above, M. B.). In their version, the Greek mythological names, e.g., Ares, Hades, Zeus, Aphrodite, Persephone, have been romanised to Mars, Pluto, Jove, Venus, Proserpina.

Pentheus, sick with disgust, but now completely under the hypnotic influence of the Stranger, is determined to go to Mount Cytheron and see for himself. The Stranger tells him that, in order not to be recognised, he must go disguised as a woman. Pentheus is horrified, but the Stranger brusquely orders him to go and change his clothing. Beroe, addressing the Stranger as Dionysus, pleads with him to spare Pentheus' life. He ignores her. Pentheus re-enters, wearing one of his mother's dresses. He calls for the Captain and tells him to line up the royal guard. Pentheus, accompanied by the Stranger, exits between their serried ranks. Left alone, Beroe breaks out into a wild lament. The Captain offers to go after Pentheus, but Cadmus says that would mean his certain death. The Captain should rest, while he and Beroe keep watch through the night. He fears they will never see Pentheus again, and, if they do, they will wish they had not. If no news has come by the morning, the Captain may go and search Mount Cytheron.

Night in the forest of Mount Cytheron. The Bassarids are heard singing a hymn in praise of Dionysus. By the light of their dancing torches Pentheus can dimly be seen, perched on the bough of a tree from which he presently descends. A chorus of maenads (women only) invoke the god. A voice answers them, saying that there is a spy in the forest whom they should hunt down. Suddenly the light of their torches discovers Pentheus and they close in. Knowing his mother to be among them, Pentheus, using the same words he used when he questioned her in the Judgement Hall, begs her to remember who she is and that he is her son. The maenads answer every appeal with the word No. They rush upon him and out of the darkness comes his final scream. The voices of the maenads are heard retreating, as they sing a song in honor of Agave the huntress.

Thebes again. Cadmus and Beroe are keeping watch. Soon Tiresias joins them. The chorus of maenads, among whom we can distinguish the voices of Agave and Autonoe, are heard approaching, singing the same song as in the last scene. Soon a crowd of Bassarids pour onto the stage. In their wake comes Agave who says: "Behold the head of the young lion whom I have hunted and brought home" and holds up the head of Pentheus. Silence. Still in a trance, Agave asks where Pentheus is. Cadmus talks to her quietly and she begins to return to a normal state. "What," he asks, "are you holding in your arms? Is it a lion?" She looks and realises what she is holding. "How did this happen and where?", she asks. Cadmus tells her. "What did we do and why?" "What you did", replies Cadmus, "you can see for yourself. Why. Ask Dionysus." The Captain and some of his guard enter, bearing the mangled corpse of Pentheus on a litter. Agave begs Cadmus to take a sword and kill her, half faints and is led to one side by Beroe. Agave, Cadmus, Beroe lament. Autonoe keeps saying "I didn't want to do it. Agave made me do it". Tiresias is smugly pleased that such a fate should have befallen the man who pulled down his house and says "The gods alone are holy, and what they will they do". The chorus deny all knowledge of what happened on Mount Cytheron. They were somewhere else and saw nothing. Aria by Agave in which she bids farewell to her dead son, saying "We both did what neither would. The strong gods are not good". The Captain and some of his men bear off the body of Pentheus. The music breaks off abruptly as the Stranger enters. He proclaims that he is the God Dionysus, decrees perpetual and separate exile to Cadmus and his daughters, and orders the Captain to set fire to the royal palace. As she is leaving, Agave turns and, in a final speech of defiance, bids Dionysus remember the fate of Uranus and Chronos. For him, too, Tartarus waits.

The stage is hidden by flames. From behind them the voice of Dionysus is heard summoning his mother Semele from the land of the dead to ascend with him to Olympus and become the goddess Thyone. The flames die down. The ruins of Thebes are seen bathed in a brilliant mediterranean light and covered with vines. Upon Semele's tomb stand two rather strange-looking statues, representing Dionysus and Thyone. In front of them the chorus prostrate themselves in blind adoration.

W. H. AUDEN
CHESTER KALLMAN

§4 AUDEN AND KALLMAN ON THE OPERA

In his letter of 20 October 1965 (see pp. 682–83), Auden, on behalf of Kallman and himself, offered to write "a technical piece, explaining what had to be done in order to turn Euripides' tragedy into an opera libretto". Two such essays, both signed by Auden and Kallman, eventually appeared, but were printed only in German translations prepared by unidentified hands. One essay, "Warum ein Meisterwerk neu schreiben?" was printed in the souvenir program book of the 1966 Salzburger Festspiele, *Salzburger Journal.* The other, "Euripides wieder aktuell", was printed in *Österreichische Musikzeitschrift,* August 1966. The contents of the two essays slightly overlap, and because a draft of the English original of "Warum ein Meisterwerk neu schreiben?" survives in Kallman's hand, it seems likely that he was primarily responsible for both.

Kallman's substantially complete draft of "Warum ein Meisterwerk neu schreiben?" is in one of his notebooks now at the University of Texas. The text printed below is taken from the draft, with the addition of a few sentences that do not appear in the draft and have been retranslated from the German. At some sacrifice of grammatical coherence, these additional passages are inserted between square brackets in the text of the English draft. Probably Kallman's final typescript differed in small syntactical details from the text of the draft, but the draft is surely closer to Kallman's final text than any possible retranslation from the German version could be. One or two words in the draft are only partly legible and have been reconstructed from the German version. Some obviously omitted words have been added silently. A few passages in Kallman's English draft do not appear in the German translation, but the cuts may not have been authorial. These passages are: third paragraph, "they are, after all . . . upon the composer"; fifth paragraph, "and, with Dionysus' announcement . . . plot in libretto form"; penultimate paragraph, "some of them taken from . . . new balance thus required" and "the new expanded . . . demanded it"; final paragraph; "as those shown" through the end. Because the draft is untitled, the title printed below is translated from the German text.

WHY REWRITE A MASTERPIECE?

BY W. H. AUDEN AND
CHESTER KALLMAN

Why not merely "adapt" Euripides' play—fill in some of the missing bits, prune the rest to the composer's requirements—didn't the conventions of Greek Drama found the conventions on which opera has developed? It might work. Frankly, though, it would have been a task for other librettists preparing a text for quite another composer.

We are not, to begin with, Greek scholars, and could not have made our own English version of the play. And Henze, once he had lived with the Euripides, and been taken with its theme, visualized a musical treatment that even the most ingenious editing of the text could not have satisfied. Furthermore, we, none of us, had the slightest wish to produce any species of that Gluck-y Greekiness which permits itself to be staged by combining the Modern Dance with the side-views of a Grecian Urn. [Given the play's structure, that was just what all too easily could be made from it. We based our changes, however, not simply on our fear of some director's ideas, but on the dramatic core of the work itself, which was not, of course, conceived as an opera libretto.]

The pivotal scenes of the play—the earthquake that frees the imprisoned followers of Dionysus, Dionysus establishing his hypnotic dominion over Pentheus, Agave returning with Pentheus' head from Cytheron, her de-intoxication and the exile of the Theban Royal House—have been taken over into the libretto; they are, after all, the situations that immediately attracted us as librettists and that urged their settable possibilities upon the composer. It remained to round these out with situations that explained them and the characters in them more fully than Euripides did in his play, or that he explained by means of narrations and choruses—verbal devices impractical for the immediate demands of operatic effect.

The matter and the mythological background of the *Bacchae* were, in any case, familiar to Euripides' audience—and the events that immediately precede the opening of the play—Dionysus' arrival in Thebes, and the populace, including Agave, falling under his spell—appear to have been dealt with by Euripides in a companion work. When Dionysus, at the opening of the *Bacchae*, announces his destructive intentions, he is not therefore kindly "giving away the plot"; but a keynote has been sounded by Euripides for his subsequent treatment: Pentheus may appear harsh and unsympathetic, the accounts of the Dionysian rites mystic and innocent: the informed audience could hear that note beneath it all.

We could not depend on a modern audience[, whose knowledge of mythology is hardly likely to be adequate and which does not believe in the reality of the events,] responding to such a device, [even though it belongs to the basic elements of tragedy. Therefore we have tried to provide dramatic supplements, which are supposed to intensify this foretaste of catastrophe. Moreover, we found ourselves confronted with an additional problem:] nor could the mass reaction to Dionysus—which obviously interested Euripides more than the personal tragedies of Pentheus, Agave and Cadmus—be kept in the foreground of an opera without its teetering over into oratorio. The mass hypnosis, however, could obviously be neither dispensed with nor cut; we therefore kept the important chorus role as a perpetual background to an individualized dramatic action, to preserve the essential ritualized atmosphere of a work dealing with the nature of a God; and, with Dionysus' announcement as our own keynote, set about reconstructing the plot in libretto form. [(Readers of the libretto can refresh their mythological knowledge with the help of the choral texts, while the intelligibility of the words in the performance necessarily gets lost.)]

Our perspective was, plainly and inevitably, historic; the variety of the characters, as a result, was pegged not only to their differing theological attitudes [(in this way Cadmus and Tiresias, who in Euripides can hardly be distinguished, become in our libretto two completely different persons)], but also to differing eras. Thus a medieval ascetic Pentheus has a French Second Empire sensual sceptic for a mother; Tiresias, a "kind" Victorian clergyman, bickers with a Cadmus who [?knew] the Gods in the time [of] pure legend, etc. Besides the aid to visual definition in a work in which the important dialectics, because of the introduction of music, was bound to be slightly blurred, this also allowed us to escape further from the Neo-Classical plaster-casts.

Then, in accord both with the conventions of Greek drama which placed, in performance, a scurrilous satyr play between the acted tragedies, and the earlier days of Opera Seria, when two acts of statuesque extended arias were relieved by a comic intermezzo, we wanted a comic interlude directly related to the central incident of the play. Here we tried not only in the name of variety to get away briefly from the intense sober air of religious disaster that envelops the rest, but to give a more immediate insight into Pentheus' psychology: He is an obsessive truth-seeker; the Interlude, his vision, is a lie. It also contributes to his falling under Dionysus' spell.

To the "new" incidents, some of them taken from the original's narration and others from Ovid and some from "new" characters to round out the new balance thus required, we added an apotheosis: the new expanded structure and the need to provide a suitable musical climax demanded it.

It had always seemed to us that the most successful (the only success-
ful?) musical works in this century on "Greek" themes, were the Strauss-
Hofmannsthal *Elektra* and the Stravinsky-Cocteau *Oedipus Rex,* and that a
good measure of their success was due to the direct look back at their
models that allowed no irrelevant reverence for mere duplication to inter-
fere with the making of a new work in a new medium [(the Strauss-
Gregor *Daphne,* despite its Tennysonian beauty, suffers somewhat from its
Hellenistic bearing)]. We can only hope our retrospective vision has been
as clear, and our talents for reconstruction as strong, as those shown in
those two works which encouraged us in our changes. The results, in any
case, we think we are justified in believing not un-Euripidean.

No manuscript survives for "Euripides wieder aktuell". A retranslation into En-
glish, made for this edition, appears below the German text. I have borrowed some
phrases from an earlier retranslation by Richard Jarman that appeared in the
program of the performance of the opera by the English National Opera, 10 Oc-
tober 1974, and in *Musical Times,* October 1974.

EURIPIDES WIEDER AKTUELL*

W. H. AUDEN—CHESTER KALLMAN

Das 18. Jahrhundert nahm es für erwiesen an, daß in einem Konflikt
zwischen Vernunft und Unvernunft die Vernunft zu siegen hatte. So hat
etwa in der *Zauberflöte,* ganz wie es sich gehört, die Königin der Nacht eine
Tochter, Sarastro bekommt einen prinzlichen Schüler, die beiden un-
schuldigen Leute verlieben sich ineinander, und alles endet in Minne.
Noch ein Jahrhundert später hätte wahrscheinlich ein Librettist oder
Komponist auf der Suche nach einem möglichen Opernstoff die *Bacchen*
des Euripides als "unnatürlich" verworfen. Solche Ereignisse, hätten sie
gedacht, mögen vor langer Zeit in primitiven barbarischen Gesellschaften

---

*[Translation:]

EURIPIDES MADE NEW
BY W. H. AUDEN AND
CHESTER KALLMAN

The eighteenth century took it for granted that in a struggle between the Rational and the
Irrational, Reason would inevitably prevail. Thus, for example, in *The Magic Flute*—as is
proper—the Queen of the Night has a daughter, Sarastro acquires a princely pupil, the two
innocent young people fall in love, and everything ends in love. Even a century later, a libret-
tist or composer searching for a possible subject matter for an opera would probably have
rejected Euripides' *Bacchae* as "unnatural". Such goings on, they would have thought, might

vorgekommen sein, aber soziale und intellektuelle Fortschritte haben es unmöglich gemacht, daß irgend etwas Ähnliches sich wieder ereignen könnte.

Heute wissen wir, daß es sich ereignen kann. Wir wissen, daß ganze Gesellschaften vom "Dämon" befallen werden können, ebensogut wie Einzelpersonen ihren Kopf verlieren können. Was ferner Psychologen uns über "Verdrängung" und deren schädliche, oft fatale Folgen gelehrt haben, läßt uns Sarastro mit kritischerem Auge betrachten. Wie Pentheus, der Held des Euripides, der sich dem Kult des Dionysos gegenübersteht, weiß Sarastro für die Auseinandersetzung mit der Königin der Nacht keinen andern Rat, als Gewalt zu gebrauchen, in seinem Fall magische Kräfte, und sie in die Unterwelt zu verbannen. Nehmen wir an, so müssen wir uns fragen, nehmen wir an, es hätte keinen Tamino und keine Pamina gegeben, um eine saubere Lösung herbeizuführen, hätte dann Sarastro seinen Triumph längere Zeit genossen? Ist es nicht wahrscheinlicher, daß er, wie Pentheus, schließlich ein gräßliches Schicksal von der Hand der wütenden Königin erlitten hätte?

Aus verschiedenen Gründen, teils musikalischen, teils dramatischen, wäre es unmöglich gewesen, die *Bacchen* so zu verwenden, wie sie geschrieben stehen. Ein Komponist wunscht mit guten Solopartien für, wenn möglich, drei männliche und drei weibliche Sänger versehen zu werden. In den *Bacchen* gibt es nur zwei bedeutungsvolle Solo-Rollen, Pentheus und Dionysos, und die einzige als Individuum auftretende Frau, Agave, erscheint erst, wenn das Stück schon beinahe vorüber ist. Die wichtigste Rolle von allen wird vom Frauenchor ausgeführt. Der Chor der griechischen Tragödie hatte zu singen und zu tanzen, obwohl so

---

have taken place a long time ago in primitive, barbaric societies, but social and intellectual progress have made it impossible that anything like that could ever happen again.

Today we know that it can happen. We know that entire societies can be seized by the "demon", just as individuals can lose their heads. Furthermore, what psychologists have taught us about "repression" and its damaging, often fatal consequences enables us to contemplate Sarastro with a more critical eye. Like Pentheus, Euripides' hero who opposes the cult of Dionysus, Sarastro knows no other way to settle his dispute with the Queen of the Night than to use force—in his case, magic powers—and to banish her to the underworld. Do we suppose—we must therefore ask ourselves—that if there had been no Tamino and no Pamina to bring about a neat solution, would Sarastro still have enjoyed his triumph for very long? Is it not more probable that, like Pentheus, he would in the end have suffered a hideous fate at the hands of the enraged Queen?

For various reasons, partly musical, partly dramatic, it would have been impossible to use the *Bacchae* exactly as written. A composer wants to be provided with good solo parts for, if possible, three male and three female singers. In the *Bacchae* there are only two important solo roles, Pentheus and Dionysos, and the only woman who makes an individual appearance, Agave, does so for the first time only when the play is already almost over. The most important role of all is performed by the chorus of women. The chorus in Greek tragedy was

gut wie nichts über die Art der Musik oder der Tanzschritte, die sie aus-
führten, überliefert wurde. In unseren Tagen ist es einfach eine Geg-
ebenheit, daß Sänger nicht tanzen und Tänzer nicht singen können.
Wenn somit eine Oper ein dramatisches Bühnenwerk sein soll, und nicht
ein statisches Oratorium, dann muß der Chor sehr sparsam eingesetzt
werden.

Vier der Szenen des Euripides—jene, in welcher Pentheus auf den ver-
kleideten Dionysos stößt, jene, in welcher Dionysos ihn hypnotisiert, so
daß er einwilligt, sich als Frau zu verkleiden und sich auf den Berg Kyth-
eron zu begeben, jene, in welcher Cadmus Agave aus ihrer Trance er-
weckt, so daß sie sich der schrecklichen Dinge, die sie tat, bewußt wird,
und die Schlußszene, in welcher Dionysos die ganze königliche Familie
aus Theben verbannt—haben uns sofort in ihren Bann geschlagen: sie
stellen ausgezeichnetes Material für eine Oper dar, und in diesen Szenen
sind wir dem originalen Text ziemlich eng gefolgt.

Um der Forderung nach Rollen entgegenzukommen, haben wir die
Partien des Cadmus und Tiresias erweitert und differenziert (bei Euri-
pides sind sie zwei eher senile Greise, die kaum auseinandergehalten
werden können), sowie drei neue Charaktere eingeführt: Beroe, Pen-
theus' alte Dienerin, den Hauptmann der königlichen Wache, und Au-
tonoe, die Schwester der Agave (bei Euripides hat Agave zwei Schwestern,
doch keine von ihnen tritt als Sprechrolle in Erscheinung). Viele Emo-
tionen und Ideen, die Euripides dem Chor anvertraut, haben wir der
einen oder anderen Hauptperson in den Mund gelegt. Und der Chor
wird, bis er, fast am Ende der Oper, vor der Bühne erscheint, als singender
Background verwendet. Wir haben ihn auch aus einem Frauenchor in

---

supposed to sing and dance, although virtually nothing has come down to us about the kind
of music or dance that was performed. In our day it is simply a given that singers cannot
dance and dancers cannot sing. And so, when an opera is supposed to be a dramatic work for
the stage and not a static oratorio, the chorus must be introduced very sparingly.

Four of Euripides' scenes—the one in which Pentheus runs into Dionysus in disguise; the
one in which Dionysus hypnotizes him, so that he agrees to disguise himself as a woman and
go up to Mount Cytheron; the one in which Cadmus wakens Agave from her trance, so that
she becomes conscious of the terrible things she has done; and the closing scene, in which
Dionysus banishes from Thebes the entire royal family—immediately fascinated us: they are
excellent material for an opera, and in these scenes we have followed the original text quite
closely.

In order to meet the need for roles, we expanded and differentiated the parts of Cadmus
and Tiresias (in Euripides they are two rather senile old men who can hardly be told apart) as
well as introducing three new characters: Beroe, Pentheus old servant; the Captain of the
Royal Guard; and Autonoe, Agave's sister. (In Euripides Agave has two sisters, but neither of
them has a speaking part.) We have put many of the emotions and ideas that Euripides
entrusted to the chorus into the mouth of one or the other main characters. And the chorus is
used to sing in the background, until, almost at the end of the opera, it appears at the front of

einen gemischten Chor verwandelt: daher der Titel *Die Bassariden,*was die Nachfolger des Dionysos bezeichnet, ohne Spezifizierung des Geschlechts.

Die *Bacchen* beginnen mit einer Ansprache des Dionysos, in welcher er dem Publikum mitteilt, was er bereits getan hat und was er zu tun gedenkt. Um Agave und die Frauen von Theben zu bestrafen, weil sie seinen göttlichen Ursprung leugneten, hat er sie bereits mit Bacchischer Raserei geschlagen. Sie sind zum Berg Kytheron gerannt. Dann kehrt Pentheus, der offenbar früher einmal König von Theben war, aus weiter Ferne zurück und erfährt zum erstenmal von dem neuen Kult. Wir fanden, daß wir die Handlung zu einem früheren Zeitpunkt anfangen lassen mußten. Daher beginnt unsere Oper gerade nach Cadmus' Abdankung zu Gunsten seines Enkels: der Kult des Dionysos steht in seinen Anfängen, aber Agave und ihre Schwester sind ihm noch nicht erlegen. Pentheus' erste Handlung als König ist die Untersagung des Kults.

Es ist klar, daß Euripides selbst nicht daran gedacht haben kann, oder auch nur wollte, daß seine Hörerschaft daran dachte, Dionysos sei ein Gott, würdig der Verehrung. Er konfrontiert uns mit einem herzlosen Monstrum, vor dem man mit gutem Grund zittert, aber das man unmöglich bewundern kann. Seine Charakterisierung des Pentheus ist zwiespältiger. Gemäß der griechischen Konzeption der Tragödie ist der schicksalhafte Sprung im Helden, der seinen Fall verursacht, immer eine Manifestation der Hybris, jener Überheblichkeit, die ihn annehmen läßt, daß er genau so wie ein Gott gegenüber allem Unglück immun sei. Euripides hält es daher nicht für notwendig, zu erklären, warum Pentheus so heftig gegen Dionysos auftritt. Für ihn und für sein Publikum genügte es,

---

the stage. We have also changed it from a women's chorus to a mixed chorus: hence the title *The Bassarids,* which indicates the followers of Dionysus without regard to their sex.

The *Bacchae* begins with a speech by Dionysus, in which he informs the public of what he has already done and what he intends to do: in order to punish Agave and the women of Thebes for having denied his divine origin, he has already struck them with Bacchic madness; they have run off to Mount Cytheron. Then Pentheus, who has evidently been King of Thebes for some time, returns from afar and learns for the first time of the new cult. We found that we had to have the action begin at an earlier point in time. Thus our opera begins just after Cadmus's abdication in favor of his grandson: the cult of Dionysus is in its early stages, but Agave and her sister have not yet succumbed to it. Pentheus's first act as king is to prohibit the cult.

It is clear that Euripides himself could not have thought or even wanted his audience to think that Dionysus was a god worthy of reverence. He confronts us with a heartless monster before whom one rightly trembles, but whom it is impossible to admire. His characterization of Pentheus is more ambiguous. According to the Greek conception of tragedy the fatal flaw in the hero, which brings about his downfall, is always a manifestation of *hubris*, that overweening pride which makes him assume that, like a god, he is proof against all misfortune. Therefore Euripides does not consider it necessary to explain why Pentheus rises up so violently against Dionysus. For him and for his public it was enough to show a mortal behaving as if he were the equal of an immortal. One could almost say that Pentheus' real objection was the result of the people of Thebes taking up the cult of Dionysus without first obtaining his

einen Sterblichen zu zeigen, der sich benahm, als ob er einem Un-
sterblichen ebenbürtig wäre. Man könnte fast sagen, Pentheus' wirkliche
Objektion resultierte daraus, daß das Volk von Theben den Kult des Di-
onysos aufgegriffen hatte, ohne zuvor seine königliche Erlaubnis dafür
einzuholen. Wir als Autoren des 20. Jahrhunderts, die wir für ein Pu-
blikum des 20. Jahrhunderts schreiben, wir fühlten die Notwendigkeit,
daß unser Pentheus—während er dieselbe Torheit der Methode wie bei
Euripides zeigt, nämlich den Versuch unternimmt, den Kult mit brutaler
physischer Gewalt zu unterdrücken—ein edleres Motiv für diesen Ver-
such haben sollte als bloße Arroganz. Wir haben deshalb aus ihm einen
platonischen Idealisten gemacht, der den alten Polytheismus zugunsten
eines philosophischen Monismus verworfen hatte, zugunsten der Ver-
ehrung eines einzigen transzendenten Guten, von dem die Menschen
Kenntnis erhalten können, indem sie ihre Leidenschaften unter Kon-
trolle halten und sich in den Gebräuchen der Kontemplation üben, das
aber seinerseits weder die Menschen kennen noch in ihr Leben
eingreifen kann.

Einem platonischen Idealisten muß Dionysos als der Feind schlechthin
erscheinen, als ein Bild aller jener irrationellen Passionen des Körpers,
die er als das Haupthindernis für ein gutes Leben betrachtet. Unser Pen-
theus erlebt seinen Fall nicht so sehr auf Grund seines überheblichen Be-
nehmens andern gegenüber, als vielmehr auf Grund seiner Unkenntnis
der eigenen Natur, einer Ignoranz, die aus einem philosophischen Irr-
tum resultiert. Seine Weigerung, die dionysischen Elemente in sich selbst
zu verstehen und sich mit ihnen zu arrangieren, macht ihn zum leichten
Opfer, sobald Dionysos seinen hypnotischen Zauber wirken läßt.

In den *Bassariden* wird die tragische Aktion durch ein komisches Inter-
ludium unterbrochen. Ein Grund dafür ist natürlich die Absicht, für

---

royal permission. We, as twentieth-century authors who write for a twentieth-century audi-
ence, felt it necessary to suppose that our Pentheus—while he shows the same madness of
method as in Euripides, attempting to suppress the cult by brute physical force—had a no-
bler motive for this undertaking than mere arrogance. Therefore we have made him into a
Platonic idealist, who has rejected the old polytheism for a philosophical monism, for the
worship of a single transcendental Good of whom human beings can have knowledge by
keeping their passions under control and practicing the rituals of contemplation. This deity,
for its part, can however neither have a knowledge of men nor intercede in their lives.
   To a Platonic idealist Dionysus must seem like the enemy itself, an image of all those irra-
tional physical passions that he considers the main obstacle to the good life. Our Pentheus
goes to his downfall not so much because of his arrogant behavior toward others as because of
his ignorance of his own nature, an ignorance that results from a philosophical error. His
refusal to understand the Dionysian elements in himself and to come to terms with them
makes him an easy victim as soon as Dionysus exercises his hypnotic magic.
   In *The Bassarids* the tragic action is interrupted by a comic interlude. One reason for this, of
course, is to provide emotional and musical variety. In the ancient Greek dramatic festivals a

emotionelle und musikalische Abwechslung zu sorgen. Bei den altgriechischen dramatischen Festspielen folgte nach drei Tragödien stets ein komisches Satyrspiel, und in den frühen Tagen der Oper wurde eine kurze Opera buffa zwischen den zwei Akten einer Opera seria eingeschoben. Ein anderer Grund für das Interludium ist der, daß es uns Gelegenheit gab, etwas von Pentheus' Vorstellungswelt zu enthüllen. Was das Publikum sieht und hört, ist das, von dem Pentheus glaubt, daß es die Anhänger des Dionysos tun, was wiederum bedeutet, daß ein Teil seines Ichs es gerne tun würde. In seinen Phantasien ist das dionysische Leben nicht, wie in der Wirklichkeit, leidenschaftlich und gefährlich, sondern dekadent und schwerlich ernst zu nehmen.

Agave ist aus andern Gründen verwundbar. Zunächst wurde sie in jungen Jahren Witwe; als eine königliche Prinzessin findet sie keinen Mann, der ihr ebenbürtig wäre und den sie heiraten könnte; und sie ist zu wählerisch, um Affären zu haben. Aber sexuelle Frustration ist nicht der wichtigste Faktor. Wie ihr Sohn, hat auch sie den Glauben an den traditionellen Polytheismus verloren; sie wurde in ihm erzogen, aber, anders als er, fand sie keinen Glauben, um ihn zu ersetzen. Folglich leidet sie unter dem Gefühl, daß ihr Leben sinnlos ist: "Sinn" ist daher das, was Dionysos ihr anzubieten scheint.

Aber wir haben uns schon zu lange verbreitet. Librettisten sollen nicht ihren Status vergessen. Was wir schrieben, wird nicht nach literarischen Meriten, wenn es darin welche gibt, beurteilt werden, sondern nach der Musik, die es in Hans Werner Henze hervorgebracht hat.

Auden wrote about the opera, in terms similar to those he used for his program notes, in *Secondary Worlds* (1968).

---

comic satyr play always followed three tragedies, and in the early days of opera a short opera buffa was inserted between the two acts of an opera seria. Another reason for the interlude is that it gave us the opportunity to reveal something of the world of Pentheus' imagination. What the audience sees and hears is what Pentheus believes the followers of Dionysus do— which in turn means that a part of himself would like to do it. In his fantasies the Dionysian life is not, as it is in reality, passionate and dangerous but rather decadent and hardly to be taken seriously.

Agave is vulnerable for different reasons. To begin with she was widowed at an early age; as a royal princess she is unable to find a man of her rank whom she could marry; and she is too fastidious to have affairs. But sexual frustration is not the most important factor. Like her son, she too has lost her faith in traditional polytheism; she was brought up in it, but, unlike him, she found no faith to replace it. As a result she suffers from the feeling that her life is meaningless; "meaning" is therefore what Dionysus appears to offer her.

But we have already gone on too long. Librettists should not forget their status. What we write will not be judged by its literary merit, if it has any, but by the music it has brought forth from Hans Werner Henze.

§5 KALLMAN'S PROLOGUE FOR THE 1968 PRODUCTION

When the first English-language production of *The Bassarids* was being planned
for the 1968 season of the Santa Fe Opera, Henze asked the librettists for a new
spoken prologue to explain the action to the audience. Auden replied on 29 Au-
gust 1967:

> Chester and I are not *absolutely* convinced that any prologue is neces-
> sary. Norse mythology is far less well-known than Greek, but Wagner
> expected [the] audience to follow *The Ring* without explanations.
> However if you *really* feel you want one, the only possible solution we
> can see is as follows:
>
> 1) Dionysus must appear before the curtain in tails (+ maybe
>   opera-hat and black cloak). To let him appear in either of his
>   stage-costumes would ruin his entries.
> 2) He must speak about himself in contemporary terms and in con-
>   temporary prose, addressing a contemporary opera audience.
>   He will tell them the Greek myth of his birth in a tone of voice
>   which makes it clear that he doesn't believe it to be true any more
>   than a modern audience does. "You may account for me", he will
>   say, "as you like, but, as you see, I exist as a force to be reckoned
>   with. What happened to Agave, Pentheus, etc. when they tried to
>   ignore or defy me, you will presently see. Let it be a warning, lest
>   something equally horrid happen to you, which, I can assure
>   you, it certainly will etc. etc." The speech must be suave, con-
>   temptuous, ironic and menacing: the audience must be scared
>   themselves.
>
> What do you think?

Kallman later supplied the following text, printed below from Kallman's typescript
now among Henze's papers in Basel. A draft is in one of Kallman's notebooks now
at the University of Texas. Henze cut the text extensively for the production. In
the second and third paragraphs, "credibility" is Kallman's error for "credulity".

PROLOGUE:
for THE BASSARIDS

[*Lights out. Spotlight reveals* DIONYSUS *before the curtain in full evening
dress—white tie, cane, etc.—holding a small "travelling" mike. He bows.*]

DIONYSUS. Ladies and gentlemen, good evening. I am, shall we say, your
. . . Master of Ceremonies. And you cannot believe with what . . . ea-
gerness I stand here before *you*, a cultivated audience,—as your very
presence here proves you. Cultivated, hence skeptical. An audience,
hence hoping for something in the way of sensation.

I hope with you, ladies and gentlemen, but for the moment my mission here is didactic. Perhaps I ought to say *purely* didactic, for being that I am Dionysus—yes, Dionysus—my mission is always in some measure didactic. *That* you will learn. Meanwhile, though you are probably thinking: "What! A god in evening dress? A god not comfortably Greek and comfortingly remote? Please don't strain our credibility!"

Well, call my costume didactic also, if you wish, and excuse me if I must strain your sensitive credibility even further by telling you something of my origins. Though you may take a little comfort in *their* remoteness.

My mother was Semele, daughter of Cadmus, founder, in prehistory, of Thebes, *Ancient* Thebes. She was extremely beautiful, beautiful enough to attract Zeus, ruler of the Olympian gods himself, and he both wooed and won her in mortal guise. Naturally, though, she well knew who he was; such things rather show. And soon there was more to be seen: Semele was obviously pregnant. To many, including her sisters Agave and Autonoe, her story of being Zeus' Paramour was greeted with an astonished giggle and much guessing about who her probable—and probably most unsuitable—successful suitor *really* was.

So it was with Semele on Earth. In the heavens of Olympus, the revealed event roused the jealous fury of Hera, Zeus' long-suffering wife. Assuming the form of Beroe, Semele's nurse, she persuaded Semele that all doubters would be silenced if Zeus appeared to her, not in mortal guise, but as himself, Zeus, god of thunder.

Poor Semele. You can imagine how she whined at and wheedled her lover when he next visited. Oh, he tried to dissuade her. She merely stamped her pretty little foot and whimpered, and he had to yield to her wish. Her last wish. Because his appearance in full glory burned her house to the ground and dazzled her into ash on the instant. And I, Dionysus, dropped unready from her womb. But Zeus—and this is my favorite bit of the story—snatched me from the ruins and improvised a new comfy womb for me in an opening in his thigh, which he then shut with a golden pin.—Of course, it had to be gold.—And from whence in due time I emerged, an infant god, to face the same mixture of hostility and disbelief that my mother had faced.

I, however, was fortunate in having Zeus for a father, so had . . . *and have* . . . more power to face it with. Why, even as a child, I halted a ship and turned its mutineering crew into dolphins when they sought to kidnap me and sell me into slavery. And I subdued the East to worship while still comparatively young. And I have now returned to . . . you. You. For tonight you are in Thebes, a chorus of eyes and ears, where your new King, Pentheus, son of that same Agave who mocked her sister's interesting condition, is determined to stamp out the remnants of compensatory worship my poor mother has been accorded in the place of my conception.

Well, that's the story to date. And, incidental symbolism apart, it's neither very pretty nor, by our own morally relaxed standards, credible. Did Euripides believe it? I doubt it. Do either Mr Auden or Mr Kallman or Mr Henze believe it? I hardly dare think so. Do *I*? [*Laughs.*] Now, you don't expect me to answer *that*, do you? No indeed. Still, the fact remains that, whatever my origins, *here . . . I . . . am.* Here I am at the gates of Thebes. Here I am about to enter the city whose King most assuredly does not believe my fantastic anecdote, who does not, in fact, believe that I, in fact, am. I will, however, be quite real to him before these curtains close, as real to him as his own flesh and blood; as real, in any case, as they should have been to him. You might put it that I shall be, in that flesh and blood, incarnate. Which will, it is true, enhance Pentheus with a deification I scarcely feel he merits. Let it pass—politics make strange deifications. The important question at present, ladies and gentlemen, is— Do *you* believe my story? *Will* you? Because *if* . . . . . .

But you know what's going to happen. You've all no doubt read the libretto. Therefore let me close with some words of mine which unaccountably do not occur in it, as they do in Euripides:

[*Slowly, deliberately accenting each syllable:*]

DO NOT IMPRISON THE GOD!

[*Pause. Then, with a little wave of his hand which both dismisses them and indicates that he wishes the curtain to rise soon, he laughs and says casually:*]

Well, you'd better not, you know.

Thank you for your attention.

Love's Labour's Lost

§1 History, Authorship, Text, and Editions

Nicolas Nabokov met Auden in 1943, joined him in the United States Strategic Bombing Survey that surveyed civilian morale in Germany in 1945, and helped arrange for the premiere of *The Rake's Progress* in Venice in 1951. Auden may have pointed Nabokov toward Rossetti's translations of Dante that Nabokov included in the program notes to the first performance of his concerto *La Vita Nuova* in 1951. In 1963 Nabokov proposed setting *The Sea and the Mirror* to music, an idea that Auden rejected because Nabokov planned to make extensive cuts in the text. Six years later, the possibility of collaborating with Auden on an opera was suggested to him by their common friend Lincoln Kirstein. As Nabokov recalled in his memoirs:

> I think it was in February 1969 when Lincoln Kirstein first said to me, "Why don't you compose an opera with Wystan and Chester? It would be good to bring them together again and have them work on a libretto. . . ."
>
> "I don't even know whether Wystan and Chester know and like my music," I demurred.
>
> "Oh, yes! Oh, yes, they do!" exclaimed Lincoln. "Wystan must like your music precisely because it is melodic and because it does not conform to fads or fashions."
>
> And after a while he added in a different tone of voice, "You know, only recently Wystan told me that the only Shakespeare play that is written like an opera and can readily be turned into an opera libretto is *Love's Labour's Lost.*"

Nabokov asked Kirstein to approach Auden, and Kirstein urged Nabokov to call Auden after reading the play. Auden's pocket diary records a visit from Nabokov on 4 February 1969.

> "Yes, of course, Nicky," said Auden that first day as I sat down in his dimly-lit, smoke-filled workroom on St. Mark's Place, "*Love's Labour's Lost* is the only Shakespeare play that will do as an opera. It is structured like an opera and so much of it is already rhymed verse."
>
> I told Auden about my struggle with the Arden [Edition] volume and with the *Love's Labour's Lost* word forms, puns, and jokes.
>
> "Well . . . I don't think we should worry about that," he said. "Some of those words can be changed, others can just as well remain. That isn't the problem. What needs to be done is to trim the play down to opera requirements. A number of secondary characters should be eliminated. Most of the comic scenes with their banter should be cut—they won't do for opera. Maybe some of the verses could be shortened, and all of the play must get leaner. I see it," he continued, "as an *opera buffa* in a fast tempo, a kind of perpetual allegro going through to the last scene. Then everything must grow solemn

and slow—that is most important," and he emphasized the word "most." "The morality-play ending of *Love's Labour's Lost* and its meaning should remain quite clear and intact."

We agreed that he should write to Chester, who was in Greece. If Chester consented to collaborate on the libretto, we could meet later that summer. Ten days later I received a postcard from Auden. It said that Chester would be glad to collaborate and that we should meet in Austria. (*Bagázh*, 1975, pp. 226–28)

In the spring, after Auden left New York for Austria, Nabokov wrote to him to make preliminary plans for the libretto. On 9 May 1969 Auden replied to a lost letter from Nabokov: "We, too, came to the conclusion that one will have to have four pairs of lovers as in the play." (Auden's letters to Nabokov are in the Berg Collection, New York Public Library.) Auden insisted that more detailed plans could only be made in person, so Nabokov visited Auden and Kallman in Kirchstetten on 15 and 16 July 1969. On 17 July Auden reported in a letter to Peter Heyworth, "Now we must start on an outline for *Loves Labours Lost*." On 23 July he wrote to Kirstein: "Nicky was here for two days to discuss *Love's Labours Lost*, and we are now busy trying to sketch out a libretto: the Bard's play has to be radically altered."

In fact, little of Shakespeare survived into Auden and Kallman's libretto beyond the opening and closing arias, the lovers' letters, and miscellaneous lines and phrases (including the speech beginning "Men have died from time to time" from *As You Like It*). Kallman told an interviewer: "We stamped Shakespeare to bits and then put it together again" (Alan Levy, *New York Times*, 8 August 1971, section 6).

Auden and Kallman sketched a scenario of the first two acts and sent it to Nabokov on 7 August 1969; in the accompanying letter Kallman told Nabokov, "We're brooding still over the Third Act, but I think only *one* scene." On 1 September they sent the typescript of Act I and reported that Act II was written and would follow shortly. Auden's pocket diary records "libretto finished" on 30 September, but the entry for 1 October also notes "libretto", so the work may have extended another day. The last page of Kallman's drafts is dated "9:38 a.m. / 30 Sept 69". Auden's pocket diary notes Nabokov's name on 6 October, probably indicating a second visit to Kirchstetten to discuss the libretto. Filippo Sanjust, the designer of the opera, visited Kirchstetten on 11 October.

Nabokov showed the libretto to the directors of the Deutsche Oper in Berlin and was commissioned by them to compose the opera. He began work on the score in the summer of 1970. The first performance was originally planned for the 1971 Edinburgh Festival, but the plan fell through when the Deutsche Oper failed to gain the necessary subsidies—apparently because of internal festival politics, Auden told an interviewer (Alan Levy, *New York Times*, 8 August 1971, section 6). The premiere was rescheduled for Berlin in 1972, but this plan also fell through, although the vocal score was published on 24 November 1972. The Deutsche Oper at last performed the work at a guest performance at the Théâtre de la Monnaie in Brussels on 7 February 1973. The musical director was Reinhard Peters and the production was by Winfried Bauernfeind. Auden and Kallman attended the premiere but did not help supervise rehearsals as they had done for their earlier operas.

Auden's drafts for his contribution to the opera are in a notebook in the Berg Collection; Kallman's drafts are in a notebook at the University of Texas, which also includes his detailed outline for the opera. Auden's drafts include a table that lists the scenes of Shakespeare's play and the corresponding scenes of the libretto. Although full manuscript evidence is lacking, Auden was probably responsible for writing or recasting the Shakespearean sections of all of I.1; in I.2, he wrote the opening and closing arias; in I.3, the first half of the scene, through the Round (p. 330); in II.1, Berowne's opening Arioso and most the second half of the scene starting probably from the Quintet (p. 337) or slightly before; all of II.2 up to the trio beginning "A Royal Highness" (p. 344), and possibly the end of the scene, from "Love us, ladies, they all cry" (p. 345); and, in III, Berowne's "Our silly game" and the litany that follows (pp. 351–52). However, Auden's notebook in the Berg Collection contains positive evidence for these attributions only in the form of partial drafts of: I.3, from the Princess's "Boy, I see mischief" through the Round (p. 330); II.1, Berowne's opening Arioso (p. 334), and much of the final section of the scene; II.2, from Boyet's entrance until Jaquenetta's exit (pp. 343–44); III, Berowne's "Our silly game" and the litany that follows (pp. 351–52).

Kallman's notebook contains full or partial drafts of the following: I.2, from Armado's "Protect me, Love" through Moth's aria "Too witless are they so to woo" and Berowne's fragmentary couplet that follows (pp. 322–26); I.3, from the King's "The hunt is up" (p. 330) through the end of the scene; II.1, from the King's first "Ah me" through Armado's "Did you give her the letter?" (pp. 334–36), and the Round (p. 340); II.2, the trio beginning "A Royal Highness" and the triplet ending "We women know what cozeners men are!" (pp. 344–45); III, from the opening through Katherine's stanzas "Blame not Boyet" (p. 351), and from the Princess's "Swear to forswear" (p. 352) through the end of the opera. Auden wrote Nabokov on 16 January 1973 [misdated 1972] about a transcript of an interview with Nabokov that Auden had received from *Intellectual Digest*: "It so happens that *every one* of the passages you quoted with approval and attributed to me were written by Chester." When the interview appeared in the April 1973 issue of the magazine the quotations were not specifically attributed to either librettist.

The typed scenario of Acts I and II (reprinted below) is in the Berg Collection, together with separate typescripts of many of the arias in the libretto and a typescript draft of I.1. Two copies of the finished typescript survive. The top copy, in the Berg Collection, includes notes by Nabokov and replies (including revisions) by Kallman. An electrostatic copy made from the same typescript at a later date, now at the University of Texas, adds a title page and dramatis personae, has a somewhat different set of revisions in the authors' hands, and substitutes four pages retyped and revised from the Berg copy. Acts I and II were typed by Auden, Act III by Kallman. The four revised pages in the Texas copy were typed by Auden, and Auden's manuscript draft of one of the revised passages is also at the University of Texas.

This edition incorporates revisions made in the Texas copy, some of them apparently based on comments by Nabokov marked in the Berg copy. Most of these revisions are incorporated silently; the untrivial ones are recorded in §3. In retyping pages for the copy now at the University of Texas, Auden sometimes dropped headings like "Aria"; these are restored here from the Berg copy. Some brief stage directions that the authors marked in the Berg copy but evidently forgot when revising the Texas copy are also incorporated silently. The authors liberally marked the typescripts with brackets to indicate lines and stanzas to be sung simultaneously. These brackets differ in the two typescripts, and I have generally incorporated brackets marked in the Berg copy but omitted in the Texas copy; the notes in §3 mention a few anomalies.

The title and subtitles of the libretto are taken from the Texas typescript, with the typescript's *Labours'* corrected to *Labour's*, the form used when the opera was performed and in the published score. In the typescript of Auden and Kallman's first essay on the libretto, printed in §4, Auden spelled the title *Love's Labours Lost*. This may have been the form Auden intended for the title, but I have somewhat reluctantly accepted the form used in the score. The libretto indifferently uses "Jaquenetta" or "Jacquenetta"; I have regularized the speech headings to use the former spelling, which is the one used in the dramatis personae. I have not, however, prevented Berowne's scroll from changing color from green (when he hands it to Moth in I.2) to blue (when Jaquenetta brings it on stage again in II.1).

The text of the opera has previously been printed only in the vocal score published by Bote & Bock in Berlin on 24 November 1972. The text in the score is incomplete and includes extensive stage directions added by the composer. The publishers dropped their initial plan to print the libretto as a separate pamphlet. The full text is published for the first time in this edition.

§2 Auden and Kallman's Scenario

An outline of the libretto appears in one of Kallman's notebooks at the University of Texas. This was the basis of a scenario of the first two acts typed by Kallman and mailed to Nabokov on 7 August 1969. Auden wrote in a covering letter:

> Herewith an outline of the first two acts, and some numbers. As you will see, Chester had what I think a brilliant idea, namely to turn Moth into a Cupid-Ariel figure who delivers the letters to the wrong ladies out of mischief. This is more dramatic and has the extra advantage of getting rid of Costard, who could not have been made a character of interest.

The "numbers" mentioned in Auden's letter are separate pages, typed by Auden, with the full text of scenes and arias. In the scenario they are referred to as "enclosures". The scenario is reprinted below, but the enclosures, which are almost identical to the final text, are omitted. The scenario and enclosures are in the Berg Collection, together with two typescripts, one of "The hunt is up", the other of "*No more!* Heartsick". This latter typescript is headed "Colcinel", which is one of Kallman's misspellings of "Concolinel", a word that appears in the Quarto version of Shakespeare's play (III.1), perhaps to represent a refrain sung by Moth. Kallman, who understood the word to be the title of a song, spells it "Colcolinel" in a parenthetical question referring to this aria in his draft outline of the opera: "Moth sings (Colcolinel? White & Red?)"; "White & Red" refers to another song Shakespeare wrote for Moth. In the typescript scenario, below, Kallman spells the word "Colconinel". Kallman's consistent misspellings in the scenario (for example, Jacquetta for Jaquenetta) are duplicated in the text below.

Act I Scene 1 in the scenario corresponds to I.1 and I.2 in the finished text, and Act I Scene 2 corresponds to I.3.

LOVE'S LABOUR LOST

ACT ONE: SCENE ONE
King, Berowne, Dumain seated about a large table. Armado to one side with papers. Moth downstage.

(See enclosure A [*i.e., Auden's draft typescript of I.1, which ends with the heading "Scene II"*])

ARIA: ARMADO
He confides in Moth his passion for Jacquetta. (See enclosure B [*i.e., Armado's "Love is a devil"*])

DUETTINO: ARMADO & JACQUETTA
Jacquetta enters carrying a basket of laundry.
1)   Armado verbosely and preciously woos her. She, uncomprehending, makes brief bewildered replies.
2)   Jacquetta is rustically loquacious, Armado brief and morose.

Jacquetta exits to see what services the ladies may require.

SONG: MOTH (Colconinel [or "White and red" *deleted*])
Armado: Warble, child.

While Moth sings Armado writes to Jacquetta on a red sheet. He rolls it up and ties it with a ribbon, then gives it to Moth to give to Jacquetta, enjoining him to hide it because he sees Berowne approaching. After all, he too has sworn off "Love". Exit Armado, and just as Moth is about to go, Berowne enters and gives him a scroll, green, and tells him to deliver it to Rosaline.

STRETTO ARIOSO: MOTH
Moth comes downstage.
Moth: Too witless are they so to woo,
                 Their vow so to belie—
             To hunt in hiding, to pursue
                 What honour should deny:

Who cheat for love will hear "Cuckoo!"
    Once they have won it. Fie!
I know what men and women do,
    But can't imagine why.
                Tu-whit to-woo (*or* Too witless woo)
                Cuckoo Cuckoo
                Goodbye Goodbye Goodbye!

(This last at a sign of impatience from Berowne who has been restlessly pacing the stage)

Exit Moth.

MONOLOGUE (Furioso): Berowne
(See inclosure C [*i.e., Berowne's "I in love"*])

ACT ONE: SCENE TWO
Princess, Rosaline, Katherine and Boyet dressed for hunting.

QUARTET AND ARIETTA
The ladies discuss the men. Boyet tells them he is certain the men are smitten with them. (See inclosure D [*i.e., Boyet's aria "Why, all their behaviours" and the dialogue preceding it*])

Enter Moth, who gives the red scroll to Rosaline.
Boyet: You see!
But when Rosaline opens it, it is of course Armado's. She reads it to general mirth.
Princess: Love does indeed blossom in this austere court, though perhaps
    too luxuriously for our taste.
Rosaline (aside): I confess I am disappointed.

The letter is returned to Moth, who pretends guilelessness.
Moth: I am too young to read.
    I can only do things by heart.
    To anything else I am blind.

ENSEMBLE
King, Berowne, Dumain and Armado enter in hunting dress.
Berowne lightly questions Rosaline to sound her reaction to his poem.
Rosaline, divining what has happened, replies:
    Today I read a coxcomb's declaration of love.
    I cannot think it truly meant for me.
Consternation of Berowne
Jacquetta enters and is briefly questioned by Armado. No reaction.

Consternation of Armado.

Armado furiously accosts Moth.

Moth reminds him that there are others present, and promises to deliver
    the scroll at the first opportunity.

King, Princess, Dumain and Katherine exchange light banter.

Boyet, aside, still believes his former observations just.

Jacquetta is puzzled:

> What is he saying to me?
>
> What does he want me to say?

this all with the briefest of transitions leads directly into

THE HUNTING MADRIGAL

then, as a cry is heard: The deer are being driven past!
to a brief

CODA

While the others turn their backs to the audience and stretch their bows,
Armado makes a sign to Moth who very covertly hands Jacquetta the
green scroll. She and Armado then also turn their backs to watch the hunt
beginning. Moth throws aside his cloak and reveals that he too is in hunt-
ing costume. With his bow taking a Cupid stance, he mimes shooting at
the backs of all, turns and kneels on one knee raising his bow.

CURTAIN

ACT TWO: SCENE ONE
(A clearing in the forest. Enter Berowne)

ARIA: BEROWNE

He is madly agitated, not only because of his love (I am toiled in a pitch)
but also because of Rosaline's seeming indifference and scorn. This all
should be more "heart-felt" than his first Act Monologue.

ENSEMBLE AND QUINTET

Berowne sees King approaching and sighing.

Berowne: Reading to himself? I must know more.

He climbs a tree. Only his head is visible.

Enter King reading his poem aloud, occasionally making emendations.

Berowne comments.

King hides in another tree on seeing Dumaine approach.

Dumaine "reads" his poem aloud.

Comments by King and Berowne.

Dumaine hides in another tree on seeing Armado and Moth approaching.
For a brief time before he enters, the others go on with their "poems".
Armado (entering):

Here we are safe. They all are hunting.

The very air seems amorous with song.

Tell me, sweet boy, Dan Cupid,

Robin Goodfellow, what did she say.

Moth: Patience, sir, she had no time.
Armado: Agony, Agony.

In the meantime, the others in the trees have broken off their poems and
    are commenting on Armado.

Then all return to their preoccupations.

(See enclosure E [*i.e., the quintet "The silver moon"*])

Dumaine then climbs down and berates Armado for breaking his oath.
King climbs down and berates both.
Berowne climbs down and mocks all three:

And I who was most unwilling

Remain the only one with will.

Moth laughs at them all.

ARIETTA: JACQUETTA

Jacquetta enters in great agitation and kneels before the King. She is
holding the green scroll.

Please, sire, the treason is not mine.

I did nothing. I encouraged no one.

And now I have this letter

And I've brought it to you as soon as I could

And though I cannot read

I can tell it is treason

Because it looks like poetry

And poetry is always about love

And love is treason in this court I know.

King takes the letter. When he sees what it is he dismisses Jacquetta.
Berowne sees the scroll is his, Armado that it is not his. Both turn furiously
to Moth who starts to repeat his lines about his innocence, while the King
begins to read Berowne's poem aloud. Distracted by this from his anger,
Berowne snatches it away and tries to tear it.

Berowne: All in the pursuit of knowledge, Sire,
    A poor literary exercise,
    An imitation of Petrarch.
    I can't imagine how the wench obtained it.
Armado (in a furious whisper to Moth):
    Where is my scroll, little Machievel?
Moth gives it to him.
The King snatches the scroll back from Berowne. Berowne confesses that he too is guilty.

ROUND: KING, BEROWNE, DUMAINE, ARMADO
      By one soft glance we were undone
      And have undone our binding vow.
      We blush to feel no shame. What plan
      Could best advance our folly now?

(During the Round Boyet enters unnoticed and seeing them all with their hands on their hearts, quickly hides behind a tree.)

King: I have a plan, come close, I'll whisper it.
    This wood has ears, we know too well.

SCHERZO: INSTRUMENTAL QUINTET
All but Moth huddle round, the 4 instruments portraying the animated character of the words we cannot hear. As Boyet leans out from his hiding-place to listen the fifth instrument, something like a bass tuba perhaps, rather clumsily on sustained notes underlines the others.

———————

The King, Berowne, Dumaine, Armado give their scrolls (all different colors) and favors to Moth.

Berowne: The whole truth's known, sweet liar, thanks to you.
    But this time let the road you take lie true.
Armado: I will make sure he does.
Moth (mockingly as he exits with A): Tu-whit To-woo!

TRIO: KING, BEROWNE, DUMAINE
(See enclosure F [*i.e., the dialogue in which the King asks Berowne to prove love lawful and the trio "Love the lowest sound can hear"*])

King: Let us go and change!
They all exit gaily with arms entwined singing:
    Tra-la-la-la Tra-la-la-la!

As this fades out in the distance Boyet steps out from behind the tree rubbing his hands.
Boyet: Aha!

[Act Two:] Scene Two

QUARTET
The Princess, Rosaline and Katherine all seated holding the open scrolls before their faces. Occasionally looking out from behind them to read excerpts and make comments like: "Juno is nothing to *me*" and "*I* am like the moon!"
Against this Jacquetta, who is standing to one side, holding her scroll away from her with one finger and peering at it suspiciously.
Jacquetta: I cannot understand.
    I thought that love was banned.
    Is he asking for my hand?
    I somehow think he's asking for
    Somewhat less and something more.

SCENA: BOYET
Enter Boyet (should Jacquetta exit?) so overcome with laughter that he can hardly speak. Bit by bit, over the music of the INSTRUMENTAL QUINTET, he tells them how he overheard plans to "amuse" and sound out the ladies by coming to them disguised as visitors from Muscovy with Armado as attendant Cossack.

———————

Princess: This does not look like seriousness.
    But if they come masked
    They shall find us the same.
    More players make a better game.
    And we shall wear our favors interchanged.

TRIO: PRINCESS, ROSALINE, KATHERINE
(All aside and *very* amoroso, belying the tartness of their words)
Princess: To woo disguised—
    How ill-advised!
    I find it worse
    Than wooing in verse.
    More than it conceals,
    What folly it reveals!
    Why play the fool

With intrigue and art,
O King, to rule
My willing heart?

Rosaline: My dear Berowne,
  Although I own
  You have my heart,
  You shall never know it
  If you needs must woo it,
  O frivolous creature,
  With so little nature
  And too much art.

Katherine: Dumaine thinks me quarry
  To hunt and to harry
  With odes and with masks.
  But I will evade him
  Until I have made him
  Fulfill harder tasks:
  That is the one art
  Which captures my heart.

QUARTET: PRINCESS, ROSALINE, KATHERINE, BOYET
Boyet: They will come from Muscovy burning
  And find ice here in Navarre.
Ladies: Men!
(See enclosure G [*i.e., the quartet "Love us, ladies"*])
Each of the ladies takes one verse, then, after Boyet's rejoinder . . .
Ladies: There speaks the man!

Then all together for a contrapuntal reprise of their complaints and Boyet's answer (All light as snowflakes, perhaps, and not too fast for the reprise, to contrast with the probably crescendoing effect of their solo renditions of the complaints.)

leading back perhaps to a tutti:
  They will come from Muscovy etc.

CURTAIN

§3 THE EVOLUTION OF THE TEXT

On 1 September 1969 Auden and Kallman sent Nabokov the typescript of Act I. Act II followed shortly thereafter. In place of a scenario for Act III, Auden provided a summary in the cover letter he sent with Act I:

1) Herewith ACT ONE.
2) ACT TWO is finished and should follow in a few days.
3) ACT THREE (one scene only). All we can tell you at the moment is that the action will go something like this. When the curtain rises, the "Muscovites", which in our version includes Don Armado, are already on stage. The Princess is disguised as Rosaline, Rosaline as the Princess, Katherine as Jaquenetta, and Jaquenetta as Katherine.

A dance, during which the ladies tease the gentlemen. Jaquenetta, courted by Dumaine, will mysteriously refuse to utter a word. Katherine, courted by Armado, will astonish him by her euphuistic language. (She may even sometimes speak in Latin.)

The dance is interrupted by the arrival of Moth, who goes straight up to the real Princess (the false Rosaline) and says that an urgent message has arrived from France. Boyet goes to get it. Naturally, Moth's action reveals to the men that they have been fooled. The ladies take off their masks, the gentlemen their Russian cloaks.

Repentance of the gentlemen.
Enter Boyet with the news of the death of the King of France.
The ladies set their lovers their respective tasks.
Grand ensemble of farewell.
All leave except Moth who sings the Winter Song.

Auden and Kallman either sent Act III to Nabokov shortly after finishing it on 30 September or 1 October, or gave it to him on his visit to Kirchstetten on 6 October. At some point Nabokov marked the entire typescript with queries and requests for cuts, and Auden and Kallman supplied most of the changes he asked for. A few of the differences between the first copy of the typescript, sent to Nabokov and now in the Berg Collection, and the copy with four revised pages, now at the University of Texas, probably result from Nabokov's suggestions, although most of the changes seem merely to be authorial second thoughts. The notes below detail most of the changes between the two copies; a few trivial changes are incorporated silently in the text.

Auden and Kallman apparently made no further changes in the text, although Nabokov, when he began work on the setting, suggested that additional lyrics might be needed. On 15 July 1970, in response to a lost letter from Nabokov, Auden wrote: "If in the end you find you need an extra verse to Biron's [Berowne's] first aria [in I.1], of course you shall have one. But our feeling was that since nothing can happen dramatically until the ladies arrive, we should keep the 'prologue' as brief as possible."

Page 317.

In Armado's first speech "spoke them" is the reading of the typescript, but "spake them" may have been intended for the sake of the rhyme in the next line.

Page 318.

Nabokov marked the repeated long "e" sounds in "The Spring is near when green geese are a-breeding" in the Berg typescript and asked Auden for a revision. In the Texas typescript Auden wrote a replacement line: "Learning takes aim that love may lie a-bleeding." The original line (quoted from Shakespeare) makes more sense of the exchange that immediately follows it. Nabokov also questioned the King's phrase "sit you out" a few lines thereafter, and Auden replaced it with "go your way" in the Texas typescript.

Page 320.

In the Berg typescript Nabokov questioned the Princess's couplet "Read this . . . fair consideration." Auden's handwritten revision in the Texas typescript adds "I fear" to the preceding line:

> I am too bold, I fear;
> Read this, I pray
> To learn the purpose of my coming here.

Page 321.

In the Berg typescript Nabokov questioned Dumaine's line "I cannot stay thanksgiving" and the phrase "Fair fall" four lines later. In the Texas typescript Auden replaced the six lines beginning with Dumaine's line with the following five lines:

> DUMAINE. At such a wish I cannot stay. [*Bows and rejoins* BOYET.]
> BEROWNE. What time of day?
> ROSALINE. The hour that fools demand.
> BEROWNE. Fair fortune grace your hand
>   And send you many lovers.

Auden's manuscript draft of the revised lines is at the University of Texas.

Page 322.

Armado's aria is printed from the version in the Texas typescript, which includes Auden's handwritten revisions. For the Texas typescript Auden retyped the opening two pages of the scene (until immediately before Moth's aria); the earlier version of the page, in the Berg copy, opens:

> Love is a devil:
> There is no evil
> Angel but love.
> But if Cupid's butt-shaft
> Proved harder than
> Hercules' club,
> It is too much odds [*etc.*]

Page 324.

Armado's list of languages ("No Spanish, Latin," etc.) lacks "English" in the

Texas typescript, but the Berg copy of the earlier version of this page includes it. The omission was probably an oversight.

Page 329.

Auden retyped the page that began with Moth's entrance. The bracketed exchange starting from Boyet's "What did I tell you?" is the revised text in the Texas typescript; the earlier version from the Berg copy, also bracketed, reads:

BOYET [*aside*]. Ah! What did I tell them? Now they must own
    How just were those observations of mine.
ROSALINE [*aside*]. A letter for me from Monsieur Berowne!
    A surprise, but a pleasing surprise, I must own.
KATHERINE [*aside*]. I wish there was also a letter for me!
PRINCESS. Monsieur Berowne is a good friend of mine.
    Take it, Boyet, and bring it to me.

In the revised Texas typescript, Auden deleted "and bring it to me" from the last line of this exchange and replaced it with "We will see what we see." This replacement phrase appears to be deleted also, but the line that apparently deletes it may in fact signify that the phrase is to be linked to the first half of the line. Lacking any better solution, I have used the replacement text in this edition. In the score the phrase reads "and give it to me", which corresponds to neither of the two typescripts.

In the line following the exchange, Auden wrote "is meant for" as a revision of "importeth" in the Texas typescript. In Boyet's recitation of Armado's letter, the Texas typescript restores Shakespeare's "commiseration" in place of the Berg typescript's "compassion".

The last word of the Princess's speech immediately before Moth's arietta, "Cannot you read, boy?" was omitted when Auden retyped this passage for the Texas typescript; the omission was probably an oversight.

Page 330.

The two speeches of the Princess and Boyet from "Boy, I see mischief" to "hunting the deer" are the replacements in the Texas typescript for this sequence in the Berg typescript:

PRINCESS. Boy, I see mischief in your eye.
    What have you done? We shall see by and by.
BOYET. Soon, ladies, I think, the lords will be here
    To join with us in hunting the deer.

Page 332.

When Auden retyped the last part of the octet and the dialogue that follows for the Texas typescript he neglected to include the break between the two stanzas for Moth and Boyet and the brackets in the speeches between the octet and the Hunting Song. These have been restored for this edition.

Pages 334–39.

In II.1 the Berg copy is more heavily marked with brackets than the Texas typescript, which has brackets only on the one page of the scene that Auden retyped after preparing the original for the Berg copy. This edition includes the brackets from the Berg copy, but follows the Texas typescript where its brackets vary slightly from those in the earlier text.

Page 336.

After Armado's line "Jaquenetta" the Berg typescript includes three additional lines linked by a bracket:

KING [*ad lib*]. O Princess!
DUMAINE [*ad lib*]. O Kate!
BEROWNE [*ad lib*]. O Rosaline!

A note and arrow in Kallman's hand indicates that these are to be "repeated ad lib against following"—that is, until Moth opens his book a dozen lines later.

Page 337.

The opening stanza of the quintet is the revised text in the Texas typescript. The Berg copy has:

> The silver Moon ne'er shone one half so bright
> As doth thy face through tears of mine give light.
> O Queen of Queens, how far thou dost excel,
> Nor thought can think, nor tongue of mortal tell.

Page 342.

The two typescripts each have different sets of brackets linking the sequence from "Rhymes! Rhymes!" through "Of huge hypocrisy!" In the Berg copy, followed here, a bracket and a vertical line (both drawn by Kallman) indicate that Jaquenetta's speech "I don't understand" is to be sung simultaneously with the rest of the sequence. The Texas typescript has two brackets (probably drawn by Auden), and makes less sense of the intended arrangement. The first bracket surrounds the first speech of the Princess, Rosaline, and Katherine; because the speech heading itself indicates that all three sing together, the bracket as written serves no function. The second bracket links all the rest of the sequence—an impractical arrangement, because the various speeches of the Princess, Rosaline, and Katherine cannot be sung simultaneously. A bracket similar to the second is deleted from the Berg copy.

Pages 352–53.

At Nabokov's request Kallman marked in the Berg copy a massive cut of the sequence from the Princess's "Swear to forswear" to the King's line beginning "What can we do or say". The entire passage was reduced to three lines:

PRINCESS. Swear to forswear! You overswear again.
KING. This is not kind. We have confessed like men.
    What can we do or say to please you, then?

Page 354.

The Princess's lines "Boyet, prepare" through "And so must we" are Kallman's revision marked in the Berg copy. The original version reads: "We leave tonight. Boyet, / Prepare. The day / Goes. So must we."

Page 355.

Next to the bracket linking Dumaine's "And your reply?" and Berowne's "Reply" Kallman added a parenthetical note: "(if wished)". The bracket and note are only in the Berg typescript.

At Nabokov's request, Kallman made two cuts in the Berg copy and replaced them with new matter. The four brief lines from Berowne's "Reply" to Katherine's "If I still love you" were cut, as was Rosaline's stanza beginning "That's the way, then". The stanza was then replaced with this dialogue:

ROSALINE. That's the way, then, to choke a gibing spirit.
BEROWNE. You loved me for my wit.
ROSALINE.   And came to fear it.
BEROWNE. Berowne grown earnest? Would you love him still?
ROSALINE. I know I could. I cannot say I will.

> [BEROWNE, *as both the* KING *and* DUMAINE *have,*
> *turns away thoughtfully.*]

Page 356.

In Armado's speech beginning "Sire, with your permission" the Berg copy (followed here) has "for" deleted in the line "To hold the plough for a term of". Three lines later, "thoughtful lords" is Kallman's replacement for "silent lords"; Nabokov had noted in the margin, "They have been talking all the time."

Page 357.

In the stage direction beginning "By now the 'costumes' of all" the sentence "The landscape has turned wintery" (following "Evening") is deleted in the Berg copy. It anticipates the similar direction in the penultimate stage direction in the libretto.

§4 AUDEN AND KALLMAN ON THE OPERA

A note on the opera, probably intended to be printed either in the program or in a libretto booklet that never appeared, was published only in Bote & Bock's journal *Tagebuch,* December 1972. The text below is taken from the typescript, now in the Berg Collection, that Auden and Kallman sent to Nabokov; the spelling of the title of the opera is emended from the typescript's "Labours". Auden typed the note, and was probably its sole author, although he and Kallman signed it.

LOVE'S LABOUR'S LOST AS A LIBRETTO

Both of us have long thought that *Love's Labour's Lost* is the only good play of Shakespeare's which a writer whose mother-tongue is English would dare think of turning into a libretto. *The Taming of the Shrew* made an excellent musical, and Vaughan Williams made an opera out of *The Merry Wives of Windsor,* but these are precisely Shakespeare's weakest works. An Italian poet could make a libretto out of one of the great plays, like *Macbeth* or *Othello,* but an English poet would not dare tamper, as a librettist must, with the magnificent spoken verse.

Love's Labour's Lost is very effective as a spoken play, but the euphuistic style in which the verse is written is not destroyed by a modification of the verbal text. Furthermore, it seemed to us that the sudden dramatic change, in the last act, from frivolity to earnestness which occurs when reality enters with the announcement of the death of the Princess's father might be even more impressive when set to music than when spoken.

Our first task, of course, was to reduce the original cast of twenty-one to a manageable number of operatic roles with a suitable range of voices. Accordingly, we eliminated Mercade, Sir Nathaniel, Holofernes, Dull, Costard, the forester, and reduced the young love-couples from four to three, that is to say, we cut out Longaville and Maria. This left us with ten characters and, since the role of Moth would be sung by a woman, gave us five male and five female voices.

The only survivors of the original sub-plot were, therefore, Armado, Jaquenetta and Moth, who had now somehow to be integrated with the main plot. Moth was no problem. With Costard gone, who was to misdeliver the letters? We decided to make Moth into a mischievous Cupid who misdelivers them, not out of ignorance, but on purpose to make trouble. In order to associate Armado and Jaquenetta more closely with the main characters, we gave the former official status as Secretary to the Court, and the latter is assigned by Ferdinand to act as laundrymaid to the ladies.

This made it possible in the Confession Scene of the male lovers to include Armado, and in the scene between the Ladies and the Gentlemen disguised as Muscovites to include Jaquenetta. In this scene Jaquenetta is disguised as Katherine, Katherine as Jaquenetta. Dumaine is puzzled because his pseudo-Katherine can hardly speak a word. Armado is enchanted because his pseudo-Jaquenetta bursts out into exclamations in Latin and Italian: he thinks she has been transfigured into the Muse.

In the spoken play, during the hunting scene (Act IV, Scene 1) only the ladies are on stage watching the men in the distance. Since we needed a big ensemble for the finale of our First Act, we made the gentlemen join them, and the final chorus is not by Shakespeare, but an anonymous madrigal from the same period.

Stage-time is never synonymous with clock-time, and in opera one can take even more liberties than in spoken drama. In the play, it would seem that, by clock-time, the action takes place in about twenty-four hours. In our opera-time it takes a year, progressing from Spring through Summer and Autumn to Winter. Thus, the opera opens with Moth entertaining the court with the song *When daisies pied and violets blue*. With the announcement of the King's death, the season turns to winter and it starts to snow. The ladies and gentlemen leave in different directions, leaving Moth, Armado and Jaquenetta on stage. Moth sings the song *When icicles hang by the wall*, after which Armado speaks the final line of Shakespeare's play: *The words of Mercury are harsh after the songs of Apollo.* (to Jaquenetta) *You that way: we this way*, and the curtain falls.

W. H. AUDEN AND
CHESTER KALLMAN

A second note, similar to the first, appeared in *Opera*, February 1973. In the fifth paragraph, "messenger" may be an error for "message".

LABOUR OF LOVE

W. H. AUDEN AND CHESTER KALLMAN

For anyone whose mother-tongue is English, there are very few Shakespeare plays with the text of which he would dare to tamper. The exceptions are his dull ones. The musical *Kiss Me, Kate*, for example, is more fun than *The Taming of the Shrew. The Merry Wives of Windsor* is, perhaps, another, but it has already been turned into a libretto more than once.

It had long seemed to us that *Love's Labour's Lost* was the one play of his which, while entertaining enough in its spoken form, could be turned into an opera without too great a sacrifice of its poetry and might even prove more effective when set to music. Anyone, reading or seeing the play, is aware of the sudden and drastic change in emotional tone which is brought about by the news of the death of the King of France. Hitherto, the characters have lived in a world of pure play, flirtation and banter, where nothing serious could happen. Now, the awareness of death as a physical fact thrusts them out into the real world, where personal relations are real and always involve suffering. Music, we felt, might make this change even more impressive.

Our first task, naturally, was to reduce the cast to a manageable size with a suitable range of voices. Accordingly we cut out those characters whom we could not imagine as "singing", namely, Sir Nathaniel, Holofernes, Dull, Costard, Mercade, and reduced the four aristocratic romantic couples to three, that is to say, we cut out Longaville and Maria. This left us with a cast of ten, the King of Navarre, Berowne, Dumaine, Don Armado, Moth, Boyet, the Princess, Rosaline, Katherine and Jaquenetta. Since the role of Moth would be taken by a woman, this gave us five male voices and five female, a practical number for a composer, and ensured that there would be no scene without at least one male or one female voice.

To make it easier for us to bring characters together whenever we wanted to, we made Armado the King's secretary, and made the King entrust Jaquenetta with the job of laundry-maid to the ladies during their visit.

With Costard gone, there was the problem of the misdirected letters. We (the idea was actually Kallman's—w.h.a.) decided to make Moth a mischievous Cupid, who misdirects them, not out of ignorance but in playful malice. Then, with Mercade gone, how was the death of the Princess's father to be announced? At the end of the comic confrontation between the masked ladies and the gentlemen disguised as Muscovites, we have Moth enter, go straight up to the pseudo-Rosaline, and address her as Princess, thus exposing the imposture, and say that a messenger from France has arrived. Boyet leaves to get it and presently, dressed in black, returns to announce the news.

For ensemble reasons we introduced both Armado and Jaquenetta into this scene, as we had included Armado in the earlier scene when the young men in turn overhear each other confessing that, contrary to their vows, they have all fallen in love. Jaquenetta is disguised as Katherine, Katherine as Jaquenetta. Taking a hint from the now defunct Sir Nathaniel, we gave Katherine Latin and Italian tags to sing, thus astounding and delighting Armado who imagines that his illiterate country maid has been miraculously transformed into the Muse.

In the play, the ladies do not appear until Act II, but, in an opera, it is essential to get the voices mixed as soon as possible, so in our libretto they enter in the first scene immediately after Berowne has reminded the absent-minded King that they are expected. Again, in the play, the ladies and gentlemen go hunting separately, but, needing a big finale for our first act, we made the latter unexpectedly join the former. Rosaline has already, thanks to Moth's machinations, received Armado's letter to Jaquenetta, and Berowne is dismayed by her mockery when he asks about his own. The scene ends with an anonymous Elizabethan madrigal "The Hunt is Up".

In the play, it would seem that the whole action takes place in not more than three days by real clock time, but dramatic time can be more fantastic without losing credibility. Accordingly, we have made our libretto cover the four seasons of the year, an assumption which the stage sets should reflect. The opera opens with Moth entertaining the court with a song

"When daisies pied and violets blue". With the announcement of the death of the Princess's father, the weather turns to winter. The ladies and gentlemen depart in opposite directions. It starts to snow. Left on stage are Armado, Jaquenetta and Moth, who now sings "When icicles hang by the wall". At the conclusion of the song, Armado turns to Jaquenetta and speaks Shakespeare's final line: "The words of Mercury are harsh after the songs of Apollo. You that way: we this way". Exeunt. Curtain.

A review of the first production in *Opera*, April 1973, prompted a reply, probably written by Kallman although signed by both librettists. It appeared in the "Readers' Letters" section of *Opera*, August 1973:

The April issue of *Opera*, containing a review by Mr John McCann of Nabokov's *Love's Labour's Lost*, composed to our libretto, has just come to our attention. Although we dislike the practice of answering critiques, this one does call for some brief comments.

Admittedly the almost unceasing verbal by-play of Shakespeare has been sacrificed and an attempt made to dramatize the light pursual of serious courtships in such a way that the composer would be able to supply his equivalent. This meant treating the play as though both it and our libretto were based on common source material. Having the play to consult, however, was hardly to our disadvantage.

Mr McCann seems in his review to be aware of what our problems were, but seems otherwise to have been both slack in his homework and naive about the production of opera. Certainly he might have commented on how much and how the Shakespeare was cut, re-arranged and added to, and might even have concluded why: To provide, for one thing, each scene with a clear musico-dramatic situation that furthered the action. ". . . Human horses in the hunting scene . . . , stripping Moth to his green *diamanté* codpiece . . . , showing the ladies changing for a bathe . . ." (stealing from Scribe, no less!!) which Mr McCann attributed to us, are hardly that, and are not in our (unfortunately not yet printed) libretto; nor were the flying kiddy-cars of other scenes. Really, the reviewer might have guessed; for when we say he seems naive we mean that he appears to know nothing of contemporary opera production.

At any rate, Mr McCann's mistakes are comprehensible. What we cannot understand is his asserting that Moth crooned "When Daisies Pied" (it was another "aria"), nor his failure to even mention David Knudsen's performance as Moth in the body of his review. Surely it was one of the most remarkable vocal performances that we have ever heard.

W. H. AUDEN AND
CHESTER KALLMAN

The Entertainment of the Senses

In 1972 Francis Routh asked John Gardner to compose an anti-masque for a pro-
duction of John Shirley's masque *Cupid and Death* planned by the Redcliffe Society.
Gardner suggested that Auden should be asked to write the libretto. Gardner and
Routh visited Auden in Oxford in January 1973 to make their proposal, which he
immediately accepted. Auden offered to work on the libretto in Austria during the
summer.

Gardner expected Auden to write a separate work that would be performed
after the masque, and expected that both works would probably be performed in
concert versions. Routh and the conductor, John Eliot Gardiner, then decided that
the masque could not be performed without some form of staging and one or two
dancers. Gardner wrote Auden on 10 July to report this and to ask how it affected
Auden's plans. Auden replied on 16 July:

> Thanks for your letter. From our discussions I gather that you only
> want one more scene, an Anti-Masque. Could you let me know how
> long you would like it to last. If we must have dancers, well we must.
>
> Incidentally, if we find we can write the thing at all, I shall be col-
> laborating with Mr Chester Kallman with whom I have always worked
> on libretti.

On 31 July Gardner asked for a work that would take about twenty minutes to
perform, using the same forces as the masque.

On 17 September Auden sent this report (the page numbers refer to the 1951
Musica Britannica edition of *Cupid and Death*):

> Mr Chester Kallman and I have nearly finished the Anti-Masque. It
> will occur between the aria in which the Chamberlain enters with two
> apes (p. 49) and the entrance of Death (p. 50). In the original, the
> apes were, presumably, real ones. We shall need five singers, dressed
> up as apes, representing the Five Senses.

Gardner replied that he thoroughly approved of Auden's decision to incorporate
the anti-masque within the masque.

Auden's pocket diary records that the anti-masque was finished on both 18 Sep-
tember (presumably the draft) and 23 September (presumably a revised type-
script). On 26 September Auden wrote Gardner in a letter signed by both Auden
and Kallman:

> This afternoon we shall be mailing you our text.
>
> It is, of course, for you to decide but it seems to us that the role of
> *Taste* should be sung by a female voice, and, possibly, the role of *Smell*.

(Smell could also be a counter-tenor.) As you will see from the irregular style of our verses, that they call for lots of syncopation.

As for the *Mild und leise* chorus, if you don't know Chabrier's *Souvenirs de Munich,* it might give you some ideas.

Auden's pocket diary records that the typescript was mailed the same day. On the night of 28/29 September, a few hours after closing the house in Kirchstetten, Auden died in Vienna.

The premiere had already been scheduled for a Redcliffe Society Concert at the Queen Elizabeth Hall in London on 2 February 1974. By November it became clear to the concert organizers that a staged performance would be too expensive and that an unstaged performance of *Cupid and Death* would make no sense. *The Entertainment of the Senses* was therefore first performed as a separate work at the concert for which the full production had originally been scheduled. The text was published in Auden's posthumous collection of poems, *Thank You, Fog,* in 1974. The music is available from the rental library of Oxford University Press.

Cupid and Death was printed and performed in 1653 and 1659. Christopher Gibbons composed the music for the first performance, some of which was retained when Matthew Locke prepared the music for the second performance. The work has the standard masque structure of five "Entries"; *The Entertainment of the Senses* is written to be interpolated near the start of the Fifth Entry.

The story of the masque has Cupid and Death spend the night in the same inn, where the Chamberlain exchanges their arrows. Until Mercury sets matters right at the end, the old people struck by Death are rejuvenated and fall in love, while the young lovers struck by Cupid are slain. At the start of the Fifth Entry, the Chamberlain has left the inn and presents a pair of dancing apes whom he has been showing at fairs. Death strikes the Chamberlain with an arrow, and he falls in love with his apes. Shirley's text for this section follows:

[*Enter* CHAMBERLAIN *leading Two Apes.*]

CHAMBERLAIN. All you that delight to be merry, come see,
 My brace of Court Apes, for a need we be three.
 I have left my old trade of up and down stairs
 And now live by leading my apes unto fairs.
 Will you have any sport?
 Draw your money, come quick, sir,
 And then come aloft, Jack,
 They shall show you a trick, sir.

[*Spoken.*] Now am I in my natural condition,
 For I was born under a wandering planet:
 I durst no longer stay with my old master,
 For fear Cupid and Death be reconcil'd
 To their own arrows, and so renew with me
 Some previous acquaintance.

[*Enter* DEATH: *he strikes* CHAMBERLAIN *and exit.*]

Oh, my heart!
Twas Death, I fear: I am paid with a vengeance.
My dear Apes, do not leave me: hah: come near.

[*Sung.*] What goodly shapes they have, what lovely faces!
Ye twins of beauty, where were all those graces
Obscur'd so long? What cloud did interpose
I could not see before this lip, this nose,
These eyes? that do invite all hearts to woo them.
Brighter than stars, ladies are nothing to them.
Oh let me here pay down a lover's duty;
Who is so mad to dote on woman's beauty?
Nature doth here her own complexion spread,
No borrow'd ornaments of white or red;
Those cheeks wear no adult'rate mixtures on them,
To make them blush as some do, fye upon them!
Look what fair cherries on these lips do grow!
Black cherries, such as none of you can show
That boast your beauty; let me kiss your a—

[*Enter a* SATYR, *who strikes him on the shoul-
der and takes away his Apes.*]

[*Spoken.*] What's that? a shot i' th' shoulder too?
What will become of me now? Oh, my Apes,
The darlings of my heart are ravished from me.

Auden and Kallman specified for Gardner the changes that would be required by the anti-masque. In Auden's letter of 17 September 1973 he wrote that the Chamberlain's first two lines should read:

All you that delight to be merry, come fix
Eyes on my five Apes, at a need we'll be six.

And his phrase "Ye twins of beauty" should read "O perfect beauties". In the typescript of the anti-masque they noted that the first part of his speech should end:

And then come aloft, Jack,
They shall show you their tricks, sirs.

The anti-masque immediately followed these lines, and the next six lines in the original text were cut. At the end of the anti-masque Auden and Kallman replaced the stage direction beginning "Enter DEATH" with "DEATH touches him on the shoulder." The Chamberlain's lines from "Oh, my heart" were retained from the original text. The last three of Shirley's lines reprinted above were replaced with these two lines, and the last line was explicitly cut:

What's that? a shot i' th' shoulder too? Ha!
What will become of me now? I have lost my senses!

Partial manuscript drafts of the anti-masque, written in the hands of both Auden and Kallman, are in the Berg Collection. Partial typescript drafts, some typed by Auden with revisions by Kallman, some typed by Kallman with revisions by Auden, are at the University of Texas and the Berg Collection. Kallman prepared the final typescript; the Berg Collection has two complete photographic copies, and John Gardner another complete copy, all with corrections by the librettists, and the University of Texas has a partial carbon copy.

In 1974, at the request of the editor of this edition, Kallman divided the authorship of the work on a copy of the typescript. The Chamberlain's first two lines are Auden's; his third line, which gives the title of the work, is Kallman's. In the speech of the First Ape, Auden wrote the lines from "Fidelity and all that" through "Merely grab"; "When you see a fair form" through "There's no sex-life"; "And there are many more new" through the end. The "*Mild und leise*" chorus, which follows this speech and the remaining speeches, is by Kallman. The speeches of the Second and Third Ape are entirely by Kallman, with the Third Ape's last line rewritten by Auden. In the speech of the Fourth Ape, Auden wrote "When Life seems dreary" through "Only aims to cause" and "For the prissy minority" through the end. In the speech of the Fifth Ape, Auden wrote "A mountain, we must confess" through "Black and white" and "Yes, we're lucky" through the end. In the final chorus Kallman noted next to the last line ("We must love one another *and* die"): "the joke was originally Cyril Connolly's". The Chamberlain's final speech and other additional speeches printed above are by Auden, except for the concluding phrase, "I have lost my senses."

Radio Plays

The Dark Valley

Although *The Dark Valley* was Auden's first radio play broadcast in America, he apparently prepared or proposed an earlier work that is now lost. At some time during 1939 he delivered a work listed simply as "Song" in the records of scripts received by the Columbia Broadcasting System. This work was to be dramatized, but no further record of it exists at CBS or anywhere else, and there is no clue to the nature of its contents.

CBS commissioned *The Dark Valley* for its Columbia Workshop drama series in the spring of 1940. Benjamin Britten was commissioned to compose music for the play, evidently at Auden's suggestion. Auden wrote the play probably in April. After it was delivered, probably around May, the script underwent some further revision and rearrangement, and was performed under the direction of Brewster Morgan on 2 June 1940 in a broadcast over the CBS network, originating from WABC in New York. Dame May Whitty performed the sole speaking part. The play seems to have been the first dramatic monologue of its kind broadcast in America.

The script first arrived at CBS under a different title from the one under which it was performed. In the network's notoriously inexact records of scripts received, the work is listed as "Psychological Reactions of the Women [*sic*] who Killed the Goose who Laid the Golden Egg". (Information supplied in 1972 by Bernard S. Krause of the CBS Radio office of business affairs.) Max Wylie, Director of Script and Continuity for CBS, recalled a slightly different version of the title in his introduction to the published text:

> The original title of the Auden piece, when it first arrived, read something like this, as nearly as I can remember: "The Psychological Experiences and Sensations of the Woman who Killed the Goose That Laid the Golden Egg." You can't get a thing like this into the newspaper listings of radio schedules. Editors look at it, blink, and just write "Drama." The Columbia Workshop changed the title to "The Dark Valley." (*Best Broadcasts 1939–40*, p. 31)

Auden evidently accepted the new title. In a letter to Elizabeth Mayer, 10 June 1940, he wrote: "Tell B[enjamin Britten] I thought the music to Dark Valley *lovely* and so did everyone else who heard it" (letter in the Berg Collection).

Early pencil drafts of the play and of the interpolated songs are in a notebook now in the Berg Collection. Some sections of the draft are written in the alliterative verse that Auden used again in 1944–46 for *The Age of Anxiety;* the corresponding sections in the final version are recognizable by their heavy alliteration. The final version, in prose except for the interpolated songs, survives in the form of two mimeographed typescripts prepared by CBS. A copy of the first, used by Benjamin Britten when composing the music, is now in the Berg Collection. (This first typescript gives the projected date of broadcast as 26 May 1940, one week earlier than the actual date.) The second typescript consists of eleven mimeographed pages retained from a copy of the first typescript and ten newly typed revised pages that replace an equal number of pages from the first version. The changes in the second typescript, which Auden made during rehearsals in order to ease the difficulty of performing the play, are for the most part large-scale rearrangements of material in the first typescript, with relatively few verbal changes. A copy of this second typescript was preserved by CBS, which deposited a microfiche copy in the Museum of Broadcasting in New York and then apparently destroyed the original. (CBS had earlier made a xerographic copy for the present editor. Neither of Auden's Columbia Workshop scripts appears to have been deposited in the Copyright Office.)

The text of this edition is based on the second typescript, with some silent emendations in places where the second clearly miscopies the first. The nonauthorial heading "SOUND" that precedes all stage directions in the typescript has been omitted, and sound effects and minor cuts and rearrangements marked in the typescript by unidentified hands have been ignored. However, changes marked in the final section of the text of this typescript seem to reflect Auden's own revisions and are incorporated in the main text; the typed version is described in the notes.

The play was published in the collection *Best Broadcasts of 1939–40*, selected and edited by Max Wylie (1940); the text was based on another marked copy of the second typescript, and includes nonauthorial stage directions and changes similar to those marked in the surviving copy of the typescript.

In a letter to Wolfgang Köhler, undated but probably late April 1939, Auden wrote: "I have been struggling to finish a radio play. It's supposed to be an old woman talking to a goose, but I believe she's really Knut Hamsun" (letter in the American Philosophical Library).

During the summer or autumn of 1940 Auden apparently planned to include the play in his book *The Double Man*, which he was preparing for publication the following year. On the rear pastedown of a copy of *The Blue Grove: The Poetry of the Uraons*, by W. G. Archer (1940), now at the University of Texas, he wrote this list:

> Letter
> Notes
> Play
> Sonnets
> Ode

Although the published version of *The Double Man* omits the play and the "Ode" (a poem written around July 1940 and first printed in 1941 as "Three Songs for St Cecilia's Day"), it contains the other items on this list, in the same sequence.

The BBC Third Programme broadcast the play on 21 January 1960. Auden wrote to P. H. Newby at the BBC on 19 August 1959: "I shall be delighted if you can do anything with *The Dark Valley*. It is very important that you get an expert in animal noises to imitate the goose. The Bells at the end should be deafening."

Britten's autograph composition sketch and nonautograph vocal and instrumental parts are in the Britten-Pears Library. In an undated letter to Britten (now in the Berg Collection), Auden wrote:

> Here is a chore for you. Here are two representative stanzas from the two songs in my radio play. Could you write two tunes.
>
> 1. Of folk-song character
> 2. Beautiful
> 3. Require no musical gift.
> 4. Gain sinister effect from being sung by an old old woman with a cracked voice.

A.   Eyes look in to the well
      Tears run down from the eye   (6. 6. 6. 6.)
      The tower cracked and fell
      From the quiet winter sky.

B.   Bribe the birds then on the branches
        Bribe them to be dumb   (8. 5. 8. 5.)
      Stare the hot sun out of heaven
        That the night may come.

A tape recording of the play can be obtained through the semi-clandestine market in recordings of radio broadcasts. Probably this tape was made from a sixteen-inch acetate recording prepared during the original broadcast in order to allow syndication later the same day in western time zones.

As he did with *Alfred,* Auden apparently wrote this new play as a single paragraph broken only by stage directions. The only point in the first typescript (the one that derives directly from Auden's lost manuscript) where a break occurs without being marked by a stage direction is on page 378, between "the darkness of a dreadful dream" and "But why am I telling you all this". On balance it seems likely that the break was introduced by the typist, so it has not been reproduced here. In both typescripts of *The Dark Valley* some pages appear to begin with the start of a new paragraph, but the appearance is the deceptive effect of the rule followed by typists at CBS that required each page of a dramatic typescript to end with a complete sentence, even if the page had adequate room to begin another sentence on the last line. This practice made it simpler to revise and replace individual pages, but the short lines at the end of some pages can be misread as the end of a paragraph that in fact continued to the next page. When some of the material in the first typescript was rearranged to create the text of the second typescript, one of the breaks represented by the stage directions disappeared. In the text of this edition, this break has been reestablished by inserting from the second typescript the pencilled-in stage direction "[*Wind.*]" (p. 371).

Some notes on revisions and emendations to the second typescript follow.

On page 373, in the eleventh sentence of the paragraph beginning "Until what", the typescripts underline "die" but the sense seems to require emphasis on "in".

On page 374, the one-sentence paragraph, "Water—at least we have water", was added to the typescript by an unidentified hand and is perhaps unauthorial.

On page 377, in the paragraph beginning "Shout yourself hoarse", the first typescript has "We've all got as much a right to do our share in the government by answering questions as he has to ask them." In revising this to the text of the second typescript ("We've all have a right to do our share in the government by answering questions and filling up forms,") the initial "We've" seems to have survived by mistake and has been emended to "We" in this edition.

On page 378, in the paragraph beginning "For those horns", this edition's "re-treating in rout" is a perhaps unnecessary emendation for the typescripts' "retreating in route".

In the second line of the song on page 379 the typescripts read "Watch you meet your love"; this edition emends "Watch" to "Would" as in all other texts of the song. The second typescript has pencilled revisions in the song that are incorporated here because they correspond to Auden's published texts: in stanza 7, "ruined" was originally "deserted", and in stanza 8 "the cobwebs from the mirror" was "the dust from the gilt mirror".

On page 380, the section beginning "It's Sunday evening" is marked in pencil in the second typescript with changes that are probably authorial and are incorporated in this edition. In the second sentence of the section "gently" was originally "comfortably"; and the fifth sentence originally read: "For business is business, and boys will be boys, and lust is a natural need like eating, and to search for the gold of grace is so tiresome, such mining is a nuisance and never pays." (This edition's text of the revised sentence emends "to search" to "the search", as does *Best Broadcasts*.)

The original text (from the first typescript) differs from the second typescript as listed below. Other differences that consist of very minor rearrangements of the order of a series of phrases are not noted here. In each extract the beginning and end corresponds to identical material in the second typescript that may be found in the main text of this edition.

Pages 371–72.

> [. . .] She's ashamed to be looked after by an old hag, a poor old woman alone in the mountains with not a neighbor near to help her, abandoned by all, her beauty gone. She'd like to live with a real lady, not someone the women whisper about in the village, and the dogs growl at if she goes near them, and the men spit as she passes by, and the children are dragged indoors by their mothers, in case she should frighten them into a fever. I know. I know. Do I feed her, care for her? What of it? What does she care? Isn't that what poor old women are for.
>
> *[Goose off.]*
>
> Na-na. There you are, you slut. Come here at once. Just wait till I catch you. I'll wring your silly neck. Alright. Stay there if you want. [. . .]

Pages 372–73.

[. . .] Yes, it's supper time, Nana, the greatest moment of the day, time for greedy little geese to stuff their guts and then bedtime. [*She is stalking the goose.*] Hushaby, sleep, sleep and such lovely dreams, flying away away away over the tree-tops, not even bothering to look back down at the poor old woman waving goodbye with tears rolling down her cheeks because now she's left all all alone with no one to care for her, but just going on and on above the forest, over the tops of the mountains, and then there it is, the fairy castle. The gate stands open. There's not a soul to be seen. Into the courtyard, through the door, up the winding stair to the tower to the little room at the very top. Knock. Knock. Who's there? Queen Nana? Come in, my dear, I've been expecting you for a thousand years. Ah, how your heart beats. At last I shall meet him, my wonderful gander, husband, my fairy prince. In you rush with a flutter of feathers, but, oh dear, something funny has happened. There's no handsome rich young gander standing there, but only the poor old woman you left behind. But what's that funny thing she's holding in her hands, so shiny and sharp. Oh, God, it's a . . . [*She grabs the goose.*]

[*Goose squawks angrily.*]

Got you. Now we'll go my way for a change. Squawking won't mend matters. There's a nice little coop of wire netting waiting for you while I get things ready. Later perhaps I shall need your help.

[*Goose being put in coop.*]

Pages 373–75.

[. . .] You'd be surprised at all the possibilities of hungry hawks and famished foxes, and stealthy stoats and lurking lynxes and bold bad bears, at all the varieties of clutch and claw and teeth and talon and snap and snatch.

[*Distant avalanche.*]

The avalanches have been falling all afternoon for the sun is still shining in the white snow peaks and the useless wastes of that world are full of useless light and heat that can do nothing. But this deep dale is dark always. Here summer has no success and short the distance of noon from night and near ever are the cold crags to this crevice where roars the glacier torrent in a gloomy twilight, wild waters in a winter dusk. Let the day break its heart on the hard heights for what it can do, the dark returns, and even up there it is autumn already. O, I am glad in this grim hole. But we must have water, Nana. I must fetch water.

[Feet on twigs then on stone steps.]

Once this valley was full of voices, effort and action, engines and men.

[Fade in stream and waterfall.]

For where a vein pointed promising the golden metal went miners like moles after, hewing into the hill their hopeful way. They sank a shaft from the surface of the earth, they drove through darkness, drifts with a purpose; in sombre stopes they scooped out ore, gold-speckled quartz with their quick hammers. They managed much, those many miners.

[Bucket in stream.]

But father was foremost, first of them all with drill and dynamite and daring hands at deeds deep down where no daylight was, and equally noble was no man living, and equally noble was no man living; for he moved like a river, riding the world. *[She has come up from the stream—the waterfall fades slightly.]* When father spoke the monsters grew mild in the sea, and the roses opened and the eagle hung spellbound over the spellbound lamb. When he smiled it was the shining spaces of summer, but when he frowned it was ages of ice, his anger ended the earth. O but *he* is ended, ended his life, lost, away, a no one, a nothing as if he never were. He perished in an explosion, his body was broken by a blast in the earth. He was drunk, they lied, the low and evil; he was killed by his lack of care they wrote, the mine owners to mother and their mean hearts were glad he was a ghost for his greatness galled them. For he was a stag among sheep, a star among tapers, alone with fools in a foul field.

[Ravens croaking overhead.]

Cry your curse from the crags, cry it again; black ravens over this ruined place. The shaft is full of water and the wind whistles through the broken buildings of an abandoned mine. For it failed soon after father died. The lode vanished—in vain they searched.

[Feet on steps continuing. Fade out waterfall.]

The gold was gone; they got nothing; they lost heart; gave up their drilling; it paid no longer; they departed poor. And none remained but mother and I on this stony farm in a stony silence. She never loved me. I knew it from the first. She was prim and pious and praying always, for father's soul and shuddered at his songs and thought him wicked and wept much. For she wanted a dummy who would drive her to church, in a blue suit; bowing to the neighbors, holy and hollow and half alive. And she could not bear me because I was like him and he knew it and loved me and would lift me up in his great hands as he imitated a lion roaring or a rutting stag. Or trot me on his knee and tell me stories of devils and dragons in dark caves and fatal love in foreign lands.

[*Goose fades in.*]

Did you think I'd forgotten about you, Nana. [. . .]

Page 376.

[. . .] And mother watched every movement I made, afraid that father's passionate blood would appear in his daughter. For he wanted no woman, but he won her; greater than parent or priest was his power and one look from his grey eyes and husbands were forgotten, for the god was his faithful friend—yes and mine. Mine also. It was he that helped me defeat my mother and made her blind, and never betrayed me but was true to his own. For he came to me in secret on soft feet, [. . .]

Page 377.

In the paragraph beginning "Look up, Nana," the first typescript has "The new man in his marvelous machine".

In the paragraph beginning "Shout yourself hoarse" the first typescript has "that plane passes over this spot, punctual to the minute"; and, later in the same paragraph, "by answering questions as he has to ask them."

THE ROCKING HORSE WINNER

Auden's first attempt to adapt a work of prose fiction for radio was an "extraction" (as such a work was called) of *Pride and Prejudice* that he prepared during the autumn of 1940, evidently on commission from the Columbia Broadcasting System's Helen Hayes Theatre. John Houseman, who was writing scripts for the series at the time, recalled it as "a very perfunctory job (since Auden was largely unacquainted with radio) which was greatly rewritten before it went on the air" (letter to Mendelson, 21 April 1972). Auden's name was used neither in the publicity for the broadcast nor in the broadcast itself on 24 November 1940. Scraps of dialogue that Auden copied or adapted from the novel are in a notebook now in the Berg Collection.

CBS gave Auden an opportunity to prepare a more successful adaptation soon afterward. From October 1940 to the summer of 1941 Auden shared a house in Brooklyn Heights with George Davis, Carson McCullers, and, at times, Benjamin Britten, Peter Pears, Golo Mann, Louis MacNeice, and Paul and Jane Bowles. Davis was literary editor of *Mademoiselle;* after accepting a short story by Davidson Taylor, a young executive at CBS, he invited Taylor to lunch at the Brooklyn house. Around this time, Taylor's wife, Mary Elizabeth Plummer, suggested to him that an effective broadcast could be made of Lawrence's story "The Rocking-Horse Winner" (first published in 1926, collected posthumously in *The Lovely Lady*, 1932). Some time after the Brooklyn lunch, Taylor invited Auden to write the adaptation.

Auden asked James Stern to collaborate, partly because Stern knew about horse racing and Auden did not. Auden had admired Stern's short stories since Isherwood recommended them in 1935, and had been a friend of Stern and his wife Tania since meeting them in Paris in 1937; the Sterns had moved to America in 1939 and resumed the friendship in New York. Auden was at first skeptical about the words Stern gave the bookies in the scene at the race course, but accepted them when Stern assured him of their authenticity. Stern's childhood home, Bective, gave its name to one of the horses in the play.

Auden delivered the script (handwritten in green ink) to Davidson Taylor early in 1941, and split his one hundred dollars with Stern. CBS commissioned Britten to write the music. After some revision, the play was performed on 6 April 1941, under the direction of Guy della Cioppa in a broadcast by the Columbia Workshop over the CBS network, originating from WABC in New York.

Auden's holograph manuscript was discarded after it was typed by Taylor's secretary. The text survives in two versions. The first is represented by a carbon copy of a typescript evidently prepared mostly from Auden's manuscript; the typist left some words blank where Auden's hand was unreadable, and the blanks have been filled in pencil by an unidentified hand that probably copied them from corrections made on the top copy, perhaps by Auden. Other corrections and changes in the same unidentified hand probably derive in a similar way from authorial changes made on the top copy. Not everything in this first typescript was prepared directly from Auden's manuscript; three lost pages in the original were replaced by a single page numbered "5–6–7", and other pages were replaced by two or more pages; the notes below provide details. Britten used this carbon copy when preparing the music, and it is now in the Berg Collection.

The second version is the mimeographed version prepared by CBS, which was apparently typed from a marked copy of the first version. Two copies of this second version survive. One, kept by James Stern, has changes in his hand. Most of these changes are also marked by an unidentified hand on the copy (stamped "as broadcast") preserved by CBS. This copy was apparently destroyed after CBS deposited a microfiche copy in the Museum of Broadcasting in New York. CBS had earlier made a xerographic copy for the present editor.

Britten's music for the play is lost, but a tape recording of the play can be obtained through the semi-clandestine market in recordings of radio broadcasts.

The text of this edition is based on the first typescript, but it incorporates the changes marked there and in the second copy, and has been checked against a copy of the recording. I have ignored the markings pencilled into the first version by the directors to indicate cues for music. Where the pencilled changes marked in Stern's copy differ from those in the CBS copy of the second version, I have preferred Stern's version. I have followed the pencilled markings in the first version in cutting some very brief passages; these are recorded in full in the note below. I have not, however, followed the pencilled deletion in the second version of the last two lines of the play; the deletion is emphatic in the "as broadcast" CBS copy and very faint in Stern's copy. The lines may have been deleted to remove an overly pious tone in the final moments, but the omission may equally have resulted from time constraints.

Both typescripts omit the hyphen in "rocking horse" in the title of the work and in all but one of the five occurrences of the word in the text itself. This evidently reflects Auden's usage, and the hyphen has been omitted in this edition. Bassett's "Manmouth 'ouse" (p. 384) may be a typist's error for "Monmouth 'ouse" but is more probably an attempt to reproduce his pronunciation.

The only extensive revisions in the text occur in the concluding verses. The main text prints the final version, taken from the second typescript as altered lightly in Stern's copy; the notes below include the text of the first version of the speech before that version was marked with corrections; the first version's corrected text was the basis of the uncorrected text in the second version.

The first typescript has scene numbers, which were mostly deleted in pencil and which do not appear (except for "Scene 1") in the second version. I have preserved them here, but instead of printing them as centered headings, I have incorporated them within the stage directions. The pages typed as replacement pages lack scene numbering, and the numbering of scenes 7, 8, and 9 has been supplied for this edition. Where the typescript is inconsistent in spelling, I have followed, wherever possible, the spelling in Lawrence's story.

Before the opening of the play as printed in the main text, the CBS copy of the second typescript has a carbon-copy page with four lines of dialogue, evidently added at the last minute:

1ST VOICE. There must be more money!
2ND VOICE. There must be more money!
1ST VOICE. This house is unlucky!
2ND VOICE. Now. Now, there must be more money—a great deal more.

In scene 3 (p. 385) the typist, in an apparent misinterpretation of Auden's manuscript, typed the first speeches of the Voices as prose rather than as verse. (The Voices' speeches are correctly laid out as verse starting with the 2nd Voice's "Ask the things you have known the longest.") I have divided the speeches into verse for this edition. The text of the fifth speech in the scene reproduces the revisions and deletion marked by James Stern on his copy. The typescripts (with the speech laid out as prose) read: "If you've no money you mayn't have a garden. You must play with the rough boys near the railway station, where the streets are dirty and the drains are bad."

A later part of the same scene was evidently abridged after Auden submitted his manuscript. In the first typescript the dialogue from the 2nd Voice's "Ask the things you have known the longest" to the same Voice's "Perhaps you have and perhaps you haven't" is on a relatively short page numbered "5–6–7"; the original versions of these three pages are lost.

Later in Scene 3 (p. 386), the speech in which Paul swears to love luck was drastically shortened by a pencilled deletion in the first typescript. The typed text reads: "I swear by the Declensions and the Conjugations, by the Prime Numbers and the Improper Fractions, by the Cyclone and the Anti-Cyclone, by Time when and Time within which, by the Plus Sign, the Minus Sign and the Decimal Point, by the Hypotenuse and the Perpendicular, by Ei with the Optative and the Optative with An, and by the Filthy Lucre to Love Luck for ever and ever. Amen." In the dialogue immediately following this speech, after the 2nd Voice's "Now mount your horse and ride", a line for the 1st Voice is deleted in the first typescript: "We will remain not and whisper the time away."

In Scene 7, in the opening dialogue at the race course (p. 390), the bets made with the 1st Bookie are numbered 448 and 449, followed by 440; presumably the authors, not the Bookie, miscounted.

In Scene 8 (p. 391), the episode of the race itself was slightly lengthened in revision: a lost original page 18 is replaced in the first typescript by pages numbered 18 and 18-A, the latter a very short page. Similarly, the dialogue among Oscar, Bassett, and Paul near the end of Scene 9 (pp. 391–92) was lengthened during revision, and a lost original page 19 was replaced by pages numbered 19, 19-A, and (a short page) 19-B.

Near the start of Scene 13 (p. 394), the first typescript has a line, deleted in pencil, that concluded the first speech of the 2nd Voice, after "always tired,": "If you need money, you'll always need it." Oscar's final speech in this scene (p. 396) ends in both typescripts "this time, though." The last word is deleted in the CBS copy of the second typescript and circled (presumably for deletion) in James Stern's copy.

The concluding verses in Scene 15 (pp. 396–97) read as follows in the first typescript, before being revised in pencil into a text corresponding substantially to the text of the second typescript:

1ST VOICE. Does she blame her luck?
2ND VOICE.   Not any more.
    Those who blame luck are full of envy,
    Those who are envious are always unlucky
    Those who love luck are in love with themselves,
    But people who weep are done with envy
    People who watch are aware of something
    People who weep know what they love
    Now at last, she weeps, she weeps and watches
    Now at last she knows that she loves her son.
1ST VOICE. Does Paul know this?
2ND VOICE.   Yes, Paul knows now.
    That's why he needn't ride any longer
    The world of Perhaps has become the Certain,
    Paul is no longer in love with luck.

1ST AND 2ND VOICES. The envy that made this house unlucky
  The envy of which we were the unwilling voices
  Is done away with. We need not whisper
  Out of the rose-bush or under the stairs.
  Sorrow has silenced envy for ever,
  Sorrow silences us. We are glad to be silent.
  Love is born from the death of this child.

Liturgical Drama and Film
Narratives

THE PLAY OF DANIEL

The New York Pro Musica Antiqua, directed by Noah Greenberg, began planning a production of the thirteenth-century liturgical drama *Ludus Danielis* around 1956. Probably around the summer of 1957 Auden wrote a verse narration to be spoken between episodes in the musical drama. The group, now calling itself the New York Pro Musica, first performed *The Play of Daniel* at the Cloisters in New York on 2–4 and 6 January 1958. The success of the production led to later performances by the New York Pro Musica in America and Europe; in performances at the Church of St Barnabas in Oxford, 1–3 June 1960, Auden, in the costume of a monk, read the narration.

Noah Greenberg sent a copy of Auden's narration to the magazine *Jubilee* on 28 October 1957; the editor of *Jubilee* had told Greenberg he was interested in publishing the text around the time of the first production, and it appeared, under the title "Daniel", in the January 1958 issue. The narration next appeared, untitled, in the booklet bound into the New York Pro Musica's recording of the work for Decca (DL 9402 and DL 7-9402), released around September 1958; then as "Daniel in the Lion's Den" in *Seventeen*, December 1958; then in the published version of the score, *The Play of Daniel: A Thirteenth-Century Musical Drama*, edited by Noah Greenberg (1959). Some of Auden's rough drafts for the narration are in a notebook now in the Berg Collection.

The text of this edition is based on a nonauthorial typescript (now in a private collection), evidently based closely on Auden's lost draft typescript and with minor corrections probably in his hand. This typescript is accompanied by a page of Auden's typescript headed "Revision of Narration IV", which nearly doubles the length of the original section IV (pp. 403–5). The original version ended:

> The princes praise the prophet Daniel
> And the Queen also for her quickness of heart.
> But the fate foretold befalls the king.
> Darius the Great who rules the Medes
> Comes forth a victor, invades the land:
> He slays Belshazzar, sits on the throne.

These lines were deleted from the full typescript when the revised version was retyped by the same typist who prepared the rest of the full typescript and the new pages were inserted. Before it was retyped, Auden deleted from his revised typescript the third line after the pause: "Care clutches him, cold are his reins;".

The printed texts of the play closely follow the typescript except for the omission of the numbers at the head of each section and some minor revisions and errors. At the end of section IV Auden's typed revision (and the nonauthorial typescript based on it) has "Slays Balshazzar, and sits on the throne", with "and" deleted. In the printed texts, "and" is restored, perhaps erroneously; this edition follows the typescript. In the printed texts the pause indicated in the revised typescript of section IV is replaced with a break corresponding to the breaks between all other sections, and in the score a passage of the musical play occurs in the break. At the end of section V the printed texts (probably mistakenly) have "relates" for the typescript's "relate". In section VIII, the printed texts have the probable revision "God sent an angel" for the typescript's "God sent me an angel". Also in section VIII this edition emends "days end" (in typescript and printed texts) to "days' end". In the last line of the play the printed texts, probably erroneously, have "people" for the typescript's "peoples". The printed texts also include some minor corrections in punctuation silently followed in this edition, and some minor errors in punctuation silently ignored.

The only differences among the printed texts are an occasional capital letter reduced mistakenly to lowercase, and the change in spelling to "Peres" in the published score from "Pheres" in all earlier versions (p. 404). The second printing of the score (1963, dated 1964) adds at the end of Section II a line that was probably written after the first performance in order to ease the transition between the narration and the music: "But first the frolic; the feast begins".

Auden had worked with Noah Greenberg and the New York Pro Musica Antiqua almost from the time the group was formed in 1953. At a concert of Elizabethan verse and music at Town Hall, New York, 30 and 31 January 1954, he read the verse and the group sang the music. In a recording that eventually grew out of this concert, *Elizabethan Verse and Its Music,* released by Columbia in 1955 (ML 5051), Auden is again heard reading the verse; he also wrote the sleeve note. Noah Greenberg edited the music and Auden and Kallman edited the text for *An Elizabethan Song Book* (1955). For the group's performance of a masque by Campion at the 92nd Street YM-YWHA in New York, 5 and 13 February 1955, Auden read Campion's Description of the masque. In September and October 1963 he tried to write a narration for the group's planned production of *The Play of Herod,* but, as he wrote to Lincoln Kirstein on 11 October:

> After making a number of attempts at a commentary for *Herod,* I have become convinced, a) that I cannot do one, b) that all which is necessary is a reading at appropriate points of the two Gospel narratives, in Luke and Matthew.
>
> The incidents have been treated in verse so often that one can only produce pastiche of already existing medieval carols. At least that is all I can do. Perhaps a Beat poet could do something.

The group eventually used a narration by Archibald MacLeish. Auden published an obituary tribute to Greenberg in *The New York Review of Books,* 3 February 1966.

RUNNER

This brief film about the Canadian runner Bruce Kidd was produced in 1962 by the National Film Board of Canada. The script and direction were by Donald Owen, the music by Don Douglas, the production by Tom Daly. Auden wrote his narration in May 1962 to accompany partly edited footage that the National Film Board sent him in Austria. In a letter of 26 May, Auden told Lincoln Kirstein that he had written "a commentary for a documentary film about a seventeen year old Canadian long-distance runner, Bruce Kidd, with which I am rather pleased—a mixture of Pindar and Beowulf." The film was completed and released in July.

Auden's original typescript is lost, but the National Film Board of Canada prepared a mimeographed transcript of the completed film, evidently based partly on Auden's typescript. Auden published a slightly different version of the text in *City Without Walls* (1969). A notebook now in the British Library (Add. MS 53772) contains partial manuscript drafts. Auden's outline for the film appears in the notebook among the drafts:

Section I	Beach sequence.	Voice A
Sec II	Warming up.	Voice B
Sect III	Slow Motion.	Voice A
Sect IV	Fast Training.	Voice B
Sect V	The Race.	Voice B
Sect VI	Epilogue.	Voice A

Tom Daly confirms that the second and third speeches of the Announcer were not written by Auden. The Announcer's first speech was perhaps written by Auden; however, it may have been adapted from lines in his lost original typescript that the Film Board replaced with the existing second and third speeches. In the fragmentary manuscript drafts these lines read as follows:

The place. East York on Dominion Day.
The event. A two mile race.
The rivals. Bruce Kidd of Canada, Lazlo Tabori of Hungary, Max Truax
    of the United States.

They're off.

Tabori Kidd Truax

Truax Tabori Kidd
Tabori Truax Kidd

Truax Tabori Kidd

One mile to go.

Kidd Tabori Truax

The winner. Bruce Kidd.
Time. 8 minutes 46 seconds.

Among the abandoned lines from the early drafts of the dialogue between the First and Second Voices appear these: "The runner does not remember / What happened during the race". Auden may have recalled these lines a year later when he wrote in "The Cave of Nakedness" that "Lovers don't see their embraces / as a viable theme for debate, nor a monk his prayers / (do they, in fact, remember them?)".

The text in this edition is based on the mimeographed transcript, emended with reference to the published text in *City Without Walls*. Auden wrote his verse commentary for two voices, but in the film (and in the Film Board's transcript) the narration is spoken by one voice only. The published text in *City Without Walls* has speech-headings for an Announcer and a First and Second Voice. The midline breaks that mark the division between the two voices in the published text are also present in the transcript (with some slight differences), and it seems almost certain that these line breaks correspond closely to the assignments to two voices in the lost original typescript. The speech headings from *City Without Walls* are used in this edition. The assignment of speeches to the two voices follows the published text except in two places: in the second part, where the published text keeps "Arms are for balance" on the same line as "Is leg-action" (p. 412), and, near the end of the third part (p. 413), where the line breaks are more frequent in the transcript than in the published text and the speech assignments are therefore somewhat conjectural. In an interview in 1971 Auden said of the film: "Unfortunately it required two speakers and only had one; it wasn't very well spoken either. I should have been there to direct it" (Elizabeth Sussex, *The Rise and Fall of British Documentary*, 1975, p. 79).

The narration is virtually unpunctuated in the transcript, perhaps following Auden's original. The initial capitals in the nouns in the last five lines are taken from the published text; the typist of the transcript probably reduced Auden's capital letters to lowercase ones. The only substantive variations between the transcript and the published text are in the passage that in the transcript reads "Trusting each other / Rivals shall ride to race together / Be firm friends / Funny is he" (p. 412). In the published text the first of these lines is absent; "should ride to the race" replaces "shall ride to race" in the second line: and "Foolish" (followed here) replaces the evidently mistaken "Funny" in the third. The published text and this edition correct Hyppokleas to Hippokleas in the opening speech.

US

This film was produced in 1967–68 for showing at the United States Pavilion at HemisFair '68, an international exposition held in San Antonio, Texas, from 6 April to 6 October 1968. The film presented documentary footage of American history and life with a narration by Auden and music by David Amram. The film, the pavilion, and the special three-screen theatre within the pavilion for which the film was designed, were commissioned by the U.S. Expositions Staff of the Department of Commerce. The film itself was directed by Francis Thompson and Alexander Hammid of Francis Thompson, Inc., in New York.

Probably late in 1967, after filming was complete, the producers phoned Auden to ask if he would be interested in writing the text. Auden visited their office and agreed to begin work. By his own choice, he wrote his narration using a timed, descriptive list of the shots included in the film. Afterward he helped shape the film during the cutting, and he and Thompson successfully held out against others in Thompson's office in insisting that the film should end on a note of challenge rather than triumph. When the cutting was complete he told Thompson, "We have made a subversive film for the U.S. Government."

Thompson recalls that Auden wrote more narrative than the producers were able to use, and that Auden urged them to cut freely. The original text is lost, but the text of the completed film was distributed by the press office of the pavilion as a photoduplicated press release under the printed heading "United States Pavilion HemisFair '68 News", probably around the time of the opening of the exposition. The text in this press release, followed in this edition, appears to descend ultimately from Auden's original typescript, and it retains some of Auden's characteristic punctuation, such as the hyphen in "good-will". At a later date the text in the press release was retyped, apparently for the files of the U.S. Department of Commerce, and photocopies of this retyped text were sent out in response to requests for copies. The retyped text omits two lines, compresses two other lines into one by omitting words, and has other minor transcription errors. With further transcription errors, this retyped text was then printed in a pamphlet, *Federal Participation HemisFair '68*, issued by the U.S. Department of Commerce in February 1971. Auden never published the text, which reuses a few lines from his 1948 poem "A Walk after Dark", printed in *Nones* (1951) and later collected editions.

INDEX OF TITLES AND
FIRST LINES

THIS index includes titles of each of the works printed or described in this edition and the first lines of each of the poems that Auden either published as separate poems or composed as separate poems before incorporating them into larger works.

Titles of works originally published as separate books or pamphlets are printed in LARGE AND SMALL CAPITALS. Other titles are in *italics*. First lines are in roman type.